THE
CIVIL WAR
IN BOOKS

THE
CIVIL WAR
IN BOOKS

An Analytical Bibliography

DAVID J. EICHER

FOREWORD BY GARY W. GALLAGHER

UNIVERSITY OF ILLINOIS PRESS

URBANA AND CHICAGO

Library of Congress Cataloging-in-Publication Data

Eicher, David J., 1961–
The Civil War in books : an analytical bibliography /
David J. Eicher ; foreword by Gary W. Gallagher.
p.   cm.
Includes indexes.
ISBN 0-252-02273-4 (cloth : alk. paper)
1. United States—History—Civil War, 1861–1865—Bibliography. I. Title.
Z1242.E57   1997
[E468]
016.9737—dc20   96-2281
CIP

For the many Civil War historians of the past,
to whom a project like this owes an incalculable debt.

CONTENTS

Soldiers

Sailors

Others

UNION BIOGRAPHIES, MEMOIRS, AND LETTERS

Politicians

Soldiers

CONTENTS

Sailors

Others

GENERAL WORKS

UNIT HISTORIES

FOREWORD

GARY W. GALLAGHER

Abraham Lincoln prophesied in his address at Gettysburg that the world would never forget what the men of the Army of the Potomac had sacrificed on that bloody battlefield. Three months earlier, Jefferson Davis had written that Robert E. Lee and the Army of Northern Virginia would become "the subject of history and object of the world's admiration for generations to come." Caught up in an upheaval of unimaginable proportion, untold thousands of other Americans North and South joined their presidents in believing they were participating in events that would resound through subsequent generations. They were correct. Books about the Civil War have accumulated at the rate of more than a title a day since fighting erupted at Fort Sumter in April 1861. No other aspect of United States history boasts a comparably large literature. Indeed, readers new to the subject, as well as many who have explored it for years, often feel overwhelmed by this massive roster of books, the size and disparate quality of which can confound and reward in about equal measure.

Books and pamphlets about the war's origins, major episodes, and leading actors had begun to appear well before peace came in 1865. Most of these titles pertained to military and political events and personalities, though some also shed light on the home fronts. Among the last category were travel accounts by foreign visitors such as the British military officer Arthur James Lyon Fremantle. His *Three Months in the Southern States: April–June, 1863*, published in Northern and Southern editions in 1864, afforded readers a gripping look behind the scenes in the Confederacy.

The two decades after Appomattox witnessed a flood of reminiscences, unit histories, and other works that usually betrayed a strongly partisan point of view. Politicians and soldiers from both sides sought to justify their activities and respective causes. For example, Jefferson Davis and Alexander H. Stephens, who as president and vice president of the Confederacy had been implacable political enemies during much of the war, offered two-volume sets of memoirs that argued the constitutional purity of the South and played down the issue of slavery as a factor in bringing secession and war (in contrast, each man had emphasized the importance of slavery in speeches and writings during the tumultuous early months of 1861). A Republican radical, Henry Wilson, provided a Northern counterpoint to Confederate writers such as Davis and Stephens in his three-volume *History of the Rise and Fall of the Slave Power in America,* a treatment of American history that placed the peculiar institution at the storm center of sectional upheaval during the 1850s and 1860s.

A number of prominent generals published their reminiscences during the first two postwar decades. Like their political counterparts, these officers often employed rancorous prose to settle scores with enemies and former comrades and to place their own campaigns in the best light. Thus did Joseph E. Johnston and John Bell Hood, successive commanders of the Confederacy's Army of Tennessee in 1864, renew their wartime infighting with one another and, in Johnston's case, with Jefferson Davis. Ulysses S. Grant used his memoirs, which enjoy a somewhat puzzling reputation as being untainted by partisanship, to argue that advantages of manpower and material wealth alone did not explain Union victory. Grant hoped to refute Jubal A. Early and other ex-rebels who, from the late 1860s through the mid-1880s, exaggerated Northern numbers and resources in various publications. Scores of other soldiers joined in this running debate about numbers, wherein they habitually overestimated the enemy's strength and minimized their own.

Much of the writing between 1865 and the mid-1880s reflected a common belief that former enemies could not be trusted to tell the truth. The war's two most famous commanders illustrate this phenomenon. Lee spoke in 1865 of writing a history of the Army of Northern Virginia "to transmit, if possible, the truth to posterity, and do justice to our brave soldiers." The following year Lee noted "misrepresentations of my words and acts" among Northern accounts and suggested that "at present the public mind is not prepared to receive the truth." In an interview in 1878, Grant expressed similar concerns about the veracity of Southern writers who explained Lee's surrender as an inevitable consequence of Northern superiority of men and goods: "The illusion that nothing but heavy odds beat him will not stand the ultimate light of history," stated Grant. "I know it is not true."

Former Confederates devoted more energy to getting their version of events into print in the two decades after the war than did their opponents. They had suffered decisive defeat on the battlefield, lost a quarter of their prewar white military-age population, witnessed wide-scale destruction of property, and seen emancipation shatter their prewar social fabric. While the victorious North applauded the outcome of the conflict as evidence that its cause had been just, Southern white writers groped toward an interpretation of the war that would impart value to their unsuccessful struggle and permit them to maintain honor in a vastly changed world. They understood the importance of establishing a "Southern" printed record because they knew future historians would draw on the writings of participants. "The history of our war has not been written," noted the keynote speaker at the convention of the Southern Historical Society in 1873, "and it devolves upon the survivors of those who participated in that war, to furnish the authentic materials for that history."

By the mid-1870s, Southern writers had constructed a reading of secession and the Confederate experiment subsequently dubbed the myth of the Lost Cause. According to this reading, 11 Southern states had seceded to protect their constitutional rights rather than to protect slavery. Once at war, heroic Confederates led by the brilliant Lee held off hordes of Northern soldiers commanded by the butcher Grant and other minimally talented officers who subsequently lied in print to cover up their mistakes on the battlefield. Undone at Gettysburg by his sulking lieutenant James Longstreet, Lee maintained an admirable resistance for nearly two more years until, his army worn out but never defeated, he surrendered to Grant at Appomattox. These Lost Cause arguments quickly became orthodoxy in the white South, eventually gained currency among many Northerners, and continue to resonate in much recent writing on the conflict.

A reconciliation movement of the late 19th and early 20th centuries influenced the tone of writings from that period. Federals and Confederates tended to ascribe bravery and high-minded motives to soldiers on both sides and to describe the conflict as a great crucible that revealed the noble qualities of all Americans. John Brown Gordon's *Reminiscences of the Civil War* typified such works. A Confederate major general and influential postwar politician in Georgia, Gordon hewed to the Lost Cause line concerning slavery and Lee's unblemished brilliance but also lavished praise on the Federals. Above all, he stressed the essential brotherhood of Federals and Confederates: "At the beginning there was personal antagonism and even bitterness felt by individual soldiers of the two armies toward one another," observed Gordon. "The very sight of the uniform of an opponent aroused some trace of anger. But this was all gone long before the conflict had ceased. It was

supplanted by a brotherly sympathy. The spirit of Christianity swayed the hearts of many, and its benign influence was perhaps felt by the great majority of both armies." This pleasant picture no doubt found a receptive audience in many quarters when the book came out in 1903, but it discloses far more about attitudes in the early 20th century than about the reality of war in 1861–1865.

Largely missing during the era of reconciliation—as it had been from earlier works—was recognition of the roles black people had played in the war. White Northerners recalled the conflict as a triumph for union and the democratic ideal rather than as a struggle that killed slavery; their Southern counterparts celebrated valorous Confederate soldiers and steadfast civilians behind the lines, mentioning Southern blacks, if at all, as loyal supporters of the Confederate cause. As early as 1870, Frederick Douglass had lamented the ease with which emancipation slipped to a position of secondary importance in the minds of white Northerners, and he devoted enormous energy through the rest of the century in a largely vain attempt to train the spotlight on freedom. Several more decades would pass before the process of emancipation, black military service, and the experiences of blacks behind the lines received full attention.

The early 20th century also brought an initial wave of scholarly studies that supplemented the more personal writings of participants. Excellent examples from the military and civilian spheres were John Bigelow, Jr.'s, immensely detailed *The Campaign of Chancellorsville: A Strategic and Tactical Study*, which still ranks among the best studies of any Civil War battle, and Emerson D. Fite's pathbreaking *Social and Industrial Conditions in the North during the Civil War*, a monograph that anticipated later scholarly attention to nonmilitary aspects of the North in wartime. Most important in terms of impact on future scholarship, the U.S. Department of War brought its 128-volume *The War of the Rebellion: A Compilation of the Official Records of the Union and Confederate Armies* to a triumphant conclusion in 1901. The single most valuable printed source on the Civil War, this set has served as the documentary backbone for countless books over the past ninety years.

The years between World War I and the end of World War II proved fruitful in various parts of the field. Douglas Southall Freeman published his seminal works on Lee and the Army of Northern Virginia, Bell I. Wiley virtually invented the field of common soldier studies, W. E. B. Du Bois produced a watershed examination of black Americans during the era of the Civil War (a book largely ignored for many decades), and other scholars similarly helped move the literature toward a higher plateau of sophistication and insight. A trickle of memoirs also appeared, though most were composed at such distance from the events described as to have only modest value.

Civil War publishing during the last half-century has developed along two quite distinct paths. Most academic scholars have focused on nonmilitary topics such as diplomacy, politics, social trends, and economics, while a few academics and a great many other writers have contributed titles on battles, campaigns, and military biography. Too often these parallel literatures take virtually no notice of one another—the nonmilitary titles conveying little sense that huge armies contended for supremacy in the Confederate countryside, and the military titles reading as if campaigns took place in a vacuum insulated from the political and social contexts.

An element of hostility between the two camps often has been detectable, most notably in the wake of the Civil War Centennial of 1961–1965. That commemoration inspired an avalanche of books, most of which explored military topics—and far too many of which relied on superficial research and lacked stylistic distinction. Academic historians rightly questioned the need for such books and suggested everything that needed to be said about the military side of the war already had been said more than once. Those with military interests responded that these critics merely envied the strong demand for military titles, insisting that much good work remained to be done on armies, generals, and the men who served in the ranks. Too many historians on both sides of this debate missed the point that the war cannot be understood without exploring the myriad reciprocal influences between the home front and battlefield.

The surfeit of titles during the Centennial soured many publishers on the Civil War. Toward the end of the 1960s and into the 1970s, the bitter American experience in Vietnam further depressed the market by casting a shadow over studies of any war. Although Shelby Foote and Allan Nevins completed their magisterial narratives of the conflict during this period and other significant and influential titles appeared, relative quiet marked the field—especially on the military side—between the mid-1960s and the early 1980s.

The last dozen years have witnessed a remarkable turnaround. The tremendous success of James M. McPherson's *Battle Cry of Freedom* in 1988, the phenomenon shortly thereafter of Ken Burns's documentary film *The Civil War,* a round of 125th-anniversary commemorations between 1986 and 1990 (what other event in United States history has been celebrated on its *125th* anniversary?), and several highly publicized threats to historic Civil War ground at Manassas, Virginia, and elsewhere all helped to fuel an astonishing growth of national interest in the Civil War. Publishers scrambled to produce books to satisfy that interest, and

readers have been treated to a feast of superior scholarship (as well as to a large number of forgettable titles that recall the excesses of the Centennial years).

Recent scholarship has widened and deepened the field. Social historians, who for years had explored the lives of common folk before and after the Civil War, belatedly recognized that rich opportunities beckoned from the nation's greatest trauma. Their efforts have expanded understanding of the roles of women, who for more than a century after the war graced the literature principally in the form of diaries (most of them from the Confederacy). Civilians in general also have come under greater scrutiny, as have their ties to the military front. Among excellent recent studies of black Americans during the war, the four volumes to date of *Freedom: A Documentary History of Emancipation, 1861–1867* give by far the fullest voice yet to slaves and free blacks. Historians such as Reid Mitchell, Michael Fellman, and Joseph T. Glatthaar have extended the pioneering work of Bell I. Wiley, employing the techniques of social history to illuminate the attitudes and actions of common soldiers and to construct sophisticated profiles of armies and smaller units.

More traditional military topics and politics—mainstays of the first century's writings about the war—also have been served well of late. Robert K. Krick, Albert Castel, John Hennessy, and Harry W. Pfanz have set a formidable standard of research and analysis in their studies of battles and campaigns. Never again will any book on a military operation that neglects to mine the extensive available manuscript sources be considered definitive or even adequate. Military biographers have produced nuanced, perceptive portraits that place their subjects within the context of their times rather than simply following them from battlefield to battlefield. On a broader canvass, Herman Hattaway and Archer Jones, Charles Royster, and others have examined strategy and conceptions of how the war should be waged with a keen eye toward the influences of politics, ideology, and logistics.

Political ideology and culture have attracted superior scholars as well. The question of the extent to which the Confederacy developed a sense of nationalism, for example, has inspired Drew Gilpin Faust, George C. Rable, and others to build on the brilliant earlier work of David Potter. Local studies have brought political tensions in counties and regions into much sharper focus. Overall, the Confederacy has benefited from recent scholarship in these areas far more than the North—a circumstance that should change as historians move to fill some of the glaring gaps in our knowledge about Northern society at war.

There never has been a better time for prospective readers to be interested in the Civil War. A daunting array of choices, which includes both new titles and scores of reprinted older ones, crowd shelves in bookstores and libraries. Where should neophytes start? Where should more seasoned students go after their initial forays into the field? Incredibly, there has been no comprehensive bibliography of Civil War materials since the publication of *Civil War Books: A Critical Bibliography* (Baton Rouge, 1967–1969). Although *Civil War Books* remains a useful guide to roughly 6000 titles, its coverage stops with books published in the early 1960s and it offers only minimal annotation. Garold L. Cole's *Civil War Eyewitnesses: An Annotated Bibliography of Books and Articles, 1955–1986* (Columbia, 1988) supplements *Civil War Books* and includes more generous annotation but treats only one part of the literature. A pair of other works, Richard B. Harwell's *In Tall Cotton: The 200 Most Important Confederate Books for the Reader, Researcher, and Collector* (Austin, 1978) and Michael Mullins and Rowena Reed's *The Union Bookshelf: A Selected Civil War Bibliography* (Wendell, 1982), were issued in very small printings and thus reached limited audiences.

In short, the field has needed precisely the type of guide David J. Eicher supplies with his roster of 1100 titles. Eicher's annotation exceeds that in any previous comprehensive bibliography and attests to his willingness to log the prodigious amount of time necessary to master such a large and disparate body of work. Although the bibliography includes only about 2 percent of the titles Eicher could have chosen, it directs users toward material in virtually every major subgenre of the Civil War literature. Casual and veteran readers alike should be thankful for Eicher's determination, care in choosing material, and his attention to detail. Here is an excellent tool with which to plot a strategy for coming to grips with the vast riches of Civil War writings.

ACKNOWLEDGMENTS

Special thanks are extended to my father, John Eicher, for the enormous amount of work he took on for this project, and to Gary Gallagher and Jim McPherson for reading the manuscript and offering detailed, helpful suggestions. Special thanks are also extended to Gary for taking the time from his busy schedule to write the foreword. I extend gracious appreciation to Richard L. Wentworth, director of the University of Illinois Press, for his valuable guidance. My copy editors at the Press, Hilda Banks and Terry Sears, have improved the manuscript immeasurably. Special thanks for encouragement and advice are also due to Robert A. Braun, Tom Broadfoot, Albert Castel, Russell Fay, Lance Herdegen, Andrew Oren, T. Michael Parrish, and Dan Weinberg. The staffs of the following libraries and institutions also offered help and encouragement: Cincinnati Historical Society, Cincinnati, Ohio; Golda Meir Library, University of Wisconsin at Milwaukee; Library of Congress, Washington, D.C.; Marquette University Libraries, Milwaukee, Wisconsin; Miami University Libraries, Oxford, Ohio; Milwaukee Public Library, Milwaukee, Wisconsin; National Archives, Washington, D.C.; U.S. Army Military History Institute, Carlisle, Pennsylvania; and the W. Norman Fitzgerald Collection, Carroll College, Waukesha, Wisconsin.

Beyond all of this, the selfless support offered by my wife, Lynda, and son, Christopher, throughout this journey has helped to keep the project on track.

INTRODUCTION

CAPTURING THE WAR ON PAPER

THE guns had been silent for nearly half a century, the smoke and pain of battle long since dissipated. An aging veteran sat in a quiet room in his home in Philadelphia, reliving the events that shook the world, events that were now memories of a vanished age. At age 72, John Page Nicholson remained fully devoted to the Civil War, surrounded by wartime friends present not in person but in the pages of several thousand books.

For Nicholson the memories of Grant and Lee, of Antietam and Gettysburg, of Lincoln and Davis were as vivid as they had been so many years before. But by 1914 the world had changed and the war between blue and gray was an event solidly lodged in the past, soon to be overshadowed by a world war. The aging Civil War veterans were answering their final roll call with increasing frequency.

During the five decades since the Civil War, Nicholson had labored to build what came to be considered by many veterans the finest Civil War library in private hands. He sought and purchased every meaningful volume he could locate and received many donations of books from the authors themselves. This was an extraordinary achievement for a man who began his wartime experience as a young boy, worked his way up through the ranks to achieve recognition, and then became one of the most energetic servants of the war's legacy.

Born on the Fourth of July in 1842, the 19-year-old Nicholson had enlisted as a private soldier in the 28th Pennsylvania Volunteer Infantry on 23 July 1861. Two days short of a year later he was commissioned first lieutenant and experienced service through an amazingly wide theater of the war, including duty in the Shenandoah Valley, Second Bull Run, Antietam, Fredericksburg, Chancellorsville, Gettysburg, Chattanooga, the Atlanta campaign, Sherman's March to the Sea, and the surrender of Gen. Joseph E. Johnston in North Carolina. For his service Nicholson was commissioned brevet captain, brevet major, and brevet lieutenant colonel of volunteers, to rank from 13 March 1865, the "omnibus day." The majority of important Union officers who substantially contributed to the Union victory received brevet commissions to rank from this date.

After the war Nicholson proved himself to be one of the most active participants in Civil War circles. He served as recorder-in-chief of the Military Order of the Loyal Legion of the United States (MOLLUS) from 1885 to his death in 1922. He compiled the registry of the Pennsylvania MOLLUS companions. He was chairman of the U.S. Gettysburg National Park Commission. He edited the two-volume work *Pennsylvania at Gettysburg* and translated into English the Comte de Paris's classic four-volume book *Historie de la guerre civile en Amérique.* But perhaps his greatest contribution to Civil War history was the foundation of his library, the outstanding model of what a 19th-century Civil War collection should include. In 1914, as he sat steeped in memories, Nicholson could be proud of having published a book about his books, *Catalogue of the Library of Brevet Lieutenant-Colonel John Page Nicholson Relating to the War of the Rebellion, 1861–1866.* The 1022-page tome, privately published in an edition of 300 copies and printed by the John T. Palmer Company of Philadelphia, is quite scarce today.

Reading through Nicholson's bibliography is a dazzling experience. Throughout the several thousand entries readers can find every important Civil War title published before 1914, many of the books bearing inscriptions from the authors—including many a general North and South—or autographic material relating to the subject or author laid in. Although most of the Nicholson collection was acquired by the Henry E. Huntington Library in California in 1927, some of Nicholson's volumes are available through book dealers and collectors. In 1991 I purchased *The "Battle Order" of the Army of the Potomac: General Order No. 10, Headquarters, Army of the Potomac, March 7, 1865,* a book originally belonging to Nicholson's library.

EVALUATING THE VAST CIVIL WAR LITERATURE

Over the next several decades a number of Civil War bibliographies appeared. They are not literal catalogs of collections but were assembled to guide the interested reader to the best literature on certain Civil War topics. Noteworthy general bibliographies include *A Military Bibliography of the Civil War* (1971–1982), by Charles E. Dornbusch, and *Civil War Books: A Critical Bibliography* (1967–1969), edited by Allan Nevins, James I. Robertson, Jr., and Bell I. Wiley. A slew of smaller general works exist—some predating the Nicholson compilation—and a number of specialized bibliographies also have been published.

In terms of coverage, Dornbusch's *Military Bibliography* is unequaled. It purports to list all books and articles of Civil War military interest, dividing them by topic. The quality of the works listed runs the gamut from good to average to outright bad. Although Dornbusch does not provide evaluative notes or reviews, he is admirably successful in including basic data for virtually all works of importance. Indeed, high-priced offerings from book dealers of rare titles "not in Dornbusch" are comic because virtually all works not listed in the compilation hardly merit a glance.

Nevins, Robertson, and Wiley's *Civil War Books* is a product of the National Civil War Centennial Commission's desire to document Civil War literature. The editors provide a brief critique (usually just a sentence or two) for each entry. Although the books are lumped into categories that produce duplicate entries, and despite the fact that the intellectual landscape of Civil War literature has changed dramatically since the era of the Civil War Centennial, *Civil War Books* will remain useful for decades to come. Indeed, this book aims to carry on the spirit of the Nevins, Robertson, and Wiley compilation by presenting somewhat more detailed criticisms of valuable books and works published since *Civil War Books* appeared. The sole surviving author of the earlier work has graced the present effort as an editorial advisor.

Garold L. Cole's *Civil War Eyewitnesses: An Annotated Bibliography of Books and Articles, 1955–1986* (1988) is extremely well done but limited in scope because it covers eyewitness accounts published between 1955 and 1986. *Travels in the Confederate States: A Bibliography* (1948), by E. Merton Coulter, is well done but limited to narratives of travel.

Other general bibliographies are interesting and useful for specialized literature searches. These include *Civil War and Reconstruction* (2d ed., 1962), by Hal Bridges; and *Civil War Books: A Priced Checklist with Advice* (3d ed., 1990), by Tom Broadfoot. Additionally, extensive bibliographic appendices appear in several general Civil War books, including *The Civil War Day by Day: An Almanac, 1861–1865* (1971), by E. B. Long; and *The Civil War and Reconstruction* (2d ed., 1961), by James G. Randall and David H. Donald.

Many specialized Civil War bibliographies exist, some of which are excellent. Five government publications are especially useful for searches concerning manuscript material. They are *Guide to the Archives of the Government of the Confederate States of America* (1968), by Henry P. Beers; *Guide to Federal Archives Relating to the Civil War* (1962), by Kenneth W. Munden and Henry P. Beers; *Special Bibliography*

#11: The Era of the Civil War, 1820–1876 (1982), edited by Louise Arnold; the U.S. War Department's *Bibliography of State Participation in the Civil War, 1861–1866* (3d ed., 1903); and *Civil War Manuscripts in the Library of Congress* (1985), edited by John R. Sellers.

Where specific battles are concerned, *The Gettysburg Campaign, June 3–August 1, 1863: A Comprehensive, Selectively Annotated Bibliography* (1982), by Richard A. Sauers, is outstanding. A later book on Antietam sources follows this example: *The Battle of Antietam and the Maryland Campaign of 1862: A Bibliography* (1990), by D. Scott Hartwig.

The area of Confederate bibliography has been particularly active. Many of the following are useful sources in researching Confederate history: *Confederate Imprints: A Bibliography of Southern Publications from Secession to Surrender (Expanding and Revising the Earlier Works of Marjorie Crandall and Richard Harwell)* (1984), by T. Michael Parrish and Robert M. Willingham, Jr.; *A Calendar of Confederate Papers with a Bibliography of Some Confederate Publications: Preliminary Report of the Southern Historical Manuscripts Commission, Prepared under the Direction of the Confederate Memorial Literary Society* (1908), by Douglas Southall Freeman; *The South to Posterity: An Introduction to the Writing of Confederate History* (1939), by Douglas Southall Freeman; *The Confederate Hundred: A Bibliophilic Selection of Confederate Books* (1964), by Richard B. Harwell; *Cornerstones of Confederate Collecting* (1952), by Richard B. Harwell; *In Tall Cotton: The 200 Most Important Confederate Books for the Reader, Researcher, and Collector* (1978), by Richard B. Harwell; and *Neale Books: An Annotated Bibliography* (1977), by Robert K. Krick. Of these, the works by Parrish and Willingham, Freeman, and Krick are notably outstanding.

Bibliographies covering the Union side of the war include *The Union Bookshelf: A Selected Civil War Bibliography* (1982), by Michael Mullins and Rowena Reed, and *The Civil War in the North: A Selected, Annotated Bibliography* (1987), by Eugene C. Murdock.

State bibliographies include *Guide to Civil War Source Material in the Department of Archives and History, State of Mississippi* (1962), by Patti C. Black; *Descriptive Bibliography of Civil War Manuscripts in Illinois* (1966), by William L. Burton; *Michigan Civil War History: An Annotated Bibliography* (1961), edited by George S. May; *The Civil War Literature of Ohio* (1911), by Daniel Joseph Ryan; and *West Virginia Civil War Literature: An Annotated Bibliography* (1963), by Charles Shetler.

A particular area of specialty interest that perennially generates many published pages is the study of Abraham Lincoln, and Lincoln bibliographies are no exception. These include *A Shelf of Lincoln Books: A Critical, Selective Bibli-*

ography of Lincolniana (1946), by Paul M. Angle; *Lincoln Bibliography, 1839–1939* (1943–1945), by Jay Monaghan; *Lincoln Bibliography: A List of Books and Pamphlets Relating to Abraham Lincoln* (1925), by Joseph B. Oakleaf; and *A List of Lincolniana in the Library of Congress* (rev. ed., 1906), by George T. Ritchey.

Specialized bibliographies exist relating to Civil War maps and photographs. These include *Civil War Photographs, 1861–1865: A Catalog of Copy Negatives Made from Originals Selected from the Mathew B. Brady Collection in the Prints and Photographs Division of the Library of Congress* (1961), by Hirst D. Milhollen and Donald H. Mugridge; the National Archives and Records Administration's *Guide to Civil War Maps in the National Archives* (2d ed., 1986); *Civil War Maps: An Annotated List of Maps and Atlases in Map Collections of the Library of Congress* (2d ed., 1989), edited by Richard W. Stephenson; *Civil War Maps in the National Archives* (1964), edited by Charlotte M. Ashby; *Civil War Newspaper Maps: A Cartobibliography of the Northern Daily Press* (1993), by David Bosse; and *Microbes and Minié Balls: An Annotated Bibliography of Civil War Medicine* (1994), by Frank R. Freemon.

EDITORIAL METHOD: THE CHALLENGE OF INCLUSION

Over the course of 135 years since the Civil War began, more than 50,000 books and pamphlets have been published on the subject (through mid-1995). How can someone interested in the Civil War—whether for light reading or through the passion of building a Civil War library—sift through this mass of printed material and discover the most important, credible, relevant, and interesting works? Although the war has generated its share of bibliographies, most having been published long after John Page Nicholson's classic, none of these is sufficiently broad, provides ample discussion, is suitably up-to-date, or credibly presents works deemed the most important books for gaining a well-rounded, objective knowledge of our most tragic national period.

The Civil War in Books: An Analytical Bibliography contains a selection of the most important 1100 books on the Civil War, which contain a total of 952,482 pages of text. The original target number of books was 1000, but as the project progressed it became clear that too many critical works would be left out, so the compilation grew by 10 percent and now includes works of interest for beginning students of the war, Civil War buffs, librarians, collectors, and historians. Of course, the criteria for selection will not be agreed on by all readers, but I have tried to include all "universally accepted" classics, those works deemed important because of their participant authors, and modern works of scholarly value. The list and many of the annotations have passed under the supervisory eyes of an editorial review board consisting of John H. Eicher, professor emeritus at Miami University; Gary W. Gallagher, professor of history at Pennsylvania State University; James M. McPherson, professor of history at Princeton University; Mark W. Neely, Jr., professor of history at Saint Louis University; Civil War expert Ralph Geoffrey Newman of Chicago, Illinois; and James I. Robertson, Jr., professor of history at Virginia Polytechnic Institute and State University. I am very grateful for their kind assistance and their many years of combined expertise.

The works in this volume cover the entire spectrum from general histories, battle and campaign books, biographies, unit histories, letters and diaries, personal narratives, reference works, picture books—and even a few works of fiction. Represented are 41 selected battles and campaigns; the biographies of 18 Confederate and 37 Union political leaders, 110 Confederate and 126 Union soldiers, 9 Confederate and 13 Union sailors, and 22 other Confederate and 30 other Union personalities of interest. The somewhat larger number of Union individuals (206) compared with Confederate individuals (159) is in part a consequence of the larger population base in the North and also is a reflection of the short existence of the Confederacy.

I personally inspected each work in a variety of places and situations, collecting notes and discussing the books at length with my father over several years. Because only slightly more than half of the works included are in my own library, I needed to locate several hundred titles in institutional libraries. An effort was made to include significant recent books in each category, which led to omitting earlier works on the same subjects that, while important in their time, have been superseded by newer books that have benefited from more recent scholarship as well as a more extensive historical perspective.

In contradiction to the guideline just stated, a few examples of very early works are included for some topics because they present the contemporary viewpoint, in some cases being penned by eyewitnesses to the events, even though the writings were made with patriotic bias and without proper historical knowledge or perspective. A few generally well known works were omitted after a search not only in my collection but in a dozen libraries, including several with outstanding collections, did not produce complete copies. If a book is nearly impossible to locate, it should first be reprinted and made available before being discussed for the readership at large.

The Civil War in Books is arranged under five broad headings, which is about as many subject categories as can allow separation without considerable overlapping. These are battles and campaigns (about 13 percent of the entries), Confederate biographies (20 percent), Union biographies (25 percent), general works (33 percent), and unit histories (8 percent). Altogether, the write-ups offer more than 290,000 words of Civil War history, approaching one word for every Federal soldier who died during the war.

The topical subdivisions are as follows. The section on battles and campaigns is subdivided into naval warfare, the war in the West, and all others (the principal category covering army operations in the East and Midwest). Biographies for both Confederate and Union individuals are grouped into four sections: politicians, soldiers, sailors, and others, the entries for soldiers amounting to 63 percent of the biographies. Where an individual held political office and served in the army, he appears as a politician. General works include 20 subdivisions with topics such as state participation, Confederate studies, politics and society, reference works, strategy and tactics, and general histories. The final category, unit histories, presents the stories of regiments and batteries as the largest subgroup. Because so many of these unit histories exist, and due to their generally poor quality and historical value, I have included only a sampling of those that offer material of interest. Within each subcategory, books are listed alphabetically by author. Indices for authors and editors and for book titles, including new and altered titles for reprint editions, are keyed to the number assigned to each entry (rather than page numbers). Because the entries are numbered sequentially, a particular individual or book title can be quickly found. The indices also include books that receive mention in the annotations but do not warrant their own entry.

A chronological analysis reveals some interesting trends. About 7 percent of the books included are contemporary with the Civil War, while about 12 percent are from the 1990s. Another 12 percent were published in 1961–1970, a period that included Civil War Centennial observances. Three periods of productive literature dominate. The first is that of the memorialization of the war from 1881 to 1910, during which many participants wrote books on the war, the most useful of which retain value for their firsthand accounts and which amount to 20 percent of the works gathered herein.

The second dominant period is that of the approach and celebration of the Civil War Centennial, from 1951 to 1970, which witnessed an explosion of publishing on the war that accounts for another 20 percent of the works in this bibliography. Although valuable works remain from the period 1911–1950, fewer came into print during that time and many of those that did have now been replaced by the works of recent generations of scholars and popularizers.

The third significant period is that of 1981 to the present, which has seen another eruption in Civil War writing, one not tied to anniversaries but to the current boost in interest in Civil War history. Fully 27 percent of the works listed have originated in this period, a rather astonishing fact with a multifaceted explanation. An increasing pool of scholars and writers turning out works has enabled many authors to claim their specialized books as the best, most recent writing on the subject. Also, the recent boom in publishing to a larger degree reflects a real increase in high-quality Civil War scholarship, a trend that appears to be continuing at full velocity. This is highly encouraging and mirrors an increased interest in the topic at large, also witnessed by television and motion picture projects, professional conferences, memberships in Civil War Round Tables, and circulations of periodicals on the subject.

The most numerous categories are those of biographies of Union soldiers (15 percent of the total work), biographies of Confederate soldiers (14 percent), battles and campaigns in the "all others" category (11 percent), reference works (9 percent), and biographies of Union politicians (6 percent). Other well-represented categories include unit histories of regiments and batteries, Confederate studies, and pictorial works. A brief look at the chronology of works that stand as important reveals some trends as well. Several areas are systematically represented in history, meaning that consistent levels of publication have occurred in these areas since the war and older works have weathered the intervening time well. This is the case with battles and campaigns (particularly the land-based "all others" category focusing on army actions in the East and Midwest), Confederate biographies, Union biographies, Confederate studies, fiction, general histories, reference works, state participation, and histories of regiments and batteries. Other areas have developed only recently or older works have lost their value, and so the areas remain in relative infancy in terms of the potential depth of publication and research: This is the case with battle and campaign studies on the war in the West, books on blacks and the war, guidebooks and essays on Civil War battlefields, the coming of the war, the common soldiers, medical aspects, the press, railroads and the war, and the war's aftermath.

A few special notes: I have listed diaries and letters under their authors, not under the names of the editors who compiled them (though the editors' names appear in parentheses). I have listed in nearly every case first editions with noteworthy subsequent editions mentioned at the end of the annotations. A few cases violate this rule, as with C. Vann Woodward's superior edition of Mary Chesnut's classic *Diary*, in which the original edition, now superseded, is given in the annotation. Save for a couple dozen of the most important works, which require lengthier discussions, my evaluations are of a reasonably brief length. For some very valuable books I include rather extensive lists of minor errors; the intent is not to damage the books' credibility of usefulness but simply to make readers aware of the pitfalls that exist even in the most solid works. For those who wish to explore other Civil War bibliographies, a short list appears as appendix 2.

The Civil War was our greatest national crisis, an event that at once split us apart and forged a single nation. As such, it provides unsurpassable stories of people and events, of a hazy time that seems incalculably distant as we approach the year 2000. Yet the war occurred only two lifetimes ago, and many of us are descendants of its participants. I hope that *The Civil War in Books* becomes a well-used guide in your exploration of those heady days when battles like Antietam and Gettysburg, Chancellorsville and Atlanta, were not sacred historic images but daily events.

BATTLES
AND CAMPAIGNS

NAVAL WARFARE (1861–1865)

1

Ammen, Daniel. **The Atlantic Coast** (vol. 2 in Scribner's series The Navy in the Civil War, 273 pp., Charles Scribner's Sons, New York, 1883)

This volume offers a balanced, straightforward account of Union naval operations along the Atlantic that judiciously includes substantive Confederate reports as well as those of the Union commanders. The book is generally well written, although it lacks in-depth analysis and a lively style that would give it more appeal to casual readers. Nine maps accompany the text.

Ammen's volume does not include material on the Union blockade—save for a criticism of its early ineffectiveness—leaving that for James Soley's companion work (*q.v.*). Instead, Ammen directs his efforts toward joint army-navy ventures that ultimately turned the tide in operations such as the Port Royal expedition, movements about Charleston, and the reduction of Fort Fisher. The author casts significant attention on operations in which he played an important role, but his treatment of himself is tastefully handled. By contrast, he attacks Secretary of the Navy Isaac Toucey for his apparent prevention of consolidating naval power before the war. Ammen builds a credible case that Confederate ironclads had a far greater psychological than substantive effect. Rear Adm. David D. Porter comes under attack for arming the expeditionary force at Fort Fisher so poorly. Although it holds few surprises, Ammen's account is solid and reliable.

(Reprinted 1989, with an introduction by Chris E. Fonvielle, Jr., 273 pp., Broadfoot, Wilmington)

2

Anderson, Bern. **By Sea and by River: The Naval History of the Civil War** (303 pp., Alfred A. Knopf, New York, 1962)

This single-volume account of the Civil War navies is readable and interesting. The author's work focuses on naval strategy with particular emphasis on the blockade and operations on the high seas. Additionally, the narrative explores the importance and success of various combined operations and the effect of the navies on possible foreign intervention.

Throughout most of the text the author offers a balanced survey of Civil War naval operations—particularly in his demonstrations of the related army-navy operations—although it sometimes inadequately treats naval efforts of the Confederacy. Anderson might have stressed in much great-er detail the importance of the North Carolina operations early in the war and the techniques and tactics of using river gunboats in the early campaigns in Tennessee. Overall, this fine survey offers much of value for readers who desire a brief summary of the naval history of the war.

(Reprinted 1989, 303 pp., Da Capo Press, New York)

3

Bearss, Edwin C. **Hardluck Ironclad: The Sinking and Salvage of the *Cairo*** (222 pp., Louisiana State University Press, Baton Rouge, 1966)

This story details the ironclad gunboat's demise on the Yazoo River in December 1862 and its salvage a century later. Beginning with the discovery of the wrecked *Cairo* in 1956, the author traces the ship's building as one of the "City class" river gunboats produced by James B. Eads, the early career of the *Cairo* on river patrol, the character of the men on the ship and its commander, Lt. Comdr. Thomas O. Selfridge, Jr., and the Vicksburg campaign that led to the ship's striking a torpedo (naval mine) and sinking. Subsequent chapters begin the story anew in the 1950s with the analysis of the *Cairo* wreck, the plans to raise her, and the (unfortunately) botched salvage attempt that cut the ship in half. The National Park Service ultimately brought up all of the major pieces and restored the ship for display at the Vicksburg National Military Park. The quickness of the ship's sinking meant that a huge cache of relics stayed on board, and these too were recovered and put on display at Vicksburg.

The well-written text describing the *Cairo*'s Civil War career by itself makes this volume a valuable addition to naval literature. The modern story of the ship's restoration, accompanied by maps and photographs, appears as a bonus, then, that adds significance and flavor to the historical story. Anyone who has seen the ship in Mississippi will certainly appreciate this work, which stands as a unique accomplishment in Civil War naval history.

(Reprinted 1980, 222 pp., Louisiana State University Press, Baton Rouge)

4

Browning, Robert M., Jr. **From Cape Charles to Cape Fear: The North Atlantic Blockading Squadron during the Civil War** (453 pp., University of Alabama Press, Tuscaloosa, 1993)

This is a fine study of a neglected area of Civil War naval history. The North Atlantic Blockading Squadron had a tremendous task before it: protecting and blockading the numerous ports and rivers stretching south to Wilmington,

North Carolina. Browning shows that after a confused first few months of operations, the squadron evolved into a highly effective force under the leadership of Rear Adm. S. P. Lee, son-in-law of Francis Preston Blair, Sr. (The author erroneously identifies Lee as the son-in-law of Montgomery Blair, who was actually Lee's brother-in-law.)

Lee commanded the squadron from 1862 to 1864 and developed a successful strategy of patrolling many bodies of water, including the Chesapeake Bay, and numerous rivers including the James, Mattapony, Neuse, Pamlico, Pamunkey, Rappahannock, Roanoke, and York. The encounters with blockade-runners form much of the interesting narrative, even if names are introduced repeatedly as if mentioned for the first time. The work's real value lies in the descriptions of naval activities in eastern North Carolina, especially the climactic capture of Fort Fisher in January 1865, a combined operation using army troops as well as naval bombardment. The story of this final port closing fittingly finishes this well-crafted work.

5

Gosnell, H. Allen. **Guns on the Western Waters: The Story of the River Gunboats in the Civil War** (273 pp., Louisiana State University Press, Baton Rouge, 1949)

Gosnell establishes a base by detailing the weird aspect of river warfare: rather than fighting ship-to-ship in a conventional style befitting the open sea, river naval warriors often battled forts, rams, torpedoes, or other gunboats in a chaos of maneuverability. The author traces the evolution of war on the Mississippi in a succession of scenes of naval action.

This work follows Union Capt. John Pope and the disastrous engagement on 12 October 1861, at Head of Passes, Mississippi, where Confederate Commodore George Hollins struck Pope's fleet of three sloops and a sidewheel gunboat in darkness. Pope's flagship, the screw sloop *Richmond*, was rammed and temporarily disabled. The author outlines the increased use of Union gunboats as floating artillery platforms in the actions against Forts Henry and Donelson, Island No. 10, and Fort Pillow.

Much of the remaining material describes the Union efforts to encroach Vicksburg and presents a superb two-part telling of the career of the Confederate gunboat CSS *Arkansas*. The author weaves narratives and reports through his story, particularly in the advances on Vicksburg, and the result is a fine description of naval warfare in the West. The book lacks a much-needed index.

(Reprinted 1993, 273 pp., Louisiana State University Press, Baton Rouge)

6

Jones, Virgil Carrington. **The Civil War at Sea** (3 vols. consisting of *The Blockaders*, *The River War*, and *The Final Effort*, 1541 pp., Holt, Rinehart and Winston, New York, 1960–1962)

A useful and entertaining general history of Civil War naval operations, the three volumes cover the naval efforts of both sides chronologically, from January 1861 to March 1862, March 1862 to July 1863, and July 1863 to November 1865. The narrative includes in brief and fast-paced style the entire story of major Civil War naval actions from the relief effort of the *Star of the West* to the last official act of the Confederacy, the striking of the CSS *Shenandoah*'s flag at Liverpool.

The work is well written and highly successful as a popular overview. But the author relies heavily on the *O.R.N.* (*q.v.*)—perhaps too heavily—and because of this he sticks squarely with describing actions, offering scant interpretation. Moreover, he neglects important areas such as naval recruiting, shipbuilding, and supplying. The lack of interpretation forces the story to exist within a universe of its own with little context attached to the overall war effort.

The battle descriptions proceed without intrusion from other areas such as politics or considerations of the war's overall strategy. The commanders operate the war on the waters, but Navy Department chiefs Gideon Welles and Gustavus Fox play an almost nonexistent role. Occasionally the author revises the importance of naval matters, such as emphasizing the operations about Island No. 10 more than those about Forts Henry and Donelson. Nevertheless, the book offers a readable and at times gripping account of many familiar naval actions and therefore can be recommended to beginning readers of Civil War naval history.

(Reprinted 1990, 3 vols., 1541 pp., Broadfoot, Wilmington)

7

Mahan, Alfred T. **The Gulf and Inland Waters** (vol. 3 in Scribner's series The Navy in the Civil War, 267 pp., Charles Scribner's Sons, New York, 1883)

Mahan traces Civil War naval warfare in the West. The chapters cover naval actions from Cairo, Illinois, to Vicksburg; from the Gulf of Mexico to Vicksburg; the opening of the Mississippi; and Texas and the Red River expedition. The major battles discussed are Forts Henry and Donelson, Island No. 10, New Orleans, Vicksburg, and Mobile Bay. Eight maps accompany the text.

Like other books in the series, the narrative is a factual journey through units and actions and dispenses a reasonably objective view as seen from the Union perspective. The volume is accurate and balanced but lacks a degree of readability that might have made it a great work. Much of the text consists of material better suited for appendices. This was Mahan's first book, a trial run for later, greater works.

(Reprinted 1989, with an introduction by William Alan Blair, 267 pp., Broadfoot, Wilmington)

8

Mooney, James L., ed. **Dictionary of American Fighting Ships** (8 vols., 5260 pp., U.S. Government Printing Office, Washington, 1959–1991)

A work that is invaluable to naval studies of all eras, Mooney's excellent history of American naval vessels is arranged alphabetically and contains extensive data, numerous photographs of ships, and bibliographies. Of special reference interest to students of Civil War navies are the following sections: Confederate forces afloat (vol. 2, appendix 2, 97 pp.); privateers (vol. 2, annex 1, 2 pp.); river defense fleet (vol. 2, annex 2, 1 p.); Texas marine department, C.S.A. (vol. 2, annex 3, 1 p.); Confederate stone fleet (vol. 2, annex 4, 2 pp.); historic ship exhibits (vol. 3, appendix 1); monitors (vol. 3, appendix 2, 36 pp. pertaining to the Civil War); Civil War naval ordnance (vol. 3, appendix 3, 23 pp.); ships of the line (vol. 4, appendix 4); and Union stone fleets of the Civil War (vol. 5, appendix 1, 19 pp.).

(2d edition of vol. 1, 1991, 520 pp.)

9

Owsley, Frank L. **The C.S.S. *Florida:* Her Building and Operations** (208 pp., University of Pennsylvania Press, Philadelphia, 1965)

This book details the life of a particularly famous ship. Second in its record only to Raphael Semmes's *Alabama*, the iron-hulled *Florida* took 33 prizes during its tenure as a Rebel vessel. The author's narrative recounts the ship's dash through the blockade to Mobile; her North Atlantic cruise; inactivity at Brest, France; her battle with the USS *Wachusett* in Brazil; and her sinking at Newport News. The work benefits from using the previously untapped "lost" remnants of the *Florida*'s log.

The author carefully examines the influence of the ship's skippers, John N. Maffitt, Joseph N. Barney, and Charles M. Morris. With such an exciting story to tell, this book might have read like a great adventure novel. Unfortunately, the style is thick and overanalytical, but readers who carry through will come out with a solid understanding of the ship's important role.

In assessing the commanders, the author contradicts various statements of his own within the work, particularly in weighing Maffitt against Morris. He overestimates Maffitt's skill during the Mobile operation and underestimates Morris by negatively assessing his successes—or lack thereof—in 1864. Still, the work is unsurpassed in terms of detailing the life of the Confederacy's second great raider.

(Reprinted 1987, 210 pp., University of Alabama Press, Tuscaloosa)

10

Perry, Milton F. **Infernal Machines: The Story of Confederate Submarine and Mine Warfare** (230 pp., Louisiana State University Press, Baton Rouge, 1965)

Perry presents the dramatic story of numerous innovations devised shortly before or during the war for use as naval weaponry. Weaving a vast sea of material on technology and invention throughout a chronological tale of Confederate seaport and river warfare, the author admirably recounts many fascinating details of this aspect of the war. The coverage centers on the role of torpedoes (naval mines), including discussions of friction models, spar torpedoes, keg torpedoes, floating torpedoes, and current torpedoes, as well as other innovations experimentally used during various actions.

The author succinctly and meaningfully describes the innovators, beginning with Matthew Fontaine Maury and moving on to others such as John M. Brooke, Hunter Davidson, Francis D. Lee, and Gabriel J. Rains. Along the way, stories of the Confederate submarines *H. L. Hunley* and the partially-submergible *David* add flavor to the thesis. Perry demonstrates how, although these devices sank or damaged 43 Union ships, they did not "contribute materially to the grand strategic effect of the war." The author might have made more exhaustive use of manuscript sources. Still, the work is ultimately successful.

(Reprinted 1985, 230 pp., Louisiana State University Press, Baton Rouge)

11

Porter, David Dixon. **The Naval History of the Civil War** (843 pp., Sherman Publishing Co., New York, 1886)

This volume contains a mammoth collection of facts, dates, and anecdotes relating to the Union's war effort on the water. It is a chronological narrative of the Union Navy and its operations in the war, from the bombardment of Sumter to the end of the war. The organization and building of the Union warships receive ample attention, as do many examples of the naval battles involving both North and South Atlantic Blockading Squadrons and on the many rivers in all theaters of the war. This massive work recapitulates many official reports and is illustrated with numerous engravings of commanders, maps, and battle scenes. The major conflicts dominate, as do actions Porter himself experienced, but the work is a general survey that covers all bases. Many summaries provide tables of command, organization of departments, prizes captured, and other interesting facts.

Unfortunately, the work is filled with inaccuracies, particularly the author's recall of dates and events. The writing lacks clarity, and the author's wandering and sermonizing reduce the impact of the narrative. There are many ambiguous references to names, a poor index, and numerous misspellings (e.g., the names of John C. Breckinridge, James D. Bulloch, George W. Cullum, Ulysses S. Grant, Josiah Tattnall, and Lloyd Tilghman, as well as place names such as Castle Pinckney, Drewry's Bluff, the Tredegar Iron Works, and the Yalobusha River). The reporting on Abraham Lincoln's visit to Richmond in April 1865, which Porter witnessed, is erroneous. Although the work is therefore unreliable on a number of counts, it shines with personal comments on commanders and battles in which Porter himself played a significant role.

(Reprinted 1984, 843 pp., Castle, Secaucus)

12

Potter, Jerry O. **The *Sultana* Tragedy: America's Greatest Maritime Disaster** (300 pp., Pelican Publishing Co., Gretna, La., 1992)

On 27 April 1865, the Mississippi River steamboat *Sultana*, jammed with liberated Union prisoners, sank after its boilers exploded near Memphis. The disaster, occurring in the wake of that most traumatic event, the assassination of Lincoln, received scant attention. This work remedies the neglect by providing a full story of the *Sultana* tragedy based on extensive and careful research. The author includes a background section on the origins of the ship and on the conditions at the prisons from which the doomed passengers came. The work describes the military situation along the Mississippi near war's end and the parole camps scattered along the river.

The story accelerates with the description of the *Sultana*'s journey. Potter incorporates human interest stories as much as he can, adding power to the tragic drama of the explosion and fire. He shows how quartermasters overloaded the ship through ignorance and perhaps payoffs. The treatment of the resulting court-martial is thin, but that

does little to detract from the capable handling of a difficult topic.

13

Pratt, Fletcher. **Civil War on Western Waters** (255 pp., Henry Holt and Co., New York, 1956)

This book establishes some important points despite its rather discouraging faults. The author competently lays the groundwork for the Mississippi's importance and establishes the strategic necessity of a controlled river to both sides, for supply as well as route of invasion. His fluent style throughout the narrative is both a blessing for readability and a liability in that it oversimplifies various situations. The text contains enough misspellings to erode the author's credibility, yet in the main he presents an engaging narrative of the many battles and skirmishes that sealed the fate of the great river.

Pratt clearly explains the relationships between Grant and Sherman and their naval comrades Farragut, Foote, and Porter. The description of the combined army-navy operations at Forts Henry and Donelson, Vicksburg, and New Orleans is vividly and accurately rendered. The complexities of these joint ventures pale, however, in comparison with the disastrous inadequacy of the Confederate naval effort. Limited to retrofitting existing ships and financing British-built rams, the Confederate Navy never had a chance—a separation of means handled ably by Pratt.

14

Robinson, William Morrison, Jr. **The Confederate Privateers** (372 pp., Yale University Press, New Haven, 1928)

A relatively early study, this work is marked by thoroughness, cautious research, and good coverage. Drawing on a wide range of printed and manuscript sources, it explores how Confederate privateering developed, the response to it, and a chronology of events and special topics related to privateering operations.

Among the more useful chapters are those treating cruises of the *Jefferson Davis*, the *Dixie*, and the *Sallie*. The "world's only submarine privateer" is outlined in an entertaining chapter. Fresh material enlightens the career of John Y. Beall. Later sections analyze how Confederate privateering evolved as the war waned and the United States dabbled in privateering. A few errors appear, as with the names of James D. Bulloch and John Slidell. The index is well done, as are illustrations and an appendix that outlines prize court procedures.

(Reprinted 1990, 372 pp., University of South Carolina Press, Columbia)

15

Scharf, J. Thomas. **History of the Confederate States Navy from Its Organization to the Surrender of Its Last Vessel: Its Stupendous Struggle with the Great Navy of the United States; The Engagements Fought in the Rivers and Harbors of the South, and Upon the High Seas: Blockade-Running, First Use of Iron-Clads and Torpedoes, and Privateer History** (824 pp., Rogers and Sherwood, New York, 1887)

This is a landmark work on Confederate naval history, written with the authority of an Confederate naval officer who experienced action in the war. It constitutes a general survey of all Confederate operations at sea and on rivers.

The author describes in detail the poor state of Confederate naval operations at the outset of war, including the organization of the Confederate Navy, the development of Confederate ironclads, and the operations of privateers. The river wars, the blockade, blockade-running, the construction of Confederate rams, various actions in Alabama, the Trans-Mississippi, Georgia, Florida, Virginia, and South Carolina, all constitute sections of real value. Additional chapters treat the Marine Corps, torpedo development, the Confederate States Naval Academy, and the cruisers. An appendix lists Confederate naval officers. A number of inaccurate names and dates are scattered throughout the work. Many of the chapters are carelessly assembled, leading to a somewhat incoherent presentation, and the work is flawed by an overzealous, partisan diatribe that surfaces from time to time. Overall, however, this book contains much of value, although the index is altogether too short.

(Reprinted 1988, 2 vols., 824 pp., Ayer, Salem)

16

Silverstone, Paul H. **Warships of the Civil War Navies** (271 pp., Naval Institute Press, Annapolis, 1989)

This is one of the finest late 20th-century works on Civil War naval warfare and is essential to any naval library. It presents the following information for all Civil War warships on each side: basic data including builder, the date each ship was laid down, dates of launch, dates of commissioning, tonnage, dimensions, machinery, complement, armament, and armor. Brief notes recount the service records of most ships, and the write-ups for many important ships include a photograph or engraving, comprising 230 altogether.

The Federal ships are divided into the following categories: armored vessels, unarmored steam vessels, acquired vessels, sailing vessels, acquired sailing vessels, the Mississippi River fleet, the U.S. Revenue Cutter Service, and the U.S. Coast Survey. The much smaller number of Confederate ships is divided as follows: ironclads, cruisers, sailing vessels, gunboats, spar torpedo boats, submarine torpedo boats, blockade-runners, the Louisiana-area Mississippi River Defense Fleet, Texas area ships, Gulf Coast area ships, Atlantic Coast area ships, Virginia area ships, and inland river vessels. Appendices list shipbuilders, and indices conveniently allow for finding Union and Confederate ship names.

17

Soley, J. Russell. **The Blockade and the Cruisers** (vol. 1 in Scribner's series The Navy in the Civil War, 266 pp., Charles Scribner's Sons, New York, 1883)

This book examines how the U.S. Navy responded to the outbreak of war in 1861 and how it later flexed its might by blockading the Confederacy. Soley's book is the best in Scribner's Navy series. It is solidly and well written, largely without bias—although the author occasionally refers to Confederates as "the enemy"—and draws insightful and elegant conclusions about the times, the men, and the actions involved. As Gary W. Gallagher points out, Soley overstates the case in some areas, such as describing the flawed Confederate ironclad CSS *Stonewall* as "formidable." To his credit, Soley does not hesitate to attack the Union Navy when warranted, most angrily criticizing the slowness of the effort at the outset of the war. Seven maps accompany the text.

(Reprinted 1989, with an introduction by Gary W. Gallagher, 266 pp., Broadfoot, Wilmington)

18

Still, William N., Jr. **Iron Afloat: The Story of the Confederate Armorclads** (260 pp., Vanderbilt University Press, Nashville, 1971)

This study contains some useful information on the poorly documented history of Confederate ironclad warfare. The author recounts in a chronological and geographical fashion how the problem-laden Confederate Navy developed a program of ironclad shipbuilding under the direction of Navy Secretary Stephen R. Mallory. The discussion ranges from the early efforts to obtain materials, design and construct ships with poor facilities, and employ the novel ideas of ironclad strategy to harass the Union war effort. The author's narrative includes insightful summaries of the careers of the CSS *Atlanta*, the CSS *Arkansas*, and the CSS *Virginia*, comprising some of the most engaging chapters of the work.

The enormous challenge of defending the rivers in the West and the harbors in the South and East merits considerable study, and this work devotes sufficient space to them. The author partially succeeds in backing his claim that the Rebel ironclads were "successful" as gunboats, although most of the 22 built were knocked out of commission before they could inflict severe damage. The reality of their psychological impact could be felt for a time, however, and is skillfully described in this work. Unfortunately a number of errors mar the text and index: "William A. Parker" is used when referring to William H. Parker, and the author misspells the names of John C. Breckinridge, Irvin McDowell, George G. Meade, Leonidas Polk, Frederick Steele, and Josiah Tattnall. The story also contains some questionable conclusions.

(Reprinted 1985, 262 pp., University of South Carolina Press, Columbia)

19

[U.S. Navy Department.] **Civil War Naval Chronology, 1861–1865** (ed. Ernest M. Eller, 1122 pp., U.S. Government Printing Office, Washington, 1971)

This volume is absolutely necessary for understanding the Civil War navies, as indispensable a reference as the *O.R.N.* (*q.v.*). Originally published in serial form during the Centennial and reissued as a single book, the work contains a mountain of documents, tables, photographs, and maps, as well as a detailed summary of naval actions for the entire war, predominantly viewed from the Federal side but also containing voluminous information on the Confederate Navy.

Five principal sections cover the war years (1860–1861, 1862, 1863, 1864, and 1865), and a sixth offers numerous appendices of great value, including essays on the makeup of Washington's naval defense force, identifying John Wilkes Booth, Lincoln's relationship with the navy (a somewhat misleading essay written from Gideon Welles's viewpoint), Marine Corps Pvt. Charles Brother's journal, Farragut at Mobile Bay, life aboard a Civil War ship, naval music of the war, a statistical summary of Confederate ships (including privateers, the river defense fleet, the Texas Marine Department, and the stone fleet), blockade-runners, salvaged and memorialized Civil War ships, and quotations relating to the naval war. Brilliantly executed, this work is a must-have for anyone with even a remote interest in the naval side of the war.

20

[U.S. Navy Department.] **Official Navy Register, 1860–1865** (6 vols., 1330 pp., U.S. Government Printing Office, Washington, 1860–1865)

This work contains the official status of U.S. Navy personnel in terms of grade and rank for the war years. The registers were published in 1860; 1 January 1861; 1 September 1862; 1 January 1863; 1 January 1864; and 1 January 1865. A volume ordered printed 1 January 1862 was internally circulated but not published for general distribution.

As with the U.S. Army registers (*q.v.*), the U.S. Navy registers contain pay tables of the officers, lists of personnel for the various bureaus and departments, lists of naval officers in the various grades, surgeons, paymasters, chaplains, professors, masters, passed midshipmen, midshipmen, boatswains, gunners, carpenters, sailmakers, Marine Corps officers, navy agents, storekeepers, engineers, naval constructors, and personnel of the Naval Academy. Additionally, the work presents resignations and casualties during the prior year, lists of vessels of war, laws of the navy, general orders, and special documents issued by the secretary of the navy.

21

[U.S. Navy Department.] **Official Records of the Union and Confederate Navies in the War of the Rebellion** (31 vols., 28,330 pp., U.S. Government Printing Office, Washington, 1894–1927)

Based in form on the *Official Records of the Union and Confederate Armies*, begun 14 years earlier, the *O.R.N.* (short for *Official Records, Navies*) contains the indispensable record of naval warfare during the war. As with the army records, the *O.R.N.* is not perfect and must be used cautiously. The records of the U.S. Navy are fairly complete, while many Confederate Navy records are missing from the compilation. Reports, letters, returns, and orders are sometimes contradictory and reflect the fallibility of individual commanders attempting to justify actions after they occurred. The set is best used by comparing all available reports on a given subject or action.

The *O.R.N.* contains 314 illustrations of representative ships, sketches, and maps. It is divided into two series and an index volume. Series 1 consists of 27 volumes and includes correspondence, reports, orders, and returns pertaining to Union and Confederate naval operations. Series 2 consists of three special volumes. Volume 1 contains statistical data on Union and Confederate ships, muster rolls of Confederate crews, Confederate letters of marque and reprisal, and Confederate Navy Department investigations. Volume 2 contains Confederate correspondence with naval agents. Volume 3 contains Confederate proclamations, appointments, correspondence, documents, reports, and logs. A single general index volume refers readers to the detailed indices in each volume for page entries.

The publication of the *O.R.N.* was authorized by an act of Congress on 7 July 1884, and the series was issued by the U.S. Government Printing Office between 1894 and 1927. The project was supervised by 10 successive secretaries of the navy. As is the case with most official government documents, the set was also published in the U.S. Government Serial set.

The impressive staff of naval personnel assigned to the task of compiling the *O.R.N.* included James R. Soley, first superintendent of the Office of Naval War Records; Lt. Comdr. F. M. Wise, second superintendent; Richard Rush, third superintendent; compiler Robert H. Woods; Edward K. Rawson, fourth superintendent; Charles W. Stewart, fifth superintendent; Comdr. George P. Colvocoresses; Capt. C. C. Marsh; Col. Harry K. White of the U.S. Marines Corps; and Capt. Dudley K. Knox.

The set has been reprinted several times (National Historical Society, Broadfoot, and Morningside). Between 1880 and 1901 the USGPO published an analogous set of official records of the Union and Confederate armies (*q.v.*).

22

[U.S. Navy Department.] **Register of Officers of the Confederate States Navy, 1861–1865, as Compiled and Revised by the Office of Naval Records and Library, United States Navy Department, 1931, from All Available Data** (220 pp., U.S. Government Printing Office, Washington, 1931)

Disappointing but without superiors, this book is an alphabetical list of Confederate naval officers with a brief annotation, birth and death dates, grade, date of rank, a short service record, and some data on paroles, captures, and woundings.

The work is incomplete and not altogether reliable, but it supersedes an earlier work, *Register of Commissioned and Warrant Officers of the Navy of the Confederate States to January 1, 1864: Including Organization of the Navy Dept., Laws of the Navy, General Orders and Circulars* (96 pp., MacFarlane and Fergusson, Richmond, 1864). The poor state of information on the Confederate Navy may be summarized by Dudley Knox's message in the 1931 work: "As data concerning Confederate naval officers is scattered and meager, this office will appreciate any authentic information leading to additional correction of errors or omissions which may have occurred."

(Reprinted 1983, 220 pp., John M. Carroll and Co., Mattituck, N.Y.)

23

Wise, Stephen R. **Lifeline of the Confederacy: Blockade Running during the Civil War** (403 pp., University of South Carolina Press, Columbia, 1988)

Wise accomplishes a fearsome task by presenting an astonishing amount of information—nearly 25 percent of the work consists of statistical appendices—and then managing to make the data readable, interesting, and highly enlightening. The many facets of running the blockade receive coverage, from the ships used to the people and companies behind them and the origins, nature, and disposition of the goods that passed through the Federal Navy. Additionally, much of interest can be found on sunken blockade-runners and the evolution of the need for breaking through the tightening grip of the North.

The work demonstrates how Southerners responded to the blockade by at first using nearly every available vessel but ultimately financing a program of designing and building blockade-runners, principally in England. The 22 appendices provide a mountain of raw data on the ships used, their construction, the dates and times of departures and arrivals, and the ships that were destroyed or fell into Union hands. This impressively detailed work will stand for a considerable time as the definitive book of its type.

CIVIL WAR IN THE WEST (1861–1865)

24

Castel, Albert E. **A Frontier State at War: Kansas, 1861–1865** (251 pp., American Historical Association and Cornell University Press, Ithaca, 1958)

This study examines the military and political aspects of Bleeding Kansas during the war years. It fills a void in a weakly covered area of the literature, and does so in an admirable way.

Castel provides a sweeping and somewhat overdrawn portrait of Kansas on the eve of the Civil War. To highlight the frontier aspect of many of its citizens, he describes the House of Representatives as an "old shack" and paints a generally deplorable picture of the land, its buildings, and the character of many of its inhabitants. He may be exaggerating, but it helps him lift a good story out of what seems like a dull and unlikely place.

Many important Kansans receive judicious discussion,

including James H. Lane, Charles Robinson, Thomas Ewing, Jr., and James G. Blunt. Lane is a recipient of particular scrutiny for his endless overtures toward Lincoln, who necessarily paid considerable attention to the senator. Much of the narrative plays off the rivalry between Lane and Governor Robinson and Lincoln's distant relationship to it.

A few errors of fact appear, such as linking John Brown with the name "Osawatomie Brown," a sobriquet given to Osawatomie businessman Orvice C. Brown. Still, the book makes a substantial contribution to understanding the nebulous role of Kansas during the war years.

(Reprinted 1992, with an introduction by Edward E. Leslie, 251 pp., Kansas Heritage Press, Lawrence)

25

Fellman, Michael. **Inside War: The Guerrilla Conflict in Missouri during the American Civil War** (331 pp., Oxford University Press, New York, 1989)

This work sets a high standard in documenting the peculiar aspects of Missouri's many minor actions. The state's unique combination of a small number of active engagements and a larger number of minor guerrilla skirmishes made it a terrifying and destructive place during the war. The author explores in this highly original work the political and economic climate of Missouri before the war, guerrilla activities on both sides, the civilian response to guerrilla warfare, the death of slavery in Missouri, Union and Confederate policies in the state, women's roles in surviving the terror, and the emergence of postwar Missouri.

Fellman draws on a wide assemblage of diaries, reports, transcripts, and depositions to piece together a comprehensive picture of the guerrilla activities, often using quotations. The result is a superb look into what the author believes was a "natural, popular war" that existed under special circumstances different from those in other areas. The book's organization results in some repetition, although much of the material cited comes from the final two years of the war. Vivid portraits of some well-known guerrillas such as "Bloody" Bill Anderson emerge, as do introductions to lesser known characters such as Missouri Militia Brig. Gen. Odon Guitar. Errors creep into the text, however, as with the misspellings of John C. Breckinridge, A. J. McRoberts, and the towns of Sedalia and Forsyth. Poor indexing created the entries "Jubal T. Early" and "Thomas E. Ewing." Such errors do little to reduce the enjoyable content of this volume, however, which belongs on every shelf devoted to the Civil War in the West.

26

Goodrich, Thomas. **Black Flag: Guerrilla Warfare on the Western Border, 1861–1865** (172 pp., Indiana University Press, Bloomington, 1995)

This volume offers a modern interpretation of the chaotic mess in the Far West. It provides a good entrance into the subject by delivering a brief yet rich narrative of the many troubles concentrated in the western states as the slavery controversy ignited. Rife with incidents in Missouri and Kansas, the book draws on a respectable collection of previously published works in addition to manuscript sources, newspaper accounts, diaries, and letters to piece together a picture of the bloody border wars with suitably vivid drama.

Goodrich delivers a picture of a vengeful war often told in the words of the participants. He surveys the massacres at Lawrence, Centralia, and Baxter Springs, enlightening the view of William Quantrill and other guerrilla leaders, bushwhackers, and desperadoes. The journey introduces readers to an assemblage of strange characters, including James H. Lane, Charles Jennison, James G. Blunt, and "Bloody" Bill Anderson. The story is infused with excitement and the author's smooth prose makes the work enjoyably readable.

27

Hall, Martin Hardwick. **Sibley's New Mexico Campaign** (366 pp., University of Texas Press, Austin, 1960)

This book casts light on a neglected aspect of the war in the Far West. It highlights in detail the primary action of the early warfare in the territories, providing a natural companion volume to the more general works of Ray C. Colton (*q.v.*), Alvin M. Josephy, Jr. (*q.v.*), and Robert L. Kerby (*q.v.*).

Hall's work offers an eloquent summary of Confederate Brig. Gen. Henry Hopkins Sibley's ill-fated plan to march his army of 3700 from Texas across Arizona and on to California. The author describes accurately the empty actions at Fort Craig and Valverde and goes on to provide the interesting details of the Confederates' fruitless attempts at plundering Albuquerque and Santa Fe, nicely building toward a description of La Glorieta Pass. Readers of the material treating the anticlimactic retreat to Texas that followed will understand why Sibley's standing among the Confederate high command sank rapidly (Sibley returned with only 1500 of his command). The author provides a significant and well-executed study that includes substantial muster rolls for the soldiers involved.

28

Josephy, Alvin M., Jr. **The Civil War in the American West** (448 pp., Alfred A. Knopf, New York, 1991)

In detailed and well-researched prose, Josephy skillfully outlines the background of the significance of the Trans-Mississippi West in the Civil War era. He then explores a large number of minor actions and several major areas of importance—Pea Ridge, Glorieta Pass, campaigns in Louisiana waged by Nathaniel P. Banks, and Indian actions in Minnesota and the Far West. This fine synthesis touches on all of the major actions of the Trans-Mississippi theater and delivers a thoughtful narrative on many personalities in the Trans-Mississippi, in Washington, and in Richmond. The material that supports the descriptions of campaigns and battles includes a recap of the political and military status of various western regions, such as details of secession in Texas and its relation to the events that followed in the area, including Glorieta Pass. An excellent map accompanies each section.

The work does have some shortcomings. Discussions of events in the Trans-Mississippi are grouped by region, leading to a somewhat difficult to interpret, nonchronological organization. The book legitimately focuses on military matters, a much-needed aspect with regard to this theater, but it comes up short on interpreting the meaning of the battles and campaigns in the larger canvas of the war, at least in political and societal terms. Much of the opportunity for new interpretation belongs to ideas on minority groups. Indians are handled well, but what about blacks in the Trans-Mississippi? Such a previously poorly documented area might have been explored more fully. The work is important, well executed, and, so far as it goes, a valuable addition to the literature of the Civil War in the West.

29

Monaghan, Jay. **Civil War on the Western Border, 1854–1865** (454 pp., Little, Brown and Co., Boston, 1955)

This is the standard work on the border struggle in Kansas and Missouri. Too often relegated to the rear of Civil War historiography, this theater conveyed psychological significance before the war and real significance during the war. As such, it deserves full and scholarly treatment, and Monaghan's work delivers nicely on that premise.

The author neatly summarizes the various clashes that made Kansas bleed and Missouri weep throughout the 1850s. The delicate balance between free-state power and proslavery forces established the terrorized mood of the border residents as war approached. Slightly more than the first quarter of the book sets this antebellum stage, and the rest accurately and insightfully describes the region's experience of civil war.

Nathaniel Lyon and his role in Missouri dominate the next sections until, of course, his death at Wilson's Creek. The author describes the actions at Lexington, Pea Ridge, Prairie Grove, Pilot Knob, and Westport. He traces the downfall of Frémont and describes the anger of the slave-holding Creek Indians who fought for the Confederacy. Monaghan briefly describes Quantrill's Lawrence Massacre and provides a contextual view from Washington and Richmond. He delivers a book that will leave students of the western war fully satisfied.

(Reprinted 1984, 454 pp., University of Nebraska Press, Lincoln)

30

Oates, Stephen B. **Confederate Cavalry West of the River** (234 pp., University of Texas Press, Austin, 1961)

Although this work is somewhat limited in scope and significance to Civil War operations, the author brings to life this arena of Rebel operations with full documentation, artistic writing, and a flair for telling the humorous anecdote.

Significant actions described include Prairie Grove, raids in Missouri by Maj. Gen. John S. Marmaduke and Brig. Gen. Jo Shelby, and Maj. Gen. Sterling Price's Missouri expedition. Oates has clearly invested meticulous research into his narrative and woven a story that, despite the theater's distance from the "real action," illuminates and engages the reader at the highest level of campaign studies. Confederate commands in the Trans-Mississippi West somehow attracted real eccentrics, and the author takes full advantage of their peculiar personalities.

(Reprinted 1992, 234 pp., University of Texas Press, Austin)

ALL OTHERS

Fort Sumter, South Carolina (12 April 1861)

31

Crawford, Samuel Wylie. **The Genesis of the Civil War: The Story of Sumter, 1860–1861** (486 pp., C. L. Webster and Co., New York, 1887)

This account of the secession crisis and the bombardment of Sumter is by the physician who was on Robert Anderson's staff during the battle. The author later served as a brigade commander through the eastern battles, commanded the Pennsylvania Reserves at Gettysburg, and rose to the grade of brevet major general in the regular army. The work concentrates on the genesis of the war, however, which required Crawford to reexamine the political and military history of the period preceding the bombardment of Sumter. Crawford studies President Buchanan's handling of the secession crisis and devotes more than 100 pages to the political scheming in South Carolina and Washington that occurred before Anderson's move to Sumter.

The focus of the work, however, is the story of the forts in Charleston harbor during 1860 and the first four months of 1861. Crawford utilizes the written record, numerous official documents and letters, his own experience, and the recollections and papers of other officers who were present at Sumter and Moultrie. He surveys the seizure of harbor forts by South Carolina authorities, the *Star of the West* incident, Lincoln's handling of the crisis, and Winfield Scott's background and views. The final 50 pages describe the bombardment itself. Although the account is enthralling and useful in places because of Crawford's participation, one wishes he would have emphasized his own experience more, rather than feeling duty bound to record the whole story in an objective way.

(Reprinted 1896, titled *The History of the Fall of Fort Sumter,* 486 pp., C. L. Webster and Co., New York)

32

Doubleday, Abner. **Reminiscences of Forts Sumter and Moultrie in 1860–'61** (184 pp., Harper and Bros., New York, 1876)

This slender volume holds more value than some of the general's other writings. Well written and immersed in first-hand recollections, the work describes the beginning of the war from the time Doubleday was stationed at Fort Moultrie to the fall of Fort Sumter, when the author left the fort with Maj. Robert Anderson and traveled north. Doubleday blames Secretary of War John B. Floyd for complicity in helping the South by arming the Southern forts, which Floyd fully expected Southerners to occupy with little resistance. The author expected David G. Farragut to be ordered south with 300 men on the USS *Brooklyn,* and seems amazed at the delayed mission of the feeble *Star of the West.* The latter was, of course, no match for Charleston's defensive batteries.

The account of the Confederate bombardment of Sumter is accomplished in magnificent detail. With insufficient gun crews and ammunition, the fort was indefensible. The author describes the inevitable surrender as ammunition ran low and the heavy attack shook the brick façade and burned

the wooden barracks. An appendix provides a roster of officers, enlisted men, and laborers present at Sumter during the bombardment and a list of Confederate commanders and their units around Charleston Harbor in April 1861.

(Reprinted 1976, 177 pp., Reprint Co., Spartanburg, S.C.)

33

Nicolay, John G. **The Outbreak of Rebellion** [vol. 1 in Scribner's series Campaigns of the Civil War, 226 pp., Charles Scribner's Sons, New York, 1881)

Nicolay's work is the first of the 13-volume set published by Scribner's in the 1880s. This book describes the opening scenes of the war as recorded by Nicolay, who served as Lincoln's private secretary.

The volume is generally well done, and covers the period from secession in South Carolina to the retreat following First Bull Run. The narrative is for the most part balanced, but Nicolay downplays the causes of the war and the force of Southern patriotism, assigning the rebellion to the minority of slaveholders who pushed the South into war. He straightforwardly asserts that Lincoln politically engineered the firing on Sumter. His view is naturally one-sided—from a window in the White House. Consequently, ex-Confederates did not appreciate the work when it first appeared. Despite this, the book retains its importance as a primary source. Eight maps accompany the text.

(Reprinted 1989, with an introduction by Gary W. Gallagher, 226 pp., Broadfoot, Wilmington; 1881 edition reprinted 1995, with an introduction by Mark E. Neely, Jr., 226 pp., Da Capo Press, New York)

34

Swanberg, W. A. **First Blood: The Story of Fort Sumter** (373 pp., Charles Scribner's Sons, New York, 1957)

Rather lightly documented and written with a literary flair, this work is generally reliable but depends on a narrow range of sources for most of its assessments. These include the *O.R.* (*q.v.*), Samuel Wylie Crawford's *The Genesis of the Civil War* (*q.v.*), and a handful of other works. Although it lacks the kind of in-depth analysis and grand review of the background political crisis that would make it a definitive work, it is a useful summary of the important actions surrounding the attack on Sumter.

The coverage ranges from the days of the November 1860 election through the attack on Sumter on 12 April 1861, and includes a brief section on the flag raising by Federal officers four years later. Swanberg characterizes many participants in the political and military game of early 1861, writing with descriptive flair and supporting most of his conclusions. But the very first page of the work signals an irritating flaw: the use of imaginary "reconstructed" conversations. This limits the credibility of the work in a number of key places, despite the documentation elsewhere. If readers can forgive this flaw, the work may be viewed as a good general summary of the Fort Sumter crisis.

First Bull Run, Virginia (21 July 1861)

35

Beauregard, G. T. **A Commentary on the Campaign and Battle of Manassas, of July 1861: With a Summary of the Art of War** (187 pp., G. P. Putnam's Sons, New York, 1891)

This book is valuable for its psychological portrait of Beauregard. An expanded article composed originally in response to writings by Joe Johnston, the work is a bitter attack on Johnston and a defense of Beauregard's actions at First Bull Run as well as a review of many disputed claims that arose over the 30 intervening years. It presents a minute examination of the campaign and battle supported by selective testimony and documents provided by Jefferson Davis, Beauregard, Johnston, and others. The aim is to show that Johnston waived command of the army on the field at First Bull Run, passing it to Beauregard; that the latter concocted the strategy that led to Confederate victory; and that Johnston maneuvered Beauregard into a position of accepting blame for a possible defeat. Moreover, the author raises many incidental questions of Johnston's truthfulness in writings about the campaign, in the *Century* magazine and in Johnston's own *Narrative* (*q.v.*).

Such a work may have been more effective if not infused with anger. Beauregard raises some fair criticisms, displays some inconsistencies on the part of Johnston, and fairly shows himself as key to the battlefield strategy at First Bull Run. But he condemns Johnston and others beyond the limits of reason, attempts to receive all credit for anything positive that occurred on the field, and egotistically appends a summary of the art of war designed to further buttress his claims. At a certain point the effect diminishes Beauregard's credibility, and readers can see that neither extreme position, that taken by Johnston or by Beauregard, can be completely true. The work contains two crude maps of the Bull Run battlefield and lacks an index.

36

Davis, William C. **Battle at Bull Run: A History of the First Major Campaign of the Civil War** (298 pp., Doubleday and Co., Garden City, N.Y., 1977)

In this book-length summary of the first major battle of the war, Davis draws on an impressively large number of primary sources and lists in the bibliography a voluminous collection of secondary sources as well. The work makes good reading and presents a generally balanced account of the battle. Coverage in the introductory sections extends as far ahead as the beginning of the war, and brief summaries introduce major characters and the military situation prior to McDowell's march southward. To its credit, the work does not merely focus on the battle but explains the related maneuvers in the Shenandoah Valley, on the Peninsula, in Washington, and in Richmond. The author has cleanly drawn a portrait that allows readers to participate in the irrepressible clash that happened to take place along Bull Run.

The tale that unfolds follows a predictable path, with McDowell coming off as a bungler and Federal commanders Dixon S. Miles, Dan Tyler, and Robert Patterson receiving harsh criticism. Pierre G. T. Beauregard receives poor marks on the Confederate side, although Davis allows more breathing room for Confederate decisions and enjoys downplaying the competence of Federal soldiers and officers, perhaps for the sake of heightened drama. The rout of the Yankees has historically and almost universally been overdrawn, and the author continues this tradition. In a strategic sense, the Federal retreat from the field represented a complete loss, but it seemed devastating mostly because the expectations were so high. Several careless misspellings appear, as with "Bernard E. Bee," "Elmer E. Ellsworth," and "Rose O'Neale Greenhow," and the book's maps are merely adequate. But overall, this is a well-researched work that delivers a handsome portrait of the war's first big affair.

37

Patterson, Robert. **A Narrative of the Campaign in the Valley of the Shenandoah, in 1861** (128 pp., John Campbell, Philadelphia, 1865)

This work attempts to vindicate Patterson from his sloppy performance during the first major campaign of the eastern war. A target of heavy criticism (and rightly so) for his poor performance, Patterson strikes back in the pages of this work, which reads like an official report. He outlines the supposed misunderstanding between him and Winfield Scott over responsibility for Patterson's actions. According to Patterson, the trouble arose over the government's deployment of three-month troops whose service period had nearly expired. He adds much of interest by inclusion of many military dispatches relating to the campaign, although the overall effect is not terribly convincing.

Wilson's Creek, Missouri (10 August 1861)

38

Bearss, Edwin C. **The Battle of Wilson's Creek** (170 pp., Artcraft Printers, Bozeman, Mont., 1975)

Based largely on the *O.R.* (*q.v.*) and a few secondary sources, this work outlines in straightforward fashion the occupation of Springfield, the engagement at Dug Springs, and the battle itself. Bearss chronicles rather well the plans and movements of units on both sides, paying particular attention to Nathaniel Lyon, Ben McCulloch, and Franz Sigel. He documents his work adequately, and delivers the story of important and not-so important events with an even-handed balance.

The workmanlike prose gains momentum as the battle erupts. The discussion of Sigel's incompetent actions and the evolution of the action on Bloody Hill is described vividly and with excellent anecdotes interjected. Several hand-drawn maps place units and camps. An appendix lists commanders, strengths, and casualties of each army engaged at Wilson's Creek.

(Reprinted 1992, 170 pp., Wilson's Creek Battlefield Foundation, Cassville, Mo.)

Ball's Bluff, Virginia (21 October 1861)

39

Farwell, Byron. **Ball's Bluff: A Small Battle and Its Long Shadow** (232 pp., EPM Publications, McLean, Va., 1990)

This work can be recommended in lieu of a fuller, more scholarly study of this small and confused action. The author writes that, "like a perfect Greek tragedy, [Ball's Bluff] had a distinct beginning, middle, and end." Suggesting that the battle had no strategic importance, Farwell nonetheless points out that the individual actions of many of its participants had great significance. He moves on to deliver a dramatic narrative of the action and to sweep across the experiences of many who fought it.

The text concentrates wholly on Ball's Bluff as a military affair. Discussion of movements, orders, attacks, and the reactions of troops is well composed yet undocumented, which leaves a nagging feeling that unsupported conjecture sneaks into the work even where the author delivers a straightforward account. Farwell examines the arrest of C. P. Stone, the examination of the battle by the Committee on the Conduct of the War, and the prisoners and casualties. Like the battle itself, however, this work in the end is unremarkable. It lacks an index and contains a selected bibliography with some questionable sources.

Belmont, Missouri (7 November 1861)

40

Hughes, Nathaniel Cheairs, Jr. **The Battle of Belmont: Grant Strikes South** (310 pp., University of North Carolina Press, Chapel Hill, 1991)

The author explores a neglected fight whose significance toward the evolving campaigns for the Mississippi is frequently underperceived. Like Hughes's earlier works, this book is built on a solid and careful job of research. The author's analysis of the events of 7 November 1861 surprisingly does not focus on Ulysses S. Grant. Instead, Grant—who directed his first battle at Belmont—shares the spotlight with Confederate commanders Leonidas Polk and Gideon J. Pillow and a host of minor officers. This is, the author suggests, in part due to Grant's peculiar report on the battle. The result is a bit surprising but in a very delightful way.

Supplemented by an array of impressive maps, the study explores the journeys of the Union and Confederate forces in southeastern Missouri and the preparations for the Confederate defense of Belmont and nearby Columbus, Kentucky. The narrative describes the battle with ample detail, often buttressed by stories of common soldiers. The discussion of Pillow's poor tactical plans and maneuvers reveals much about this pathetic figure. The author's description of the depletion of Grant's army after pushing away the defenders is first-rate. Hughes makes clear the sometimes confused way in which the clash unfolded, in part because of the heavily wooded terrain. The work rightly criticizes Union Navy Comdr. Henry Walke for inadequate support at crucial times and Polk, of course, for failed opportunities in not striking back at Grant and possibly inflicting significant losses. The work is clear and detailed and serves to reverse the long-standing neglect of this interesting action.

Forts Henry and Donelson, Tennessee (6–16 February 1862)

41

Cooling, Benjamin F. **Forts Henry and Donelson: Key to the Confederate Heartland** (354 pp., University of Tennessee Press, Knoxville, 1988)

In a well-written, meticulously researched, and properly documented study, Cooling concludes that the campaign of Forts Henry and Donelson began a domino effect that led to Shiloh and the deep penetration into the Mississippi River Valley that ultimately broke the western theater of the Confederacy. Therefore, the author argues, Forts Henry and Donelson played a much more important role than they have typically been credited with and deserve significant treatment. Fortunately, they receive a beautiful summary in this book, as does Grant's first major victory and its effects on his rising stature in the minds of War Department officials.

The early earthwork fortifications constructed along the Tennessee and Cumberland Rivers were poorly situated given Kentucky's early neutrality. The author shows that Confederate defenders did nothing to improve or relocate the defenses, in part because they did not perceive a serious threat to the area. Cooling's narrative of the campaign begins in February with Grant's and Flag Officer Andrew H. Foote's movement on Henry, which easily overtook the position. He skillfully describes one of the Union Navy's first signal triumphs, as their gunboat bombardment reduced the fort before Grant's troops became involved.

Cooling contends that panic in the Confederate chain of command exacerbated the situation and that a measured, determined approach might have successfully driven Grant's army from Donelson. He chastises Albert Sidney Johnston for abandoning his theater and describes in detail the nearly comic passing of command from Floyd and Pillow and their subsequent flight. There are annoying misspellings of names, such as those of John C. Breckinridge, Mary Chesnut, Justin Dimick, John Buchanan Floyd, Stephen Hurlbut, and Leonidas Polk, and Cooling not only confuses William Nelson Pendleton with his son Alexander ("Sandie") but often confuses the reader by using abbreviated names or initials rather than full names. The work is a significant success, however, despite these rather minor flaws.

42

Force, Manning F. **From Fort Henry to Corinth** (vol. 2 in Scribner's series Campaigns of the Civil War, 204 pp., Charles Scribner's Sons, New York, 1881)

This book describes the early war in the West, including Grant's capture of Forts Henry and Donelson and the battles of New Madrid, Island No. 10, Shiloh, and Corinth. The great asset of this work is Force's painstaking research that places units and strengths accurately and substantiates the conclusions he draws. More than half the book gives a detailed description of Shiloh, a battle in which the author participated under Maj. Gen. Lew Wallace. Disappointingly, Force's reluctance to assess his superiors prevents him from shedding light on Wallace's controversial late arrival on the Shiloh battlefield. The chief drawback of the work is a narrative that plods along. Eight maps accompany the text.

(Reprinted 1989, with an introduction by Allen C. Guelzo, 204 pp., Broadfoot, Wilmington)

Pea Ridge, Arkansas (4–8 March 1862)

43

Shea, William L., and Earl J. Hess. **Pea Ridge: Civil War Campaign in the West** (417 pp., University of North Carolina Press, Chapel Hill, 1992)

This is a wonderful book that fills a big gap in the literature. The authors trace the movements of Union Maj. Gen. Samuel R. Curtis's Army of the Southwest and Confederate Maj. Gen. Earl Van Dorn's Army of the West, their clash at Pea Ridge, and what the battle meant in the larger picture of the war. In treating this largest Trans-Mississippi Civil War battle, the authors offer penetrating portraits of the commanders, a detailed and engaging description of the battle, well-done maps, and modern photographs of important sites on the field.

To liberate Missouri, Van Dorn pieced together forces under Sterling Price and Ben McCulloch. The resulting battle was essentially two engagements, at Leetown and at Elkhorn Tavern. The authors describe the deaths of McCulloch and Brig. Gen. James M. McIntosh and the resulting chaos in the Confederate command structure in the Elkhorn Tavern area. The Leetown battle was also a Confederate rout, and the descriptions of Indians participating in the fighting are handled in a most interesting fashion. The authors show how the dual catastrophe for the Confederate forces resulted in hopelessness in regaining control of Missouri and also, ultimately, the loss of Arkansas. It was a disaster for the

South. This work is a gem that provides all the significant characteristics of a well-executed battle study.

USS *Monitor* vs. CSS *Virginia,* Hampton Roads, Virginia (8 March 1862)

44

Davis, William C. **Duel between the First Ironclads** (201 pp., Doubleday and Co., Garden City, N.Y., 1975)

This book constitutes a history of the evolution of ironclad warfare, the building of Ericsson's *Monitor,* the reconfiguring of the USS *Merrimack* into the CSS *Virginia,* an account of the major characters involved, and a compelling and accurately rendered story of the famous battle. Amazingly, the author has delivered this in a compact package that makes use of an economy of language, absorbing writing, and a first-rate job of research.

The narrative describes the difficult and intriguing personalities of John Ericsson and the *Monitor*'s commander, Lt. John L. Worden. Davis shows that Worden was a capable if not outstanding ship's captain, and details the problematical designing and construction of the revolutionary *Monitor.* Elevating Ericsson to a position of genius, the author shows how the Swedish-born inventor devised a ship that made effective use not only of armor plating but of a shallow draft, fair speed, and the revolving turret that resulted in a revolutionary change in naval tactics. Davis also covers Confederate naval officer John M. Brooke's rebuilding of the *Merrimack* and suggests it resulted in an "ersatz ironclad" that could not effectively withstand the *Monitor*'s superior design. He skillfully details the subsequent destruction of the *Virginia,* the loss of the *Monitor,* and the legacies of both ships.

Peninsular Campaign, Virginia (17 March– 1 July 1862)

45

Dowdey, Clifford. **The Seven Days: The Emergence of Lee** (380 pp., Little, Brown and Co., Boston, 1964)

Dowdey has compiled a military history of the Seven Days battles from the Confederate side. The result is a work that explores some old themes and offers a solid and interesting narrative. Describing the actions at Seven Pines and Fair Oaks, the author outlines Joe Johnston's command of the campaign until his serious wounding. He then introduc-es readers to Robert E. Lee's handling of the remainder of the campaign and, through lively and lightly documented prose, reconstructs the Seven Days battles themselves.

Clearly Dowdey is devoted to Lee, and he occasionally overlooks the larger picture of events in the Confederate and Union armies. He suggests that Stonewall Jackson's poor performance should be attributed to overstress in the wake of the Valley campaign. Nonetheless, this depiction of the many small actions that made the Seven Days succeeds admirably.

(Reprinted 1993, with an introduction by Robert K. Krick, 400 pp., University of Nebraska Press, Lincoln)

46

Sears, Stephen W. **To the Gates of Richmond: The Peninsula Campaign** (468 pp., Ticknor and Fields, New York, 1992)

Written in an enjoyable style and the product of tight research, this work has much to recommend it. It analyzes the genesis of the movement up the Peninsula, explores in admirable detail the siege of Yorktown, the battle of Williamsburg, the battle of Seven Pines, the advance of Stonewall Jackson into the picture, Stuart's ride, the entrance of Robert E. Lee as army commander, and the Seven Days battles. Sears accomplishes all of this by drawing on a wide range of sources from both armies and offering an opinionated critique of an astonishing number of commanders and decisions made along the way. The text remains balanced on both sides, and the accompanying maps, engravings, and photographs add greatly to the readers' grasp of a doomed Union strategy.

The author's works relating to George McClellan establish a basis for his interpretation of the general offered here. "Little Mac" comes away badly bruised, most often rightly so. Surprisingly, however, so do some of his subordinates, including such generally capable officers as Fitz John Porter. Conversely, the tarnished reputation of Stonewall Jackson receives delicate treatment, an interpretation many readers might quarrel with. The completeness of the story and the masterful grasp of characters and events boost this volume into a superior position, making it one of the better campaign studies.

47

Smith, Gustavus W. **The Battle of Seven Pines** (202 pp., C. G. Crawford, New York, 1891)

The work is a rarity in that it presents a detailed narrative of the first major battle on the Peninsula in 1862 from the pen of a Confederate major general who commanded the battle briefly following the severe wounding of Joe

Johnston. Taken with caution, Smith's book, with its accusations and apologies, is a valuable addition to the literature on the bungled action that permitted Robert E. Lee to rise to prominence. The opportunity provided by a separated Federal Army might have proved valuable for Johnston, commanding the Confederate forces, and he ordered an attack on the two corps south of the James, those commanded by Erasmus D. Keyes and Samuel P. Heintzelman. Although a good idea in principle, the attack was a complete failure, planned poorly, executed in an uncoordinated, piecemeal fashion, and badly supported. It failed, and in the process Johnston was wounded, yielding the command to Smith, the author of this work.

Smith strongly defends Johnston and blames others, most notably James Longstreet, for failing to press the attack sufficiently. Longstreet in turn blames Benjamin Huger, who did not carry out his orders effectively, and Johnston, for sluggish direction. Meanwhile, Smith himself was clearly to blame for a significant delay in employing his own division during the attack. Despite the roundtable of allegations, careful readers will find much of value in this work if they can uncover the facts, which in most instances are present but buried beneath the accusations.

(Reprinted 1974, 202 pp., Morningside, Dayton)

48

Webb, Alexander S. **The Peninsula: McClellan's Campaign of 1862** (vol. 3 in Scribner's series Campaigns of the Civil War, 219 pp., Charles Scribner's Sons, New York, 1881)

This work is an all-facts military description of the movements and engagements of the armies. It is reliable and evenhanded and remains, as it was at the time of publication, one of the best sources on the campaign. As an experienced artillerist and William F. Barry's acting inspector general, Webb played a role in the campaign that established the potential for a great story, which shines through in the descriptions of several of the Seven Days battles, particularly Gaines's Mill and Malvern Hill.

Webb gingerly assigns blame to the president for certain elements of the failed campaign, particularly the use of McDowell to protect the Shenandoah Valley and to screen Washington. And he solidly criticizes McClellan. Webb's narrative is objective, generally fair in its conclusions, and reveals a slight bedazzlement by the Confederates and their commanders. Eight maps accompany the text.

(Reprinted 1989, with an introduction by William F. Howard, 219 pp., Broadfoot, Wilmington)

Shiloh, Tennessee (6–7 April 1862)

49

Sword, Wiley. **Shiloh: Bloody April** (519 pp., William Morrow and Co., New York, 1974)

This is a detailed and splendidly written blow-by-blow assessment of the conflict on the Tennessee River that draws heavily on both the *O.R.* (*q.v.*) and a wide-ranging array of memoirs, letters, and reports scattered in a great variety of places. Unfortunately, the work is flawed. Sword views the battle primarily from the Confederate standpoint in terms of strategy, while the driving strategy of the Union penetration southward was the important factor in the theater at that time. Moreover, by not using some significant available sources relating to the western theater, he sometimes oversimplifies. He also does not seize the opportunity to shed new light on the controversies of Shiloh, such as Lew Wallace's arrival and performance on the field.

These disappointments aside, Sword provides a gripping story of Shiloh that makes excellent use of the human aspects of war, its suffering, terror, and meaning (or lack thereof). Because of this, his book, which is among the more interesting modern works on a significant battle, should be read by all students of the war.

(Reprinted 1993, with a new introduction by the author, 519 pp., Morningside, Dayton)

Fort Pulaski, Georgia (10–11 April 1862)

50

Gillmore, Quincy A. **Official Report to the United States Engineer Department of the Siege and Reduction of Fort Pulaski, Georgia, February, March, and April 1862** (96 pp., D. Van Nostrand Co., New York, 1862)

This relatively brief military report nonetheless contains much of value on the historic fall of Fort Pulaski. The event showed that brick masonry forts were no match for the new rifled cannon, and Gillmore's direction of the batteries that breached Pulaski is here described in minute detail. The report, sent to Chief Engineer Joseph G. Totten, consists of 55 percent of the work. The author presents the story of the reduction of the fort, highlighting the bombardment, its planning, and the effects of what it meant to brick forts.

Lengthy appendices offer a letter of Gillmore's to William T. Sherman, leading the expeditionary forces, and special orders outlining the batteries involved, including Stanton, Grant, Burnside, Sherman, Halleck, and Totten.

The work presents elaborate, hand-colored maps but lacks an index.

(Reprinted 1988, 96 pp., Thomas Publications, Gettysburg)

Andrews's Raid, Georgia (12 April 1862)

51

Angle, Craig. **The Great Locomotive Chase** (354 pp., published by the author, Rouzerville, Pa., 1992)

In stark contrast to Pittenger's book (*q.v.*), this study contains a description of the origin of the raid, a lengthy narrative of the operation itself, and a discussion of the fates at the gallows and in prison of the raiders who did not escape. Angle presents lengthy connective material, but describes the story largely in the words of the surviving raiders themselves, drawing on testimony they provided to the War Department after reaching Washington. A significant cache of material from the pursuing Confederates also appears, providing a running account of the details of the raid as it unfolded.

The testimony contributes a more meaningful set of material than that in Pittenger's highly emotional work. In Angle's book, Pittenger himself describes much about the raid, as do Daniel Dorsey, William A. Fuller, Anthony Murphy, Jacob Parrott, John R. Porter, William H. Reddick, and J. Alfred Wilson. Angle's extensive treatment of prison life for the captured and spared raiders is quite good. Photographs and maps add much to this volume, which fills a gap concerning one of the most dramatic adventures of the war.

52

Pittenger, William. **Daring and Suffering: A History of the Great Railroad Adventure** (288 pp., J. W. Daughaday, Philadelphia, 1863)

In gripping, first-person, and often highly partisan language, Pittenger recounts the story of Andrews's Raid, and as one of the raiders drawn from the 2d Ohio Infantry, one of the six survivors exchanged in March 1863. His story, occasionally containing re-created "conversations" and written with the appropriate spirit of youth, conveys the experience of joining James J. Andrews's gang of 22, who were ultimately captured, traveling south from Chattanooga under aliases, and capturing the General at Big Shanty. The real excitement of the work of course lies in the ensuing chase, and the bare facts here are sound. The experiential nature of the account gives it tremendous power despite frequent overdramatization. Equally as valuable are the tales of prison life in Chat-

tanooga, Knoxville, Atlanta, and Richmond. The eyewitness account of the last experiences of the eight condemned prisoners is valuable if brief. Overall, a superb story resides in this work despite the intrusion of unappealing qualities. The work lacks an index.

Many subsequent editions of this tale have appeared, each containing additional and reworked material, but none capture the sense of immediacy of the original. Variant titles include *The Great Locomotive Chase: A History of the Andrews Railroad Raid into Georgia* and *Capturing a Locomotive: A History of Secret Service in the Late War*.

(Reprinted 1982, 288 pp., Time-Life Books, Alexandria, Va.)

New Orleans, Louisiana (18–25 April 1862)

53

Hearn, Chester G. **The Capture of New Orleans, 1862** (292 pp., Louisiana State University Press, Baton Rouge, 1995)

From a strategic point of view, the loss of New Orleans was a crucial blow to the Confederate effort in the West and was arguably a blow the Confederate military effort never fully recovered from. In this well-documented and well-researched volume, Hearn outlines the echoes of an occupied New Orleans: the loss of the Trans-Mississippi from the eastern war effort, a tightening of the blockade's effects on the Southern home front, and the devastating psychological setback of losing control of the South's largest city. The capture of New Orleans may not have lost the war, but it certainly was a milestone on the path toward defeat.

This work offers a solid discussion of wartime New Orleans and excels at detailing Farragut's journey from Ship Island to the battles of Forts Jackson and St. Philip. The account of the pre-invasion bombardment and the headlong rush beyond the *Manassas* is absorbing. The author's analysis of Farragut's destruction of the Rebel fleet and the resulting surrender is first rate.

Jackson's Valley Campaign, Virginia (May–17 June 1862)

54

Allan, William. **History of the Campaign of Gen. T. J. (Stonewall) Jackson in the Shenandoah Valley of Virginia, from November 4, 1861, to June 17, 1862** (175 pp., J. B. Lippincott and Co., Philadelphia, 1880)

Like Allan's later work (*q.v.*), his history of Jackson's Valley campaign is a solid, relatively balanced, gripping account of one of the great campaigns of the war. Although much briefer than the *Army of Northern Virginia* (*q.v.*), this book focuses on Jackson's early strategy and successful dodging and interrupting of Union generals and thus makes it an important work of Confederate history. That Allan was a staff officer for his fallen chief gave him the ability to recall from firsthand experience the critical details of operations, and he recounts them straightforwardly.

(Appears in the *Southern Historical Society Papers* [*q.v.*], vol. 43, pp. 111–294, 1920; reprinted 1987, with an introduction by Gary W. Gallagher, 175 pp., Morningside, Dayton; reprinted 1995, with Allan's *The Army of Northern Virginia in 1861–1862* [*q.v.*], with an introduction by Robert K. Krick, 537 pp., Da Capo Press, New York)

55

Tanner, Robert G. **Stonewall in the Valley: Thomas J. "Stonewall" Jackson's Shenandoah Valley Campaign, Spring 1862** (436 pp., Doubleday and Co., Garden City, N.Y., 1976)

In a properly researched and documented volume, Tanner lays down the story of Jackson's operations in the Valley from November 1861 through the conclusions of his Valley campaign, viewing the events predominantly from the Confederate side. The author's lucid style and clear perception of the importance of Jackson's strategy and tactics make this a worthwhile campaign history that adds much to the understanding of Jackson and his army.

The discussion of the Valley campaign wisely encompasses matters of strategy and tactics outside the Valley, enabling readers to glean a sense of the campaign's importance as it progresses. Tanner deals intelligently with the detour of McDowell's troops from Fredericksburg to the Valley, placing their deployment into a realistic context. Lincoln did not panic and fear for the safety of Washington, readers learn, but earnestly wished to destroy Jackson's army and free the Valley. Moreover, the author realistically treats Jackson himself, detailing his mistakes as well as his triumphs. The result is a superior work on one of the preeminent military campaigns of the war.

56

Wayland, John W. **Stonewall Jackson's Way: Route, Method, Achievement** (244 pp., McClure Printing Co., Verona, Va., 1940)

Containing a well-researched text accompanied by 186 photographs and 56 maps, this work traces Jackson's Civil War years. The emphasis lies in the Valley campaigns, although the author begins with a tribute to Jackson's early years by examining Clarksburg and Lexington. The maps are suitably detailed to show many prominent houses that stood or still stand in historic areas. The photographs, many taken during the last decade or two of the 19th century or the first several decades of the 20th century, show many structures of interest.

Wayland continues the Jackson story by examining Harpers Ferry and First Bull Run, Winchester and Romney, and, in great detail, the Valley campaign of 1862. He effectively interweaves historical facts about Jackson with a travelogue that stops at certain fascinating sights. Jackson's part in the Peninsular campaign, Cedar Mountain, Second Bull Run, Harpers Ferry and Antietam, Massanutten Gap and Fisher's Gap, Fredericksburg, Chancellorsville, and the return of Jackson's remains to Lexington are all covered. This charming book is recommended for those interested in Jackson's legacy.

(Reprinted 1984, with a foreword by James I. Robertson, Jr., 244 pp., Morningside, Dayton)

Cedar Mountain, Virginia (9 August 1862)

57

Krick, Robert K. **Stonewall Jackson at Cedar Mountain** (472 pp., University of North Carolina Press, Chapel Hill, 1990)

The research and documentation of this work are mightily impressive—clearly such a neglected battle long needed an account written with zest and backed by interjections of numerous soldiers and commanders. The detail of the author's research clearly shows in many of the accounts of various units participating in the battle, complete with specific times and descriptions of small unit actions. For this alone the work ranks as one of the more impressively researched battle books and deserves wide reading.

While the account of Cedar Mountain is focused and detailed enough to allow readers to understand the battle thoroughly, the context of Cedar Mountain in a strategic sense—both following Lee's post–Peninsular campaign period and before Second Bull Run—loses some focus. Unfortunately, this failure to place the battle in context prevents readers from appreciating fully what Cedar Mountain meant for both sides, an argument skillfully developed in part in the words of many soldiers who fought in the battle. Moreover, the author severely criticizes Pope for his civilian order, but his shock and dismay defy acknowledgment that a rebellion was taking place. In fact, some of Krick's passages are so charged with caustic adjectives that his credibility is weakened, as with his description of numerous Federal acts as "savage." Despite such sectionalism, the work offers a thorough examination of Cedar Mountain while casting the spotlight on Jackson.

Second Bull Run, Virginia (29–30 August 1862)

58

Hennessy, John J. **Return to Bull Run: The Campaign and Battle of Second Manassas** (607 pp., Simon and Schuster, New York, 1993)

This is a smoothly composed, masterfully researched, and entertainingly written book. Rescuing Second Bull Run from its also-ran status, the author describes this important battle wherein much was at stake. Beginning in the wake of Cedar Mountain, a detailed picture emerges of the maneuvering of the two armies, placed nicely within the larger military context of the summer of 1862. The discussions on corps, division, brigade, and regimental levels wind through the maneuvering and subsequent actions along the old Manassas battlefield between 28 and 30 August. The author also provides a full and thoughtful analysis of the battle and what it accomplished.

In describing the battles, Hennessy reveals much about the commanders on both sides. He shows Irvin McDowell as incompetent for interference that helped collapse the Union line on 30 August. He holds a traditional view of the poorly abled Union commander John Pope, but goes beyond tradition by showing that Pope reasoned politically as well as militarily in designing strategy. Fitz John Porter comes off as less than sterling but still essentially railroaded by Pope. The author suggests that Halleck, McClellan, and Pope all contributed to the Union failure at Second Bull Run. He finds that Lee fought a great strategic battle there and lightly criticizes Stonewall Jackson for slow support of James Longstreet, whom he praises for caution and careful planning. Characterized by fine scholarship, this work is one of the best modern campaign studies on the war.

59

Ropes, John Codman. **The Army under Pope** (vol. 4 in Scribner's series Campaigns of the Civil War, 229 pp., Charles Scribner's Sons, New York, 1881)

This work treats the eastern theater action following McClellan's Peninsular campaign. The disastrous tenure of Pope as field commander provides a theme as the author explores Cedar Mountain, Jackson's Valley campaign, Groveton, Second Bull Run, and Chantilly. The book is generally well written and livelier than some in the set.

Ropes soundly criticizes Pope for Second Bull Run, labeling him "a brave and zealous officer, but destitute of military judgment." He squarely blames Halleck for the lack of support given Pope by McClellan's army and vigorously supports Fitz John Porter, subsequently cashiered as Pope's scapegoat. The book's undue attention to the case helped spark the eventual clearing of Porter's reputation. Although the majority of the work is unclouded by prejudice, Ropes does criticize Jackson and is reluctant to praise Confederate ingenuity. Eight maps accompany the text.

(Reprinted 1989, with an introduction by William Alan Blair, 229 pp., Broadfoot, Wilmington)

Antietam Creek, Maryland (17 September 1862)

60

Frassanito, William A. **Antietam: The Photographic Legacy of America's Bloodiest Day** (304 pp., Charles Scribner's Sons, New York, 1978)

Like the author's works on Gettysburg (q.v.) and the May campaign (q.v.), this book documents the battlefield photography that occurred in the wake of the fight and describes the photographers, the field, and the basic maneuvers and outcome of the battle. Following an introductory essay on Civil War photographic methods, the author describes the surviving Antietam photographs and the photographers who made them shortly after (and one perhaps during) the battle. In the course of his discussion, he introduces the reader to the admirable characters Alexander Gardner and James F. Gibson.

The chapters that follow describe the 95 surviving images made around the Antietam field during September and October 1862. The photographs are grouped using simple maps into the following regions surrounding Sharpsburg: the East Bank and Antietam Bridge (the Middle Bridge), the David R. Miller Farm, the West Woods, Bloody Lane, Burnside Bridge (the Lower Bridge), and miscellaneous views that include photographs of the town.

Frassanito has painstakingly tracked down precise camera positions for most of the photographs and presents a well-written narrative of the battle as it relates to each area. The modern companion views make the work valuable as a guidebook for visiting the field. He exercises superb judgment in assessing the meaning of the photographs. In the case of the famous picture made from the Philip Pry House (image I-2) allegedly during the battle, the author contends that it could not have been taken during the battle because the nearby inactive artillery unit "probably belonged" to Humphreys's division, which did not arrive on the field until 18 September. However, the disposition of 5th Corps reserves on the afternoon of the battle, the smoke and haze over the field in the image, and the apparent interest of the soldier with field glasses aimed toward the center of the field suggest the image may indeed depict the field as the battle raged. The question may never be settled, but such close investigations make Frassanito's book a superb addition to the literature.

61

Gallagher, Gary W., ed. **Antietam: Essays on the 1862 Maryland Campaign** (102 pp., Kent State University Press, Kent, 1989)

This work offers five brief but revealing articles on various aspects of the campaign. Gallagher presents an overview of the military situation as the first Confederate raid into the North unfolded. He introduces the objectives of Lee and McClellan and surveys the opportunities afforded both sides in the operations. He argues that Lee miscalculated the abilities of his army and that McClellan, given the chance for decisive action, did nothing. Dennis E. Frye examines the action at Harpers Ferry during the campaign, outlining the dreadful performances of Cols. Dixon S. Miles and Thomas H. Ford, and McClellan's mistake of failing to reinforce the position.

In a revisionist exercise, Robert K. Krick writes about why the Army of Northern Virginia "should not have been at Sharpsburg." After reviewing the entire campaign as viewed from the Southern perspective, he concludes that fighting at Antietam was a bad decision by Lee, "probably his worst of the war." A. Wilson Greene investigates McClellan's performance during the campaign and shows how the battle not only demonstrated once and for all that McClellan was not a

field commander but helped transform the war into a more desperate, "total" war. Gallagher then nicely summarizes the campaign in a concluding chapter that underscores the bitter political and diplomatic outcome for the Confederacy.

62

Luvaas, Jay, and Harold W. Nelson, eds. **The U.S. Army War College Guide to the Battle of Antietam: The Maryland Campaign of 1862** (310 pp., South Mountain Press, Carlisle, Pa., 1987)

This is the first in a series of four such works that serve as a historical summary of important battles and in a general way as a guide to reconnoitering the ground over which these battles were fought. The other volumes treat Fredericksburg and Chancellorsville (*q.v.*), Gettysburg (*q.v.*), and Chickamauga (*q.v.*). This work employs 10 stops along the South Mountain battlefield, one Crampton's Gap summary, a discussion of the fall of Harpers Ferry, and 18 stops along the Antietam battlefield to summarize the operations of the campaign. It contains 1 area map and 23 detail maps showing troop movements, along with a smattering of contemporary and Civil War era photographs to supplement important areas.

The maps, which show troop movements during the various phases of the campaign, are overlaid with important geographical landmarks and a few modern roads to show where the armies were positioned during significant moments of battle. The editors draw almost exclusively on the *O.R.* (*q.v.*), presenting battlefield reports of commanders to summarize the big picture of what was happening. The result is a fine tour of where the waves of blue and gray washed over areas of the field. An excellent appendix by Charles R. Shrader covers field logistics of the war, and a fine order of battle also appears.

63

Palfrey, Francis W. **The Antietam and Fredericksburg** (vol. 5 in Scribner's series Campaigns of the Civil War, 228 pp., Charles Scribner's Sons, New York, 1882)

This book tells the story of Lee's Maryland Campaign in September 1862 and the Federal response, the subsequent reorganization of the Army of the Potomac, and the battle of Fredericksburg. Like most other volumes in the Scribner's set, Palfrey's is a straightforward narrative of military operations. He is fair in his narrative, criticizing McClellan for the handling of the army at Antietam and Hooker for his movement of troops. He chastises Burnside for failing to ford the Rappahannock at Stafford Heights near Fredericksburg and bitterly attacks Halleck as "confused and scared" during the period. Palfrey criticizes Lee for failing to follow up after Fredericksburg, despite the short attention to details of the Confederate high command. Four maps accompany the text.

(Reprinted 1989, with an introduction by A. Wilson Greene, 228 pp., Broadfoot, Wilmington)

64

Sears, Stephen W. **Landscape Turned Red: The Battle of Antietam** (431 pp., Ticknor and Fields, New Haven, 1983)

This is the standard work on Antietam, engagingly written, well researched, and comprehensive in its coverage. Drawing on primary and a large number of secondary sources, Sears reconstructs the political and military situation of the weeks prior to Antietam and discusses intelligently the timing of the potential issuance of the Emancipation Proclamation. The characters are brought into play with great care and literary skill. The spotlight falls most often on McClellan and Lee, and the author's extensive research on the former enables him to present a very harsh treatment of the Federal commander.

The story of the armies' movements, the details of action around and on South Mountain, and the blow-by-blow description of Antietam itself are handled expertly. The battle's three major phases receive equal scrutiny, with much of the narrative comprised of extracts from reports and postwar reminiscences. This works exceedingly well save for perhaps relying on suspect sources too heavily, even reusing recreated "conversations" in places to heighten the dramatic effect. The maps are superb, showing troop movements down to regimental level. The author delivers a fine analysis of Burnside's actions at the famous bridge attack and a synopsis of the Lost Order and its significance, in addition to an order of battle. A few misspellings appear, as with Lawrence O'Bryan Branch, Abram Duryée, Jacob Duryée, William Gates LeDuc, and William T. Poague.

Corinth, Mississippi (3–4 October 1862)

65

Dudley, G. W. **The Lost Account of the Battle of Corinth and Court-Martial of Gen. Van Dorn** (ed. Monroe F. Cockrell, 78 pp., McCowat-Mercer Press, Jackson, Tenn., 1955)

This is a hodgepodge of material covering the campaign of Corinth and the resulting investigation of Van Dorn. It is based on a careful study of the *O.R.* (*q.v.*), discussions with a variety of participants in the battle and campaign, and some 50 letters written by participants. Dudley's book was composed around the turn of the century but not published until 50 years later. One copy was allegedly printed in 1899, but no others have surfaced; thus, the book did not come into circulation until the McCowat-Mercer edition was published.

Dudley's examination of the proceedings of the Court of Inquiry into Earl Van Dorn's conduct does not stand up as well as the previous sections, as the entire affair is covered in full in the *O.R.* Dudley also presents a roster of Confederate troops engaged in the battle and a biographical sketch of Col. William P. Rogers, the most significant casualty, contributed by Rogers's daughter. Cockrell adds a summary of the battle, making this work a useful addition to the literature on the war in Mississippi.

(Reprinted 1987, 88 pp., Broadfoot, Wilmington)

Perryville, Kentucky (8 October 1862)

66

McDonough, James Lee. **War in Kentucky: From Shiloh to Perryville** (386 pp., University of Tennessee Press, Knoxville, 1994)

This work centers on the strategic importance of Kentucky and Bragg's campaign of 1862. It draws on an assortment of obvious sources blended with diaries, letters, and reminiscences. McDonough examines the command theory of both sides, closely scrutinizing Bragg's plans and battlefield record as well as those of Don Carlos Buell, C. C. Gilbert, Henry W. Halleck, Alexander M. McCook, John Hunt Morgan, William Nelson, Leonidas Polk, Lovell H. Rosseau, Edmund Kirby Smith, George H. Thomas, and Earl Van Dorn—all of which adds much to the value of this work.

The author describes the Union attempt to capture Chattanooga, the Confederate movement through Tennessee, and the complex invasion of Kentucky launched by Bragg. Descriptive accounts of the battles at Richmond, Munfordville, and particularly the bloody encounter at Perryville highlight this study. McDonough smartly recounts the aftermath of Perryville and analyzes the strategic importance of the state's control for the Federal government. He contends that this battle, indeed the invasion, supports the idea that 1862 was the decisive year of the war.

Fredericksburg, Virginia
(13 December 1862)

67

Gallagher, Gary W., ed. **The Fredericksburg Campaign: Decision on the Rappahannock** (243 pp., University of North Carolina Press, Chapel Hill, 1995)

This study provides a selective, analytical view of aspects of a major battle that is otherwise poorly documented in the literature. Following the format of several other volumes in the series Military Campaigns of the Civil War, this work contains an editor's summary overview of the battle and campaign and sections written by experts on particular phases of the campaign. William Marvel's examination of Ambrose Burnside at Fredericksburg attempts to exonerate the much-maligned commander but succeeds only in part. He convincingly asks for forgiveness for Burnside relative to Robert E. Lee, whose terrible frontal attack at Gaines's Mill is forgotten. But do two poorly managed battles make them each forgivable, or even wise in the context of the time?

Alan T. Nolan's essay on Confederate leadership at Fredericksburg also contains some fascinations. Nolan finds the fight Lee's best of the period and marvels over the difference in conclusions Lee and Longstreet reached after the battle. George C. Rable summarizes the awful carnage that occurred on the field and searches for meaning in it. Carol Reardon explores Brig. Gen. Andrew A. Humphreys's Pennsylvania division at Fredericksburg. Gallagher reviews the range of Confederate interpretations of the battle. William A. Blair investigates the effects of the Union Army on the civilians caught in the crossfire. A. Wilson Greene outlines the month following the battle for the Army of the Potomac. With so many experts contributing such a variety of essays, this work is a must-read for anyone interested in what happened at Fredericksburg.

68

Luvaas, Jay, and Harold W. Nelson, eds. **The U.S. Army War College Guide to the Battles of Chancellorsville and Fredericksburg** (360 pp., South Mountain Press, Carlisle, Pa., 1988)

This work continues in the fine tradition of the U.S. Army War College series that also examines Antietam (*q.v.*), Gettysburg (*q.v.*), and Chickamauga (*q.v.*). Following the formula employed in the earlier volumes, the editors present a battlefield guide based on lengthy extracts from the *O.R.* (*q.v.*), supplemented by maps showing troop maneuvers and a small number of historical and contemporary photographs. An area map shows the region and the highways that provide access to it, while 23 detail maps cover important areas and crucial times during the battles of Fredericksburg (7 maps) and Chancellorsville (16 maps). Altogether, the reports from field commanders dictate stopping 12 times on the Fredericksburg battlefield and 23 times on the Chancellorsville field.

While not a tour of all the features one can see on these battlegrounds, this work skillfully describes the motions and clashes of the opposing units on various areas of the field, reconstructing the battle supported by the after-battle reports of the most significant commanding officers. The directions given are convoluted because of recent changes made at the parks. Very fine appendices cover intelligence in the Chancellorsville campaign, provide a detailed order of battle, and supply casualty figures for both armies.

Stones River, Tennessee
(31 December 1862–2 January 1863)

69

Bickham, William D. **Rosecrans' Campaign with the Fourteenth Army Corps, or the Army of the Cumberland: A Narrative of Personal Observations, with Official Reports of the Battle of Stone River** (476 pp., Moore, Wilstach, Keys and Co., Cincinnati, 1863)

Bickham recounts his experience as a journalist with William S. Rosecrans's army from October 1862 through the battle of Stones River. Correspondent for the *Cincinnati Commercial*, the author warmly supported the Ohioan Rosecrans and arrived at Bowling Green in October 1862. The work consists of Bickham's account of his activities in the field throughout three months.

Stones River clearly caught the correspondent completely off guard. He was astonished by the enormity of the conflict and the staggering numbers of casualties. About two-thirds of this work describes the battle and its immediate aftermath, with Bickham staunchly defending some fairly indefensible actions on the part of his hero, the army's commander. Nonetheless, spirited descriptions of many of the incidents along Stones River and in Murfreesboro emerge from this study.

70

Cozzens, Peter. **No Better Place to Die: The Battle of Stones River** (281 pp., University of Illinois Press, Urbana, 1990)

Stones River has lacked significant treatment for more than a century and receives a careful analysis in this work, which uses the *O.R.* (*q.v.*) and a number of primary and secondary sources to re-create the tactically confused and strategically ambiguous struggle near Murfreesboro. Generally the work is sound, providing a solid and detailed chronological account of the battle and the personalities of commanders on both sides who shaped it. Rosecrans and Bragg receive significant attention, of course, but so do John C. Breckinridge, Thomas L. Crittenden, William J. Hardee, Alexander M. McCook, Leonidas Polk, and Philip H. Sheridan. While the details of the battle of 31 December and 2 January are full and told quite adequately, the interpretation of Stones River in light of the larger strategic issues of the hour is relatively light.

The work suffers somewhat from a writing style that ranges from rigidly passive to overwrought with metaphors. There are a few misspellings, such as with Arthur J. L. Fremantle, and misinterpretations, such as indexing Edmund Kirby Smith under *K*. Some factual errors appear, as with the contention that the 8th Tennessee's casualties at Stones River represented the highest percentage for a Confederate regiment in a single battle. These are minor criticisms, however, that do not detract substantially from the work's usefulness.

Grierson's Raid, Tennessee, Mississippi, and Louisiana (17 April–2 May 1863)

71

Brown, D. Alexander. **Grierson's Raid: A Cavalry Adventure of the Civil War** (261 pp., University of Illinois Press, Urbana, 1954)

This is by far the best lengthy work on this stirring episode of the western theater. Written with the zest of an enjoyable novel yet impressively researched and adequately documented, the book fairly sets forth the story of Col. Benjamin H. Grierson's diversionary raid that damaged the Vicksburg railroad and diffused the pressure on Grant by thoroughly confusing the Confederate defenders. The author nicely summarizes the military situation in the theater before introducing Grierson and the other important participants of the 6th and 7th Illinois Cavalry who made the two-week ride.

This book draws on the *O.R.* (*q.v.*), Grierson's autobiography, and the letters and journals of Stephen Alfred Forbes, a raider, to create an almost diary-like account of the expedition. The planning and start of the raid are thus offered as exciting moments, and readers can follow the exploits of the raid and the pursuers on the plunge south through Mississippi with great interest, highlighted by the railroad attack and the

celebration in Baton Rouge. In places Brown offers reconstructed "conversations" which may strain credibility, but in general he delivers a most enthusiastic and reliable package.

(Reprinted 1981, 261 pp., Morningside, Dayton)

Chancellorsville, Virginia (29 April–14 May 1863)

72

Bigelow, John, Jr. **The Campaign of Chancellorsville: A Strategic and Tactical Study** (528 pp., Yale University Press, New Haven, 1910)

Built around 44 three-color maps showing troop movements and several battle plans, this work objectively and dispassionately sets down the historical record of the Chancellorsville campaign, allowing readers to understand clearly troop movements down to a minute level and thereby comprehend the brilliant maneuvers by general officers like Stonewall Jackson and the incomprehensible actions by commanders like Joe Hooker.

The possibilities for criticism when writing of the Chancellorsville campaign are striking, yet Bigelow finds a good balance in assessing the actions of Federal and Confederate officers. He explains the tactical movements of artillery and infantry but also expertly details the campaign's cavalry operations, including those by Fitzhugh Lee, Grumble Jones, and John S. Mosby, which add excitement to the story.

(Reprinted 1991, 528 pp., Morningside, Dayton)

73

Doubleday, Abner. **Chancellorsville and Gettysburg** (vol. 6 in Scribner's series Campaigns of the Civil War, 243 pp., Charles Scribner's Sons, New York, 1882)

This is the worst volume in the Scribner's set. Doubleday commanded a division at Chancellorsville, although his troops stayed in reserve throughout the fight. At Gettysburg he temporarily assumed command of the 1st Corps when its commander, John F. Reynolds, fell dead on the field. When Doubleday failed to receive permanent command of the corps, his anger flared—and it consumes a potentially useful book in a veil of hatred against numerous fellow officers, particularly Meade and Maj. Gen. Oliver O. Howard, who erroneously reported that during the battle Doubleday's corps "gave way."

To say the book lacks documentation would be a grievous understatement. The narrative on Chancellorsville focuses on discrediting Howard for his tardiness in preparing his corps and goes on to blame Howard for the defeat. The attacks on Meade for Gettysburg are even sharper, painting the commanding general as without plans and without a stomach to fight. Commenting on the unbiased spirit, impartial historical judgment, and scholarly research generally found in the Scribner's set, a reviewer for the *Nation* wrote in 1882 that "this uniformity is now sharply broken by a book which is conspicuous for the absence of every one of the good qualities above referred to." Indeed, Doubleday's book fails to enlighten the reader on Chancellorsville or Gettysburg but it does provide insight into Doubleday himself. Twelve maps accompany the text.

(Reprinted 1989, with an introduction by Richard A. Sauers, 243 pp., Broadfoot, Wilmington; 1882 edition reprinted 1994, with an introduction by Gary W. Gallagher, 243 pp., Da Capo Press, New York)

74

Furgurson, Ernest B. **Chancellorsville, 1863: The Souls of the Brave** (405 pp., Alfred A. Knopf, New York, 1992)

This is a balanced account of a major battle that has long needed a modern study. It draws on a wide variety of sources, from the *O.R.* (*q.v.*) to many diaries, letters, and secondary accounts, to re-create the greatest tactical success fought by Robert E. Lee. The action unfolds in this work at corps, division, brigade, and regimental levels, allowing readers to sample the many experiences of soldiers and officers. The author provides succinct evaluations of commanders on both sides, judiciously offering interpretations that agree with the conventional wisdom: Chancellorsville was a great victory for Lee (although it may have emboldened him too greatly), Hooker was incompetent and did not make clear judgments when the situation seemed clear to others, and the South suffered a terrible loss with the accidental mortal wounding of Stonewall Jackson.

Aside from detailing the terrain and providing 18 fine maps, Furgurson interprets the battle so that even readers who have not visited Chancellorsville can imagine why things unfolded the way they did. On the Union side, the roles of many subordinate commanders are nicely treated, as with Darius Couch; on the Confederate side, the narrative's momentum builds through Jackson's daring flank march. The author chastises Jeb Stuart for poor performance as an infantry commander at the battle, an out-of-assignment role he found himself playing. An occasional misspelling appears, as with the names of Philippe de Trobriand and Alexander Schimmelfennig, but overall this is a balanced, sufficiently detailed, and pleasing work in its coverage of a highly significant Civil War engagement.

Vicksburg, Mississippi (18 May–4 July 1863)

75

Bearss, Edwin Cole. **The Campaign for Vicksburg** (3 vols. consisting of *Vicksburg Is the Key* [769 pp., 1985], *Grant Strikes a Fatal Blow* [689 pp., 1986], and *Unvexed to the Sea* [761 pp., 1986], 2219 pp., Morningside, Dayton, 1985–1986)

The author provides an exhaustive account of the fighting for the Mississippi's primary fortress. The three volumes trace Grant's strategy for capturing Vicksburg and the unfolding siege from November 1862 to the city's fall. Bearss supplies a condensed version of the *O.R.* (*q.v.*) that readers can digest, although a number of other sources are also employed. Although analysis and interpretation are sparse, details of many actions—not all of them important—are abundant, often to a miniscule level.

The first volume carries the story through March 1863, when the Federal frustration for the campaign's lack of success required a rethinking of tactics. Volumes 2 and 3 carry the reader through the many small actions and larger attacks that punctuated the tedium of the siege. The second volume continues through 17 May 1863, giving readers a wonderful summary of Grant's river crossing, the march to Jackson, battles at the capitol and at Raymond, Big Black River, and Champion's Hill, and the beginning of the siege. The final volume completes the story through the Confederate surrender.

The author sometimes concludes that an action was not important to the campaign after spending pages examining it, which can be frustrating for the reader. But those who want a comprehensive story of the Vicksburg campaign beyond the official reports will find this lengthy set highly useful.

76

Fiske, John. **The Mississippi Valley in the Civil War** (368 pp., Houghton Mifflin Co., Boston, 1900)

Fiske examines the military significance of the Mississippi Valley at the outbreak of the war and the campaigns that unfolded in the ensuing four years. Long considered a classic, this work is the result of a number of lectures developed by the author and sharpened over some years before setting them down in print. It offers a useful synopsis of the significance of the Mississippi Valley as a region and the delicate nature of states like Missouri and Kentucky in the political balance of the war. Despite the fact that the author relied on sources predating the *O.R.* (*q.v.*), he succeeds in assembling the story of the early incidents of the West, from the capture of Camp Jackson in 1861 to the campaigns along the Mississippi to the closure of the waterway to the Trans-Mississippi West.

As a thoughtful analysis on some characters, the book stands up reasonably well. Significant attention is given to Frank P. Blair, Jr., a number of war governors, and regional personalities who helped define the distinctly different psychologies of the states and territories in question. The author makes significant blunders, however, in assessing Lincoln's military competence (which he underestimates) and the abilities of a variety of commanders by deemphasizing the accomplishments of Grant and Sherman.

(Reprinted 1994, titled *The War in the West: The Mississippi Valley in the Civil War*, 2 vols., 368 pp., Archive Society, Harrisburg, Pa.)

77

Greene, Francis V. **The Mississippi** (vol. 8 in Scribner's series Campaigns of the Civil War, 276 pp., Charles Scribner's Sons, New York, 1882)

This book's coverage includes operations about Iuka and Corinth, the extensive movements on and siege of Vicksburg, and the fight for Port Hudson. It is one of the better volumes of the Scribner's series, a straightforward, factual narrative. Although it lacks color and anecdotal material, Greene's story of military movements is clear and sober. Thirteen maps accompany the text.

(Reprinted 1989, with an introduction by Terrence J. Winschel, 276 pp., Broadfoot, Wilmington)

78

Walker, Peter F. **Vicksburg: A People at War** (235 pp., University of North Carolina Press, Chapel Hill, 1960)

Although the title suggests that this work treats the war period fully, instead it analyzes Vicksburg's citizenry up to the city's fall. The author carefully follows the evolution of the townspeople's feelings toward civil war and documents the rapid shift to secession aided by Jefferson Davis's personal influence and Lincoln's call for volunteers. The book is valuable for showing the full array of types of people in a typical Mississippi town, as much of the story's appeal comes from learning about the characters inhabiting the town rather than from Vicksburg's special role in a strategic sense.

Walker's skill in painting a social picture does not always carry over into the military aspects of Vicksburg's story. He errs occasionally relating to military operations in the vicinity, such as the occupational status of Jackson, the nature of railroads in Jackson and Port Gibson, and the dates of Mississippi's secession and the fall of New Orleans, and he con-

tends that the Army of Tennessee's right wing was "shattered" at Mill Spring—11 months before the army was created. Unfortunately, the work does not follow Vicksburg's role through the final two years of the war, neglecting the important Union operations that occurred in the area.

(Reprinted 1987, 235 pp., Broadfoot, Wilmington)

Port Hudson, Louisiana (21 May–9 July 1863)

79

Cunningham, Edward. **The Port Hudson Campaign, 1862–1863** (174 pp., Louisiana State University Press, Baton Rouge, 1963)

Carefully documented and well researched, this work examines the role of the town defended by 7000 troops under Franklin Gardner in the spring of 1863. The author demonstrates the value of Farragut's exploratory action on 14 March 1863, and the resulting strategy of attacking Port Hudson by land. As the siege of Vicksburg began to the north, Maj. Gen. Nathaniel P. Banks attempted to take Port Hudson with two major attacks before settling into his own siege that lasted until Port Hudson capitulated on 9 July.

Cunningham has carefully used a rich mine of sources to describe the actions at Port Hudson and thus creates a picture of military events usually overshadowed by the siege of Vicksburg itself. This is a worthwhile and capably executed work.

(Reprinted 1994, 174 pp., Louisiana State University Press, Baton Rouge)

80

Hewitt, Lawrence L. **Port Hudson: Confederate Bastion on the Mississippi** (232 pp., Louisiana State University Press, Baton Rouge, 1987)

This book adds to the story of Port Hudson by delivering a blow-by-blow account of the action there. The author believes that Port Hudson has been unfairly overlooked by historians and cites the battle's influence in drawing black soldiers into the war and reducing the stature of Maj. Gen. Nathaniel P. Banks, thereby helping to elevate Grant. Because of this, Hewitt contends, Port Hudson was "a turning point of the war."

While this may be overstating the case, the detailed and carefully executed description of the activities around Port Hudson is commendable. The author's narrative begins with the occupation of Port Hudson in August 1862, the efforts to fortify the city through the rest of that year, Banks's unsuccessful attempts at capture, Farragut's naval passage, and the fall of Port Hudson on the heels of the fall of Vicksburg.

The discussion of military aspects is fine, and the analysis of strategy and tactics comes through in most cases with great clarity. The book's final section speculates on Banks and Grant by stating that if Banks had taken Port Hudson in an early attempt, he would have taken credit for the resulting fall of Vicksburg and overshadowed Grant, becoming the leading general of the Union Army in the West. Here the author resorts to wild conjecture, as unlimited what-if speculations on all aspects of the war could be asked and one cannot intelligently predict what might or might not have happened if things had been different. When one considers the reputations of Grant and Banks with the War Department in 1862 and early 1863, it is difficult to accept that Banks may have been headed for supreme command.

Charleston, South Carolina (mid–1863)

81

Gillmore, Quincy A. **Engineer and Artillery Operations against the Defences of Charleston Harbor in 1863: Comprising the Descent upon Morris Island, the Demolition of Fort Sumter, the Reduction of Forts Wagner and Gregg: With Observations on Heavy Ordnance, Fortifications, etc.** (354 pp., D. Van Nostrand Co., New York, 1865)

Gillmore's report contains a description of the buildup of artillery power on the islands surrounding Charleston harbor by the officer who directed the Federal bombardment. This work describes in plain narrative fashion the movement onto Morris Island from Folly Island and the removal, under the supervision of Brig. Gen. Israel Vogdes, of 47 heavy guns to Morris. The engineering feat on Morris Island, supervised by Gillmore, leaps out in this work as a critical operation of the war, with the precise descriptions of ammunition, construction of parapets, bombproofs, and magazines providing sufficient detail to enable the reader to comprehend the enormity of the movement.

Gillmore's correspondence is absorbing. It does not admit criticism of subordinates, particularly relating to John A. B. Dahlgren. The report on the attack of the 54th Massachusetts Infantry on Fort Wagner is clumsy and filled with politically driven diplomacy. The subsequent reports of T. B. Brooks, Edward W. Serrell, and Peter S. Michie are equally valuable, and the material covering the artillery pieces themselves is meticulous and illuminating. The

many plates showing guns, especially those that exploded, are fascinating. Two maps provide superb graphical coverage of Charleston harbor and the approaches to Fort Wagner. The work lacks a much-needed index.

(Reprinted 1868, titled *Engineer and Artillery Operations against the Defences of Charleston Harbor in 1863; with a Supplement*, 486 pp., D. Van Nostrand Co., New York)

82

Wise, Stephen R. **Gate of Hell: Campaign for Charleston Harbor, 1863** (312 pp., University of South Carolina Press, Columbia, 1994)

The author presents a detailed look at this critical and eventful year in the Charleston area. He outlines the defenses of Charleston, covering Du Pont's unsuccessful attack of 1863, and discusses the U.S. monitor force. The narrative expands into an interesting analysis of the Union command structure and various personalities, including David Hunter and Samuel F. Du Pont, Quincy A. Gillmore and John A. B. Dahlgren, Israel Vogdes, George C. Strong, and Alfred H. Terry. The work outlines Hunter's organization of U.S.C.T. units, including Col. Thomas W. Higginson's 1st South Carolina Infantry and Col. Robert Gould Shaw's 54th Massachusetts Infantry. The famous raid by Col. James Montgomery on Darien, Georgia, receives coverage. Wise also delivers vivid descriptions of the preliminary actions on James Island as well as Colquitt's attack on the 54th Massachusetts at River's Causeway on 16 June 1863.

This work nicely delivers a grand explanation of the famous attack on Fort Wagner of 18 July 1863. After 9000 rounds of Federal artillery failed to soften the fort's 1600 defenders, 10 Union regiments charged in a frontal attack led by Shaw's 54th Massachusetts. The fight lasted from 7:30 P.M. until 1:00 A.M. the following morning, and the 54th Massachusetts suffered 42 percent casualties. An officer of the 48th New York Infantry dubbed the fort "gate of hell."

Wise provides far more analysis of Charleston's tumultuous year of 1863. He describes the siege of Fort Wagner as Gillmore advanced by regular approaches covered by gun emplacements; much about Gillmore's engineering and the abandonment of the fort on 7 September 1863; the reduction of Fort Sumter to a pile of brick dust and rubble; and, in closing, how Charleston was effectively shut down as a port and simply sat inactive until Sherman's approach forced evacuation in the spring of 1865. A few errors appear, such as photo captions listing Truman Seymour and Alfred Terry as major generals and the consistent misspelling of Israel Vogdes. These are minor problems in a splendid and thorough job of research and writing.

Gettysburg, Pennsylvania (1–4 July 1863)

83

Coddington, Edwin B. **The Gettysburg Campaign: A Study in Command** (866 pp., Charles Scribner's Sons, New York, 1968)

Massively documented and systematically even in its telling of the campaign, this work ranks as one of the best on a Civil War military campaign. The narrative begins with Lee's plan for a summer raid northward and concludes, 574 pages later, with the Army of Northern Virginia's retreat and the timid pursuit of Meade's army. The voluminous notes appear at the back of the book, following a detailed order of battle for each army.

Coddington so thoroughly researched his topic that he has produced a brilliantly detailed synopsis with the proper emphasis in all the right places. Moreover, he utilizes a wealth of previously untapped sources to add glimmers of fresh insight to several important aspects of the battle and the campaign, elevating George Meade to his rightful position of significance for his leadership days after receiving the assignment as commander of the Army of the Potomac. Coddington elucidates the well-oiled machinery of the Union Army's various levels of command that made possible a stunning Federal victory; surveys the reactions of Pennsylvania farmers as war draws onto their landscape; and describes the logistics and equipment involved with admirable clarity. The study picks up steam in describing the second and third days of the battle (the first day receives somewhat lesser attention). Overall, this work is a necessary and wholly successful element of Civil War literature.

(Reprinted 1984, 866 pp., Scribner's, New York)

84

Dowdey, Clifford. **Death of a Nation: The Story of Lee and His Men at Gettysburg** (383 pp., Alfred A. Knopf, New York, 1958)

This work retains some value as a story of Gettysburg principally seen through the eyes of the Southern commanders and soldiers. It relies on a large cache of sources but is undocumented, leaving many questions as to the reliability of certain sections. Furthermore, the evaluations of battlefield performance strongly favor Robert E. Lee, Virginians, and the Confederacy, in that order. The Federal troops and commanders are mentioned rarely, and so readers see the campaign and battle from the tent level of the Confederate command and soldiers.

Despite these drawbacks, the discussion of military ma-neuvers and the engagement provides a stirring narrative from the outset of the campaign. Dowdey sketches the first day of battle, examines the chaos of the second day, and builds to the standard climax of Pickett's Charge. The praise for Lee comes at the expense of others, most predictably James Longstreet and Richard S. Ewell. An appendix provides an order of battle for the Army of Northern Virginia at Gettysburg. A few spelling errors appear, as with George Cary Eggleston, Clement Anselm Evans, Philip Kearny, Moxley Sorrel, Bell Irvin Wiley, and John H. Worsham.

(Reprinted 1992, 383 pp., Butternut and Blue, Baltimore)

85

Frassanito, William A. **Gettysburg: A Journey in Time** (248 pp., Charles Scribner's Sons, New York, 1975)

The foremost work on the historic photographs made in the wake of the battle, this book follows the author's formula employed in his studies of Antietam (*q.v.*) and Grant's May Campaign (*q.v.*). Frassanito's selection of 104 Gettysburg images establishes a foundation for analysis of the battlefield and its earliest photographers. Hand-drawn maps show the field and the photographers' positions.

Frassanito has matched modern views with those of Alexander Gardner, Mathew Brady, Charles and Isaac Tyson, and others. The photographs are arranged chronologically relative to the progress of the battle—Willoughby's Run and McPherson's Ridge, Cemetery Hill, Cemetery Ridge, Little Round Top and the Devil's Den, and the Rose Farm. The work is marvelously successful at tying the images to the modern-day field, and a few curiosities are examined, such as the contrivance of the dead Confederate sharpshooter lying among the rocks in the Devil's Den. A significantly alluring sequel may be found in *Early Photography at Gettysburg,* by William A. Frassanito (436 pp., Thomas Publications, Gettysburg, 1995).

86

Gallagher, Gary W., ed. **The First Day at Gettysburg: Essays on Confederate and Union Leadership** (173 pp., Kent State University Press, Kent, 1992)

This work is a reexamination of several crucial aspects of the first day's fight at Gettysburg. The four essays briefly examine topics of classical controversy. They are an assessment of Robert E. Lee's performance on the first day of battle, by Alan T. Nolan; a review of the records of corps command by A. P. Hill and Richard S. Ewell, by Gary W. Gallagher; an evaluation of Oliver Otis Howard's leadership of the 11th Corps, by A. Wilson Greene; and a description by

Robert K. Krick of three Confederate failures of brigade leadership on Oak Ridge during the first day. Although the work examines Union and Confederate leadership, the overwhelming emphasis is on the Confederates.

The first essay argues persuasively that Lee's movement northward across the Potomac was poor strategy and that he must receive the blame for failures Southern writers have pushed onto others. Lee's vagueness of orders to Ewell, for example, hardly allows placing the failure to take Culp's Hill and Cemetery Hill on Ewell's shoulders. The author also rescues Jeb Stuart and A. P. Hill from blame for absence and for transforming a small skirmish into a full engagement. Gallagher's essay on Hill and Ewell continues this inspection. He finds them shy of Stonewall Jackson's abilities as a corps commander but hardly deserving of the blame they have received, blame that rightfully rests with Lee. Greene revives the reputation of Howard and the 11th Corps from its historical level of pity. Krick argues that poor leadership on Oak Ridge reveals much about the mid-level commanders of the Army of Northern Virginia at the time of Gettysburg. The work is valuable, informed, and reflective.

87

Gallagher, Gary W., ed. **The Second Day at Gettysburg: Essays on Confederate and Union Leadership** (209 pp., Kent State University Press, Kent, 1993)

These selections follow the format of the similar work on the first day's action (*q.v.*). The five essays herein comprise a heartier blend of large-scale controversies and neglected aspects of the day than does the first volume. They are a summary of Robert E. Lee's actions on the second day, by Gary W. Gallagher; a study of Daniel Sickles's controversial movement of his 3d Corps into the Peach Orchard, by William Glenn Robertson; an evaluation of James Longstreet on the second day of battle, by Robert K. Krick; a view of Henry Warner Slocum and the 12th Corps, by A. Wilson Greene; and a smaller-scale study of John C. Caldwell's Federal division in the Wheatfield, by D. Scott Hartwig.

The scholarship in this volume is outstanding. Gallagher's question centers on whether Lee's offensive stance on the second day was reasonable. He writes that Lee clearly "ruled out defensive maneuvers that might have opened breathtaking possibilities," and concludes in a rational manner that Lee gambled and erred in taking the offensive, but that the risks were not entirely unreasonable. Robertson argues that although Sickles's decision was a mistake, it might have had beneficial results in destabilizing the Confederate movements, but such a move would have been far more beneficial had it been coordinated with the other large Federal

units. Krick's essay delivers a mixed bag on Longstreet, siding neither entirely with Longstreet nor his detractors, but leaning toward the latter. Greene finds that Slocum's "vacillation and oversights" might have caused a pathetic reputation for the commander, but the errors did not result in any serious setbacks. Hartwig offers a sympathetic and praiseful portrait of Caldwell.

88

Gallagher, Gary W., ed. **The Third Day at Gettysburg and Beyond** (217 pp., University of North Carolina Press, Chapel Hill, 1994)

This book continues the examination of specific commanders at Gettysburg established in two earlier works with similar formats (*q.v.*). The final day of the battle provides controversial topics: Gary W. Gallagher surveys the effect of the loss at Gettysburg on Lee's army and the Southern home front; William Garret Piston revives the controversy surrounding Lee and Longstreet on the final day; Carol Reardon covers Pickett's Charge; Robert K. Krick delivers a tale of Lewis Armistead and Richard Brooke Garnett; Robert L. Bee examines Sgt. Ben Hirst's narrative of the third day; and A. Wilson Greene comments on Meade's sluggish pursuit of Lee following the battle.

As with the previous volumes, the intelligent analysis in these essays is admirable. Gallagher shows that Confederate soldiers received a "jolt" at Gettysburg but that neither they nor their kinfolk at home saw the loss as a symbol of eventual doom. Piston finds Longstreet more at fault on the third day than on the second day. Reardon's essay constitutes a significant sorting of fact from fiction relative to the charge. Krick's essay mourns the loss of Armistead and Garnett while it weaves their friendship into an interesting story. Bee's presentation of a Connecticut soldier's notes on Gettysburg asks why he recorded the battle as he did. Greene finds the criticism of Meade's caution unfounded.

89

Hoke, Jacob. **The Great Invasion of 1863; or, General Lee in Pennsylvania: Embracing an Account of the Strength of the Armies of the Potomac and Northern Virginia: Their Daily Marches with the Routes of Travel, and General Orders Issued: The Three Days of Battle: The Retreat of the Confederates and Pursuit of the Federals: Analytical Index: With an Appendix Containing an Account of the Burning of Chambersburg, Pennsylvania, a Statement of the General Sickles Controversy, and Other Valuable Historic Papers** (613 pp., W. J. Shuey, Dayton, 1887)

Hoke offers an eyewitness account of the Pennsylvania

campaign by a Chambersburg businessman, along with supporting material drawn from many official documents. Curious for its patriotic Northern viewpoint and a respectable job of research by an amateur writer, the work serves today as an entertaining source on the campaign.

The author sets the stage by examining the disposition of the Federal and Confederate armies in Virginia and their northward marches. Hoke's greatest contribution may be in describing the reaction of Pennsylvanian citizens to a coming raid as well as the reaction of local defense forces. The literary style is rather dry, and the book contains a great deal of factual minutiae, along with a relatively standard description of the three days' fight and the resulting retreat and pursuit. Concluding material surveys the Gettysburg battlefield and what it meant to locals in 1863 and 20 years later. The index is poor and employs ambiguous references for many names.

(Reprinted 1992, 613 pp., Stan Clark Military Books, Gettysburg)

90

Longstreet, Helen D. **Lee and Longstreet at High Tide: Gettysburg in the Light of the Official Records** (346 pp., published by the author, Gainesville, Ga., 1904)

This is a defense of James Longstreet by his second wife and is based mostly on the *O.R.* (*q.v.*). The well-known accusation that Longstreet disobeyed Lee's orders at Gettysburg and cost the Army of Northern Virginia the battle (and perhaps the war) was vigorously asserted by Virginians in the years following Lee's death. This work attempts to review the official documents surrounding the case and end Longstreet's status as scapegoat. The introduction by none other than Daniel E. Sickles sets the stage for what is generally a successful analysis.

Although much of the work consists of a loose body of tributes and reminiscences from those who knew or were associated with Longstreet, the evidence central to the Gettysburg controversy eventually surfaces. The case is strong in Longstreet's favor. Contradictions of the charges lodged in the *Southern Historical Society Papers* (*q.v.*) and other influential sources abound. The work serves effectively to answer, if not silence, most of the criticism lodged against Longstreet, even if it damages Lee and others in the process.

(Reprinted 1989, with an introduction by Carl W. Breihan, 360 pp., Broadfoot, Wilmington)

91

Luvaas, Jay, and Harold W. Nelson, eds. **The U.S. Army War College Guide to the Battle of Gettysburg** (240 pp., South Mountain Press, Carlisle, Pa., 1987)

The authors offer an outstanding summary of the after-battle reports from Gettysburg. Although this book matches the style of three others in a series covering Antietam (*q.v.*), Fredericksburg and Chancellorsville (*q.v.*), and Chickamauga (*q.v.*), it is somewhat thin relative to the others, considering the tremendous importance and complexity of the three day battle at Gettysburg. Nonetheless, it conveys summaries of the major phases of the action drawn principally from the *O.R.* (*q.v.*) and is supplemented by maps showing troop movements during portions of the battle. Thus, the work functions as a guide to the battle and a battlefield tour book presenting the most significant areas of fighting for those on the spot.

The book presents 25 stops along the battlefield in three large sections covering each day of battle. Some of the directions are inaccurate because of recent changes at the parks. The reports come from Robert E. Lee, George G. Meade, and a long list of subordinate commanders on both sides. They provide excellent commentary on the major phases of action, and the editors' narrative ties the reports together nicely. The maps show units down to the regimental level and help one visualize the action as it unfolded. Modern and historical photographs supplement the text. An excellent appendix treats capabilities and doctrine in the Civil War and includes an order of battle and summary of casualties.

92

Mosby, John S. **Stuart's Cavalry in the Gettysburg Campaign** (222 pp., Moffat Yard and Co., New York, 1908)

Mosby delivers an analysis of Jeb Stuart's activities in late June and early July 1863 with the intention of clearing the subject from blame for absence from Robert E. Lee's army. The early supporters of Lee's reputation heaped a large part of the blame for the disaster at Gettysburg onto the shoulders of Stuart, who was riding around the Union Army and therefore out of touch with Lee and unable to provide the commanding general with intelligence regarding the Federal corps. This contention evolved in many works produced by Lee supporters, most notably those of Henry Heth (*q.v.*), A. L. Long and Marcus Wright (*q.v.*), Charles Marshall (*q.v.*), and Walter Taylor (*q.v.*). This work, by a Virginian well known in his own right, attacks the contention by showing that Stuart was simply following Lee's orders. Moreover, the engagement planned by Lee shifted to Gettysburg because Heth and A. P. Hill disobeyed orders. Had Stuart been on hand, little else probably would have unfolded differently.

The author covers the period from Chancellorsville to the withdrawal from Gettysburg on 4 July. By drawing on documents and correspondence from most of the principal parties, Mosby demonstrates that Heth precipitated the battle and that the absence of cavalry was, indeed, no justification for him to move toward Gettysburg. Further, Lee attempted to rescue Heth and Hill once the booming of cannon started. The resulting reconnaissance in force became a general engagement when the enemy resisted in force. The author demonstrates that two of Lee's reports disagree with each other, and Mosby believes the general may have signed one without reading it, or was simply supporting his subordinates Hill and Heth in their errors. As an argument, the work succeeds in removing at least Stuart as a cause for Southern defeat in Pennsylvania. For a modern updating of Mosby that agrees with nearly all of his conclusions, see *Saber and Scapegoat: J. E. B. Stuart and the Gettysburg Controversy,* by Mark Nesbitt (227 pp., Stackpole Books, Mechanicsburg, Pa., 1994).

(Reprinted 1987, 228 pp., Olde Soldier Books, Gaithersburg, 1987)

93

Norton, Oliver Willcox. **The Attack and Defense of Little Round Top, Gettysburg, July 2, 1863** (350 pp., Neale Publishing Co., New York, 1913)

A detailed story of the critical fight at Gettysburg drawn largely from the *O.R.* (*q.v.*), this work attempts a reexamination of the fight on 2 July for Little Round Top some 50 years after the battle by analyzing the various accounts, official and otherwise, that touched on this important phase of the battle. Norton's research was supported in part by his presence on Little Round Top during the battle; at the time he was bugler of the 83d Pennsylvania Infantry, Col. Strong Vincent's old regiment. Vincent was the brigade commander who was killed shortly after action along the crest erupted.

This book examines many secondary accounts, including those of William Swinton (*q.v.*), Abner Doubleday (*q.v.*), Francis A. Walker (*q.v.*), Henry J. Hunt (in *Battles and Leaders* [*q.v.*]), and William H. Powell (*q.v.*). In comparing these records, the author finds that "no two agree in their details" of what transpired during the most critical moments of the battle. He largely supports the reports of Maj. Gen. Gouverneur K. Warren and disputes many little details in the words of others' versions of the day. Misspellings and misinformation occasionally surface, as with the names of

Evander M. Law and others. Unfortunately, the work lacks an index.

(Reprinted 1983, with a foreword by John J. Pullen, 350 pp., Morningside, Dayton)

94

Nye, Wilbur Sturtevant. **Here Come the Rebels!** (412 pp., Louisiana State University Press, Baton Rouge, 1965)

This is a documentary describing the local and regional reaction to Lee's invasion of the North. Although it begins as a relatively routine campaign history, it abruptly leaves the larger military picture of the Gettysburg campaign to examine Pennsylvania's reaction to war washing onto its soil, from Governor Andrew Curtin's raising of emergency forces to the employment of militia to protect an impressive number of towns, roads, and bridges. The result is a very different focus on a familiar story, and one that succeeds with its special goal.

Nye provides excellent summaries of the early cavalry actions in the campaign, including Brandy Station, Aldie, Middleburg, and Upperville. We ride alongside Stuart during his famous maneuver and, supported by the author's analysis, come to see that perhaps the historical record has treated him too harshly for his actions during the campaign. Conversely, the author is critical—too much so—of Pleasonton. The work examines Ewell's capture of Winchester and the chaotic mess of the skirmish at Stephenson's Depot. And then Lee's army rolls into Pennsylvania and the state's guards seem ready.

The author reconstructs the defenses of Harrisburg and details the employment of militia, national guard, and the invalid corps. He relates many incidents involving his characters and does so with the authoritative flavor of one who knows the landscape he is describing. The book ends before the big battle begins, and so it serves as an illuminating preface to the many studies of Gettysburg.

(Reprinted 1988, 412 pp., Morningside, Dayton)

95

Pfanz, Harry W. **Gettysburg: Culp's Hill and Cemetery Hill** (507 pp., University of North Carolina Press, Chapel Hill, 1993)

This is a deserving partner to the same author's earlier work on the battle's second day (*q.v.*). The fantastic detail may overwhelm those who are not serious students of the battle, but the author's thorough knowledge of the ground, the commanders, and the actions of units makes it an invaluable read. He meticulously examines the fighting on the second and third days of the contest at Culp's Hill and Cemetery Hill, focusing exclusively on these controversial and important areas.

Pfanz summarizes Ewell's operations and finds that although Howard's decision to take the hill was advantageous—and Ewell's decision not to take it was a disaster—Union mistakes nearly created the possibility for significant Confederate gains in these critical areas. The work surveys the fighting in the town of Gettysburg, the fight between Federal cavalry and the Stonewall Brigade, which was kept away from Edward Johnson's assault on Culp's Hill, and the skirmishes that erupted south of the town along Cemetery Ridge. The author outlines in great detail the poor coordination of the Confederate tactics on both 2 July and 3 July, showing the action on the Confederate right and left on 2 July did not coincide well, and the 3 July attack on Culp's Hill was out of phase with Pickett's Charge. Massively documented, thoughtful, and researched with insight, this work will stand as a monument to these important aspects of the Gettysburg fight.

96

Pfanz, Harry W. **Gettysburg: The Second Day** (601 pp., University of North Carolina Press, Chapel Hill, 1987)

As battle studies of strategy and tactics go, this work is among the most complete, scholarly, and well documented. Pfanz's knowledge of the attack he details is overwhelming and the level of discussion so minute that readers will feel they have experienced the action. The narrative sets the stage with the Confederate and Union preparations for large-scale battle and the haphazard growth of the Gettysburg conflict on 1 July. The detailed analysis begins, however, with the Union 3d Corps' salient movement, the attack of Longstreet's corps, the action in the Peach Orchard, the Wheatfield, Devil's Den, and Little Round Top, and the subsequent repulse of Longstreet's attack by Union forces. Although he omits analysis of the actions at Culp's Hill and Cemetery Hill, Pfanz concentrates on the crucial actions of the battle's second day, the decisive fight of the battle. Curiously, he believes that Ambrose R. Wright's Confederate brigade occupied a part of Cemetery Hill, contradicting most earlier writers and raising the possibility of a tide turning except for Meade's decisive leadership.

The massive detail that accompanies each chapter provides a concrete and thorough understanding of the battle for readers, but—to his credit—the author does not push the limits of scholarship beyond what is reasonable: he makes clear where evidence runs out and conjecture takes over. Mysteries linger: the reporting of dormancy by Lee's scouts

in an area swimming with Union activity remains cloudy. Where Pfanz does have the full clarity of the historical record, he assesses the performance of commanders on both sides, giving high points to George Meade while evaluating Lee's performance as weak and unimaginative. Although he may have had better strategic ideas, Longstreet's uncooperative nature further impaired Lee's ability, as did A. P. Hill's lackluster performance. Of course, Dan Sickles, on the Federal side, receives harsh criticism for his reckless maneuver of 2 July.

97

Sauers, Richard A. **A Caspian Sea of Ink: The Meade-Sickles Controversy** (194 pp., Butternut and Blue, Baltimore, 1989)

A Caspian sea of ink has been shed in descriptions of [Gettysburg's] various details and monuments," wrote an editor of the *New York Tribune* in 1886. As Gettysburg controversies go, the irrational disagreement between Maj. Gen. George G. Meade and Maj. Gen. Daniel E. Sickles is second to none. Sickles's movement of his 3d Corps on 2 July not only jeopardized it and may have risked the battle, but it created a firestorm of debate that rages on today. As Sauers adeptly describes, Sickles launched a defensive campaign to justify his actions before the pain of his amputation waned.

Sauers's study is his revamped master's thesis from Pennsylvania State University, set in typescript and aided by an appendix of 6 maps and 10 photographs. The writing is factual, straightforward, and linear, and constitutes a superb job of well-documented historiography. The author clearly demonstrates that Meade was right and his flamboyant corps commander was in error. Sauers's work is the definitive study of this curious aspect of the battle.

98

Stewart, George R. **Pickett's Charge: A Microhistory of the Final Attack at Gettysburg, July 3, 1863** (354 pp., Houghton Mifflin Co., Boston, 1959)

Covering a mere 15 hours centered on the final attack at Gettysburg, Stewart's work presents a careful analysis of the circumstances and events of the charge. The author's use of primary materials and his judicious application of secondary sources have created a valuable work. Although parts of the study are weakly documented, such as where the author offers supposed conversations, overall the effect is balanced and the research sound.

This work should be read as a plain story of the events surrounding Pickett's Charge. The author is on weaker ground when it comes to interpretation. Suggesting that the divisions under Pickett, Pettigrew, and Trimble had a reasonable chance at success bespeaks a misunderstanding of the military tactics involved and the strength of the Union cannonade (Stewart wrongly states, for example, that 10,500 men participated in the charge). He more accurately reflects the facts concerning Lee and Longstreet and does justice to Pickett.

(Reprinted 1983, 354 pp., Morningside, Dayton)

Lawrence, Kansas, Massacre
(21 August 1863)

99

Goodrich, Thomas. **Bloody Dawn: The Story of the Lawrence Massacre** (207 pp., Kent State University Press, Kent, 1991)

Goodrich describes the famous raid on a Kansas town accomplished by the guerrilla William Clarke Quantrill on 21 August 1863. This work is the finest of its kind in describing the details of the raid and the raiders, as well as the response to Black Friday, as it came to be known. The author's background chapter outlines the Bleeding Kansas period of the 1850s and the various jayhawker raids from Kansas into Missouri. By 1862 one of the retaliatory bands of raiders from Missouri was headed by Confederate soldier Quantrill, who targeted Lawrence because of its abolition sentiment.

The author's description of the raid itself is first-rate. The narrative of the more than 400 raiders and their journey more than 60 miles into Kansas is well spun. The recounting of the many atrocities committed during the Lawrence raid—murder, arson, robbery, beatings—adds up to a tale of savagery exceeded by only a few other accounts of the war. The destruction lasted nearly half a day, and after it was over 150 lay dead, numerous homes were wrecked, stores looted, and the citizens of Lawrence stunned. The author's description of these stark facts and the Federal response belongs in collections covering the war in the West.

Chickamauga Creek, Georgia
(19–20 September 1863)

100

Cozzens, Peter. **This Terrible Sound: The Battle of Chickamauga** (675 pp., University of Illinois Press, Urbana, 1992)

This single-volume history of the greatest battle of the western theater is an assemblage of hundreds of vignettes of the experiences of soldiers and commanders set against the events of 18, 19, and 20 September 1863 and therefore does not supply a full analysis of the campaign or its significance in the scheme of the larger war. Rather, it focuses on the terrain of the Chickamauga field and the action of the battle on regimental and brigade levels. This formula works relatively well in that it immerses readers in the thick of the action on two levels: the fighting of the soldiers and the thinking of the commanders, primarily, of course, Rosecrans and Bragg but also many subordinate officers. The reliance on both primary and secondary sources translates into a story that rises and falls in reliability throughout the text.

More troubling are a number of errors that permeate the narrative. The author does not always place troops correctly on the otherwise very fine maps. The treatment of Longstreet's breakthrough attack at the Brotherton Field receives scant analysis, leaving the story of the gap created by Wood's division—the most significant moment of the battle—relatively unexamined. Factual errors are many. Cozzens states erroneously that John C. Pemberton was born in New York; that Col. James Sheffield commanded Evander M. Law's brigade on 20 September; and that States Rights Gist's brigade arrived on the field from Mississippi. He also misplaces Robertson's Texas brigade on 20 September. Misspellings crop up (Jacob Goodson, for example), and occasionally the same story is told in two different places as if for the first time. Despite these problems, the work brings together a huge mass of information on Chickamauga and offers a reasonable story of the battle.

101

Gracie, Archibald III. **The Truth about Chickamauga** (462 pp., Houghton Mifflin Co., Boston, 1911)

Composed by the son of Confederate Brig. Gen. Archibald Gracie, Jr., who was killed at Petersburg, this work seeks a reappraisal of the performance of certain commands during what the author terms the high point of the Confederate war effort. He examines in microscopic detail the actions of 20 September 1863, centered on the areas of Horseshoe Ridge and Kelly Field. A study of postwar political wrangling between former officers as well as a history drawn from the *O.R.* (q.v.), this work treats some commanders fairly and attacks others. The author feels no sympathy toward Henry Van Ness Boynton, but he defends the actions of Philip H. Sheridan, with whom Boynton had an ongoing controversy.

In a style reminiscent of a massive legal brief, Gracie attacks the reputations of William S. Rosecrans, Gordon Granger, and John M. Brannan. The material drawn from the *O.R.* is buttressed by conversations with many survivors of the battle, who verified a mass of information, particularly on the final action around Snodgrass Hill. George H. Thomas retains the luster of having staved off the Confederate push until the Army of the Cumberland could retreat in relative order, but a significant collection of analysis on other commanders sheds much light at a lower level of commands. Confusingly, the work occasionally mentions a companion volume on Petersburg that was never written. The maps are detailed and plentiful and add a deep level of understanding to the sometimes labored text. Numerous photographs of officers provide a valuable collection of Chickamauga-related images.

(Reprinted 1987, with an introduction by William Glenn Robertson, 462 pp., Morningside, Dayton)

102

Spruill, Matt, ed. **The U.S. Army War College Guide to the Battle of Chickamauga** (290 pp., University Press of Kansas, Lawrence, 1993)

This work continues the formula presented first in the companion volumes on Antietam (*q.v.*), Gettysburg (*q.v.*), and Fredericksburg and Chancellorsville (*q.v.*)., which serve as historical summaries of important battles and in a general way guidebooks to reconnoitering the ground over which these battles were fought. The Chickamauga volume contains 24 stops at which the narrative explains the action during an important phase of the battle. Nine illustrations and 19 maps help the interpretation of important battle actions.

The maps, which show troop movements during the various phases of the battle, are overlaid with important geographical landmarks and a few modern roads to show where the armies were positioned during significant moments of battle. For its text, the volume draws almost exclusively on the *O.R.* (*q.v.*), presenting battlefield reports of commanders to summarize the big picture of what was happening. The result is a fine tour of where the Federal and Confederate troops fought over areas of the field.

Chattanooga Campaign, Tennessee (October–November 1863)

103

Cozzens, Peter. **The Shipwreck of Their Hopes: The Battles for Chattanooga** (515 pp., University of Illinois Press, Urbana, 1994)

Cozzens's book provides a detailed description of the campaign beginning with the deplorable condition of the Union Army in Chattanooga and focuses on the actions at Brown's Ferry, Orchard Knob, Lookout Mountain, and Missionary Ridge. The Union effort to open the "cracker line" to supply the hungry troops receives careful analysis. The author skillfully explains the various military affairs with a natural emphasis on the decisive (and amazing) assault of 25 November on Missionary Ridge. That this highly significant campaign has not been treated with more analysis by most historians is puzzling.

Basing his account on the *O.R.* (*q.v.*) and many secondary sources, Cozzens rightfully stings Braxton Bragg for his lethargic performance—and foolish decisions, such as dispatching Longstreet to Knoxville—that if successful might have had far-reaching effects on the North. Bragg thus weakened his army and did not renew the offensive, allowing the Federal Army to strengthen in the process. The author effectively portrays Ulysses Grant and William T. Sherman, exposing the nuggets of their strategy, and supplies much-earned credit to Hooker for the strategic importance of capturing Lookout Mountain. The narrative of the grand assault on Missionary Ridge is superb, along with its analysis of the effects of many units and their commanders involved in the charge. This work is the principal study of a vital campaign.

104

Hoobler, James A. **Cities under the Gun: Images of Occupied Nashville and Chattanooga** (224 pp., Rutledge Hill Press, Nashville, 1986)

This work competently represents a type of book we should like to see more often—a detailed photographic history of a prominent and relatively neglected campaign. While most of these images have been published elsewhere, Hoobler brings together 347 photographs of Nashville, Chattanooga, and environs and creates a useful portrait of the Chattanooga and Nashville campaigns. Photographers represented include George N. Barnard, Nashville photographer T. M. Schleier, and many whose identifications are lost. Beyond the 169 images of Chattanooga and 129 of Nashville, the author includes a section of 49 views of railroad trestles.

105

Sword, Wiley. **Mountains Touched with Fire: Chattanooga Besieged, 1863** (430 pp., St. Martin's Press, New York, 1995)

The author provides a storylike version of the events around the embattled city. Although this book appeared shortly after Peter Cozzens's detailed study on the same subject (*q.v.*), it takes a somewhat different perspective and so the two works complement each other nicely, both adding to the understanding of a veritable crisis for the Federal high command.

Sword describes the situation at hand for the Federal armies following the defeat at Chickamauga and casts a lengthy view on the panic that characterized Washington and that led to the grand movement of two army corps southward and to Grant's supervision of the campaign. The author establishes a lengthy and interesting basis for analyzing the Confederate side of things as well, affording much interpretation into Braxton Bragg's inabilities to take advantage of the situation. The narrative brings into play a beautiful array of sources, though the tenor of the story is so escalated toward maximizing the drama that the greatness of every little event becomes somewhat exaggerated. Sword explores a huge array of characters and the developing situation before providing a detailed story of the three-day fight around Lookout Mountain, Orchard Knob, and Missionary Ridge. There are a few careless errors, as with the misspellings of Mary Chesnut and Orlando B. Willcox. Overall, however, this work is nearly spotless and is a fine addition to the literature.

Mine Run Campaign, Virginia (November–December 1863)

106

Humphreys, Andrew A. **From Gettysburg to the Rapidan: The Army of the Potomac, July, 1863, to April, 1864** (86 pp., Charles Scribner's Sons, New York, 1883)

Because of the length of Humphreys's book on the Virginia campaign of 1864 and 1865 (*q.v.*), the publisher issued the opening chapters as a brief and distinct work. This slim volume is not as clearly composed as the larger work, does not provide many important anecdotes of the Federal Army during the period in question, and supplies insufficient detail for the matters it covers. Further, it does not supply numbers for the armies during this period. Much of the last part of the work transforms into a defense of George G. Meade for falling back to Centreville and for the ill-devised Mine Run campaign. There is a satisfactory handling of Kilpatrick's raid on Richmond and an intelligent discussion of the Dahlgren papers, but the work falls far short of what it might have been. There is no index.

(Reprinted 1987, 86 pp., Butternut and Blue, Baltimore)

Meridian Campaign, Mississippi (3 February–5 March 1864)

107

Bearss, Margie Riddle. **Sherman's Forgotten Campaign: The Meridian Expedition** (363 pp., Gateway Press, Baltimore, 1987)

This study effectively mines the *O.R.* (*q.v.*) and a number of other sources to present a detailed story of the plan under which Sherman hoped to capture a wide corridor of Mississippi, restrict Confederate operations south of Memphis, and cut off much of the remaining rail transport supplying Confederate armies in the area. The typescript work, sponsored by the Jackson Civil War Round Table, reflects an enthusiastic author. "Sherman torches central Mississippi in his first use of total warfare," reads the heading for the book's first, lengthy section. The second part investigates the Federal occupation of Yazoo City and the resulting battle.

Bearss summarizes Sherman's action, which the general himself called "unsatisfactory," and provides a numbing amount of detail on actions of great interest and of small consequence, resulting in what seems to be a lengthy official report peppered with anecdotes. The index contains an annoying number of repetitous and sometimes erroneous entries referring to the same person or place, as with "Edward C. Nye," "Edward G. Nye," and "Master's Mate Nye," all referring to the same person. There are 17 page references under "L. Sull Ross" and 10 under "Colonel Lawrence Sullivan 'Sull' Ross." Nonetheless, this work fills a gap in the coverage of an overlooked military operation.

Kilpatrick-Dahlgren Raid, Virginia (28 February–4 March 1864)

108

Jones, Virgil Carrington. **Eight Hours before Richmond** (180 pp., Henry Holt and Co., New York, 1957)

Beset by inactivity and always ready to propose a daring plan of action, Brig. Gen. Judson Kilpatrick set off on 28 February 1864, with a band of raiders to liberate Union prisoners held in Richmond at Libby Prison and on Belle Isle. Among the participants was the one-legged Col. Ulric Dahlgren, son of Union Rear Adm. John A. B. Dahlgren. Shortly after the raid began the plan fizzled, as the weather turned bad, Kilpatrick lost contact with Dahlgren, and the innermost advance of the horsemen turned out to be the outskirts of the city.

Jones's narrative delivers the details of the story well and summarizes the factors that led to the raid's abandonment. The only lasting significance was the death of Dahlgren, who was ambushed and died outside the city; Kilpatrick and the others fled to the safety of Butler's lines. The author attributes the raid's failure to a lack of coordination between the commands and a poor understanding of the military situation about Richmond, as well as to the impetuous nature of Kilpatrick himself.

The controversy over the "Dahlgren papers," documents allegedly found on Dahlgren's body that indicated a plot to assassinate Confederate leaders, receives a detailed examination by Jones. A memorandum book, a letter of orders to a subordinate, and an address to the raiders constitute the papers in question. The originals are lost; the only known copies are photostats in the National Archives, which Jones examined. Despite the fact that the address misspells Dahlgren's name, Jones concludes that the papers were genuine. The weight of the evidence is very much in doubt, and the controversy rages on. Despite that, Jones's narrative is a good one that makes a real contribution to a rather unimportant but fascinating raid of the war.

Red River Campaign, Louisiana
(10 March–22 May 1864)

109

Johnson, Ludwell H. **Red River Campaign: Politics and Cotton in the Civil War** (317 pp., Johns Hopkins University Press, Baltimore, 1958)

Scant material exists on the Red River campaign itself, and Johnson's study leads the way in analyzing a messy and ultimately futile operation of the war's latter months. The author carefully documents the various reasons for the Red River campaign, from Northerners' desires to invade cotton-rich Texas to the political aspirations of Maj. Gen. Banks. Johnson shows how the opportunity, as ill fated as it was, drew support away from none other than Ulysses S. Grant during a time of important possibilities at Mobile. The campaign did move forward, and this work handles Banks's adventures in Louisiana, including a frustrating loss at Sabine Crossroads dealt by Dick Taylor, with clarity and excitement.

The second phase of the campaign, the Camden Expedition, receives more cursory treatment. Johnson supposes that Frederick Steele improvised the move on Camden rather than carrying out a predetermined plan. Maps would have helped readers understand the logistics of the events as they unfolded. Overall, this work offers a good survey of a campaign nearly forgotten.

(Reprinted 1993, with a new preface, 317 pp., Kent State University Press, Kent)

Atlanta Campaign, Georgia
(1 May–8 September 1864)

110

Castel, Albert. **Decision in the West: The Atlanta Campaign of 1864** (665 pp., University Press of Kansas, Lawrence, 1992)

This ambitious tome delivers a detailed examination of the outcome at Atlanta, one that moves far beyond the classic work by Jacob Cox (*q.v.*). It is written in a powerful style and with the keen insight of one who clearly envisions the full depth of his characters, the military situation at the outset and during the campaign, and the strategic and tactical reasons behind the planning and execution of the many battles for Atlanta.

Supported by massive documentation and an opinionated outlook, Castel's book concludes that the only hope for saving Atlanta lay in preserving Joe Johnston as commander of the Army of Tennessee. Hood inherited a hopeless situation, the author believes. Sherman at first fought cautiously, despite his overwhelming numerical superiority, and in the summer of 1864 the Federal commander turned up the heat on capturing Atlanta because of the touchy political situation. According to the author, Forrest's cavalrymen played an insignificant part in jeopardizing Sherman's supply lines. On larger matters, Castel believes that Sherman passed up opportunities to "crush" Confederate forces in the state. Some of the author's conclusions, however, such as Sherman's March demonstrating that he "did not like to fight," may stretch the bounds of credibility.

The mass of impressive analysis finds an unusual, and somewhat distracting, method of delivery: the work is written in the present tense. Some of the interpretations are peculiar as well, as with the author's technique of bringing Robert E. Lee into the picture and proclaiming that Lee, had he been commanding the Southern army, would have saved Atlanta and beaten or stalled out Sherman, turning the tide in the autumn election. This seems weird at best, and the kind of hypothetical what-if history that serves no coherent purpose. The book possesses many great qualities and is supplemented by wonderful maps and photographs and excellent biographical summaries. Its workmanlike descriptions of the battles and skirmishes north of and around Atlanta will stand for years to come as an impressive achievement.

111

Cox, Jacob D. **Atlanta** (vol. 9 in Scribner's series Campaigns of the Civil War, 274 pp., Charles Scribner's Sons, New York, 1882)

This work is outstanding and one of the best volumes in the Scribner's set. Its author not only commanded a division in the battles for Atlanta but was well trained in literature, military affairs, and politics. Maj. Gen. Cox's great skill as an independent thinker and wordsmith shines clearly here. Like other volumes in the series, this book takes the Union viewpoint of military affairs. Cox's narrative is nonetheless balanced in tone and as meaningful as it could have been prior to the publication of the *O.R.* (*q.v.*).

Because Cox drew on personal experience, his narrative is predominantly one sided—we see the campaign principally from the Union point of view. Cox concentrates on his own army's activities, again a natural tendency because he knew more about them. Cox downplayed the relevance of the Confederate cavalry's disorganization during the campaign and ignored outright the political importance of the fall of Atlanta. Yet the book offers a precise look at the Union movements toward Atlanta from the pen of an important participant, and for that it remains worthwhile. Seven maps accompany the text.

(Reprinted 1989, with an introduction by Richard M. McMurry, 274 pp., Broadfoot, Wilmington; 1882 edition reprinted 1994, titled *Sherman's Battle for Atlanta*, with an introduction by Brooks D. Simpson, 274 pp., Da Capo Press, New York)

112

Dodge, Grenville M. **The Battle of Atlanta and Other Campaigns, Addresses, etc.** (183 pp., Monarch Printing Co., Council Bluffs, Iowa, 1910)

A miscellany of essays and an address related to the war's campaigns in the West, this work contains Dodge's recollections of and reflections on the southwestern campaign that began in May 1861 in St. Louis and moved toward the battle of Wilson's Creek in August 1861 and Pea Ridge, where Dodge led a brigade, in March 1862. The accounts of these western actions are well worth reading. The selections also cover the Indian campaigns of 1864 and 1865, the battle of Atlanta, and many miscellaneous aspects of the author's life as a soldier, capped with an address to the Army of the Tennessee.

The incidents touched on by Dodge make the work useful today. The author's railroading skill comes alive in the passages relating to the rebuilding of the road from Decatur to Nashville. The discussion of Atlanta is the most valu-

able aspect of the work and illuminates fully and realistically Dodge's decisive and risky actions involving his command during the conflict.

(Reprinted 1965, 181 pp., Sage Books, Denver)

May Campaign, Virginia (4 May–14 June 1864)

113

Dowdey, Clifford. **Lee's Last Campaign: The Story of Lee and His Men against Grant, 1864** (415 pp., Little, Brown and Co., Boston, 1960)

Dowdey provides a story of the Wilderness campaign through the end of the war as viewed through the eyes of the Confederate high command. Probably the best of Dowdey's works, this book presents a detailed picture of the operations at the Wilderness, Spotsylvania, Cold Harbor, Petersburg, and Five Forks. It is undocumented but contains a fine bibliographical essay and shows evidence of a respectable variety of sources.

The author casts Robert E. Lee into the Freemanesque role of superhero, while throwing significant attention onto Jefferson Davis, Dick Ewell, James Longstreet, and many others. Dowdey discredits the behavior of some Confederate officers who were at odds with Lee, perhaps most prominently Pierre G. T. Beauregard. The tactical and strategic dominance of the Federal army is downplayed, of course, and Lee comes off practicing legendary generalship despite Grant's repeatedly successful flanking maneuvers. A number of odd errors appear, as with the statement that George Meade held "nominal" command of the Army of the Potomac. Spelling errors also occur, as with Junius Daniel. Still, this is a carefully woven story, accurate in most respects, and well worth reading.

(Reprinted 1993, with an introduction by Robert K. Krick, 415 pp., University of Nebraska Press, Lincoln)

114

Frassanito, William A. **Grant and Lee: The Virginia Campaigns, 1864–1865** (442 pp., Charles Scribner's Sons, New York, 1983)

The author presents a wonderful collection of images from the campaigns and analyzes the photographers and the images (including the dates, times, and camera positions for most of them). He includes modern images to match those historic, familiar scenes from the final campaigns of the eastern theater. Frassanito's well-written text presents an introduction to the campaigns and their primary battles in addition to summarizing the photographic history they left behind.

The narrative focuses on eight area groups: the Rapidan crossing, Belle Plain, and Fredericksburg; Spotsylvania, Massaponax Church, and the North Anna River; Cold Harbor and White House Landing; the James River crossing and the battle of Petersburg; City Point and the Petersburg siege; the James River operations; the "beginning of the end" at Forts Mahone and Sedgwick; and the cities of Richmond and Petersburg.

The commentary is crisp and insightful, highlighting the work of Alexander Gardner's employees and those of Andrew J. Russell. Unfortunately, the photographic coverage is highly uneven for the final eastern campaigns: numerous views in the forts encircling Petersburg chronicle casualties in the early forms of trench warfare, but almost nothing remains of the North and South Anna battles or the struggle at Cold Harbor. The interpretation is solid, however, with only a few minor faults. Is the Fredericksburg Sanitary Depot building gone, as the author says? A building near its presumed location seems to match what the camera recorded. And Grant's last meeting with Lincoln did not occur in Petersburg, as the author states. Nonetheless, this work stands as a great achievement.

115

Humphreys, Andrew A. **The Virginia Campaign of 1864 and 1865** (vol. 12 in Scribner's series Campaigns of the Civil War, 451 pp., Charles Scribner's Sons, New York, 1883)

This is the largest and one of the best of the Scribner's set. As Meade's chief of staff, Humphreys had access to all the best data that could be obtained for such a work, and he experienced the entire campaign as few could. Like other volumes in the set, this one takes the Union viewpoint, yet considering his position, Humphreys took great pains to present a balanced story.

The chief drawback is the author's propensity toward a giant official report. Humphreys's writing is hardly polished, yet the terse, tense style builds a degree of excitement as readers follow the army. The book begins with the army's crossing of the Rapidan at Germanna Ford and describes the battles of the Wilderness, Spotsylvania, Drewry's Bluff, Cold Harbor, and the siege of and various battles around Petersburg. The narrative concludes with the fall of Richmond and the surrender of Lee's army at Appomattox as well as the surrenders of other Confederate armies. Ten maps accompany the text.

(Reprinted 1989, with an introduction by Chris Calkins, 451 pp., Broadfoot, Wilmington; 1883 edition reprinted 1995,

titled *The Virginia Campaign, 1864 and 1865*, with an introduction by Brooks D. Simpson, 451 pp., Da Capo Press, New York)

116

Matter, William D. **If It Takes All Summer: The Battle of Spotsylvania** (455 pp., University of North Carolina Press, Chapel Hill, 1988)

Matter has authored one of the more likeable books on a Civil War battle. Entertainingly written, splendidly researched, and proper in its scope and focus, this is an important and necessary work for any student of the Civil War in Virginia. The study begins with the aftermath of the bloody Wilderness battle and the subsequent race southward to a destination that became the battlefield outside Spotsylvania Court House. Providing ample details of strategy, tactics, logistics, and the command and soldier levels of both sides, the author re-creates the southward movement and Confederate fortification of the Mule Shoe at the Bloody Angle. A terrifically detailed and enthralling discussion of the nearly month-long action around Spotsylvania ensues, with emphasis on Upton's attack, the huge thrust of 12 May 1864, and the final breakthrough and retreat of Lee's army toward the North Anna River.

The complexity of the details involved with a battle like Spotsylvania is staggering, and it is difficult at best to keep all aspects balanced for readers. But Matter accomplishes just such a difficult feat, making this work outstanding and highly recommended. The book's 22 maps are notably well executed, detailed, and clear in presentation.

117

Rhea, Gordon C. **The Battle of the Wilderness, May 5–6, 1864** (512 pp., Louisiana State University Press, Baton Rouge, 1994)

This is by far the most thorough, best researched, and most interestingly composed narrative of the Wilderness fight to date. The research is meticulous, extending beyond the usual sources into relatively obscure manuscript collections, and the result is a valuable book that offers fresh insights into the campaign. It presents the evidence showing that Robert E. Lee failed tactically by not delaying Grant's movement into the Wilderness to the point where Lee might have taken decisive steps to smash Grant's front. Furthermore, Lee placed much of his own army in an endangered position during the early stages of the battle. Rhea documents the confusion on the side of the Federal high command that resulted in the hesitation in Grant's movement and the battle where it occurred.

The narrative contains a highly detailed picture of the fighting as it unfolded. The author examines the details of the relationships between Lee and his subordinate commanders as well as the Grant-Meade alliance and its effects on the Union battle plans. Despite such an amazing amount of detail, the work is engagingly written and will be enjoyed by even casual readers. The maps are efficiently presented and show the topography clearly. The analysis and enjoyable presentation set a high standard for future scholarly studies of battles only weakly covered in the present literature.

118

Robertson, William Glenn. **Back Door to Richmond: The Bermuda Hundred Campaign, April–June 1864** (284 pp., University of Delaware Press, Newark, 1987)

This revisionistic essay upsets the applecart on the traditional interpretations of the Bermuda Hundred campaign. Scholarly and well documented, the treatment is likely to provoke prolonged argument over several central issues of the campaign, most revolving around the controversial Federal Maj. Gen. Benjamin F. Butler.

The author argues that Butler has received unfair treatment from past historians of the Federal movement on Richmond in 1864. Rather than Butler's being "bottled up" and wasting his time, the author feels that Butler accomplished some strategic goals during the campaign, such as gaining possession of City Point, wrecking Confederate supply lines in the area, and holding off a much larger Confederate Army until Grant was able to position himself. Robertson provides many small actions in unparalleled detail, including Drewry's Bluff, Port Walthall Junction, Swift Creek, Chester Station, and Flat Creek Bridge. From the author's research these minor battles, formerly relegated to the *O.R.* (*q.v.*), come alive in impressive and meaningful detail, accompanied by excellent maps.

The narrative does not limit itself to Federal operations. Arguments between Confederate high commanders such as Robert Ransom and Seth Barton, and also Henry A. Wise and William H. C. Whiting, document a confused defense against Butler's campaign.

(Reprinted 1991, 284 pp., Louisiana State University Press, Baton Rouge)

119

Schiller, Herbert M. **The Bermuda Hundred Campaign** (375 pp., Morningside, Dayton, 1988)

This study takes a more traditional view of Butler's operations around Petersburg than that of William Glenn Rob-

ertson on the same campaign (*q.v.*). The focus here lies in documenting Butler's lost opportunities, which the author covers in detail as the campaign unfolds. The traditional view that Butler was "bottled up" at Bermuda Hundred and wasted critical time in which he might have moved on Richmond receives support. Schiller describes the difficult relationships between Butler, in command of the Army of the James, and his two corps commanders, Quincy Gillmore and Baldy Smith. Smith's aim to take over command of the army and his superior's attempts to dislodge Gillmore, the author shows, consumed a great deal of time and effort that might have gone into military successes.

Butler's wasting of seven days after landing at Bermuda Hundred was his critical error, he contends. In describing the Confederate side of the campaign, the author shows many difficulties relating to Jefferson Davis, Samuel Cooper, Pierre G. T. Beauregard, and George Pickett that tend to support the thesis that Butler squandered an opportunity. Whether the political general could have taken Richmond and shortened the war, however, as the author contends, is a tenuous assertion grounded only in speculation.

120

Scott, Robert Garth. **Into the Wilderness with the Army of the Potomac** (236 pp., Indiana University Press, Bloomington, 1985)

In nine major sections, the author details the military events that unfolded between Grant's crossing of the Rapidan on 4–5 May 1864, and the beginning of the southward movement toward Spotsylvania on 7 May. The narrative is based largely on the *O.R.* (*q.v.*), with a number of primary and secondary sources added to the fray. The result is a lightly documented, easily readable, and successful account of a very bloody fight.

While the narration is written in a lively style, the book is light on interpretation. The author clearly understands the proper context of Grant's strategy and the tactical chaos that erupted in the Wilderness; indeed, he provides a good summary of the fighting on a small unit scale and admirable capsule biographies of many of the commanders in the fight. The lack of analysis means we receive no opinion on the consequences of Meade's tardiness on 4 May or on Phil Sheridan's temperamental demonstration over the use of cavalry in the Wilderness thickets. The author does go so far as to proclaim that George W. Getty's arrival on the Brock Road was a key to Union success as much as Longstreet's attack was a key to Confederate success. The simple and useful order of battle is partly confused by headings that mislabel Confederate forces as if they were part of the Army of the Potomac. In the end, Scott shows the Wilderness fight for what it was: a bloody and cruel wrestling match between armies that were desperate in very different ways.

121

Trudeau, Noah Andre. **Bloody Roads South: The Wilderness to Cold Harbor, May–June, 1864** (354 pp., Little, Brown and Co., Boston, 1989)

Trudeau compresses a great deal of history about the Wilderness, Spotsylvania, North and South Anna, and Cold Harbor battles into a relatively compact package. This work skillfully outlines the campaign, its objectives, and the events of each day largely in the words of the major and minor participants on both sides.

The technique of weaving numerous accounts together in chronological fashion is effective in creating a readable text. The author handles both large, pitched engagements such as the Wilderness, Spotsylvania, and Cold Harbor, and lesser actions, such as the fighting along the North Anna River and at Bethesda Church. But the approach also creates problems, as with Trudeau's oversimplification of various parts of the campaign and assessments that are misleading, such as his depiction of Lincoln as a military neophyte.

The author is often short on much-needed interpretation that could help his readers better to understand what is happening and its significance. The repeated quotations of a large number of primary authors without such analysis presents some problems, such as contradictory views that are left to the reader to interpret. Trudeau fails to adequately place the campaign in the larger context of the war, and the few maps are not particularly helpful. Still, the work ably offers a clear view of what the battle of the Wilderness must have been like for many common soldiers and a number of officers.

New Market, Virginia (15 May 1864)

122

Davis, William C. **The Battle of New Market** (249 pp., Doubleday and Co., Garden City, N.Y., 1975)

Davis showcases the campaign and battle of New Market that ended Franz Sigel's attempt to dominate the Shenandoah Valley in the spring of 1864. Although somewhat slim in size, this book contains a wealth of detail and its author has used copious sources. This is among the better studies of actions in the Valley, covering the campaign in brief and spending most of its energy with a detailed description of

the battle of 25 May 1864. The author fairly and astutely describes the character of Sigel and the relationship of his force to the other three attack forces simultaneously in motion during the spring campaign. Davis also diligently sketches the competence of John C. Breckinridge, who used a force smaller than Sigel's to ward off the clumsy Federal movement.

The author's description of the battle at New Market is exactly related. The narrative describes the action and shows that the critical fighting erupted along the Valley Turnpike rather than at the Bushong Farm. Although he demonstrates a predisposition toward overdramatizing the role of the Virginia Military Institute cadets in the battle, in the end the author fairly describes their actions and moderate significance.

Some misinterpretation involving the importance of the campaign appears. Davis unjustifiably feels that Sigel, having beaten Breckinridge and crossed the Blue Ridge Mountains, posed a major threat to Lee's army. He also errs by stating that Lee's command did not include that of Brig. Gen. John D. Imboden. The few slips aside, however, this is a first-rate campaign history that nicely relates the story of a fabled encounter.

Brice's Cross Roads, Mississippi (10 June 1864)

123

Bearss, Edwin C. **Forrest at Brice's Cross Roads and in North Mississippi in 1864** (382 pp., Morningside, Dayton, 1979)

This work originated with the writer Glenn Tucker and was essentially redone by Bearss after Tucker's death. Relying heavily on the *O.R.* (*q.v.*) and other primary sources and documents, the author traces the period of Forrest's activities from April through August 1864 with a special focus on the battle at Brice's Crossroads. The research is thorough and the writing will satisfy those who enjoy digging deep into campaigns: the text is saturated with details that Civil War buffs will appreciate. At times the material betrays evidence of poor editing, but the slips are minor.

The work fairly assesses Forrest's success at Brice's Crossroads while it sheds light on the bungled performance by Samuel Sturgis and other Federal commanders in the vicinity of Guntown. Bearss uses a great deal of space to assess matters from Forrest's point of view, but he does not fall into hero worship. On the contrary, he harshly deals with Forrest and Stephen D. Lee for the botched encounter at Harrisburg on 14 July. He also blames Lee for a failed strategy to counter Sherman's attempts to prevent Forrest from breaking the Federal supply lines.

Petersburg Campaign, Virginia (15 June 1864–2 April 1865)

124

Pleasants, Henry, Jr. **The Tragedy of the Crater** (110 pp., Christopher Publishing House, Boston, 1938)

Written by the cousin of Lt. Col. Henry Pleasants, commander of the 48th Pennsylvania Infantry, this work uses the letters and records of the elder Pleasants. The author had a fantastic story to work with, that of his cousin's role in creating the mine at Petersburg that resulted in the ill-fated Battle of the Crater in July 1864. The book offers both the story of the Crater and biographical material on Lt. Col. Pleasants; unfortunately, it accomplishes only a mediocre job of the former.

The author's underlying research is relatively limited, and his ability to describe the details surrounding the Crater—particularly the countermining by Confederates—falls short. Not only did he miss valuable and interesting sources on Confederate attempts to thwart the Union tunneling and the attempt to set off a charge in Gracie's Salient, but he also neglected easily available material like that contained in the *O.R.* (*q.v.*). Still, this book provides insight on Pleasants and adds some material to a story that lacks a thorough, documented study.

(New edition 1961, titled *Inferno at Petersburg,* by Henry Pleasants, Jr., and George H. Straley, 181 pp., Chilton Co., Philadelphia)

125

Sommers, Richard J. **Richmond Redeemed: The Siege at Petersburg** (670 pp., Doubleday and Co., Garden City, N.Y., 1981)

Confusingly titled, this work actually treats Grant's Fifth Offensive, which began on 29 September 1864 and ostensibly lasted four days. That the author could devote 449 pages of text, an exhaustive order of battle, amazingly detailed maps, appendices, and notes to a four-day period bears witness to the impressive research that went into this book. It also suggests the level of detail contained within: a minutely documented study of a small portion of the Petersburg offensive that will greatly interest those specifically researching that four-day span but is essentially too limited in scope

for anyone who wants a general survey of the Petersburg campaign.

The focus is slightly tipped toward the Union Army, although the author describes actions from the Confederate standpoint as well. Most of the work consists of a blow-by-blow accounting of where virtually all participants in the Fifth Offensive were at each moment of the four days, what they were doing, and what effect they had on the fighting of the moment. Sommers does not interpret much along the way, saving his analysis for a final chapter. Disturbingly, he infrequently refers to timing: pages roll by before a reference to date and time comes along, making it confusing to place endless details in context. In the end, Sommers shows that the Fifth Offensive captured some ground but failed to take Petersburg. The work contains some valuable military assessments.

126

Trudeau, Noah Andre. **The Last Citadel: Petersburg, Virginia, June 1864–April 1865** (514 pp., Little, Brown and Co., Boston, 1991)

The author provides a smoothly written work on the campaign of Petersburg that concentrates on important periods of the siege, provides chronological summaries of events at headquarters and in the field on important dates throughout the siege, and makes good use of well-known primary and secondary sources, including those from many officers and enlisted men.

The following periods in 1864 receive extensive coverage: 9, 15–18, and 21–23 June; 22 June–1 July; 30 July; 14–21 and 25 August; 15–16 September; 29 September–2 October; 27 October; and 7–12 December; and in 1865: 5–7 February; 25 March; and 2 April. The text relies heavily on the *O.R.* (*q.v.*), extracts from Grant's reports, and a number of other contemporary sources. Such a focus on significant actions that broke the drudgery of the campaign brings the important characters and clashes to light, but it tends to bury the monotonous nature of the ongoing siege. Nor are all of the relatively significant actions described, as with Second Darbytown Road, the Confederate countermine, and operations south of Hatcher's Run. Thus the actions brought in the reader's attention do not provide a comprehensive understanding of the campaign.

Occasional errors may be found in the text, relating to commanders and units, and in the order of battle and the bibliography. The interpretation of what various actions meant is shallow—the story is here, but its meaning often goes unstated. Despite these flaws, some of plan and some of execution, this work offers the best single-volume summary of the siege in print. Thus, it is a necessary part of the battles and campaigns bookshelf.

Early's Raid on Washington
(27 June–7 August 1864)

127

Cooling, B. F. **Jubal Early's Raid on Washington, 1864** (344 pp., Nautical and Aviation Publishing Co., Baltimore, 1989)

Cooling examines the famous campaign in which Early skirted Washington and produced alarm in the city during the final full summer of the war. This work is the best summation of a much-overlooked series of minor engagements; it contains careful descriptions of the clashes and commanders involved that include valuable writings not only on Early, but also on David Hunter, Phil Sheridan, and Lew Wallace.

This work opens with an exposé of Early's victory over Hunter at Lynchburg, carries on through the relatively important clashes at Monocacy Creek and at Fort Stevens just outside Washington, and concludes as the Confederates retreat across the Potomac. The author tells the tale of Lincoln under fire at Fort Stevens, and he provides a meaningful summation of Wallace's role at Monocacy in checking the Confederate advance.

Unfortunately, Cooling overestimates the significance of Early's raid, claiming that it extended the war by "nine months," a contention that stands against a mountain of contradictory evidence. He also exaggerates both the size of Early's force and the likelihood that he might have "captured" Washington—a good trick under the circumstances. Misspellings in the text detract from the work's credibility, such as those of Ely S. Parker, Leonidas Lafayette Polk (not to be confused with the Confederate general officer), Robert Ransom, Roger Taney, and Elihu B. Washburne. Still, this work remains the best single synthesis of a curious if not terribly important raid. For another, similarly interesting and more compact treatment, see *Jubal's Raid: General Early's Famous Attack on Washington in 1864,* by Frank E. Vandiver (198 pp., McGraw-Hill, New York, 1960; reprinted 1988, 198 pp., University of Nebraska Press, Lincoln).

128

Worthington, Glenn H. **Fighting for Time; or, The Battle That Saved Washington and Mayhap the Union: A Story of the War between the States, Showing How Washington Was Saved from Capture by Early's Army of Invasion and How That Achievement Contributed to the Preservation of the Union, with Many Stories of the Invasion Hitherto Untold** (306 pp., published by the author, Frederick, Md., 1932)

This constitutes an adequate story of the fight at Monoc-

acy Creek. As the title indicates, the author contends that had Early not been checked by Wallace at Monocacy, Washington would have been occupied and disaster would have befallen the Union. That is exceedingly unlikely to have occurred, however, as Early would not have risked having his small force hemmed in on three sides. Indeed, Maj. Gen. John B. Gordon, along on the adventure, later wrote that all the commanders present at Early's many councils of war agreed that Washington would not be entered.

Despite the strategic embellishment inherent in this work, it provides a linearly factual story of how Early and his raiders struck a psychological blow to the populace of the city. The author develops the characters of Jubal Early and Lew Wallace and demonstrates how Wallace's clash at Monocacy was indeed impressive, given his force. Based on the *O.R.* (*q.v.*) and a scattering of small sources, this work will stand as a useful part of the literature until a compelling version of the story appears. Several maps, photographs, and an index complete the work.

(Reprinted 1985, with an additional material and an introduction by Brian C. Pohanka, 306 pp., Beidel, Shippensburg, Pa.)

Mobile Bay, Alabama (3–23 August 1864)

129

Bergeron, Arthur W., Jr. **Confederate Mobile** (271 pp., University Press of Mississippi, Jackson, 1991)

Scholarly in its outlook and written in a fine style, this work merits the close inspection of anyone interested in the Confederate defenses of Mobile from the early captures of the city's forts to the surrender at the end of the war in May 1865. Bergeron first establishes the strategic relevance of Mobile to the Confederacy by examing its status as a port and origin of supply to the Confederate interior. He then surveys the various commanders involved in defending the city and the Union efforts to capture it. Excellent summaries of the character of John H. Forney, Dabney H. Maury, and Jones M. Withers emerge, as do comments on Edward R. S. Canby, David G. Farragut, and Gordon Granger.

The point of view in this work leans heavily toward the Confederate defenders, but readers expect that from a book focused squarely on Mobile. Other questions of balance are handled superbly, as with the coverage of both army and navy maneuvers, the early fortifications of Morgan and Gaines, and the fierce struggle on both sides during the battle of Mobile Bay. The author's examination of the Confederate response to an endangered Mobile reveals a more complex and competent preparation than previously recorded in one volume. Likewise, the treatment of the final months of the conflict in a war-weary city adds much of significance to the story of an important locale in the Deep South.

Sheridan's Valley Campaign, Virginia (7 August 1864–2 March 1865)

130
Gallagher, Gary W., ed. **Struggle for the Shenandoah: Essays on the 1864 Valley Campaign** (120 pp., Kent State University Press, Kent, 1991)

This work contains five thoughtful reflections on various aspects of the campaign. Gallagher provides an overview of the Shenandoah Valley in 1864, introducing the dominant figures of Jubal Early and Philip Sheridan and lamenting the relative lack of analysis inspired by the second great Valley campaign relative to Stonewall Jackson's campaign of two years earlier. Jeffry D. Wert examines Early and concludes that his handling of the campaign was stacked against long odds and that the Federals could afford risks whereas Early could not; indeed, he says Union forces "with their numerical superiority decisively defeated the Rebels." Wert finds Early a "flawed man and general."

A. Wilson Greene examines Union generalship in the campaign and finds Sheridan's performance indeed commendable, but he suggests that a gallery of others deserve significant credit—Abraham Lincoln, Ulysses S. Grant, and such stellar performers on the individual fields as George Crook, Horatio Wright, George Custer, Wesley Merritt, Emory Upton, and George Getty. Robert K. Krick examines Jubal Early's use of cavalry during the campaign and finds that he did not use it very effectively. Dennis E. Frye discusses the role of John S. Mosby in the 1864 Valley campaign, one that irritated Federal authorities but never significantly affected the course of events. Indeed, Frye writes, Mosby chose to play a bold game "and lost."

131
Pond, George E. **The Shenandoah Valley in 1864** (vol. 11 in Scribner's series Campaigns of the Civil War, 287 pp., Charles Scribner's Sons, New York, 1883)

Pond details actions throughout the Valley from April 1864 to March 1865. The principal focus is Maj. Gen. Philip H. Sheridan's successful campaign. Written by the former editor of *Army-Navy Journal* (and ex-officer of the 45th

Massachusetts Infantry), this work is more readable than others in the Scribner's set, very nearly reading like a novel.

The book covers Cloyd's Mountain, New Market, Maj. Gen. David Hunter's campaign, Maj. Gen. Jubal Early's raid toward Washington, Kernstown, Fisher's Hill, Cedar Creek, and Waynesboro. Despite his literary ability, Pond was so thrilled with the Federal commanders that he gave only slight attention to Confederates. Consequently, the work is far from balanced. Additionally, Pond occasionally slips with facts and figures. Eight maps accompany the text.

(Reprinted 1989, with an introduction by Jeffry D. Wert, 287 pp., Broadfoot, Wilmington)

132
Wert, Jeffry D. **From Winchester to Cedar Creek: The Shenandoah Campaign of 1864** (324 pp., South Mountain Press, Carlisle, Pa., 1987)

A competently researched treatment of Sheridan's campaign in the Valley, this work surveys events from Sheridan's assignment to invade the Valley in the summer of 1864 to the battle of Waynesboro on 2 March 1865, the demoralizing finish to Early's depleted army. In between lie vivid accounts of Third Winchester, Fisher's Hill, and Cedar Creek, as well as a number of scattered, smaller activities in the campaign. The narrative derives from research in the *O.R.* (*q.v.*) plus a number of secondary accounts that enliven the work at critical places.

The author offers sound evaluative comments on a variety of commanders, not limiting his analysis to Sheridan and Early. He also wisely interprets the actions of the Valley in the larger context of the ongoing war, particularly the Petersburg siege to the south, and touches on the political situation of that summer, a critical aspect in recognizing the importance of Sheridan's campaign to the overall Union war effort. The text is skewed slightly toward the Union side, which may be appropriate for viewing the events that climaxed with Sheridan's ride and Cedar Creek. The maps are adequate though unspectacular; the index is rather brief.

Hampton-Rosser Cattle Raid, Virginia (16 September 1864)

133
Boykin, Edward C. **Beefsteak Raid** (305 pp., Funk and Wagnalls, New York, 1960)

The author provides a fast-paced, readable telling of one of the war's more adventuresome operations. As the Union

Army's noose around Petersburg tightened in late summer 1864, food shortages inside the lines in the Army of Northern Virginia became critical. Armed with intelligence that nearly 2500 head of Federal cattle at Coggins's Point were poorly guarded, Maj. Gen. Wade Hampton launched a cleverly executed raid to capture them.

The colorful and adventurous story might appear to be embellished were it not for the author's care with the facts. Readers fairly ride through the Virginia night along with Hampton's 4000 horsemen as they make their way to Dinwiddie Court House and then, the following night, move on Coggins's Point. The narrative details Brig. Gen. Thomas L. Rosser's spearheading attack and the Confederates' capture of the cattle, as well as the story of their return to safety within the Petersburg lines. In just three days Hampton's troopers had resupplied their comrades in heroic fashion.

Pilot Knob, Missouri
(24–28 September 1864)

134

Peterson, Cyrus A., and Joseph Mills Hanson. **Pilot Knob: The Thermopylae of the West** (324 pp., Neale Publishing Co., New York, 1914)

This succinct account of a nearly forgotten battle presents the military conditions in Missouri in 1864, describes the early phases of Price's raid, and sets the stage for the relevance of the action at Pilot Knob. The remainder of the work consists of a tapestry woven from more than 100 accounts by Federal soldiers relating to the battle, a handful of Confederate reminiscences, and excisions from official documents.

Although the analysis is rather lean and the organization is sometimes haphazard, a great cache of useful material may be found by paging through this work. The best chapters cover preparations of Union defenders at Fort Davidson, the Confederate attack, the defense of Leasburg, and a brief summary. In the final section the authors conclude that a nominal tactical victory was won by the Confederates, but strategically the Federals triumphed because of the casualties inflicted on Price's army. The authors hence lean toward sympathies with the Union, and they do more than lean when they conclude that Pilot Knob was "one of the greatest as well as one of the most decisive conflicts of the terrible internecine struggle of half a century ago." The work lacks an index.

(Reprinted 1964, 324 pp., Ramfre Press, Cape Girardeau, Mo.)

Sherman's March to the Sea, Georgia, and Carolinas Campaign
(15 November 1864–26 April 1865)

135

Barrett, John G. **Sherman's March through the Carolinas** (325 pp., University of North Carolina Press, Chapel Hill, 1956)

After introducing the basics of Sherman's life and character, the author picks up the story of Sherman's final campaign beginning in January 1865. The book presents a chronological narrative of events of the march and includes moderately detailed coverage of the burning of Columbia, the battle of Bentonville, and the surrender at Durham Station. The author adeptly describes Grant's role in the surrender process following the first Sherman-Johnston meeting. The level of detail in certain spots and anecdotal reminiscences drawn from a wide variety of sources is particularly pleasing. This is a campaign book with an exciting story to tell, and the mission is carried off splendidly.

Barrett's story is balanced and quite objectively told. He resists classic exaggerations of Sherman's character and the destruction that followed in the wake of his army. He also understands the concept of "total war" and its inventor, and the emotional reactions to it by those who experienced Sherman's March are carefully documented. The reader comes away with an appreciation of life as a bummer, the difficulties of moving an army through the Carolina wilderness, the peculiar friendliness of Sherman toward Johnston, and the exploits of many colorful soldiers such as Judson Kilpatrick and Smith D. Atkins.

(Reprinted 1996, 325 pp., University of North Carolina Press, Chapel Hill)

136

Cox, Jacob D. **The March to the Sea: Franklin and Nashville** (vol. 10 in Scribner's series Campaigns of the Civil War, 265 pp., Charles Scribner's Sons, New York, 1882)

Cox continues here where his previous Scribner's volume on Atlanta (q.v.) leaves off. Like that book, this work is outstanding as one of the best early campaign books on the war. Maj. Gen. Cox's intimate knowledge of military tactics and both superior and inferior officers shows here with great merit.

Although the book is written predominantly from the Union point of view, Confederate officers and actions receive fair and objective treatment, with the exception of Cox's overestimation of Confederate forces employed during the

March. Cox played a key role in defeating Confederate Gen. John B. Hood's army at Franklin and Nashville, a fact Cox's modesty barely allows to enter the story. His treatment of Schofield and Thomas is balanced, though he infers that Thomas was clearly slow in moving against Hood—a sentiment powerfully seconded by Grant. The rest of the work describes Fort Fisher, Kinston, Savannah, and Bentonville. The narrative of the army's march through the Carolinas is both cramped and electrifying. Ten maps accompany the text.

(Reprinted 1989, with an introduction by Nathaniel Cheairs Hughes, 265 pp., Broadfoot, Wilmington; 1882 edition reprinted 1994, titled *Sherman's March to the Sea, Hood's Tennessee Campaign, and the Carolina Campaigns of 1865*, with an introduction by Brooks D. Simpson, 265 pp., Da Capo Press, New York)

137

Glatthaar, Joseph T. **The March to the Sea and Beyond: Sherman's Troops in the Savannah and Carolinas Campaigns** (318 pp., New York University Press, New York, 1985)

Unlike other works on the campaign, Glatthaar's approaches the concept of inventing total war and conquering the Deep South from the perspective of common soldiers. As such he supports this work with a mountain of soldier diaries and letters as well as many standard sources, providing a foot soldier's bible of experiences during battles and life on the march and in camp. Because Glatthaar carried off this approach so skillfully, the work is particularly enjoyable.

Sherman's army, the author makes clear, was an army of grizzled veterans. The shirkers and the faint of heart were long gone. The Georgia campaigners enjoyed bringing war to central Georgia, and one senses through their letters that they understood in many cases the value of bringing the pain of war on the populace, of defeating the Confederacy by killing its spirit. The author does not provide a significantly new thesis or novel interpretation in this work, but his collection of battlefield anecdotes, brought onto paper by the pens of those who marched to the sea, warrants a place in collections covering battles and campaigns. A superbly executed, more recent work by Lee Kennett, *Marching through Georgia: The Story of Soldiers and Civilians during Sherman's Campaigns* (418 pp., HarperCollins, New York, 1995), supplements Glatthaar's book nicely because of its emphasis on soldiers and civilians.

138

Lucas, Marion Brunson. **Sherman and the Burning of Columbia** (188 pp., Texas A&M University Press, College Station, 1976)

The author's clear chapters survey the events at Columbia on 17 and 18 February 1865, as well as they can be reconstructed, in addition to providing a thoughtful analysis of the fire's origins and outcomes. The work is well documented, written in a straightforward, factual manner, and provides enough background in terms of the city's evacuation, capture, and destruction to clearly see through the smoke on this emotionally distorted topic.

Lucas finds that the potential for trouble clearly remained intact when Confederate authorities left behind large amounts of liquor and also evacuated as burning bales of cotton stood scattered through the town. Much of the responsibility for the resulting fire therefore must rest on the Rebels, the author shows, particularly when Federal commanders could hardly find it feasible to risk the lives of dozens or hundreds of soldiers in hostile territory to fight the fire. Still, the work shows that Union officers might have retained order in a better fashion than they did. Lucas notes that rioting and looting by drunken Federal troops occurred on a relatively small scale, and that many Union soldiers helped to protect civilians and homes from the wind-driven inferno. Two appendices list ordnance stores captured by the Federals on 17 February and a directory of Confederate officers in the town. All those who wish to know the details of this much-publicized incident in Sherman's final campaign should consult this work.

139

Nichols, George Ward. **The Story of the Great March, from the Diary of a Staff Officer** (394 pp., Harper and Bros., New York, 1865)

Nichols joined Sherman's staff as aide-de-camp in Atlanta, where this narrative commences, and recorded his impressions of the Georgia countryside, the men in the march, and many little incidents of the commanders. He provides detailed observations of Sherman, Howard, Mower, and Blair. The coverage extends from Allatoona, through the burning of Atlanta, to the march itself, through the Carolina campaign and up to Johnston's surrender. The fact that Nichols took voluminous notes along the way and based this work on those notes gives the narrative an immediacy that other works lack.

The author presents revealing scenes of the capture of Milledgeville, the arrival at Millen, the storming of Fort

McAllister, the evacuation of Savannah, the march on Columbia and its monumental fire, the capture of Fayetteville, the battle of Bentonville, and the surrender at Durham Station. Some of the material is worked into high drama, as evidenced by the manufactured quotations. For the most part this work is reliable and presents a soldier's view of the march and the Carolinas campaign.

(Reprinted 1972, 394 pp., Ayer, Salem)

Franklin and Nashville, Tennessee
(30 November–15 December 1864)

140

Cox, Jacob D. **The Battle of Franklin, Tennessee: November 30, 1864** (351 pp., Charles Scribner's Sons, New York, 1897)

This remains valuable as a well-composed and judicious commentary on a battle in which Cox played a pivotal role. The work both answered and generated controversy at the time of publication. For example, Cox asserts that the fight justified William T. Sherman's division of his forces and March to the Sea; that George D. Wagner's poor performance resulted from violating Cox's orders; and that by virtue of being the overall commander on the battlefront Cox deserves credit for the splendid Union victory.

While this work may not definitively solve any of the three controversies, it does deliver a blow-by-blow account of the action in which Hood's frontal attack demolished much of his army. Written with Cox's usual outstanding literary skill, it provides an overview of the campaign; the march to Franklin; the assault on Wagner's rear guard; the eruptive fighting at the center, left, and right of the Union line; the battle after darkness; Wilson's cavalry engagement; and the Federal retreat from the field. Subsequent chapters examine Franklin in the wake of the battle, provide extensive discussions of Schofield and Wagner, a recapitulation of the fight at the Carter House, a statistical summary of the casualties, and Henry Stone's and David Stanley's criticisms of the battle. Appendices present official reports.

(Reprinted 1983, with an introduction by Michael A. Hughes, 351 pp., Morningside, Dayton)

141

Hay, Thomas Robson. **Hood's Tennessee Campaign** (272 pp., Neale Publishing Co., New York, 1929)

This retains value as a relatively early, scholarly study of an important series of battles. Reasonably well researched and documented with adequate notes and a useful index, it lives on as a source both on Hood and on the campaign, principally from the Confederate viewpoint. It covers the opening of the campaign, the disposition of Hood and Thomas, the relationship between Sherman and Thomas, Hood's preparations, the delay at Tuscumbia, and Hood's advance.

The straightforward narrative accelerates in interest with the failure at Spring Hill, Schofield and Wilson's exploits at Spring Hill, the battle of Franklin, and two long analytical sections on the battle of Nashville. Hay concludes with a discussion of the retreat from Nashville and the lost cause of the Confederacy following the loss of Hood's army. He also faults Hood for poor strategy and tactics. The book contains crude but detailed maps. The final sections lament the Army of Tennessee and the sinking of the Confederate cause.

(Reprinted 1976, with an introduction by Robert Womack, 272 pp., Morningside, Dayton)

142

Horn, Stanley F. **The Decisive Battle of Nashville** (181 pp., Louisiana State University Press, Baton Rouge, 1956)

The author has much to say about the downfall of the Army of Tennessee. Hood's drive northward following the disaster in Atlanta signaled a rather desperate attempt to demonstrate offensive action that was aided for a time mostly by the inaction of Federal Maj. Gen. George Thomas. Of course, the Army of Tennessee discovered the horrors of frontal attacks at Franklin at the end of November 1864 and was demolished two weeks later at Nashville, and this later action, rather poorly covered in the literature, forms the focus of Horn's book.

Although Horn describes the motives of the commanders and the actions that unfolded rather well, his interpretation of the battle's significance seems clouded by imaginary scenarios. If several things had happened differently, the author argues, then the general's "daringly conceived plan" might have succeeded, tipping the balance of the war. A simple investigation of the military situation at that time refutes any such claim, and the evidence to render the assertion without foundation exists in the author's own work. Apart from such occasional interjections of unrestrained hope for Hood, this is a solid contribution to understanding the smaller details of the battle. The book lacks a much-needed index.

(Reprinted 1991, 181 pp., Louisiana State University Press, Baton Rouge)

143

Sword, Wiley. **Embrace an Angry Wind: The Confederacy's Last Hurrah—Spring Hill, Franklin, and Nashville** (499 pp., HarperCollins, New York, 1992)

Sword delivers a clear summary of the final battles of the West principally from the Confederate viewpoint in this well researched and zestfully written book. As such, he makes a significant contribution to the literature on the Tennessee campaign of 1864.

The first third of the work examines the events leading up to Hood's movement into Tennessee and generally provides a sound interpretation of the fumbled strategy employed by the embattled commander. However, viewing the events primarily from the Confederate side results in a relatively naïve recounting of the Union war aims employed as Sherman marched to the sea and Thomas supervised Federal forces in Tennessee. The peculiar bias leads to some unclear and garbled narrative, but generally the reader emerges from this section realizing the desperation of the Confederate cause and the foolishness of the tactics employed at Spring Hill and Franklin.

The accounts of the march to Franklin and the disastrous frontal attack there are clear and well presented. The author skillfully brings into play an increasing number of characters as Hood's beaten army makes a final stand at Nashville and, defeated decisively by Thomas, effectively ceases to exist. It becomes obvious that by the end of the year the Confederacy no longer has an effective force of resistance outside the Army of Northern Virginia, itself sapped in strength. The author's account deserves a spot on the battles and campaigns bookshelf.

Fort Fisher, North Carolina
(15 January 1865)

144

Gragg, Rod. **Confederate Goliath: The Battle of Fort Fisher** (343 pp., HarperCollins, New York, 1991)

The author provides a competently researched and written account of the second attack on Fisher, a story loaded with interesting and ironic events. Gragg's text briefly sets the stage for the strategic importance of Wilmington and examines Washington's increasing need to blockade and capture that city. Thereafter the author sketches the first, unsuccessul attack on Fisher, increasing the momentum toward the core of the book, which is a detailed narration of Terry's attack and how the Federal Navy assisted it.

The work is balanced by suitable background material on the Confederate defenses at Fort Fisher and a detailed story of Col. William Lamb and other notable officers in gray. The author recounts the enormous size and physical nature of the fort and provides exhilarating detail describing the attack of 15 January. He draws on a battery of primary sources to support his own narrative. The background material necessary to place the attack in context is relatively brief, however, and the work stops short of interpreting the meaning of Fort Fisher in the larger context of the closing weeks of the war. Still, this lively book merits widespread attention.

Wilson's Selma Raid, Alabama
(22 March–20 April 1865)

145

Jones, James Pickett. **Yankee Blitzkrieg: Wilson's Raid through Alabama and Georgia** (256 pp., University of Georgia Press, Athens, 1976)

This competent and enjoyable study sheds light on a large-scale operation that has received little analysis in the Civil War literature.

Wilson's raid began on 22 March 1865 as Confederate resistance was caving in everywhere. The strongest area of the Deep South remained the area in eastern Mississippi, Alabama, and western Georgia, encompassing Montgomery, Selma, Meridian, and Macon. Maj. Gen. Wilson's 13,480 troopers constituted the largest cavalry force of the war as they began their 525-mile journey. A month later, after destroying the Confederate naval foundry and ordnance works in Selma, scattering what remained of Nathan Bedford Forrest's command, fighting six battles, capturing more than 6000 prisoners, and seizing vast quantities of field pieces, longarms, railroad boxcars, and supplies, the raiders ended their mission in Macon.

The author describes the raid and in a precisely documented fashion details the encounters and the spoils captured by Wilson's army. The focus is naturally on the Federal side, both because Wilson's men were the aggressors and because few organized Confederate forces remained. The story is one that illuminates the dying days of the Confederacy from an unfamiliar stage and provides a cohesive picture of what was happening as Sherman pursued and caught Johnston and the Petersburg lines unraveled. Along the way readers receive interesting details of cavalry tactics, weapons, and strategy.

(Reprinted 1987, 256 pp., University of Georgia Press, Athens)

Appomattox Court House, Virginia, and Beyond (9 April 1865–   )

146

Chamberlain, Joshua Lawrence. **The Passing of the Armies: An Account of the Final Campaign of the Army of the Potomac, Based on Personal Reminiscences of the Fifth Army Corps** (392 pp., G. P. Putnam's Sons, New York, 1915)

This is one of the finest accounts of a campaign penned by a Federal soldier. The wide range of battle experience for this former teacher created a singular position from which he participated in the surrender ceremonies at Appomattox by accepting the flags and rifles of the vanquished Army of Northern Virginia. Such a milestone in Chamberlain's career, one for which he was commissioned brevet major general of volunteers, added luster to his clear and precise recording of the final campaign of the war, from the last days of fighting at the Petersburg front, along the White Oak Road and elsewhere, through Five Forks, the flight of Lee's tattered army, the slipping of Southern hope at Amelia Courthouse, the disaster at Sayler's Creek, and the surrender at Appomattox. The work also includes a narrative of the Grand Review and the closure of Sherman's march northward to Washington and concludes with the disbanding of the armies.

Chamberlain's intelligence and literary ability enabled him to compose a work of superior quality, from the precision of the facts cited to the prose with which he has woven them together. The story is supplemented by excellent maps, though it lacks an index. Most valuable, perhaps, are the illuminations concerning Five Forks and the Sheridan-Warren dispute, the focus on Grant's pursuit of Lee after the lines broke, and the on-the-spot eyewitness material relating to the several days around Appomattox. Additionally, the author casts interesting reflections on the relationships between the two Federal armies and their commanders. This is a stellar work of Civil War history—a classic.

(Reprinted 1986, with a foreword by John J. Pullen, 392 pp., Morningside, Dayton)

147

Hanna, A. J. **Flight into Oblivion** (306 pp., Johnson Publishing Co., Richmond, 1938)

With careful documentation and astute writing, the author has pieced together a narrative that allows the chaos of the times to shine through. An embellished story is not necessary here: the insanity and confusion of the events themselves provide a powerful witness to the last weeks of the Confederate government.

Hanna's book begins as Richmond falls. The narrative follows the flight of Jefferson Davis, Judah Benjamin, John C. Breckinridge, Robert A. Toombs, George Davis, and their entourages south to Burkeville, Danville, Greensboro, and Charlotte. Hanna reveals Davis's deluded thinking and the contrasting survival mentality of most other refugees. The capture of Davis in Irwinville is expertly recounted, as are the capture of George Davis at Key West and the journeys of Toombs to Havana and of Breckinridge and Benjamin to England. This is a first-class description of the unraveling of the civilian Confederate high command.

(Reprinted 1959, with a new preface, 306 pp., Indiana University Press, Bloomington)

148

Tremain, Henry E. **Last Hours of Sheridan's Cavalry: A Reprint of War Memoranda** (ed. John Watts de Peyster, 563 pp., Bonnell, Silver and Bowers, New York, 1904)

Tremain's work remains useful as a primary resource relating to the final actions in the East. The author was an aide-de-camp on the staff of Maj. Gen. George Crook. As such, he was centrally placed during the 11-day campaign surrounding Richmond and Petersburg through the Confederate retreat to Appomattox. After the surrender of Lee, the author formulated his notes on the campaign in camp while awaiting the Grand Review in Washington. The combination of privileged perspective and freshness of material combine to make this volume an enthralling eyewitness record of the eastern war's final days.

In the years after the war, the author (and subsequently his editor) added and amended much material from the *O.R.* (*q.v.*), greatly improving the historical record of the original narrative. But the primary value of the work lies in the personal reflections on the campaign surrounding the writer. The story is told with great charm.

149

Trudeau, Noah Andre. **Out of the Storm: The End of the Civil War, April–June 1865** (470 pp., Little, Brown and Co., Boston, 1994)

This is the third in a trilogy of works by this author covering the Virginia campaigns of 1864 and 1865. As with the previous works (*q.v.*), this book is well researched and written with zeal, presenting a chronological story of the important actions that it covers by moving circularly from the fronts to the command posts and capital cities of both sides. The coverage in this work extends from the Federal destruction of the railroads and resulting fall of Petersburg through the Appomattox campaign, the surrender of the Army of Northern Virginia, and the final scenes of war as Lincoln is assassinated and the remaining Confederate forces eventually capitulate.

The strength of Trudeau's approach lies in the fine writing and organization and the sweeping coverage in terms of geography and time that result in a compelling story. The research is impressively evident, although the work is not formally documented but instead contains general notes on sources for each chapter. Some careless errors occasionally result, as with the misspelling of Mary Chesnut's name and use of the antiquated name Fortress Monroe. These are minor flaws, however, in a book that offers casual readers an enjoyable synopsis of the final weeks of the war.

CONFEDERATE BIOGRAPHIES, MEMOIRS, AND LETTERS

POLITICIANS

Judah Philip Benjamin (1811–1884)

150

Meade, Robert Douthat. **Judah P. Benjamin: Confederate Statesman** (432 pp., Oxford University Press, New York, 1943)

In this well documented and composed narrative, Meade illuminates the character of the man who served as Confederate secretary of war, secretary of state, and attorney general. He explores how Benjamin's Jewish ancestry affected his performance in the midst of the attitudes that pervaded much of the South and how his special, close relationship with Jefferson Davis, a symbiotic pairing that benefited both parties, aided his performance. Meade examines Benjamin's ironic attitudes toward slavery, as Benjamin owned slaves of his own yet came to press for emancipation in exchange for military service.

The author's careful study reveals Benjamin's quixotic personality, allowing readers to see a clear picture of Benjamin the man. Meade draws on a suitable array of sources and provides a section of analysis on Benjamin's escape from Federal authorities and his subsequent legal career in England. This work offers a balanced view of the controversial "brains of the Confederacy."

(Reprinted 1975, 432 pp., Arno Press, New York)

Joseph Emerson Brown (1821–1894)

151

Parks, Joseph H. **Joseph E. Brown of Georgia** (612 pp., Louisiana State University Press, Baton Rouge, 1977)

Well researched and incredibly detailed, this book is likely to stand as a respectable piece of Confederate political literature for years to come. Parks successfully sketches Brown's support of Confederate war aims and his simultaneous adherence to state rights policies and nearly continuous battles with Jefferson Davis. The treatment of Brown's complex relationship with the Confederate leader and with other Richmond politicians is handled nicely, with thoughtful and extensive analysis.

The tense maneuvers between Brown and Davis over supplying troops from the Georgia militia and war materiel from within Georgia are scrutinized. The author carefully analyzes the postwar activities of Brown, who accepted defeat, transformed into a Republican, and made a fortune in business, dropping the state rights ideals as rapidly as he had abandoned slavery. The work concludes with an examination of Brown's conversion back to the Democratic party and his later years in the U.S. Senate.

A few misspellings are scattered throughout the text, as with the names of Lafayette McLaws, Wager Swayne, and Henry Wirz. The bibliography lists an impressive array of primary and secondary sources, some of which should be used with care, and the index is well done.

Jefferson Finis Davis (1808–1889)

152

Bledsoe, Albert T. **Is Davis a Traitor; or, Was Secession a Constitutional Right Previous to the War of 1861?** (263 pp., published by the author, Baltimore, 1866)

According to Bledsoe, the answer to the first question is of course no; to the second question, yes. This is a brief and partly persuasive legalistic argument that echoes in more compact form much of the later work by Alexander H. Stephens (*q.v.*). Bledsoe's work began in 1863 when Davis himself proposed a constitutional defense of the Confederacy, and the author carried out much of the research in the British Library. The argument amounts to showing the Confederates as the inheritors of the Founding Fathers' dream.

Bitterly partisan and composed in the fury of Confederate defeat, the work's most lasting influence may have been to help release Davis from prison. Bledsoe delivers discourses on the Constitution as a compact between the various states, the language of the Constitution, the opinions of Alexander Hamilton, James Madison, and others, and presumed inconsistencies in the speeches of Daniel Webster. He offers a demonstration of the "absurdity" that the Constitution was made by one people as a nation, an examination of the causes of secession, and a discourse on the legislators of the Constitution as political prophets. Bledsoe makes selective use of material to strengthen his case and includes much that is illogical, but he does demonstrate how the Confederate high command attempted to justify the war in the days immediately following surrender. Bledsoe concludes by stating that in the end, British tyranny would have been more tolerable to the South than losing to the Yankees.

(New edition 1915, titled *The War between the States; or, Was Secession a Constitutional Right Previous to the War of 1861–65?*, 242 pp., J. P. Bell Co., Lynchburg)

153

Davis, Jefferson. **The Papers of Jefferson Davis** (ed. Haskell M. Monroe, James T. McIntosh, Lynda Lasswell Crist, Mary Seaton Dix, and Kenneth H. Williams, 8 vols. to date, 5116 pp., Louisiana State University Press, Baton Rouge, 1971–)

This indispensable set is of great value to all Civil War students. The work in part supersedes the earlier compendium *Jefferson Davis, Constitutionalist: His Letters, Papers, and Speeches,* by Jefferson Davis (ed. Dunbar Rowland, 10 vols., 5841 pp., Mississippi Department of Archives and History, Jackson, 1923), although some of the later volumes in this ongoing project provide relatively small numbers of full, annotated documents. The Rowland set contains significant numbers of letters to Davis as well as those written by him, along with articles, speeches, transcripts of official documents, and so on. The earlier set nonetheless will remain useful in tandem, despite its occasional inaccuracies.

The eight volumes so far published cover the following periods: 1808–1840, 1841–1846, 1846–1848, 1849–1852, 1853–1855, 1856–1860, 1861, and 1862. Doubtlessly teased by the superb execution of these volumes, students of the Civil War await the volumes covering the remaining war years with bated breath. There is much of value, of course, in that which already exists.

Two brief autobiographies open the first volume. Numerous letters both to and from Davis appear, as well as ancillary documents relating to Davis and his career. Each volume contains a chronology of important Davis-related events. Miscellaneous documents of lesser importance follow the main work. Surveying the work reveals much about Davis's character, as we experience his strained relationship with father-in-law Zachary Taylor, assorted medical problems, the death of his first wife, and his burgeoning military career, including his complaint of nonpromotion to first lieutenant sent to Secretary of War Cass and his court-martial in 1835.

The volumes that follow contain extensive material of interest. The courtship and marriage of Jefferson Davis and Varina Howell appear in letters scattered throughout the second volume, as well as substantial material on his development as a young, exceedingly ambitious politician. A vast account of Davis's Mississippi political wranglings appears, as do details of life on his estate, Brierfield, near Vicksburg. Volume 2 concludes with the raising of the Mississippi Rifles and Davis's departure to begin his Mexican War service. The next two volumes illuminate his Mexican War service and career in the U.S. Senate. This period chronicles Davis's alarmist views toward abolition sentiment and his genuine hope of avoiding sectional conflict.

As the conflict approaches, volumes 5 and 6 reveal Davis's rising national prominence, his staunch support of slavery, and his views on loyalty to his home state. Volume 7 contains the first of what will be a trove of important wartime documents, including 124 reproduced in full and some 2500 listed in calendar form. The period encompassing Davis's ascension to the Confederate presidency, his reactions to the formation of the burgeoning Confederate government, and his incisive attention to military affairs is highly enlightening. Volume 8 presents 133 documents in full and an extensive calendar. Elements of Davis's dissatisfaction with various commanders and his embattled dealings with the Congress shine through as prominently as his happiness with the Confederate military successes that marked key periods of the year.

154

Davis, Jefferson. **The Rise and Fall of the Confederate Government** (2 vols., 1515 pp., D. Appleton and Co., New York, 1881)

This pseudo–magnum opus of the Confederacy is a lengthy and ponderous justification of the maneuvers of Davis throughout his career and the war effort of the Southern states. Disappointing in all respects, the volumes offer an overdrawn and often illogical attempt at legal defense, ranging from the origins of the African slave trade to the meaning of the Constitution to the whys and wherefores of Confederate military failure. Had Davis attempted a history of his experience in the secession crisis and Civil War sprinkled with reminiscences of individuals he worked with and fought with, the work might have been intrinsically valuable. Unfortunately, this alternative history of the United States and of Africa often clashes with reality or employs piecemeal arguments stretched or distorted to make a point in a long equation of frustration. As if the historical legal brief were not enough, however, the lengthy history of the war itself, which consumes part of the first volume and almost all of the second, is riddled with outright errors.

Apart from the books' distracting and destructively bitter tone, their content is often at odds with the truth. One who knew nothing about the war and read this work would conclude that the Southern armies had won essentially all of the battles and would be left wondering how they could have lost the war. Many single incidents are wholly inaccurate, as with the author's contention that General Sherman burned Columbia. Davis also takes time to swipe at his internal enemies with distorted passages, perhaps the prime target being Joe Johnston. The work of course downplays the significance of slavery as a cause, despite official papers of the author and other notables such as Alexander Stephens and Howell Cobb contradicting that claim. The cloak of deception ranges far and wide. Davis exaggerates the strategic significance of Southern victories and finds Gettysburg "a check." He believes the Federal government instituted a reign of terror in the border states that mirrored that of the French revolution. History does not live in this book, though a valuable portrait of the postwar psychological state of Jefferson Davis most certainly does.

(Reprinted 1958, with a foreword by Bell I. Wiley, 2 vols., 1515 pp., Thomas Yoseloff, New York; 1881 edition reprinted 1990, with an introduction by James M. McPherson, 2 vols., 1515 pp., Da Capo Press, New York)

155

Davis, Varina Howell. **Jefferson Davis, Ex-President of the Confederate States of America: A Memoir by his Wife** (2 vols., 1638 pp., Belford Co., New York, 1890)

Davis's second wife provides a glimpse into the private life of the Confederate leader in this overly sentimental but warm and literate recollection of the war and of the Davises. Undoubtedly written with Davis's assistance—the Confederate president may have contributed portions of the text—the work retains far more value than Davis's own defensive adventure into constitutionalism (*q.v.*). The greatest value comes from the recollections of the personal and social life of the Davises within the Confederate White House during the war.

These two volumes draw on an intimate knowledge of Richmond society and the influential characters of Confederate political and military circles. Readers will find valuable portraits of leaders, remembrances of events within the city, and a measure of the spirit of the Confederacy waning around the Davises as the war drew on. Many of the opinions, of course, reflect Jefferson Davis's feelings, toned down significantly for public consumption. The work lacks an index.

(Reprinted 1990, with an introduction by Craig L. Symonds, 2 vols., 1638 pp., Nautical and Aviation Publishing Co., Baltimore)

156

Davis, William C. **Jefferson Davis: The Man and His Hour** (784 pp., HarperCollins, New York, 1991)

The author attempts a sweeping modern interpretation of the difficult personality of the Confederate president. In the introduction, he suggests that the story of Jefferson Davis is straightforward and clear, and he sets out to record it for posterity—a feat not achieved by previous biographies. The author then serves up a detailed narrative on the career of Davis and also attempts to explain his personality, based almost exclusively on contemporary sources. He admirably explores Davis's antebellum years and provides a significantly detailed analysis of the war years, offering a massive amount of minutiae along the way. Moreover, the clear and engaging writing style makes this work a pleasure to read.

The author's attempt at interpretation is sometimes reckless. Without consulting a number of other recent works that might have been helpful, he uses a commonsense approach to explain various actions in Davis's life and in the lives of those around him. This frequently amounts to unsupported guesswork. The author concocts a thesis based on Davis's alleged insecurity to explain many actions throughout his life, which allows him to make such statements as Davis's failure "may have been preordained." Such overwrought fatalism is hard to accept. A large number of other interpretive statements rely on assumptions and draw conclusions the author could not concretely know as fact. Occasional trivial errors slide through, such as misspelling the names of Daniel Ammen, Albert T. Bledsoe, Abraham Buford, Mary Chesnut, Ethan Allen Hitchcock, Lucius Quintus Cincinnatus Lamar, and Metairie Cemetery.

Davis sometimes interjects significant observations that contradict his psychological portrait of the president. Jefferson Davis was impatient, we are told, yet in dealing with Joe Johnston he was "too patient." In the end, the author damns his subject with faint praise—Davis's assets "somewhat outweigh" his liabilities. Readers are not given a clear and definitive portrait of Davis in this work, and we must conclude that the introduction is faulty. Davis is indeed a complex and difficult person to know after all.

157

Eckert, Edward K. **"Fiction Distorting Fact"**: *Prison Life*, **Annotated by Jefferson Davis** (168 pp., Mercer University Press, Macon, 1987)

A modified edition of John J. Craven's *Prison Life of Jefferson Davis: Embracing Details and Incidents in His Captivity, Particulars concerning His Health and Habits, Together with Many Conversations on Topics of Great Public Interest* (377 pp., Carleton, New York, 1866), this work examines the credibility of the earlier work and contains, as the title promises, annotations by Davis himself. Echoing the analysis by William Hanchett in his splendid work *Irish* (*q.v.*), Eckert provides ample evidence for the contention that the author of the earlier and widely read work was not Bvt. Lt. Col. Craven but the well-known journalist Charles G. Halpine, whose intention it was to pad his pocket and assist Andrew Johnson with the struggle for Reconstruction.

Partly because *Prison Life* exposed Davis as a suffering and caring man who was not the devil incarnate, the former president of the Confederacy received freedom about a year after the book's publication. Despite the political assistance offered by the book, Davis read a copy while still imprisoned at Fort Monroe and made numerous criticisms of inaccurate and fictional passages. The copy used for the present work is that annotated by Davis, and so the book is absorbing from a historical standpoint and curious for the test of Davis's own pen.

158

Jones, J. William. **The Davis Memorial Volume; or, Our Dead President: Jefferson Davis and the World's Tribute to His Memory** (672 pp., B. F. Johnson and Co., Richmond, 1890)

This useful sourcebook on the Confederate president consists of two primary sections, an outline of the life and character of Jefferson Davis, and an account of his sickness, death, funeral obsequies, and the "world's tribute to his memory." Among the most valuable portions of the work are Davis's autobiography written at Beauvoir in November 1889; his inaugural addresses of 18 February 1861 and 22 February 1862; and a great store of personal information gleaned from Jones's friendship with Davis and the recollections of many others. The work is essentially a laudatory and sympathetic review by the longtime secretary of the Southern Historical Society and includes extensive quotations from the *Southern Historical Society Papers* (*q.v.*) and Davis's own *Rise and Fall of the Confederate Government* (*q.v.*).

Jones presents several papers attempting to show that Davis was not a traitor to his country but "the greatest patriot and statesman of his time." Many of the passages in this work might be challenged, as with the claim made to the General Assembly of Virginia by Sen. John W. Daniel in 1890 that "even at Andersonville, where the hot summer Sun was of course disastrous to men of northern clime, well nigh as many of their guard died as of them." Time and again, Jones employs a variant of the standard early explanation for Southern defeat, "that the Federal armies were largely recruited from our Negro population, and by means of large bounties and other inducements, they drew from the dense populations of Europe a very large proportion of their levies." Overwhelming numbers of the invaders then caused the downfall of the South.

The author also indulges in wishful thinking in the form of might-have-beens. Had not Albert Sidney Johnston been killed at Shiloh, he would have captured Grant's entire army. Had not Stonewall Jackson been killed at Chancellorsville, he would have destroyed Hooker's army. Had Robert E. Lee's orders been fully executed at Gettysburg, Meade's army would have been defeated. Such rationalizations cloud the usefulness of a work that despite them contains much of interest.

159

Patrick, Rembert W. **Jefferson Davis and His Cabinet** (401 pp., Louisiana State University Press, Baton Rouge, 1944)

Patrick's study contains material still of use to readers concerned with the highest political circles of the Confederacy. The work revolves around Davis, to whom the author rightly devotes most of the spotlight, and the "brains of the Confederacy," Judah P. Benjamin. Additionally, this most helpful survey includes summaries of the 17 individuals who held posts in Davis's cabinet as well as chapters that illuminate wartime life in the capital cities of Richmond and Montgomery.

The author provides analysis of the personalities integral to the operations of Confederate policy, although he treats several subjects rather gingerly and occasionally presents Davis in a too-favorable light. However, on the whole this work remains a contribution that deserves wide reading.

(Reprinted 1976, 401 pp., Louisiana State University Press, Baton Rouge)

William Woods Holden (1818–1892)

160

Harris, William C. **William Woods Holden: Firebrand of North Carolina Politics** (332 pp., Louisiana State University Press, Baton Rouge, 1987)

An early Whig and editor of the *North Carolina Standard* in Raleigh, Holden ran for governor as a Democrat in 1858 but lost. Influential nonetheless in the party, he preached Union sentiment until Lincoln called for troops. Although he promoted secession vigorously, he nevertheless helped to form the Conservative party in North Carolina during the war. Following Gettysburg, he called for a negotiated peace, after continually harassing the Confederate government in Richmond. Holden supported Zeb Vance in the gubernatorial election but became dissatisfied with Vance and ran himself, eventually being appointed provisional governor by Andrew Johnson in 1865. Defeated in the regular election, he switched parties again and was elected as a Republican, only to be impeached in 1871.

Such a roller coaster of a career in the divisive arena of wartime North Carolina shapes a book that runs off in many directions. On top of documenting a great deal of minutiae regarding the Tarheel state's wartime politics and its occasional bouts with Richmond, Harris portrays a little-remembered figure of the war who deserves examination. The narrative runs along sympathetically, alleging that Holden was basically doing what was right and made genuine contributions to the reformation of North Carolina politics. Although its subject had a curious and not altogether successful career, the book shows that behind apparent failures, this unusual man contributed to the moderation of support for the war and served well in the early days of Reconstruction.

Samuel Houston (1793–1863)

161

Houston, Sam. **The Writings of Sam Houston, 1813–1863** (ed. Amelia W. Williams and Eugene C. Barker, 8 vols., 4164 pp., University of Texas Press, Austin, 1938–1943)

Useful for American historiography during the Texas revolution and Mexican War periods, the work's value to students of Civil War history lies chiefly in the final two volumes. These tomes cover 1 March 1858 to Houston's death; included are Houston's senatorial writings. Despite the decline in the quality of his writing with increasing age, the tough fighter of the past shines through, sensitive and reactive to those opposing his ideals.

The 450 documents treating his reign as Texas governor are vitally illuminating. Houston's extreme adherence to national unity could not sway his constituents, who strongly supported secession. Dislodged from office on a "revolutionary technicality," he bitterly disagreed with the course of *his* Texas and made infrequent public pronouncements, offering some analysis on Texans in the Confederacy. The final letter, written two months before his death, advises friends that "under no circumstances will I permit my name to be used as a candidate" for the governorship of a Confederate Texas.

Robert Mercer Taliaferro Hunter (1809–1887)

162

Hunter, Martha T. **A Memoir of Robert M. T. Hunter, by Martha T. Hunter (His Daughter): With an Address on His Life (Prepared for the Hunter Monument Association) by Col. L. Quinton Washington** (166 pp., Neale Publishing Co., Washington, 1903)

This slim, highly eulogistic volume holds tributes and memorials to the Confederate secretary of state. In addition, it contains a large number of Hunter's letters relating to his family and many letters received by Hunter. The Civil War coverage is relatively brief but includes valuable official documents and a narration of the subject's views on the Confederate cabinet, logistics of supplying the Confederate war effort, and aspects of Confederate statesmanship. The work thus provides a fine, sympathetic overview of Hunter's life, including his ancestry, childhood and youth, life as a student, marriage and political career, letters written to his wife, political messages of the 1850s, Confederate diplomatic career, and postwar years. The address by Washington is a lament for a lost colleague.

163

Hunter, Robert M. T. **Correspondence of Robert M. T. Hunter, 1826–1876** (ed. Charles Henry Ambler, 383 pp., U.S. Government Printing Office, Washington, 1918)

The *Correspondence* was published as volume 2 of the *Annual Report of the American Historical Association for the Year 1916*. Unfortunately, many of the author's letters, particularly those relating to the war years, were destroyed at the end of the war. Thus, this book contains few of Hunter's own missives and many that reflect on Virginia politics in the decade preceding the Civil War. The letters from James A. Seddon, Roger A. Pryor, and Lewis E. Harvie elucidate the factions in the state's political makeup that took hold of regional Democratic party politics.

The work illuminates the political forces in Virginia in the approaching secession crisis. It shows how Stephen A. Douglas lost support from the state's operators, largely due to his break with James Buchanan. Seddon's 1852 letter describing how the South should establish and control presidents instead of electing their own men is fascinating.

(Reprinted 1971, 383 pp., Da Capo Press, New York)

John Beauchamp Jones (1810–1866)

164

Jones, John B. **A Rebel War Clerk's Diary at the Confederate States Capital** (2 vols., 893 pp., J. B. Lippincott and Co., Philadelphia, 1866)

This work, long hailed as a classic, provides a rare glimpse of the inner workings of the Confederate government. Editor of the Philadelphia proslavery paper *The Southern Monitor*, Jones slipped south four days before the firing on Sumter. Serving as clerk in the Confederate War Office, he compiled a daily diary that is one of the richest sources on life in Richmond. Moreover, it is peppered with assessments of numerous personalities of the Confederate government. Along with the diary of Richard Garlick Hill Kean (*q.v.*), this work is a must for grasping details and incidents of wartime Richmond.

Jones's entries are pedestrian in style, sometimes reflect misunderstandings, and assess issues from a restricted viewpoint. However, working for war secretaries Walker, Benjamin, Randolph, Seddon, and Breckinridge did allow the author to see many important politicians and officers and record his opinions of them. He draws a sympathetic portrait of Davis yet recounts the petty faults of his five bosses to a level of pure triviality.

Extending from the war's first days to the fallout from Lincoln's assassination, the diary mirrors the evolution of thought of the plain folk of the Confederacy. At the outset, Jones is eager, buoyant, exhilarated. Hopes are high for smashing military victories, smooth workings between Davis and Congress, foreign intervention, and signs of a weakening Northern spirit. As hopes fade, the bitter realities of the Confederacy's decline imprint heavily on the author. He portrays the death, starvation, and ruin of war with all its blemishes, unable to delude himself on behalf of Davis or anyone else any longer. The work is a necessary chronology of the Confederacy, its early aspirations as well as its demise.

(Reprinted 1982, 2 vols., 872 pp., Time-Life Books, Alexandria; abridged edition 1958, ed. Earl Schenck Miers, 545 pp., Sagamore Press, New York; 1958 edition reprinted 1993, 545 pp., Louisiana State University Press, Baton Rouge)

Lucius Quintus Cincinnatus Lamar (1825–1893)

165

Murphy, James B. **L. Q. C. Lamar: Pragmatic Patriot** (294 pp., Louisiana State University Press, Baton Rouge, 1973)

A Georgia lawyer and teacher, Lamar held firm to the Union during the early months of sectional conflict but abandoned his loyalty to the Federal government on the election of Lincoln. The first few months of war saw Lamar in a military career as lieutenant colonel of the 18th Mississippi Infantry, resigning after suffering an "apoplectic stroke." Serving briefly as Jefferson Davis's special commissioner to Russia, Lamar returned to serve as judge advocate of the 3d Corps of the Army of Northern Virginia. His varied career included postwar service as Grover Cleveland's interior secretary and six years of service as associate justice of the U.S. Supreme Court.

This well-researched study is a full biography that focuses on the more important phase of Lamar's career, his Reconstruction-era political activities. Murphy views his subject realistically, seeing an orator and propagandist who lacked the high intellectual capacity to contribute substantially to the Confederate cause. The author shows that Lamar's actions during Reconstruction, including his eulogy of Charles Sumner, helped to secure home rule and legitimize Lamar's role as a nationalist. A final chapter summarizes the subject in rather glowing terms.

John Letcher (1813–1884)

166

Boney, F. N. **John Letcher of Virginia: The Story of Virginia's Civil War Governor** (319 pp., University of Alabama Press, Tuscaloosa, 1966)

Unlike his counterparts in Georgia and North Carolina, Letcher cooperated remarkably well with the national government of Jefferson Davis that shared Richmond during the war. Boney shows how Letcher worked tirelessly to prevent the state's western counties from siding with the Union and supported Davis on such touchy issues as impressment and conscription. He raised the Virginia militia that included its sterling officers Robert E. Lee and Thomas J. Jackson and nationalized it into Confederate service faster than the other states did their militias. On the negative side, however, the author shows how Letcher micromanaged details and, in part because of his difficult personality, grew apart from the legislature in much the same way Davis did with the Confederate Congress.

The author treats his subject realistically, faulting Letcher for his lack of imagination and his negligence concerning major issues of state in favor of detail management. Having established a background of thorough research and documentation, Boney supports his summary of Letcher as a "pillar of the Confederacy." He concludes by describing the governor's declining postwar years. Ruined by the war, Letcher lived out a relatively insignificant existence.

Stephen Russell Mallory (1813–1873)

167

Durkin, Joseph T. **Stephen R. Mallory: Confederate Navy Chief** (446 pp., University of North Carolina Press, Chapel Hill, 1954)

Durkin's task with this project was complicated by the destruction of Mallory's notes and journals following the war. Despite this, the author has created a useful portrait of one of the ablest and most influential of the Confederate cabinet officers.

Mallory was well educated, somewhat arrogant, charming, and skilled in political wrangling. These traits served him well not only in antebellum days but also as he faced the difficulties of managing the infant Confederate Navy. Shortages of materiel and monies and an initial abundance of senior officers stunted early progress. The resources for shipbuilding were available in the South but could not easily be extracted for use. The Confederacy had few shipyards. The path became clear: with all available money, the Confederate Navy must purchase ships abroad and rework captured vessels into serviceable warships. The navy would necessarily be small and fragile throughout its four-year life. Mallory's founding of the Confederate Naval Academy and its exercises on the James is in itself a superb and infrequently told story.

Although Mallory could hardly have foreseen it, he erred by adopting a policy of attacking the blockade with raiders. The vast reserve of the Union Navy could afford to lose a few ships to such a policy with virtually no loss in effectiveness. Despite this, Mallory's navy pioneered change and innovation, driven by the lure of a miracle weapon. His support of submarine warfare, torpedoes, ironclad armor, and other innovations helped usher in a new era of naval warfare, even if such innovations failed to help the Southern cause.

The story of Mallory's postwar exploits pales in comparison, offering the disappointing tale of a man in decline.

Furthermore, the author fails to place much of what Mallory did accomplish in perspective. The meaning of Mallory's career must be interpreted for oneself. Still, this is the best source on Mallory and a valuable narrative on Confederate naval operations.

(Reprinted 1987, 446 pp., University of South Carolina Press, Columbia)

Christopher Gustavus Memminger (1803–1888)

168

Capers, Henry D. **The Life and Times of C. G. Memminger** (604 pp., Everett Waddey Co., Richmond, 1893)

Despite severe problems, this remains a useful source on the Confederate secretary of the treasury. Written by the chief clerk in the Confederate Treasury Department, the work is poorly organized, overly praiseful of its subject, and badly written. Because of Memminger's key role in the financial history of the Confederacy, the work necessarily contains a great deal of interest relating to these matters. His background as a South Carolinian, a secession commissioner to Virginia in 1860, and one who had been opposed to Calhoun's nullification ideals gives the study interesting possibilities for analysis.

Showing great imbalance, the author attempts to document that the Confederate Congress rather than Memminger was responsible for nearly all of the financial mistakes of the Confederate policy. Particularly illuminating sections treat the Confederate cabinet and local aspects of Reconstruction. An appendix of nearly 200 pages presents many documents of high value, including six official reports issued by Memminger.

George Wythe Randolph (1818–1867)

169

Shackelford, George Green. **George Wythe Randolph and the Confederate Elite** (240 pp., University of Georgia Press, Athens, 1988)

This is a well-written, scholarly biography. A grandson of Thomas Jefferson, Randolph organized the Richmond Howitzers at the outbreak of hostilities, was commissioned brigadier general in the spring of 1862, and served as Confederate secretary of war for most of the remainder of that year. Angered by Jefferson Davis's micromanagement, Randolph resigned before his health declined and left for France to recover. Resigning his commission in 1864, the Confederate high commander died in 1867.

Shackelford's carefully documented full biography examines Randolph's entire life. About 64 percent of the work treats the wartime years, however, when Randolph's career approached greatness before abruptly ending. Despite Davis's dominance of the war secretaries, the author views his subject's brief tenure as highly important. According to Shackelford, rather than "drifting" like predecessors Walker and Benjamin, Randolph revamped the war office and explored innovative ways to deal with the challenges ahead. Shackelford documents Randolph's appointments that drew from "elite" connections and believes that these appointments represented a new Southern aristocracy that helped counter logistical and economic problems that beset the Confederacy, extending its life into 1865.

The author overstates the case when it comes to Randolph's significance; indeed, he appears to worship his subject at times. He analyzes at length the unimportant plan to liberate New Orleans that Randolph hoped would come to fruition and seems preoccupied with genealogy, pushing the concept of the aristocracy quite far—as with the "First Families of Virginia"—against a time frame during which Southern aristocracies were crumbling. A few errors occur, such as repetitions and misspellings, as with Danville Leadbetter's name.

John Henninger Reagan (1818–1905)

170

Reagan, John H. **Memoirs, with Special Reference to Secession and the Civil War** (ed. Walter Flavius McCaleb, 351 pp., Neale Publishing Co., New York, 1906)

The first portions of the *Memoirs* recount the author's early life in Texas, his frequent hardships on the frontier, his employment as an overseer, and his congressional activities in the years immediately prior to the war. Reagan's blunt style lends credibility to his statements and makes the work valuable in sketching out his activities. The book candidly traces Reagan's effective operation of the postmaster's work despite bickering with the War Department and a flurry of troubles he could control only in part.

The most worthwhile passages relate to Reagan's participation in Confederate cabinet meetings and his relationships with Jefferson Davis and other Confederate leaders. He records acts of compassion by Davis that ought to reduce the impression of a cold, uncaring man. He also treats Recon-

struction most effectively, including the famous Fort Warren letter that brought many ex-Confederates into cooperation with Andrew Johnson and elicited the wrath of many others. Nine extensive appendices spanning 100 pages record congressional speeches made by Reagan as well as his prison missives. The editing is admirable. This book represents an important source on the Confederate cabinet.

(Reprinted 1968, 351 pp., University of Texas Press, Austin; reprinted 1973, 351 pp., AMS Press, New York)

171

Proctor, Ben H. **Not without Honor: The Life of John H. Reagan** (361 pp., University of Texas Press, Austin, 1962)

This excellent study delivers a calculated and meaningful summary of Reagan. The author demonstrates how Reagan held moderate views during his antebellum tenure as a U.S. senator and, at the outbreak of war, resisted secession until it became inevitable. As an adoptive Texan, Reagan offered his services to the new Confederate president and received the postmaster generalship, a post he may not have had in mind and one that would present innumerable frustrations during the course of the war.

Proctor expertly communicates Reagan's wartime exploits and his involvement with the often improvised postal system, a service that greatly affected morale at home and especially on the front. The story, with all its sadness, offers much societal history of the Confederacy as it also demonstrates Reagan's competence. The cabinet member's military background was scant, but he nevertheless offered sound judgments that often were not, but should have been, listened to. These included a warning about the Gettysburg campaign and the much-repeated plea for military reinforcement at Vicksburg. This is a fine contribution to Confederate history.

Robert Barnwell Rhett (1800–1876)

172

White, Laura A. **Robert Barnwell Rhett: Father of Secession** (264 pp., Century Co., New York, 1931)

White's work resulted from a 20-year search for material on the politician and journalist who helped spark South Carolina's split from the Union. While the result is a full picture of Rhett, the limitations faced by the author in not finding more papers relating to Rhett prevented her from writing a completely satisfying book. The work examines all phases of the subject's career, with two events providing special focus: the Nashville convention of 1850 and the resulting secession scare, and Rhett's behavior during the war itself.

White argues that Rhett was a Southern nationalist and that he believed early on that states with economic interests in common ought to band together. His opposition to Jefferson Davis and his furious refusal to permit a strong central government form a strong thesis for the war years. Unfortunately, this section is far too brief, leaving the door open for future biographers of this fascinating politician.

Alexander Hamilton Stephens (1812–1883)

173

Schott, Thomas E. **Alexander H. Stephens of Georgia: A Biography** (552 pp., Louisiana State University Press, Baton Rouge, 1988)

Schott has taken a complex subject and written with zest and a splendid sense of detachment in analyzing the peculiar career of Stephens. About 30 percent of this massive work treats the war years; most of the remainder examines Stephens's antebellum political career in Georgia and in the U.S. House of Representatives. Using a wide range of sources magnificently culled and employed, the author examines Stephens's sickly childhood, the early death of his mother, and his relationships with his half-brother Linton (a close one) and his stepmother (not so close). The author details the interesting stories attached to the early life of a man who, despite his ill health and diminutive form, fairly quickly rose to prominence in Georgia.

His pro-Union stance notwithstanding, Stephens bowed to secession and played a prominent part in the politics of the early Confederacy, becoming its vice president when support for him as provisional president was shattered. The author carefully and rightfully demonstrates that the testy relationship between Davis and Stephens came about through both of their shortcomings, and he details the amazing tale of Stephens's absences from Richmond. Partially abandoning the Southern cause after the first year or two of war, Stephens stuck to his principles and his continuing influence helped to lessen Georgia's cooperation with the Richmond government. Schott concludes his valuable study by depicting the declining years in which Stephens became governor of Georgia even though he was a frail relic of a past age.

174

Stephens, Alexander H. **A Constitutional View of the Late War between the States: Its Causes, Character, and Results** (2 vols., 1481 pp., National Publishing Co., Philadelphia, and Zeigler, McCurdy and Co., Chicago, 1868–1870)

This is the Confederate vice president's magnum opus, a companion volume to Davis's *Rise and Fall of the Confederate Government* (*q.v.*). Like Davis, who might have delivered a reminiscence of real value, Stephens presents a defensive and illogical rationalization and apologia for the actions of the Confederacy. This work is reminiscent of Galileo's *Dialogo*, utilizing 24 colloquies in the Socratic style, casting the author in imaginary discussions with "Judge Bynum," "Professor Norton," and "Major Heister," who collectively are no match for Alexander Stephens. The writing is verbose, ponderous, and redundant.

The introduction contains the seeds of Stephens's argument, that the federalism held by the state rights group was more in line with the Constitution than the nationalism of the Northern radicals. Furthermore, the issue of slavery was introduced only to placate the Northern abolitionists.

The colloquies center on the following 24 topics: the United States was a federation of sovereign states; the Articles of Confederation was its basis; an analysis of the Articles of Confederation; the Constitution was devised for the states, by the states; an analysis of the Constitution; state constitutions examined; a peek at Daniel Webster; John C. Calhoun's Constitution as compact; Jefferson Davis's claim that states are independent sovereignties; nullification is constitutional; the compact is a federalism and not a nationalism; the many successful confederations in history; South Carolina rightfully took Fort Sumter; the Constitution permitted the retention of slaves; a justification of the Missouri Compromise; speeches of Toombs, Clay, and Calhoun; debates in the Senate and the House; correspondence with Lincoln and Stephens's "Union" speech of 14 November 1860; the Provisional Congress in Montgomery; Lincoln's call for militia; the character of the Civil War; prisoner exchanges; the Hampton Roads Conference; and Andrew Johnson was responsible for Reconstruction.

The conversations carry on through this defensive history. Nineteen appendices cover a myriad of topics. Stephens believes that all of his debators were mistaken in their facts and that all of his claims are based on obvious truths. A careful reading of the work, if it can be carried out, demonstrates the errors of these beliefs. It is interesting to note that the critics of this monumental two-volume work are assailed by Stephens in his 1872 book, *The Reviewers Reviewed: A Supplement to the "War between the States," etc., with an Appen-*

dix in Review of "Reconstruction," So Called (273 pp., D. Appleton and Co., New York).

(Reprinted 1994, 2 vols., 1481 pp., Sprinkle Publications, Harrisonburg, Va.)

175

Stephens, Alexander H. **Recollections of Alexander H. Stephens: His Diary Kept When a Prisoner at Fort Warren, Boston Harbour, 1865: Giving Incidents and Reflections of His Prison Life and Some Letters and Reminiscences** (ed. Myrta Lockett Avary, 572 pp., Doubleday, Page and Co., New York, 1910)

This work contains a moving record from the pen of the imprisoned Confederate vice president. Arrested in Crawfordville, Stephens was taken to Fort Warren and imprisoned from 25 May 1865 through late October of that year. His damp, dark cell was solitary save for the occasional visits of a mouse, which he pathetically recorded in his diary with great glee.

The chief interest lies in the attention Stephens gives to the problem of freed slaves in the South. Genuinely concerned and feeling they could not face the transition without his counsel, he dreamed of them often and attempted to offer advice, even to President Johnson. Ultimately undergoing great mental anguish, Stephens was greatly reduced in physical health during the five months of his imprisonment and, as the diary entries show, beset by terrible anxiety that reduced his ability to cope with the outside world. The only method of keeping his mind employed was to write about the unfolding events of the day, and the record therefore constitutes a fascinating account.

(Reprinted 1971, 572 pp., Da Capo Press, New York)

Robert Augustus Toombs (1810–1885)

176

Thompson, William Y. **Robert Toombs of Georgia** (281 pp., Louisiana State University Press, Baton Rouge, 1966)

Thompson gives us a clear and penetrating picture of a violent and influential man. Filled with ambition, egotism, and old-world conservatism, Toombs very nearly became president of the Confederate States. He did not, however, and the parts he did play in the Confederate nation, the author demonstrates, amounted to little in the end.

This work shows that Toombs never recovered from his anger over Davis's election. His months early in the war as secretary of state proved him completely unsuited for the office, and the author shows how petty squabbles and personality defects clouded his subject's ability to think clearly, let alone deal with others in a rational way. The military career that followed also led to disaster. Toombs retained his congressional seat as he fought in the Seven Days battles and at Antietam, where he was wounded severely. During all his service as brigadier general he attacked the military policies of the Confederacy through his congressional connections. How could he expect either venture to succeed?

The author's depiction of Toombs's 1863 resignation and his deteriorating relationship with everyone but himself rounds out this scholarly study. If nothing else, the work sparks wonder at the disasters that might have occurred had Toombs become the premier Confederate leader.

177

Toombs, Robert A., Alexander H. Stephens, and Howell Cobb. **The Correspondence of Robert A. Toombs, Alexander H. Stephens, and Howell Cobb** (ed. Ulrich B. Phillips, 759 pp., U.S. Government Printing Office, Washington, 1913)

This collection appeared as volume 2 of the *Annual Report of the American Historical Association* for 1911. The editor intended to "enable the student to put himself in the places of these men and see current affairs of their time through their eyes." The work partly succeeds. Unfortunately, it contains only half of the known correspondence between these parties, the portions not published before 1913. A full calendar of the correspondence appears in the volume, but the letters published here, by virtue of not appearing in early, important works, tend to be the more trivial correspondence.

The collection spans the years 1844–1882. The correspondence spanning the war years sheds some light onto the individuals involved, but it adds relatively little fresh information to other parties or events. Toombs is revealed as terribly jealous of West Point generals, and his attitude toward Jefferson Davis is reprehensible. Stephens partakes in the Davis bashing as well, of course, but the letters show that Toombs and Stephens did little with anti-Davis parties other than privately fume over their leader's perceived faults.

(Reprinted 1970, 759 pp., Da Capo Press, New York)

Zebulon Baird Vance (1830–1894)

178

Vance, Zebulon B. **The Papers of Zebulon Baird Vance** (ed. Frontis W. Johnston, 475 pp., North Carolina State Department of Archives and History, Raleigh, 1963)

Of particular interest is wartime governor Vance's endless dispute with Jefferson Davis and the centralized government of the Confederacy, a legendary relationship adeptly documented in this work. Unfortunately, the work extends only through 1862. It contains 338 letters, only 88 of which were written by Vance, the remainder being letters he received. Although the coverage in the first volume spans 1843–1862, about 75 percent of the material relates to Vance's Civil War governorship, which began in 1862. Additional volumes apparently were not published.

The Vance-Davis struggle comes alive in these pages, and the editor of this work builds a case that Vance's associations and actions significantly damaged the Confederate war effort. A documented and intelligent introduction summarizes the feisty executive's career.

Henry Alexander Wise (1806–1876)

179

Simpson, Craig M. **A Good Southerner: The Life of Henry A. Wise of Virginia** (450 pp., University of North Carolina Press, Chapel Hill, 1985)

This work is readable and serves as a kind of register of the history of Virginia during the decades prior to the Civil War and throughout Reconstruction. Wise's term as governor coincided with the secession crisis, with its pivotal events such as John Brown's raid. When the war came, he was appointed a brigadier general in the Confederate Army and served in the western Virginia campaign under Robert E. Lee. The work contains much of military interest relating to Wise's service in North Carolina, at Charleston, and in the final months of the war in the Petersburg defensive lines.

Simpson craftily shows how Wise served as a military commander with the politics of his state always in mind. He decided to fight against the "usurpations" of the Federal government once it became clear that although not all Virginians supported state rights, they were unified in their fear of abolitionists and in the cause of protecting their property from governmental intervention. Wise realized that if war broke out "every Union man of Virginia would be a south-

ern man." He was more or less correct, but the book shows how the Confederate military ran into many troubles it did not anticipate. Simpson carefully treats Wise's battles with white conservatives. He does not shy away from criticizing his subject and therefore delivers a balanced and considerate portrait.

SOLDIERS

Edward Porter Alexander (1835–1910)

180

Alexander, Edward Porter. **Fighting for the Confederacy: The Personal Recollections of General Edward Porter Alexander** (ed. Gary W. Gallagher, 664 pp., University of North Carolina Press, Chapel Hill, 1989)

This significant memoir remained unpublished for 80 years before the manuscript was discovered, assembled, and edited. This "private" version stands as a valuable companion to Alexander's *Military Memoirs of a Confederate: A Critical Narrative* (634 pp., Charles Scribner's Sons, New York, 1907, reprinted 1993, with an introduction by Gary W. Gallagher, 634 pp., Da Capo Press, New York). The two works complement each other very well. *Military Memoirs* is a superb history of Lee's army with some of Alexander's own actions in it. *Fighting for the Confederacy* was intended only for family and close friends and constitutes a superb personal narrative with a good deal of analysis of Lee's operations thrown in. Hence, this version of Alexander's recollections is dramatic and revealing, an important source on the general, his fellow officers, and the Army of Northern Virginia.

Alexander relates encounters with many Confederate officers he knew and leaves the reader with a precise idea of what many critical points in the conflict must have been like. The work spans the entire war, including lengthy and interesting reminiscences of Bull Run, the Seven Days, Second Bull Run, Antietam, Fredericksburg, Chancellorsville, Gettysburg, Chickamauga, Chattanooga, Knoxville, the Wilderness, Spotsylvania, Drewry's Bluff, Cold Harbor, Petersburg, and Appomattox. The eyewitness accounts of action and discussion include such scenes as the commander's narrative of the artillery barrage that preceded Pickett's charge at Gettysburg; Alexander's horse being hit by a shell fragment as he reeled in the saddle at the Wilderness; and Robert E. Lee's insistence to surrender at Appomattox and avoid a guerrilla struggle, telling Alexander, "we must consider only the effect which our action will have upon the country at large."

181

Klein, Maury. **Edward Porter Alexander** (279 pp., University of Georgia Press, Athens, 1971)

This scholarly and well-researched effort explores the meaning of one of the finest young Confederate artillerists. The author divides this full biography into three primary sections: Alexander's prewar plantation life and development as a soldier at West Point, his Confederate career and evolution into a brilliant artillerist, and his postwar years up to his death in 1910.

Because of the span of years covered and the work's overall length, the author does not provide as much detail on Alexander's Civil War service as does Alexander's own memoir. Yet Klein's dispassionate recounting of the many battles Alexander experienced in the Army of Northern Virginia is valuable and objective. He skillfully examines Alexander's early service at First Bull Run, which led to his rise to chief of ordnance of the Army of Northern Virginia and then Longstreet's artillery chief. Klein describes Alexander's participation in the army's many early battles, the pivotal moments of crisis at Gettysburg, the subsequent actions at Chickamauga, Knoxville, and the final battles of the eastern theater. He shows that Alexander, while loyal to his native South, eventually realized the futility of fighting against what emerged as a modern American civilization.

Joseph Reid Anderson (1813–1892)

182

Dew, Charles B. **Ironmaker to the Confederacy: Joseph R. Anderson and the Tredegar Iron Works** (345 pp., Yale University Press, New Haven, 1966)

Dew's work consists of a biography of a Confederate brigadier general whose field command was cut short by his skills in industrial management. It is also a detailed history of Anderson's factory, the Tredegar Iron Works in Richmond, one of the most crucial sources of munitions for Confederate armies in the field.

The author traces the rise of Tredegar from its 1837 founding to the years before the war, when Anderson forged the operation into the premier foundry of the South. Dew draws on the Tredegar records to portray a company that teetered on the brink of bankruptcy before subsidies and the need for cannon, iron plating, munitions, and artillery carriages allowed Tredegar to reap healthy profits. Anderson's year-long field command interweaves with his return to the company in 1862 to direct its business. Staffed in part by slaves, the factory turned out astonishing numbers of supplies under Anderson's directorship, and the author shows that Anderson was highly loyal both to the cause of the Confederacy and to profitability. Dew makes several intriguing claims, including the possibility that the outcome at Gettysburg may have been affected had Tredegar not been damaged by fire and halted from producing long-range Parrott guns.

This work is valuable as a life of Anderson, a chronicle of a man whose time was divided between military and industrial service, and a behind-the-scenes look at the South's best military supplier.

Turner Ashby (1828–1862)

183

Avirett, James B. **The Memoirs of General Turner Ashby and His Compeers** (408 pp., Selby and Dulany, Baltimore, 1867)

This book consists of a hodgepodge of material relating to the Virginia colonel whose death cut short the career of a skilled cavalryman (Ashby was never confirmed as a general officer). The author's service as chaplain of the 12th Virginia Cavalry, Ashby's unit, brought him into close contact with the cavalryman and a large number of associates who knew Ashby well. Drawing on his own experiences and from contributions by many others, Avirett presents a jumble of recollections, notes, anecdotes, and papers relating to Ashby and his service and untimely death at Harrisonburg. Much of limited value exists within these pages, yet the work offers a sourcebook of material on Ashby worth consulting.

(Reprinted 1984, 428 pp., Olde Soldier Books, Gaithersburg)

John B. Bannon (1829–1913)

184

Tucker, Philip Thomas. **The Confederacy's Fighting Chaplain: Father John B. Bannon** (254 pp., University of Alabama Press, Tuscaloosa, 1992)

Tucker presents a full and well-researched biography of a little-known religious figure of the Confederate Army. The work is scholarly and provides an enriching story of an Irish priest who settled in St. Louis and served as chaplain of the 1st Missouri Confederate Brigade in the western theater. He later traveled to Richmond to undertake a diplomatic mission for the Confederate government. The story is an interesting one mainly because it is so unusual, and the narrative contains much of interest relating to Bannon's tending to the wounded, preaching to the troops, and participating in battle.

The coverage of Bannon's journeys to gain diplomatic recognition from Pope Pius IX is dramatic. He hoped through his dealings with the papacy to increase the odds for achieving Confederate recognition from Britain and France. Bannon also traveled to Ireland to help stem the tide of Irish immigrants flooding into the Northern states and the Federal Army during the middle period of the war. Neither scheme worked, of course, but the opportunities afforded Bannon create a highly interesting story related in fine order in this novel work.

George Baylor (1843–1902)

185

Baylor, George. **Bull Run to Bull Run; or, Four Years in the Army of Northern Virginia: Containing a Detailed Account of the Career and Adventures of the Baylor Light Horse, Company B, Twelfth Virginia Cavalry, C.S.A., with Leaves from My Scrap Book** (412 pp., B. F. Johnson Publishing Co., Richmond, 1900)

This military narrative, which highlights the author's service in the eastern theater, is peppered with official documents and anecdotal reminiscences of minor incidents. The work is chiefly a memoir, but it serves adequately as a unit history of the Baylor Light Horse, Company B, 12th Virginia Cavalry, commanded by the author's father, Robert W. Baylor. The younger Baylor first tasted battle at First Bull Run and ended his war service in a minor action near the old Bull Run battlefield as part of John S. Mosby's rangers. The narrative of the intervening years contains much of interest from an intelligent Virginia infantryman who turned horse soldier during the war.

Although written long after the war, the narrative is well supported by documents and is balanced, factual, and for the most part dispassionate. Baylor recalls service in Jackson's Valley campaign, Antietam, his capture near Porter's Factory, imprisonment at Fort McHenry and Fort Delaware (where his father was also imprisoned), and a subsequent journey to Fort Monroe, City Point, and exchange. The battle narrative begins anew with scattered actions in West Virginia, minor actions in Virginia, and the Wilderness campaign. Excellent descriptions of activities in the Shenandoah Valley in 1864 and recollections of Mosby round out this worthwhile book. The work lacks an index.

(Reprinted 1983, with an index added, 427 pp., Zenger Publishing Co., Washington)

Pierre Gustave Toutant Beauregard (1818–1893)

186

Roman, Alfred. **The Military Operations of General Beauregard in the War between the States, 1861 to 1865: Including a Brief Personal Sketch of His Services in the War with Mexico, 1846–8** (2 vols., 1285 pp., Harper and Bros., New York, 1883)

This "authorized" biography was written in substantial part by Beauregard himself. Where the writing was not literally Beauregard's, Roman used the general's notes to compose presentable prose. The result is a work with an agenda that is heavily slanted yet fascinating. The biography reflects the vibrance of a writer who was on the spot—Roman was Beauregard's aide-de-camp and inspector general. It is unncessarily long and too frequently repetitive. Great sections consist of a legal brief in defense of Beauregard relating to his differences with Jefferson Davis.

The book not only sympathizes with Beauregard but shows him to be nearly uniformly perfect in his military judgment. Still, the careful reader will see how Beauregard's French-Creole background and overestimated confidence conspired to create mistrust among the older Anglo-Saxon commanders of the Confederacy. The work does provide a detailed and entertaining description of Beauregard's many activities during the war, in both theaters and in Virginia as well as the Deep South. The minute details are occasionally too thick. The attacks on Davis mar the thin interpretation the author attempts. Yet this is a valuable source on the first victor of the Confederacy. Useful appendices contain official documents, and there is a serviceable index.

(Reprinted 1994, with an introduction by T. Michael Parrish, 2 vols., 1285 pp., Da Capo Press, New York)

187

Williams, T. Harry. **P. G. T. Beauregard: Napoleon in Gray** (345 pp., Louisiana State University Press, Baton Rouge, 1954)

Williams carefully and competently re-creates Beauregard's career and, with the dispassionate eye of objective history, concludes that indeed Beauregard was a good general but not a great one. Of course, the hero worship experienced by Beauregard and his own egotism confined his career and produced problematical relationships with Davis and most of the Confederate high command—even though Beauregard was perhaps the only officer legitimately appointed a brigadier general in the field, at First Bull Run, by President Davis himself. Williams's book is a full biography, treating Beauregard's early years and Mexican War service, Civil War career, and postbellum life during Reconstruction. The author's emphasis on the war (more than half the book examines this period) and his careful scholarship give this work lasting value.

The Napoleonic honor of Beauregard never waivered. Following his prewar superintendency of West Point, Beauregard's supreme confidence never broke. That led to his resentment of Lee during the war years and the self-actuated feeling that at times he knew better than Davis and his cabinet. This, of course, deteriorated the relationship between Beauregard and Davis shortly after Manassas, a relationship that Williams details capably in his narrative. The highlights of the work are Shiloh, Charleston, and Petersburg, reflecting the highlights of Beauregard's career. After reading this book, one wonders what Beauregard might have become had his relations with Davis, Lee, and others been different.

(Reprinted 1995, 345 pp., Louisiana State University Press, Baton Rouge)

Berry Benson (1843–1923)

188

Benson, Berry. **Berry Benson's Civil War Book: Memoirs of a Confederate Scout and Sharpshooter** (ed. Susan Benson Williams, 203 pp., University of Georgia Press, Athens, 1962)

These memoirs contain valuable tales relating to service in the Army of Northern Virginia. Thirteen years after the war's end, Benson composed this work from diaries he and his brother Blackwood kept, with the addition of a few letters. Fighting under Stonewall Jackson and later in a company of sharpshooters attached to Maxcy Gregg's 1st South Carolina Infantry, Benson experienced a wide range of battle in the eastern theater. The book is enjoyable for its three areas of coverage: reminiscences of battle, Benson's experiences reconnoitering as a scout, and descriptions of his five-month stay in New York's Elmira Prison. The work also contains much on the life of a common soldier in the Army of Northern Virginia, and it recounts the boredom that characterized that life save for a few terrifying interruptions.

Benson's most enthralling writing follows his experiences during the Seven Days, Second Bull Run, Antietam, Fredericksburg, Spotsylvania (where he was captured), and the

final days around Petersburg. The book would have benefited from an index.

(Reprinted 1992, with a foreword by Herman Hattaway, 203 pp., University of Georgia Press, Athens)

William Edwin Bevens (1841–1924)

189

Bevens, William E. **Reminiscences of a Private: William E. Bevens of the First Arkansas Infantry, C.S.A.** (ed. Donald E. Sutherland, 282 pp., University of Arkansas Press, Fayetteville, 1992)

Published in a brief and inferior edition in 1914, this simple work was penned long after the war. Nevertheless, it is straightforwardly written without extensive embellishment and provides an account of service with the 1st Arkansas Infantry from First Bull Run to the destruction of the Army of Tennessee at Nashville.

The author's candid recollections are folksy and recall much about the relaxed attitude of soldiers in the Army of Tennessee toward discipline. Bevens's stories of agitating his officers along with fellow members of the regiment go a long way toward explaining the character of the western soldier. The author's recollections of various battles hold one's interest, even if they contain illogical assertions (e.g., Shiloh would have been won if Albert Sidney Johnston had lived, etc.). The details of engagements are sometimes short—and some misspellings such as "Alatoona," and "Kenesaw" appear—but the editing goes a long way to make up for the original manuscript's shortcomings.

Charles Minor Blackford (1833–1903)

190

Blackford, Charles Minor. **Memoirs of Life in and out of the Army in Virginia during the War between the States** (ed. Susan Leigh Colston Blackford, 2 vols., 571 pp., J. P. Bell Co., Lynchburg, 1894–1896)

The main portion of this work consists of letters from Charles Minor Blackford, a captain in the 2d Virginia Cavalry, written mainly to his wife. Mrs. Blackford's letters to her husband also appear, as do diary entries from the soldier's father, William M. Blackford. (An intriguing companion volume exists in Charles Blackford's brother William's war reminiscence of serving under Jeb Stuart [q.v.].)

Charles Blackford's material relates to his cavalry service

and later staff position as judge advocate general for James Longstreet's 1st Corps, Army of Northern Virginia. Much activity focuses on the region around the Potomac River, First Bull Run, Fredericksburg, Gettysburg, campaigns in eastern Tennessee, and the decisive battles around Richmond and Petersburg. The account of Appomattox is superlative. Excellent descriptions of wartime Virginia appear in the work, with scenes of mansions and desperate lives recorded in vivid detail. The author is an astute observer of Lee, Longstreet, Edmund Kirby Smith, Braxton Bragg, Jefferson Davis, and Jeb Stuart. He also shows Stonewall Jackson as a less than perfect man.

(Abridged edition 1947, *Letters from Lee's Army; or, Memoirs in and out of the Army in Virginia during the War between the States*, ed. Charles Minor Blackford III, 312 pp., Charles Scribner's Sons, New York)

William Willis Blackford (1831–1905)

191

Blackford, William W. **War Years with Jeb Stuart** (322 pp., Charles Scribner's Sons, New York, 1945)

The author, from a distinguished Virginia family that produced another entertaining reminiscence of the war by Charles Minor Blackford (*q.v.*), offers his recollections as a staff officer with Stuart. Written sometime prior to 1896, the work consists of family letters and notes buttressed by memories that flavor the narrative. Blackford served as adjutant in Stuart's command and rose to lieutenant colonel and chief engineer on Stuart's staff, giving him the opportunity to witness nearly all the major battles in the eastern theater.

Unfortunately, the author was not present at Yellow Tavern when Stuart was mortally wounded, eliminating a potentially superb description of that fateful battlefield. Rather, in the spring of 1864 Blackford was transferred to the engineering staff of Col. T. M. R. Talcott, a former Lee staffer, and thereafter witnessed the Petersburg and Richmond battles that led to war's end. Blackford's contention that a bout of diarrhea struck and incapacitated Robert E. Lee at Gettysburg has not stood as a factor in the history of the battle. The writing is stylistically compelling and bears the marks of credibility throughout. Occasional misspellings surface in the text, as with the names of Laurence Simmons Baker and Martin Witherspoon Gary. The index is adequate, and the introduction by Douglas Southall Freeman is very helpful.

(Reprinted 1993, 322 pp., Louisiana State University Press, Baton Rouge)

Johann August Heinrich Heros von Borcke (1835–1895)

192

Borcke, Heros von. **Memoirs of the Confederate War for Independence** (2 vols., 641 pp., W. Blackwood and Sons, Edinburgh, 1866)

This is a lively and highly entertaining reminiscence of Civil War service by a storytelling Prussian soldier of fortune who built a reputation for wearing a huge broadsword and being a jokester. As such, it should be read with caution.

Running the Charleston blockade and traveling north, the author charmed the Richmond authorities and found a staff position with Jeb Stuart. He fought alongside the cavalry great from Seven Pines until being severely wounded at Upperville on 19 June 1863. The story of his year-long stint with Stuart and of Borcke's further exploits, such as returning to England on a Confederate mission in 1864, form a spritely narrative, though the author does not always separate what he saw personally from secondhand accounts. The book focuses on the military aspects of Borcke's experiences. Many narrow escapes and heroic actions are almost certainly exaggerated, but they do little to detract from an unusual and valuable piece of writing.

(Reprinted 1985, 438 pp., Morningside, Dayton)

Braxton Bragg (1817–1876)

193

Hallock, Judith Lee. **Braxton Bragg and Confederate Defeat, Vol. 2** (298 pp., University of Alabama Press, Tuscaloosa, 1991)

This work continues the narrative begun by McWhiney (*q.v.*). The account begins following the battle of Stones River and explores the growing problems Bragg encountered with both subordinates and superiors throughout the actions at Tullahoma, Chickamauga, and Chattanooga. Marked by a balanced tone, the work both compliments and criticizes Bragg. Hallock applauds Bragg for his handling of Chickamauga and blames Polk and Longstreet for their actions in the campaigns of November 1863. She finds that Bragg served ably in Richmond but faltered significantly by pushing for the removal of Joe Johnston and the assignment of John Bell Hood to command the Army of Tennessee as Sherman approached Atlanta. The author is harshly critical of Bragg for his defensive actions at Wilmington as the war came to a close.

The book includes a brief summary of Bragg's postbellum life and a soul-searching assessment of Bragg the commander. Hallock finds Bragg was dedicated, hardworking, and generally competent—after all, he "achieved more successes with the Army of Tennessee than did any other western general." Because Bragg occasionally lost his level-headedness in the heat of battle and lacked the short-term tactical clarity required, his actions sometimes won plaudits but also proved disastrous, as at Chattanooga.

194

McWhiney, Grady. **Braxton Bragg and Confederate Defeat, Vol. 1: Field Command** (421 pp., Columbia University Press, New York, 1969)

This is the first of two volumes written by two different people, the second published more than 20 years after the first (see the companion volume by Hallock). McWhiney's book summarizes the general's life through 1862. About two-thirds of this work focuses on the first two years of Bragg's Civil War command, the remainder dealing mainly with Bragg's Mexican War service. In balanced, scholarly fashion, the author assesses Bragg's performance on the field and finds that he was neither incompetent nor particularly outstanding, depicting Bragg as essentially unqualified for the tasks he was asked to accomplish.

The author explores Bragg as commander and as human being and maintains that although Bragg held an important assignment as commander of the Army of Tennessee, he "made a major contribution toward Confederate defeat." McWhiney shows how Bragg, like many Civil War officers, failed to comprehend the revolutionary innovations of warfare that were rapidly outstripping his tactical education. He seemed incapable of learning from his many mistakes, was rash, argumentative, and sometimes impossible toward others, and yet he often retained the upper hand because of his friendship with Jefferson Davis.

(Reprinted 1991, 421 pp., University of Alabama Press, Tuscaloosa)

John Cabell Breckinridge (1821–1875)

195

Davis, William C. **Breckinridge: Soldier, Statesman, Symbol** (744 pp., Louisiana State University Press, Baton Rouge, 1974)

A full biography deserving of its subject, this work rates among the better Confederate studies of its time de-

spite the fact that it draws on many secondary sources, puts forth some questionable assertions, and is rather lightly documented.

Breckinridge, the grandson of Thomas Jefferson's attorney general, has always vexed historians, if for no other reason than his precipitous fall from such a high pillar to his final years of mediocrity. His skill as a politician resulted in his election as vice president under James Buchanan, despite turning down the nomination when it first came. Sympathetic and sometimes praising of his subject, Davis recounts Breckinridge's early years and rise to political prominence. He contends that Breckinridge was a "secret opponent of slavery" although he ran as a candidate for Southern extremists in 1860 and stayed on in Washington after Lincoln's election to aid proslavery interests. As Kentucky teetered on secession, Breckinridge resigned and was commissioned brigadier general and major general C.S.A. in rapid succession.

The author skillfully outlines Breckinridge's military involvement, even if he consistently overrates his subject's command capabilities. The stories of Breckinridge's command of the Reserve Corps at Shiloh, his service at Vicksburg, a bright spot at Stones River, and disaster at Missionary Ridge provide exciting battle reports. Davis admiringly tells of Breckinridge's victory at New Market and his part in Early's raid on Washington before detailing his subject's brief role as Confederate war secretary.

A very brief postwar treatment touches on Breckinridge's flight from prosecution (having been vice president, he was mortified by charges of treason) and early death in Kentucky. An occasional error creeps in, as with the author's statement that Horace Greeley died during his presidental campaign.

(Reprinted 1992, 687 pp., Louisiana State University Press, Baton Rouge)

Simon Bolivar Buckner (1823–1914)

196

Stickles, Arndt M. **Simon Bolivar Buckner: Borderland Knight** (446 pp., University of North Carolina Press, Chapel Hill, 1940)

This is a well-researched study that provides a detailed picture of the various phases of Buckner's life, although the writing is workmanlike and hardly rises to the interesting nature of its subject. Buckner's early life in Kentucky, his West Point days, and his experience in the Mexican War are described and reasonably documented. The chapters on Buckner's Civil War service are more inspiring, but the author does not always lift the local and regional interests of various actions into perspective on the national scene.

Stickles follows Buckner's first major action, his role as victim at Fort Donelson, with sound explanation. After being exchanged, Buckner received a hodgepodge of assignments that led to Perryville, the defenses of Mobile, Chickamauga, and service as chief of staff to Edmund Kirby Smith. The postwar coverage is adequate, describing the bases of Buckner's Kentucky governorship and his unsuccessful run for national office. The book nicely reflects the importance of Buckner's role in Confederate veterans' affairs. This sound work will stand as a legitimate source until a more analytical book is published.

Henry King Burgwyn, Jr. (1841–1863)

197

Davis, Archie K. **Boy Colonel of the Confederacy: The Life and Times of Henry King Burgwyn, Jr.** (406 pp., University of North Carolina Press, Chapel Hill, 1985)

Davis chronicles the short life of a distinguished North Carolina Confederate officer. Burgwyn gained fame by being mortally wounded on the first day at Gettysburg, shot through the lungs, and dying at the head of a celebrated regiment, the 26th North Carolina Infantry. With a considerable degree of sympathy toward his subject, the author explores the fairly uneventful life of Burgwyn prior to his command of the 26th and his untimely death.

Davis provides a picture of a spoiled young lad who, failing to gain admission to West Point, chose an education at the Virginia Military Institute and pursued a military career. Selfish and utterly without moral considerations for slavery or other problems, Burgwyn pushed his ambition hard and won commissions as lieutenant colonel and colonel of the regiment, succeeding Zebulon Vance. The narrative provides a discussion of the many battles of the 26th following Burgwyn's entrance into the organization, including accounts of New Bern, Gaines's Mill, Malvern Hill, Rawls's Mill, and Gettysburg. These are based in part on the diary kept by Burgwyn during his war service. The story is well told, the exploits of the 26th North Carolina worthy of research, but the character and motivation of Harry Burgwyn remain elusive.

John Overton Casler (1838–1926)

198

Casler, John O. **Four Years in the Stonewall Brigade** (495 pp., State Capital Printing Co., Guthrie, Okla., 1893)

This is a superb tale of a common Confederate soldier's wartime service. Written at a basic level and composed nearly three decades after the war, this work nevertheless espouses with some bitterness the experiences of a private in the 33d Virginia Infantry as he fought through most of the eastern battles of the Army of Northern Virginia. Important accounts include those of Antietam and Gettysburg. The work's general reliability rests on the author's use of a fragmentary diary to reconstruct most of his narrative. In January 1865 the author enlisted in the 11th Virginia Cavalry, and his abrupt change in daily life led to an interesting experience during the final weeks of the war. Captured and imprisoned at Fort McHenry, the author sat out war's end and recorded his thoughts for posterity.

Much of Casler's praise centers on Stonewall Jackson, whose performance at First Bull Run is adequately described. The Peninsular campaign rolls by without criticism of Jackson's lackluster behavior, and a subsequent section of interest deals with Chancellorsville. The author harshly criticizes Jubal Early for incompetence and offers personal views on many others, along with detailed recollections of marches, foraging, fighting, and his unpleasant captivity.

(New edition 1906, 495 pp., Appeal Publishing Co., Girard, Kans.; 1906 edition reprinted 1982, with notes by James I. Robertson, Jr., 362 pp., Morningside, Dayton)

John Hampden Chamberlayne (1838–1882)

199

Chamberlayne, John H. **Ham Chamberlayne, Virginian: Letters and Papers of an Artillery Officer in the War for Southern Independence, 1861–1865** (ed. Churchill G. Chamberlayne, 440 pp., Dietz Printing Co., Richmond, 1932)

This overlooked book holds great interest. The author, a journalist, enlisted as a private soldier in the 21st Virginia Infantry in April 1861 and emerged as captain of Chamberlayne's Battery in Hill's Corps of the Army of Northern Virginia. The work consists largely of letters written by Chamberlayne to his mother, sister, brother-in-law, and a close woman friend. They describe all the experiences of common soldier life, from marches, camps, battles, and even prison, as Chamberlayne found himself in Fort Delaware, Johnson's

Island, and Point Lookout. The many battle anecdotes range from Acquia Creek, Cheat Mountain in western Virginia, the Peninsular campaign, Second Bull Run, Antietam, Fredericksburg, Chancellorsville, Gettysburg, the battles for Richmond and Petersburg, and the final days of the war as the author fled toward North Carolina.

The letters are particularly good and are published exactly as they were written. The work contains other personal papers of Chamberlayne's and a magnificent group of photographs of persons relevant to the story. Many of the letters were composed in great haste, which gives them the flavor of the immediacy of Civil War battle. This is an enjoyable book that deserves recognition.

(Reprinted 1992, 440 pp., Broadfoot, Wilmington)

Patrick Ronayne Cleburne (1828–1864)

200

Buck, Irving A. **Cleburne and His Command** (382 pp., Neale Publishing Co., New York, 1908)

Written by Cleburne's assistant adjutant general, this narrative features the reminiscences of one who observed Cleburne for a period of nearly two years, from December 1862 to Cleburne's wounding at Jonesboro on 2 September 1864. Buck's work consists almost entirely of a wartime discussion of his commander, save for a brief introduction treating Cleburne's early life, for which Buck consulted published sources. He likewise used secondary accounts to cover the three-month period before Cleburne's death.

Buck's work was composed over a period of years, probably beginning in the 1880s. Certainly the young staff officer revered and adored the great general. Nevertheless, the book contains a solid account of Cleburne's wartime adventures, one that makes it valuable today. The accounts of Shiloh, Stones River, Chickamauga, Missionary Ridge, Ringgold, and Atlanta are particularly revealing.

(New edition 1958, with a foreword by Bell I. Wiley and a 53-page biographical essay titled "Pat Cleburne, Stonewall Jackson of the West," ed. Thomas Robson Hay, 378 pp., Mc-Cowat-Mercer Press, Jackson, Tenn.; 1958 edition reprinted 1985, 378 pp., Morningside, Dayton)

201

Purdue, Howell, and Elizabeth Purdue. **Pat Cleburne, Confederate General: A Definitive Biography** (498 pp., Hill Junior College Press, Hillsboro, 1973)

The authors chronicle the life and Civil War career of the famous commander using a wide range of sources. They have produced a study marked by extensive research but little interpretation. The sources range from published accounts to Cleburne's own letters and journals, which gives the account validity and at the same time renders it rather dull. The exhaustive detail provided by the authors calls out for interpretation of Cleburne's importance and documentation for the conclusions they make, but they fail to provide either one.

The work summarizes the commander's early days around Bowling Green, where his winning personality endeared him to his men. As the western war crystallized, Cleburne's tenacity at Shiloh demonstrated his effectiveness as a field commander. The Purdues competently describe Cleburne's actions at Richmond, where he was grievously wounded in the face; Perryville, where he was wounded again; and Ringgold, where he won great recognition. Moved north to help John Bell Hood invade Tennessee, he was among the six general officers killed or mortally wounded at Franklin. The authors' narrative provides a specific and detailed account of these and other actions. Its unscholarly quality aside, it contains much of value.

Thomas Reade Rootes Cobb (1823–1862)

202

McCash, William B. **Thomas R. R. Cobb: The Making of a Southern Nationalist** (356 pp., Mercer University Press, Macon, 1983)

This study is objective, detached from its subject, and thoroughly documented. Overall it is a fine work of historical scholarship. However, the author makes an enormous error, referring to Cobb as a brigadier general when in fact he died a colonel. The Senate of the Confederate States never confirmed Cobb's commission as brigadier general, which had been forwarded by Davis. McCash neglects this, even titling a chapter "Confederate General." He also makes a glaring error with respect to a verifiable Confederate brigadier general, John Rogers Cooke, stating that he was killed along with Cobb. Wounded at Fredericksburg, Cooke survived until 1891. Indeed, the general was among the founders of the Confederate Soldiers Home in Richmond.

John Esten Cooke (1830–1886)

203

Cooke, John Esten. **Wearing of the Gray: Being Personal Portraits, Scenes, and Adventures of the War** (601 pp., E. B. Treat and Co., Baltimore, 1867)

This is a beautifully written and most enthralling reminiscence of the war and the author's experiences in it. Much of the material appeared first in the *Southern Illustrated News*, a Richmond newspaper, during the war. After the war's close, Cooke edited much of the material, molding it into a less-caustic diatribe. Hence, this book lacks much of the original and authentic wartime spirit of the Confederate soldier fighting for his independence. The softer, more romantic tales are nonetheless gems that belong on every Confederate bookshelf.

Cooke's observations of Jeb Stuart predominate, but there are other valuable insights in this work: comments on Jackson, Ashby, Mosby, Early, Beauregard, and Lee. The author's description of life in the cavalry arm of the Army of Northern Virginia includes a vivid account of the Gettysburg campaign. The most entertaining section, "Outlines from the Outpost," contains much of value on the life of a common soldier in the South's greatest army. Additional material describes the adventures of the scout Frank Stringfellow and the war's final operations.

(New edition 1959, ed. Philip Van Doren Stern, 572 pp., Indiana University Press, Bloomington; 1867 edition reprinted 1993, 563 pp., Olde Soldier Books, Gaithersburg)

Sumner Archibald Cunningham (1843–1913)

204

Simpson, John A. **S. A. Cunningham and the Confederate Heritage** (246 pp., University of Georgia Press, Athens, 1994)

Simpson describes the eventful career of the young Tennessee soldier who registered a mediocre Civil War career but rose to fame after the war by founding and editing the *Confederate Veteran* (q.v.). The full-length biography explores Cunningham's youth and Civil War record but focuses strongly on the editor's influence as a builder of the Lost Cause mythology. Less than one-third of the work describes Cunningham's exploits in the 41st Tennessee Infantry, including a humiliating baptism of fire at Fort Donelson, where he was captured and sent to Fort Morton. After scattered fighting in Mississippi, Cunningham again tasted an objectionable military role at Port Hudson and in the Vicksburg, Chattanooga, and Atlanta campaigns.

The sections on the subject's postwar activities are more enlightening and propose that Cunningham was driven by his inglorious war record to bolster the Confederate image. The *Veteran* was for some years a leading voice of Confederate memorialization and the voice of the United Confederate Veterans, if its contents were not always realistic. The work contains some sloppy errors, as with "William J. McPherson" for James B. McPherson, but overall it presents an interesting appreciation of a forgotten Confederate populist.

Francis Warrington Dawson [Austin John Reeks] (1840–1889)

205

Dawson, Francis W. **Reminiscences of Confederate Service, 1861–1865** (180 pp., News and Courier Book Presses, Charleston, 1882)

This slim book holds high value for its sharp telling of artillery service in the Army of Northern Virginia. Thinly documented, the work surveys Dawson's unusual career, in which he left his native England, changed his name, and entered Confederate service. Before joining the artillery, however, Dawson served on the CSS *Nashville* and as a master's mate on the ironclad *Louisiana*, and the mixture of naval and army experiences give this work an unusual flavor.

Dawson's journalistic talents and his position on James Longstreet's staff enabled him to pen recollections that are literate and valuable for the campaigns in which he participated. The treatment of the battle of Mechanicsville, his brief imprisonment at Fort Delaware, and service at Fredericksburg, Gettysburg, and the Knoxville campaign are particularly worthwhile. The accounts are not limited to battles, however, as many anecdotes of soldier life enliven the text. The author supports the high estimates of Longstreet by most witnesses and delivers complimentary portraits of many other officers, including Fitzhugh Lee and Dick Anderson. After the war he married Sarah Morgan, the future author of another valued work, *A Confederate Girl's Diary* (q.v.). This work lacks a much-needed index. An appendix presents wartime correspondence between Dawson and his family and friends in England.

(New edition 1980, ed. Bell I. Wiley, 214 pp., Louisiana State University Press, Baton Rouge)

James Dinkins (1845–1939)

206

Dinkins, James. **1861–1865 by an Old Johnnie: Personal Recollections and Experiences in the Confederate Army** (280 pp., Robert Clarke Co., Cincinnati, 1897)

Dinkins has authored a curious and fanciful Confederate reminiscence. He served as a private soldier in Barksdale's brigade through the first two years of war, was commissioned a lieutenant in April 1863, served on the staff of James R. Chalmers, and for the last year of the war closely watched Nathan Bedford Forrest's activities, participating in some of the great cavalryman's raids. This third-person narrative is sprinkled with tall tales and reconstructed "conversations" the author remembered long after the war. Thus, it should be read with extreme caution.

Despite the occasional stretch of credibility, the book hangs together nicely and offers much of value relating to Dinkins's personal experiences. Highlights include Antietam, critical observations of D. H. Hill, Fort Pillow, the capture of Oxford, the battle of Nashville, and many little incidents and anecdotes told with a dose of humor that will delight readers.

(Reprinted 1975, with a foreword by Ken Bandy, 280 pp., Morningside, Dayton)

John Edward Dooley (1842–1873)

207

Dooley, John. **John Dooley, Confederate Soldier: His War Journal** (ed. Joseph T. Durkin, 244 pp., Georgetown University Press, Washington, 1945)

A lad of 18 from a busy Richmond family, Dooley enlisted with the 1st Virginia Infantry as a private soldier and kept a journal of battle experiences from 2 August 1862 to 3 July 1863. Enriched with the youthful optimism of a soldier defending his country, the diary delivers much on the war itself and many characters in it. Perhaps most valuable are its observations of soldier life in the Army of Northern Virginia.

The author's diary embraces a period of being brigaded under the command of Brig. Gen. James L. Kemper, in Longstreet's corps. With his regiment's participation in Second Bull Run, Antietam, Fredericksburg, and Gettysburg, Dooley eventually rose to be commissioned a major in the unit. He was wounded and captured in Pickett's Charge and spent the following year and a half in prison. The prison notes are il-

luminating and conclude with the officer's description of the Confederacy after his release: "steeped in a fatal lethargy."

Henry Kyd Douglas (1840–1903)

208

Douglas, Henry Kyd. **I Rode with Stonewall: Being Chiefly the War Experiences of the Youngest Member of Jackson's Staff from the John Brown Raid to the Hanging of Mrs. Surratt** (401 pp., University of North Carolina Press, Chapel Hill, 1940)

This book was written soon after the war from diaries kept by Douglas throughout his campaigns with Jackson and supported by notes collected after the war. It contains material of interest but unfortunately distorts and misrepresents many recollections. Many of Douglas's former comrades, including Jed Hotchkiss and Jubal Early, insisted that Douglas lied about a number of episodes, inflated his own importance, and generally proved himself untrustworthy. Assembled for publication in 1899, the book was nonetheless not widely distributed until its formal publication 41 years later.

Douglas recalls his encounter with John Brown prior to the Harpers Ferry raid, his lengthy service as Jackson's assistant adjutant general and assistant inspector general, and his observation of the hanging of the Lincoln conspirators in Washington. Many anecdotes of Jackson and other officers are buried within this text and are well worth searching out. The discussions of Jackson's Valley campaign of 1862, the Maryland campaign, Gettysburg, Douglas's imprisonment at Johnson's Island, the Valley campaign of 1864, and Appomattox are all engrossing. A few misspellings appear, as with the names of Philip Kearny, Joseph B. Kershaw, Lafayette McLaws, Alfred Pleasonton, James B. Ricketts, and Albin F. Schoepf. The work contains a short biographical essay on Douglas by Fletcher M. Green.

(Reprinted 1987, 401 pp., University of North Carolina Press, Chapel Hill)

Basil Wilson Duke (1838–1916)

209

Duke, Basil W. **Reminiscences of General Basil W. Duke, C.S.A.** (512 pp., Doubleday, Page and Co., Garden City, N.Y., 1911)

This book supplies the loosely constructed but occasionally fascinating life story of the young Kentuckian who rode with John Hunt Morgan and became Morgan's brother-in-law during the war. Composed in a storylike fashion for a popular audience, it contains some suspicious tales and much about the grievous horrors of war. The work stretches through all of Duke's life, providing background on his early days in Kentucky, the outbreak of the war, and his weeks in Missouri during the mounting tensions of the border warfare.

The narrative accelerates in interest with the author's deepening involvement in the Confederate cause. The story of his marriage dissolves into anecdotal material presenting reminiscences of M. Jeff Thompson, his return to Kentucky, and service with the 2d Kentucky Cavalry. Stories of guerrilla warfare, profanity, and soldier life on the march and in camp add much to this narrative. The author works in many associations, not only with Morgan but also with such notable officers as Humphrey Marshall, John C. Breckinridge, Roger W. Hanson, Braxton Bragg, and William Preston. He touches on such topics as blacks before and during the war, Southern hospitality, religion in the armies, life in prison with Morgan, and an analysis of Jefferson Davis. Postwar life in Louisville and reflections on the war conclude this uneven and intermittently valuable tome.

Jubal Anderson Early (1816–1894)

210

Early, Jubal A. **Autobiographical Sketch and Narrative of the War between the States** (496 pp., J. B. Lippincott and Co., Philadelphia, 1912)

This useful memoir was written by one of Lee's most controversial general officers. Although the majority of it reads like a stiff official report, it offers a look inside the mind of one of the South's important field commanders and stands as a respectable source on Early's Shenandoah Valley campaign of 1864. Filled with the characteristic tone of hating all things Northern, the narrative offers a catalog of insights into the commander who after the war constructed much of the Lee mythology and who died as one of the last outspoken unreconstructed Rebels. Relatively unimaginatively written, the text delivers an important factual chronology of Early's activities in virtually all the major engagements of the Army of Northern Virginia from the army's inception to Cold Harbor, where the newly minted lieutenant general took command of Ewell's Corps.

The book's strongest section treats the 1864 Valley campaign in which Early defeated David Hunter, broke through the Federal position at Monocacy Creek, and approached the

city of Washington before being driven back. Here the author appears at his zenith, terrorizing the Yankees and commanding his own semi-autonomous force before his defeat at the hands of Sheridan at Cedar Creek. The final sections attempt to rationalize Early's defeat through the numerical superiority approach. Although little appears in this book that touches the experience of common soldiers and much of it interprets various activities through a thick lens of bias, it remains fittingly important as a window to the commander himself. In 1867 Early published the second edition of an inferior work, *A Memoir of the Last Year of the War for Independence, in the Confederate States of America, Containing an Account of the Operations of His Commands in the Years 1864 and 1865* (135 pp., C. W. Button, Lynchburg, 1867).

(New edition 1960, titled *War Memoirs: Autobiographical Sketch and Narrative of the War between the States*, with an introduction by Frank E. Vandiver, 496 pp., Indiana University Press, Bloomington; 1912 edition reprinted 1989, titled *General Jubal A. Early: Autobiographical Sketch and Narrative of the War between the States*, with an introduction by Gary W. Gallagher, 496 pp., Broadfoot, Wilmington; 1912 edition reprinted 1989, titled *Jubal Early's Memoirs: Autobiographical Sketch and Narrative of the War between the States*, with an introduction by Craig L. Symonds, 496 pp., Nautical and Aviation Publishing Co., Baltimore)

211

Osborne, Charles C. **Jubal: The Life and Times of General Jubal A. Early, CSA** (560 pp., Algonquin Books, Chapel Hill, 1992)

This work is well documented, draws on the *O.R.* (*q.v.*), Early's own memoir (*q.v.*), and a large array of other primary and secondary sources. It is a full biography, although the antebellum coverage, including both political and military aspects, represents only 7 percent of the narrative and the postwar years a mere 16 percent. Thus the work is primarily a Civil War biography that focuses on Early's abandonment of his Union stance, emergence as a Confederate officer, and cantankerous relationships with a range of Confederate officers.

Osborne spends much of his effort examining Early's role in various battles, from First Bull Run through Salem Church and the Gettysburg campaign. The work nicely examines the Wilderness, Cold Harbor, and the frequently recounted raid on Washington in 1864, with particular emphasis on Monocacy. The Chambersburg raid and the subsequent Valley campaign against Sheridan in the autumn of 1864 receive balanced, critical analysis. There are a few misspellings (as with the names of Daniel D. Bidwell and Jeffry D. Wert) and some errors in the index (one entry for D. H. Hill under "Daniel Harvey" and other entries for him repeated in two places). The maps are well done. The net result is a book of value to the literature of the Confederacy.

Clement Anselm Evans (1833–1911)

212

Evans, Clement A. **Intrepid Warrior: Clement Anselm Evans** (ed. Robert Grier Stephens, Jr., 598 pp., Morningside, Dayton, 1992)

A collection of the wartime letters and diaries of the general officer and historian are presented. Compiled by the general's grandson, the great-great nephew of Alexander H. Stephens, the work is a welcome addition to Confederate literature. Some 245 letters written by Evans and his wife, Allie, appear in the volume, illuminating a wide range of matters relating to common soldiers, commanders, camps, marches, battles, and the psychology of war. The smaller, simpler matters of a marriage in the period are fairly discussed in this correspondence. The material covering Evans's political career in Georgia during the secession crisis is valuable, nearly as much as the battlefield letters. The author's activities in the Army of Northern Virginia are clearly described in vivid detail beginning in the summer of 1862.

The correspondence covers nearly every major engagement of the eastern theater from the Peninsular campaign through Appomattox and is composed with intelligence and observational candor. The portions covering the Shenandoah fighting, Gettysburg (where he did not record the fight as a great Confederate loss), Monocacy, and Cedar Creek are particularly valuable. His observations of commanders, such as admiration for John B. Gordon or disgust for Jubal Early, frequent the pages. An occasional mistake surfaces, as with describing the position of Brawner's Farm at "Grovetown" and misspelling Shippensburg, Pennsylvania, and the names of Nathan G. Evans, Edmund Kirby Smith, and Josiah Tattnall. Generally, however, the book is accurate and the index is helpful.

Richard Stoddert Ewell (1817–1872)

213

Ewell, Richard Stoddert. **The Making of a Soldier: Letters of General R. S. Ewell** (ed. Percy Gatling Hamlin, 161 pp., Whittet and Shepperson, Richmond, 1935)

This is a brief but highly interesting account of Ewell's developmental years. Along with *Old Bald Head* (q.v.), this work forms a valuable chronicle of Ewell's military and personal life. The more than 50 letters "represent the bulk of General Ewell's private correspondence," the editor claims. All but two are by Ewell and are addressed to his brother Benjamin Stoddert Ewell or his brother's daughters. More than half the letters cover the antebellum era, from Ewell's admittance into West Point to the onset of the secession crisis. They uncover much about the dirty and unenviable life in the frontier army.

The coverage relating to the Mexican War is highly interesting. As the Civil War approached, Ewell wrote: "The truth is in the army there are no sectional feelings and many from extreme ends of the Union are the most intimate friends." This may have been true, but the war gave Ewell his glory with the Confederacy. Ten letters describe his wartime service—a disappointingly small number, yet they are gems. Comments on service with Jackson in the Valley and at Second Bull Run, where he lost a leg, are illuminating. Ewell's confinement in Fort Warren also provides worthwhile observations. One only wishes the collection were far larger.

214

Hamlin, Percy Gatling. **Old Bald Head (General R. S. Ewell): The Portrait of a Soldier** (216 pp., Shenandoah Publishing House, Strasburg, Va., 1940)

This work focuses almost exclusively on Ewell's Civil War career, with a scant introduction treating his early years and only six pages covering the period after the war until his death. The story, delivered without flourish, is steeped in well-researched fact. The lengthy discussions of military movements bog down the narrative at times and could have benefited from well-drawn maps. Despite the heavy leaning on military campaigns, Ewell's personality emerges in this work, and it is one the reader will find amusing and bewildering.

The disagreement between Ewell and Jubal Early receives only brief attention. Thoughtful analysis attempts to show that Ewell's error at Gettysburg was not in failing to capture Cemetery Hill on the first day but in failing to shift his corps to the right on the first night. The collection of manuscript sources employed for this work, including a diary and wartime journals, serves to make the book worthwhile today. The index and appendices add little to the bulk of the work and might have been expanded into more useful extensions.

(Reprinted 1988, 377 pp., R. Van Sickle, Gaithersburg, with both Ewell's letters and Hamlin's monograph)

William Andrew Fletcher (1839–1915)

215

Fletcher, W. A. **Rebel Private Front and Rear: Experiences and Observations from the Early Fifties and through the Civil War** (193 pp., Press of the Greer Print, Beaumont, Tex., 1908)

This work offers entertaining reading based on the wartime experiences of a youngster in Hood's Texas brigade. Written nearly 40 years after the war ended, it bears the marks of much-embellished stories and so must be used and viewed with caution. While a private soldier in the 5th Texas Infantry, the author recorded much about the simple life of a soldier in camp and battle. In the summer of 1864, Fletcher was transferred to the 8th Texas Cavalry, a part of Terry's Texas Rangers, and experienced a very different final year of action. Admittedly hazy in his recollection, Fletcher checked his experiences against known facts and produced a memoir whose value lies in capturing the spirit of the Confederate resistance as felt by a common soldier.

Much of the work recounts Fletcher's participation in battles such as Second Bull Run and Chickamauga, where he was wounded. A highlight of the account consists of Fletcher's 1864 capture and escape, after which he saw much of the Carolinas during the war's final days. Regrettably, many copies of the first edition of this work were destroyed in a fire in 1924.

(New edition 1954, titled *Rebel Private Front and Rear*, ed. Bell Irvin Wiley, 162 pp., University of Texas Press, Austin; reprinted 1995, with an introduction by Richard Wheeler, 223 pp., E. P. Dutton, New York)

Nathan Bedford Forrest (1821–1877)

216

Henry, Robert Selph, ed. **As They Saw Forrest: Some Recollections and Comments of Contemporaries** (306 pp., McCowat-Mercer Press, Jackson, Tenn., 1956)

This is a curious auxiliary work that is nonetheless quite valuable. Consisting of a miscellany of comments on Forrest

from his contemporaries, it constitutes a gigantic appendix to Henry's 1944 biography (*q.v.*). Yet this miscellany contains a mountain of useful material and makes us wish similar works had been produced relating to other notable commanders.

Forrest's exploits and reputation created intense worship from Confederates and intense hatred from Yankees. The selection presented here echoes that separation admirably and offers much to ponder, not only concerning Forrest, but also the Tennessee area in which he practiced war. The primary selection is an appraisal by the English soldier Garnet Joseph Wolseley of Forrest as an untarnished military genius. (This paper also appears in volume 20 of the *Southern Historical Society Papers*.) Wolseley's assessment was based on research rather than a personal intimacy. More substantial accounts follow in which soldiers recount their participation in battles served under Forrest. Gilbert V. Rambaut's tale of service on Forrest's staff at Shiloh, William Witherspoon's recollections of Brice's Crossroads, and James Dinkins's account of Forrest's Memphis raid on 21 August 1864 are valuable commentaries.

In many cases the praise for Forrest's legendary traits is overburdened. "A massive brain, an inflexible purpose, unflinching courage, tireless energy, and a will that could brook no opposition" characterized Forrest, according to John W. Morton, his former chief of artillery. Although poetic tributes occasionally dominate the narrative, this volume contains value for modern students.

(Reprinted 1987, 306 pp., Broadfoot, Wilmington)

217

Henry, Robert Selph. **"First with the Most" Forrest** (580 pp., Bobbs-Merrill Co., Indianapolis, 1944)

Useful despite fine books that have followed, this wartime biography of the cavalry great provides a chronological narrative of his battles, yielding only a brief introductory chapter on Forrest's prewar life and two short chapters on his postwar exploits. The highlights of coverage include discussions of Fort Donelson, Shiloh, the Tennessee campaigns of 1862 and 1863, the defense against Streight's Raid, Chickamauga, Fort Pillow, Brice's Crossroads, Spring Hill and Franklin, and the shattering of Forrest's command before Wilson's Selma raid. The narrative is thorough and well conceived, and conflicts are described in sufficient detail to satisfy those grounded in following tactics and strategy. The maps are poorly done, and the book lacks photographs.

Henry's experience with railroad history has produced a work that treats the transportation problems with more than the usual ability. The chief problem with this otherwise impressive work is the author's transparent admiration for his subject, which colors the interpretation delivered to the reader. The work minimizes Forrest's shortcomings and failures, excuses his flights (as with Donelson), and suggestively ignores the massacre at Fort Pillow.

(Reprinted 1969, 580 pp., McCowat-Mercer Press, Jackson, Tenn.; 1969 edition reprinted 1987, 580 pp., Broadfoot, Wilmington)

218

Jordan, Thomas, and J. P. Pryor. **The Campaigns of Lt.-Gen. N. B. Forrest, and of Forrest's Cavalry** (704 pp., Blelock and Co., New Orleans, 1868)

This early, so-called authorized biography of the cavalry great makes heavy use of the general's papers and was written with his collaboration. Although the work was completed far too early to take advantage of the *O.R.* (*q.v.*) and other important references, and despite a strong Southern bias, this collection of papers and notes merits continued inspection. Users of this book should be aware of the considerable number of factual errors and consider themselves warned that the authors omitted a significant amount of material not favorable to Forrest. Despite these rather substantial inadequacies, the work is a sourcebook of primary material on Forrest's generalship because of his contributions and involvement in this project.

Former Confederate general officer Jordan served on the staffs of Beauregard, Johnston, and Bragg and therefore knew Forrest well. Pryor, his primary collaborator, was a newspaperman, as was Jordan after the war. Their task, with Forrest's help, was to lay down the record of command and to set forth the legend of the Confederate cavalryman. Controversial items that should have been illuminated, such as disputes with Earl Van Dorn and Braxton Bragg, are passed over with little comment. Yet the work contains a solid and relatively unembellished narrative of Forrest's exploits throughout the war, and the authors present a mountain of firsthand data on their subject. Indeed, subsequent biographies of Forrest, despite the availability of many other sources, have drawn heavily on this still-useful work.

(Reprinted 1988, with an introduction by Ezra J. Warner, 704 pp., Morningside, Dayton)

219

Wills, Brian Steel. **A Battle from the Start: The Life of Nathan Bedford Forrest** (457 pp., HarperCollins, New York, 1992)

Two chapters in this work examine the prewar life of Forrest, serving admirably to sketch the subject's financial rise and military interests. Two final chapters treat the former Confederate general's activities with the Ku Klux Klan and as a railroad executive, again sketching briefly Forrest's exploits and providing a minimum of interpretation. The substance of this work are the 12 chapters that examine Forrest's wartime performance. Using a variety of primary and a few secondary sources, Wills provides a nice retelling of Forrest's campaigns, written in a far more lively style than earlier works.

The standard battles are here: the escape from Fort Donelson, Shiloh, Forrest's Tennessee raids, the Chickamauga campaign, the capture of Fort Pillow and the resultant massacre, Brice's Crossroads, Forrest's 1864 raids, the chaos of the Nashville campaign, and the scattering of Forrest's forces in the path of Maj. Gen. James H. Wilson's Selma raid. While the battles and campaigns are credibly described, little significant detail or analysis thrusts forward to enlighten readers. Two erroneous references appear in the work, incorrectly providing the names of William Brimage Bate and George Baird Hodge. This competent life story of Nathan Bedford Forrest, notable for its prewar and postwar discussions, may be of significant use to students.

220

Wyeth, John Allan. **Life of General Nathan Bedford Forrest** (655 pp., Harper and Bros., New York, 1899)

Wyeth provides one of the more interesting turn-of-the-century works of Confederate biography. The author's wartime experience as a young trooper of the 4th Alabama Cavalry invests this work with its strengths and its weaknesses. Wyeth was able to write about many wartime events with the authority of one who had lived through them, and he relates stories of Forrest with a candor and perception that often entertain the most casual reader. However, young Wyeth's adoration of his commander clouded his vision in crucial ways. The author often exaggerates the importance of Forrest's actions, as with Longstreet's statement on the famed telegram to Bragg following Chickamauga, and the inconsequential railroad raid in September 1864. He downplays Forrest's role in the Fort Pillow massacre. He erroneously suggests that Forrest captured a strategically placed battery at Shiloh and goes on to proclaim that had Forrest's superiors heeded his words Grant might have been demolished before Buell reached the field. The author naturally reduces the significance of Forrest's involvement in the Ku Klux Klan following the war.

Despite Wyeth's hero worship, the work contains much of value. For instance, the author establishes a logical argument supporting the contention that Forrest was perhaps the only Confederate commander thinking clearly at Fort Donelson.

(New edition 1959, titled *That Devil Forrest: Life of General Nathan Bedford Forrest*, with a foreword by Henry Steele Commager, 614 pp., Harper and Bros., New York; 1959 edition reprinted 1989, with a foreword by Albert Castel, 614 pp., Louisiana State University Press, Baton Rouge)

Samuel Gibbs French (1818–1910)

221

French, Samuel G. **Two Wars: An Autobiography of General Samuel G. French: Mexican War: War between the States, a Diary: Reconstruction Period, His Experience: Incidents, Reminiscences, etc.** (404 pp., Confederate Veteran, Nashville, 1901)

This work leaves us with the reminiscences of an officer whose spotty record and medical difficulties during the war prevented an outstanding reputation. Nonetheless, the work is well composed, told with enthusiasm, and provides significant commentary on a large number of officers on both sides of the Civil War and in the Mexican War as well. The most valuable portions cover French's participation in a string of operations, highlighting service around Richmond and Petersburg, Jackson, Mississippi, and the career history of the Army of Tennessee commencing with the Atlanta campaign.

The work draws on a wartime diary regularly kept up to date. Few surprises emerge from the characterizations: apparently unreconstructed, French blasts the Yankees for nearly everything wrong in civilization, and the bitter partisanship of many passages mars the work's credibility. He also flagrantly attacks John Bell Hood for the Tennessee campaign of 1864, and he fires shots at John J. Pettus and Leonidas Polk too. French charges William J. Hardee with deliberately plotting his downfall, and the casualty figures he quotes in many instances are wildly inaccurate. The lengthy appendix relating French's ideas on numbers and statistics is worthless. What does remain useful in this work are the author's diary accounts and recollections of the military campaigns and battles he witnessed.

John Brown Gordon (1832–1904)

222

Eckert, Ralph Lowell. **John Brown Gordon, Soldier, Southerner, American** (367 pp., Louisiana State University Press, Baton Rouge, 1989)

Gordon's amazing war record provides the focus of this study, 31 percent of which consists of coverage of the war years. Gordon's rapid rise in the ranks from a captain to major general commanding a corps in the Army of Northern Virginia are impressive enough, but the reader will find many other uniquely interesting experiences throughout Gordon's various campaigns.

Eckert skillfully describes Gordon's war experiences and finds him highly impressive as an officer. The role of his subject in postwar years transforms into a more complex being, as Gordon takes on leadership in both the Ku Klux Klan and the U.S. Senate and eventually becomes governor of Georgia. Ultimately, the aging Civil War hero found his place as leader of the United Confederate Veterans, a group he worked tirelessly to promote and that itself promoted sectional healing even as it glorified the Lost Cause.

Making good use of the sources that remain, the author has produced a valuable study of a war hero and a politician who enjoyed popularity but accomplished relatively little for his constituents. John Brown Gordon was a failure as a businessman and a hero as a soldier. Parts of his life vaguely echo parts of Grant's life. Nonetheless, Gordon was staunchly Southern and proud of it, and this study details his life in a winning manner.

223

Gordon, John B. **Reminiscences of the Civil War** (474 pp., Charles Scribner's Sons, New York, 1903)

A vividly written if severely exaggerated record of the great commander's Civil War service. Spanning the period of Gordon's raising of troops in Alabama to his celebrated participation in the surrender ceremonies at Appomattox, the work lays down a heroic story of one who played an influential role in many of the Army of Northern Virginia's key actions. Along the way Gordon interjects many lively anecdotes, from observing families divided by the war to comments on many Confederate officers to gripping accounts of battles. This last category includes the famous passages describing Gordon's hours in the Sunken Road at Antietam, where he was hit five times and nearly drowned in his own blood. Often, these anecdotes are the product of the general's fertile imagination.

Still, some material of value lies within this book. The author comments on the performance of field commanders and common soldiers at First Bull Run, the Peninsula, Chancellorsville, Gettysburg, Vicksburg, Chickamauga, Chattanooga, the Wilderness campaign, the Valley campaign of 1864, the Petersburg siege, and the final campaign. Frequently Gordon's luck and personality cast him into crucial parts of battles, and his sterling record of promotion attests to his competence. The author's outstanding career, keen military insight, and enjoyable style make this a highly important work.

(Reprinted 1981, 474 pp., Time-Life Books, Alexandria, Va.; reprinted 1993, with an introduction by Ralph Lowell Eckert, Louisiana State University Press, Baton Rouge; 1904 edition reprinted 1993, 474 pp., Morningside, Dayton)

Thomas Jewett Goree (1835–1905)

224

Goree, Thomas J. **Longstreet's Aide: The Civil War Letters of Major Thomas J. Goree** (ed. Thomas W. Cutrer, 239 pp., University Press of Virginia, Charlottesville, 1995)

At the tender age of 25, T. J. Goree began his involvement in the Civil War as a volunteer aide-de-camp to Brig. Gen. James Longstreet. The author remained with Longstreet through the entire war, rising to the grade of major and participating in and writing about numerous actions, including the Peninsular campaign, Second Bull Run, Antietam, Fredericksburg, Gettysburg, Chickamauga, Knoxville, Petersburg, and Appomattox. Written mostly to family members, the letters are often long and revealing, frank and earnest in their observations. The result is a kaleidoscopic view of many personalities in the Army of Northern Virginia, most prominently Longstreet himself but also Robert E. Lee, Edward Porter Alexander, Moxley Sorrel, George Pickett, and Micah Jenkins. Among the most absorbing descriptions of battle in the letters are those covering Blackburn's Ford, Seven Pines, Yorktown, Williamsburg, Fredericksburg, and Chickamauga.

The work presents 51 wartime letters of Goree, several letters written to him from other officers, and a travel diary that he kept during his 1865 trip accompanying Longstreet from Virginia to Talladega, Alabama. Postwar letters to and from Goree reflect on a variety of wartime situations. The editor has done a fine job assembling this material into an impressive volume that will be highly prized by collectors of material relating to the Army of Northern Virginia.

Josiah Gorgas (1818–1883)

225

Gorgas, Josiah. **The Journals of Josiah Gorgas, 1857–1878** (ed. Sarah Woolfolk Wiggins, 305 pp., University of Alabama Press, Tuscaloosa, 1995)

This finely edited and comprehensive volume of Gorgas's diaries is a welcome addition to the Confederate bookshelf. The diary was kept primarily for family members, including Gorgas's son William (who would become the renowned physician), and for the most part contains few revelations of vital interest. The entries typically cover the minutiae of everyday life in the Confederacy, generally without any special insights into the personalities of some famous characters whom Gorgas knew. The occasional mentions of ordnance department business generally amount to self-congratulation.

Despite the mundane nature of the work, some glimpses of interest shine through. Illuminating passages reflect on notables such as Jefferson Davis, whom Gorgas did not like. The work shows that the Confederate cause sometimes appeared weak to Gorgas because of widespread Union sentiment. The author, originally a Northerner, did not approve of South Carolina, and of Charlestonians in particular. Despite this, Gorgas held out for longshot Confederate victories on the battlefield until the very end of the war. The skillful editing makes the work valuable, although one wishes the content lived up to its potential as a keystone source. The work effectively supersedes an earlier edition, *The Civil War Diary of General Josiah Gorgas* (ed. Frank E. Vandiver, 208 pp., University of Alabama Press, University, 1947).

226

Vandiver, Frank E. **Ploughshares into Swords: Josiah Gorgas and Confederate Ordnance** (349 pp., University of Texas Press, Austin, 1952)

Vandiver has written a stimulating and well-composed biography of the ordnance chief. The work begins slowly and accelerates as the subject's career expands, ultimately delivering a balanced and wise assessment of this tragic and talented figure. The coverage of Gorgas's Northern birth, cranky personality, and early days in the army establishes a pattern for years to come. The disagreements with superiors in the antebellum Ordnance Department of the U.S. Army, the author shows, gave Gorgas ample opportunity when the secession crisis arrived to journey south and assume responsibility.

The author's portrayal of Gorgas's Confederate career is

magnificent, providing readers with substantial background material on ordnance operations and a capsule history of the Confederate Ordnance Department as well as a biography. The work overstates the subject's importance by a longshot, however, claiming he contributed "more than than any other man" save for Robert E. Lee to the Confederate war effort. Many may dispute that, but they will not dispute the value of the numerous details in this work, which assemble a clear picture of what Gorgas did to serve the South during the war.

(Reprinted 1994, 349 pp., Texas A&M University Press, College Station)

George St. Leger Grenfell (1808–?)

227

Starr, Stephen Z. **Colonel Grenfell's Wars: The Life of a Soldier of Fortune** (352 pp., Louisiana State University Press, Baton Rouge, 1971)

While this work brings to life a rather obscure but intriguing figure, it offers some dubious suppositions about the subject's role in the larger picture of the war. Although Starr's research resources were necessarily scant, he explains that soldier of fortune Grenfell rose to prominence riding with John Hunt Morgan throughout the Kentucky raids of 1862. Filled with Southern sympathy and the taste for adventure and battle, Grenfell delighted in giving Union forces the slip and generally wreaking havoc amid the Kentucky landscape. The author contends that Grenfell then withdrew from military service to partake in the Northwest Conspiracy, a plot that would disrupt the Union governments of Indiana, Illinois, Missouri, and Ohio, liberate Confederate prisoners in the North, and promote Copperhead activities to draw the war to a speedy close while preserving the Confederacy.

In describing the conspiracy, the author repeats misinterpretations of the past by affording considerable significance to actions of the Copperhead leaders, particularly Clement L. Vallandigham. Grenfell was captured and sentenced to be executed. Escaping from the Dry Tortugas, Grenfell was apparently lost at sea. This nebulous end to Grenfell's life also marks the nature of the author's thesis. Still, the work adequately describes a peculiar and fascinating personality and some of his exploits with John Morgan.

Bryan Grimes (1828–1880)

228

Grimes, Bryan. **Extracts of Letters of Major-Gen'l Bryan Grimes to His Wife, Written While in Active Service in the Army of Northern Virginia: Together with Some Personal Recollections of the War, Written by Him after Its Close, etc.** (ed. Pulaski Cowper, 137 pp., Edwards, Broughton and Co., Raleigh, 1883)

This constitutes a succinct record of a North Carolina officer who became the last major general commissioned in the Army of Northern Virginia. Containing notes and letters spanning virtually the entire length of Grimes's service, the work offers insights into Chancellorsville, the Valley campaign of 1864, and the Appomattox campaign. The reflections on a long list of Confederate officers include passages on George B. Anderson, Stonewall Jackson, Robert E. Lee, and Stephen Dodson Ramseur.

The editor offers a brief overview of Grimes's service in the eastern theater. The remainder of the work includes a hodgepodge of sources, including Grimes's own partial notes on his career through Chancellorsville, official reports relating to Gettysburg and Cedar Creek, letters of Grimes and John B. Gordon relating to the Appomattox campaign, and Grimes's letters to his wife covering the final year of the war.

(Reprinted 1986, with an introduction by Gary W. Gallagher and an index, 143 pp., Broadfoot, Wilmington)

Silas T. Grisamore (1825–1897)

229

Grisamore, Silas T. **The Civil War Reminiscences of Major Silas T. Grisamore** (ed. Arthur W. Bergeron, Jr., 227 pp., Louisiana State University Press, Baton Rouge, 1993)

This account offers a glimpse into a Louisiana officer's experience in the Trans-Mississippi theater of war. A native Hoosier who moved to Louisiana during the Mexican War period, Grisamore joined a company that was incorporated into the 18th Louisiana Infantry. He served as regimental quartermaster and then took on that assignment at brigade and division levels, so that his narrative, based on now-lost diaries and written shortly after the war, retains value. The author's account includes garrison duty in Mississippi and Alabama, a transfer west of the Mississippi, and the end of the war in Louisiana.

The author's sober insight into problems of supply casts a worthwhile light on the problems of the western Confederate armies, even shortly after the outbreak of war. The accounts appeared first in the *Weekly Thibodeaux Sentinel* between December 1867 and April 1871. A variety of obscure actions receive treatment, as with Alfred Mouton's command at the battle of Labadieville, his death at Mansfield, and the actions of Henry H. Sibley and others at Bisland. Rare comments on the equipage of his units, encompassing tents, clothing, food, ammunition, and other items, along with a curious sense of humor, give this account permanence.

Johnson Hagood (1829–1898)

230

Hagood, Johnson. **Memoirs of the War of Secession, from the Original Manuscripts of Johnson Hagood, Brigadier-General, C.S.A.** (ed. U. R. Brooks, 496 pp., State Co., Columbia, 1910)

This memoir ranks among the more valuable reminiscences of a South Carolinian. Divided into two parts, it treats Hagood's service as colonel of the 1st South Carolina Infantry and his subsequent command of a brigade. After some newspaper testimonials and a sketch of the general's life, the book presents reminiscences based on Hagood's wartime papers, his retained copies of reports and memoranda, and diaries and newspapers. The sketches are exciting, written with intelligence, and filled with detail at certain points along Hagood's career. At the very outbreak of war Hagood participated in the bombardment of Sumter, after which he fought with the 1st South Carolina at First Bull Run.

After the unit's baptism of fire, it returned to Charleston. The following text details much of interest not only relating to military affairs but also to the condition of the city during the ensuing months. The diary of conditions during the siege of Charleston is supported by many abstracts from official documents. The narrative makes almost no mention of the character of the 54th Massachusetts, the leading regiment of the most celebrated attack on Fort Wagner, and does not contain Hagood's bitter reply to the request for Shaw's body. Material follows relating to the activities of Hagood's brigade around Petersburg. Several crude maps are included. A number of misspellings appear throughout the text, as with the names of James Chesnut, John A. B. Dahlgren, Joseph Finegan, and Quincy A. Gillmore. The text misidentifies Robert Gould Shaw as a general officer. Several pages of errata precede the first chapter. Appendices provide a roster of Hagood's brigade, poetry, and photographs of the Hagood Brigade Monument near the Weldon Railroad site south of Petersburg.

(Reprinted 1989, 496 pp., J. J. Fox, Camden, S.C.)

Wade Hampton III (1818–1902)

231

Wellman, Manly Wade. **Giant in Gray: A Biography of Wade Hampton of South Carolina** (387 pp., Charles Scribner's Sons, New York, 1949)

This is a serviceable biography of the wealthy politician who became a legendary cavalryman. The work opens at the close of war, moves back to survey Hampton's heritage and early days, provides a short synopsis of the subject's antebellum career, and proceeds with a lengthy discussion of the Civil War years. Written in a spritely, almost novelistic style, the biography is adequately documented and draws on mostly printed sources (a few contain dubious information) and a few manuscript sources. The result is a work that will remain useful until a more detailed, scholarly treatment arises.

The book focuses not only on Hampton's military adventures but also the political and social aspects of this aristocrat's Civil War. Allegedly the wealthiest landowner in the South, Hampton at once raised his legion of South Carolinians and participated at First Bull Run and in the Peninsular campaign before transforming into a cavalry commander. The analysis of tactics and strategy is rather light, and a disturbing number of conversations directly quoted on the battlefield appear. Wellman clearly admires his subject, and this occasionally stands in the way of credibility. Still, the descriptions of Hampton's part at Gettysburg and of his exploits as corps commander following Jeb Stuart's death are related with excitement. The work continues with a fine series of chapters describing Hampton's political triumphs in South Carolina and in Washington in the postwar years. Another title worthy of inspection is *Family Letters of the Three Wade Hamptons, 1782–1901*, by Wade Hampton III et al. (ed. Charles Cauthen, 181 pp., University of South Carolina Press, Columbia, 1953). This book includes a large selection of letters from the Confederate general.

(Reprinted 1980, 387 pp., Morningside, Dayton)

William Joseph Hardee (1815–1873)

232

Hughes, Nathaniel Cheairs, Jr. **General William J. Hardee: Old Reliable** (329 pp., Louisiana State University Press, Baton Rouge, 1965)

This is an outstanding Confederate biography. Hardee's career offers bountiful opportunities for interpretation, and the author takes full advantage of his subject. Hughes argues that Hardee made a superb corps commander who shied away from command of an army (the Army of Tennessee) because his personality contained an element of "failure of will." The author also asserts that Hardee's competence as a corps commander was checked by a strong adherence to conventional military tactics. Despite these shortcomings, Hughes demonstrates how Hardee performed capably in many situations and established a record as one of the more successful Confederate commanders at his level.

The small cache of Hardee papers available meant the author had to rely heavily on the *O.R.* (*q.v.*) and other well-known primary sources. Despite this, the brief story of Hardee's early life and Mexican War experience and the lengthy discussion of Hardee's Civil War career succeeds in great style and with penetrating analysis. The author describes Hardee's successes, as with saving the Army of Tennessee following Missionary Ridge, and controversies, such as Hardee's role in ousting Bragg as the army's commander. This work has much to say about Hardee's character, his performance on the field, and the war in the West. The author has created a solid and reliable work.

(Reprinted 1987, 329 pp., Broadfoot, Wilmington; reprinted 1992, 329 pp., Louisiana State University Press, Baton Rouge)

Alexander Cheves Haskell (1839–1910)

233

Haskell, Alexander Cheves. **Alexander Cheves Haskell: The Portrait of a Man** (ed. Louise Haskell Daly, 224 pp., published by the author, Norwood, Mass., 1934)

The wartime letters and recollections of Haskell, a South Carolina soldier, contain much on family matters, a sizable section on the author's childhood and early years, and lengthy postwar anecdotes. The core of the work treats the war years. Haskell enlisted in the 1st South Carolina Volunteers and soon served as military secretary to Col. Maxcy Gregg, followed by staff duty with Brig. Gen. Samuel McGowan. The eyewitness description of the bombardment of Fort Sumter is particularly fine, as are comments on service in the Army of Northern Virginia. The staff duties positioned Haskell to view many important officers and situations, and these are related most vividly in the letters and sometimes in the recollections, penned many years later.

The accounts of Antietam and Fredericksburg, where Haskell was wounded, are informative. Wounded at Chancellorsville, he missed Gettysburg but was the following

spring commissioned lieutenant colonel of the 7th South Carolina Cavalry. Subsequently promoted to colonel, Haskell commanded the regiment at Drewry's Bluff, about Petersburg, and surrendered at Appomattox Court House. The letters form a valuable and enjoyable collection. Another title worthy of inspection is *The Haskell Memoirs,* by John Cheves Haskell (ed. Gilbert E. Govan and James W. Livingood, 176 pp., G. P. Putnam's Sons, New York, 1960). John's memoirs contain many passages relating to Gettysburg, the Wilderness, and other actions.

(Reprinted 1988, ed. Lee A. Wallace, Jr., 267 pp., Broadfoot, Wilmington)

William Williston Heartsill (1839–1916)

234

Heartsill, William W. **Fourteen Hundred and 91 Days in the Confederate Army: A Journal Kept by W. W. Heartsill, for Four Years, One Month, and One Day; or, Camp Life: Day-by-Day, of the W. P. Lane Rangers, from April 19th 1861, to May 20th 1865** (264 pp., published by the author, Marshall, Tex., 1876)

Published in an edition of 100 copies and printed by the author on a tabletop press, the original edition featured photographic prints sent to Heartsill by members of his company, the W. P. Lane Rangers, and pasted in by hand. Thirteen copies are known to have survived. Readers are fortunate that a new edition was edited by Bell I. Wiley (332 pp., McCowat-Mercer Press, Jackson, Tenn., 1953). In the 1980s Broadfoot acquired the original manuscript and published an edition with a single holographic page tipped in.

As a member of the 2d Texas Cavalry, Heartsill experienced a variety of Civil War adventures that make his narrative well rounded and enthralling. These included frontier duty, prison time at Camp Butler in 1863, a peculiar exodus to serve in the Army of Tennessee (which resulted in experiencing Chickamauga), and a wartime journey from Georgia to Texas that offers observations of the Southern home front. He also guarded Federal prisoners at Tyler in 1864. This is a gem among Confederate narratives.

(1953 edition reprinted 1992, 336 pp., Broadfoot, Wilmington)

Henry Heth (1825–1899)

235

Heth, Henry. **The Memoirs of Henry Heth** (ed. James L. Morrison, 303 pp., Greenwood Press, Westport, 1974)

These are the reminiscences of one of the most liked officers of the Army of Northern Virginia (Heth was the only man Lee addressed by his given name). Heth's rise to prominence took some unusual turns. Having ranked near the bottom of his West Point class, the Virginian entered Confederate service as colonel of the 45th Virginia Infantry, serving in the early campaigns in western Virginia. He joined the Army of Northern Virginia in 1863, after participating in the Kentucky campaign, and as a brigadier general was central in bringing on the engagement at Gettysburg. Wounded at Gettysburg (and attacked by some for disobeying orders), he nonetheless shared in the many battles to come in 1864 and surrendered at Appomattox.

Heth's manuscript, which remained unpublished for the better part of a century, makes an interesting addition to Confederate literature, although the narrative focuses on Heth's more glamorous and successful actions and dismisses others with little comment. The memoirs describe Heth's days at West Point and his friendships with Grant, Lee, John Reynolds, and others; his antebellum days fighting Indians on the frontier; and, most prominently, his Civil War service. The editor shows that although Heth was an aggressive fighter, he was also typically careless. (Heth remarks on touching off the battle of Gettysburg in a single paragraph.) Heth's more valuable reminiscences cover Perryville, Chancellorsville, the Wilderness, Spotsylvania, and the surrender at Appomattox. The editor has added a sound introduction.

Ambrose Powell Hill (1825–1865)

236

Robertson, James I., Jr. **General A. P. Hill: The Story of a Confederate Warrior** (382 pp., Random House, New York, 1987)

Elusive in death as well as life, Hill has presented biographers with a difficult job, but the present work accomplishes a superb depiction of Powell Hill and many of the battles he fought before an untimely and almost accidental death outside Petersburg in the war's final weeks. Although the work ostensibly attempts to present a full biography, it centers heavily on Hill's Civil War career. Prominent in the narrative are accounts of Hill's commands at Williamsburg, the Peninsular campaign, Cedar Mountain, Antietam, Fredericksburg, Chancellorsville, Gettysburg, the Wilderness campaign, and the closing scenes of Hill's life at Petersburg. The treatment is scholarly, extremely well researched, written with balance as well as admiration, and thoroughly entertaining to read.

In addition to documenting Hill's many successes, Robertson uncovers the answer to a longstanding puzzle over Hill's health: he suffered from gonorrhea, which he contracted at West Point in 1844. The author speculates repeatedly on Hill's mental health and makes a few errors, stating that Hill was Lee's third subordinate early in 1863 (p. 171), suggesting that James J. Pettigrew succeeded Dorsey Pender at Gettysburg (p. 219), saying that the Shenandoah River is east of Ashby's Gap (p. 41), and placing the Howlett Line west of Petersburg (p. 316). Other errors include misspelling the names, in the text or the index, of Romeyn Beck Ayres, James Barnet Fry, Winfield Scott Hancock, Wladimir Krzyzanowski, and Dixon Stansbury Miles. Despite these flaws, this work offers the current definitive picture of Powell Hill.

Daniel Harvey Hill (1821–1889)

237

Bridges, Hal. **Lee's Maverick General: Daniel Harvey Hill** (323 pp., McGraw-Hill, New York, 1961)

Blessed by great purpose and talents as a military commander, Hill could not restrain his sarcastic and bitter criticisms of anything that failed to suit him. He fits into the common mold of an excellent subordinate commander who lacked the administrative and leadership qualities to coordinate large-scale strategy and tactics. His carping eventually led to his dismissal from the Army of Northern Virginia, along the same path marched on by a number of difficult general officers before and after.

Bridges traces a clear portrait of Harvey Hill's Civil War career. Sympathetic to his subject, he establishes reasons for the major clashes in Hill's military record and sides with Hill rather than his detractors, even when it comes to Robert E. Lee. This handling of the analysis may lean too favorably in Hill's direction, but it provides enlightening, scholarly reading about one of the South's most celebrated, and enigmatic, commanders.

(Reprinted 1991, with an introduction by Gary W. Gallagher, 323 pp., University of Nebraska Press, Lincoln)

Thomas Carmichael Hindman (1828–1868)

238

Neal, Diane, and Thomas W. Kremm. **The Lion of the South: General Thomas C. Hindman** (319 pp., Mercer University Press, Macon, 1993)

While this work provides a reasonable synthesis of Hindman's life, it focuses heavily on the Civil War years, providing only 85 pages on the general's antebellum days and a brief section on his postwar life and murder. This may be warranted, as Hindman's political career in Arkansas is relatively one-dimensional and therefore does not require extensive analysis. But one wishes the coverage of the subject's Civil War command were grounded in more recent scholarship, interpreted more for the reader, and offered a clearer sense of Hindman's value to the Confederacy.

The narrative centers on Prairie Grove, Chickamauga, the Atlanta campaign, and Hindman's flight as the Confederacy crumbled. How did the subject's caustic personality affect his battlefield decision making? The authors hint at trouble here and there and offer a discussion of Hindman's resignation, offered in February 1864 but rejected. Did Hindman feign disgust to win a new command? Was he assassinated by the radicals of the Loyal League? This work provides a satisfactory story of Hindman's life; a fuller analysis will come in some later volume.

John Bell Hood (1831–1879)

239

Dyer, John P. **The Gallant Hood** (383 pp., Bobbs-Merrill Co., Indianapolis, 1950)

This is a serviceable portrait of the much-maligned Confederate commander. The difficulty with a military biography of Hood lies in the scarcity of source materials. Most of Hood's papers were lost, and those that survived were widely scattered and have never been published as a collection. Thus, much of the support in untangling this enigmatic figure is not available, and Dyer therefore worked principally from the *O.R.* (*q.v.*) and a sizable collection of primary and secondary sources.

The story focuses on Hood's Civil War career, with brief treatment of the antebellum life and postwar decline of this tragic figure. The author examines Hood's battlefield performance sympathetically, while realizing the occasional success and ultimate grand failure that Hood represents. He shows that Hood's pursuit of flattery and of political

assistance helped to unravel his personality and his performance on the field. The work unfairly attacks James Longstreet, assessing his performance on several fields in old, stereotypical ways, and astonishingly purports that "no battle" took place at Resaca during the Atlanta campaign. Overall, though, Dyer delivers a fair and much-needed assessment of Hood.

(Reprinted 1993, 383 pp., Konecky and Konecky, New York)

240

Hood, John Bell. **Advance and Retreat: Personal Experiences in the United States and Confederate States Armies** (358 pp., Hood Orphan Memorial Fund, New Orleans, 1880)

As is the case with such memoirs, the objective is to rewrite the credentials of the author and knock down those who opposed him. In this case the primary target is Joe Johnston. Unfortunately, the careless and untruthful way in which Hood set about this shameless goal accomplished little. Although proceeds from the book did help to support his 11 orphaned children following Hood's premature death from yellow fever, in the eyes of historians the book only makes Hood appear foolish.

Early in the war John Bell Hood behaved competently. His fall from grace resulted from his disabling wounds and from being placed into a situation requiring more than his ability. Hood repeatedly ducked responsibility for unfolding actions and occasionally placed others in command during times of risk. He may have intentionally neglected his duties at various times, including at Cassville, to make his superior, Johnston, look bad. When he did take command of the Army of Tennessee, he did nothing except ultimately ruin it by folly in the Tennessee campaign of 1864. The net result was a career that faltered and the destruction of one of the South's great armies. Hood's memoir is riddled with rationalizations and misinterpretations. It is worthwhile reading only to shed light on the confused mind of its author. To add insult to injury, the maps are badly flawed.

(New edition 1959, ed. Richard N. Current, 376 pp., Indiana University Press, Bloomington; 1959 edition reprinted 1990, 376 pp., Kraus Reprints, Millwood, N.Y.; 1880 edition reprinted 1993, with an introduction by Richard M. McMurry, 368 pp., Da Capo Press, New York)

241

McMurry, Richard M. **John Bell Hood and the War for Southern Independence** (239 pp., University Press of Kentucky, Lexington, 1982)

This is the most modern and intelligent treatment of a controversial soldier. McMurry's well-documented study examines Hood's paradox as a highly effective brigade commander in the Peninsular campaign and at Second Bull Run, as well as his outstanding divisional command at Antietam and his utterly disastrous command of the Army of Tennessee in the critical campaign before Atlanta and in Tennessee in 1864. The author meticulously shows that Hood's primary blunder was a lack of organizational skill, preventing sufficient planning before a campaign or battle occurred.

In a careful and thoughtful analysis of Hood's actions at Atlanta, McMurry shows that Hood failed to supervise his subordinate commanders. The author assigns Hood a fatalistic view: once an action began, Hood felt, his boys would bring him out of it as the winner. It was a belief that equaled abandoning his responsibilities as army commander during a fight. The work also surveys the relationships between Hood and his common soldiers, Jefferson Davis, and general officers including Joe Johnston and Braxton Bragg. A single misspelling was found, the name of Francis Asbury Shoup, Hood's chief of staff in the 1864 campaign.

(Reprinted 1992, 239 pp., University of Nebraska Press, Lincoln)

Jedediah Hotchkiss (1827–1899)

242

Hotchkiss, Jedediah. **Make Me a Map of the Valley: The Civil War Journal of Stonewall Jackson's Cartographer** (ed. Archie P. McDonald, 352 pp., Southern Methodist University Press, Dallas, 1973)

As topographical engineer on the staffs of a battery of Confederate general officers, Virginian Hotchkiss became the most celebrated military mapmaker in the Southern armies. Many of his products appear in the *Atlas to Accompany the Official Records* (q.v.), and a portion of the present book—his journal from August 1864 to May 1865—appears in the *O.R.* itself (q.v.). *Make Me a Map of the Valley* brings the complete work into easy availability and was skillfully edited and annotated, making it a superbly enjoyable work of Confederate biography.

Hotchkiss's journal spans a three-year period beginning in March 1862, when during the Valley campaign Jackson asked Hotchkiss to make a map of the Valley of the Shenandoah. Hotchkiss's subsequent service included Second Bull Run, Antietam, Chancellorsville, Gettysburg, and the Virginia campaigns of 1864. His journal includes much about the battles as well as important data on topographical reconnaissance and field mapmaking, and observations of many important Confederate officers he knew and served under. These included not only Jackson but Lee, Dick Ewell, Jubal Early, and Lunsford L. Lomax. The editor includes a biographical introduction. A few errors occasionally mar this and the notes within the manuscript itself. Also consult William J. Miller's excellent *Mapping for Stonewall: The Civil War Service of Jed Hotchkiss* (176 pp., Elliott and Clark, Washington, 1993).

(Reprinted 1988, 352 pp., Southern Methodist University, Dallas)

McHenry Howard (1838–1923)

243

Howard, McHenry. **Recollections of a Maryland Confederate Soldier and Staff Officer under Johnston, Jackson, and Lee** (423 pp., Williams and Wilkins Co., Baltimore, 1914)

This splendid memoir is filled with much of interest to those following Maryland soldiers in the war and in the Army of Northern Virginia. At the outbreak of war, 22-year-old Howard, a Marylander and grandson of Francis Scott Key, joined the 1st Maryland Infantry (Confederate) and participated in First Bull Run. Thereafter he joined the staff of Brig. Gen. Charles S. Winder as an adjutant and served under Stonewall Jackson in the Valley campaign of 1862. Following Winder's death, he served on the staffs of Brig. Gens. George H. Steuart and Isaac R. Trimble and finally on Steuart's staff again. Captured at Spotsylvania, Howard remained in Fort Delaware until the last few months of war, only to be recaptured at Sayler's Creek.

Howard's memoir provides a solid account of many great actions, including First Bull Run, the Valley campaign, the Seven Days battles, Cedar Run, Mine Run, the Wilderness campaign, and Spotsylvania. His account of prison life in Fort Delaware and at Johnson's Island is particularly valuable, and his reflections on the final weeks of war as Lee's army scattered westward form an engaging narrative. Soundly based on letters and journals, the work bears the marks of care and reliability despite its completion long after the war. The author's descriptions of Ewell, Jackson, Edward Johnson, Custis Lee, Robert E. Lee, and of course Winder, Steuart, and Trimble are particularly worthwhile.

(New edition 1975, ed. James I. Robertson, Jr., with notes and corrections that significantly improve the earlier work, 483 pp., Morningside, Dayton)

Alexander Hunter (1843–1914)

244

Hunter, Alexander. **Johnny Reb and Billy Yank** (720 pp., Neale Publishing Co., New York, 1905)

This oddly titled account relates a common soldier's experience in the Confederate Army. Hunter was a member of the 17th Virginia Infantry until the spring of 1863; thereafter he joined the 4th Virginia Cavalry as a horse soldier. The work is intelligently composed, and although written long after the war, it seems more or less reliable. Hunter's regimental commanders included Cols. Montgomery D. Corse and William Henry Fitzhugh Payne; his regiments' battles included First Bull Run, the Peninsular campaign, Second Bull Run, Antietam, Fredericksburg, Chancellorsville, Brandy Station, Gettysburg, the Wilderness campaign, Petersburg, Five Forks, and Appomattox.

The book's real value lies in the calm, unaffected descriptions of camp life among common soldiers. The many observations of ordinary events are engaging, as are the author's evaluation of Confederate defeat. He blames Jefferson Davis and the Confederate leader's choice of friends as commanding generals, the irrationality of the War Department, Jubal Early's independent command, and the failure to arm the slaves. The index is inadequate, and spelling errors can be found throughout the text.

John S. Jackman (1841–1912)

245

Jackman, John S. **Diary of a Confederate Soldier: John S. Jackman of the Orphan Brigade** (ed. William C. Davis, 174 pp., University of South Carolina Press, Columbia, 1990)

This is an interesting narrative account of a typical Confederate soldier of the West. It has two major strengths: the diary was composed during the war and written into final form by 1867, and the author was a relatively perceptive observer of events around him and did not seem to need embellishment to draft his story. Thus the material reliably gives us a good view into the campaigns of the 1st Kentucky Brigade, John C. Breckinridge's unit of border state Confederates who lost their home during the war to

Union occupation (see *The Orphan Brigade*, by William C. Davis [*q.v.*]).

Jackman's account includes material on Shiloh, the defenses of Vicksburg in 1862, Stones River, Chickamauga, Chattanooga, the Atlanta campaign, and the end of the struggle. Most of the daily entries are quite short, and many are peppered with the minutiae of soldier life and of discussions of fellow soldiers and relatives and acquaintances at home. The several sections that cover Jackman's experiences in battle and on the march make this diary worthy of close reading.

Thomas Jonathan Jackson (1824–1863)

246

Chambers, Lenoir. **Stonewall Jackson** (2 vols., 1133 pp., William Morrow, New York, 1959)

Stripping away much of the mythology that characterized earlier works, Chambers offers Jackson the man and Jackson the soldier in place of Jackson the legend. The result is a comprehensive biography of Jackson that travels a long distance toward setting the Jackson record straight and restoring an accurate assessment of an often exaggerated personality and military record.

Chambers casts Jackson's odd personality traits as characteristic of a prude, a hypochondriac, an eccentric oddball, and a religious zealot. Moreover, Jackson could be a guiltless killer—even of his own soldiers—over relatively small infractions of discipline. However, viewed in the character of the times, none of these traits should be particularly shocking. In the 1850s and 1860s numerous people brimmed with religious fervor, believed in unwaivering discipline without exception, had strange beliefs about their bodies, and seemed generally eccentric. Stonewall Jackson just happened to be one of them.

The study's more important elements, of course, deal with Stonewall's military history. Chambers does not fall into uncritical hero worship. He properly evaluates Jackson's role as a tactician and strategist as brilliant, particularly in describing the Valley campaign and the daring risks such as the flank march at Chancellorsville. What of Jackson's peculiar failures? Chambers suggests during the Peninsular campaign that his subject was ill and exhausted. He does not explain Jackson's behavior at Fredericksburg. How good was Jackson as a commander? He was a great commander, and even great commanders are not perfect. Chambers's book is a worthy reflection of one of the towering figures of the Confederacy.

(Reprinted 1988, 1133 pp., Broadfoot, Wilmington)

247
Cooke, John Esten. **Stonewall Jackson: A Military Biography** (470 pp., D. Appleton and Co., New York, 1866)

Highly romanticized and containing significant quantities of embellished dialogue, the work is nonetheless valuable for communicating the popular Southern feeling of the day regarding its dead hero of the battlefield. The biography is not particularly valuable, then, as military history, and many of the anecdotes of Jackson are simply repackaged as secondhand lore. Its high degree of eulogistic worship accentuates the bitterly partisan nature of the work, as one would expect a piece written during the war to be, and much of the anecdotal material is offered repeatedly.

Superficial aspects of Jackson as hero come forth with fair strength, although the analysis of Stonewall's tactics and strategy is weak. Within this work exist the seeds of much of the Jackson mythology, including the statement that Barnard Bee uttered on Henry House Hill: "There is Jackson standing like a stonewall! [*sic*] Let us determine to die here, and we will conquer! Follow me!" Other such romanticized moments make up much of this story, which offers a superb record of wartime heromaking for the sake of propaganda. Appendices contain official reports relating to the Antietam campaign and a tribute to the Stonewall brigade. The work lacks an index. Earlier, inferior editions include the first, *The Life of Stonewall Jackson from Official Papers, Contemporary Narratives, and Personal Acquaintance, by a Virginian* (305 pp., Ayres and Wade, Richmond, 1863).

(1863 edition reprinted 1971, 305 pp., Books for Libraries, Freeport, N.Y.)

248
Farwell, Byron. **Stonewall: A Biography of General Thomas J. Jackson** (560 pp., W. W. Norton and Co., New York, 1992)

This biography falls short of a definitive treatment. While it offers a highly readable narrative of the general's life, it is lightly documented and presents little fresh analysis. The work includes a brief synopsis of Jackson's early life, reasonably good material on his West Point and antebellum years in Virginia, and good coverage of the Mexican War period. The Civil War chapters cover the Valley campaign of 1862 with special closeness, relating a well-written grasp of the details of Winchester, Cross Keys, and Port Republic and a forgiving recollection of Jackson's performance on the Peninsula.

The invasion of Maryland, Fredericksburg, and Jackson's triumph and subsequent mortal wounding at Chancellorsville round out the narrative. A large number of sources are employed, some reliable and others not, and the annoying disposition to cast "conversations" between major figures in the battles surfaces too many times. The work contains a number of trivial but disturbing errors, as with the incorrect spellings of Wladimir Krzyzanowski, Thomas T. Munford, Adolph Wilhelm August Friedrich von Steinwehr, and Alexander Hamilton Stephens. Farwell's study may serve as a casual summary of Stonewall's military life for less serious readers, but a definitive and scholarly biography remains to be written.

249
Greene, A. Wilson. **Whatever You Resolve to Be: Essays on Stonewall Jackson** (186 pp., Butternut and Blue, Baltimore, 1992)

Greene presents five retrospections on Jackson's performance at three controversial battles or campaigns—the Seven Days, Second Bull Run, and Fredericksburg—and two general essays that introduce the man and the legend and conclude how we should view him based on the three actions under analysis. Careful, thoughtful, well documented, and controlled in their interpretations, the essays succeed admirably, providing a valuable addendum to reading a Jackson biography like that by Lenoir Chambers (*q.v.*). Greene's opening essay provides a balanced view of the man, exploring his religious, military, and personal habits and separating exaggerated myths from the facts.

The chapter on the Seven Days reviews Jackson's poor health following the Valley campaign, suggests he made errors and did not function well as a subordinate without an independent command, but proposes that in no way do these facts compose a basis for condemning his generalship during the week of battle. The author demonstrates how Jackson's performance at Second Bull Run eliminated any remaining fears about his competency. Jackson's critical albeit imperfectly played role at Fredericksburg contributed substantially to the Confederate victory, which was costly and of limited strategic significance. In concluding this insightful volume, the author suggests that Jackson, despite a set of unusual characteristics and his problems relating to other people, deserves the high acclaim accorded him since the war.

250
Henderson, G. F. R. **Stonewall Jackson and the American Civil War** (2 vols., 975 pp., Longmans, Green and Co., London, 1898)

This was for years the standard biography of the Confederate commander. A sweeping narrative of Jackson's background, character, and pivotal role in the first two years of war, the work contains an abundance of intelligent writing and careful reviews of Jackson's performance on the battlefield. The author succeeds admirably in establishing a clear picture of Jackson the man and how he operated with his subordinate commanders. He does not fare so well with objectivity when it comes to assessing Jackson's successes on the field or the political and military means of the Federal government. In this regard the work shows a clear bias toward the Southern point of view, as the discussions of the causes of the war and the Emancipation Proclamation demonstrate.

The biography nicely uncovers the complexity of Jackson's personality, showing him to be not merely a religious fanatic but a far-sighted tactician. A risk taker, he asked everything of his junior commanders and established a psychological relationship with them that strained their performance. A strict taskmaster, Jackson often was uncommunicative to the point of jeopardizing his operations, and he laughed off such concerns by declaring, "If I deceive my own friend I can make certain of deceiving the enemy." The commander's steely lack of regard for other people also created problems, such as his spectrum of harsh punishments inflicted on everyone from common soldiers to major generals who might have disagreed with him or committed a slight infraction. Such a relationship did little to help his troops function well, as the present study shows. A number of misspellings appear, as with the name of Philip Kearny. The author incorrectly identifies Dudley Donnelly as a brigadier general.

(Reprinted n.d., 2 vols., 975 pp., Blue and Grey Press, Secaucus; 1898 edition reprinted 1988, with an introduction by Thomas L. Connelly, 737 pp., Da Capo Press, New York)

251

Jackson, Mary Anna. **Life and Letters of General Thomas J. Jackson (Stonewall Jackson)** (479 pp., Harper and Bros., New York, 1892)

This book provides a glimpse into Jackson the man and contains a surprising amount of useful material relating to his career in the field. Compiled by Jackson's widow, the lengthy tome consists of a chronological narrative of Jackson's life that offers much on the officer's antebellum years. The widow's reminiscences, interleaved through the chronology, sometimes add insight and occasionally glut the work with sentimentality. Some value lies in the details of Jackson's home life, his professorial duties, and his relationships with servants. But the overriding value of the work lies in the letters written by Jackson from the battlefield and published here for the first (and in many cases only) time. Additionally, 17 essays composed by Confederate soldiers

who served with Jackson supply enjoyable reading. The work's high points include discussions of the Valley campaign of 1862; the battles of Antietam, Fredericksburg, and Chancellorsville; and the sad tale of Jackson's lingering final days in the Chandler Farm Office at Guinea's Station.

(New edition 1895, titled *Memoirs of Stonewall Jackson by His Widow, Mary Anna Jackson*, with additional material, 647 pp., Prentice Press, Louisville; 1895 edition reprinted 1993, with an introduction by Lowell Reidenbaugh, 647 pp., Morningside, Dayton)

252

Vandiver, Frank E. **Mighty Stonewall** (547 pp., McGraw-Hill Co., New York, 1957)

A full biography, this analysis of Jackson squarely centers on the war years but delivers an impressive section of 132 pages covering the officer's early life, campaigns in Mexico, professorial duties at the Virginia Military Institute, and home life with each of his wives and his family. The material was carefully researched and the narrative skillfully crafted, making this section a solid contribution to the literature. Fortunately, the biography's high caliber continues through the discussion of Jackson's service in the Army of Northern Virginia.

Vandiver describes with great clarity and precision the battles and campaigns fought by Jackson, yet he manages to maintain a high level of excitement throughout the text. He follows Douglas Southall Freeman's lead in ascribing Jackson's poor performance on the Peninsula to exhaustion and interjects a previously overlooked dispatch to explain his subject's halt at Grapevine Bridge. In recounting the successes of the man, particularly the risky maneuvering at Chancellorsville, the author concludes that indeed Jackson was a great battlefield tactician and among the most capable of Civil War general officers. The material drawn together by Vandiver is impressive and solidly documents the career of Lee's most promising officer.

Bushrod Rust Johnson (1817–1880)

253

Cummings, Charles M. **Yankee Quaker, Confederate General: The Curious Career of Bushrod Rust Johnson** (417 pp., Fairleigh Dickinson University Press, Rutherford, 1971)

A native Ohioan, Johnson migrated to Nashville before the war and was commissioned colonel of engineers C.S.A. soon after Sumter. His career as a general officer contained some memorable experiences, such as being captured at Fort Donelson and wounded at Shiloh. Johnson served in both the western (Perryville, Stones River, Chickamauga, and Knoxville) and eastern (Drewry's Bluff, Petersburg, Sayler's Creek, and Appomattox) theaters.

In giving us a clear and well-documented biography of Johnson, Cummings also provides a picture of an average general officer—neither spectacularly successful nor unsuccessful. Throughout his exhaustive narrative of Johnson's military actions, the author only occasionally explains the meaning of his subject's character. This may not be Cummings's fault, however, but probably reflects the somewhat dull and unreflective nature of Johnson himself.

(Reprinted 1993, with an endnote by Noble K. Wyatt that describes the general's 1975 reinterment in Nashville's City Cemetery, 436 pp., General's Books, Columbus)

Albert Sidney Johnston (1803–1862)

254

Johnston, William P. **The Life of Gen. Albert Sidney Johnston, Embracing His Services in the Armies of the United States, the Republic of Texas, and the Confederate States** (755 pp., D. Appleton and Co., New York, 1878)

This sympathetic portrait of the Confederate general was written by his son. The eulogistic treatment highlights Johnston's early life, career in the Black Hawk War, days at Jefferson Barracks, the Texas revolution, the Mexican War years, and the subject's role in the Mormon rebellion. The author analyzes Johnston's role as a militarist reasonably well, although the early, pre-*O.R.* (*q.v.*) nature of the discussion relating to Civil War service sometimes results in muddled descriptions.

The work strives for a balanced portrait of Johnston and attacks Grant and Confederates in dispute with Johnston, chiefly Beauregard. A singular goal of the Civil War coverage is to show Johnston as a capable battlefield commander, something that his death and the strategic loss at Shiloh make difficult. Following discussions of Johnston's activities relating to the West, at Bowling Green, Belmont, and Forts Henry and Donelson, five long chapters treat Shiloh, accompanied by crude maps. The study attempts to show Johnston's overriding brilliance. Partisan in many places, it fails to solidify its case for Johnston's spectacular reputation, but it remains valuable for its discussion of the general's antebellum life and for personal anecdotes. A brief, general index is included.

255

Roland, Charles P. **Albert Sidney Johnston: Soldier of Three Republics** (384 pp., University of Texas Press, Austin, 1964)

Controversial in life and death, Johnston received both praise and harsh criticism for his short Civil War career. This biography is full, scholarly, and systematic in its treatment of Johnston's antebellum army career and life, providing a superb account of his command of the Texas army and his years as a United States officer. It is most useful and appealing, however, in its coverage of Johnston's Civil War record.

Roland methodically assesses Johnston's role by emphasizing his subject's high character and intelligence. The dilemma of this task is to judge Johnston and his wartime tactics and strategy based on the high esteem he garnered from Jefferson Davis and the plain folk of the Confederacy and also based on his achievements. For all his received praise and high character, Johnston was nonetheless a general who lost the first battle he commanded and was mortally wounded in the process. The many what-ifs of Civil War history, often invoked in Johnston's case, are irrelevant to a rational understanding of his actual importance to the Confederate cause.

The author describes Johnston's failed line of defense in Kentucky and the movements south by Grant and Halleck. Johnston's reorganization around Corinth and his strategy of attacking Grant before he could be reinforced seemed sound enough, but the fortunes of war robbed Johnston of a real opportunity to prove himself a great Confederate leader. The author has captured a balanced portrait of Johnston, succeeding where both sides have previously failed.

(Reprinted 1994, 384 pp., University of Texas Press, Austin)

Joseph Eggleston Johnston (1807–1891)

256

Symonds, Craig L. **Joseph E. Johnston: A Civil War Biography** (450 pp., W. W. Norton and Co., New York, 1992)

This work is a full biography with emphasis on the Civil War years. The author describes Johnston's early years, West Point education, frontier actions, Mexican War record, and service in the 1850s. The antebellum coverage amounts to 25 percent of the manuscript, and the postbellum discussions make up 12 percent. Symonds pays considerable attention to details and provides thoughtful analysis of Johnston's controversial role in the Confederate Army.

One can quickly learn the author's view of Johnston's career from his handling of a few critical situations. Does he side with Johnston in the key disputes? Is he a Jefferson Davis backer? Fortunately, Symonds presents a thoughtful, balanced, and intelligent treatment of Johnston's field command and the political squabbling behind it. For those who would fault Johnston for the loss of Vicksburg, Symonds shows how Pemberton, Davis, and even the self-centered eastern field commanders bore the brunt of the blame. He describes the rift between Johnston and Davis over Johnston's rank, a bone of contention at the war's very beginning. The long shadow from this unfortunate circumstance, in which Davis was legally correct, colored the history of the Peninsular campaign and later the Army of Tennessee. A number of spelling errors appear, as with the names of Mary and James Chesnut, Sandie Pendleton, Persifor Smith, and Tishomingo Creek, Mississippi.

257

Johnston, Joseph E. **Narrative of Military Operations, Directed, during the Late War between the States, by Joseph E. Johnston, General, C.S.A.** (602 pp., D. Appleton and Co., New York, 1874)

This is one of the early classic narratives by a senior commanding general of the Confederate armies. Bitterly partisan and constructed to attack the credibility of charges brought against him, Johnston's narrative contains little that illuminates the military history of the battles he commanded. The heat of passion is directed most intensely at Jefferson Davis and serves to address the tension between Johnston and Davis that arose from practically the first day of the war, when Johnston felt snubbed by his low rank as a general officer. Uninventive, legalistic, and bitter, the work is a great disappointment. It does manage to illuminate some aspects of Johnston's personality and unwittingly comments with great alacrity on a number of actions, but it achieves little compared with what it might have done.

Miscommunication and distrust characterized the growing relationship between Johnston and Davis in the spring of 1862. Much of the work rationalizes Johnston's actions and attacks those of the President. Johnston's poor performance and lack of coordination during the Vicksburg campaign further alienated him, and the failure to protect Atlanta was the last straw. Johnston claims to have planned on protecting Atlanta "forever," a remark made with appropriate hindsight.

The estimates of troops involved in various battles are way off, typically underestimating the Confederate numbers and overestimating those of the Union. A lengthy appendix provides official documents relating to Johnston's various commands and his relationship with Davis. A few errors appear, as with the ascription of Turner Ashby as a brigadier general and the misspellings of Abraham Buford, James H.

Wilson, and the Yalobusha River. The author sometimes confuses events, as with several incidents in the Vicksburg campaign.

(New edition 1959, with an introduction by Frank E. Vandiver, 621 pp., Indiana University Press, Bloomington; 1959 edition reprinted 1990, 621 pp., Kraus Reprints, Millwood, N.Y.)

Robert Garlick Hill Kean (1828–1898)

258

Kean, Robert Garlick Hill. **Inside the Confederate Government: The Diary of Robert Garlick Hill Kean** (ed. Edward Younger, 241 pp., Oxford University Press, New York, 1957)

Kean's is an essential Confederate narrative. The nephew of George Wythe Randolph, the author enlisted in the 11th Virginia Infantry at the outbreak of war and the following spring was commissioned captain and assistant adjutant general on his uncle's staff. Shortly thereafter Randolph became secretary of war, and his highly skilled nephew went to Richmond with him as chief of the Bureau of War. Kean outlasted his uncle's tenure and stayed on in the bureau until the end of the war. The diary, in fact, continues through the end of 1865.

Such a position afforded a spectacular view of wartime events in the highest circles of the Confederacy, and Kean's diary, begun in September 1861, records many fascinating events and evaluations of military officers and politicos. The author illuminates the poor relations between Davis and a host of others, including Randolph, Joe Johnston, Beauregard, Alexander Stephens, and the Confederate Congress. He thought Davis "the worst judge of men in the world." In the war office itself, the revolving door of secretaries prompted the author to ascribe the real competence and power to Assistant Secretary John A. Campbell. Of Samuel Cooper, Kean thought little: he never made any decisions of importance and was "out of his office most of the time."

Military commanders often came under Kean's scrutiny. Bragg had "repulsive traits" yet retained his command because of his relationship with Davis. Joe Johnston emerges as "a very little man" who was "morbidly jealous of Lee and all his superiors." Robert E. Lee receives less than perfect marks, too, as Kean believes he ran the Army of Northern Virginia in self-centered fashion and issued communications that were "brief and jejune." A multitude of other relevant and important assessments lie scattered throughout these pages. Kean's diary makes a good companion with that of the war clerk John B. Jones (*q.v.*).

(Reprinted 1993, 241 pp., Louisiana State University Press, Baton Rouge)

Robert Edward Lee (1807–1870)

259

Connelly, Thomas Lawrence. **The Marble Man: Robert E. Lee and His Image in American Society** (249 pp., Alfred A. Knopf, New York, 1977)

Most of this work examines the Lee mythology expressed chiefly by members of the Southern Historical Society in the years immediately following Lee's death and the eulogistic and often unreal image of Lee that has taken hold in the public consciousness. A single chapter examines the general during the war itself. Consequently, this is not a work that everyone will enjoy reading or necessarily agree with in all respects. However, it raises and answers many issues and addresses misinterpretations attached to Lee that cannot be ignored.

Connelly offers a psychoanalytical portrait of Lee—a man who felt himself a failure as an officer, a father, and a husband. While the author's thesis may be stretched on some accounts, it does raise salient points that in many cases fit the Lee whose desperation allowed him to selfishly operate the Army of Northern Virginia with little regard for the Confederacy as a whole and to prosecute the Southern war long after he probably knew the struggle could not be won. Certainly some of Lee's morose scratchings during the war reflected feelings of the moment, yet the significant part of the book is the assessment of Lee's generalship relative to the postwar mythology.

The author's documentation of Lee's overblown competence in his followers' eyes is striking. Connelly clearly explores Lee's precipitous change from Unionist to Rebel. He also astutely shows how Lee lived most of the war without the kind of hero worship attached to many other generals and how Jubal Early, J. William Jones, and others reordered his image through a conspiracy of sorts throughout the 1870s and 1880s. The mythmakers attacked convenient scapegoats, such as Longstreet and Stuart, out of context, ignored facts, invented others, and generally carried on in any way possible to elevate their idol to demigod status. This study breaks down many misconceptions still in force, and for that alone it is important.

(Reprinted 1991, 249 pp., Louisiana State University Press, Baton Rouge)

260

Cooke, John Esten. **A Life of Gen. Robert E. Lee** (577 pp., D. Appleton and Co., New York, 1871)

Cooke's biography became an early classic on the Southern hero, published shortly after Lee's death and in the fury of the formulation of Lee mythology. The work is eulogistic and supportive of the Lee myths, although it upset the Virginia supporters of Lee by including significant praise for Stonewall Jackson, who had arguably been a larger hero during the war. Cooke's association with Lee in the field during the last months of the war gives the work a certain usefulness, and the tone is respectful and affectionate. Strongly pro-Confederate, the biography nonetheless avoids partisan bitterness that characterizes so much of the literature from this period. From a literary viewpoint the book stands up rather well, as do the rest of Cooke's writings.

The author examines Lee's early life then abruptly moves to the war near Richmond, where Lee rose to prominence. Subsequent chapters examine the movements on the Chickahominy, the advance northward, Lee's invasion of Maryland, Chancellorsville and Gettysburg, the final campaign of 1863, the last campaigns and Lee's last days, and tributes to the fallen hero. In most of the analyses by Cooke, Lee can do no wrong, and the author often attacks others while exaggerating Lee's battlefield effectiveness.

261

Dowdey, Clifford. **Lee** (781 pp., Little, Brown and Co., Boston, 1965)

While this book serves as an admirable correction to some of the military discussions in Douglas Southall Freeman's monumental work (*q.v.*), it has serious shortcomings. It is unrealistic in characterizing a number of military and political personages, both North and South (but mostly North), to the credit of Lee and the expense of others. This exaggerated and biased outlook extends at times to the point of historical fraud, which is most obvious during the discussion of Lee's life during Reconstruction. Dowdey also misrepresents the wartime activities of radical Republicans in Washington, particularly their efforts on behalf of emancipation, and he appallingly misrepresents the significance of Abraham Lincoln's activities regarding the efforts toward emancipation.

Such serious flaws do not squander the usefulness of the work, however. Dowdey's command of battlefield topography and the military relevance of various campaigns is generally solid, and his narrative works these themes rather well. This book should be consulted with caution, however, as even the primary themes relating to Lee are contradictory. Variously, Lee appears as the grandfatherly man of perfection as well as the "hot-tempered, ambitious, and aggressive" soldier. The author further characterizes Lee's visionary comprehension and excuses his miscalculations with stories of sickness and confusion. Will the real Lee please stand?

(Reprinted 1991, 781 pp., Stan Clark Military Books, Gettysburg)

262

[Pulitzer Prize, 1935]

Freeman, Douglas Southall. **R. E. Lee: A Biography** (4 vols., 2398 pp., Charles Scribner's Sons, New York, 1934–1935)

This classic work, characterized by brilliant writing, is a necessary part of any Confederate bookshelf. A tribute to Lee, the biography is marked by a high degree of scholarship and is comprehensive in scope. The four volumes cover Lee's entire life and also provide background on the illustrious Lee family. The overwhelming bulk of this study naturally covers Lee's Civil War career, with volume 1 ending in the spring of 1862, volume 2 carrying the story through the death of Stonewall Jackson, volume 3 concluding with the start of 1864, and the last volume describing the final campaigns and Lee's years after the war. Useful appendices attack in detail a variety of complex or controversial subjects, including Lincoln's supposed offer of Union Army command, the composition of Lee's staff, Jackson's sluggishness on the Peninsula, the flank march at Chancellorsville, Jeb Stuart's alleged failure during the Gettysburg campaign, the supply problem during the movement to Appomattox, and Lee's decline and death.

The overwhelming and impressive research exerted in this work is evident on nearly every page. Exactness and extensive precision with documentation and weighing contradictory evidence are its great strength, yet the book offers much of the great story aspects of Sandburg's *Lincoln* (*q.v.*). Freeman's vast knowledge of military matters and of the terrain in Virginia permit a first-class narrative, with abundant detail, of the many battles and campaigns Lee fought. The book additionally delivers a store of personal details on the man as well as his actions, and so the most complete portrait of Lee in existence emerges from the many pages of text. The author is certainly sympathetic to Lee, at times outright glorifying his subject, but this generally does not present major problems. Occasional might-have-beens obscure the relevance of the ongoing story; at other times the author glosses over imperfections in Lee, as with his too generous assessment of the handling of the May campaign of 1864 and the connective downplaying of Grant's success. As a whole, however, this work is stellar.

263

Jones, J. William. **Life and Letters of Robert Edward Lee, Soldier and Man** (486 pp., Neale Publishing Co., New York, 1906)

This is an early and eulogistic portrait of the Confederate commander but one that is historically valuable nonetheless. Jones served in the 13th Virginia Infantry as a soldier and then as regimental chaplain. Through his staff association with A. P. Hill, his residence in Lexington after the war, and his secretaryship of the Southern Historical Society, Jones came to study Lee's character and observe him on many occasions (although mostly after Appomattox). Several introductory sections recount the story of Lee's early life, establish his character, and describe his Mexican War activities and army life during the 1850s. The bulk of the work, however, focuses on the Civil War years and offers reminiscences, reflections, letters, reports, and anecdotal material chosen and organized to elevate the subject's standing as one of the world's great men. The narrative of Civil War operations does not stand out as enviable for its accuracy.

Despite the book's uncritical nature, it does contain information of specific value not easily located elsewhere. This is particularly true of the sections treating Lee's postwar activities in Lexington, when the author could draw on his own experience without relying on secondary material. Many of the letters included do appear elsewhere. The book lacks an index. Another work by the same author, *Personal Reminiscences, Anecdotes, and Letters of Gen. Robert E. Lee* (509 pp., D. Appleton and Co., New York, 1874), is a highly partisan, eulogistic, and poetical hodgepodge of material that exhaustively attempts to document Lee's absolute perfection (reprinted 1989, 509 pp., United States Historical Society Press, Richmond).

(Reprinted 1986, 486 pp., Sprinkle Publications, Harrisonburg, Va.)

264

Lee, Fitzhugh. **General Lee** (433 pp., D. Appleton and Co., New York, 1894)

This story of the legendary commander retains value largely because it was written by Robert E. Lee's nephew. Of course highly worshipful of its subject, the book echoes the themes set forth by George Cary Eggleston—that Virginians had honor, a sense of duty, and high ideals not found elsewhere in the Confederacy. In lamenting the Confederate defeat, the work parallels that of Eggleston and others by suggesting the populace was essentially misguided by politicians. Despite this, the author composed a chapter in which he offers Lee's reasons for supporting the Confederacy. This section transforms into a longwinded Constitutional discussion of the Southern states' right to secede, with little supporting evidence of Lee to justify the material. In fact, the material quoted from Lee's letter apparently contradicts what the author is attempting to establish.

Nonetheless, the portion that does reflect on Lee is well done and interesting, particularly those events of which the author had personal knowledge. The work essentially offers a military history of the Civil War in the East, and the author at times fails to hide echoes of partisanship by complimenting Federal officers with liberal views toward the Confederacy. Estimates of troops engaged and casualties should not be relied on. A number of errors occur, as with naming Thomas R. R. Cobb a brigadier general and misspelling the names of Henry W. Halleck, Philip Kearny, Persifor F. Smith, George J. Stannard, David A. Weisiger, and Henry Wirz.

(Reprinted 1989, 433 pp., Broadfoot, Wilmington; 1894 edition reprinted 1994, with an introduction by Gary W. Gallagher, 433 pp., Da Capo Press, New York)

265

Lee, Robert E. **Lee's Dispatches: Unpublished Letters of General Robert E. Lee, C.S.A., to Jefferson Davis and the War Department of the Confederate States of America, 1862–1865, from the Private Collection of Wymberley Jones de Renne, of Wormsloe, Georgia** (ed. Douglas Southall Freeman, 400 pp., G. P. Putnam's Sons, New York, 1915)

This is a cornerstone collection that stands as a necessary companion to *The Wartime Papers of R. E. Lee* (q.v.). The work presents 204 dispatches written from Lee to President Davis from the period of Lee's inheritance of the command of the Army of Northern Virginia on the Peninsula to the issuance of an evacuation warning on 1 April 1865. The material is significantly valuable and together with the previously mentioned work forms the closest set in print covering Lee's wartime correspondence.

This book sheds valuable light on several campaigns, particularly the abundance of material on the May campaign of 1864. Clearly the commander knew that his army was falling into a less-enviable position with each of Grant's flanking maneuvers, yet there was little the great commander could do. It was a painful time for Lee.

The editing is capable, often outstanding, but sometimes slips into judgmental blunders, always favoring the central subject. Despite this, Lee's own words show him as deeply human and highly admirable despite his imperfections. A generalized foldout map of Lee's Virginia campaigns appears at the end of the book. An occasional slip appears, as with

"Richard Henry Anderson" rather than Richard Heron Anderson. and the usual wartime misspellings of John C. Breckinridge, Franz Sigel, and others.

(Reprinted 1957, ed. Grady McWhiney, with 10 new dispatches, 416 pp., G. P. Putnam's Sons, New York; 1957 edition reprinted 1994, 416 pp., Louisiana State University Press, Baton Rouge)

266

Lee, Robert E. **The Wartime Papers of R. E. Lee** (ed. Clifford Dowdey and Louis H. Manarin, 994 pp., Little, Brown and Co., Boston, 1961)

This necessary work deserves high praise. A mammoth project of the Virginia Civil War Centennial Commission, the volume offers 1006 wartime papers of the Confederate commander, most containing notable and highly interesting military material. Altogether, about one-sixth of Lee's letters and battlefield reports appear in this volume.

Separated by chronology and illustrated with pertinent maps, the papers cover a wide range of important subjects and campaigns. The Lee of legend emerges from this work, living up to the superhuman qualities of understanding, caution, forgiveness, and fatherly doting. So too the Lee who occasionally issued vague orders and restrained supplies and manpower for his own army at the expense of others makes an appearance. In short, the real Lee is here, unclouded by the embellishment of biographers and presented clearly for those to interpret independently his actions and recorded thoughts.

Unfortunately, the work is poorly annotated, which to a degree limits its usefulness as a significant research device. Despite this, all students of the war should relish this invaluable companion.

(Reprinted 1987, 994 pp., Da Capo Press, New York)

267

Lee, Robert E., Jr. **Recollections and Letters of General Robert E. Lee** (461 pp., Doubleday, Page and Co., New York, 1904)

Although much of the material in this work has been superseded by a superior treatment in Dowdey and Manarin's *Wartime Papers* (q.v.), this volume by Lee's son retains its charm and usefulness because of the spectrum of anecdotal material sprinkled throughout. Young Lee recalls his father's antebellum days in a brief introduction and then proceeds to outline the chief events of his father's Civil War career. The son's narrative, scattered between the documents, contains occasional comments of interest. Great value exists in the story of Lee's family life and his experiences after the war, which consumes more than half the book.

(Reprinted 1926, with 10 pages of new material added by William Taylor Thom, 471 pp., Garden City Publishing Co., Garden City, N.Y.; 1926 edition reprinted 1960, titled *My Father, General Lee*, ed. Philip Van Doren Stern, 473 pp., Doubleday and Co., Garden City, N.Y.)

268

Long, A. L., and Marcus J. Wright. **Memoirs of Robert E. Lee: His Military and Personal History, Embracing a Large Amount of Information Hitherto Unpublished** (707 pp., J. M. Stoddart and Co., New York, 1886)

Written by the blinded staff officer Armistead Lindsay Long, painstakingly scratched onto a slate and buttressed with substantial official documents, the book captures a fair amount of minutiae relating to Lee's early life as well as recollections of the war years. The effort is most valuable in those instances—few and far between—that relate information from Long's personal knowledge. That the work is ostensibly a substitute for Lee's autobiography, a claim Long makes, is ridiculous.

The outlook toward Lee is deeply anchored in the Virginia-centric view of Lee as infallible hero. Unfortunately, much of the material relating to Lee's early life and military career is not newly presented in this work but is echoed from a variety of earlier sources, most prominently J. William Jones's *Life and Letters of Robert E. Lee, Soldier and Man* (*q.v.*). Long incorrectly claims that Lee prepared no formal report on the operations of 1864. A spurious letter appears, supposedly written by Lee to his son Custis (pp. 464–465). The work contains the misstatement that Gordon's men refused to go into battle unless Lee went to the rear on 10 May 1864 rather than 12 May 1864. The recollections of Lee fortified by Long's personal experience, the story of Lee's early life, and his Mexican War career are treated well.

(Reprinted 1983, 707 pp., Blue and Grey Press, Secaucus)

269

Maurice, Frederick. **Robert E. Lee: The Soldier** (313 pp., Houghton Mifflin Co., New York, 1925)

Although written with a British perspective and containing some seemingly contradictory conclusions, this book retains its value. The stimulating nature of the essay comes from Maurice's military expertise and his keen interest in the American war. He believes that Lee's achievements in the campaign of 1862 were "supreme in conception and have not been surpassed, as examples of strategy, by any other achievement of their kind by any other commander in history." Clearly the analyst is impressed by Lee's generalship, further calling his handling of the 1864 campaign against Grant "fifty years ahead of its time."

Maurice's analysis of the major battles commanded by Lee contains numerous smaller insights of value. The author also criticizes Lee, noting that some of his greatest victories resulted despite bungled, vague orders that sometimes got him into trouble—implying Lee may have been lucky on some occasions. The work, while steeped in the aura of Lee's greatness, remains engaging because of its foreign viewpoint.

270

Meredith, Roy. **The Face of Robert E. Lee in Life and Legend** (143 pp., Charles Scribner's Sons, New York, 1947)

This photographic study of the Confederate commander, with annotations of the images, is the best available. Covering all phases of Lee's life, the work draws on 47 photographs and photographic variants, 32 portraits and paintings, 30 engravings, and 15 photographs of sculpture to provide an impressive collection of Lee imagery. A smaller collection of Lee images exists than of others of the era (most notably Lincoln), yet Meredith achieves a competent contribution to understanding Lee and the Lee mythology.

The book divides almost equally into selections from life and those from after Lee's death, when he passed into legend. The reproduction is satisfactory, and the book will stand as a valuable study until another, more modern photobiography of Lee eclipses it.

271

Nolan, Alan T. **Lee Considered: General Robert E. Lee and Civil War History** (231 pp., University of North Carolina Press, Chapel Hill, 1991)

The author looks beyond the historical mythology surrounding Lee and, with his lawyer's calm, calculated argument, unveils Lee the man. The process, begun with Thomas Lawrence Connelly's *The Marble Man* (*q.v.*), has upset a large number of Civil War historians and buffs who prefer Robert E. Lee the way he used to be. However, one might argue that truth stands above all men, and in this work, the truth about Robert Edward Lee is made starkly plain, at least with regard to several aspects of his character and performance as a general officer.

Nolan investigates Lee's views toward slavery, his relationship with secession, his performance on the battlefield, his eventual defeat, and his postwar decline. The sifting of data necessarily constitutes a major evaluation of the vast Lee literature, and so much of the work evaluates specific points made by previous authors who have rightly or (often) wrongly assembled the current vision of Lee that Civil War students work with. Nolan knocks down many myths, some of them first attacked by Connelly. For instance, he lays to rest the misconception that either Lincoln or Winfield Scott offered Lee "command of the Union Army." The author shows, as alert students have known for ages, that Scott's discussion pertained to the command of what became Irvin McDowell's army that marched to Bull Run. The author soundly and straightforwardly re-creates the myth building by Jubal Early and others of the early Southern Historical Society to cement their former commander's name in the annals of history. He demonstrates how early Northern writers allowed this skewing of history because it fit their own agenda of an antebellum past with grand social connections. Northern racism, too, supported this vision.

The author demythifies Lee in other ways. He shows that Lee indeed embraced standard Southern values including the sanctity of slavery, in practice if not fully in principle. He approved of capturing free blacks and returning them to slavery and of executing blacks who wore blue in battle. Not a profound political strategist, Lee was characterized and restrained by paranoid feelings toward a host of subjects, from non-whites to the eroding Southern political base. Additionally, the author shows that Lee had a poor grand strategy in mind on the battlefield, fought illogically in some cases (as at Gettysburg), and in extremely self-centered fashion reserved men and supplies for his own army without thinking of the Confederate cause as a whole. He thought in terms of offense yet almost always fought defensively.

Lee often referred to the enemy as "those people," believing the Yankees were barbaric and inferior. Despite grandfatherly feelings toward his own troops, however, the most damning evidence against Lee comes from a matter of timing. If Lee knew the war could not be won in early 1864, as the evidence suggests, why did he continue on for another year, needlessly sacrificing thousands of lives?

This is one of the most important books in recent times on any Southern personality. It resets the playing field to an investigation of Lee the man and prevents students of the war from living in a fantasy world when it comes to understanding one of the war's key figures. Although it has harsh critics, this work cannot be ignored.

272

Snow, William P. **Lee and His Generals** (2d ed., 473 pp., C. B. Richardson, New York, 1867)

This book is useful as an expression of the growing sentiment for Lee immediately after the war. It essentially constitutes a defense of Southern generalship during the war, examining not only Lee but a wide spectrum of Confederate field commanders: Stonewall Jackson, Pierre G. T. Beauregard, Joe Johnston, Samuel Cooper, James Longstreet, Braxton Bragg, Richard S. Ewell, Jeb Stuart, A. P. Hill, John Bell Hood, Albert Sidney Johnston, Leonidas Polk, Sterling Price, Edmund Kirby Smith, John Hunt Morgan, William J. Hardee, and Wade Hampton III.

Biographical sketches of the generals in question are presented along with extensive analysis of the campaigns operated by each officer. The volume is rather stuffy, justifies the Southern loss using the standard "overwhelming numbers" defense, and rationalizes many what-if situations. Snow employs some official documents, dispatches, and much hearsay evidence. The author concludes that every Southern general, none more powerfully than Lee, was a great hero, and he backs up this conclusion by including poetry and some fraudulent information, as with Lee's alleged letter to his son written from Arlington in 1852. The inferior first edition is titled *Southern Generals: Who They Are, and What They Have Done* (473 pp., C. B. Richardson, New York, 1865).

(Reprinted 1982, 473 pp., Fairfax Press, New York)

273

Thomas, Emory M. **Robert E. Lee: A Biography** (472 pp., W. W. Norton and Co., New York, 1995)

The author tackles a major job of delivering a fresh, scholarly biography of the great Confederate, and he succeeds admirably. Researching in a spate of institutions and employing many manuscript sources in addition to those used previously, Thomas offers a psychological portrait that suggests that Lee existed in a kind of personal balance that kept him from loosening up and enjoying his life. This self-tension of Lee's clearly appears to have manifested itself in certain situations, and the author suggests and cleverly documents in some cases that this self-limiting psychology was always present in Lee's mind.

The author has delivered a full biography. The Civil War years represent 45 percent of the manuscript. Thomas skillfully describes Lee's early life and his troubles over his father's failures. The sections on Lee's military education, his duty in the Mexican War and on the frontier, and his days at West Point are handled very capably. The author clearly admires Lee, occasionally falling for the mythological revisionism of the Southern Historical Society, but he makes an effort to present a fair and balanced portrait unaffected by the writings that occurred long after the events he describes. The Civil War chapters, of course, hold paramount interest; they are well done, as detailed as could be expected, and present controversial issues with a balanced eye. A few minor spelling errors appear, as with the names of Mathew Brady, Roswell S. Ripley, and Walter Herron Taylor, and the author employs the peculiar usage "West Point Military Academy." However, the study is superbly executed overall and will make a longstanding significant contribution to the Civil War bookshelf.

Stephen Dill Lee (1833–1908)

274

Hattaway, Herman. **General Stephen D. Lee** (283 pp., University Press of Mississippi, Jackson, 1976)

Stephen D. Lee played a significant role throughout the war, primarily in the western theater, and has received little attention in the literature aside from his activities as a politician and commander of the United Confederate Veterans after the war. Because Lee's wartime exploits deserve great attention, it is fortunate that Hattaway, known for his great care, winning style, and thorough understanding, should have tackled Lee as a subject.

Lee began his Confederate service as an aide to Pierre G. T. Beauregard and rose to the grade of brigadier general by late 1862. He commanded Pemberton's artillery at Vicksburg, was captured, and then promoted to major general after his exchange. He was switched from artillery to cavalry and then took over Hood's old corps of the Army of Tennessee in 1864, in time to see it demolished the following winter. He surrendered with Johnston at Durham Station.

Hattaway's study is a success. The narrative reflects an understanding of the strategy and tactics at play throughout the campaigns Lee participated in, and it offers insights into the western war and into the destruction of the Army of Tennessee during the war's final months. Good maps and a number of photos accompany the text. One curious error: an engraving of Fitzhugh Lee presented as an image of the subject.

St. John Richardson Liddell (1815–1870)

275

Liddell, St. John R. **Liddell's Record: St. John Richardson Liddell, Brigadier General, C.S.A., Staff Officer and Brigade Commander, Army of Tennessee** (ed. Nathaniel C. Hughes, 216 pp., Morningside, Dayton, 1985)

Not a particularly likeable man, St. John R. Liddell nevertheless served as staff officer and then brigadier general in two theaters of war, the West and the Trans-Mississippi West. A lost manuscript penned by Liddell before he was murdered constitutes this work. Although it is not particularly extensive in its treatment of Liddell's record, this slim volume offers what amounts to the subject's autobiographical narrative of the war.

A West Point dropout, the author entered the war by virtue of volunteering to serve on Brig. Gen. William J. Hardee's staff in the autumn of 1861. Although sometimes colored by bitterness and often relating skewed appraisals of fellow commanders, Liddell's reminiscences of his experience at Corinth, Perryville, Stones River, and Chickamauga, are fascinating. Sufficient detail accompanies most of the battle accounts, and the narrative picks up some interest by virtue of a few similar accounts after Liddell's transfer west of the Mississippi. At that time and through 1864 and the spring of 1865, he participated in the Red River campaign and defended Mobile, where he was captured at Fort Blakely. The unreconstructed officer surged with wartime alacrity as he penned these thoughts shortly after the war.

James Longstreet (1821–1904)

276

Eckenrode, H. J., and Bryan Conrad. **James Longstreet: Lee's War Horse** (399 pp., University of North Carolina Press, Chapel Hill, 1936)

A brief chapter outlines Longstreet's prewar life before presenting more detailed discussions of the Peninsular campaign, Second Bull Run, Antietam, Fredericksburg, Gettysburg, Chickamauga, Knoxville, the Wilderness campaign, and the Appomattox campaign. The discussion of Longstreet's battlefield performance is generally sound and often puts forth valuable reflection on a battery of Longstreet's more controversial actions, even if such discussion is not always adequately supported.

The larger problem with this work is the overdrawn portrait of Longstreet's personality traits during the war, which the authors contend colored his abilities. Longstreet may have been highly ambitious and stubborn, but those qualities resulted most often in success for Lee's highly valued corps commander. Indeed, Longstreet's preferred strategy at Gettysburg would probably have resulted in a better outcome for the Confederacy, and his many singular triumphs—as with the breakthrough attack at Chickamauga—mark some of the tactical successes of the Army of Northern Virginia.

Eckenrode and Conrad unfairly criticize their subject on a number of crucial points, making him a scapegoat in the tradition of the postwar Virginians. Such assertions are only weakly supported by use of the *O.R.* (*q.v.*) and Longstreet's memoirs (*q.v.*), which damage their case. The work contains some good descriptions of Longstreet's command activities but does not deserve to be followed when estimating the man.

(Reprinted 1986, with a foreword by Gary W. Gallagher, 399 pp., University of North Carolina Press, Chapel Hill)

277

Longstreet, James. **From Manassas to Appomattox: Memoirs of the Civil War in America** (690 pp., J. B. Lippincott and Co., Philadelphia, 1896)

Although one of the most important Confederate reminiscences, Longstreet's memoirs are often defensive in tone and are written in the uninventive, dry style characteristic of a 19th-century soldier. His explanation of Gettysburg includes charges made by various officers and refutations of those charges, countercharges by other generals and refutations of the countercharges. This military bickering rolls on for more than 40 pages and often presents a too-angry and relatively ineffective defense of Longstreet's actions, particularly relating to the second day at Gettysburg.

Despite this, Longstreet's tome is a milestone of great importance in Confederate literature. It tells the story of the war in first person from one of the great generals of American history, allows him to make his case, and at least on some accounts quiets the armchair strategists who have faulted Longstreet too severely. In the main, Longstreet is correct with most of his assertions, and the well-documented inflation of the Lee side of the Gettysburg controversy can be traced through the pages of the *Southern Historical Society Papers* and elsewhere. Longstreet here provides ample documentation of his close relationship with Lee, although his language is sometimes blunt and egotistical. The references to the *O.R.* (*q.v.*) as the "rebellion record" may be confusing.

(Reprinted 1960, ed. James I. Robertson, Jr., 692 pp., Indiana University Press, Bloomington; 1960 edition reprinted 1990, 692 pp., Kraus Reprints, Millwood, N.Y.; 1896 edition reprinted 1992, with an introduction by Jeffry D. Wert, 690 pp., Da Capo Press, New York)

278

Piston, William Garrett. **Lee's Tarnished Lieutenant: James Longstreet and His Place in Southern History** (252 pp., University of Georgia Press, Athens, 1987)

In a lengthy essay encompassing Longstreet's military involvement in the war, Piston analyzes the general's battlefield performance relative to many of his detractors, beginning with the Southern Historical Society of the 1870s. The first half of the work straightforwardly assesses Longstreet's Civil War history; the second half scrutinizes the postwar evaluation of Longstreet by others.

The effort is not simply to reconstruct Longstreet's image. The author finds fault with his subject in several key areas, such as the general's performance at Seven Pines and the bitter tone of Longstreet's memoirs (*q.v.*). Piston clearly feels the importance of Longstreet, however, declaring him the "best corps-level commander of the war." That may be an overstatement, but James Longstreet certainly was among the most skilled Confederate strategists and was slandered repeatedly by apologists for Confederate defeat. The author's generally fair and well-backed argument clarifies much that others have distorted about this key Confederate officer over the years. A number of small errors crop up with names, as with Irvin McDowell, misidentifications (of Alexander Pendleton), and dates (the capture of Winchester during the Gettysburg campaign). However, these do not detract from the work's mission of showing that the Southern historical treatment of James Longstreet has been, for the most part, distorted.

279

Wert, Jeffry D. **General James Longstreet, the Confederacy's Most Controversial Soldier: A Biography** (508 pp., Simon and Schuster, New York, 1993)

This study offers a modern and correct view of this much-maligned commander. Unlike the traditional school that supports the Lee-Jackson mythology and bashes Longstreet, this biography provides a full look at Longstreet's life with the predictable (and proper) heavy emphasis on the war years. It does not view Longstreet altogether sympathetically, instead casting a realistic light on the situations Longstreet found himself in on and off the battlefield. The commander is criticized for his lethargic role at Seven Pines, Lookout Mountain, and Knoxville.

Wert's detailed descriptions of Longstreet at Second Bull Run, Antietam, Fredericksburg, Gettysburg (where his controversial reluctance to attack haunted him), Chickamauga (where his frontal assault swept the field), and the Wilderness (where he was severely wounded) show Longstreet's impressive and highly competent record. It is no wonder that Lee called Longstreet "my war horse." In his interpretation of Longstreet's performance, the author sides with other revisionist works, and he documents the politically motivated postwar attacks on Longstreet that Southerners perpetuated to build up Lee and Jackson. The author goes even further, stating that "Longstreet, not Jackson, was the finest corps commander in the Army of Northern Virginia." After exploring this chronicle of Longstreet's battlefield decisions, his rapid action, and grasp of terrain and tactics, readers may find it difficult to disagree.

William Mahone (1826–1895)

280

Blake, Nelson M. **William Mahone of Virginia: Soldier and Political Insurgent** (323 pp., Garrett and Massie, Richmond, 1935)

Blake provides not just the military and political details of Mahone's life but also a biographical summary of his subject's activities as a railroad executive. The author's careful research using the Mahone papers and a store of previously published sources makes this work reliable and illuminating. The study is sympathetic toward Mahone but not unduly so, and the facts leap from the page in a well-organized, workmanlike fashion. Readers can glean much about Mahone's antebellum engineering and railroading activities, his participation in the capture of the Norfolk Navy Yard, his role in constructing the fortifications at Drewry's Bluff, and his long career with the Army of Northern Virginia, his most famous moment coming at the battle of the Crater.

After the war the focus returns to railroading, and this work documents it well. The construction of the would-be Norfolk and Western system and Mahone's rise as party boss constitute interesting sections. The work examines Mahone's political conversion in detail, casting light on his Republican friendships, the reactions of old Confederates, and his influence as a Southern liberal.

Bartlett Yancey Malone (1838–1890)

281

Malone, Bartlett Yancey. **Whipt 'Em Everytime: The Diary of Bartlett Yancey Malone, Co. H, 6th N.C. Regiment** (ed. William Whatley Pierson, Jr., 131 pp., McCowat-Mercer Press, Jackson, Tenn., 1960)

Thin and written to the horror of grammarians, this book nevertheless contains entertaining insights into the adventures of a young private who rose to the grade of sergeant in the Army of Northern Virginia. The diary was published originally in volume 16 of the James Sprunt Studies in History and Political Science (North Carolina Historical Society, Chapel Hill, 1919). Made widely available in the 1960 edition, this work surveys Malone's service in the 6th North Carolina from January 1862 to his capture in Virginia in November 1863. Paroled in February 1865, he went home and married, tired of prison life at Point Lookout.

The narrative serves primarily to demonstrate the semiliteracy of many soldiers on both sides and is highly instructive if painful to read at length. "At nite we had to bild ous sum brest works," wrote Malone on 15 December 1862. "Our cavalry had a littel fite in the eavning," reads another account. The spelling is atrocious but typical of many soldiers, and the entries are short and generally strung together with dozens of "and then we . . ." constructions. Still, if one can contend with the adventure of wading through this work, the simple story of a simple soldier emerges, punctuated with numerous recordings of the weather on dozens of days. Malone honestly sets forth his experiences without declaring why he was fighting and without expressing any real hatred of the Yankees. For this, the work deserves a quick read.

(Reprinted 1991, 131 pp., Broadfoot, Wilmington)

Arthur Middleton Manigault (1824–1886)

282

Manigault, Arthur M. **A Carolinian Goes to War: The Civil War Narrative of Arthur Middleton Manigault** (ed. R. Lockwood Tower, 344 pp., University of South Carolina Press, Columbia, 1983)

Written one year after the close of the war, the narrative encompasses Manigault's service from staff duty around Charleston to his severe wounding at Franklin, which removed him from field command. Skillfully edited, these memoirs cast an illuminating light on the operations of the

Army of Tennessee, in which Manigault served as regimental and brigade commander following the battle of Shiloh. The author's observations of and conclusions about a variety of operations and commanders provide valuable reading and should be considered important and insightful if not always unique.

The author experienced the chaos of the army following Shiloh and found it difficult to believe in his superiors. Although he initially served under P. G. T. Beauregard in Charleston Harbor, he found the successor to Albert Sidney Johnston unable to manage troops and organize movements effectively. He believed Braxton Bragg to be as difficult as most of Bragg's other subordinates did, although he thought Bragg superior to Joe Johnston in terms of thinking in the field. Manigault's characterization of Johnston as weak in the face of Sherman's Atlanta campaign may be overly harsh, but his assessment of John Hood's incompetence rings true, even if the statement that Hood's assignment before Atlanta may have "caused" the Confederacy's defeat is overdrawn. Within the clear characterizations are many superb accounts of battle as a brigade commander saw them, which permit Manigault to conclude that the failure of subordinate commanders led to the Army of Tennessee's doom.

Edward Manigault (1817–1874)

283

Manigault, Edward. **Siege Train: The Journal of a Confederate Artilleryman in the Defense of Charleston** (ed. Warren Ripley, 364 pp., University of South Carolina Press, Columbia, 1986)

Manigault's manuscript is a sleeper among Confederate diaries. In fact it is one of the best recently published diaries of the Civil War. Skillfully edited, well produced, and enthralling in content, it offers a spellbinding view of activities centered on Charleston Harbor. The author, brother of Brig. Gen. Arthur Middleton Manigault, began his 13-month-long diary on the day of the Federal attack on Folly Island, 10 July 1863.

"At 5h. 5m. A.M. the Yankee batteries on Little Folly Island opened upon southern end of Morris Island," Manigault recorded on 10 July. "The fire was very heavy (said to be from 44 pieces in Battery) and in a few hours the enemy landed and took possession of the southern half of the island." Entries range from the routine to the spectacular, from ordinary military matters to riveting descriptions of battle. A great lesson in Confederate artillery awaits the reader. For

example, in the final entry Manigault describes in detail the various batteries under his command.

Many drawings from Manigault's diary accompany the text. Among the maps are two large foldouts showing Charleston Harbor and its batteries and fortifications. Appendices cover the battle of Grimball's Causeway on 10 February 1865 and provide a useful index of units discussed in the book.

Charles Marshall (1830–1902)

284

Marshall, Charles. **An Aide-de-Camp of Lee, Being the Papers of Colonel Charles Marshall, Sometime Aide-de-Camp, Military Secretary, and Assistant Adjutant General on the Staff of Robert E. Lee, 1862–1865** (ed. Frederick Maurice, 287 pp., Little, Brown and Co., Boston, 1927)

Marshall's close association with Lee from March 1862 to war's end provided him with access to Lee's plans, his military policies, and his thoughts on the performance of the Army of Northern Virginia. The author relates how Lee advocated his defensive war by protecting Richmond and threatening Washington to the point where "the defense of Richmond controlled all other considerations." Lee feared a Federal advance up the James River most of all, which could bring supplies and men to the limits of the city in quick time. The author further relates that Lee's invasion of Maryland came about because Lee could not stay put: he either had to go forward and procure supplies or retreat and endanger Richmond by a Federal movement.

The author's comments on other characters will enthrall or inflame readers. He lays blame on Jeb Stuart and Lee's corps commanders for the failure at Gettysburg. He comments on Stonewall Jackson's poor performance on the Peninsula. He details Lee's conception of the flanking maneuver at Chancellorsville. The author witnessed the front parlor scene at Appomattox, and so his recollection of the end is particularly valuable. Only the editor adds occasional blame on Lee, faulting him most for his famously vague orders.

Dabney Herndon Maury (1822–1900)

285

Maury, Dabney H. **Recollections of a Virginian in the Mexican, Indian, and Civil Wars** (279 pp., Charles Scribner's Sons, New York, 1894)

The author presents a chatty remembrance of the Old South and the wide-ranging Civil War service of an easterner who served primarily in the West. The work begins with charming reminiscences of Maury's boyhood in Fredericksburg, the city's traditions of Lee and Washington, and the author's many relations of note, including Matthew Fontaine Maury and Capt. John Minor Maury. The entertaining narrative continues through the West Point years, with mostly lighthearted anecdotes of Grant, McClellan, Stonewall Jackson, and others. The Mexican War coverage and that of antebellum service on the plains contain many more reminiscences about officers who would be famous, including Winfield Scott Hancock, William B. Franklin, and George G. Meade.

The Civil War coverage sketches Maury's career and includes material on Joe Johnston at First Bull Run, the author's Trans-Mississippi service, the retreat from Corinth, Van Dorn's Mississippi campaign, and Maury's move to Mobile. Some of the recollections do not square with other, more reliable sources. The many portraits of Civil War officers before and during the war are quite valuable, and material of significance appears late in the work regarding Nathan Bedford Forrest and Dick Taylor. The book, accomplished without bitterness, contains some re-created conversations and many recollections of the author's long career. A conversation with Forrest recalls the Fort Pillow massacre, in which Maury claims Forrest told him the shooting began because the black troops did not surrender after the Confederate flag was raised and so Forrest's men fired. The old cavalryman, according to Maury, regretted the scene.

Carlton McCarthy (1847–1936)

286

McCarthy, Carlton. **Detailed Minutiae of Soldier Life in the Army of Northern Virginia, 1861–1865** (224 pp., C. McCarthy and Co., Richmond, 1882)

First serialized in the *Southern Historical Society Papers* (*q.v.*) in various issues from 1876 to 1878, this work consists of scenes drawn from Pvt. McCarthy's experiences in the Richmond Howitzers, 2d Corps, Army of Northern Virginia. Too young to enlist in the field at the outset of war, the author served in the home guard in Richmond until 1864, when he was mustered into the artillery regiment. Drawing on the experiences of his brother, who was killed at Cold Harbor, and many friends and acquaintances, he composed this work nearly two decades after the conflict. Its homespun tone and generic descriptions of how Confederate soldiers walked, ate, fought, spoke, and what they wore and carried offer much to re-create the genuine feel of Confederate soldier life.

Written in the florid language of the late 19th century and characterized by unflattering attitudes, the work denegrates slaves in the few places it mentions them and rationalizes poor behavior on the part of Southern soldiers. Nevertheless, McCarthy offers an authentic look at Confederate soldier life. The excellent illustrations that accompany the text were drawn by William L. Sheppard, a well-known soldier-artist who belonged to the same unit. The book lacks an index.

(Reprinted 1982, 224 pp., Time-Life Books, Alexandria, Va.; reprinted 1993, with an introduction by Brian Steel Wills, 224 pp., University of Nebraska Press, Lincoln)

Ben McCulloch (1811–1862)

287

Cutrer, Thomas W. **Ben McCulloch and the Frontier Military Tradition** (402 pp., University of North Carolina Press, Chapel Hill, 1993)

Cutrer gives us a clear view of this western commander who met his end at Pea Ridge. The work casts McCulloch as an "old school" soldier who learned how to fight against a typical set of enemies on the western frontier. This background gave him positive and negative qualities. During his Mexican War and Civil War duty, McCulloch knew how to strategize in unconventional ways, an occasional asset. However, McCulloch's lack of military education set him back as the Civil War approached and the benefits of a West Point schooling became more significant.

The frontier military tradition ultimately failed McCulloch, the author shows. Although the subject studied arduously and sought promotion, he was passed over repeatedly by junior officers with formal training. The author explores McCulloch's career and his psychology and how they relate to his performance in the wartime West, including the battles of Wilson's Creek and Pea Ridge, where he died in the fight around Elkhorn Tavern.

Randolph Harrison McKim (1842–1920)

288

McKim, Randolph H. **A Soldier's Recollections: Leaves from the Diary of a Young Confederate, with an Oration on the Motives and Aims of the Soldiers of the South** (362 pp., Longmans, Green and Co., New York, 1910)

This is a Confederate classic. The youthful soldier, a student of religion at the University of Virginia, enlisted in the 2d Virginia Infantry, followed the regiment through several fights, and rose to first lieutenant before gaining a staff assignment as aide de camp to Brig. Gen. George H. Steuart. Rising to the occasion at critical moments during the Valley campaign of 1862, the fight at Stephenson's Depot, and the Culp's Hill action at Gettysburg, McKim served meritoriously throughout the first two years of war. He then resigned to obtain a chaplaincy from the Episcopal church and joined the 2d Virginia Cavalry as its chaplain in August 1864.

Although it was written more than four decades after the war, the author's narrative is based on a wartime diary and exercises a careful, scholarly approach in recalling the war's events. Thus the work sheds light on the battles McKim fought in and the units he was attached to, in addition to presenting recollections of Steuart and other important officers. The sections on Jeb Stuart's absence in the Gettysburg campaign (a response to John Mosby's criticism of Robert E. Lee), the Culp's Hill fight, and the battles of the Valley campaign are particularly useful. The oration is not especially valuable, but it plays a small part in an otherwise largely worthwhile book.

(Reprinted 1984, 362 pp., Time-Life Books, Alexandria, Va.)

Edward Alexander Moore (1842–1916)

289

Moore, Edward A. **The Story of a Cannoneer under Stonewall Jackson, in Which Is Told the Part Taken by the Rockbridge Artillery in the Army of Northern Virginia** (315 pp., Neale Publishing Co., New York, 1907)

Moore offers an above-average narrative of artillery service in the eastern theater. In early 1862 the author interrupted his studies at Washington College in Lexington, Virginia, to enlist in the famous Rockbridge Artillery. The book follows Moore's service with the unit from the war's second spring through Appomattox. Particularly valuable sections describe the author's service at Antietam, where

he was wounded, and in the Shenandoah Valley campaign of 1864.

The narrative centers on military aspects and includes vignettes of the lives of common soldiers and officers in Moore's unit and within the Army of Northern Virginia. Recollections of William N. Pendleton, William T. Poague, Stonewall Jackson, and others provide entertaining reading. Assembled 40 years after the war, however, the story evokes a shadow of dubiousness with occasional manufactured "conversations" and spurious remembrances. Still, it makes enjoyable reading. Introductions by Robert E. Lee, Jr., and Henry St. George Tucker are included. The work lacks an index but appends a roster of the Rockbridge Artillery.

(Reprinted 1983, Time-Life Books, Alexandria, Va.)

John Hunt Morgan (1825–1864)

290

Ramage, James A. **Rebel Raider: The Life of General John Hunt Morgan** (306 pp., University Press of Kentucky, Lexington, 1986)

The author has thoroughly and thoughtfully researched the somewhat difficult record and personality of Morgan and delivered a superbly professional account of his exploits, free of exaggeration and mistreatment. Such an accomplishment is difficult with a controversial subject such as Morgan, and it is to Ramage's credit that he achieved such a solid book—one that is also filled with the adventure of Morgan's raids and other activities.

The narrative places into context the guerrillalike activities of Morgan and his command by assessing more modern warfare with various interjections. The author evaluates Morgan's achievements as a guerrilla and finds his importance was more symbolic than strategic, an assessment that might be extended to lesser Confederate guerrillas such as John Mosby. Extensive research allows the author to recount many transgressions committed by Morgan and his command, such as shooting Federal pickets, robbing civilians, and disguising themselves as Federals. Such unheard-of tactics seemed horrifying at the time and diminish the luster of Morgan's legend.

Ramage believes that much of the cavalryman's behavior can be explained by his periodic bouts of depression, his gambler's personality, and his overriding justification that Southern victory should be achieved by any means. The Union occupation of Kentucky, the author convincingly contends, broke Morgan's spirit and drove him to desperate measures—at least until his marriage in 1862. The security provided by this arrangement, the author finds, may have contributed to weaker performance on the field and even possibly cost the rebel raider his life.

John Singleton Mosby (1833–1916)

291

Jones, Virgil Carrington. **Ranger Mosby** (345 pp., University of North Carolina Press, Chapel Hill, 1944)

Researched admirably and presented with a writer's flair, this full-length biography of the Confederate ranger remains respectable though it takes liberties for the sake of the story. Relatively scant coverage examines Mosby's early life and his declining postwar years; the emphasis is on Mosby's four years as a military adventurer, and the narrative of war events rests primarily on the *O.R.* (*q.v.*). Jones makes good use of Mosby's own *Memoirs* (*q.v.*), an occasionally suspicious source; he also consulted the horseman's wartime letters and presents excerpts. The result is a serviceable biography that explains all the major aspects of this fabled Confederate partisan.

The story of Mosby's rather pedestrian service throughout the first two years of war transforms into an enthralling tale as Mosby discovers partisan warfare. The coverage of Chantilly, the Gettysburg campaign, and Mosby's high-spirited antics in the Shenandoah Valley contribute much of great value, although the author overdramatizes Mosby's significance in the Valley campaign of 1864. He also uses a disturbingly large number of "conversations" to dramatize the story, something the author in many cases could not possibly know as reliable. One typographical error was noticed, the misspelling of Alfred Pleasonton's name. The work stands up rather well, though, and shall continue as a source on Mosby until a thorough, scholarly work appears.

(Reprinted 1989, 347 pp., EPM Publications, McLean, Va.)

292

Mosby, John S. **The Memoirs of Colonel John S. Mosby** (ed. Charles Wells Russell, 414 pp., Little, Brown and Co., Boston, 1917)

This reminiscence consists of a series of recollections compiled by Mosby during his last years and edited by his brother-in-law. The recollections are based on writings and lectures delivered by Mosby and gleaned from newspaper accounts of his wartime exploits. Most of them are interesting and cover Mosby's career as a private in William E. Jones's company of cavalry, which became a part of Jeb

Stuart's 1st Virginia Cavalry. The most legendary aspects of Mosby's career are those of his days as an independent scout in 1862 and starting in 1863 as a captain of partisan rangers. Mosby's most publicized raid was the affair on 9 March 1863 when he startled and captured Federal Brig. Gen. Edwin H. Stoughton at Fairfax, Virginia. Other incidents shine through this work, however, as with the discussion of Stuart's movements during the Gettysburg campaign. Mosby vigorously defends his old chief against allegations of failing his superiors.

Mosby produces some amazing errors in his work, as with the statement that at the battle of First Bull Run, Irvin McDowell had 153,682 men. A number of names are misspelled, including those of Arthur J. L. Fremantle and Alfred Pleasonton. Much the same ground is covered in a less valuable work published in 1887, John S. Mosby's *Mosby's War Reminiscences, and Stuart's Cavalry Campaigns* (264 pp., Dodd, Mead and Co., New York; reprinted 1958, 264 pp., Pageant Book Co., New York).

(1917 edition reprinted 1959, with a foreword by Virgil Carrington Jones, 414 pp., Indiana University Press, Bloomington; 1959 edition reprinted 1990, 414 pp., Kraus Reprints, Millwood, N.Y.; 1917 edition reprinted 1990, 414 pp., Olde Soldier Books, Gaithersburg)

293

Scott, John. **Partisan Life with Col. John S. Mosby** (492 pp., Harper and Bros., New York, 1867)

This is an early, highly partisan account of life with the cavalry raider who was transformed into legend by this and other works. Endorsed by Mosby himself, this authorized biography sets forth the life story of the Confederate partisan ranger through the Civil War, almost certainly embellishing many stories and at times utilizing a strongly biased tone and interpretation. Nevertheless, it presents the record of one who helped to invent tactics of harrassment during the war. The aim with the early material is clearly to mythologize Mosby, whose misfortune in shooting another man and serving a six-month jail sentence is transformed into high adventure. The early Civil War service is also made romantic in an adventurous sense, with Mosby constantly trying to unleash his peculiar brand of warfare but essentially confined to playing scout for William E. Jones and Jeb Stuart.

By the second year of the war, the narrative suggests, Mosby secured information as a prisoner that enabled the Confederates to shape the campaign of Second Bull Run by moving away from McClellan and concentrating on Pope days earlier than they might have otherwise. The following year, Mosby received the opportunity to begin his partisan guerrilla activities by banding together men who would fight, steal, and harrass the Federals at short notice and quickly disappear into the country homes. The techniques certainly proved bothersome to the Union Army in Virginia, but the significance of Mosby's exploits is here presented, as it is elsewhere, with exaggeration.

George Dallas Mosgrove (1844–1907)

294

Mosgrove, George Dallas. **Kentucky Cavaliers in Dixie; or, The Reminiscences of a Confederate Cavalryman** (271 pp., Courier-Journal Job Printing Co., Louisville, 1895)

This highly entertaining memoir, though rambling and variously presenting an embellished story or a set of official documents, overall has a charm that will delight readers of the western theater. The approach is pro-Confederate, exaggerates the glories of Kentuckians as opposed to Southern soldiers from other states, and frequently manifests the author's wistfulness for the Old South. Despite these characteristics, the book offers much valuable coverage on operations in Kentucky and Tennessee.

Mosgrove presents material chiefly centered on the 4th Kentucky Cavalry, C.S.A., a unit raised near Owenton in late 1862 that surrendered at Mt. Sterling on 30 April 1865. The narrative also reflects on the other units variously brigaded with the 4th Kentucky. Actions include those at Blue Springs, Rogersville, Laurel Gap, and Saltville. The author reflects much on the regiment's officers, chiefly Henry L. Giltner and Moses T. Pryor, and offers much of value on John Hunt Morgan. There are a few misspellings, as with the names of George Crook and Lloyd Tilghman.

(Reprinted 1957, with an introduction by Bell Irvin Wiley and an index, 281 pp., McCowat-Mercer Press, Jackson, Tenn.; 1957 edition reprinted 1991, 281 pp., Broadfoot, Wilmington)

George Michael Neese (1839–1921)

295

Neese, George M. **Three Years in the Confederate Horse Artillery** (362 pp., Neale Publishing Co., New York, 1911)

Neese's work is based on a wartime diary but was much embellished before publication. A competent gunner in Chew's Virginia Battery, which was eventually placed in the Army of Northern Virginia, the author participated in many eastern actions and recorded both important and trivial events for posterity. Neese covers much of the ordinary life of a Confederate artillerist, the Shenandoah Valley campaign of 1862, Crampton's Gap, Brandy Station, the cavalry actions about Gettysburg, the Wilderness campaign, and prison life at Point Lookout from October 1864 to the close of the war.

Marked by a florid style and literary sidetrips that wander, the work nonetheless contains excellent descriptions of Brandy Station, Port Republic, Poolesville, and Jeb Stuart's great cavalry review in June 1863. The author was chief of artillery of the cavalry corps for the Army of Northern Virginia by the time of his capture, and he offers many recollections of the details of artillery.

(Reprinted 1988, with an introduction by Lee A. Wallace, 396 pp., Morningside, Dayton)

James Cooper Nisbet (1839–1917)

296

Nisbet, James Cooper. **Four Years on the Firing Line** (445 pp., Imperial Press, Chattanooga, 1914)

Nisbet provides valuable and engaging recollections of a Georgia soldier's experience in the Army of Northern Virginia. A company commander at age 22, Nisbet participated with the 21st Georgia Infantry as a part of the Doles-Cook brigade throughout much of the early war in the East. The battles he describes include Winchester, the Peninsular campaign, Second Bull Run, Antietam, and Fredericksburg. As part of Stonewall Jackson's Corps, Nisbet's regiment saw heavy action at most of these engagements, and the author's recollections include the rock fight at the Deep Cut during Second Bull Run and temporary regimental command during the Peninsular campaign and at Antietam.

In 1863 Nisbet was commissioned colonel of the 66th Georgia and led it through the Chattanooga and Atlanta campaigns. He describes his capture at Atlanta in riveting detail, and his subsequent stay at Johnson's Island provides a second level of depth in this worthwhile account. The memoir includes a description of the author's trip home in September 1865. Although Nisbet apparently did not keep a diary, his account bears the mark of trustworthy, serious writing and contains many useful observations on events and commanders that brushed alongside this Georgia soldier's Civil War career.

(Reprinted 1963, ed. Bell I. Wiley, 267 pp., McCowat-Mercer Press, Jackson, Tenn.; 1963 edition reprinted 1991, 267 pp., Broadfoot, Wilmington)

Robert Patrick (1835–1866)

297

Patrick, Robert. **Reluctant Rebel: The Secret Diary of Robert Patrick, 1861–1865** (ed. F. Jay Taylor, 271 pp., Louisiana State University Press, Baton Rouge, 1959)

This work contains an unusually good soldier's account of the war in the West. Literate and with a refreshingly good sense of humor, Patrick begins his story with the experience of traveling from Port Hudson to New Orleans in the opening days of the war and continues with discussions of several major actions.

The author was a member of the Hunter Rifles of the 4th Louisiana Infantry, a unit mustered in at Camp Moore on 25 May 1861 whose colonels included Henry Watkins Allen. Patrick's ability to describe the conditions of common soldiery and the larger issues of organization, logistics, tactics, and supply make this a superior account. His early descriptions of battle at Shiloh are well composed. The pace slackens during the regiment's duty on picket during the siege of Vicksburg. At Baton Rouge and during the encampment and siege of Port Hudson the author again produces a satisfying picture of the Civil War in the Southwest. Many worthwhile entries appear during the regiment's move east to join the Army of Tennessee during the Atlanta campaign. Discussions of Johnston's retreat to the city and the subsequent actions at Peachtree Creek, Ezra Church, and Jonesboro are nicely described.

Elisha Franklin Paxton (1828–1863)

298

Paxton, Elisha F. **Memoir and Memorials, Elisha Franklin Paxton, Brigadier-General, C.S.A.: Composed of His Letters from Camp and Field While an Officer in the Confederate Army** (ed. John G. Paxton, 114 pp., published by the editor, Independence, Mo., 1905)

This difficult-to-procure book has a peculiar publication history in that the remaining stock of this privately printed work was purchased in 1907 by the Neale Publishing Company, Washington and New York, which sold it beginning in 1907. A new edition in 1978 with an introduction by Harold B. Simpson, titled *The Civil War Letters of General Frank "Bull" Paxton, C.S.A., a Lieutenant of Lee and Jackson* (102 pp., Hill Junior College Press, Hillsboro), is the one most easily obtainable today.

The letters included cover Paxton's service as a lieutenant in the 27th Virginia Infantry in 1861 and then his exploits as assistant adjutant general on Stonewall Jackson's staff, beginning with the 1862 campaigns. The letters change markedly when in late 1862 Paxton took command of the Stonewall brigade as a brigadier general. His writing reflects his activities at Fredericksburg and up to the time when he was killed at Chancellorsville. Material added by Paxton's son explains the general's activities and death at his final battle. The letters span the period April 1861–April 1863 and were penned to Paxton's wife, so they contain personal as well as military information. The 1978 edition contains much information added by Simpson, including an appendix of official records and a bibliography.

William Ransom Johnson Pegram (1841–1865)

299

Carmichael, Peter S. **Lee's Young Artillerist: William R. J. Pegram** (209 pp., University Press of Virginia, Charlottesville, 1995)

Willie Pegram was adored as one of the great young soldiers of the Army of Northern Virginia. Had he not been mortally wounded during the final days of the eastern war at Five Forks, he might have been remembered as a greater hero than he is. This book, a biography of Pegram focused cleanly on the Civil War years, admirably captures Pegram's record. After a very brief treatment of the antebellum years, Carmichael examines in detail Pegram's role in the Seven Days fighting, at Cedar Mountain, Harpers Ferry, Fredericksburg, Chancellorsville, Gettysburg, Spotsylvania, Petersburg, and Five Forks. The descriptions of artillery service at various battles are detailed and valuable, providing ample reading for students of the Army of Northern Virginia and its artillery strategy and tactics.

The work is made more insightful by the focus on Pegram's meaning within his generation. The text explores how Southern society by the 1850s established firmly the notion that support of slavery was a Christian duty for white Southerners. The author describes how Pegram's fervent belief in a God in support of Southern ideals was shattered with the realization of Confederate defeat. He suggests that, rather than showing signs of a crushed Southern morale, Pegram and many others in his generation staunchly supported the Confederate military and its philosophical aims until the religious outlook collapsed at war's end.

John Clifford Pemberton (1814–1881)

300

Ballard, Michael B. **Pemberton: A Biography** (250 pp., University Press of Mississippi, Jackson, 1991)

In his full biography with extensive and extremely helpful coverage of Pemberton's prewar exploits, Ballard fortunately describes this Northern-born Confederate lieutenant general with an objective eye. The only previous full-length work is a sympathetic apologia composed by Pemberton's grandson; Ballard's study renders the former obsolete and offers some curious and well-supported reflections on the path of Pemberton's career.

The author's splendid discussion of Pemberton's early life, relationship with his Southern-born wife, and Mexican War service establish a credible and detailed background for his subject's Civil War experience. Placed in a difficult position and not adequately supported by those at Richmond, Pemberton essentially had no hope of prevailing against Sherman and Grant in the Vicksburg campaign. The author explores Pemberton's tight friendship with Jefferson Davis, but he does not fully explain why the Confederate government poorly sustained the defense of Vicksburg. Ballard finds that Pemberton made substantial strategic and tactical errors throughout the campaign, at times perhaps judging his subject too harshly. The Civil War career of Pemberton was eclipsed after the fall of Vicksburg, and his postwar exploits were unspectacular. Still, the author accomplishes a superb feat in describing them with style and detail, and the work will no doubt stand as a solid piece of Confederate history.

William Dorsey Pender (1834–1863)

301

Pender, William Dorsey. **The General to His Lady: The Civil War Letters of William Dorsey Pender to Fanny Pender** (ed. William W. Hassler, 271 pp., University of North Carolina Press, Chapel Hill, 1965)

Moderately successful in his West Point class of 1854, the North Carolinian was commissioned colonel of the 3d North Carolina at the outbreak of war and rose to major general before his death. Fearless and outstanding at Seven Pines, Cedar Mountain, Antietam, Fredericksburg, and Chancellorsville, Pender was struck by a shell fragment on the second day at Gettysburg. He considered the leg wound unimportant long enough for infection to set in, and he did not survive the subsequent amputation.

Pender's letters offer a close view into the mind of such a young major general. They contain a great deal of personal gossip and musings but also much of military interest. His observations of Lee, Jackson, A. P. Hill, and D. H. Hill are valuable and add significantly to the body of works on the Army of Northern Virginia. Indeed, Douglas Southall Freeman quoted from the letters liberally in *Lee's Lieutenants* (*q.v.*). The editor of this volume might have annotated the letters in a significant and helpful way; this notwithstanding, it is still an excellent book.

(Reprinted 1987, 271 pp., R. Van Sickle, Gaithersburg)

Alexander Swift Pendleton (1840–1864)

302

Bean, W. G. **Stonewall's Man: Sandie Pendleton** (252 pp., University of North Carolina Press, Chapel Hill, 1959)

What might have happened to Sandie Pendleton had he survived the Valley? Bean nearly answers that question and speaks to the societal downfall of the members of Pendleton's generation who did survive battle. As a mere 21-year-old at war's beginning and the son of Lee's artillery chief, Sandie Pendleton had an elevated view of his generation and its war aims. Moreover, young Pendleton found himself an assistant adjutant general on Stonewall Jackson's staff.

Bean offers a capable portrait of Pendleton and throws light on his involvement in the Valley campaign and, following Stonewall's death, his assignment as Ewell's chief of staff. He does not limit the narrative to the rigors of war, however; much material traces Pendleton's romance with Kate Corbin. The author's treatment of Pendleton's death could be applied to the whole of the young Confederacy to summarize its overwhelming grief.

(Reprinted 1987, 252 pp., Broadfoot, Wilmington)

William Nelson Pendleton (1809–1883)

303

Lee, Susan Pendleton. **Memoirs of William Nelson Pendleton, D.D., Rector of Latimer Parish, Lexington, Virginia: Brigadier-General C.S.A.: Chief of Artillery, Army of Northern Virginia** (490 pp., J. B. Lippincott and Co., Philadelphia, 1893)

This volume reflects on the wartime period and antebellum life in Virginia. Composed with great reverance for the subject by his daughter (and the wife of Confederate Brig.

Gen. Edwin G. Lee and sister of Alexander S. Pendleton), the *Memoirs* draw together notes, diary entries, and letters of Pendleton along with the author's connective material to form what is part biography and part autobiography. The work is of course sympathetic in tone and praiseful toward Pendleton, but it also delivers a mountain of unusual and interesting material on the operations of the Army of Northern Virginia. Pendleton served as nominal chief of artillery for the army. He therefore discusses much of interest relating to artillery matters as well as the usual reminiscences of battle and of commanders.

The biography succeeds largely because of the valuable pool of material from which it was drawn. Pendleton was present at nearly all the major battles of the Army of Northern Virginia from First Bull Run to Appomattox. He therefore knew the army and how it worked exceptionally well, and his background as a religious figure helped to temper his military career. The many recollections about Robert E. Lee and Stonewall Jackson are particularly valuable, as Pendleton was close to both men. Along the way, Pendleton criticizes the handling of many battles and adds controversy to many individual incidents.

(Reprinted 1991, 537 pp., Sprinkle Publications, Harrisonburg, Va.)

James Johnston Pettigrew (1828–1863)

304

Wilson, Clyde N. **Carolina Cavalier: The Life and Mind of James Johnston Pettigrew** (303 pp., University of Georgia Press, Athens, 1990)

This ambitious and highly successful biography illuminates one of the more interesting characters from South Carolina to fight in Lee's army. Nephew of the famous Unionist James L. Petigru, Pettigrew nonetheless took up arms for his adopted state and rose to the grade of brigadier general by the spring of 1862, serving under Joe Johnston in the Peninsular campaign until wounded and captured at Seven Pines. Two months later he returned to the field and played a significant part in Gettysburg, where his division formed part of Pickett's Charge. He survived but was mortally wounded during Lee's retreat southward.

Pettigrew's Civil War service forms the backdrop for Wilson's broad description of the antebellum and wartime South. The author makes a well-supported case that Pettigrew embodied the ideals of the Old South cavalier and that he viewed himself with a great deal of detachment and self-irony because of it. Expertly skilled in a variety of subjects,

Pettigrew was most certainly a valuable asset to the Confederate cause, yet Wilson shows he ultimately never ascended to significance as a general officer. The narrative occasionally exaggerates the importance of Pettigrew as representative of the Old South culture and the overall significance of that culture itself, but in the main this work is impressive.

Gideon Johnson Pillow (1806–1878)

305

Hughes, Nathaniel Cheairs, Jr., and Roy P. Stonesifer. **The Life and Wars of Gideon J. Pillow** (455 pp., University of North Carolina Press, Chapel Hill, 1993)

This narrative examines the record of an amazingly incompetent Tennessee general officer in two wars. Finely written and researched, the book neither aspires to elevate Pillow to anything more than his record suggests nor to ascribe his failures to some psychological portrait of malfunction. Rather, it straightforwardly describes the failed career of a man who through his association with James Knox Polk obtained a commission as major general during the Mexican War despite his incompetence at Cerro Gordo and Contreras. Hughes and Stonesifer devote a fair amount of space and energy to providing a significant analysis of Pillow's life before the Civil War, portions of the work that contain much of reader interest.

During the capably handled Civil War chapters, the familiar portrait of Pillow emerges, though in finer detail than previously offered. The subject's relationship with the Confederate War Department receives excellent treatment, as do his early activities in the West. Sufficient testimony from other wartime figures provide a damning assessment of Pillow's character and his total lack of military skill, which was amply demonstrated by his abandonment of the command at Fort Donelson. The authors' insights into this poorly executed campaign and Pillow's postwar decline add much of value to this volume. Useful maps and a small selection of photographs accompany the text.

William Thomas Poague (1835–1914)

306

Poague, William Thomas. **Gunner with Stonewall: Reminiscences of William Thomas Poague: A Memoir, Written for His Children in 1903** (ed. Monroe F. Cockrell, 181 pp., McCowat-Mercer Press, Jackson, Tenn., 1957)

A lawyer who was elected lieutenant of the 1st Rockbridge Artillery in 1861, Poague rose to the grade of lieutenant colonel before war's end. In addition to shedding light on artillery operations in the Army of Northern Virginia, Poague's work includes superb descriptions of Jackson's Valley campaign, Second Bull Run, Fredericksburg, Gettysburg, the May campaign, and Appomattox.

The book was written from memory nearly 40 years after the war, yet the narrative is lucid, articulate, and unembellished. The work includes remembrances of Lee, Jackson, Johnston, Polk, and Pendleton and may be particularly valuable for the last, considering the small store of material relating to Lee's chief of artillery. Poague recounts being slightly scolded by Lee at Gettysburg over the vague nature of his report on troop movements. He remembers a mystifying order of Jackson's at Fredericksburg, and he recalls the admirable and caustic character of D. H. Hill. Many such nuggets characterize the work and make it an enjoyable contribution to the literature of the Army of Northern Virginia.

(Reprinted 1989, 181 pp., Broadfoot, Wilmington)

Leonidas Polk (1806–1864)

307

Parks, Joseph H. **General Leonidas Polk, C.S.A.: The Fighting Bishop** (408 pp., Louisiana State University Press, Baton Rouge, 1962)

Much of the allure of this work comes from the remarkable personality of its subject, which Parks describes in admirable detail. This full biography presents an adequate and sometimes revealing treatment of Polk's antebellum career as a planter and preacher, documenting his rise toward appointment in 1841 as the first Episcopal bishop in Louisiana. Nearly 40 percent of the work analyzes Polk's prewar years, the remaining narrative examining Polk's three Civil War years.

Although readers glean a significant and detailed portrait of Polk's life, the author has not provided a proper interpretation of Polk's military significance. Overly sympathetic toward his subject and mired in using the bishop's own papers—be they important or trivial—Parks exaggerates when assessing Polk's relative importance. He proclaims his subject a "competent" corps commander, a judgment one could exhaustively unravel, and suggests Polk made up for his lack of understanding of tactics and strategy by his good spirit. The author would have readers believe Polk was an effective general officer who might have achieved even greater accomplishments had he not been struck by the shell on Pine Mountain.

What of Polk's rise to military command? The author fails to make the case that Polk won his generalship by virtue of his friendship with Davis, a significant factor at the very least. Such lack of analysis hurts the work for those familiar with Polk's record and dismisses the truly intriguing possibility of a modern biography that objectively places Polk in the military context of the Confederate Army.

(Reprinted 1992, 408 pp., Louisiana State University Press, Baton Rouge)

308

Polk, William M. **Leonidas Polk: Bishop and General** (2 vols., 791 pp., Longmans, Green and Co., New York, 1893)

This lengthy tribute from son to father was prepared with the substantial assistance of William S. Perry and E. J. Biddle. The biography remains valuable by virtue of employing family correspondence and official documents, many of which are provided in full. The story treats Polk's military and ecclesiastical career, although its great drama lies within the three years of Polk's Civil War activities. The author shows relative care, literary skill, and a balanced viewpoint with regard to controversial subjects.

The first volume covers Polk's life to the Civil War. The second volume covers the war years, Polk's relationship with Jefferson Davis, his commissioning as major general, and his rapid rise to lieutenant general. The story of Polk's troubles with Braxton Bragg receives careful analysis and is handled in a mature and dignified way. Polk's battlefield performance receives both sympathetic and realistic treatment, and of course the bishop's death at Pine Mountain while covering Johnston's retreat receives significant and tender coverage. A few errors of fact appear, as with the incorrect dates for the publication of *Memoirs of General Greene* and the misstatement that George E. Badger was a North Carolina Supreme Court justice. The index is nicely prepared and serves the reader well.

Sterling Price (1809–1867)

309

Castel, Albert. **General Sterling Price and the Civil War in the West** (300 pp., Louisiana State University Press, Baton Rouge, 1968)

This study exclusively treats Price's controversial Civil War career and produces a detailed, scholarly, and fair assessment. The work begins by setting the stage for Price's role with a background on Missouri at the outbreak of war and follows Price's involvement in the campaigns that followed. Castel delivers excellent summaries of Wilson's Creek, Lexington, Pea Ridge, Iuka, Corinth, Helena, Little Rock, Jenkins's Ferry, Pilot Knob, and Westport. Throughout the narrative of Price's involvement—his few successes and many failures—the author shares his knowledge and analysis openly and in so doing allows the reader to reap a clear view of the Confederacy's poor standing in the Trans-Mississippi West.

Few mistakes can be found in Castel's depiction of Price's military career. He does erroneously refer to Maj. Thomas Price as the general's son, and he sheds little light on the relationship between Price and Jefferson Davis and other members of the Confederate high command. Yet this work intends only to describe Price's role in the western battles, which it accomplishes in superb fashion.

(Reprinted 1993, 300 pp., Louisiana State University Press, Baton Rouge)

310

Shalhope, Robert E. **Sterling Price: Portrait of a Southerner** (311 pp., University of Missouri Press, Columbia, 1971)

Unlike Castel's work (*q.v.*), Shalhope's book is a full-fledged biography of Price that devotes over half its space to his antebellum life. The author capably shows that Virginia-born Price, who moved to Missouri at a relatively early age, evolved into a farmer, marketer, and politician. To his political fame he added service on the frontier in New Mexico Territory, and these exploits led to a term as governor of Missouri beginning in 1853. Price's tenure during the critical period of violence in the area was marked by periodic support of proslavery interests.

Shalhope contends that Price worked to preserve neutrality as the secession crisis erupted despite his pro-Southern activities with the Missouri State Guard. The author believes that his subject dealt fairly with William S. Harney in the wake of the Camp Jackson takeover by Union troops and that he was clearly a moderate when compared with ultrase-

cessionist legislator Claiborne F. Jackson. Price's Civil War career receives less critical and detailed study than in Castel's work but each retains a useful place in the literature.

William Clarke Quantrill (1837–1865)

311

Castel, Albert. **William Clarke Quantrill: His Life and Times** (250 pp., Frederick Fell and Co., New York, 1962)

Castel brings an objective treatment to a subject often described in subjective terms. Moreover, this account incorporates the previously untapped Smith Manuscript, a recollection of Quantrill and his exploits written by Frank Smith, a fellow bushwhacker who penned his memories many years after the fact. Although the Smith papers may be slightly embellished, in many cases they fill voids left unexplored by previous biographers.

Quantrill's exploits not only provide an interesting study of one band of angry young men but typify the violence of many others in the Kansas-Missouri theater. The author's narrative makes clear that prior to the Lawrence Massacre and the resulting Order No. 11, selective murder in Missouri and raids into Kansas characterized Quantrill's activities. Order No. 11 effectively stopped the Kansas raiding. Castel quite successfully portrays the life of a notorious guerrilla and the flavor of the area in which his lawlessness reigned.

Stephen Dodson Ramseur (1837–1864)

312

Gallagher, Gary W. **Stephen Dodson Ramseur: Lee's Gallant General** (232 pp., University of North Carolina Press, Chapel Hill, 1985)

Gallagher chronicles the short life of one of the Confederacy's young general officers. A North Carolina native who was commissioned colonel of the 49th North Carolina Infantry in 1861, Ramseur acquired a reputation for daring during the Seven Days battles when he was wounded severely. Fighting again at Chancellorsville, where he was again wounded, Ramseur adhered to the Southern cause and gained recognition from a host of senior commanders, including Stonewall Jackson, A. P. Hill, and even Robert E. Lee. In 1864 Ramseur was assigned to Jubal Early's army in the Shenandoah and became the youngest major general in the Confederate service. Mortally wounded at Cedar Creek, Ramseur died the following day.

What are we to make of the life of a Stephen Dodson Ramseur? The author makes effective use of Ramseur's family papers to find an answer. A brief prewar introduction leads to well-spun military accounts peppered with excerpts from Ramseur's correspondence with relatives and with Ellen Richmond, his wife during his final year. These allowed Gallagher to portray Ramseur in a thoroughly documented way, reporting on his subject's life with clarity and alacrity. Ramseur was certainly a capable soldier, brave and noble throughout his service. He fervently believed in secession ideals and the South's right to kill Yankees. Yet in the end, Ramseur's nature keeps the meaning of his life somewhat elusive.

William Johnson Seymour (1832–1886)

313

Seymour, William J. **The Civil War Memoirs of Captain William J. Seymour: Reminiscences of a Louisiana Tiger** (ed. Terry L. Jones, 162 pp., Louisiana State University Press, Baton Rouge, 1991)

This book provides a brief but interesting memoir of an officer from the Trans-Mississippi West who joined the Army of Northern Virginia and tasted combat in the East. A journalist and editor of the New Orleans *Commercial Bulletin*, Seymour served as an aide to Brig. Gen. Johnson K. Duncan and stayed at Fort Jackson until the fall of the Crescent City. After his imprisonment at the fort and subsequent pardon, Seymour secured a staff position with Brig. Gen. Harry T. Hays. In the Louisiana brigade of the Army of Northern Virginia, the author experienced the battles of Chancellorsville, Gettysburg, and the Wilderness and the Shenandoah Valley campaign of 1864. The narrative ends following the battle of Cedar Creek.

Tapping his journalistic background, Seymour views clearly the actions taking place around him and weaves an engaging story. He is often as critical of Confederate actions as those of the Union commanders and offers no illusions about the glory of war. The editing of this volume is adequate but sometimes draws on secondary sources of dubious value, and the introduction and epilogue stop short of interpreting much of what Seymour has to say. Still, the volume offers a useful glance into the war experiences of a Louisiana officer who made an unusual journey through the 1860s.

Joseph Orville Shelby (1830–1897)

314

O'Flaherty, Daniel. **General Jo Shelby: Undefeated Rebel** (437 pp., University of North Carolina Press, Chapel Hill, 1954)

O'Flaherty covers Shelby's early days in Kentucky, his business activities, partisan actions in the Kansas-Missouri conflicts of the 1850s, and of course his famous Civil War cavalry career. Additionally, the author focuses on Shelby's postwar business ventures. The work employs a smattering of sources, curiously ignoring many of value while using some nearly worthless material. The result is a fair record of Shelby's life but one littered with a disturbing number of errors.

Many flaws concerning geography can be found, as with the misplacement of Dover, the erroneous inclusion of Howard and Lafayette Counties in the famous Order No. 11, and the characterization of Missouri's western border counties as being composed of secessionists. The description of the battle of Carthage is bungled in several respects, most glaringly by claiming that the Missouri forces were amateurs, Sigel's army consisted of well-trained professionals, and the armies were of roughly equal size. The work is well written, and where it succeeds in interpretation it casts some light on the character of Jo Shelby.

Henry Hopkins Sibley (1816–1886)

315

Thompson, Jerry D. **Henry Hopkins Sibley: Confederate General of the West** (399 pp., Northwestern State University Press, Natchitoches, 1987)

Thompson contributes an interesting evaulation of a Confederate commander who sank into total failure early in the war. The author sets up Sibley's strange Civil War career by briefly recounting his early life and Mexican War service. By all accounts Sibley was poised for a significant command in the Confederate Army, enjoying the confidence of Jefferson Davis and marred only by a love of alcohol. Unfortunately, the author has been shackled in his portrait because Sibley's personal papers were lost or destroyed. Nonetheless, the present work sketches Sibley's entrance into the Confederate service as a colonel and his peculiar plan to push Federal forces from the Rio Grande Valley, opening a pathway to California, where the Confederate government naively hoped for cooperation and supply.

Thompson's description of Sibley's New Mexico campaign is well documented and written with sufficient detail to merit interest, but he overestimates the importance of the campaign. The plan turned diastrous for the Confederates following the battles of Valverde and Glorieta Pass when the Confederates found they could not subsist in the barren desert. Sibley lost a third of his army and never again saw a significant command. The following year he narrowly escaped conviction in a court-martial brought on by Dick Taylor. His career subsequently evaporated.

The work does contain annoying grammatical, typographical, and syntactical errors. A psychological portrait of Sibley does not emerge clearly. However, as the single worthwhile biography of this tragic figure, Thompson's work shows that a pathetic historical character can provide a curious story.

Edmund Kirby Smith (1824–1893)

316

Parks, Joseph H. **General Edmund Kirby Smith, C.S.A.** (537 pp., Louisiana State University Press, Baton Rouge, 1954)

The author draws on a wide variety of primary sources to judiciously deliver a portrait of this controversial commander. Supported by access to the family's papers, this study stands as an impressive achievement in Southern biography. The work devotes about 23 percent of its space to Kirby Smith's antebellum career, focusing on the family's background, and provides a rigidly chronological story of the subject's Mexican War service, his professorship at West Point, and the frontier military duty that preceded the secession crisis.

The story, of course, gains momentum with the coming of the war. The analysis shines when focused on Kirby Smith's activities as a commander in the Trans-Mississippi West. Parks documents how Kirby Smith dealt with all manner of problems, from angry subordinates to inadequate supplies and funds to omnipresent rumors of impending attack from Union forces. Although often gentle with his subject, the author faults Kirby Smith for failures during the Red River campaign and shows how his chief critic, Dick Taylor, benefited from the sloppy generalship of Nathaniel Banks. The short section on Kirby Smith's postwar life is well worth reading.

(Reprinted 1992, 537 pp., Louisiana State University Press, Baton Rouge)

Gilbert Moxley Sorrel (1838–1901)

317

Sorrel, G. Moxley. **Recollections of a Confederate Staff Officer** (315 pp., Neale Publishing Co., New York, 1905)

This is an exceptionally fine Confederate memoir of a youthful Georgian who enlisted in a cavalry unit before the war erupted, so anxious was he to serve his home state. Following First Bull Run, Sorrel gained a position as aide-de-camp on Longstreet's staff, in which capacity Sorrel, who eventually was commissioned brigadier general and chief of staff of the 1st Corps, Army of Northern Virginia, witnessed much of the war in the East as well as Longstreet's involvement in the battles at Chickamauga, Chattanooga, and in eastern Tennessee.

Sorrel's competent narrative ability and closeness to Longstreet and other important commanders make this memoir an exciting source from start to finish. The author's reflections on particular generals such as Lee, D. H. Hill, Early, Pendleton, Stuart, Jackson, Pickett, Bragg, and Toombs are priceless and for the the most part objective and careful evaluations. Sorrel's writing is detached enough from partisan feelings to include balanced appraisals of Federal commanders, and his intimate knowledge of strategy and tactics shows in balanced analyses of various battles. Here is an author who knew or saw many of the war's chief participants and wrote about them honestly. His close relationships did not bend his judgment, either. Writing on Gettysburg, Sorrel thinks that Longstreet's plan may have been better than Lee's but "it was too late to alter [Lee's plans] with the troops ready to open fire on each other." Moreover, Longstreet "lacked the fire and point of his usual bearing on the battlefield." Sorrel's candor does not permit him to avoid criticizing his old chief.

Although probably written at the turn of the century, Sorrel's recollections stand with the best of those written by an influential officer on either side. This book is necessary for any Civil War library.

(Reprinted 1978, with an introduction by Edwin C. Bearss, 333 pp., Morningside, Dayton; new edition 1958, ed. Bell I. Wiley, 322 pp., McCowat-Mercer Press, Jackson, Tenn.; 1958 edition reprinted 1991, 322 pp., Broadfoot, Wilmington)

Robert Stiles (1836–1905)

318

Stiles, Robert. **Four Years under Marse Robert** (368 pp., Neale Publishing Co., New York, 1903)

Stiles's artillery and staff service provide an engaging perspective from which to recall his widespread activity in the eastern theater. The author composed his work long after the war and some recollections are undoubtedly spurious, yet the work retains charm and value in showing the highlights of this young officer's career and the psychology of why many young Southerners went to war in the first place.

The descriptions of life within the Richmond Howitzers form splendid reading. Of high value is the material relating to a large number of battles and evaluations of many commanders, notably Richard S. Ewell. The book contains significant and seemingly avoidable errors, as with the estimates of troops involved at various actions. Strangely, the author shows some affection for George McClellan throughout parts of the work. Stiles echoes the sentiment of George Cary Eggleston that Virginians stood apart morally and intellectually from the rest of the Confederacy. The work exaggerates the worshipful qualities of Robert E. Lee. Not always reliable, Stiles's book is nonetheless always entertaining in the most valuable sense.

(Reprinted 1988, with an introduction by Robert K. Krick, 378 pp., Morningside, Dayton)

James Ewell Brown Stuart (1833–1864)

319

McClellan, H. B. **The Life and Campaigns of Major-General J. E. B. Stuart, Commander of the Cavalry of the Army of Northern Virginia** (468 pp., Houghton Mifflin Co., Boston, and J. W. Randolph and English, Richmond, 1885)

The author has written a book that is partly biography of Stuart and partly autobiography of Henry Brainerd McClellan, who served as adjutant general to the Confederate cavalry legend. The work's reminiscences of the capture of John Brown, the campaign and battle of First Bull Run, and the military adventures of Stuart through the Wilderness campaign are spirited and permeated with details of great value. The book achieves significance despite being composed 20 years after the war and without the use of many valuable records relating to Stuart. Although the prose is often labored or stilted and many official documents interrupt the more enjoyable anecdotal material, this eyewitness account succeeds admirably in providing a credible portrait of Stuart and his campaigns. The material covering Brandy Station, Gettysburg, the early portions of the Wilderness campaign, and Stuart's mortal wounding at Yellow Tavern is quite worthwhile.

The work's appendix presents official documents relating to Brandy Station. A number of errors or distortions appear, mainly in the guise of defending Stuart against criticism by others, and are addressed in full in the modern edition cited below, which contains an appendix of valuable notes by the editor that correct or clarify a number of McClellan's comments. A few misspellings include the names of Elon J. Farnsworth, Maxcy Gregg, and Robert Patterson.

(Reprinted 1958, titled *I Rode with Jeb Stuart*, ed. Burke Davis, 455 pp., Indiana University Press, Bloomington; 1958 edition reprinted 1990, 455 pp., Kraus Reprints, Millwood, N.Y.; 1958 edition reprinted 1994, 455 pp., Da Capo Press, New York)

320

Thomas, Emory M. **Bold Dragoon: The Life of J. E. B. Stuart** (354 pp., Harper and Row, New York, 1986)

This book attempts to analyze Stuart as a man as well as a soldier and devotes some 30 percent of its space to the prewar years on the frontier. In offering a portrait of Stuart significantly deeper and more human than the caricature of a dashing horseman, Thomas has provided a valuable service. Stuart is portrayed as a calculating and talented officer whose rise to fame and glory is accompanied not only by dashing bravery but also by skill in military tactics, a man thoughtful and decisive in war. The author also shows that Stuart was not particularly thoughtful outside of war, apparently feeling nothing about slavery or moral or ethical issues at large. His decision to side with Virginia was one of simple residence.

The author believes that his subject's personal friendship with Lee was highly significant in the development of Stuart's career in the Army of Northern Virginia. Thomas floats little analysis of Stuart's military campaigning in crucial spots where it is needed, as with the alleged misuse of time during the Gettysburg campaign or the loss at Brandy Station shortly before. The narrative treats Stuart sympathetically, coming to the well-deserved conclusion that his abilities tower above those of the often more celebrated Forrest, Morgan, or even Mosby.

There are a few errors and slips of fact. The author uses such cavalier phrases as "with Stuart's star," showing an apparent lack of understanding of the insignia for Confederate generals. Carelessness with names sometimes occurs, as with the misspellings of George St. Leger Grenfell, Irvin McDowell, and Orlando M. Poe, and even Philip St. George Cooke and Philip St. George Cooke Stuart, Jeb Stuart's father-in-law and son. The index includes such improprieties as listing Chancellorsville's Hazel Grove under "Grove, Hazel." Overall, though, this work contains much of interest for those investigating Jeb Stuart.

Richard Taylor (1826–1879)

321

Parrish, T. Michael. **Richard Taylor: Soldier Prince of Dixie** (553 pp., University of North Carolina Press, Chapel Hill, 1992)

This is the only modern biography of this important Confederate general officer, and it is brilliantly executed, providing a detailed and thoughtful analysis of Taylor's life backed by ample research from a wide array of sources. Further, it is well written and offers a winning combination of narrative and interpretation. Taylor's early life as the son of the military hero and president Zachary Taylor and his later life as a field commander provide ample material of interest, taken full advantage of by the author.

The focus of the work is Taylor's Civil War service, but Parrish reveals a clear portrait of his subject's antebellum and postbellum life as well. As Zachary's son and Jefferson Davis's brother-in-law, Taylor clearly was going to receive a significant command in the Confederate Army. The author artfully sketches Taylor's rise from an advisor to Bragg at Pensacola to colonel of the 9th Louisiana Infantry and his rapid promotion to command of the Louisiana brigade. The descriptions of Taylor's service in Jackson's Valley campaign and the Peninsular campaign are first-rate. His shift to the Trans-Mississippi West marked a major jump in Taylor's career and creates an increasingly enthralling momentum in Parrish's book.

The handling of the Red River campaign of 1864 is superb and incorporates a smattering of sources into a cohesive narrative account. Taylor's role at the overlooked battles of Mansfield and Pleasant Hill receives nice treatment, as does his evolving and difficult relationship with Edmund Kirby Smith. On the latter point the author does not back away from criticizing his subject for irrational behavior. The account of Taylor's final weeks of war and his postwar life reveals much about the man, clearly presented in this very fine work.

322

Taylor, Richard. **Destruction and Reconstruction: Personal Experiences of the Late War** (274 pp., D. Appleton and Co., New York, 1879)

The son of Zachary Taylor, brother-in-law of Jefferson Davis, and a lieutenant general in the Confederate Army, Taylor had a unique position from which to observe events both military and political during the war. His memoir will not disappoint its readers in the least, for it provides a superb analysis of numerous commanders, politicians, and engagements and surprisingly is composed with an exceptional writing style lacking in most old soldier's reminiscences.

Taylor's story follows his career in the East at First Bull Run and at the Peninsular campaign, then switches theaters to the West to describe the war in Louisiana, the defense of Vicksburg approaches, and the Red River campaign. Along the way Taylor interjects valuable comments on military operations and how they unfolded. Despite his connections with Davis, Taylor delivers an objective treatment of many individuals who were not so well connected, including Joe Johnston. Devoted to Lee, Taylor nonetheless criticizes some of the great general's strategy.

In a reflective chapter following a description of surrender, Taylor subtly blames Longstreet for the loss at Gettysburg, laments over the lost opportunity of Shiloh, and writes that if any single individual could have saved the cause of the South, it was Albert Sidney Johnston.

(Reprinted 1983, 274 pp., Time-Life Books, Alexandria, Va.; new edition 1955, ed. Richard Barksdale Harwell, 380 pp., Longmans, Green and Co., New York; 1879 edition reprinted 1995, with an introduction by T. Michael Parrish, 274 pp., Da Capo Press, New York)

Walter Herron Taylor (1838–1916)

323

Taylor, Walter H. **General Lee, His Campaigns in Virginia, 1861–1865: With Personal Reminiscences** (314 pp., Press of Braunworth and Co., Brooklyn, N.Y., 1906)

Taylor's book contains an early account of life on General Lee's staff. A former cadet of the Virginia Military Institute, Taylor served as adjutant to Lee throughout the war, giving him an exceptional position from which to view many activities. The work includes much material about the personal traits of Lee and of Taylor himself and stands up well to analysis from other sources. Valuable descriptions pertain to the Peninsular campaign, Second Bull Run, Antietam,

Chancellorsville, Gettysburg, and the 1864 campaigns in Virginia. Much exists here beyond the military narrative, however, as interpretations of Lee's attitudes about tactics and subordinate commanders fill many pages. The tone is skewed significantly, at times straining credibility, which is understandable considering Taylor's youth and closeness with Lee during the war. Lee was never at fault according to Taylor, and errors were always made by others. This unquestioning loyalty aside, the work remains a valuable source.

A less-detailed and inferior work was published in 1877, Walter H. Taylor's *Four Years with General Lee: Being a Summary of the More Important Events Touching the Career of General Robert E. Lee, in the War between the States: Together with an Authoritative Statement of the Strength of the Army Which He Commanded in the Field* (199 pp., D. Appleton and Co., New York; reprinted 1962, ed. James I. Robertson, Jr., 218 pp., Indiana University Press, Bloomington).

(Reprinted 1975, 314 pp., Morningside, Dayton; reprinted 1994, with an introduction by Gary W. Gallagher, 314 pp., University of Nebraska Press, Lincoln)

324

Taylor, Walter H. **Lee's Adjutant: The Wartime Letters of Colonel Walter Herron Taylor, 1862–1865** (ed. R. Lockwood Tower, 343 pp., University of South Carolina Press, Columbia, 1995)

This insightful work contributes a collection of 110 letters written by Taylor between 15 May 1862 and 27 March 1865. The youthful officer wrote frequently to his fiancée, Elizabeth Selden Saunders, and to various members of his family, recording events of soldier life on the staff of Gen. Robert E. Lee. The work is well edited and contains sufficient detail to be enthralling in various parts for students of the Army of Northern Virginia. Not only does Taylor illuminate the simple, inelegant life of Lee in camp, but he casts light on the command decisions Lee made on the battlefield. The author's choicest letters cover the period during which Lee commanded on the Peninsula, the weeks following the defeat at Gettysburg, and the drudgery of the campaigns of 1864.

Taylor characterizes youthful Confederate soldiers in his frequent lashing out at all things Yankee. The letters occasionally illuminate areas beyond the battlefield, as with various religious and social concerns of the day. Beyond his hatred of the enemy, Taylor betrays an ill-defined purpose for the fight. That the enemy must be beaten is clear, but why he must be beaten, beyond the line of simple duty, is not always clear. Simple maps accompany the text. The editor added appendices on Taylor's end-of-the-war wedding and genealogies of Taylor and his wife.

Meriwether Jeff Thompson (1826–1876)

325

Thompson, M. Jeff. **The Memoirs of M. Jeff Thompson** (eds. Donal J. Stanton, Goodwin F. Berquist, and Paul C. Bowers, 310 pp., Morningside, Dayton, 1988)

This memoir provides unusual insight into the terror-laden experience of Missouri and Arkansas in the Civil War. Serving as a partisan most of the time but holding a commission as a brigadier general in the Missouri State Guard, Thompson rose to his sobriquet as the "Swamp Fox of the Confederacy" at Plum Run Bend and as a staff officer for Edmund Kirby Smith. He ended his Confederate service by participating in Sterling Price's latent Missouri raid and valiantly led his brigade through the battle of Westport near Kansas City.

The renegade soldier's memoirs were haphazardly composed as a sort of outline for a future, grander work that was never attempted. Characterized by a surprisingly well written and at times humorous depiction of Thompson's peculiar exploits, the *Memoirs* are probably frequently embellished and always view events through the partisan eyes of a guerrilla. Egotism and rationalization aside, interesting accounts in this work offer glimpses into obscure actions in the Trans-Mississippi West. The biographical discourse added by the editors works nicely and presents a stark contrast to the opinionated monologue of this dramatic figure.

Earl Van Dorn (1820–1863)

326

Hartje, Robert G. **Van Dorn: The Life and Times of a Confederate General** (363 pp., Vanderbilt University Press, Nashville, 1967)

Characterized by acceptable research and a generally sound writing style, this work undertakes to deliver the record of Van Dorn's military life despite the relative scarcity of papers relating to the general. Van Dorn's life provides a confusing basis for interpretation. He repulsed the Federal armies at Vicksburg in 1862, but his most critical battles, Pea Ridge and Corinth, were Confederate losses. More capable as a cavalry commander than as an infantry leader, the chagrined Mississippian took charge of Pemberton's cavalry during 1863 before his exploits with Mrs. Jessie Peters led to his violent death by retribution. Disliked by most Confederates, he was buried in Port Gibson in a corner of the local cemetery and has gone largely unremembered.

In bringing forth a story of Van Dorn's Civil War career, Hartje attempts to reconstruct his image. Occasionally overwritten, the study is also lightly documented and the bibliography not overly helpful. However, careful stories of the two main battles, Pea Ridge and Corinth, emerge, or at least Van Dorn's undistinguished role in them does. Careless with tactics, poor with his reconnaisance, and unable to execute control over his army, Van Dorn gives us a summary of how not to command. His personal life was equally as dangerous, as his early death attests.

(Reprinted 1994, 363 pp., Vanderbilt University Press, Nashville)

William Henry Talbot Walker (1816–1864)

327

Brown, Russell K. **To the Manner Born: The Life of General William H. T. Walker** (411 pp., University of Georgia Press, Athens, 1994)

Brown's is the first full-length life of this ill-fated Confederate general officer. The author employs Walker's papers, letters, diaries, and official documents to forge a complete picture of his subject. The biography examines the officer's Seminole and Mexican War activities but places emphasis squarely on his Civil War career. Walker emerges as one who argued with his superiors frequently, was beset by wounds that nearly incapacitated him, and floated through the dullness of peacetime army life. The work pays special attention to the youthful Walker's court-martial and his planting and business ventures.

The Civil War coverage is especially good. Walker's peculiar service at Pensacola and in northern Virginia and his subsequent resignation are reviewed carefully. The author casts much light on Walker's service as a militia general, his return to service in the Confederate Army in 1863, and his rapid rise in importance because of Joe Johnston's intervention. The coverage of Lay's Ferry suggests that Walker was unable to lead troops effectively at the battle. The work examines in spectacular detail the Atlanta campaign, during which Walker was killed by a minié bullet. Brown demonstrates that Walker was a careful organizer handicapped by his difficult personality and lack of political judgment.

Admirably, only one typographical error appears, a misspelling of Edward Johnson's sobriquet of Allegheny. Appendices cover the general's staff and the units he commanded. The index is quite nicely done; the notes and bibliography are impressively full. This finely crafted book was long overdue.

Joseph Wheeler (1836–1906)

328

DuBose, John Witherspoon. **General Joseph Wheeler and the Army of Tennessee** (476 pp., Neale Publishing Co., New York, 1912)

This historical relic offers an experiential record of Wheeler's adventures and the campaigns of the great western army. It is part biography and part tribute to the army. The former does not succeed very effectively; the latter is marked by deficiencies but contains more of measured value. The bulk of the work focuses on the campaigns of 1864 and rather severely criticizes Braxton Bragg. The work contains a good number of official documents as well as writings from officers in the army recounting their glories.

The book may be valuable, then, as a reminiscence of old soldiers, but in many places it is not particularly valuable as history. False assertions appear relating to Abraham Lincoln and other topics, including the events surrounding Sumter, and a general bitter partisanship mars much of the low-level interpretation of actions. If one can swallow the hatred that accompanies this work, much of it forged long after the war, some small pieces worthy of reading stand out.

329

Dyer, John P. **"Fightin' Joe" Wheeler** (417 pp., Louisiana State University Press, University, 1941)

Not limited to the general's Civil War career, this work provides a splendid insight into the diminutive cavalry commander who became one of the younger generals on the Confederate side to amass such an impressive record. The author's narrative obviously shows a great familiarity with and affection for Wheeler. However, Dyer wisely avoids the common stumbling block of marrying his fortunes with those of his subject, and the storybook charm of Wheeler's career reads smoothly and credibly.

The author provides a reasonably detailed account of Wheeler's activities at Stones River, Chickamauga, Chattanooga, and Knoxville, and he details the almost comically frustrating weeks of the March to the Sea campaign, in which Wheeler's tiny force nearly singlehandedly attempted to oppose Sherman's army. Wheeler's faults come through clearly, the most important being his apparent lack of organizational skill and his inability to lead troops independent of his superiors.

The book concludes with Wheeler's service in the Spanish-American War, a strange episode in which the now major general U.S.V. argues with his superiors and conducts a turn-of-the-century media campaign.

(Abridged edition 1961, titled *From Shiloh to San Juan*, 275 pp., Louisiana State University Press, Baton Rouge)

John Henry Winder (1800–1865)

330

Blakey, Arch Frederic. **General John H. Winder, C.S.A.** (304 pp., University Presses of Florida, Jacksonville, 1990)

Strict and bookish, Winder displayed a signal contempt for anything that violated absolute military rule, perhaps in overcompensation for his father's failed military career and in hopes of redeeming the family name. Blakey treats his subject rather sympathetically, suggesting that Winder has received treatment too harsh for his record. To accomplish this, the author devotes 80 percent of the text to discussing the war years.

Winder's controversial role began immediately after the war commenced when he was appointed provost marshal of Richmond and made responsible for a succession of duties including enforcing martial law, establishing price controls, creating a passport system, and looking after the Confederacy's prisons—in and out of Richmond. The author outlines the hopeless nature of looking after the prisons, although he tends to rationalize Winder's incompetence, blaming the problems in part on Jefferson Davis, Samuel Cooper, and even Grant and Lincoln for the suspension of the exchange. The latter point ignores a key reason for this: the Confederate refusal to treat black soldiers equally in such exchanges.

While the details of much of Winder's activities are here, Blakey's interpretation stumbles. Clouded by an overestimation of Winder's abilities, the author feels that his subject was highly capable, a contention negated by mounds of contrary evidence. Further, he frequently speculates on might-have-beens, a fruitless exercise. The story suffers from a confusingly nonchronological organization. A number of misspellings pepper the text, as with the names of Milledge Luke Bonham, Castle Pinckney, Judson Kilpatrick, Irvin McDowell, and Truman Seymour (who appears as "Thomas Seymore"). Despite the author's contentions, one gets the feeling after reading this work that Winder was indeed lucky to have died before being captured.

John Henry Worsham (1839–1920)

331

Worsham, John H. **One of Jackson's Foot Cavalry: His Experiences and What He Saw during the War, 1861–1865, Including a History of "F" Company, Richmond, Va., 21st Regiment Virginia Infantry, Second Brigade, Jackson's Division, Second Corps, A.N.Va.** (353 pp., Neale Publishing Co., New York, 1912)

Twenty-two years of age at the outbreak of hostilities, Worsham enlisted in the 21st Virginia and proceeded to experience much of the war in the East, recording his thoughts on battle, camp life, marches, and a galaxy of personalities including many important officers. The result is a Confederate classic that should adorn the shelf of every Civil War library.

Worsham took part in Jackson's Valley campaign, Second Bull Run, Antietam, Mine Run, the Wilderness campaign, and Monocacy. Particularly good accounts of the action appear relating to Gaines's Mill, Williamsport, the Wilderness, and Spotsylvania, where the author was struck twice by spent balls while defending the Mule Shoe, and Second Winchester, where a bullet shattered his left knee. His observations of officers are splendid, including hateful remarks thrust on Banks, Pope, and Sheridan, and laudatory comments for Jackson, Lee, Gordon, and Early. The narrative's misspellings and occasional lapses of fact (placing Jefferson Davis at Gaines's Mill, for example) are relatively minor.

(Reprinted 1982, 353 pp., Time-Life Books, Alexandria, Va.; new edition 1964, titled *One of Jackson's Foot Cavalry*, ed. James I. Robertson, Jr., 215 pp., McCowat-Mercer Press, Jackson, Tenn.; 1964 edition reprinted 1991, 215 pp., Broadfoot, Wilmington)

John Allan Wyeth (1845–1922)

332

Wyeth, John Allan. **With Sabre and Scalpel: The Autobiography of a Soldier and Surgeon** (534 pp., Harper and Bros., New York, 1914)

This book contains the lifelong recollections of the well-known and respected author of the more famous work *Life of General Nathan Bedford Forrest* (*q.v.*). The autobiography is highly conversational, contains much of importance and a great deal of minutiae, and might be considered as useful for its details of medical history as for its anecdotes of Civil War history. Slightly more than one-quarter of the text treats the war years, so readers find a great store of data on the author's early life in Alabama, his interest in medicine and surgery, recollections of antebellum conditions in the Deep South, and a lengthy narrative on Wyeth's postwar career as a doctor.

The wartime coverage is entertaining. It presents stories of the author's days at La Grange Military Academy, a recollection of seeing the USS *Tennessee* pass on the Tennessee River, and a more involved narrative describing the author's membership in Morgan's cavalry. After this brief service is described, the author's story develops significantly as he recalls service with the 4th Alabama Cavalry, some of which overlaps with the content of the author's life of Forrest. The finest section treats Chickamauga (including a wonderfully detailed, early map), but other worthwhile material relates to the Tullahoma campaign and the author's capture and subsequent imprisonment at Camp Morton. The author occasionally slips into partisan bitterness, but for the most part the recollections remain objective.

Bennett Henderson Young (1843–1919)

333

Young, Bennett H. **Confederate Wizards of the Saddle: Being Reminiscences and Observations of One Who Rode with Morgan** (633 pp., Chapple Publishing Co., Boston, 1914)

Young provides a treasure trove of enlightening information on western cavalry greats intermingled with superfluous chatter. The author's stirring tale centers around his service in the 8th Kentucky Cavalry in which he participated in several actions in the Kentucky campaign of 1862 and had occasional contact with Brig. Gen. John Hunt Morgan. Captured with Morgan in July 1863, Young sat in prisons in Columbus and Chicago before escaping in January 1864. Thereafter, the story relates the adventure of the author's command of the St. Albans Raid, the northernmost action of the war.

The volume centers on the exploits of Morgan and a handful of other cavalry greats, including Nathan Bedford Forrest, Joseph Wheeler, and, in more minor fashion, Wade Hampton III, Jeb Stuart, and John S. Mosby. The work's two dozen chapters are chaotically organized, and praise of Young's Confederate horseback heroes reaches florid heights throughout the text. As a conglomeration of events in which Young participated and those he simply wanted to record for later generations, this work stands as an interesting if somewhat confused narrative.

(Reprinted 1988, with an introduction by E. B. Long, 633 pp., Morningside, Dayton)

Felix Kirk Zollicoffer (1812–1862)

334

Myers, Raymond E. M. **The Zollie Tree** (200 pp., Filson Club Press, Louisville, 1964)

This work tells the story of Felix Zollicoffer, an important figure in Tennessee and an early influence on Confederate strategy in the West until his death at Mill Spring. (The book's title refers to the tree under which Zollicoffer died and which stood until 1995 near the mass grave of Confederates who died under his command.) Myers clearly describes the contradictions in his subject's character. Zollicoffer was an educated editor who rose to political prominence as a Whig and who despised secession until midsummer 1861. When it became clear that Tennessee was predominantly pro-Confederate, Zollicoffer offered his services and was commissioned a brigadier general in Tennessee's provisional army.

The author nicely traces Zollicoffer's assignment to eastern Tennessee, where Confederate officials hoped he could persuade pro-Unionists to support the South. As a brigadier general C.S.A., he helped to fortify Cumberland Gap and approached Mill Spring. The author's finest battle writing appears in the final section, in which his subject is killed by none other than Col. Speed Smith Fry, the Kentuckian who would become a Union brigadier general. The author dutifully describes the Confederate disaster at Mill Spring before closing the curtain on the significance of Zollicoffer's life. Myers shows that Zollicoffer's death and the loss at Mill Spring helped seal the fate of southeastern Kentucky and Cumberland Gap.

SAILORS

James Dunwoody Bulloch (1823–1901)

335

Bulloch, James D. **The Secret Service of the Confederate States in Europe; or, How the Confederate Cruisers Were Equipped** (2 vols., 918 pp., R. Bentley and Son, London, 1883)

Bulloch's work offers the best source for Confederate naval operations in Europe. His position as agent for the financing, purchasing, and construction of Confederate warships in England and France gave him a valuable outlook on this influential aspect of Confederate naval planning. Extensive discussions of the work in England on the *Alabama* and the *Florida* are provided, based on Bulloch's retained correspondence relating to his duties. The story of the ships, simple but elegantly written, entertains as well as informs. For the most part the work is balanced and devoid of partisan distortions.

The account presents valuable details relating to Bulloch's other major achievements, including his piloting of the *Fingal* through the blockade, his purchase of other blockade-runners, the construction of the Laird rams, the procurement of the French-built *Stonewall*, and the purchase of the *Shenandoah*, a vessel destined to be the last ship to surrender. The work loses objectivity in some of its passages relating to more general history, as with the discussions of slavery, nullification, and the assessments of Northern leaders, particularly William Henry Seward. However, these are minor points, peripheral to the more specific value of Bulloch's work. The book, which lacks an index, is an important primary source covering this aspect of the Confederate Navy.

(Reprinted 1959, with an introduction by Philip Van Doren Stern, 2 vols., 918 pp., Thomas Yoseloff, New York; reprinted 1972, 2 vols., 918 pp., Burt Franklin, New York)

George Townley Fullam (1841–1879)

336

Fullam, George Townley. **The Journal of George Townley Fullam, Boarding Officer of the Confederate Sea Raider** *Alabama* (ed. Charles G. Summersell, 229 pp., University of Alabama Press, University, 1973)

Fullam's journal is among the more interesting and useful sources on Confederate naval history. This British sailor joined the crew of the *Alabama* with an eye on prize money and in short order was transformed into an enthusiastic Confederate. His journal spans the period July 1862 to the destruction of the ship in 1864. Massively enhanced by the editor, the manuscript is a delight to readers fascinated with Confederate naval operations and particularly the much-storied career of Semmes's *Alabama*.

As boarding officer of the raider, Fullam temporarily commanded many of the 76 vessels captured by the *Alabama*, collected and transferred the crews, and burned the prizes after unloading them of worthy supplies. Many famous actions are described within Fullam's journal, as well as a multitude of observations on shipboard life, other offi-

cers of the *Alabama*, events, and places visited. This is a worthy contribution to Civil War naval history.

John Newland Maffitt (1819–1886)

337

Shingleton, Royce. **High Seas Confederate: The Life and Times of John Newland Maffitt** (160 pp., University of South Carolina Press, Columbia, 1994)

In presenting this brief but illuminating sketch of the adventurous officer of the CSS *Florida*, the author draws on a cache of Maffitt's letters and papers and gives us a full biography centering on the sailor's Civil War service. Shingleton also provides details on Maffitt's ancestry, early life in North Carolina and New York, and his antebellum naval career. The author examines Maffitt's duties cruising in the Gulf of Mexico, first marriage, service at the Pensacola Navy Yard, and hydrographic work in Boston and North Carolina. The survey work and Maffitt's second marriage set a casual tone for the 1850s, a decade that builds to chaos by its close. The war years offer the most interesting material. Early staff duty with Robert E. Lee gives way to blockade-running adventures and service on the CSS *Florida*. An appendix provides data on captures by Maffitt during the first cruise of the *Florida* and a list of the officers who served on the ship.

The coverage of the *Florida* holds greatest interest. Converted from the British steamship *Oreto*, the ship took on a crew that brushed with yellow fever before sailing the high seas as a raider. From Havana, the ship cruised to Mobile where it languished for repairs after fighting its way through the blockade. After several attempts, the ship escaped on 16 January 1863 and began a cruise. She usually raised a British or American flag until overtaking an American merchant ship and hoisting the stars and bars, classifying her as a pirate vessel in the eyes of the Federal government. Suffering from ill health, Maffitt had to leave the ship in the summer of 1863. He made his way back to Richmond, was assigned briefly to the *Albemarle*, but returned to blockade-running. After the war he established a farm near Wilmington. In reflecting on the war and his service, Maffitt thought the Confederacy's greatest mistake was neglecting the navy early in the war.

Matthew Fontaine Maury (1806–1873)

338

Williams, Frances Leigh. **Matthew Fontaine Maury: Scientist of the Sea** (720 pp., Rutgers University Press, New Brunswick, 1963)

This biography is much aided by a truly appealing subject: the young U.S. naval officer who, crippled in an accident, takes to his desk and becomes one of the finest hydrographers of the century. Williams follows this line in tracing Maury's life and details his achievements and publications in naval ordnance, meteorology, astronomy, and oceanography. The author describes the military and political considerations of Maury's tenure as superintendent of the U.S. Naval Observatory and of the Depot of Charts and Instruments, as well as his postwar adventures in Mexico, England, and at the Virginia Military Institute. The discussion of poor relations with the U.S. Navy explains much about Maury's character and that of the prewar navy. The author explores the nebulous relationships between Maury and many leading figures of science who came from far different backgrounds and held markedly different stations in life. In this the author errs by always sympathizing with Maury.

The brief core of this heavily researched volume treats Maury's wartime years in Richmond and in England as a naval agent. The author describes Maury's poor relations with Jefferson Davis and Secretary Mallory, his peculiar (and highly valuable) tinkerings with naval innovations in Richmond, and his efforts to buy ships and supplies on behalf of the Confederacy. Maury's poor standing in Richmond arose from several factors, among which were unrealistic schemes such as building a coastal defense force of small ships fitted with heavy caliber guns. Many details extend the story and make it stand among the best biographies of Civil War naval personnel.

James Morris Morgan (1845–?)

339

Morgan, James M. **Recollections of a Rebel Reefer** (491 pp., Houghton Mifflin Co., Boston, 1917)

Morgan, a distant relative of Varina Davis, has written an amusing and interesting memoir of a midshipman who experienced a wide range of action in the Confederate Navy. The work is highly chatty, written long after the war, and utilizes re-created "conversations" reported as exact interchanges of dialogue. Despite this, it retains value because of the author's emphasis on the war and his service on many Confederate vessels. About half of the lengthy work covers the war years; the remainder consists of a brief introduction relating the author's background and detailed discussions of postwar adventures in Egypt and many other parts of the world.

The Civil War material recalls Morgan's service on the CSS *McRae*, the CSS *Alexandria*, and other vessels. The finest parts of the work treat the naval battle at Drewry's Bluff in 1862, actions around New Orleans, and the cruise on the *Georgia* under William L. Maury. Anecdotal material covers Morris's activities in Richmond, his membership in the party fleeing south with Jefferson Davis, and the author's subsequent arrest. Morgan was a brother of Sarah Morgan, author of a famous Confederate narrative (*q.v.*), and brother-in-law of Francis W. Dawson, who left yet another work of interest on the Confederacy (*q.v.*).

William Harwar Parker (1826–1896)

340

Parker, William Harwar. **Recollections of a Naval Officer, 1841–1865** (372 pp., Charles Scribner's Sons, New York, 1883)

The author presents a superb account of a Confederate naval officer's exploits before and during the war. A Northerner, Parker fought gallantly during the Mexican War in the U.S. Navy and recounts his part in support of the engagements at Resaca de la Palma, Palo Alto, and Vera Cruz. The period between wars receives careful scrutiny as well, a fact made more palatable by the author's engaging style. The account of Parker's life at the early naval academy is a valuable contribution.

The Civil War coverage is of paramount interest. Despite his Northern birth, Parker's heritage reached far back into Virginia and he sided with the Confederacy. Commanding the CSS *Beaufort*, Parker participated in the battles at Hampton Roads on 8 March 1862 and witnessed the clash between the USS *Monitor* and the CSS *Virginia* the next day. His account is one of the principal sources of data on this storied action. As executive officer of the ironclad CSS *Palmetto State*, the author battled Federal ships about Charleston harbor and was appointed superintendent of the Confederate Naval Academy at Drewry's Bluff near Richmond. The sketch of operations relating to this service is invaluable. Parker's supervision of Confederate treasury funds in the government's flight south from Richmond provides a bracing interruption of the story and offers a first-person account of the chaos as the Confederacy collapsed. The study is valuable and should be consulted by those interested in Southern naval operations.

(Reprinted 1985, with an introduction by Craig L. Symonds, valuable notes, and a brief index, 403 pp., Naval Institute Press, Annapolis)

Raphael Semmes (1809–1877)

341

Semmes, Raphael. **Memoirs of Service Afloat, during the War between the States** (833 pp., R. Bentley and Son, London, 1869)

This is a genuine classic. Several attributes combine to make this work a valuable tome filled with the spirit of high adventure. Semmes's text is very well written. His exploits with the *Alabama* carried him across an amazing arena of territory. Semmes's crew included interesting characters. The various actions are described in alluring detail. Unfortunately, parts of the book act as a defensive rationalization of the Confederacy rather than an autobiography. But for the most part the work stands up well enough to hold readers' interest.

Over the couse of its cruise throughout the Atlantic, the *Alabama* sank, burned, or captured 65 Federal vessels, a record untouched by any other Confederate warship. After delivering rather trite discourses on the constitutionality of secession and the effects of slavery on the coming of the war, Semmes commences his narrative. The accounts of battle are worth careful reading, and the ultimate action off Cherbourg is described with great aplomb. Equally as valuable as the military reminiscences, an array of travelogues provides readers with valuable descriptions of many ports of call in exotic places (by 1860s standards). Final chapters provide a straightforward telling of Semmes's return to the United States and his brief involvement with the Confederate Army before his arrest. A careful reading of this work should not escape anyone with Civil War interest.

(Reprinted 1987, 833 pp., Blue and Grey Press, Secaucus; abridged edition 1948, titled *Rebel Raider: Being an Account of Raphael Semmes's* Memoirs of Service Afloat, *Written in the Year 1869*, ed. Harpur Allen Gosnell, 218 pp., University of North Carolina Press, Chapel Hill; new edition 1962 , titled *The Confederate Raider* Alabama, ed. Philip Van Doren Stern, 464 pp., Indiana University Press, Bloomington)

342

Taylor, John M. **Confederate Raider: Raphael Semmes of the *Alabama*** (317 pp., Brassey's, McLean, Va., 1994)

This is by far the most valuable work relating to the legendary Confederate naval hero. Taylor makes the most of the scanty materials available to biographers of Semmes and rounds out his sound judgment and careful research with an engaging style of writing. The result is a work that adds greatly to the standard volume on Semmes, his own autobiography (*q.v.*). The book makes use of letters written by Semmes as well as his memoir but draws a significantly detailed picture of the man over and above the relatively few words he left on paper. The analysis is admirable and intellectual, and Taylor gives us the most complete and well-rounded picture of Semmes to date.

As enjoyable as it is, Taylor's book does not approach a full biography. A mere 17 percent of the work treats Semmes's antebellum career and only 12 percent covers his postwar activities. The work is overwhelmingly focused on the Civil War years and on Semmes's cruise aboard the CSS *Alabama*. This plays well into the interests of Civil War readers, of course, and the handling of the story of Semmes's famous ship is finely accomplished. The author's excitement over his subject may carry too far on occasion, as his admiration for Semmes shines through strongly. But the detailed analysis stands up handsomely. An appendix lists the prizes of the CSS *Sumter* and *Alabama*.

Arthur Sinclair IV (1837–1925)

343

Sinclair, Arthur. **Two Years on the *Alabama*** (352 pp., Lee and Shepard, Boston, 1895)

Sinclair's is a controversial Confederate naval memoir. Together with the works of Raphael Semmes (*q.v.*) and John M. Kell, the book constitutes a narrative of the cruise of the CSS *Alabama*, the most famous ship of the Confederacy. The Virginia-born author was an officer on the ship during its entire career, having earlier served as a volunteer aide to Franklin Buchanan and participated in the USS *Monitor*–CSS *Virginia* fight at Hampton Roads. His memoir concentrates wholly on the *Alabama* and offers an interesting story that in places one must use cautiously because it was composed so long after the war.

On its publication the work was attacked by a number of Sinclair's contemporaries because of the repetition of material that had appeared earlier in Semmes's book. Kell launched several disputes with Sinclair's recollection of key events. Sinclair's narrative disagrees with that of Semmes in critical places, however. The negative reactions may have come as a defense of criticism toward Semmes. The author certainly exaggerates his importance in the crew of the *Alabama*, romanticizes events and persons on the ship, claims to have known more critical information than he could have during the war, and draws on a sometimes failing memory. Admirably, only one misspelling was found, the name of James D. Bulloch.

(Reprinted 1989, with an introduction by William N. Still, Jr., 303 pp., Naval Institute Press, Annapolis)

John Taylor Wood (1830?–1904)

344

Shingleton, Royce G. **John Taylor Wood: Sea Ghost of the Confederacy** (242 pp., University of Georgia Press, Athens, 1979)

This is a significantly appealing book, although not a complete biography, as Shingleton chose to focus on Wood's wartime years. In March 1862 he participated as a second lieutenant aboard the CSS *Virginia* in the famous "battle of the ironclads" against the USS *Monitor*. After scuttling the *Virginia*, Wood led her crew in the difficult task of arming the gun emplacements at Drewry's Bluff above the James River, successfully preventing McClellan's movement toward Richmond in the Peninsular campaign. In late 1862 Wood began a series of night raids on Yankee ships that earned him the sobriquet Sea Ghost, and in early 1863 he became an aide to his relative, President Davis.

In early 1864 Wood received the Confederate Thanks of Congress for capturing the USS *Underwriter*, and during the following year he harassed the eastern seaboard, seizing or wrecking more than 30 ships. After escaping Richmond with the president, he was captured along with Davis in May 1865. But unlike Davis, Wood escaped by bribing a guard and made his way to Cuba, along with John C. Breckinridge. Few participants of the Civil War experienced such adventures, and Shingleton's book succeeds greatly with the daunting task of portraying the life of the Sea Ghost.

OTHERS

William Gannaway Brownlow (1805–1877)

345

Brownlow, William G. **Sketches of the Rise, Progress, and Decline of Secession: With a Narrative of Personal Adventures among the Rebels** (458 pp., George W. Childs, Philadelphia, and Applegate and Co., Cincinnati, 1862)

This collection presents the controversial author's speeches, correspondence, editorials, and life experiences. Editor of the Knoxville *Whig*, Brownlow favored slavery but violently opposed secession. He so savagely attacked the Confederate war aims and secession government in Tennessee that he was eventually exiled to the North. This extraordinarily partisan and hostile book is valuable for analyzing Brownlow's political views and influence in the region. It contains an autobiographical sketch, arguments on the right of secession, a pronouncement of the African slave trade as piracy, and discussions of the nullification crisis of 1832. The author further explores the state of South Carolina, its history, and why it was hostile to the Union.

Brownlow analyzes threats made against him and his paper and describes the "reign of terror" in the South. The author includes an exposition on the clergy of the North and the South and draws some remarkable contrasts. Describing in detail the work of the secessionists at Knoxville, he asks, "Which side is God on?" (the Union, according to the author). The book includes much on the politics of eastern Tennessee, explores the cessation of his paper, and describes prison life.

(Reprinted 1969, 458 pp., Da Capo Press, New York)

346

Coulter, E. Merton. **William G. Brownlow: Fighting Parson of the Southern Highlands** (432 pp., University of North Carolina Press, Chapel Hill, 1937)

A biographical record of the vitriolic editor, this book lays down most successfully the facts of Brownlow's career. Readers can trace the suppression of his pro-Union paper in 1861, his banishment to Federal territory, and his return to Knoxville and the press after Burnside captured the area, renaming the paper the *Knoxville Whig and Rebel Ventilator*. Coulter shows how influential Brownlow and his paper were in raising Union sentiment in eastern Tennessee, pushing for Union elections and a loyal government for the state.

The biography contains all these facts and shows the incredible means Brownlow employed to achieve them. The study is marred by an overdrawn picture of Brownlow as a villian, a notion that surfaces repeatedly from the author's pen. Coulter succeeds with the details of Brownlow's career but fails on occasion to place these in the context of the times. The study examines Brownlow's terms as governor of Tennessee beginning in 1865 and his tenure as a U.S. senator. Too much of this material comes from newspaper sources and not from diaries and letters, and the author is frequently too judgmental.

(Reprinted 1971, with an introduction by James W. Patton, 432 pp., University of Tennessee Press, Knoxville)

Mary Boykin Miller Chesnut (1823–1886)

347

[Pulitzer Prize, 1982]

Chesnut, Mary. **Mary Chesnut's Civil War** (ed. C. Vann Woodward, 886 pp., Yale University Press, New Haven, 1981)

Chesnut's long and eloquent manuscript was masterfully edited and annotated by Woodward, whose modern version supersedes the first edition titled *A Diary from Dixie, as Written by Mary Boykin Chesnut, Wife of James Chesnut, Jr., United States Senator from South Carolina 1859–1861, and Afterward an Aide to Jefferson Davis and a Brigadier-General in the Confederate Army* by Mary Chesnut (ed. Isabella D. Martin and Myrta Lockett Avary, 424 pp., D. Appleton and Co., New York, 1905).

Woodward's research into the diary's origins and the resulting discovery that Chesnut's manuscript was composed in the 1880s does not detract significantly from the work's usefulness. Indeed, the author had attempted three novels before using the wartime notes to spin her "diary." The material, though somewhat embellished, paints a fair picture of life in South Carolina during the war by one whose high connections allowed her to see far more than the average Confederate and whose intelligence and candor permitted a firm grasp of what transpired around her.

The annotations in many cases provide a clear sense of what comes from the original wartime diary and from an 1870s version, allowing readers to sort through the additions. Following a bibliographical essay on the diary, the editor adds a biographical sketch of Chesnut and a literary exploration of her apparent hatred of slavery. The following pages bring readers the complete and annotated diary, a masterpiece of Civil War literature. Not only do we experience the low-country feel of 1860s South Carolina but also the noisy clatter of war in Charleston's streets. The passages relating to the bombardment of Sumter are legendary, as are many accounts following great battles and many estimations of politicians and military officers on both sides, not the least of which are comments on Jefferson Davis. Chesnut also defines, even if somewhat unwittingly, the upper-class woman in the slaveholding South. The result is an invaluable portrait of a remarkable individual, one of the finest records of wartime life on the home front, a sterling commentary on the Confederacy, and a definitive work that belongs in every Civil War collection.

An interesting comparison may be made by reading Mary Chesnut's *The Private Mary Chesnut: The Unpublished Civil War Diaries*, edited by C. Vann Woodward and Elisabeth Muhlenfeld (292 pp., Oxford University Press, New York, 1984). This supplementary work provides the exact text of the original diaries as they were written during the war.

348

Muhlenfeld, Elisabeth. **Mary Boykin Chesnut: A Biography** (271 pp., Louisiana State University Press, Baton Rouge, 1981)

This superb telling of Chesnut's life makes a wonderful companion to the Woodward edition of the diary (*q.v.*). Muhlenfeld's description serves as an astute biography of the woman who documented wartime life in Charleston. It also provides a biography of life in antebellum Charleston and a penetrating look at James Chesnut, Jr., the attorney who Mary Miller married at age 17.

The antebellum portion of this document reveals the high place in Charlestonian society occupied by the Chesnuts. As secession approaches, the story accelerates and uncovers much about the subject. The author shows how Chesnut believed herself generally superior to those around her and how her keen intelligence and friendships in what would become the highest circles of the Confederacy allowed her to perceive what was happening as the war deepened. Muhlenfeld also fairly assesses and comments on many diary passages from the war years, making this conversational book a solid success.

Virginia Clay-Clopton (1825–1915)

349

Clay-Clopton, Virginia. **A Belle of the Fifties: Memoirs of Mrs. Clay, of Alabama, Covering Social and Political Life in Washington and the South, 1853–66** (ed. Ada Sterling, 386 pp., Doubleday, Page and Co., New York, 1904)

This is a volume of Lost Cause sentimentality from a Richmond socialite and friend of the Confederate First Family during the war. The memoirs cover a period during which the South transformed from old to new, and thus the progression of events and scenes described offers much of value. The tone and style are lighthearted, present a great deal of embellished conversation, and depend on the memory of an aging woman. Thus, the details often cannot be relied on. However, the work does offer literate and reflective observations that remain valuable, particularly for the antebellum Deep South, prewar Washington, and especially Civil War Richmond.

The narrative treatment of the author's childhood and youthful marriage to Clement C. Clay, Jr., gives way to material of deeper interest as she visits Washington in the 1850s with her husband, a U.S. senator. The descriptions of the prewar city and its occupants are vivid and absorbing. Glimpses of lasting value are to be found in her travel narratives as war approaches and in her descriptions of Richmond, her husband's political and espionage activities for the Confederate government, her social connections with the Davises and other Confederate elite, and other matters. Misspellings abound, as with the names of Mary Chesnut, Ulric Dahlgren, Samuel G. French, Stephen A. Hurlbut, George B. McClellan, Edmund Kirby Smith, and James E. B. Stuart, and the index is poor.

(Reprinted 1969, 386 pp., Da Capo Press, New York)

Thomas Conolly (1823–1876)

350

Conolly, Thomas. **An Irishman in Dixie: Thomas Conolly's Diary of the Fall of the Confederacy** (156 pp., University of South Carolina Press, Columbia, 1988)

A member of the British Parliament drawn to the magical story of the Confederacy (and needing to line his pockets), Conolly hatched a scheme in 1864 to come to the Confederate States and initiate investments in blockade-running. He set up shop and purchased a steamer for the venture, only to have it damaged in a storm, grounding his plans. His diary of travels in the Confederate States begins near Wilmington on 27 February 1865, and he records the scenes he witnessed during the final weeks of the Confederate resistance.

Journeying through the North Carolina wilderness ahead of Sherman's army provided safe passage to Richmond, where the visitor met Jefferson and Varina Davis, observed Confederate ships at Drewry's Bluff, spent time at Lee's headquarters, and moved on to Maryland before the fall of Richmond. Conolly's observations of great leaders and the societal collapse of the Confederate military machine are

generally uninspired but nevertheless provide some interesting reading. The author's artwork illustrates the text, as do photographs appropriate to the journey, forming a neat package that offers a very different view of a well-known time.

Kate Cumming (1835–1909)

351

Cumming, Kate. **A Journal of Hospital Life in the Confederate Army of Tennessee, from the Battle of Shiloh to the End of the War: With Sketches of Life and Character, and Brief Notices of Current Events during That Period** (199 pp., J. P. Morton and Co., Louisville, and W. Eveyln, New Orleans, 1866)

In April 1862 Kate Cumming, in her late 20s, traveled to Okolona, Mississippi, to nurse wounded Confederates transported there from the Shiloh battlefield. She stayed with the field hospitals of the Army of Tennessee to the close of the war and recorded her experiences.

Although occasional lapses into poetry and philosophical musings mar parts of the record, Cumming's narrative is much better than most nursing diaries for several reasons. The author was intelligent, serious, uninterested in romance, and attentive to events surrounding her. She rarely became discouraged, and the resulting narrative reflects a balanced, objective view even as her cause began to collapse. The sole trigger of emotion seems to be an attack on the character of female nurses who followed the armies.

(New edition 1959, titled *Kate: The Journal of a Confederate Nurse*, ed. Richard Barksdale Harwell, 321 pp., Louisiana State University Press, Baton Rouge)

Sarah Morgan Dawson (1842–1909)

352

Dawson, Sarah Morgan. **A Confederate Girl's Diary** (439 pp., Houghton Mifflin Co., Boston, 1913)

A resident of Baton Rouge, young Sarah faithfully recorded her impressions of wartime Louisiana from 10 January 1862 to 15 June 1865. Early on, the Morgan family shows divided loyalties. Sarah is loyal to her home state but controlled in passion until, after the battle of Baton Rouge, the Federals pillage her home. She then is transformed into a fire-breathing Southerner, her widowed mother and sisters in tow.

Adventure heightens as the family abandons home and stays variously with friends in nearby plantation homes and at Clinton. Sarah then journeys around Lake Ponchartrain and seeks refuge in New Orleans. The narrative is detailed, articulate, passionate, and at times very feminine. The result is one of the best home-front diaries of the period and certainly the best treating the war in Louisiana.

(Reprinted 1960, ed. James I. Robertson, Jr., 473 pp., Indiana University Press, Bloomington; new edition 1991, titled *The Civil War Diary of Sarah Morgan*, ed. Charles East, 688 pp., University of Georgia Press, Athens; 1991 edition reprinted 1992, titled *Sarah Morgan: The Civil War Diary of a Southern Woman*, 626 pp., Touchstone, New York)

Thomas Cooper DeLeon (1839–1914)

353

DeLeon, Thomas Cooper. **Four Years in Rebel Capitals: An Inside View of Life in the Southern Confederacy, from Birth to Death, from Original Notes, Collated in the Years 1861 to 1865** (376 pp., Gossip Printing Co., Mobile, 1890)

This book presents the experiences of a Southern journalist who spent much of the war in Richmond but also traveled throughout the South. Parts of the work appeared originally in serial form in the Mobile *Sunday Times*, the Louisville *Courier-Journal*, and the Philadelphia *Times*. DeLeon claims to have composed most of the material in this volume "almost immediately" after the war and based it on extensive notes. Highly partisan and at times openly bitter, the account nevertheless manages to convey a good deal of useful information.

A South Carolinian by birth, DeLeon spent the first tense weeks of 1861 in Washington, where he observed and noted the political attitudes of parties on both sides of the question. Early chapters on Montgomery and the formation of the Confederate government are highly interesting. Despite the author's patriotic fervor, he manages to shed light on some difficulties with Jefferson Davis and the workings of the infant Confederate government that would haunt it much later. The accounts of travel through important cities such as New Orleans and lengthy diatribes on social and political considerations in Richmond have much to offer. Lighter reminiscences focus on literature, the arts, and humor as a means of coping during the war.

(Reprinted 1962, with an introduction by E. B. Long, 416 pp., Collier Books, New York; 1890 edition reprinted 1983, 376 pp., Time-Life Books, Alexandria, Va.)

Isabella Buchanan Edmondson (1840–1873)

354

Edmondson, Belle. **A Lost Heroine of the Confederacy: The Diaries and Letters of Belle Edmondson** (ed. William and Loretta Galbraith, 239 pp., University Press of Mississippi, Jackson, 1990)

The exploits of a courier, spy, and smuggler in western Tennessee are documented here. Young Belle found romance and adventure in Memphis early in the war years and, after the battle of Shiloh, nursed Confederate wounded in the city. Her active support of the Confederate cause expanded when Memphis was occupied and she began regular smuggling and intelligence operations. The book consists of several brief diaries covering 1863 and 1864 and letters received from a variety of correspondents. The diary entries mirror a despondent individual caught up in a depressive spiral and apparently dependent on drugs.

The work accelerates in tempo in 1864 as the author flees Memphis and settles on a plantation in Mississippi, her native state. The commentary on a number of Confederate officers of note forms interesting reading, and these occasionally quoted diaries appear here together for the first time. An occasional typographical error pops up, as with the misspellings of Frank C. Armstrong, Augustus L. Chetlain, and Tunnel Hill, Georgia, but these do not detract from the curious and entertaining charm of this work.

Catherine Ann Devereux Edmondston (1823–1875)

355

Edmondston, Catherine Ann Devereux. **"Journal of a Secesh Lady": The Diary of Catherine Ann Devereux Edmondston** (ed. Beth Gilbert Crabtree and James W. Patton, 850 pp., North Carolina Division of Archives and History, Raleigh, 1979)

Kate Edmondston's diary reveals the inner thoughts of the wife of a wealthy planter in North Carolina. Although it has drawn comparisons with Mary Chesnut's *Diary* (q.v.), this work is very different in character. The author draws few conclusions about the war raging on the distant fields—indeed, the author of this manuscript is primarily concerned with her own plantation and its immediate surroundings. She did have contacts with some prominent personalities of the Confederacy, such as Leonidas Polk and Josiah Turner, but the focus here is a reflection of Confederate plantation society. The work is thus as articulate as Chesnut's but substantially less intellectual and revealing.

Still, the diary makes good reading and delivers a wonderul chronicle of plantation life in North Carolina during the war. Voluminous, carefully edited and assembled, and complete in presentation, it will delight readers. The author fully expects male acquaintances to serve in the Confederate Army but sanctimoniously is relieved after her husband's commission is cancelled. The plantation lifestyle of walking, gardening, reading, and relaxing marches on throughout the exigencies of war. The author's comments on slaves suggest that she believes she knows what they need most; at the same time she shows little personal familiarity with any of them.

George Cary Eggleston (1839–1911)

356

Eggleston, George Cary. **A Rebel's Recollections** (260 pp., Hurd and Houghton, New York, 1875)

First serialized in the *Atlantic Monthly*, this collection established a landmark psychological portrait of Virginians as distinct from the rest of the Old South. The Hoosier teacher composed the series of articles with romantic themes in mind, painting a tribute to his beloved Virginia. The work suggests that the special education, social status, and grace of Virginians included a love for the Federal Union. Virginians had duty, honor, and other high ideals lacking in other parts of the Confederacy but were simply misguided. Thus, Eggleston sought to decriminalize Virginians and set them aside as distinct from the rest of the Confederacy in the eyes of the Northern public.

In terms of his autobiographical tone, the author is almost reluctant to offer any sort of strong feeling on many issues to support the thesis at hand. The "recollections" are thus impersonal, and his observations of many unusual characters as well as Confederate leaders are highly successful. Clear and abrupt in style, the work contains much of interest in addition to its rather famous agenda.

(Reprinted 1959, with an introduction by David Donald, 187 pp., Indiana University Press, Bloomington)

Arthur James Lyon Fremantle (1835–1901)

357

Fremantle, Arthur J. L. **Three Months in the Southern States: April–June, 1863** (316 pp., W. Blackwood and Sons, Edinburgh, 1863)

The young British officer's leave from the Coldstream Guards provided the opportunity to witness great moments of the Confederate war effort and paint vivid pictures of some of its greatest characters. Fremantle's unique treatment resulted from a desire by politicians to establish a bond with its greatest potential supporter, England. In addition, Fremantle enjoyed the confidence of Confederate officers because of his military reputation.

The author's journey from Texas, Louisiana, and Mississippi provides a superb backdrop for experiencing the Southern home front during the spring of 1863. His comments on such figures as Louis Octave Hébert, States Rights Gist, and Edmund Kirby Smith provide glances into the minds of important officers. The journey continues through Alabama, Tennessee, South Carolina, Virginia, and on to Gettysburg, where Fremantle experienced the battle sticking close to Longstreet and Sorrel. He made his way to New York in time to witness the draft riots before departing for England. After Gettysburg and the fall of Vicksburg, Fremantle still predicted a Southern victory. His outlook was certainly influenced greatly by the many notable figures he met and commented on. Some of the most valuable of these passages treat Davis, Benjamin, Lee, Polk, Hardee, Ewell, and Beauregard.

(Reprinted 1954, titled *The Fremantle Diary: Being the Journal of Lieutenant Colonel James Arthur Lyon Fremantle, Coldstream Guards, on His Three Months in the Southern States*, ed. Walter Lord, 304 pp., Little, Brown and Co., Boston; 1864 New York edition [309 pp., John Bradburn] reprinted 1991, with an introduction by Gary W. Gallagher, 329 pp., University of Nebraska Press, Lincoln; 1863 edition reprinted 1984, 316 pp., Time-Life Books, Alexandria, Va.)

Parthenia Antoinette Vardaman Hague (1838–?)

358

Hague, Parthenia Antoinette. **A Blockaded Family: Life in Southern Alabama during the Civil War** (176 pp., Houghton Mifflin Co., Boston, 1888)

This work offers a useful look at life on the home front in a remote section of the Confederacy. A schoolteacher,

Hague resided on a wealthy slaveholding plantation near Eufala, Alabama, and her views on a number of touchy subjects are predictable. Written long after the war, the author's memoir consists of a defensive and often wistful recollection of the destruction of her antebellum lifestyle. She makes no apology for participating in the slave economy or for outwardly racist views. Instead, she bitterly and occasionally sadly recalls the hardships caused by the Union blockade and the raids of Benjamin Grierson and James H. Wilson, events that worsened the already miserable state of affairs in rural Alabama during the war years.

The most valuable and interesting parts of these recollections lie in the clear impressions of how a Southern woman dealt with hardships in the home or on the plantation. The author's descriptions of experimentation with household chemistry, weaving, food supplies, and substitutions for lost common pleasures make a significant, if folksy, contribution. The work lacks an index.

(Reprinted 1991, with an introduction by Elizabeth Fox-Genovese, 176 pp., University of Nebraska Press, Lincoln; reprinted 1995, 176 pp., Applewood Books, Bedford, Mass.)

Constance Cary Harrison (1843–1920)

359

Harrison, Constance Cary. **Recollections Grave and Gay** (386 pp., Charles Scribner's Sons, New York, 1911)

Written long after the war by the wife of Jefferson Davis's personal secretary, Burton N. Harrison, this book echoes the earlier thesis of George Cary Eggleston, that Virginians were superior to other Southerners and that despite their sense of duty, honor, and devotion to the Union, they had been misled by politicians who fueled secession. Although most of the work covers the war years, the author also describes the Harrisons' postwar life in New York and elsewhere. Virtually all of the story relies on the author's memory, and many "conversations" appear, suggesting a lack of credibility on details in many places.

Still, Harrison's recollections provide a window into the chaos that ruled Richmond during the war. The remembrances of little things, the difficulty of obtaining supplies, the rugged determination of Confederate spirit, the grim electricity that pervaded the city when battles drew close, gives this volume great value. Many minor errors occur, as with the attribution of brigadier general grades to Turner Ashby and Francis S. Bartow and the misspellings of Mary Chesnut, Arthur J. L. Fremantle, Albin F. Schoepf, and Frank Vizetelly. The index is poor.

Emma Edwards Holmes (1838–1910)

360

Holmes, Emma Edwards. **The Diary of Miss Emma Holmes, 1861–1866** (ed. John F. Marszalek, 496 pp., Louisiana State University Press, Baton Rouge, 1979)

In the spring of 1861 Emma Holmes was a 22-year-old resident of Charleston, South Carolina. Filled with partisan patriotism, intelligent, and positioned to witness events that would be memorable in the war's history, Holmes left a valuable diary covering the period 13 February 1861–7 April 1866. The manuscript was carefully edited into an enthralling narrative that may be considered a companion to the more eloquent and authoritative diary of Mary Chesnut (*q.v.*). After the great fire of 1861, the Holmes family left Charleston for Camden, South Carolina. There Emma reported on a wide range of societal issues, events of daily life, often-exaggerated war news, and reflections on the Confederate cause.

The most valuable aspects of this work are the reflections Holmes cast on herself. "We, the free-born descendants of the Cavalier," she wrote, "to submit to the descendants of the witch burning Puritans, whose God is the Almighty Dollar. Never!" The diary proceeds to describe Holmes's tenure as a schoolteacher, an effort at defining her role in the crumbling world around her, and the approach of Sherman's army late in the war. This is by no means equal to Chesnut's diary, but it does offer reading of value.

(Reprinted 1994, 496 pp., Louisiana State University Press, Baton Rouge)

Charles Colcock Jones, Sr. (1804–1863)

361

Jones, Charles Colcock, Sr., Charles Colcock Jones, Jr., et al. **The Children of Pride: A True Story of Georgia and the Civil War** (ed. Robert Manson Myers, 1845 pp., Yale University Press, New Haven, 1973)

The Rev. Charles Colcock Jones, Sr., and his educated and insightful family lived a comfortable plantation life in Liberty County, Georgia, southeast of Savannah. Their voluminous letters cover the period 1854–1868, revealing much about antebellum plantation life, the oncoming secession crisis, the participation in the war of a wealthy family, and the earliest years of Reconstruction. The letters come from the pens of several relatives and friends who fought in the war and one, Charles Colcock Jones, Jr., who would become a historian of the war, producing contributions for the *Southern Historical Society Papers* (*q.v.*).

About 40 percent of the family letters date from antebellum days. In many instances these focus on the plantation's 3600 acres and 129 slaves. The editor shows that despite such material wealth the family was occasionally strapped for cash, and plantation life meant close ties to religion, frequent brushes with sickness, and hardships over poor weather. The religious dominance of thought colored the family's attitudes toward slavery and about catastrophes such as the deaths of Charles Jr.'s young wife and son.

Letters from the war period illuminate the epic of the Confederacy, from the excitement of the early months to the slow realization that the war would not be won. Charles Jr. stayed near Savannah to lead an artillery company, while another son, Joseph, served as a surgeon in the army. Their existence seems to spiral apart as Sherman's march targets the Savannah region. Those on the home front have already known poverty and now know refugee life and terror. Daughter Mary Jones Mallard describes much of the Atlanta campaign from a residence in that city.

The editor has made extensive annotations and notes wherever he believes some light can be cast on an aspect of the correspondence, and the index offers mind-boggling detail. However, the depth of the editor's knowledge sometimes gives out, permitting careless errors. For example, in the biographical section on page 1694, he refers to Jeb Stuart as the son-in-law of Philip St. George Cocke and goes on to describe details of Cocke and his relatives. He has mistaken two general officers with similar names serving on different sides. Despite such occasional sloppiness, the letters form a valuable and vivid picture of wartime life in Georgia. Several much inferior reprints are abridgments.

Joseph LeConte (1823–1901)

362

LeConte, Joseph. **'Ware Sherman: A Journal of Three Months' Personal Experience in the Last Days of the Confederacy** (146 pp., University of California Press, Berkeley, 1937)

This brief and entertaining journal recounts the experiences of civilians in the path of Sherman's final campaigns. Unclouded by partisanship and composed with keen intelligence, this work chronicles the efforts of LeConte, a chemist with the Confederate States Nitre and Mining Bureau, to remove family members and various supplies from the area endangered by Sherman's movements. As the Federal Army approached Savannah, LeConte traveled to Charleston and then to a point near Savannah but found the railroad cut.

After a perilous journey from Columbia to Augusta, Milledgeville, Macon, Albany, and Doctortown (near his relatives), the chemist retrieved the relatives and returned northward. The story is peppered with interesting observations. LeConte reached Columbia immediately before Sherman's army and had to flee again. The editing is well done, and this brief but enticing story is a gem.

A related title of lesser interest is Emma LeConte's *When the World Ended: The Diary of Emma LeConte* (ed. Earl Schenck Miers, 124 pp., Oxford University Press, New York, 1957; reprinted 1987, with a foreword by Anne Firor Scott, 124 pp., University of Nebraska Press, Lincoln).

Cornelia Peake McDonald (1822–1909)

363

McDonald, Cornelia Peake. **A Diary with Reminiscences of the War and Refugee Life in the Shenandoah Valley, 1860–1865** (ed. Hunter McDonald, 540 pp., Cullom and Ghertner Co., Nashville, 1935)

McDonald delivers a diary account of the war as seen from her home in Winchester, Virginia. The work was expanded and written 10 years after the war (but not published until 1935), giving it a fullness it previously lacked, and apparently not diminishing the truthfulness of what it contains. Living in one of the most frequently occupied and counteroccupied towns of the war allowed this woman to witness much of significance. Her observation of Confederate and Union forces continued until the summer of 1863, when she became a refugee and lived in several Virginia towns with relatives and friends. One such location, Lexington, allowed her in 1864 to see David Hunter's burning of the Virginia Military Institute. The record of McDonald's experience is engaging, contains significant eyewitness observations, and stands as a fine memoir. Some errors of spelling occur, as with the names of Francis Stebbins Bartow, Barnard E. Bee, Gustave P. Cluseret, John C. Frémont, Maxcy Gregg, and William S. Rosecrans.

(Abridged edition 1992, titled *A Woman's Civil War: A Diary, with Reminiscences of the War, from March 1862*, ed. Minrose C. Gwin, 303 pp., University of Wisconsin Press, Madison)

Samuel Alexander Mudd (1833–1883)

364

Mudd, Samuel A. **The Life of Dr. Samuel A. Mudd, Containing His Letters from Fort Jefferson, Dry Tortugas Island, Where He Was Imprisoned Four Years for Alleged Complicity in the Assassination of Abraham Lincoln: With Statements of Mrs. Samuel A. Mudd, Dr. Samuel A. Mudd, and Edward Spangler Regarding the Assassination: Also "Diary" of John Wilkes Booth** (ed. Nettie Mudd, 326 pp., Neale Publishing Co., New York, 1906)

Presenting the life story of the physician caught in aiding the Lincoln conspirators, this book is a historical footnote that nonetheless unfolds an interesting tale. In addition to the brief background material on Mudd, there is a long, labored discussion of the Lincoln murder and the conspirators.

The work's chief thesis is that Mudd was not guilty of knowingly aiding President Lincoln's murderers. Whether or not that was true (see the works by Hanchett [*q.v.*] and Bryan), many documents appear in this work along with legal discussions of Mudd's case. The book's most absorbing parts are letters written from Fort Jefferson, which provide engrossing minutiae. The work lacks an index.

(Reprinted 1975, with additional material on Mudd's genealogy and related subjects, 383 pp., Continental Book Co., Linden, Tenn.)

Phoebe Yates Pember (1823–1913)

365

Pember, Phoebe Yates. **A Southern Woman's Story** (192 pp., G. W. Carleton and Co., New York, 1879)

This volume contains potent observations of the Confederacy's largest hospital (indeed, at the time, the world's largest hospital) from a woman of unusual background and character. Born in Charleston, the author moved to Savannah in the 1850s and married Thomas Pember, who subsequently died. The relatively young widow was left with a strong sense of mission. In 1862 her relatives sought refuge in Marietta, Georgia, but Pember found the surroundings unhappy ones. In 1862, through friendships she had forged in high places, Pember moved to Richmond and became chief matron of Hospital No. 2 at Chimborazo, one of five hospitals that formed the Confederacy's great camp of wounded.

The narrative, composed from memory between 1865 and 1879, has much of value on hospital life, social aspects of Richmond, the qualities of common folk of the South, scarcity of goods, and inflation. The story is related with a peculiar humor. The narrative is engaging but includes a number of exact "conversations" that likely could not have been recalled with such high precision. The author recounts the great skill of many nurses and surgeons, the red tape that often hindered hospital operations, incompetence of various officials, and struggles over control of the supplies of whiskey. This last battle became a major political fight, others not appreciating the strict control of such a commodity by a woman. A number of personalities are mentioned, including Jefferson Davis, Jeremy F. Gilmer, Alexander R. Lawton, and George Wythe Randolph.

(Reprinted 1959, titled *A Southern Woman's Story: Life in Confederate Richmond*, ed. Bell I. Wiley, 199 pp., McCowat-Mercer Press, Jackson, Tenn., with nine wartime letters written from Pember to her sister Eugenia and Mrs. Jeremy F. Gilmer, a close friend in Charleston)

Sarah Ann Brock Putnam (1828–1911)

366

Putnam, Sallie Brock. **Richmond during the War: Four Years of Personal Observation** (389 pp., G. W. Carleton and Co., New York, 1867)

This book stands out among civilian narratives of wartime life in a Confederate city. Consisting of both a narrative concentrating on the military fortunes of the Confederacy and a detailed commentary on the social aspects of Richmond, the work contributes valuable insight into wartime life in the capital city. Putnam was in her 30s during the war and wrote about military aspects with a fair degree of clarity and understanding. The rigors of everyday life are more detailed, of course, and provide a measuring rod on the difficulty of Confederate existence. Based on Putnam's diaries and notes made during the war, the book was completed just months after Lee's surrender, giving it a freshness and lack of embellishment that is quite valuable.

Not only do hopeful summations of the news from the front persist throughout the work, but also incidents involving refugees, the sick and wounded, prisoners, the difficulty of obtaining basic supplies, and incidents in the city. Particularly enriching sections treat the period of the Peninsular campaign and the final weeks of the war. The work lacks an index.

(Reprinted 1983, 389 pp., Time-Life Books, Alexandria, Va.)

FitzGerald Ross (1825–?)

367

Ross, FitzGerald. **A Visit to the Cities and Camps of the Confederate States** (300 pp., W. Blackwood and Sons, Edinburgh, 1865)

An experienced cavalry officer of the Austrian Army, Ross traveled through the South between June 1863 and April 1864, making a wide range of detailed observations. The author was certainly strongly drawn to the Southern cause and his observations are therefore partial, yet taken in that context they form a valuable record of a foreigner's impression of the experiment that was the Confederacy. The material first appeared in *Blackwood's Magazine*.

The most alluring part of the work occurs as Ross observes the Gettysburg campaign in its early days and describes Southern soldiers and their march northward as well as Northern civilians in the wake of the invading army. After the campaign, Ross sought adventures in cities throughout the Southeast, and his comments are less valuable from a military standpoint but illuminating on conditions in the larger populated areas of the South. The narrative gains force as Ross describes the residue from the battle of Chickamauga and the conditions around Chattanooga in the autumn of 1863.

(Reprinted 1958, ed. Richard Barksdale Harwell, 262 pp., University of Illinois Press, Urbana, with notes drawing useful comparsions with the similar narrative by Fremantle [q.v.]; these two works form an outstanding pair)

Edmund Ruffin (1794–1865)

368

Ruffin, Edmund. **The Diary of Edmund Ruffin** (ed. William K. Scarborough, 3 vols., 2266 pp., Louisiana State University Press, Baton Rouge, 1972–1989)

This diary imparts an exhaustively detailed look into the mind of one of the South's great fire-eating civilians. The three bulky volumes cover the coming of the war (*Toward Independence*, October 1856–April 1861), the war's first two years (*The Years of Hope*, April 1861–June 1863), and the final two years of war (*A Dream Shattered*, June 1863–June 1865). The editor's presentation of Ruffin's voluminous scratchings and his meticulous annotations make the work exceedingly valuable to students of South Carolina's role in the war crisis and to understanding the thinking of the most rabid secessionists.

Despite Ruffin's violent prosecession philosophy, volume 1 of his diary somewhat surprisingly reveals him as a literate and reflective man. Evidently hoping to see a Southern Nation as quickly as possible, Ruffin greeted every action that helped to precipitate war with the greatest possible joy. He triumphed over Harpers Ferry and traveled to witness the hanging of John Brown. Ruffin later participated in the bombardment of Sumter.

The second volume outlines Ruffin's return to Virginia and his exploration of the war as it erupted about him. His extremist views are both fascinating and at times bizarre; occasionally he recorded views on strategy with insight. The first event to shock Ruffin appears to have been the fall of New Orleans, a disaster Ruffin believed "most momentous— and still worse consequences must follow." Yet illusions remained. The diary's author believed slavery would live on, even after the shocking realization that some of his own slaves had fled toward freedom.

The final volume adds a growing sense of despair to the record of Ruffin's life. Indeed, both the diary itself and the editor's excellent annotations paint a vivid portrait of self-delusion, of an old man clinging to the past even after he witnessed it unraveling around him.

Sarah Katherine Holmes Stone (1841–1907)

369

Stone, Sarah Katherine Holmes. **Brokenburn: The Journal of Kate Stone, 1861–1868** (ed. John Q. Anderson, 400 pp., Louisiana State University Press, Baton Rouge, 1955)

This extensive diary records the war impressions of an intelligent young woman on a cotton plantation in northeast Louisiana. Brokenburn was a 1260-acre plantation with about 150 slaves. Twenty years old when the war broke out, Kate Stone began her journal in May 1861 and carried it through September 1868, providing not only wartime details of events near Vicksburg but also glimpses of Reconstruction Mississippi. The diarist's scope on the war mirrors the view of many on the home front. In the first year of war she displayed unbridled optimism and confidence in the Southern war effort. When the battlefields moved closer to home, however, she reflected a strong hatred of anything Yankee and deliberated in her pages on the evil gunboats that restricted travel and communication with her brothers in the Confederate army. She professed outrage at P. G. T. Beauregard's order to destroy the cotton remaining at Brokenburn so the Yanks would not capture it.

Tension rose as Federal forces moved closer to Vicksburg

in the summer of 1862 and heightened as the Union movement proceeded and ultimately failed to produce a siege. At the new year, however, Grant's deployment of Federal forces in what became the Vicksburg campaign created a swarm of foraging parties that raided, among other places, Stone's Brokenburn. The family fled to Texas in the summer of 1863.

Primitive life there did not play well with the Stones. They lived in Texas through the end of the war, hearing as many rumors as facts. The diary's reflections on daily life leave a valuable record.

(Reprinted 1995, with an introduction by Drew Gilpin Faust, 400 pp., Louisiana State University Press, Baton Rouge)

UNION BIOGRAPHIES, MEMOIRS, AND LETTERS

POLITICIANS

Charles Francis Adams, Sr. (1807–1886)

370

Adams, Charles Francis, Charles Francis Adams, Jr., and Henry Brooks Adams. **A Cycle of Adams Letters, 1861–1865** (ed. Worthington Chauncey Ford, 2 vols., 579 pp., Houghton Mifflin Co., Boston, 1920)

This collection captures highlights of the correspondence of three Adamses during the war years. The interplay between Minister Adams, his son and private secretary, and cavalry officer Adams allows a penetrating look at the role of Britain during the war and how the military perceived its importance.

The enlightened viewpoints of the writers make the Adams letters revealing, much more so than most wartime correspondence. The volumes' first letter finds Charles Jr. on garrison duty at Fort Warren in Boston Harbor in May 1861, writing his mother revelations on the uncomfortable life of a soldier. The work concludes with the same writer's letter of 2 May 1865 to his brother J. Q. Adams, relating his experiences after being arrested for disobeying orders and his subsequent release by Maj. Gen. Ord. In between lie many tidbits worthy of close investigation.

371

Duberman, Martin B. **Charles Francis Adams, 1807–1886** (525 pp., Houghton Mifflin Co., Boston, 1961)

While many biographers sympathize with their subjects, painting an overly rosy picture of their abilities and accomplishments, the reverse is true in Duberman's portrait of Charles Francis Adams. In thorough and scholarly fashion, the author describes Adams's privileged youth and rise to his own power. The biographer's analysis of Adams's major diplomatic contributions during the war is well executed and meticulously documented.

Unfortunately, Duberman highlights the stereotypical and exaggerated view of Adams as cold, austere, and unfeeling, and this colors much of the story. Certainly Adams was reserved, formal, quietly intellectual, and conservative, but to characterize him as possessing "little charm or magnetism" is unduly severe. So too is it harsh to suppose that Adams's achievements came from unrelentingly tiresome devotion and single-minded purpose rather than vision, intellect, and ability. These notions are cast asunder by an examination of Adams's handling of several wartime incidents, most notably that of the *Trent* affair.

John Albion Andrew (1818–1866)

372

Pearson, Henry G. **The Life of John A. Andrew, Governor of Massachusetts** (2 vols., 682 pp., Houghton Mifflin Co., Boston, 1904)

Written with authority and a heavy reliance on Andrew's official papers and speeches, this work carries the tone of a doctrine but occasionally moments of humor surface. The picture of Andrew's life as governor explains why he died shortly after the war: his exhaustive schedule, numerous state affairs, and the multitudinous complexities of vigorously supporting the Lincoln administration's war policy were certainly grave and daunting responsibilities. Several stories weave through the narration of official policy and acts, as with the raising of the 54th Massachusetts Infantry, the first Northern-trained black regiment, Andrew's advice and communications with the regiment's colonel, Robert Gould Shaw, and one of the governor's proudest moments in office, seeing off the 54th for the South Carolina shore.

The ponderous reflection on Andrew's record is at times too serious and overwrought by minutiae. A great deal of attention focuses on the governor's squabbles with Benjamin F. Butler and Edwin M. Stanton. The work admirably addresses the great questions of Massachusetts's role in prosecuting the war and contains a significant summary of Andrew's early thoughts on Reconstruction. Not a biography in a modern sense, the work nonetheless offers much of value on one of the busiest Northern war governors.

Edward Bates (1793–1869)

373

Bates, Edward. **The Diary of Edward Bates, 1859–1866** (ed. Howard K. Beale, 685 pp., U.S. Government Printing Office, Washington, 1933)

Published as volume four of the *Annual Report of the American Historical Association for 1930*, this work is a compilation of intermittent notes that does not form a smooth and continuous narrative but comments on developments in brief bursts. This diary by Lincoln's attorney general is valuable for reflections on the secession crisis politics of Washington, numerous legal issues, the writer's evaluations of Lincoln, posturing on administration policies, and affairs relating to Missouri and Reconstruction.

The editor adds much of value, with lengthy, encyclopedic comments on nearly every page. Interpretation thus surfaces relating to Bates's political background and his attitudes toward a multitude of problems. The work shows that Lincoln occasionally accepted the suggestions of his attorney general and that Bates offered sound opinions as well as poorly judged advice. An appendix contains six letters by Bates published in the *Missouri Democrat* in 1865.

(Reprinted 1971, 685 pp., Da Capo Press, New York)

374

Cain, Marvin R. **Lincoln's Attorney General: Edward Bates of Missouri** (361 pp., University of Missouri Press, Columbia, 1965)

Although he lacked importance as a Lincoln advisor and had few qualities to endear him to others in the wartime capital, Edward Bates emerges as a significant Northern figure because of his revealing diary (*q.v.*). Therefore, it is important to gain a significant understanding of this elderly member of Washington's political high command.

Cain draws on a variety of sources to provide a full biography of Bates. Based on many of his subject's papers, the narrative displays Bates's frequent inconsistencies that often limited his associations in Washington. The author details Bates's opposition to emancipation and to the creation of West Virginia, as well as his support of the suspension of the writ of habeas corpus and of the Southern blockades. The work is scholarly and adequately executed.

John Bigelow (1817–1911)

375

Bigelow, John. **Retrospections of an Active Life** (5 vols., 2967 pp., Baker and Taylor Co., New York, 1909–1913)

This work contains the autobiographical musings of the man who served as consul at Paris and minister to the court of Napoleon III. It covers the author's life in New York from 1835 to 1861, when he went to Paris, and his tenure as an observer and participant in European attitudes toward the American war, particularly those in France. As a journalist, the author lacked the typical qualifications as a diplomat, but he drew the assignment as one who could be counted as a loyalist and advisor to William Henry Seward.

The portion of this work that bears on Civil War history relates to France's reaction to the war, Bigelow's involvement in mediation between the nations, and the French experiment in Mexico. The work conveys many details of the French affairs of state and includes large numbers of documents but unfortunately presents little of value relating to

Louis Napoleon's venture in Mexico. The collapse of the Mexican experiment and Napoleon's hesitancy to recognize the Confederacy unless signal victories were achieved (like capturing Washington) made French intervention a near impossibility. Despite the less than outstanding evaluation of this in Bigelow's work, significant sketches of many of the personalites emerge, including Lincoln, Seward, Louis Napoleon, Palmerston, Charles Sumner, and William Howard Russell.

James Buchanan (1791–1868)

376

Klein, Philip Shriver. **President James Buchanan: A Biography** (506 pp., Pennsylvania State University Press, University Park, 1962)

This offers a detailed and full rendering of the president who did nothing to avert civil war. The great range of Buchanan's career dictates a study that culminates with the subject's tenure in the White House, an unhappy period clouded by indecision that nearly makes the previous years as representative, senator, and secretary of state more enlightening. Nevertheless, the present study is skillfully produced and adds much to the understanding of this much scorned leader.

About 25 percent of the book covers Buchanan's presidential term. The chief fault of this study may be an oversympathetic tone that paints its subject as a victim of the times. Klein does not fault Buchanan's treatment of the impending crisis but compassionately describes his efforts to maintain a fragile administration composed in large part of Southern politicians. The author demonstrates that his subject lacked the skills necessary for greatness in leadership. One comes away from this book thinking that even if Buchanan were extremely talented in understanding people, his stuffy and humorless personality still would have limited his effectiveness.

Simon Cameron (1799–1889)

377

Bradley, Erwin S. **Simon Cameron, Lincoln's Secretary of War: A Political Biography** (451 pp., University of Pennsylvania Press, Philadelphia, 1966)

Bradley examines the Pennsylvania politician who held brief tenure in Lincoln's cabinet. This unusual work focuses almost exclusively on Cameron's political life without analyzing the man himself. Having sifted through letters and manuscript sources, the author rather harshly assesses his subject—in agreement with previous studies—despite verging on somewhat revisionistic conclusions about his perplexing protagonist.

Cameron presents biographers with a difficult and not very rewarding job. Not only was he an incompetent war secretary under Lincoln but also a U.S. senator, minister to Russia, and U.S. senator again. The problem is that in a varied political career often in influential positions, he did little of consequence. Rather than analzying his wartime role in the War Department in depth and offering a confident analysis of Cameron, this biography reflects its subject in that it concludes little about many small matters. However, it remains the best study available on Cameron.

Salmon Portland Chase (1808–1873)

378

Chase, Salmon P. **The Salmon P. Chase Papers.** Vol. 1: **Journals, 1829–1872** (ed. John Niven, 789 pp., Kent State University Press, Kent, 1993)

This is the first of a planned series presenting the works of Chase. The impressively researched first volume makes a great cache of Chase material widely available and will add insight to his actions, particularly in the less-studied antebellum days. The 19 journals cover the period from January 1829 through 1872, a few months before Chase's death. Necessarily, then, they reflect on such a vast canvas of time that one can glean interesting minutiae relating to the administration of John Quincy Adams or read about the troubles of the Grant presidency. Coverage of the Civil War years begins in December 1861 and extends through more than 40 percent of the book.

Thus, a great deal of interest appears relating to Chase's cabinet participation, his dealings with Lincoln, Washington society during the war, the controversial activities of Chase's daughter Kate, and Chase's political aspirations and eventual appointment as chief justice. The material is terribly important as Chase is, of course, candid and highly literate and reflective. A few minor errors appear, as with reporting Jefferson Davis's capture at "Irwindale, Georgia" and the misspelling of Theodore Fitz Randolph. This work is a much-needed and extremely valuable addition to the literature. The second volume, *The Salmon P. Chase Papers: Vol. 2, Correspondence, 1823–1857* (489 pp., Kent State University Press, Kent, 1995) provides an enlightening glimpse into

Chase's legal and private activities as the war clouds approach. The work supersedes several earlier editions, most notably *Inside Lincoln's Cabinet: The Civil War Diaries of Salmon P. Chase,* by Salmon P. Chase (ed. David H. Donald, 342 pp., Longmans, Green, New York, 1954), and an edition published in 1903 in the *Annual Report of the American Historical Association for the Year 1902* (vol. 2, 527 pp., U.S. Government Printing Office, Washington; reprinted 1971, 527 pp., Da Capo Press, New York).

379

Niven, John. **Salmon P. Chase: A Biography** (546 pp., Oxford University Press, New York, 1995)

Niven presents the most balanced and analytical account of Chase's full life both in politics and with his family. Although the author treats his subject sympathetically—at times too sympathetically—the portrait that emerges here provides a clear view into the mind and activities of one of the key players in the Union high command. The work is a full biography that carefully and with great documentation inspects Chase's early life. Despite this, Niven manages to devote nearly 40 percent of the book to the Civil War era, the period in which Chase's presidential ambitions were quelled and his valuable financial contributions to the war effort blossomed. As the author develops a portrait of Chase, he provides readers with a penetrating view of his subject's difficult youth, profound religious beliefs, abolition views, and almost limitless ambition.

The discussion of Chase's cabinet activities is superb, providing a view of the war and its politics from an important and often forgotten viewpoint. The book adeptly examines Chase's career as chief justice, vividly balancing it against Chase's lust for power, and thus delivers a full, fresh picture of an important Civil War figure. There are a few errors, such as the pesky misspellings of David K. Cartter and Irvin McDowell.

Schuyler Colfax (1823–1885)

380

Smith, Willard H. **Schuyler Colfax: The Changing Fortunes of a Political Idol** (475 pp., Indiana Historical Bureau, Indianapolis, 1952)

Smith presents the best story to date of a political figure who deserves greater recognition for his Civil War service in the U.S. House than he has received. The outgrowth of a doctoral dissertation, this scholarly, balanced work is based on manuscripts, governmental repositories, and newspaper accounts. It is a full biography that emphasizes the subject's role as a longtime member of the House, elected from St. Joseph County, Indiana. The focus also illuminates Colfax's close relationship with Lincoln, Lincoln's consideration of Colfax as a possible cabinet member, and Colfax's six year tenure as Speaker of the House, which began in December 1863. Further, the work examines Colfax's vice presidency under Grant and the latter's dissatisfaction with him.

This is a capable and sometimes enlightening biography. The author adequately treats the early years of Colfax and his evolution through journalism and into politics. The analysis of political voting and the stance taken by Colfax on certain issues during the war is clearly presented, and the book's outstanding chapter deals with Colfax's role in the Credit Mobilier scandal. Smith fairly estimates Colfax's involvement in the scandal and defensiveness when accused of wrongdoing and asks for forgiveness on behalf of his subject.

John Jordan Crittenden (1787–1863)

381

Kirwan, Albert D. **John J. Crittenden: The Struggle for the Union** (514 pp., University Press of Kentucky, Lexington, 1962)

Crittenden's political activities in Kentucky included service in the legislature and as secretary of state and governor. On the national scene, Crittenden acted as U.S. senator, U.S. district attorney, and as attorney general for William Henry Harrison and later Millard Fillmore. He rose to the brink of national influence as civil war approached, but as events unfolded his Crittenden Compromise was voted down and the Kentucky lawyer fell away from greatness, dying less than three years later. Crittenden's influential family and its standing in Kentucky politics promises intrigue, as two sons became Civil War general officers, one Union and the other Confederate.

Kirwan believes his subject inherited the legacy of fellow Kentuckian Henry Clay and worked under the latter's doctrine to avert war. He believes that the Republicans in power erred by not fully supporting the Crittenden Compromise. The proposition suggested restoring the old line of the Missouri Compromise, forbidding the federal government from abolishing slavery, prohibiting abolition in the District of Columbia, and preventing the government from interfering with slave trading.

Such a plan could not have been acceptable to the Republicans in 1860, as the author suggests. Lincoln would not have preserved the Union at the expense of everything he stood for. The author has captured what Crittenden represented but does not fully interpret those qualities for his readers. Thus, we have a useful biography of the man and his times, but judgments and characterizations of others in the story are not balanced enough to be fair.

Charles Anderson Dana (1819–1897)

382

Dana, Charles A. **Recollections of the Civil War: With the Leaders at Washington and in the Field in the Sixties** (296 pp., D. Appleton and Co., New York, 1898)

Dana's memoir contains the war record of the journalist who turned militarist by serving as assistant secretary of war and acting as eyes and ears for the War Department as U. S. Grant remained in the field. The author acted as confidential reporter for Edwin M. Stanton in the period from Shiloh to Vicksburg and afterward in his official capacity. Although the book was composed long after the war, it is based on definitive sources and a sound memory and serves as an eyewitness record of many exciting moments in the field. Dana stayed at army headquarters, knew of all high-level decisions and plans, made tours of inspection, and sat in on councils of war. Reflective, though not always fair, portraits of Stanton, Grant, Rosecrans, Sherman, and others emerge from this work, which may have been ghostwritten by the journalist Ida M. Tarbell based on Dana's notes.

The dispatches sent by Dana are meticulous and literary in composition and content. He sometimes judged too harshly, as when at Chattanooga he telegraphed Washington that Chickamauga had been a monstrous disaster, thus fanning the flames of panic before hearing about Thomas's stand. But by and large Dana was reflective, careful, loyal to Washington but watchful of Grant, and performed his duty admirably. The present work offers much of great value. Many of Dana's dispatches appear in the *Rebellion Record* (*q.v.*).

(Reprinted 1963, with an introduction by Paul M. Angle, 255 pp., Collier Books, New York)

383

Wilson, James Harrison. **The Life of Charles A. Dana** (544 pp., Harper and Bros., New York, 1907)

The author provides a complementary study to Dana's *Recollections of the Civil War* (*q.v.*). Unlike the autobiography, this work provides a full analysis of Dana's deeds but conveys little about his personality or personal life. The whole life appears here, from Dana's early interest in literature, hustling through Harvard, hard work at Brook Farm, and studious work on editing despite his poor eyesight. The nearly 200 pages covering the war years are the most enthralling, however, and chronicle the unfolding importance of Dana to the Union war effort.

Based in part on papers loaned to Wilson by Dana's family, the work nicely shows the complex relationship Dana developed with Edwin M. Stanton. It portrays Dana's usefulness as the eyes of the War Department in the field, accompanying Maj. Gen. Grant. Evidence of Dana's value in building the credibility of the Republican party is provided, although after his falling out with Grant in 1869, Dana abandoned the party. Material relating to the newspaper business in midcentury America is also included, as are important reflections on Dana's old boss, Horace Greeley.

Alfred Ely (1815–1892)

384

Ely, Alfred. **Journal of Alfred Ely, a Prisoner of War in Richmond** (ed. Charles Lanman, 359 pp., D. Appleton and Co., New York, 1862)

Ely's journal preserves the prison experience of a New York congressman who was captured at First Bull Run and held captive in the Confederate capital city. To report on the training and efficiency of Federal troops, Ely accompanied the 13th New York Infantry to Bull Run and found himself separated from his party. His carriage broke down, forcing him to hide in the woods, but after a short time he surrendered to a Confederate captain. He was subsequently taken to Manassas and on to Richmond, where he became one of the war's first prisoners. Ely was not released as were most civilian captives. The congressman kept a journal during his captivity that offers insight into the prison conditions in Richmond and the early days of the Confederate government, as well as reflections on fellow prisoners.

With the other Bull Run prisoners, Ely found himself in Liggon's Tobacco Warehouse in the Rocketts section of the city, designated C.S.A. Prison No. 1. The author received many visitors from the city who were interested in interviewing him, including John Letcher, John H. Winder, John C. Breckinridge, John H. Reagan, and William Preston. Ely commented daily on such visitors, on prison life, and on many newspaper reports from the Richmond dailies he received. A fellow civilian prisoner who fell ill, Calvin Huson, was transferred to the house of Mrs. John Van Lew, a wealthy widow, who looked after Yankees. After Huson died in October 1861, Ely was allowed to visit Mrs. Van Lew and her daughter, Elizabeth Van Lew. Other prisoner friends of Ely's included Michael Corcoran, William Raymond Lee, and Paul J. Revere. On Christmas Day 1861 Ely was exchanged for Charles J. Faulkner, a former representative from Virginia who had been arrested in Washington. An appendix lists a prisoner-of-war roster compiled by Ely containing the names of 124 officers and about 2700 enlisted men and civilians.

William Pitt Fessenden (1806–1869)

385

Fessenden, Francis. **Life and Public Services of William Pitt Fessenden, United States Senator from Maine, 1854–1864: Secretary of the Treasury, 1864–1865: United States Senator from Maine, 1865–1869** (2 vols., 741 pp., Houghton Mifflin, Boston, 1907)

This study is valuable as an historical curiosity for its discussion of the war years and the subject's controversial role in the Johnson and Grant administrations. Composed by Fessenden's son, who rose to major general of volunteers, the work offers a reflection on the politician-father along with numerous letters, papers, and speeches. Written with compassion and clear insight into the characters and the times, the volumes contain something of value on Fessenden's tenure in the Civil War Senate and his work as treasury secretary.

The narrative may show that Fessenden was somewhat out of place as a conventional, statesmanlike thinker in an arena dominated by radicals. Many enlightening documents bear on Fessenden's reluctance to impose suffrage for blacks on the former rebellious states. It contains significant coverage of Fessenden's reluctance to convict Andrew Johnson, one of several stances that brought him severe criticism from the radicals. While it may not restore Fessenden's image in the eyes of many, the work helps to define the man in stark terms.

(Reprinted 1970, 2 vols., 741 pp., Da Capo Press, New York)

386

Jellison, Charles A. **Fessenden of Maine: Civil War Senator** (294 pp., Syracuse University Press, Syracuse, 1962)

Jellison incorporates a solidly researched, modern biography of Fessenden. The author contends that Fessenden's reserved, austere, and sometimes confusing personality stemmed from the fact that he was born out of wedlock, which "streaked across his soul" throughout his life. Whether or not such feelings of inadequacy tainted Fessenden's public activities, the author delivers a charming and well-written description of Fessenden's Civil War senatorial activities, his brief tenure as Lincoln's secretary of the treasury, and his activities before and after.

In contrast to previous studies, Jellison contends that Fessenden was not a radical Republican but more of a moderate and that Lincoln himself declared Fessenden a radical devoid of the "fretfulness" of many radicals. The author describes Fessenden's activities in wartime Washington and postwar involvement as chair of the Senate Committee on Reconstruction. He outlines the senator's position as one of the seven who would not vote to impeach President Johnson. The details are so clear that perhaps their context in the bigger picture is clouded, and we are left wondering, in some fundamental ways, just what kind of a difference Fessenden made in the end.

Benjamin Brown French (1800–1870)

387

French, Benjamin Brown. **Witness to the Young Republic: A Yankee's Journal, 1828–1870** (ed. Donald B. Cole and John J. McDonough, 675 pp., University Press of New England, Hanover, 1989)

The New Hampshire politician worked as a clerk in the U.S. House of Representatives from 1833 to 1847 and thereafter served as commissioner of public buildings in Washington during periods of the 1850s and 1860s. This published work contains about one-third of Brown's voluminous journal, with 24 percent covering the Civil War years. During this time French enjoyed the confidence of many Washingtonian politicians and officers, and so his narrative holds interesting accounts of personalities and events. An old-line Democrat, French became a Republican in 1856. The author's commentary on such figures as Abraham and Mary Todd Lincoln, Ulysses Grant, and Franklin Pierce will interest all readers.

Gustavus Vasa Fox (1821–1883)

388

Fox, Gustavus Vasa. **Confidential Correspondence of Gustavus Vasa Fox, Assistant Secretary of the Navy, 1861–1865** (ed. Robert Means Thompson and Richard Wainwright, 2 vols., 932 pp., Naval History Society, Washington, 1918)

This work of signal importance consists of 10 large sections that offer correspondence between Fox and a large number of naval personnel, particularly collections of interchanges with Samuel F. Du Pont, Louis M. Goldsborough, David G. Farragut, Charles Henry Davis, David Dixon Porter, and S. P. Lee. An introductory chapter details Fox's efforts to discover the situation concerning Fort Sumter in the first days of crisis, and supplementary chapters in each volume contain miscellaneous correspondence.

In some cases these volumes eclipse the value of the *O.R.N.* (*q.v.*), in that the letters herein were written with strict secrecy in mind and are therefore completely candid. The letters cover the period 1861–1864, and highlights concentrate on Du Pont's Port Royal expedition, Goldsborough's activities in North Carolina, Farragut's opening of the lower Mississippi, and Foote's actions in the upper Mississippi. The letters are not annotated, complicating certain aspects of their use by researchers, but they remain a tremendously important primary source. Unfortunately, this worthwhile book lacks an index.

(Reprinted 1972, 2 vols., 932 pp., Books for Libraries, Freeport, N.Y.)

James Harlan (1820–1899)

389

Brigham, Johnson. **James Harlan** (398 pp., State Historical Society of Iowa, Iowa City, 1913)

Highly sympathetic toward Harlan, this work contains a useful set of materials drawn from the Harlan papers as well as other manuscript collections, chiefly from Iowa. Harlan's election to the U.S. Senate in 1855 cast him in a role as a moderate, but by the time of his reelection in 1861 Harlan leaned toward the radical Republicans on most issues. A staunch supporter of the Lincoln administration, Harlan befriended the president and ultimately became the administration's secretary of the interior. The study examines these activities with satisfying detail, even if it fails to examine Harlan critically.

The work's discussion of the Homestead Act of 1862 and

Harlan's role in it is worthwhile, as is the illumination of Harlan's attitudes and activities toward the prosecution of the war. The expansion of the Union Pacific Railroad and postwar land speculation are described, but again with little critical analysis from the author. The work is adequate, showing the basics of this politician's influence and contribution to the politics of Washington in the Civil War era.

John Milton Hay (1838–1905)

390

Hay, John. **Lincoln and the Civil War in the Diaries and Letters of John Hay** (ed. Tyler Dennett, 348 pp., Dodd, Mead and Co., New York, 1939)

Although much of this material appears in Nicolay and Hay's *Abraham Lincoln: A History* (*q.v.*), the Hay diary is in itself a significant work that should be read straight through by students of the war.

As the president's assistant secretary, young Hay had the opportunity to observe Lincoln almost daily throughout the entire war. Fortunately, Hay possessed an astute and analytical mind and generally recorded events and interpretations with great objectivity. Hay's letters also offer valuable insights into the Lincoln White House and the Northern political and military operations throughout most of the war's crucial periods. Several gaps in coverage exist, but overall the work stands as a significant primary resource for understanding Lincoln as politician and commander-in-chief.

(Reprinted 1972, 348 pp., Greenwood Press, Westport; reprinted 1988, 348 pp., Da Capo Press, New York)

Andrew Johnson (1808–1875)

391

Johnson, Andrew. **The Papers of Andrew Johnson** (ed. LeRoy P. Graf, Ralph W. Haskins, and Paul H. Bergeron, 10 vols. to date, 7781 pp., University of Tennessee Press, Knoxville, 1967–   )

The coverage thus far consists of the following: volume 1 (1822–1851), volume 2 (1852–1857), volume 3 (1858–1860), volume 4 (1860–1861), volume 5 (1861–1862), volume 6 (1862–1864), volume 7 (1864–1865), volume 8 (May–August 1865), volume 9 (September 1865–January 1866), and volume 10 (February–July 1866). Each volume contains an introduction and overview, the papers themselves, and a summary of Johnson's career for the period covered. The work is skillful-

ly edited and ably documented, providing a basic source work for an important wartime general officer, military governor of Tennessee, and accidental president.

The greatest drawback of the Johnson set relative to the other scholarly volumes of collected works such as those of Lincoln (*q.v.*), Davis (*q.v.*), and Grant (*q.v.*) is the slim volume of papers actually created by Johnson. The collected works of Johnson are slender either because the man created little correspondence (he found writing physically painful and was not notably literate) or because much of that produced has been scattered and lost. Whatever the problems, this small amount of correspondence caused the editors to include a great deal of material written to Johnson rather than by him. They have also scanned and excerpted newspaper accounts of Johnson speeches from the *Congressional Globe* and other secondary sources. The result is a highly useful work, but the tiny fraction of primary Johnson letters produces the feeling of viewing Johnson from afar as one pages through the collection.

Volume 6 sheds some light on Johnson's career as military governor of Tennessee. Twenty percent of the papers in this volume are by Johnson, the rest sent to him or consisting of newspaper reports of his speeches. The papers and the volume's introduction help explain just how Johnson interacted with Washington and how such an apparently unlikely figure received the nod as a vice presidential candidate.

The most crucial period of Johnson's career is covered in volume 7. Unfortunately, the papers written by Johnson are scarce and so offer limited insight into the mind of the vice president and man who suddenly was thrust into the presidency at one of the great moments of crisis in American history. A mere 86 of the 657 papers included come from the pen of Johnson, and many others are newspaper accounts of his speeches. Still, much of value lies within, particularly relating to the subject's last months as military governor of Tennessee. The introduction by the editors is excellent.

Volume 8 covers Johnson's ascendancy to the presidency and his first weeks in office. The larger volume of Johnson papers during his tenure as president allowed a greater use of material. Still, only 70 of the approximately 800 documents were written by Johnson; the majority are missives written by friends, associates, supporters, office seekers, and ex-Confederates who wished to do Johnson great bodily harm. The subsequent volumes carry on the story of Johnson's tenure after the war, characterized by a flood of problems and a variable degree of success dealing with them.

A useful supplementary volume exists in *Advice after Appomattox: Letters to Andrew Johnson, 1865–1866* (ed. Brooks D. Simpson, LeRoy P. Graf, and John Muldowny, 259 pp., University of Tennessee Press, Knoxville, 1988), containing 38 letters of Salmon P. Chase, Ulysses S. Grant, Carl Schurz, Benjamin C. Truman, and Harvey M. Watterson sent to Johnson from May 1865 to January 1866. The president's special correspondents—particularly Chase and Schurz—reported on conditions in the South and the progress of Reconstruction.

392

Trefousse, Hans L. **Andrew Johnson: A Biography** (463 pp., W. W. Norton and Co., New York, 1989)

A full and scholarly treatment emerges in this carefully researched and soundly written work, 28 percent of which treats the Civil War years. Using in large measure documents from *The Papers of Andrew Johnson* (*q.v.*), Trefousse has pieced together an admirable account of Johnson's unremarkable antebellum life and his somewhat unlikely rise to political prominence. The early chapters explore the contradictions in Johnson's career, in which proslavery views and self-inadequacy clashed and created an anti-aristocratic sentiment in many of Johnson's actions. The author shows that what Johnson stood for could certainly be brought into question at many times, as indeed it was. Johnson's adherance to views unpopular with other Southern senators made him a virtual outcast whose spotty record appeared to be philosophically inconsistent.

The work's narrative reveals how Johnson "jumped ship" as the sectional crisis approached and threw his support solidly behind the Union. By doing so he became a Northern hero and vigorously supported emancipation as military governor of Tennessee. Many of Johnson's stances had more valuable psychological effects than real ones, but his place of origin and the popularity of this peculiar man made him an appealing ticket-balancer in 1864.

This sound work assesses its subject as a basically competent politician whose career as president was disastrous partly because it was out of his control and partly because of his anachronistic outlook. Further, the work demonstrates concretely that Johnson most certainly left a legacy of racism behind that he could have done far more to reduce or eliminate.

Samuel Jordan Kirkwood (1813–1894)

393

Clark, Dan Elbert. **Samuel Jordan Kirkwood** (464 pp., State Historical Society of Iowa, Iowa City, 1917)

Born in Maryland, matured in Ohio, and an Iowa pioneer by the mid-1850s, Kirkwood attained the executive reins of Iowa as a conservative Republican in 1859. The biography details Kirkwood's efforts to raise monies for the state's prosecution of the war, his attitudes toward conscription, and his activities in combatting Copperheads in Iowa. The narrative is plainly sympathetic toward its subject and lacks in-depth analysis.

Clark details Kirkwood's inheritance of the vacant senate seat in 1866 and investigates only superficially Kirkwood's attitudes toward Reconstruction during his 14 months in the Senate in 1866–1867. The work, then, provides an adequate portrait of a rough-hewn man whose influence materially aided Iowa during the war and who occasionally rose to national significance.

Abraham Lincoln (1809–1865)

394

Bates, David Homer. **Lincoln in the Telegraph Office: Recollections of the United States Military Telegraph Corps during the Civil War** (432 pp., Century Co., New York, 1907)

Despite inadequacies, this work is enjoyable reading because it offers a glimpse of an important station in the wartime administration where Lincoln spent a good deal of time. Bates used a war diary and added significant recollections to fashion a story of Lincoln's visits to the military telegraph office. The narrative additionally draws on the reminiscences of Thomas T. Eckert, Charles A. Tinker, and Albert B. Chandler, Bates's fellows in the War Department telegraph office.

The text is most valuable as a portrait of Lincoln drawn by those seeing Lincoln almost on a daily basis during the war and conversing with him about matters important and trivial. Much minutiae unrelated to Lincoln also appears, as do many errors of fact. The author states that McClellan's failure to destroy Lee following Antietam caused Lincoln to bring the Emancipation Proclamation before his cabinet. The author also overstates Lincoln's estimate of Francis P. Blair's diplomatic mission in 1865, an exercise Lincoln privately ignored while he entertained Blair's wishes. Despite its blemishes, this work offers an interesting depiction of Lincoln and his close association with the telegraphers who brought him the news from the front lines.

(Reprinted 1995, 432 pp., University of Nebraska Press, Lincoln)

395

Bruce, Robert V. **Lincoln and the Tools of War** (368 pp., Bobbs-Merrill Co., Indianapolis, 1956)

This book holds great value for Lincoln students and those fascinated with the rise of technological weaponry during the war years. Far from being a story based wholly on Lincoln, many others—principally ordnance chief James W. Ripley and Rear Adm. John A. Dahlgren—play important roles. Lincoln, Ripley, and Dahlgren all had what the author terms "engineer's minds," as even Lincoln, lacking the proper training to perform an engineer's duty, had a remarkably keen mind and sense of things mechanical.

Lincoln's technological interests made possible the testing of numerous innovations even when his generals or flag officers had no concern with them. Bruce tells the story of how Lincoln himself tested rifles and accoutrements on what is now the Washington Mall. Lincoln also traveled to the Navy Yard to see the latest in naval technology, including Dahlgren's extensive tests of armor plating. Along the way, readers gain a concise history of army and navy ordnance. Bruce examines Ripley's reluctance to take on new inventions and Lincoln's delicate and occasionally amused handling of the situation. A virtual catalog of amazing inventions passes under the reader's eye in addition to the important details relating to successful tools such as a variety of breech-loading cannon, carbine rifles, and the forerunners of machine guns. This is a beautifully executed work on a much-neglected aspect of the Federal war effort.

(Reprinted 1989, with a new preface, 368 pp., University of Illinois Press, Urbana)

396

Carpenter, Francis B. **Six Months at the White House with Abraham Lincoln: The Story of a Picture** (359 pp., Hurd and Houghton, New York, 1866).

Toward the end of the year of Jubilee, the young artist Carpenter received permission to visit Lincoln regularly to make character studies for a painting depicting the signing of the Emancipation Proclamation. Carpenter clung to Lincoln throughout a portion of 1864, creating the pieces and perfecting the approaches that ultimately produced that famous piece of art.

Along the way Carpenter observed the Lincolns and their administration from a unique position, and his work reflects the experiences he captured during the last full year of Lincoln's life. The work is partly embellished using material from several contributors including William H. Herndon. Yet Carpenter's keen sense of what transpired around him and ability as a wordsmith produce enjoyable reading that contains some famous scenes etched in Lincolniana. These include Lincoln's fondness for certain poems, the relations among Lincoln's inner circle (including Mary Todd), behavioral aspects of cabinet members, seemingly endless crowds of favor seekers crowding the Executive Mansion hallways, and Lincoln's own recollection of his decision to emancipate the slaves. Subsequent editions are titled *The Inner Life of Abraham Lincoln.*

397

Donald, David Herbert. **Lincoln** (660 pp., Simon and Schuster, New York, 1995)

Scholarly, richly documented, and fully researched, this tome will long stand as the best single-volume biography of Abraham Lincoln. The work focuses most strongly on Lincoln's political career and his machinations as commander-in-chief during the war years. It is a full biography, delivering crisp coverage of Lincoln's early years and avoiding much of the speculative mythology that permeates the Lincoln literature. Emphasis is squarely on the war years, however, with fully half of the book's narrative devoted to this four-year span.

Donald succeeds admirably in delivering a summary of the crucial and interesting aspects of Lincoln's life in something Lincoln himself practiced, an economy of language. Much information lies packed into the book's pages, yet the author's prose communicates the Lincoln story effectively in today's language and with a general tenor of relaxed quiet. The author highlights Lincoln's early independent, strong-willed thought and his simple, logical character. The period of Lincoln's enormous political growth following the Mexican War through the middle 1850s is covered at length, handled superbly and with a plain narrative style. The author resists attempts at glorifying or glamorizing the Lincoln story: wisely, he lets the simple facts speak for themselves.

Chiefly through the political looking glass, the author expertly weaves a simple story of Lincoln's handling of the war years. He surveys on broad canvas the politics, war milestones, sociological pulse, and technological evolution of Lincoln's America at war. The book may not always hold the depth that Lincoln scholars will need, but for the great majority of the reading public it is a great achievement.

398

Donald, David. **Lincoln Reconsidered: Essays on the Civil War Era** (200 pp., Alfred A. Knopf, New York, 1956)

Donald offers an original analysis of fundamental questions of the war, interpreted in the context of Lincoln's role, but not limited to it. The author's introductory "Getting Right with Lincoln" assesses the public's beliefs about Lincoln the man in the wake of his assassination and foreshadows the chapters to come. The material that follows shows careful reflection on a variety of topics, from Lincoln's unquestioned ability as a statesman to the causes of sectional crisis and the reasons for Northern victory.

Donald successfully reduces the Lincoln of legend by exposing the party politician who worked tirelessly and the idealist who existed miles away from the abolitionist elite. Among the work's most significant sections is the discussion of Lincoln's famous remark, "My policy is to have no policy." That Lincoln mastered the politics of Washington and its influential radicals without compromising direction, that he indeed variously used them or ignored them, shows a significant aspect of Lincoln's mind. In fact, Donald asserts that he wishes to raise the radical Republicans from their evil reputations, a goal fairly accomplished in certain sections of this work.

(Reprinted 1972, 2d ed., with some new material, 250 pp., Alfred A. Knopf, New York)

399

Hamilton, Charles, and Lloyd Ostendorf. **Lincoln in Photographs: An Album of Every Known Pose** (Rev. ed., 421 pp., Morningside, Dayton, 1985)

This collection offers all known photographs of the 16th president. The first edition of this work (409 pp., University of Oklahoma Press, Norman, 1963) itself superseded the first great photographic book on Lincoln, *The Photographs of Abraham Lincoln,* by Frederick Hill Meserve and Carl Sandburg (30 pp. + 95 plates, Harcourt, Brace and Co., New York, 1944). Meserve and Sandburg's book employed "Meserve numbers" to identify each unique photograph. (Meserve published his first analysis of Lincoln photographs in 1915.) The present work utilizes Lloyd Ostendorf's collection and a system of "Ostendorf numbers" for the 126 authentic Lincoln photos. Several spurious Lincoln photos are presented with commentary.

400

Hanchett, William. **The Lincoln Murder Conspiracies: Being an Account of the Hatred Felt by Many Americans for President Abraham Lincoln during the Civil War and the First Complete Examination and Refutation of the Many Theories, Hypotheses, and Speculations Put Forward since 1865 Concerning Those Presumed to Have Aided, Abetted, Controlled, or Directed the Murderous Act of John Wilkes Booth in Ford's Theater the Night of April 14** (303 pp., University of Illinois Press, Urbana, 1983)

The most rational and complete study in a field swimming with irrationality, this is the first book one should turn to for an analysis of the assassination. Hanchett suggests that many groups and individuals indeed had sufficient motive to kill Lincoln. After a discussion of the assassination itself, the author investigates changing perceptions of the crime— first as Confederate grand conspiracy, then as a simple conspiracy, and finally as a reinflamed, irrational grand conspiracy, fueled by the writings of Otto Eisenschiml. Hanchett demonstrates to conspiracy theorists that one angry, troubled man indeed can alter U.S. history.

401

Herndon, William H., and Jesse W. Weik. **Herndon's Lincoln: The True Story of a Great Life** (3 vols., 638 pp., Belford, Clarke and Co., Chicago, 1889)

The standard biography for years, this work has nonetheless stood under a cloud of controversy since it was first published. Immediately after Lincoln's death, former law partner Herndon began the task of compiling a thorough biography to supersede the thin, uncritical works published during Lincoln's presidential campaign and administration. Herndon's research and Weik's writing had the potential for greatness, but Herndon's motives skewed many aspects of the Lincoln story.

The basis for severe criticism of Herndon and Weik's biography is to be found in the following portrayals: the arguable illegitimacy of Lincoln's mother, an overwrought interpretation of Lincoln's frontier childhood, the exaggerated romance with Ann Rutledge, a blinding overemphasis or invention of Lincoln's stormy relations with Mary Todd, and a poorly interpreted telling of Lincoln's progressive religious views. Yet for 20 years Herndon worked with Lincoln as closely as anyone else, and part of his story remains useful and important even if it stumbles repeatedly during the critical years of civil war, when Herndon did not know Lincoln.

(Reprinted 1942, titled *Herndon's Life of Lincoln,* 511 pp., World Publishing Co., Cleveland)

402

Holzer, Harold, Gabor S. Boritt, and Mark E. Neely, Jr. **The Lincoln Image: Abraham Lincoln and the Popular Print** (234 pp., Charles Scribner's Sons, New York, 1984)

The advertising media of the 1860s, photographs and engravings used in newspapers, books, and journals or as campaign pieces, played a vital role in the public perception of a leader. In Lincoln's case, photography was becoming widespread as the art of engraving and the process of lithography were being perfected, all at the time of the onset of the great American war. Lincoln recognized the practical value of posing for photographs and hence helped to make himself the most visible U.S. president up to that time.

The authors of this work chronicle Lincoln's photographs and engravings, providing a history of Lincoln in the media during his presidential campaigns and during the war itself. According to the authors, engraved political cartoons played a significant part in public perceptions of the war, and the book presents many pro-Lincoln and a few anti-Lincoln examples. Despite Lincoln's almost comical homeliness, the authors contend, prints and photographs boosted Lincoln's image. After the assassination, prints helped to mold Lincoln into an American demigod. The collection of prints within this volume is alone valuable; the perceptive text that accompanies it makes it doubly worthwhile.

403

Kunhardt, Dorothy Meserve, and Philip B. Kunhardt, Jr. **Twenty Days: A Narrative in Text and Pictures of the Assassination of Abraham Lincoln and the Twenty Days and Nights That Followed: The Nation in Mourning, the Long Trip Home to Springfield** (312 pp., Harper and Row, New York, 1965)

This work serves as souvenir and explanatory document of the weeks that followed the assassination. Drawing on the vast Meserve collection of images and including a richly detailed popular text, the authors examine the murder of Lincoln and then trace the investigation, the characters involved, and the 20-day journey of Lincoln's body back to Springfield for burial.

The memoir includes 317 photographs and engravings (mostly photographs) that in essence trace Lincoln's life backward as he returns to his old home. Various friends, associates, and family members appear in context as the funeral train tours the Midwest and the vivid events of the assassination night are reconstructed. Many rare images of funeral obsequies from cities in the East and Midwest appear, as do images associated with those convicted and implicated in the conspiracy. This work skillfully re-creates with stark imagery some of the nation's darkest hours.

404

Lewis, Lloyd. **Myths after Lincoln** (367 pp., Harcourt, Brace and Co., New York, 1929)

This is a fascinating book. Lewis successfully develops an argument that the apotheosis of Lincoln sprouted a wealth of American folk legends reflecting their lost hero. Not only is Lincoln escalated to demigod status by such beliefs, but the murderer often lives on because an easy death would be unsatisfactory.

Transparently visible in this work's text is the instant change in Northern popular opinion from a kind homecoming after the trials of war to the vilification of the South and punishment of Reconstruction. Indeed, Lincoln's death served as the lightning rod for this change, which altered the presumably tender management of the "erring states" by Lincoln to the iron-fisted control of the radical Republicans.

The work contains a riveting set of stories from the chaos and despair of the Lincoln funeral journey to the ironic, seething anger of the ministers on "Black Easter" to the unfortunate loss of mental balance that seemed to plague survivors of the night at Ford's Theater. Tales verging on the comic appear as well, including the botched attempt to steal Lincoln's body and the several "Booths" who survived into the 20th century.

(Reprinted 1941, with an introduction by Carl Sandburg, 367 pp., Press of the Reader's Club, New York; reprinted 1994 as *The Assassination of Lincoln: History and Myth*, with an introduction by Mark E. Neely, Jr., 367 pp., University of Nebraska Press, Lincoln)

405

Lincoln, Abraham. **The Collected Works of Abraham Lincoln** (ed. Roy P. Basler, 11 vols., 5254 pp., vols. 1–8 and index volume, Rutgers University Press, New Brunswick, 1953–1955; vol. 10, Greenwood Press, Westport, 1974; vol. 11, Rutgers University Press, New Brunswick, 1990)

Together these volumes present thousands of Lincoln autograph letters, speeches, documents, and many letters signed by the president. The coverage spans the few scraps of Lincoln's sum book (1824–1826) through the final days of his presidency. The work omits many legal documents currently being compiled into a separate work, but provides substantial material relating to Lincoln's most prolific years, those of the war, which comprise seven of the volumes.

The most reliable texts of Lincoln's great works, the Gettysburg Address, the inaugural addresses, the military communications, and many political letters and messages all appear in these volumes. So do many letters and writings of lesser immediate historical significance but of great personal relevance that reveal much about Lincoln's character. Reading them enlightens one about Lincoln and his world as much or more than the best biography could hope to do. The thoroughness of the collection of important papers and the annotation and editing of this massive project is highly professional and leaves little to be desired. The discovery of more Lincoln documents necessitated the supplements, but the decreasing importance of those included in the final two volumes suggests that virtually all of the most important works have been found, both from institutional collections and those in private hands. By its very nature, this work is an absolute must for the bookshelf of any Civil War library and will be used for reading as well as reference.

406

McPherson, James M. **Abraham Lincoln and the Second American Revolution** (173 pp., Oxford University Press, New York, 1990)

McPherson describes Lincoln's renewal of the American society in a second revolution that transformed old America into modern America. The work's economy of language delivers a short and tightly knit argument in the opening chapter that such a revolution occurred. It then proceeds to define Lincoln's central role in making that revolution happen. The author solidly demonstrates that Lincoln was hardly a conservative but a revolutionary who coordinated the policy of his military commanders, the Republican party, opposition politicians, and ultimately the conquered South.

The author convincingly outlines how Lincoln cleverly communicated the onset of this new revolution to both Northern and Southern civilians. He proceeds to examine how emancipation changed American society, how the military loss of the Confederacy drastically altered the balance of political power in Washington, and how the Civil War Congress passed an astonishingly large amount of revolutionary legislation. Although brief, this expertly woven work is impressive.

407

Mearns, David C., ed. **The Lincoln Papers: The Story of the Collection, with Selections to July 4, 1861** (2 vols., 681 pp., Doubleday and Co., Garden City, N.Y., 1948)

This group of correspondence comes from the Robert Todd Lincoln papers, kept unopened in the Library of Con-

gress until 26 July 1947, as ordered by Robert Lincoln's will. The full collection consists of 18,000 documents bound in almost 200 folio books, including some 900 documents written entirely in Lincoln's hand. Small parts filtered into books before 1947. Hay and Nicolay used some of the papers for their 10-volume *Abraham Lincoln: A History* (*q.v.*). Many of the documents written by Lincoln were included in the early incarnations of Lincoln's *Collected Works* (*q.v.*).

Mearns, then director of the reference department of the Library of Congress, compiled the present work, which begins with an entertaining 136-page introduction. The letters that follow, written by others and sent to Lincoln, were chosen for their freshness and widely scattered views to illustrate the problems of Lincoln's campaign and first weeks of his presidency. Arranged chronologically, the correspondence wonderfully illustrates the minutiae as well as the great drama involved in conducting the Civil War. Prewar letters are also included.

The grim nature of the weeks preceding war comes alive in a series of letters from Southerners threatening Lincoln's life. The last letter in the book, written on 6 July 1861 by a woman in Philadelphia, suggests dispensing copies of Lincoln's war message to southern camps by means of Thaddeus S. C. Lowe's balloon. It is easy to imagine Lincoln's thoughts after receiving such a blend of support and violent opposition, and to better appreciate his state of mind as the country came apart.

408

Miers, Earl Schenck, ed. **Lincoln Day by Day: A Chronology, 1809–1865** (3 vols., 1119 pp., Lincoln Sesquicentennial Commission, Washington, 1960)

Compiled by Lincoln scholars William E. Baringer and C. Percy Powell, this work is based in part on earlier research by Harry E. Pratt, Benjamin P. Thomas, and Paul M. Angle. However, Miers's *Lincoln Day by Day* includes material from the Robert Todd Lincoln papers, made public only in 1947, and Basler's *Collected Works* of Lincoln (*q.v.*), published in 1953–1955. Hence, the completeness of the material in this work is impressive, and the final volume is irreplacable as a reference to check circumstances of Lincoln's actions as commander-in-chief during his 1504 days in the White House.

The present volumes outline Lincoln's daily activities in the periods 1809–1848 (vol. 1), 1849–1860 (vol. 2), and 1861–1865 (vol. 3). The authors drew on a vast array of published and primary sources, and of course the earlier volumes are sketchier than the third, massive Civil War volume. The editorial tone is neutral; only the facts appear, as interpretation would have ballooned the work into a far more massive study. Yet the coverage of documents, trips, meetings, and reactions to wartime events is impressive: of the 1566 days of Lincoln's life covered in volume 3, only 41 pass without any entries.

(Reprinted 1991, with an introduction by Ralph G. Newman, 1119 pp., Morningside, Dayton)

409

Nicolay, John G., and John Hay. **Abraham Lincoln: A History** (10 vols., 4706 pp., Century Co., New York, 1890)

Hay and Nicolay knew Lincoln during the Springfield years but far more important acted as secretaries to the president during his administration. Consequently, they observed Lincoln during the most critical period of his activities. Moreover, they drew on the voluminous Lincoln papers on loan from Robert Todd Lincoln, something Herndon and Weik (*q.v.*) could not do. To form the basis for such a work, Nicolay made extensive notes and Hay kept a diary (*q.v.*) during the latter part of the war specifically to buttress just such a biography.

When it first appeared, serialized in the *Century* magazine, Nicolay and Hay's work clearly established a definitive claim to objectivity and balance. Neither author may have regarded Mary Todd Lincoln with affection, but they were not about to grind axes. Some early reviewers criticized the fact that Robert Todd Lincoln read and approved each page. Yet this does not seem to have prevented a fair history of either Lincoln or the war, for this work is a mammoth description of the war as much as a biography of the war's central figure.

Although much of the material used by Nicolay and Hay has since been published elsewhere, this biography presents a dizzying array of sources chronologically, and the interpretation is solid and well documented, though occasional bursts of partisan rancor color certain sections. Many sources used as secondary material appear only in this work, including Nicolay's memoranda, many letters received at the Executive Mansion, Winfield Scott's daily reports, and numerous personal papers now in repositories. More than a century after its publication, Nicolay and Hay's work remains an important record of the war.

(Abridged edition 1966, ed. Paul M. Angle, 394 pp., University of Chicago Press, Chicago)

410

Paludan, Philip Shaw. **The Presidency of Abraham Lincoln** (384 pp., University Press of Kansas, Lawrence, 1994)

This is a highly worthwhile work for the Lincoln bookshelf. The author examines 15 critical periods in Lincoln's presidency to reveal aspects of Lincoln's character and his leadership during the war. Superbly researched, deeply reflective, and intelligent in its conclusions, the study offers much of great value. Paludan sets the stage by introducing the war clouds of the winter of 1860 and proceeds by describing the cast of characters in Lincoln's administration. The author insightfully offers brief and superb assessments of Seward and Chase, in particular. The chapter on the Sumter crisis summarizes the most recent scholarship on Lincoln's motives during this critical period. The work claims forcefully that the goals of preserving the Union and abolishing slavery were linked and cannot be considered as separate issues.

The book becomes increasingly engrossing as the war progresses. The author deals expertly with congressional actions, the gathering of resources and manpower for war, and controversies over Maj. Gen. McClellan and emancipation. Fine writing characterizes these sections in that complex ideas are summarized and presented with admirable economy. The remaining chapters, also engagingly written, examine such themes as dissent in the North, the beginnings of Reconstruction, Federal military victories, the drama of a wartime election, and Lincoln's sudden death. The coverage seems less detailed as the work draws to an end, thinning during the last weeks of Lincoln's presidency. Many passages in this work are highly original and valuable; others are not quite so but neatly present old and important ideas in a fresh and exciting way. A few typographical errors were found, as with misspellings of John C. Breckinridge, Irvin McDowell, and William S. Rosecrans.

411

Peterson, Merrill D. **Lincoln in American Memory** (482 pp., Oxford University Press, New York, 1994)

This highly intelligent analysis examines the changing views on Abraham Lincoln in American society from his death and martyrdom to the present day. The apotheosis of Lincoln, Peterson argues, swept over not only Washington and Springfield but over the American nation, even the South and other countries in the years following the president's demise. The resulting social, cultural, and political reactions to Lincoln over time reveal much about Lincoln himself but even more about the evolution of American society. Lincoln, as a mirror, is exceptionally clear and revealing.

The author surveys Lincoln's early biographers, uncovers their amateurish biases, and describes how serious historians climbed onto the Lincoln bandwagon very late in the game. He examines how blacks have perceived Lincoln over time and how that perception has ranged from redeemer to villain. The author broadly defines five Lincolns of American memory: the savior of the Union, the great emancipator, the man of the people, the first true American, and the self-made man. The spread of each of these Lincoln themes allows most people to see Lincoln and his influence through a certain filter. The author marvelously compares the perceived Lincoln with the historical Lincoln and in so doing examines a broad range of interesting facts about Americans past and present.

412

Randall, James G., and Richard N. Current. **Lincoln the President** (4 vols., 1722 pp., Dodd, Mead and Co., New York, 1945–1955; consisting of *Springfield to Gettysburg*, vol. 1, 395 pp., 1945; *Springfield to Gettysburg*, vol. 2, 439 pp., 1945; *Midstream*, vol. 3, 467 pp., 1952; and *Last Full Measure*, vol. 4, 421 pp., 1955)

Although more recent works have appeared, Randall and Current's voluminous set summarizes the important revisionist aspects of Lincoln historiography dominating the post–World War II era.

The first two volumes, *Springfield to Gettysburg*, and the third, *Midstream*, were completed by Randall. Much of the work of the final volume, *Last Full Measure*, was finished by Current after Randall's death. The emphasis throughout the volumes stays focused on political matters. Military aspects are presented as secondary material. Although the title suggests the work is completely engrossed in Lincoln's presidency, much about the antebellum years appears in the first two volumes. Here Randall established his revisionist approach by rejecting the Ann Rutledge story, concluding that the fundamental differences between Lincoln and Douglas were slight and, of greatest importance, that war could have been avoided.

Randall's characterization of most inhabitants North and South as complacent and peaceful, only to be cast into war by small numbers of extremists on both sides, continues to be compelling. Indeed, the analysis of this and other issues relating to Lincoln's presidency includes arguments and counterarguments so that readers can weigh the evidence accordingly. Throughout the wartime coverage, Lincoln appears as both central character and one dropped into the background while the authors analyze actions of the other major players in Lincoln's administration. So the book is more than a biography of Lincoln, constituting a general work on the times. This study has outlasted many similar views of Lincoln and will continue to be counted as an important accomplishment far into the future.

(*Last Full Measure* reprinted 1991, with an introduction by Richard N. Current, 421 pp., University of Illinois Press, Urbana)

413

[Pulitzer Prize, 1940]
Sandburg, Carl. **Abraham Lincoln: The Prairie Years** and **Abraham Lincoln: The War Years** (6 vols., 3465 pp., Harcourt, Brace and Co., New York, 1926–1939, consisting of: *The Prairie Years*, vol. 1, 480 pp., 1926; *The Prairie Years*, vol. 2, 482 pp., 1926; *The War Years*, vol. 1, 660 pp., 1939; *The War Years*, vol. 2, 655 pp., 1939; *The War Years*, vol. 3, 673 pp., 1939; and *The War Years*, vol. 4, 515 pp., 1939)

Not reliable for historical accuracy, this work is nonetheless a masterpiece of poetic biography. Sandburg's success in portraying the themes of Lincoln's life is unexceeded. Readers receive not only a biography of Lincoln the man but also a kaleidoscopic view of the great changes sweeping across America from the 1830s through the 1850s. The work's final four volumes offer an intimate journey through Lincoln's wartime Executive Mansion. The overall effect is a great success in that readers come away with a genuine feeling for and understanding of Lincoln's mind.

However, Sandburg's Lincoln is not true to history. Many periods of Lincoln's early life lack documentary evidence, and often Sandburg imagined a story line to fill the gaps. Many other stories in Sandburg's book are just that—stories, including the embellished romance with Ann Rutledge (and the use of forged documents and relics relating to it). In this and other cases, Sandburg embraced the Herndon doctrine. Other parts of the work ramble on with a threadbare connection to Lincoln. More disturbing, perhaps, Sandburg paints a too conservative picture of Lincoln and his dealings with the radicals.

The four volumes of this set devoted to the war years are better history than the first two. Here, of course, Sandburg could rely on a vast historical record of documentary sources lacking for much of Lincoln's antebellum career. This permitted an objectivity missing from the bulk of the first two volumes but pushed the wartime discussion away from the compelling prose of the earlier volumes. Together, the six volumes contain some of the best writing about Lincoln. They are not always reliable, but offer a monumental assessment of the elusive character of Lincoln the commander-in-chief.

414

Tidwell, William A., James O. Hall, and David Winfred Gaddy. **Come Retribution: The Confederate Secret Service and the Assassination of Lincoln** (510 pp., University Press of Mississippi, Jackson, 1988)

Both exhilarating and ultimately disappointing, this is the first modern investigation of the role of Confederate clandestine activities during the war. Separated into three parts, the work explores the Confederate intelligence "machinery," the potential use of that machinery against President Lincoln, and the secret plan to kidnap Lincoln that degraded into murder. The authors have completed an impressive amount of research into many sources, some previously untapped, and contend through a construction of mostly circumstantial evidence that Jefferson Davis and other high Confederate officials were behind the assassination of Lincoln and were engaged in other "terrorist" activities.

With such a momentous claim and such inherently absorbing material, the book might have bewitched readers with a polished, professional style. Unfortunately, it is a conglomeration of separate efforts rather clumsily pieced together, making plodding through it difficult. The construction of an argument implicating high Confederate officials as directors of Booth's pistol at times appears convincing, at other times distinctly speculative. Organization suffers, resulting in a confused walk through the story. That notwithstanding, the book contains many nuggets of interest and value. The study's most interesting section describes a plot to blow up Lincoln inside the Executive Mansion, one of a number of activities planned to be carried out with the help of John Mosby's cavalry. It is clear that ties existed between Booth and the Confederate agents of espionage. Although this work stops well short of demonstrating that orders to kill Lincoln came from Richmond, it suggests that something more than a simple conspiracy of small time hoodlums may have stood behind the Booth gang.

Mary Todd Lincoln (1818–1882)

415

Baker, Jean H. **Mary Todd Lincoln: A Biography** (429 pp., W. W. Norton and Co., New York, 1987)

A difficult subject to reduce to some 400 pages, Mary Lincoln has been treated many times in the past, usually with limited success. The present work, however, assembles a detailed history of the times filled with a sound and scholarly depiction of Mary Lincoln's life. This full biography

devotes some 20 percent of its space to the war years. Still, the prewar and postwar analysis of Mary Lincoln's complex character adds greatly to the understanding of a much mythologized figure in Civil War Washington.

Baker portrays Mary Lincoln as one who time and time again felt significant loss in her life until it was too much to bear. As a child she lost the spotlight of being the baby of the family, she lost an infant brother, and when Mary was six, she lost her mother. Her sensitivity and loneliness were further heightened by Abraham Lincoln's frequent absences from home as he rode the judicial circuit. She lost Edward and William Lincoln as young sons, and of course sat beside President Lincoln as he was assassinated. Additionally, Mary lost Tad after the war. According to the author, the longing to feel important and secure, never truly realized, continued until it built to explosive proportions during the war years.

This work demonstrates that many of Mary Lincoln's erratic activities seem to have been attempts to compensate for the elusive sense of belonging. In other respects the author shows that as a politically astute and generally intelligent woman, Mary may have been ahead of her time in supporting her husband and effectively playing political partner. The portrait of Mary Lincoln that emerges from this significant work is one of balance, importance, and of course tragedy.

416

Lincoln, Mary Todd. **Mary Todd Lincoln: Her Life and Letters** (ed. Justin G. Turner and Linda Levitt Turner, 750 pp., Alfred A. Knopf, New York, 1972)

The result of a mammoth research job and careful, scrupulous editing, this key work on the controversial First Lady of the wartime North presents 609 letters spanning the period July 1840–March 1882. The majority of the letters reside in institutions, but many were uncovered from private collectors. The result is a life story of Mary Todd that reflects much on antebellum life in Kentucky, the rising aspirations of this spirited woman, her marriage and relationship with Abraham Lincoln, and Civil War Washington. The downward spiral of Mary Lincoln's postwar years is fresh and occasionally stunning in this volume, which transforms into a psychological portrait as her world seemingly crumbles.

The work's greatest value may lie in revealing Mary Todd as a historical figure, disavowing some of the mythology that surrounds her. The author's attitudes and evaluations of Civil War personalities including U. S. Grant, Julia Grant, Edwin M. Stanton, Salmon P. Chase, and others is highly compelling. Perhaps the most revealing letters are from Mary to those with whom she felt close friendship, as they are candid and often comment on matters that shed light on the author's personality.

Hugh McCulloch (1808–1895)

417

McCulloch, Hugh. **Men and Measures of Half a Century** (542 pp., Charles Scribner's Sons, New York, 1888)

The author presents his varied recollections as secretary of the treasury during the last weeks of the war, throughout Andrew Johnson's presidency, and later under James A. Garfield. The narrative stretches the entire canvas of McCulloch's life, introducing the young New Englander who relocated in Indiana where he learned finance at a bank in Fort Wayne. The author's financial prowess comes across in his reflections on managing the Indiana State Bank through the financial dips of the 1850s.

The work accelerates in interest with the years of Civil War, although the focus largely remains on finance. The discussion of McCulloch's relationship with Chase and McCulloch's eventual about-face on the national banking bill receives a respectable treatment. The material on cultural, political, and social aspects of the war increases as McCulloch acquaints himself with wartime Washington. Much of interest may be found regarding his relationships with those in the administration and his reluctant issuance of greenbacks, an act that once completed could never be undone, as McCulloch realized years later.

(Reprinted 1970, 542 pp., Da Capo Press, New York)

Edward McPherson (1830–1895)

418

McPherson, Edward. **The Political History of the United States of America during the Great Rebellion, from November 6, 1860, to July 4, 1864: Including a Classified Summary of the Legislation of the Second Session of the Thirty-sixth Congress, the Three Sessions of the Thirty-seventh Congress, the First Session of the Thirty-eighth Congress, with the Votes Thereon, and the Important Executive, Judicial, and Politico-Military Facts of That Eventful Period: Together with the Organization, Legislation, and General Proceedings of the Rebel Administration** (440 pp., Philip and Salomans, Washington, 1864)

Clerk of the U.S. House of Representatives and owner of a farm made famous on the Gettysburg battlefield,

McPherson composed this lengthy political treatise which retains value for its flavor of the times. The work is chaotically arranged and contains a mountain of useful data. It is slanted heavily toward the Federal side of the war and offers a massive amount of political information.

The work presents a chronological summary of the secession legislation of the Southern states with many quotations of official documents and lists of members of the interstate commissions and the Confederate congresses. Included are congressional debates and reactions to the secession crisis, slavery, and the bombardment of Fort Sumter. An analysis of the constitutions of the United States and the Confederate States appears, as do Lincoln's inaugural addresses and messages to Congress. Much of interest may be found in the congressional debates and resolutions on habeas corpus, confiscation, emancipation, and the fugitive slave laws. Material appears from debates on the enrollment acts, the employment of black troops, the plans for Reconstruction, and documents relating to foreign affairs and finance.

Valuable sections on the 1864 political campaign highlight activities of the Baltimore convention, the radical meeting in Cleveland, and the Democratic meeting in Chicago. The volume also includes election results of the 1864 contest and many other tidbits of political interest.

(Reprinted 1865, with an appendix with the principal political facts of the campaign of 1864, a chapter on the church and the rebellion, and the proceedings of the 2d Session of the 38th Congress, 653 pp., Philip and Salomons, Washington; 1865 edition reprinted 1876, titled *The Political History of the U.S.A. during the Civil War*, 653 pp., Philip and Salomons, Washington; 1876 edition reprinted 1972, with an introduction by Harold M. Hyman and Hans L. Trefousse, 440 pp., Da Capo Press, New York)

Edwin Denison Morgan (1811–1883)

419

Rawley, James A. **Edwin D. Morgan, 1811–1883: Merchant in Politics** (321 pp., Columbia University Press, New York, 1955)

This is a simple and undecorated biography of a colorful politician and major general of volunteers. A full treatment, it covers the business, political, and military aspects of Morgan's career, drawing on a wide variety of sources including the Morgan papers, official documents, and even newspapers. The account is workmanlike in that it delivers the facts without digressions into the human side of its focus, which will disappoint many readers. The full documentation and capable organization makes this a valuable compilation, even if it stops short of revealing much about the whys of E. D. Morgan.

Rawley investigates Morgan's New England upbringing and ventures into politics, describing fairly the work as chairman of the Republican National Committee. Also illuminated is Morgan's governorship of New York throughout the secession crisis and into the middle of the war, when he is commissioned a major general by Lincoln for his sterling efforts in raising troops and supplies. The narrative adequately sketches Morgan's performance in the Senate. Rarely judgmental, Rawley allows readers to divine the value of Morgan's career for themselves.

Oliver Hazard Perry Throck Morton (1823–1877)

420

Foulke, William Dudley. **Life of Oliver P. Morton, Including His Important Speeches** (2 vols., 1081 pp., Bowen-Merrill Co., Indianapolis, 1899)

This set remains of high interest for studies of Civil War Union governors and Indiana's role in the war. Foulke fairly assesses Morton's role in the wartime years without undue sympathy, documenting his subject's rise in Republican politics and aggressive and militant personality. The work illuminates Morton's work toward creating a device by which the Republican majority in the Indiana Senate could oust a Democratic member whose seat was contested. The scheme worked and solidified Morton's standing in Indiana politics.

During the war, the volume shows, Morton's governorship vigorously supported the Lincoln administration and its war policies. The work reflects on the bill of 1862 in which Democrats attempted to curtail the governor's power to organize state militia forces. Acting under Morton's leadership, however, Republicans broke the quorum. The result was that Morton assumed grand powers to pass other laws, borrowing monies from the Federal government and state banks to enact his war measures. The author concludes that Morton "was" the state of Indiana during this politically turbulent period. The work casts a needed bright light on this leader who by dictatorial measures supported his party's causes during the conflict.

Francis Harrison Pierpont [Peirpoint] (1814–1899)

421

Ambler, Charles H. **Francis H. Pierpont, Union War Governor of Virginia and Father of West Virginia** (483 pp., University of North Carolina Press, Chapel Hill, 1937)

In this strong, detailed, well-written work, Ambler provides a scholarly evaluation of the first leader of West Virginia. Pierpont (Peirpoint during the war years, before the name change in 1881) contributed materially to the Union political scene. The author carefully explains how the major differences of western Virginians made a split during the war inevitable. He documents fully Pierpont's views on state rights, secession, and slavery. The simplistic and inflexible views on these questions drove Pierpont to a vigorous plan for organizing Union sentiment in Virginia, particularly after the issuance of the Emancipation Proclamation.

The narrative eloquently approaches Pierpont's activities with the restored Virginia government, headquartered at Alexandria in 1863. Bitterly hated by Virginia Confederates, the subject nonetheless removed to Richmond after the war and fought for leniency toward those who took part in the rebellion. Although the Federal government had maintained that Virginia had a loyal government and was never outside the Union, Pierpont ran into trouble with the radical Republicans in Congress and his political career terminated in 1868. Ambler skillfully and interestingly delivers this story.

Albert Gallatin Riddle (1816–1902)

422

Riddle, Albert Gallatin. **Recollections of War Times: Reminiscences of Washington, 1860–1865** (380 pp., G. P. Putnam's Sons, New York, 1895)

The wartime notes of an Ohio congressman form the basis for this volume. A single brief chapter provides the background on Riddle's life up to 1861, when he removed to Washington and entered the U.S. House, emerging in the first weeks of war as an inexperienced Republican. The narrative focuses well on the war years, providing excellent anecdotal material on the Federal rout at Bull Run and the ensuing panic in Washington. Recollections of politics and politicians on Capitol Hill, some of which are quite valuable, fill many of the work's pages.

Many sections of interest address such subjects as Lincoln's relations with the Congress, emancipation measures, the Committee on the Conduct of the War, the investigation of Ball's Bluff, and disloyalty in Washington. In 1863 the author traveled south to serve as consul at Matanza, Cuba, and his discussions of politics there and of blockade-runners carry some interest. Further material evaluates Lincoln's secretaries Cameron and Stanton and provides insight into early Reconstruction measures. The work concludes with anecdotes of July 1865, and appendices contain tributes to John Brown and Edwin M. Stanton.

Frederick William Seward (1830–1915)

423

Seward, Frederick W. **Reminiscences of a War-Time Statesman and Diplomat** (489 pp., G. P. Putnam's Sons, New York, 1916)

Despite being composed long after the war, this book contains some interesting material. As the assistant secretary of state during the conflict, remembered as the victim of Lewis Powell during the night of assassination at war's end, Frederick Seward observed a wide latitude of both statesmanship and military aspects of the Civil War. He also witnessed many scenes of great interest in wartime Washington.

While it contains useful reminiscences on some aspects of the war, this volume is ultimately disappointing. Although somewhat more than one-quarter of the book treats the Civil War era, few surprises emerge from the narrative, which mostly resembles a collection of vignettes rather than a tightly focused, serious chronology of the war's diplomatic history. The best portions are based on wartime notes. In other sections Seward rambles on about his early history in New York state and the growing clouds of tension prior to the firing on Sumter and engages in lengthy recollections on various post-war exploits including the purchase of Alaska. The style occasionally wanders rather far afield and many "conversations" are presented with incredible accuracy. In short, the work presents glimpses of interest, including much about the author's father and the assassination night. The index is poorly done and loaded with ambiguous references.

William Henry Seward (1801–1872)

424

Seward, William Henry. **The Works of William H. Seward** (ed. George H. Baker, 5 vols., 3216 pp., J. S. Redfield, New York, 1853–1884)

This work traces the entirety of Seward's lengthy public career. Volume 5 holds the bulk of the papers related to the Civil War. Official documents, letters, speeches, and messages pertaining to Seward's Civil War career trace his activities from the assumption that on his selection as U.S. secretary of state he would essentially run the government in Lincoln's stead. The evolution of a positive working relationship with Lincoln and a realization of their interactions comes through the many documents, as do characterizations relating to numerous Union officials and Seward supporters and antagonists, including Thurlow Weed, Horace Greeley, Edwin M. Stanton, John A. Dix, and a host of diplomats.

The goal of preserving the Union is clearly the sole fixation for Seward throughout the war's early months, yet Seward realized on Lincoln's election that slavery would be abolished. The diplomatic crises were generally minor save for that of the *Trent* affair, and the correspondence during this period is particularly revealing. The diplomatic diary and correspondence in volume 5 greatly illuminate the character of the war, despite their focus on the general progress of events and diplomatic concerns. The author's recognition of the weaknesses of the Confederacy undoubtedly aided Lincoln greatly as their relationship matured. Perhaps the most striking quality of Seward's messages is the absolute boldness and firmness with which he acted.

425

Taylor, John M. **William Henry Seward: Lincoln's Right Hand** (340 pp., HarperCollins, New York, 1991)

This work nicely complements Van Deusen's earlier biography (*q.v.*). Written for a popular audience yet documented superbly and composed with great flair, it is the most readable biography of the Union secretary of state. Taylor uncovered fresh archival material including family letters and combined them into a portrait that reappraises Seward's role as a politician, advisor to Lincoln, and husband and father. The book lacks the exhaustive political analysis set in a scholarly monologue of Van Deusen's work, but it offers significantly more modern analysis of Seward the man and will satisfy all but the most detail-oriented readers as a general survey of Seward's life.

About half of the text covers Seward's Civil War years,

which allows the author to construct a credible and highly entertaining portrait of Seward's rise to political prominence. The postwar activities of Seward receive significant coverage too, but the relationship with Lincoln takes center stage. The author dispassionately places his subject into a balanced light, blaming him where necessary and avoiding siding with his subject in the early months of tension with Lincoln. The analysis is clear and cogent, the interpretation of events evenhanded. The result an enjoyable, modern view of a complex and ultimately embittered personality.

426

Van Deusen, Glyndon G. **William Henry Seward** (666 pp., Oxford University Press, New York, 1967)

Exhaustive and meticulous in detail, this book offers a splendid, full picture of the Union secretary of state. Drawing on the rich collection of the Seward papers at the University of Rochester, Van Deusen reconstructs Seward's life with a moderate degree of sympathy. Slightly more than one-quarter of the book treats Seward's wartime role in which the ambitious former governor found himself subordinate to Lincoln. The author sympathetically but realistically covers Seward's changing relationship with his president, documenting his vigorous support of the chief executive.

The author shows how Seward skillfully handled many crises without the egotistical character typical of his first weeks in office. Indeed, Seward provided valuable political service in directing many activities such as the handling of the *Trent* affair. The full picture and appreciation of Seward's abilities and his balancing of ideals and realities thus emerge strongly. Van Deusen contends that throughout his many victories his subject lacked the personal vigor to ignite the fires of the populace behind him, or was simply shackled by conservatism. Still, Van Deusen's book supplies an accurate, deserved, and impressive view of William Henry Seward.

John Sherman (1823–1900)

427

Sherman, John. **John Sherman's Recollections of Forty Years in the House, Senate, and Cabinet: An Autobiography** (2 vols., 1239 pp., Werner Co., New York, 1895)

This is a highly valuable and often neglected source on the politics of wartime Washington. The work contains many excerpts of speeches and other official documents of the Ohio senator, a staunch Republican and the younger

brother of Maj. Gen. William T. Sherman. The narrative offers much of value relating to the political circles of the Civil War Senate. The most valuable aspects relate to financial matters and the senator's deep involvement in military affairs, emancipation measures, and such key legislation as the Legal Tender Act, the national banking system, and the Federal income tax, all cleverly and vigorously supported by Sherman's basically conservative agenda.

More than one-quarter of the first volume treats the war years. Although much of the narrative linking speeches and documents recalls events of 30 years earlier, the work seems steadfastly reliable. Many facsimiles of letters and official documents appear, as do photographs of significant players in the political and military machines of the Federal war effort. A large store of material covers Sherman's significant postwar activities, consuming much of the first volume and the entire second volume. The discussions of Sherman's role in Reconstruction will interest all students of that tragic period. A few errors of spelling appear, as with the names of Galusha A. Grow and Donn Piatt.

Edwin McMasters Stanton (1814–1869)

428

Thomas, Benjamin P., and Harold M. Hyman. **Stanton: The Life and Times of Lincoln's Secretary of War** (642 pp., Alfred A. Knopf, New York, 1962)

A full, soundly researched biography, this work devotes about half its space to the war years. The early years of Stanton's life come alive in detail for the first time as does his path toward legal high circles and the replacement of Cameron as secretary of war. By the time the Civil War comes into focus and Stanton settles into his autocratic career, it is clear that the authors are recounting a superbly told story and that they are somewhat partial toward their subject.

However, the book does not go blindly into the night. The authors carefully document conclusions and use a wide range of evidence to support their pro-Stanton stance. Only occasionally do they clearly stop short of critical analysis or make outright errors, such as misspelling the name of Lewis Paine and mistaking some details relating to the Lincoln assassination and Stanton's early efforts to deal with it. On the whole, this book remains an important contribution that can be trusted and read with the expectation of balanced, rational insight.

Thaddeus Stevens (1792–1868)

429

Brodie, Fawn M. **Thaddeus Stevens: Scourge of the South** (448 pp., W. W. Norton and Co., New York, 1959)

Brodie examines the career of this cantankerous Northern politician. About three-fourths of the work examines the Civil War and Reconstruction years, with splendidly researched analysis on Stevens's voting records, accomplishments, political associations, and battle for suffrage for blacks. The study focuses on a wide range of actors on the Civil War era stage, so it is not closely a biography of just Stevens but also deals with a number of his associates and enemies.

Although it records the career information of Stevens, the narrative amounts to a general history of the wartime era and adds little to that published previously. The biography investigates Stevens's early life far more effectively than have earlier studies, however, showing how physical disability and overreaching responsibilities molded his personality at an early age. The work is generally sympathetic but does not hesitate to attack its subject for a number of faults. Too much may have been made of party politics in assessing Stevens's career, but the book delivers a generally sound summary that stands as the best single work available.

Charles Sumner (1811–1874)

430

[Pulitzer Prize, 1961]

Donald, David H. **Charles Sumner and the Coming of the Civil War** (392 pp., Alfred A. Knopf, New York, 1960) and **Charles Sumner and the Rights of Man** (595 pp., Alfred A. Knopf, New York, 1970)

Together, these volumes comprise a detailed, scholarly, and heavily researched portrait of the Massachusetts senator's entire life in and out of politics. The first volume examines the subject's early life and career through the eve of the war. The second, massively detailed volume outlines Sumner's involvement in the politics of war and his relatively brief career in postbellum years.

The work allows a penetration into Sumner's mind to such a level that readers can see the full extent of his fight for emancipation and for equality during Reconstruction. The author deftly illuminates the way in which Sumner used his clout as chair of the Committee on Foreign Relations to win colleagues over to his progressive social views. The au-

thor also demonstrates in detail how Sumner cooperated with Lincoln more frequently than he often gets credit for, occasionally manipulated Andrew Johnson, and outright blocked some of Grant's ideas.

Donald places much of Sumner's actions in the context of Massachusetts political tradition. That allows him to answer the whys of many complex actions, although the answers—as with Sumner's criticism of the Fourteenth Amendment—may not always satisfy. Indeed, the author may overinterpret a personality who was if nothing else an enigma to those who knew him. Donald's work creates a significant picture of one of the most powerful senators of the war period. In doing this he illuminates many aspects of wartime politics in a superb way.

431

Sumner, Charles. **The Selected Letters of Charles Sumner** (ed. Beverly Wilson Palmer, 2 vols., 1246 pp., Northeastern University Press, Boston, 1990)

This magnificently edited work is greatly important for both antebellum and wartime senatorial analysis, and it forms a significant narrative of important wartime events in Washington City as well. Sumner wrote more than 7000 letters during his life, many of which still exist in repositories, libraries, and private collections. The editor chose more than 900 letters to appear in this work and extensively annotated them to form a very usable compilation. There are 244 letters covering the war period itself.

The senator's correspondents included Abraham Lincoln, Francis Lieber, Salmon P. Chase, John A. Andrew, Thomas Wentworth Higginson, George Bancroft, William Lloyd Garrison, and many other famous politicians and reformers of the period. The list was not confined to Americans but also included such Englishmen as John Bright and Richard Cobden. The extensive coverage of the published Sumner letters allows one to follow Sumner's thoughts and actions at critical periods, including his prewar caning, his return to the Senate, his interactions with the Lincoln administration, and his private thoughts about various politicos and military commanders. The ability to explore Sumner's correspondence provides valuable insight for readers. Moreover, the high standard of the editing makes the set even more useful, as Palmer tracked down and defined obscure references, filled in a multitude of facts, and generally made the letters as usable as possible to a wide audience. This set is a magnificent addition to the literature.

Roger Brooke Taney (1777–1864)

432

Steiner, Bernard C. **Life of Roger Brooke Taney, Chief Justice of the United States Supreme Court** (553 pp., Williams and Wilkins Co., Baltimore, 1922)

The life of this controversial jurist is chronicled in sometimes too much detail. Taney's lifespan coincides with the evolution of ancient America, dating from nearly the Declaration of Independence to the forging of modern America to the seeds of Reconstruction policies during the final year of the Civil War. Such a long life allows the author to portray Taney's almost fanatical devotion to his principles and work ethic against the background of 19th-century law. Particularly interesting material relates to Taney's involvement with the Jackson administration and of course his legal interpretation of matters relating to slavery. Black Americans had "no rights which the white man was bound to respect," Taney wrote.

While not quite a full biography, this work analyzes Taney's legal career at length and particularly his tenure as chief justice of the U.S. Supreme Court. The focus on *Scott vs. Sanford* is handled well, although Steiner overstates Taney's lack of communication with James Buchanan. The work misstates the case with respect to Virginia and Maryland's forbidding the importation of slaves; the state constitutions were in question, not the U.S. Constitution. Six justices believed the Missouri Compromise void, not four as stated in these pages. The study does not fully explore the relationship between Taney and Lincoln. But it stands as the best collection of material relating to this political figure who found himself overwhelmed by revolutionary change and ignored by Abraham Lincoln.

Clement Laird Vallandigham (1820–1871)

433

Klement, Frank L. **The Limits of Dissent: Clement L. Vallandigham and the Civil War** (351 pp., University Press of Kentucky, Lexington, 1970)

The Copperhead agitator Clement L. Vallandigham presented problems for nearly everyone during the war, not the least of whom was Lincoln, who banished him to the South. He also presents problems for biographers because of an unlikable personality whose negative influence bred controversy and a general lack of rich material to work with. Although the biography suffers from some of these maladies, this is the most suitable assessment of Vallandigham.

Klement depicts Vallandigham's role as a U.S. representative and newspaper owner who opposed the war, voted against conscription, and vigorously attacked the Republicans. Arrested for speaking out in sympathy toward the enemy, Vallandigham was tried by a military court, denied a writ of habeas corpus, and released into the countryside south of Murfreesboro, Tennessee.

The author describes Vallandigham's trial adequately, although he does not analyze the many complex issues at hand. In measuring Vallandigham's tests of the limits of dissent, the author erroneously supports the Roger Taney view on the habeas corpus writ. Readers do not glean how Vallandigham viewed the limits of dissent, nor how his contemporaries saw the chaos of a disorganized Federal government transform into one with procedures for national security. Despite this "crackdown" on dissent, in the long run the war expanded the civil and political liberties of Americans. Klement does not show the full picture here but concentrates so much on his subject that one might feel his story typifies the Lincoln administration's treatment of dissenters.

Benjamin Franklin Wade (1800–1878)

434

Trefousse, Hans L. **Benjamin Franklin Wade, Radical Republican from Ohio** (404 pp., Twayne Publishers, New York, 1963)

As chairman of the Commitee on the Conduct of the War, Wade exercised great power in affecting the ways in which Washington interpreted strategy, tactics, and commanders. One of the most vocal aspirants of emancipation, Wade helped to thrust forward the cause of blacks during the war and afterward. This study, much more complete than previous biographies, contains full coverage of the Civil War years but also relishes Wade's varied roles in Reconstruction.

In portraying Wade's own somewhat tarnished image, Trefousse may have gone somewhat too far. Empowered by noble causes, Wade seemingly attempted to use any means he could to achieve the goals in mind, and in this the author seems to approve. Although the author stops short of complete sympathy toward his subject, the portrait that emerges seems somewhat slanted in favor of the senator. This aside, the work clearly tops the previous studies of Wade's life as it sets its subject in a clearer and more favorable light.

Elihu Benjamin Washburne (1816–1887)

435

Hunt, Galliard. **Israel, Elihu, and Cadwallader Washburn: A Chapter in American Biography** (397 pp., Macmillan Co., New York, 1925)

Hunt records the diverse activities of three brothers who made significant contributions to Civil War America. Well researched from the Library of Congress and other manuscript collections, this remembrance of the Washburns consists of three biographical sections preceded by a brief chapter on the brothers' births and upbringing in Livermore, Maine. Israel receives 37 percent of the attention; 35 percent of the book examines Elihu B. Washburne's career (Elihu changed the family name); and brother Cadwallader receives coverage amounting to 25 percent of the book's space.

The work consists chiefly of letters and documents linked by a minimal narrative. Altogether, about two-thirds of the chapters consist of this source material rather than narration. The primary value is high, then, but the book functions more as a reference than a story. It amply illuminates the careers of the three Washburns but does not even approach casting them in a personal light. Cadwallader's settlement in Wisconsin and his military career unfold in the documents, supplying material to the story of his commands at Vicksburg, at Memphis, and in Missouri. His terms as U.S. congressman and governor of Wisconsin receive significant attention. Many documents appear relating to Israel's tenure as governor of Maine. Elihu's friendship with Lincoln and sponsorship of U. S. Grant make his section revealing. The work is not intimate but provides a documentary record of three influential brothers of the wartime period.

(Reprinted 1969, 397 pp., Da Capo Press, New York)

Gideon Welles (1802–1878)

436

Niven, John. **Gideon Welles: Lincoln's Secretary of the Navy** (676 pp., Oxford University Press, New York, 1973)

Although not a full biography, Niven's book offers a detailed and impressively documented study of Welles's prewar career as a newspaper editor and politician as well as extensive material on the Civil War and Reconstruction years. About 35 percent of the work covers the war years and Welles's important and influential work as secretary of the navy.

Welles's background in Connecticut receives critical and detailed treatment by the author, who recounts his subject's role in shaping the state's political parties, including the Jacksonian, Free Soiler, and Anti-Nebraska Democrat and Republican contingencies. What emerges from this is a clear view of Connecticut's part in New England politics and the secession crisis that loomed as the 1850s drew to a close.

The most valuable aspects of the book arise from the descriptions of Welles's median activities in shaping the wartime Navy Department, his involvement with recruiting, supervising the blockade, shipbuilding, and participating in sessions on naval strategy. The author shows that despite criticism for delegating too much and awarding civilians hefty contracts, Welles played the central part in decision making within the department. Although Niven does not fully involve Welles's personality and shys away from placing him into context within the Lincoln administration, readers get the impression that Welles stood outside the cabinet's inner circle and harped on Stanton and others as a defense mechanism. A number of typographical errors and a relatively inadequate index do not significantly harm the book's overall usefulness.

(Reprinted 1994, 676 pp., Louisiana State University Press, Baton Rouge)

437

Welles, Gideon. **The Diary of Gideon Welles** (3 vols., 1943 pp., Houghton Mifflin Co., Boston, 1911)

This classic American diary is a necessary source for students of the Lincoln administration, wartime Washington, and New England thinking about the war. The diary contains a narrative of events during the first weeks of war and commences with daily entries on 10 August 1862. These entries, full of valuable information and opinions relating to virtually all important governmental officials, general officers, political decisions, and military campaigns, continue throughout the war. The diary closes with an entry on 6 June 1869.

Like other famous wartime diaries, however, Welles's published manuscript is not an exact copy of the diary. After the war the navy secretary penned corrections, additions, and an introductory chapter covering the war's first year. Moreover, Welles's son Edgar altered some material and so did the editors at Houghton Mifflin. The result is a historical document that occasionally strays from the original intent. As Richard N. Current pointed out in 1960, some large sections added after the war appear as if they are contemporary, as with the Lincoln conversation of 13 April 1865.

Still, most of these changes are minor, and most simply clarify the original document. The work offers a cornerstone source of many famous scenes and evaluations, including the failures of McClellan, the caustic nature of Secretary Stanton, the first tidings of emancipation, and the assassination of Lincoln. Great historical value is to be found in the wealth of information contained in Welles's jottings.

(Reprinted 1960, with editorial inserts correcting some of the "original" changes, ed. Howard K. Beale, 3 vols., 1943 pp., W. W. Norton and Co., New York)

SOLDIERS

Henry Livermore Abbott (1842–1864)

438

Abbott, Henry Livermore. **Fallen Leaves: The Civil War Letters of Major Henry Livermore Abbott** (ed. Robert Garth Scott, 266 pp., Kent State University Press, Kent, 1991)

Readers will explore the 139 extant letters written during the war by a bright young Massachussetts officer who rose to brevet brigadier general of volunteers. Abbott was graduated from Harvard in 1860 and promptly joined the 20th Massachusetts Infantry (the "Harvard regiment") in 1861, receiving a commission as second lieutenant. He participated with the regiment in many pitched battles of the Army of the Potomac and went through the full range of experiences of a junior officer before being killed in action at the Wilderness.

The letters, written to Abbott's father and other relatives, reveal the author's judgment with great candor. Abbott holds McClellan in extremely high regard. With Abbott's New England background of wealth and influence (but not abolition philosophy), he scoffs at the Emancipation Proclamation and occasionally makes rude observations about the less fortunate and foreigners. Despite these blemishes of character, Abbott holds the preservation of the Union as the principle for which he is fighting and makes insightful observations about camp life, the soldiers he commanded, and politics. A fine job of editing, maps, 33 photos, and an introduction and epilogue round out this rewarding collection.

Charles Francis Adams, Jr. (1835–1915)

439

Adams, Charles Francis, Jr. **Charles Francis Adams, 1835–1915: An Autobiography** (224 pp., Houghton Mifflin Co., Boston, 1916)

Characterized by candor and perhaps a lack of self-realization, the volume sets forth the exploits of this brevet brigadier general, railroad executive, and historian. Without the common illusions about his accomplishments, the narrative is refreshingly clear about Adams's record in the war and afterward. He perhaps too freely criticizes others, however, and occasionally the work swims in a tone of apology for the writer's outwardly gruff demeanor. The author's estimates of his achievements are modest, giving the volume a somewhat self-effacing quality that sometimes distracts.

Despite this, the narrative pertaining to the war years is well worth reading. Nearly a third of the work treats the years 1860 and 1861, with a riveting story of the young Adams taking a campaign journey with William Henry Seward and spending the critical month of mid-February through mid-March 1861 in Washington. From the spring through autumn of 1861, the author gradually moved toward entering the service and finally was commissioned a cavalry officer, distinguishing himself in a number of campaigns that are inadequately described here as they appear in the author's previous writings, chiefly for the Massachusetts Historical Society. Because the work was published posthumously, Worthington Chauncey Ford added a short section completing the last years of Adams's life, appended with a memorial address by Henry Cabot Lodge.

Adelbert Ames (1835–1933)

440

Ames, Blanche Ames. **Adelbert Ames, 1835–1933: General, Senator, Governor: The Story of His Life and Times and His Integrity as a Soldier and Statesman in the Service of the United States of America throughout the Civil War and in Mississippi in the Years of Reconstruction** (625 pp., published by the author, North Easton, Mass., 1964)

This volume is the best work on Ames. The Union general's daughter compiled a work that naturally casts Ames in a favorable light and downplays the political turmoil he found himself in during his tenure in Reconstruction Mississippi. Consisting largely of letters and reminiscences, the book has a folksy tone. Illustrations include three-color maps and a collection of rare photographs that show old America passing into new America—from Adelbert Ames as West Point cadet in 1861 to Adelbert Ames playing golf in his nineties with John D. Rockefeller.

Those wishing to investigate Ames further may wish to consult *Chronicles from the Nineteenth Century: Family Letters of Blanche Butler and Adelbert Ames.* Compiled in 1935 by Ames's widow, this work consists of 1408 pages in two volumes. It was privately published by Jesse Ames Marshall in Clinton, Massachusetts, in 1957.

Nicholas Longworth Anderson (1838–1892)

441

Anderson, Nicholas Longworth. **The Letters and Journals of General Nicholas Longworth Anderson: Harvard, Civil War, Washington, 1854–1892** (ed. Isabel Anderson, 320 pp., Fleming H. Revell Co., New York, 1942)

Anderson's work contains the record of one of Ohio's youthful commanders. Consisting of three distinct parts, the collection presents the Harvard journals of the Cincinnati student during the years 1854–1858, Anderson's wartime notes and diaries, and letters to his wife and son written during the last year of the war and for the remaining 30 years of his life, spent mostly in Washington among a circle of influential friends. The Civil War coverage, then, consumes about one-fifth of the work.

During this period Anderson rose from first lieutenant and regimental adjutant of the 6th Ohio Infantry to the same unit's colonel, and was eventually brevetted brigadier general and major general on the "omnibus day" of 13 March 1865 for heroism at Stones River and Chickamauga. The brief diaries, though presented without much interpretation and often containing only a sentence or two per day, present material of interest for particular events of the western theater. Moreover, they constitute a kind of running narrative of events in the life of the 6th Ohio and contain brief comments on many officers.

William Woods Averell (1832–1900)

442

Averell, William Woods. **Ten Years in the Saddle: The Memoir of William Woods Averell, 1851–1862** (ed. Edward K. Eckert and Nicholas J. Amato, 443 pp., Presidio Press, San Rafael, Calif., 1978)

This work recounts experiences that might have made Averell a cavalry legend, yet during the upswing of his prominence in the middle of the war he abruptly faded into the background. Often poised on the brink of success, Averell hesitated at crucial moments, was twice relieved of command, and in May 1865 resigned from the army. Nevertheless, memoirs of Union cavalry officers are scarce, and although the rambling style in this one is sometimes annoying, the memoir sheds valuable light on some topics.

The first 236 pages of Averell's work cover his prewar years; only 148 pages cover the war, and the memoirs abruptly stop with the end of the Peninsular campaign. (Hurt by Hooker and Sheridan's actions of removal, which Averell felt were undeserved, the general never finished the work.) The sections on First Bull Run and the Peninsula offer vivid detail from a firsthand perspective, and Averell has written a lucid account of training the 3d Pennsylvania Cavalry. A final wartime chapter, "Conduct of the War," broods over McClellan and has the flavor of someone who watched much of the war from the sidelines. Unfortunately, the memoir does not include Averell's wartime experiences during 1863 and 1864, nor does it shed light on the dispute between Sheridan and Averell at the time of Fisher's Hill, after which Averell's career effectively ended.

Willoughby Babcock (1832–1864)

443

Babcock, Willoughby. **Selections from the Letters and Diaries of Brevet-Brigadier General Willoughby Babcock of the Seventy-fifth New York Volunteers: A Study of Camp Life in the Union Armies during the Civil War** (ed. Willoughby M. Babcock, Jr., 110 pp., University of the State of New York, Albany, 1922)

This collection chronicles the wartime career of a New York officer who served gallantly before being mortally wounded at Winchester in October 1864. Skillfully edited by the fallen officer's grandson, the work presents 201 letters, arranged in 12 groups, written by Babcock to his wife. The groups document the subject's career as a first lieutenant in the 3d New York Infantry, a lieutenant colonel of the cavalry division, Department of the Gulf, and lieutenant colonel of the 75th New York Infantry. Babcock was brevetted brigadier general posthumously for his service at Winchester.

The letters are exceptionally well composed and offer superb insights into Babcock's personality and activities, the soldiers he knew and commanded, and life in the South during the war. Highlights include material covering the organization of the 3d New York, life at Camp Hamilton, Virginia, a tour of duty and sickness at Fort McHenry, a journey to Santa Rosa Island, Florida, life in occupied New Orleans, the 75th New York's Louisiana expedition, action at Donaldsonville and Thibodeaux, and the Shenandoah Valley campaign of 1864. There is no index.

Lafayette Curry Baker (1826–1868)

444

Baker, Lafayette C. **History of the United States Secret Service** (704 pp., published by the author, Philadelphia, 1867)

This odd Civil War figure has provided a curious and unreliable memoir. The author's inability to fashion a truthful story on several well-publicized public questions casts a distinct haze over this work, which offers an overdramatized story with Baker cast in the role of self-appointed hero. Allegedly based in part on notes made by Baker at various times, the account examines his career in the "secret service" during the war (as a spy and later special provost marshal) and his controversial involvement in Andrew Johnson's administration in the two years following the war.

Baker traces his early life before exploring his adventures for the government, including an interview with Winfield Scott, an attempt to visit Richmond as a spy, and an interview with Jefferson Davis, along with some letters of Davis, Toombs, and Walker. The author further describes his experiences in the North as a "Confederate spy" and his activities searching out corruption in the war effort, highlighting fraud among postmasters, stealing and smuggling in the army, suspicions of corruption abroad, investigations of the Treasury Department, and so on. He does not document his own fraud.

Highly sensationalized in places and containing re-created conversations, the work is undependable. The narrative also contains much about Baker's part in tracking down the Lincoln conspirators and addresses the capture of Southern leaders, as well as Baker's postwar legal calamities. Useful only for light entertainment, the book lacks an index. Several retitled and embellished variants appeared between 1874 and 1894.

Nathaniel Prentiss Banks (1816–1894)

445

Harrington, Fred Harvey. **Fighting Politician, Major General N. P. Banks** (301 pp., University of Pennsylvania Press, Philadelphia, 1948)

Studiously researched, comprehensive in its coverage, and intelligent in its interpretation, this work admirably examines the army career of a political general who remained greatly influential despite his succession of failures. Although it lacks a generally enjoyable style, the book successfully follows Banks's rather amazing antebellum career as a Massachusetts politician, analyzing his governorship and tenure in the Massachusetts and U.S. Houses (briefly as speaker of the latter), all compressed into the hectic decade of the 1850s.

Harrington's calculated and moderate evaluation continues through the war years, wherein the author does not hesitate to praise Banks for his accomplishments and bash his poor judgment that was perhaps caused by a certain lack of principle. Banks was shoved about the Shenandoah Valley and at Cedar Mountain by Stonewall Jackson, ordered terrible and probably unnecessary assaults at Port Hudson, and commanded the ill-fated Red River campaign. Exacting in its examination of these actions and of Banks's postwar career, this work is likely to stand as an important contribution for some time to come.

William Francis Bartlett (1840–1876)

446

Bartlett, William Francis. **Memoir of William Francis Bartlett** (ed. Francis Winthrop Palfrey, 309 pp., Houghton, Osgood and Co., Boston, 1878)

A useful tribute to the young Massachusetts brigadier general, this volume consists largely of Bartlett's diaries and letters from the war and the relatively brief postbellum life he enjoyed. The work thus manages to avoid eulogistic nonsense but lacks both analysis and an adequate unifying narrative from the editor. It is a sourcebook, then, whose greatest value lies in the general's own reflections on his Civil War career.

The story is one of pathos. Bartlett held the South in high esteem, and his many Southern friends made his decision to enlist difficult. In the U.S. Army, however, he gallantly participated and lost a leg at Yorktown. He was wounded in almost every major battle in which he fought, Confederate sharpshooters taking special aim at the Yankee horseman.

The diary reveals a young man of great character despite his constant suffering. The account of Bartlett's wounding and capture at the battle of the Crater and subsequent life in Libby Prison is valuable. The postwar coverage consists of letters written from Europe and others touching on business and political matters. The last few pages constitute a tribute from Palfrey.

John Beatty (1828–1914)

447

Beatty, John. **The Citizen-Soldier; or, Memoirs of a Volunteer** (401 pp., Wilstach, Baldwin and Co., Cincinnati, 1879)

This is a minor classic narrative of soldier life from a Federal brigadier general. The Ohioan's career in the 3d Ohio Infantry, which included wide service in McClellan's campaign in western Virginia, Mitchel's raid in Tennessee and northern Alabama, and the battle of Perryville, gave this soldier a mixed bag of wartime experience. Reminiscences focus on Beatty's command of brigades at Stones River, Chickamauga, Chattanooga, and Knoxville.

Beatty's keen insight and literary intelligence provide a work that holds up dependably today. In addition to the battles described, he also reflects on politics, nature, the Southern whites and blacks he observed (with interesting observations on their attitudes toward Unionism), and the alternately brilliant and deplorable actions of Union soldiers in the South. A good deal of material relates to Murfreesboro and Huntsville, Alabama, where he spent considerable time. The diary terminates with Beatty's resignation in January 1864. An appendix contains the narrative of the capture and escape of Beatty's fellow inmate, Bvt. Brig. Gen. Harrison C. Hobart. The index is skimpy.

(Reprinted 1946, titled *Memoirs of a Volunteer, 1861–1863*, with an introduction by Lloyd Lewis, ed. Harvey S. Ford, 317 pp., W. W. Norton and Co., New York; 1879 edition reprinted 1983, 401 pp., Time-Life Books, Alexandria, Va.)

Alfred Bellard (1843?–1891)

448

Bellard, Alfred. **Gone for a Soldier: The Civil War Memoirs of Private Alfred Bellard** (ed. David Herbert Donald, 298 pp., Little, Brown and Co., Boston, 1975)

English born and a resident of New Jersey at war's commencement, Bellard enlisted as a private in the 5th New Jer-sey Infantry, a unit commanded by Cols. Samuel H. Starr and William J. Sewall. The unit's duty was typical of an eastern three-year regiment: the Peninsular campaign, Second Bull Run, Fredericksburg, Chancellorsville, Gettysburg, the Virginia campaigns of 1864, and disbandment in November of that year. During the war the author kept a journal and sent letters home once a week to his father; about 15 years later he compiled this record into a lengthy and richly illustrated log of his Civil War service.

The battle accounts are splendidly accomplished. They include the regiment's actions through Chancellorsville, where the author was wounded and subsequently transferred to the Veteran Reserve Corps. The accounts of common soldier life are most enriching, illustrated (as they were drawn) in color, and serve to throw light onto the concerns of a typical foot soldier. Food, comfort, and marches were much on the mind, as were the wounded and combatting boredom in camp. In the latter pages of the book, describing duty in Washington, the author records the daily routine in the capital city as the final, gruesome year of conflict ground on. Unfortunately, there is only a slim "biographical index."

John Davis Billings (1842–1933)

449

Billings, John D. **Hardtack and Coffee; or, The Unwritten Story of Army Life, Including Chapters on Enlisting, Life in Tents and Log Huts, Jonahs and Beats, Offences and Punishments, Raw Recruits, Foraging, Corps and Corps Badges, the Wagon Trains, the Army Mule, the Engineer Corps, etc.** (406 pp., George M. Smith and Co., Boston, 1887)

In this favorite classic among reminiscences of soldier life in the Civil War, a veteran of the 10th Massachusetts Artillery recounts in simple language not so much the battles and leaders but the trivial and daily aspects of soldier life in the Federal Army. The style is conversational, the latitude of topics covered enormous, and the result forms a valuable introduction to what soldier life in the Army of the Potomac must have been like.

Anecdotes marked by clarity and honesty pepper the recollections of routine things. Billings surveys the plan and practical parts of a camp, lists the tents used, describes methods for creating fireplaces, and outlines the drudgery and boredom of camp life. His scenes re-create the realities of guards, army rations, punishments, assembly, drill, foraging, and inventions of the common soldier's war. Marching, wagon trains, bridge building, flags, torches, badges—all receive scrutiny. This establishes a neat picture of the many things that a soldier would have carried in his mind into battle.

Six color plates and more than 200 engravings by Charles W. Reed illustrate the volume, adding a great deal of character. There is no index.

(Reprinted 1960, titled *Hardtack and Coffee: The Unwritten Story of Army Life*, ed. Richard Harwell, 483 pp., Lakeside Press, Chicago; 1887 edition reprinted 1982, 408 pp., Time-Life Books, Alexandria, Va.; 1887 edition reprinted 1993, with an introduction by William L. Shea, 413 pp., University of Nebraska Press, Lincoln)

David Bell Birney (1825–1864)

450

Davis, Oliver W. **Life of David Bell Birney, Major-General United States Volunteers** (418 pp., King and Baird, Philadelphia, 1867)

This early and complete biography of Birney is divided into 51 concise chapters, an appendix of official reports, a list of Birney's staff officers, and an index. A few of the first chapters discuss Birney's family, especially his father, James G. Birney, who became a Southern planter and then an abolitionist and a third-party candidate for the presidency in 1844. David Bell Birney was born in Huntsville, Alabama, but soon moved to Cincinnati and by 1848 had settled in Philadelphia.

The author surveys Birney's lengthy Civil War career by focusing on his early militia service, participation in the 23d Pennsylvania Infantry, and early commission as a brigadier general. The narrative follows Birney's service in the Peninsular campaign, his service on a Washington court-martial board, and his frustration in having two subordinates, Daniel E. Sickles and Hiram G. Berry, promoted ahead of him. The discussion provides much detail about camp life in the spring of 1863 complete with horse races, dances, and picnics. Chancellorsville and Gettysburg represent a strengthening of Birney's role as he inherited the 3d Corps at the latter battle when Sickles was carried from the field. The text traces Birney's incorporation into Hancock's 2d Corps in the spring of 1864 and Birney's command of the corps during Hancock's absence. By midsummer Birney was shuffled into the Army of the James near Deep Bottom, and the following autumn he fell ill with malaria, dying at the age of 39.

Davis provides a serviceable narrative of Birney's career while making a few of the standard errors of dates, names,

and facts found in such early compilations. He supposes that Union Col. George W. Willard, killed at Gettysburg, was a general. He contributes many spelling errors and misidentifications, such as "General Gherardie" for Confederate Col. Victor J. B. Girardey. The author also employs a few contrived dialogues and engages in some what-if speculations about things that may have changed the course of the war.

(Reprinted 1987, 418 pp., R. Van Sickle, Gaithersburg)

Charles Harvey Brewster (1833–1893)

451

Brewster, Charles Harvey. **When This Cruel War Is Over: The Civil War Letters of Charles Harvey Brewster** (ed. David W. Blight, 366 pp., University of Massachusetts Press, Amherst, 1992)

The 137 letters collected here chronicle the author's war record between July 1861 and October 1864. Serving with the 10th Massachussetts Infantry until the last summer of the war, Brewster experienced a wide range of actions before recruiting black soldiers in Norfolk, Virginia. Very fine accounts of the siege of Yorktown, the battle of Seven Pines, Gettysburg, the Wilderness campaign, and the first weeks of the Petersburg siege fill these pages. The letters quite elegantly record the typical range of a soldier's experience, and the editor focuses in his annotations on the social and psychological aspects of the life of this common soldier. Because of this, the ironies of a Massachusetts soldier stand out strikingly: Brewster felt slavery should be abolished but did not think highly of blacks.

The emphasis on Brewster's social experience results in only a casual attempt at explaining the military aspects of his letters. The background information is thin concerning the organizations that Brewster was involved in, the commanders and other soldiers he comments on, and the explanation of the battles mentioned. The book lacks an index, limiting its usefulness as a research tool.

John Hill Brinton (1832–1907)

452

Brinton, John H. **Personal Memoirs of John H. Brinton, Major and Surgeon U.S.V., 1861–1865** (361 pp., Neale Publishing Co., New York, 1914)

Brinton's memoirs contain the outstanding recollections of an officer who experienced the war in the West. As a physician, Brinton had the opportunity to experience the aftermath of several major battles in the West and to make the acquaintance of important commanders, including U. S. Grant, Phil Sheridan, William S. Rosecrans, and Henry W. Halleck. Brinton carefully recorded his wartime experiences, and although the work was composed long after the war, he accurately recalls what he had seen. The memoirs recount the growing war spirit in Philadelphia, the author's travel to St. Louis, and early recollections of John C. Frémont and the chaotic politics of Missouri.

The author presents significant reflections on a Civil War surgeon's life, describes the Mound City hospital, recalls his first meeting with Grant, describes a malaria infestation, and sketches his appointment as medical director of the Army of the Tennessee. The work describes scenes of ghastly surgery following Belmont and the battle of Shiloh, service in the surgeon general's office, and war experiences in the East. Brinton's take on South Mountain, Antietam, and Fredericksburg is superb, as are recollections of seeing Lincoln, Sheridan's Valley campaign, and a return to the West under Rosecrans. The tone is serious, the narrative is well written, and the collection contains much of interest to medical studies of the war.

Wiley Britton (1842–1930)

453

Britton, Wiley. **Memoirs of the Rebellion on the Border, 1863** (458 pp., Cushing, Thomas and Co., Chicago, 1882)

Britton provides a rare narrative glimpse of the war in the far West from a member of the 6th Kansas Cavalry. The author's portrait focuses on army movements, guerrilla activities, Indian affairs, and the state of the civilian population in the area of southwestern Missouri, northwestern Arkansas, eastern Kansas, and eastern Oklahoma. The work is a simple narrative that infrequently sets off on literary detours. For the most part, however, the author intertwines meaningful discussions of events of certain interest with lighthearted anecdotes, as the discussion of stargazing in camp illustrates.

The work betrays a careful mind without partisan bitterness and reflects acts of kindness toward citizens from the author and his comrades. Britton also highlights depredations by Union soldiers, the political nature of commands, the bloody aspects of the guerrilla war, and the general futility of war as a whole. Composed after the war, the memoirs nonetheless read credibly. Unfortunately, the volume lacks an index.

(Reprinted 1993, with an introduction by Philip T. Tucker, 458 pp., University of Nebraska Press, Lincoln)

Ambrose Everett Burnside (1824–1881)

454

Marvel, William. **Burnside** (504 pp., University of North Carolina Press, Chapel Hill, 1991)

Such a biography was much needed for this difficult figure, one who played a significant part in several battles in the East before becoming one of the worst commanders of the Army of the Potomac and displaying striking ineptness strategically and tactically at Fredericksburg. Marvel apparently surveyed a wide range of sources and employs a simple and straightforward style of prose.

The biography centers on Burnside's Civil War years, with more than half the work devoted to the general's post-Fredericksburg career. The brief discussion of Burnside's antebellum days is sketchy. That which follows is more detailed, the sections on Antietam and Fredericksburg dominating. Unfortunately, the discussions of First Bull Run and the North Carolina expedition lack sufficient detail.

All of these sections are characterized by subjectivity: Marvel apparently adores Burnside, and this colors the interpretation of events. The narrative rationalizes Burnside's incompetence by proposing conspiracies against the commander who himself admitted he was "unfit for high command." An example: after extensively attempting a proof that Burnside did not receive the bridge attack order from McClellan at Antietam until 10 A.M. (instead of 9:10 A.M.), he does not ask why Burnside waited long after 10 A.M. to advance and then only hesitatingly moved forward. The author suggests that at Antietam, McClellan was ultimately responsible for his subordinates; at Fredericksburg he suggests the subordinates let down Burnside. Burnside himself ducks responsibility in both cases. Occasional misspellings occur, as with Edward Porter Alexander, Isaac P. Rodman, and Alexander P. Stewart. Much good information exists here; however, it is clouded in a tale of the great Burnside and those who worked their sinister ways against him.

Benjamin Franklin Butler (1818–1893)

455

Butler, Benjamin F. **Autobiography and Personal Reminiscences of Major-General Benj. F. Butler: Butler's Book** (1154 pp., A. M. Thayer and Co., Boston, 1892)

This widely distributed self-tribute might be characterized as a defense of the writer against most of the other participants in the Civil War. The cockeyed general had difficulty seeing eye to eye with just about everyone—superiors, subordinates, and the Confederates—and this lengthy memoir demonstrates that abundantly. Despite his difficulties and many failures as one of the war's worst political general officers, Butler remained in a powerful position through nearly the entire conflict. He did achieve successes, and these are described in lengthy detail, as with the North Carolina expedition at Hatteras in the war's first summer and the generally successful governing of New Orleans.

Other events are recounted with higher degrees of self-justification, including the bungled handling of troops at Big Bethel, the "bottling up" of the Army of the James at Bermuda Hundred, the futility of the Dutch Gap canal project, the poorly planned and executed first attack on Fort Fisher, and the giant error of propaganda in issuing the "woman's order" at New Orleans. Filled with many letters and statistics (which are useful in themselves), much of this work has little more to offer beyond showing the nature of how, three decades after the war, Ben Butler persisted in espousing a mountain of twisted truths.

456

Butler, Benjamin F. **Private and Official Correspondence of Gen. Benjamin F. Butler, during the Period of the Civil War** (5 vols., 3303 pp., Plimpton Press, Norwood, Mass., 1917)

This companion to the previous work was edited and published by family members to preserve Butler for posterity. Extracted from Butler's wartime letterbooks, his correspondence, and many passages from the *O.R.* (*q.v.*), the work offers a valuable compilation of materials relating to the controversial politician-general. Unfortunately, the editing is poor, leaving users with few annotations where many are required, and there is a general lack of precision in transcribing and evaluating material. Nonetheless, the voluminous collection touches on all phases of Butler's wartime relations, and for that alone it casts much light on his successes and many controversies.

The work contains letters by and to Butler, official war-related documents, and many newspaper accounts relating

to the subject. The frequent letters to and from Butler's wife provide a backdrop against which the many other sources interplay, and the result is gratifying if mainly for its thoroughness. Letters from Abraham Lincoln, Salmon P. Chase, Frank Blair, and John A. Andrew constitute much of value on political matters as well as the military situations Butler created, particularly in the long summer of 1864 and the war's final spring. Each volume contains a flawed index.

457

Trefousse, Hans Louis. **Ben Butler: The South Called Him Beast!** (365 pp., Twayne Publishers, New York, 1957)

This is an important work, for it provides a carefully documented and objective analysis to one of the more influential Federal political generals. Without a modern study, one might be left to the severely skewed telling of Ben Butler's role in the war provided by his own works (*q.v.*).

Trefousse demonstrates the odd themes of Butler's character. A successful and patriotic politician (he had been governor of Massachusetts and a U.S. congressman), he was nevertheless reckless with his thinking and careless and cantankerous with his personal encounters. A careful analyst of emancipation policy, he was foolish and unthinking as the time for arming black soldiers approached. Unpopular with the general officers he served, Butler was ultimately a powerful politician who became more trouble than he was worth. That he stayed on as a major general and commanded the Army of the James had more to do with Lincoln's sense of political balance than Butler's ability as a soldier. Butler's story is nevertheless an important one, and Trefousse presents it capably.

Daniel Butterfield (1831–1901)

458

Butterfield, Julia L. S., ed. **A Biographical Memorial of General Daniel Butterfield, Including Many Addresses and Military Writings** (379 pp., Grafton Press, New York, 1904)

This privately published memoir chronicles the career of an influential staff officer during the first two years of the war. A successful political militia colonel, military confidant of George McClellan, and chief of staff of the Army of the Potomac from the Peninsula through Gettysburg, Butterfield warrants close inspection despite his removal from command before the decisive battles and his poor evaluation by many important commanders. The present volume is a tribute but is not marred by that fact in that it contains a great deal of useful information regarding Butterfield's military career.

The book's more entertaining passages cover such innovations by Butterfield as corps badges, the use of military music to identify the members of his brigade, and identification markings for artillery trains and headquarters locations within the army. The work includes much correspondence and official documents tracing Butterfield's rise from colonel of the 12th New York State Militia to his association with McClellan and later activities, notably the position on Hooker's staff in early 1864. The work repeats material occasionally and is anything but concise. Much detail of note appears regarding McClellan's Peninsular campaign, although with some inaccuracies, as with the statement that McDowell and his 40,000 men at Fredericksburg failed to reinforce McClellan, a judgment perhaps made with less than gracious motives in mind. McDowell's 30,000 men were required to stay because of Jackson's movement down the Valley; in fact, McClellan moved his forces toward the Valley to protect Washington. Lines 6 and 8 on page 374 are transposed.

Robert Goldthwaite Carter (1845–1936)

459

Carter, Robert Goldthwaite. **Four Brothers in Blue; or, Sunshine and Shadows of the War of the Rebellion: A Story of the Great Civil War from Bull Run to Appomattox** (509 pp., Gibson Brothers Press, Washington, 1913)

The author was a private in the 22d Massachusetts Infantry. His brothers also served in the Army of the Potomac: Eugene as first lieutenant and quartermaster of the same regiment, Walter as sergeant major of the 22d, and John H. as a sergeant in the 1st Massachusetts Heavy Artillery. Their letters, woven together with narrative by Robert Carter, form an unbroken chronicle of life in the army throughout some of the heaviest fighting of the eastern theater. Because the brothers were observant and literate, the work is a splendid source for life on the march, in camp, and in battle with the Massachusetts men.

Prior to the wartime discussion, Robert Carter's narrative describes his days at West Point immediately before the war broke out. The wartime letters contain commentary on two commanders of the 22d, Cols. Henry Wilson and William Tilton, and those of the 1st Heavy, William B. Greene and Thomas R. Tannatt. The finest portions of the work describe the brothers' great range of experiences in battle: First Bull Run, the Peninsular campaign, Antietam, Fredericksburg, Chancellorsville, Gettysburg, Mine Run, the

Wilderness, Spotsylvania, Cold Harbor, Petersburg, City Point, and Appomattox. The letters are filled with interesting minutiae such as stories of Philadelphia's Cooper Shop, captures of prisoners, an execution, a narrow escape from capture, rearguard fighting, drunkenness, camp music, the death of friends, rotten food, and numerous points of interest on many battlefields.

(Reprinted 1978, with an introduction by John M. Carroll and a foreword by Frank Vandiver, 537 pp., University of Texas Press, Austin)

Joshua Lawrence Chamberlain (1828–1914)

460

Trulock, Alice Rains. **In the Hands of Providence: Joshua L. Chamberlain and the American Civil War** (569 pp., University of North Carolina Press, Chapel Hill, 1992)

The emphasis in this work is overwhelmingly on the war years, with just brief treatments of the antebellum and postbellum days adding some insight into the subject's character. This is the case despite Chamberlain's significant accomplishments in education and politics following the war. Nevertheless, the work treats the Gettysburg hero's war years in well-researched detail, providing readers with a clear and balanced narrative of this professor-turned-fighter.

Chamberlain's service as lieutenant colonel of the 20th Maine Infantry commenced five weeks prior to Antietam, where he fought bravely and impressed his superiors. Trulock's description of Chamberlain's performance in the Army of the Potomac is first rate, drawing on letters and other material owned by the subject's descendants and previously untapped. The chilling and disheartening experiences of Fredericksburg and Chancellorsville, famous from passages written by Chamberlain himself, come alive in this lucid and well-supported text. The description of the celebrated charge of the 20th Maine with Chamberlain as its colonel in the hollow between Round Top and Little Round Top at Gettysburg is as tightly executed and riveting as any presented in the best battle and campaign studies. Subsequent moments of drama, such as the terrible wounding at Petersburg and the final participation in the surrender ceremony at Appomattox, add a luster to this work that makes it among the better recent Union biographies.

A few errors appear, as with the misspellings of B. Gratz Brown, Lysander Cutler, and Philip Kearny. These minor blemishes do not detract from a solid, comprehensive work that adds greatly to Chamberlain's own campaign reminiscence, *The Passing of the Armies* (*q.v.*).

Cyrus Ballou Comstock (1831–1910)

461

Comstock, Cyrus B. **The Diary of Cyrus B. Comstock** (ed. Merlin E. Sumner, 408 pp., Morningside, Dayton, 1987)

This diary records the soldier life of a young West Pointer who would become one of U. S. Grant's most trusted staff officers. Comstock's engineering background and skilled military judgment manifest themselves early in this diary, which covers the period 13 December 1850 to Grant's funeral in 1885. Most of the detail focuses on two four-year periods, Comstock's days at West Point and his Civil War service. Thus the diary offers a great and detailed view of life at West Point from 1851 to 1855 and includes minute comments on the customs of West Point life and on the curriculum. The author routinely mentions the activities of many who would be important officers in the war, giving this section a rare fascination.

The great value of the book comes from the wartime coverage, which amounts to just over one-quarter of the narrative. Good reportage of the early operations after Sumter gives way to a gap in the diary from August 1861 to June 1862. The author records sketchy but interesting accounts of activities in the Peninsular campaign before another gap occurs between September 1862 and April 1863. Much of great interest to engineering operations appears in the following entries as Comstock's duties carry him to the western theater. The coverage in 1864, after Comstock's appointment on Grant's staff, is much fuller and provides intimate descriptions of the May campaign and of Grant and his associates.

The work contains a number of errors of spelling, as with the names of George Burgwyn Anderson, Laurence Simmons Baker, Alvan Cullem Gillem, Joseph King Fenno Mansfield, and James Brewerton Ricketts. An uncomfortably large number of words in the diary are omitted as they were indecipherable, owing to Comstock's small, difficult handwriting. These minor criticisms aside, the work is a splendid one for students of Grant and the final operations of the war.

Alonzo Cooper (1830–1919)

462

Cooper, Alonzo. **In and Out of Rebel Prisons** (335 pp., R. J. Oliphant, New York, 1888)

Cooper's narrative offers an account of captivity during the war's final year. Composed almost a quarter-century after the war, allegedly with the help of a prison diary, the account covers the period from capture in April 1864 to February 1865, when the author was sent to Richmond and exchanged. The work contains a small amount of apparently contrived dialogue but in the main appears reliable upon checking with other sources on major accounts. The author served briefly as first lieutenant in the 12th New York Cavalry before being captured at Plymouth, North Carolina. His narrative details in interesting fashion the battle of Plymouth, his capture, and the execution-style deaths of black troops captured by Confederates under Brig. Gen. Robert F. Hoke.

The narrative that follows focuses on the little incidents of Cooper's march and transport to prison and contains relatively little about the deprivations of prison life. He describes his episodes of escape and recapture and offers interesting observations of the people along the route as well as the Confederate military hosts. The author's range of prison experience carried him from Macon to Savannah, Charleston, Columbia, and finally Danville. After his exchange in February 1865, he made his way down the James River, north to Annapolis, and ultimately joined the final days of Sherman's exploits in North Carolina. An appendix lists prisoners held at Macon during 1864. The work lacks an index.

(Reprinted 1983, 335 pp., Time-Life Books, Alexandria, Va.)

William Corby (1833–1897)

463

Corby, William. **Memoirs of Chaplain Life by Very Rev. W. Corby: Three Years Chaplain in the Famous Irish Brigade, "Army of the Potomac"** (391 pp., La Monte, O'Donnell and Co., Chicago, 1893)

Corby, who was chaplain of the Irish Brigade during part of its service with the Army of the Potomac, lacked a diary or letters in composing these memoirs, written from memory nearly 30 years after the war. Despite this, the work is realistic and appears to deliver a faithful view of the author's service with the boys in blue.

Apart from a standard and rather laborious narrative of the author's minor experiences with the army—and repeated misspellings of names and places—some interesting observations are uncovered. Corby greatly admired McClellan, whom he staunchly defends, and had mixed feelings about a number of other officers. The book naturally focuses on Fr. Corby's work with the wounded, and his descriptions of sick and ailing soldiers in the wake of several battles vividly re-create the horror of war. The author's recollections are peppered with admonitions against those who were bigoted against Catholics. Intermingled with these warnings are a great many accounts of life in the field with the common soldiers, remembrances of marches, camp scenes, poor food, sickness, lice and other insects, and dire suffering.

(Reprinted 1992, titled *Memoirs of Chaplain Life: Three Years with the Irish Brigade in the Army of the Potomac,* ed. Lawrence Frederick Kohl, 412 pp., Fordham University Press, New York)

Samuel Eckerman Cormany (1838–1921)

464

Cormany, Samuel Eckerman, and Rachel Bowman Cormany. **The Cormany Diaries: A Northern Family in the Civil War** (ed. James C. Mohr, 597 pp., University of Pittsburgh Press, Pittsburgh, 1982)

A pair of diaries kept by sweethearts from 1858 to 1865 provides the basis for an interesting book. The Cormanys met at Otterbein College in Ohio in 1858, began their diaries, and recorded an immense collection of data as they experienced the war in different ways. Samuel and Rachel's courtship and marriage, the birth of their first child, and the war consume the bulk of these pages. Between 1862 and 1865 Samuel served in the 16th Pennsylvania Cavalry, and Rachel lived with relatives in Chambersburg.

Many of the entries cover aspects of soldier life and life on the home front in a small Pennsylvania town. The religious nature of both parties infuses a certain evangelical tone into parts of the diaries. Serving as a horse soldier with J. Irvin Gregg's regiment, Samuel provides excellent accounts of Chancellorsville, Gettysburg, Mine Run, and Petersburg. Rachel's superb writings include an eyewitness account of the burning of Chambersburg. The diaries are split and alternate to provide a rough chronology in this worthwhile book.

Jacob Dolson Cox (1828–1900)

465

Cox, Jacob D. **Military Reminiscences of the Civil War** (2 vols., 1145 pp., Charles Scribner's Sons, New York, 1900)

Written with great attention to detail, these memoirs stand with the best of those penned by Federal general officers. One of the highly capable political generals, Cox compiled his reminiscences long after the war but supported them with his own wartime papers and those of many fellow officers. The author's literary experience gives the work a quality rarely seen in memoirs by a commander, and thus they are enjoyable as well as informative to read. Commissioned a brigadier general in May 1861, Cox took part in the early campaigns in western Virginia. Despite his friendship with George McClellan, the author recalls that the credit for Rich Mountain belonged to the junior officers. Subsequent battle accounts shed additional light on other fellow officers. Ambrose Burnside fares well for his activities at Antietam, supported in this account by the poor orders of McClellan. Yet despite the level analysis of McClellan's faults (as with the perpetual overestimation of the enemy's size), Cox treats his old commander with tenderness and respect.

The author feels that the distinction between regular army officers and volunteers should have been "abolished," as many capable officers who were not outstanding students had the natural capability to lead effectively in the field (witness Ulysses S. Grant), whereas those with preeminent schooling (Halleck) did not. The portions of text treating Atlanta and the battles of Franklin and Nashville echo to a degree the author's works on those conflicts (*q.v.*), but much of interest may be found regarding the final days of the campaigns in North Carolina. The narration relating to many Federal officers who fought along with Cox remains highly valuable.

George Crook (1828–1890)

466

Crook, George. **General George Crook: His Autobiography** (ed. Martin F. Schmitt, 326 pp., University of Oklahoma Press, Norman, 1946)

This narrative examines Crook's military exploits up to 1876. Although it emphasizes Crook's activities as an Indian fighter, including just 58 pages of coverage on the commander's Civil War duty, the autobiography contains a valuable record of Crook's war service. Additional materials prepared by the editor conclude Crook's story. Crook begins his Civil War reminiscences by describing his trip eastward from San Francisco and the belief, after hearing of initial success by Federals at Bull Run, that the war would be "over before we reached Washington."

The following chapters nicely summarize Crook's involvement in Civil War battles ranging from the early actions as colonel of the 36th Ohio Infantry in western Virginia through the conclusion of the war. The narrative is serious and focused on large-scale military operations Crook experienced, so it lacks detail that might have made it a richer story. Nonetheless, the author's discussions of South Mountain, Antietam, and his subsequent cavalry commands are worth reading. The narrative offers significant recollections of Chickamauga and fighting in West Virginia, the Shenandoah Valley, and Maryland late in the war, including the embarrassing incident of capture by McNeill's rangers. Crook's exchange enabled him to participate in the Appomattox campaign, which he succinctly recalls in this work. One typographical error was found, a misspelling of Nelson Appleton Miles.

(Reprinted 1960, with a foreword by Joseph C. Porter, 326 pp., University of Oklahoma Press, Norman; reprinted 1986, 326 pp., University of Oklahoma Press, Norman)

Alonzo Hereford Cushing (1841–1863)

467

Brown, Kent Masterson. **Cushing of Gettysburg: The Story of a Union Artillery Commander** (330 pp., University Press of Kentucky, Lexington, 1994)

Brown offers a well-researched view of the Wisconsin youth who became a hero after his death in Pickett's Charge. The author uses an impressive array of manuscript sources as well as reliable primary printed works to produce the first detailed portrait of this nearly forgotten soldier. Other, secondary sources used sometimes verge on the completely unreliable. The work presents a lengthy military narrative of Cushing's Civil War exploits without much dramatic style.

The author examines Cushing's full life, devoting a respectable two chapters to the antebellum years in Wisconsin and at West Point. There is detailed, workmanlike coverage of Cushing's part at First Bull Run, in the Peninsular campaign, at Antietam, Fredericksburg, Chancellorsville, and of course Gettysburg. The interpretation is often good, sometimes oversteps its bounds, and occasionally illuminates fresh ideas. A disturbing number of errors are scattered throughout the book, as with the misspellings of Barnard E.

Bee, Catharinus P. Buckingham, William H. Emory, Willis A. Gorman, Philip Kearny, Wladimir Krzyzanowski, Alexander R. Lawton, and Henry Warner Slocum. The index occasionally contains two different sets of entries for the same person. While most of these errors do not cloud the meaning of events, they do not inspire confidence in the text.

George Armstrong Custer (1839–1876)

468

Custer, George A., and Elizabeth Custer. **The Custer Story: The Life and Intimate Letters of General George A. Custer and His Wife Elizabeth** (ed. Marguerite Merington, 339 pp., Devin-Adair Co., New York, 1950)

The wartime letters between Custer and his wife were assembled by the friend and literary executrix of Elizabeth Custer. The work contains excerpts from family correspondence arranged in approximate chronology and treating thematic aspects of Custer's career and the Custers' relationship. More than one-third of the book covers the Civil War years, and although in most cases only short sections of letters appear, much material of value lies within them.

Custer's widespread staff duty, including early service with George B. McClellan and Alfred Pleasonton, provided a position from which Custer made spirited assessments of the fights he was in and the commanders he encountered. His command of a brigade in Kilpatrick's division and involvement in the cavalry fight at Gettysburg produces superb material in the letters. Of greatest interest to Civil War readers, however, may be Custer's sterling performance in the Appomattox campaign. Apart from the military aspects of this work, many details of Custer's family life appear and are worthy of close inspection. The editing leaves something to be desired, as interpretation is scant and errors lie scattered throughout the work. Particularly annoying errors of spelling mar the names of William Woods Averell, Jenny Lind, Thomas Taylor Munford (misidentified as a brigadier general), Alfred Pleasonton, William Starke Rosecrans, and Julius Stahel.

469

Monaghan, Jay. **Custer: The Life of General George Armstrong Custer** (469 pp., Little, Brown and Co., Boston, 1959)

Often overblown and misinterpreted, Custer's participation in the war was marked by success as a "boy general" but also by a number of characteristically foolish actions that won glory at the great risk of disaster. Fortunately, Brig. Gen.

Custer found his moment at Appomattox when his "road-block" helped entrap the final Confederate battle line of the Army of Northern Virginia. Before that point the officer served on the staffs of McClellan and Pleasonton until receiving command of a cavalry brigade just prior to Gettysburg. Custer's performance was dashing and frequently successful throughout many of the major battles of the final two years of war.

Custer brings to the reader a painstakingly researched description of its subject's life with a significant emphasis on the Civil War years. Written with clarity and verve, the author's narrative allows the reader to explore Custer's vivacious and self-indulgent personality while fairly assessing his contributions to the war. The research is adequately documented, and a fine selection of photographs adds a great deal to the text. The author commits a few odd errors, as with the description of Paul Semmes's capture at Sayler's Creek, whereas in reality he had been mortally wounded nearly two years before at Gettysburg.

(Reprinted 1971, 479 pp., University of Nebraska Press, Lincoln)

Philippe Régis Dénis de Keredern, comte de Trobriand (1816–1897)

470

de Trobriand, Régis. **Four Years with the Army of the Potomac** (ed. George K. Dauchy, 757 pp., Ticknor and Co., Boston, 1889)

Assembled here are the recollections of the French officer who entered service as colonel of the 55th New York Infantry and rose to brevet major general of volunteers by war's end. Originally published in 1867 as *Quatre ans de campagnes à l'Armée du Potomac* and later translated into this first English edition, the recollections concentrate on the service and officer corps of the Army of the Potomac and contain valuable glimpses into many characters of high grade and rank. The narrative is remarkably frank, describing both heroics and blunders of the army, greatly praising some officers while criticizing others. The credibility of this work is therefore quite high, and de Trobriand's judgments are for the most part valuable.

The author describes his part during the Peninsular campaign and his brigade command in the 3d Corps at Fredericksburg, Chancellorsville, and Gettysburg. The glimpses of battle are fresh, based on de Trobriand's wartime notes and immediate postwar recollections. Among the more interesting sections are those touching on the final weeks of the war

about Petersburg and the movements toward Appomattox. Interspersed with the fine military dialogue are comments on a variety of related social and political issues, such as emancipation, morale on the home front, and occupation. The work lacks an index.

(Reprinted 1988, 757 pp., R. Van Sickle, Gaithersburg)

John Adams Dix (1798–1879)

471

Dix, Morgan. **Memoirs of John Adams Dix** (2 vols., 823 pp., Harper and Bros., New York, 1883)

The life story of the ranking major general of volunteers during the war is told. Armed with the numerous military and political achievements of the subject, Dix's son presents a chronological summary of his father's life without a great deal of focus on the war years, or at least without revealing much astounding information about Dix's Civil War command. Nonetheless, the work neatly offers a detailed picture of Dix's youthful service in the War of 1812, his suppression of the New York City draft riots, his term as adjutant general of New York, and his political appointments as New York's secretary of state, governor, minister to France, U.S. senator, and James Buchanan's secretary of the treasury.

The spotlight remains focused on Dix throughout these pages. Little interpretation of his actions or placement into a larger context occurs. The author does show how Dix, as a Jacksonian Democrat, reigned with great confidence during the secession crisis. His greatest legacy, indeed, may be the statement, "If any one attempts to haul down the American flag, shoot him on the spot." Dix's command of the Middle Department was relatively uneventful, the field commanders taking most of the decisive action. Still, this work records the career of a high-ranking and influential member of the Union high command.

Grenville Mellen Dodge (1831–1916)

472

Dodge, Grenville M. **Personal Recollections of President Abraham Lincoln, General Ulysses S. Grant, and General William T. Sherman** (237 pp., Monarch Printing Co., Council Bluffs, Iowa, 1914)

This slim volume contains some comments of interest from an aged former Federal commander. The book's three parts review Dodge's acquaintances with each of the three victors of the war and offer some insight into their character. The recollections of Lincoln seem typical and lack distinct vision, in accordance with Dodge's slight relationship with the president during the war. Dodge recalls his own military service and role in the expansion of military railroads and sheds some light on late-war service in Missouri and his correspondence with Lincoln in the war's final months.

The sections on Grant and Sherman are more immediate. Reviewing Grant's career, Dodge staunchly defends his old chief against Henry Halleck, before and during Corinth, where Dodge commanded a division. The discussion contains much of interest relating to intelligence gathering. The author defends Sherman's decision to assign Oliver O. Howard in place of John A. Logan to placate George Thomas.

(Reprinted 1965, 237 pp., Sage Books, Denver)

Lucius Fairchild (1831–1896)

473

Ross, Sam. **The Empty Sleeve: A Biography of Lucius Fairchild** (291 pp., State Historical Society of Wisconsin, Madison, 1964)

The author restores this Federal brigadier general to proper historical perspective. Usually remembered for his tantrum directed at Grover Cleveland, who in 1887 ordered the return of Confederate battle flags to the South, Fairchild played a significant military role in the war itself. Ross chronicles this soldier's service as a private and then as captain of the 1st Wisconsin Infantry and his subsequent commission as lieutenant colonel of the 2d Wisconsin. As such, Fairchild participated as an important officer in the Iron Brigade's struggle at Second Bull Run. Promoted to colonel, he led the regiment at South Mountain, Antietam, Fredericksburg, and Chancellorsville. Fairchild's left arm was shattered during the first day at Gettysburg, ending his military career.

The author skillfully and dispassionately describes Fairchild's participation in the war and presents an eloquent discussion of his subject's wartime tenure as Wisconsin's secretary of state. The book is a full biography, carrying the story on into Fairchild's postbellum career as a politician.

Wilbur Fisk (1839–1914)

474

Fisk, Wilbur. **Anti-Rebel: The Civil War Letters of Private Wilbur Fisk, 1861–1865** (ed. Emil Rosenblatt and Ruth Rosenblatt, 383 pp., published by the editors, Croton-on-Hudson, N.Y., 1983)

The Fisk letters represent an impressive and full collection describing the war experience of this soldier of the 2d Vermont Infantry. Fisk sent the letters home for publication in the Montpelier *Green Mountain Freeman* (written by "Anti-Rebel"); as such, they brought the war news and experiences of a hometown regiment in the Army of the Potomac to the local populace.

The many accounts of battle stretch from Fisk's enlistment to the siege of Petersburg, and the commentary on battles and campaigns is outstanding. Further, the author found himself attached to the depot hospital at City Point for a time and describes its activities as well. Caution should be exercised, however. Because Fisk intended the letters for publication, he sometimes embellished them to put his experiences and those of his comrades into the best light. Read with care, these letters offer a great view of the camps, battles, and marches of the 2d Vermont and its participation on the eastern front.

(Reprinted 1992, titled *Hard Marching Every Day: The Civil War Letters of Private Wilbur Fisk, 1861–1865*, with a new introduction, 383 pp., University Press of Kansas, Lawrence)

Michael Hendrick Fitch (1837–1930)

475

Fitch, Michael H. **Echoes of the Civil War as I Hear Them** (368 pp., R. F. Fenno and Co., New York, 1905)

This book recalls the Civil War service of a Wisconsin officer. Based on a wartime diary, the memoir traces the author's experiences as a first lieutenant in the celebrated 6th Wisconsin Infantry of the Iron Brigade and his subsequent service as lieutenant colonel of the 21st Wisconsin. Although the work was written 40 years after the close of the war, it stands up reasonably well, offering anecdotes and glimpses of soldier life in addition to recollections of battles and skirmishes. Because of the author's association with the 6th Wisconsin, in which he served until July 1862, he brushed up against such characters as Lysander Cutler, Edward S. Bragg, and Rufus R. Dawes.

The narrative covers a wide variety of western engagements, including Perryville, Stones River, Chickamauga, Chattanooga, the Atlanta campaign, the March to the Sea, and Bentonville, as well as the author's subsequent return to Milwaukee. The portion of the work recounting life in the 21st Wisconsin contains reminiscences about the notable officers Benjamin J. Sweet and Harrison C. Hobart.

John Charles Frémont (1813–1890)

476

Rolle, Andrew. **John Charles Frémont: Character as Destiny** (351 pp., University of Oklahoma Press, Norman, 1991)

Frémont gained his notoriety as the pathmarker of the West and as the first (and unsuccessful) Republican presidential candidate. But Frémont's status as a high-ranking major general and his renegade actions early in the war—such as the private emancipation activities—keep him important as a controversial Civil War figure. Of course, Frémont's influence ended abruptly as he tangled with his commander-in-chief, but during the first months of the war he towered over other general officers as a leading figure of the war in the West.

The author carefully documents Frémont's wartime activities and offers a psychological interpretation of Frémont's checkered career. The illegitimate son of the Frenchman Charles Frémont and the unhappy Anne Pryor, young John Charles traveled nearly constantly with his family until settling in Charleston. His father died when John was only five years old. Consequently, according to the author, Frémont grew up in a fantasyland wherein he concocted grandiose personality traits. Later, unusual relationships with wife, Jessie Benton, and father-in-law, Thomas Hart Benton, heightened his sense of adventure, at which he excelled, even as his loner status deepened. His wife staunchly and at times irrationally defended everything Frémont did, and this potent combination ultimately brought him into trouble. Battling both Lincoln and the Blairs, Frémont found himself continuously in trouble in the summer of 1861 until he stepped over his line of authority once too often.

An occasional incorrect spelling crops up, as with Benjamin F. Butler and James Shields. However, these minor errors do not diminish the value of this full biography of one of the Civil War's most powerful and troubled officers.

James Abram Garfield (1831–1881)

477

Garfield, James A. **The Wild Life of the Army: Civil War Letters of James A. Garfield** (ed. Frederick D. Williams, 325 pp., Michigan State University Press, East Lansing, 1964)

Garfield's successful and important tenure as a Civil War officer comes alive in this work. Although in the end Garfield's career was simply a path to political election, his important service, literate nature, and sensible observations of critical actions and personalities make these letters valuable.

The editor has selected and annotated more than 200 letters written between April 1861 and the closing days of 1863, when Garfield resigned to take his seat in the U.S. House. The letters reveal much about Garfield and document the successes of his military campaigns. Garfield's involvement in Kentucky in early 1862, in facing and defeating Humphrey Marshall at Middle Creek and Pound Gap, receive illuminating attention. Letters also portray the less triumphant involvement at Shiloh and Corinth and Garfield's election to the U.S. House, as well as his involvement in the court-martial of Fitz John Porter. In 1863, as Rosecrans's chief of staff, Garfield both supported his commander and criticized him in correspondence, politically sheltering himself while building associations with Chase and other radical Republicans. Finally, the disaster at Chickamauga ruined Rosecrans and Garfield left for Washington.

478

Peskin, Allan. **Garfield** (716 pp., Kent State University Press, Kent, 1978)

Garfield's religious youth, political aspirations, postwar presidency, and assassination have typically dominated his earlier biographies, with relatively shallow attention paid to his military activities. This work, however, devotes nearly one-quarter of its space to the wartime period, covering Garfield's field service and his headstrong entrance into the U.S. House in 1863. The book delicately treats Garfield's youth and early years in Ohio, his days at Hiram College, and his burgeoning career as a religious thinker. The author successfully portrays the complex contradictions in Garfield's clouded personality, suggesting how his subject could be a "pacifist turned soldier" and a "man racked by self-doubts who was, at the same time, convinced of his high destiny."

Peskin does not shy away from criticizing his subject. He describes Garfield marrying his wife while in love with another woman, wrangling his opponents for control of the Western Reserve Eclectic Institute, and approaching involvement with scandals several times, including the Credit Mobilier and DeGolyer cases. The author finds that Garfield's wavering loyalty to his Civil War commander, William S. Rosecrans, demonstrated "disingenuous" behavior on Garfield's part. The depth of this work is impressive—more so than the man it undertakes to examine.

John White Geary (1819–1873)

479

Geary, John W. **A Politician Goes to War: The Civil War Letters of John White Geary** (ed. William Alan Blair, 259 pp., Pennsylvania State University Press, University Park, 1995)

The editor makes a solid contribution to the literature that was begun by Bell Irvin Wiley more than 15 years earlier. The nearly 200 letters in this volume, written mainly to Geary's wife, constitute a major source of interest for students of the Federal command and the war in Pennsylvania. Not only do the missives often reflect much about the battles and campaigns Geary was currently entangled with and the personalities of other Union commanders, but they also reflect much of the lives of common soldiers and Geary's personal life aside from the battlefield. The result is a volume worthy of all Civil War libraries.

Although the letters center on the war years, readers get a flavor for Geary's earlier political career in the Democratic party, as mayor of San Francisco, and as governor of Kansas Territory. The politician was commissioned colonel of the 28th Pennsylvania Infantry and led it into the field before being commissioned brigadier general of volunteers. The letters are most interesting during the months beginning in 1862 when Geary was elevated to brigade command. Discussions of the actions at Cedar Mountain, Chancellorsville, and Gettysburg are a high point. Geary's famous defense of the night actions at Wauhatchie, his participation in the March to the Sea, and his governorship of Savannah all contribute materially to this enjoyable volume.

John Gibbon (1827–1896)

480

Gibbon, John. **Personal Recollections of the Civil War** (426 pp., G. P. Putnam's Sons, New York, 1928)

This superb memoir is by the sometime commander of the Iron Brigade and the stand-in for Winfield Scott Han-

cock's 2d Corps at Gettysburg. The Union major general rose rapidly from chief of artillery for Irvin McDowell to division commander and, after his wounding and corps command at Gettysburg, again commanded a division in the Army of the Potomac until near the end of the war, when he received his own corps command, that of the 24th Corps of the Army of the James. Such a career carried Gibbon through some of the most dramatic moments of the war from a position of battlefield authority, and this important memoir, composed in 1885 from Gibbon's diary, letters, and notes, contributes lasting value about the war in the East.

The accounts relating to Second Bull Run, Antietam, Gettysburg, the Wilderness, Petersburg, and Appomattox are particularly appealing. The Gettysburg account contains a classic record of Meade's council of war held in the Leister House on the night of 2 July 1863. Other periods are buttressed with letters from fellow commanders, mostly Union and sometimes Confederate, to substantiate or reflect on the narrative. The author largely glosses over his dispute with Hancock over the attack order of 6 May 1864, at the Wilderness, a minor disagreement that brought together Gibbon and Francis C. Barlow. Reconstructed "conversations" may be somewhat embellished but are presumably based on the author's diary. The work lacks an index.

(Reprinted 1988, with an introduction by Don Russell, 426 pp., Morningside, Dayton)

Willard Worcester Glazier (1841–1905)

481

Glazier, Willard W. **Three Years in the Federal Cavalry** (339 pp., R. H. Ferguson and Co., New York, 1870)

This is an early account infused with great patriotism and fervor for the war. Although overwritten, embellished, and containing manufactured "conversations," the story of this soldier's experiences during a multitude of battles is worthwhile. Glazier is especially strong in relating many little incidents of soldier life, as he entered service in Troy, New York, and worked his way into the reorganized Harris Light Cavalry, the 2d New York Cavalry. The narrative describes episodes of mounted drill, the bugle corps, Confederate guerrilla activities, Virginia weather and citizens, and the regiment's advance to the Rappahannock. Incidents of march and picket duty add to the discussions of Fredericksburg, Thoroughfare Gap, and the end of the Peninsular campaign.

The author recounts much of what a soldier experienced in his discussions of the deaths of comrades, trading around camp, marching in the mud, and picket duty; he narrates his unit's part in Pope's campaign in Virginia, the Confederate advance into Maryland, payday, letter writing, laying pontoons under fire, and the reorganization of the cavalry corps. The work includes a highly dramatic account of Chancellorsville, Stoneman's raid, Yorktown, Falmouth, Brandy Station, and Gettysburg. Glazier describes the death of Col. Benjamin F. Davis of the 8th New York Cavalry at Beverly Ford and discusses Kilpatrick's gunboat expedition. The book concludes with Glazier's capture at Cedar Run and imprisonment, at which point readers are referred to his prison diary, a less interesting work published as *The Capture, the Prison Pen, and the Escape: Giving a Complete History of Prison Life in the South, Principally at Richmond, Danville, Macon, Savannah, Charleston, Columbia, Belle Isle, Millin, Salisbury, and Andersonville, Embracing, also, the Adventures of the Author's Escape from Columbia, South Carolina, His Recapture, Subsequent Escape, Recapture, Trial as a Spy, and Final Escape from Sylvania, Georgia* (422 pp., United States Publishing Co., New York, 1868). The work lacks an index.

James Henry Gooding (1837–1864)

482

Gooding, James Henry. **On the Altar of Freedom: A Black Soldier's Civil War Letters from the Front** (ed. Virginia M. Adams, 139 pp., University of Massachusetts Press, Amherst, 1991)

Although brief, this book offers a rare view of a black soldier's experience of Civil War combat. With his naval background, Gooding made an unusual member of the celebrated 54th Massachusetts Infantry, the early black unit led by Col. Robert Gould Shaw. From 3 March 1863 to 8 February 1864, Gooding wrote 48 letters that were published originally in the New Bedford *Mercury*. The letters of this 26-year-old enlistee began during the training period of the 54th, prior to their journey south that would result in the famous attack on Fort Wagner in Charleston Harbor. The letters ended before Gooding was captured at Olustee. The author later died in Andersonville prison.

These 48 letters provide a valuable view of the 54th from the soldier's level, and the able editing enhances their value. The subjects range from the standard fare of soldier life in camp and on the march to the remarkable unity of the men of the 54th and the infrequent terror of battle such as the Wagner attack. Gooding bitterly criticizes black Americans who would not serve in the ranks, complains of hardships such as low pay and ridicule experienced by the men,

and offers high praise for the regiment's officers, including Shaw and Lt. Col. Edward N. Hallowell. A fine introduction complements the letters, as do illustrations and six poems Gooding penned at sea.

George Henry Gordon (1823–1886)

483

Gordon, George H. **Brook Farm to Cedar Mountain in the War of the Great Rebellion, 1861–62: A Revision and Enlargement (from the Latest and Most Authentic Sources) of Papers Numbered I., II., and III., Entitled, "A History of the Second Massachusetts Regiment" and the "Second Massachusetts Regiment and Stonewall Jackson"** (376 pp., James R. Osgood and Co., Boston, 1883)

These recollections of the first two years of war from the colonel of the 2d Massachusetts Infantry, consisting of papers written for reunions of his regiment, form a coherent whole that is precise and laced with occasional humor. Essentially a detailed narrative of the part played by the 2d Massachusetts and its commander throughout the first 14 months of the conflict, the work nicely recounts service at Harpers Ferry, on the Potomac, through the Shenandoah Valley against Jackson, at the battle of Winchester, and at Cedar Mountain. Gordon offers a highly critical evaluation of Nathaniel P. Banks's command at Cedar Mountain.

The narrative is focused tightly on the activities experienced by this regiment but also serves as a strong autobiography of Gordon and a reflection of the larger war around the 2d Massachusetts. Some re-created "conversations" are reported verbatim. A few maps and illustrations highlight significant actions and aspects of the unit. Appendices cover organization of the Federal forces and casualties from the battle of Cedar Mountain. The index is adequate. The work contains an occasional misspelling, as with Franz Sigel.

484

Gordon, George H. **History of the Campaign of the Army of Virginia, under John Pope: From Cedar Mountain to Alexandria, 1862** (498 pp., Houghton, Osgood and Co., Boston, 1879)

This is a continuation of Gordon's *Brook Farm to Cedar Mountain* (q.v.), following Gordon and the 2d Massachusetts Infantry from the close of Cedar Mountain through Second Bull Run. The work is well documented and draws on many official documents. The organization occasionally lacks coherence, and the great amount of material employed to cover an interval of only about three weeks might have been significantly cut down to heighten the overall effect.

The chief attribute of this history is the enormous amount of detail presented on the regiment, Gordon, related officers, and the campaign, though such a highly detailed narrative might not interest most readers. The quality of writing occasionally suffers as well, as if the book were rushed to publication. Still, there is good— though harsh— analysis of Pope's inadequacy as a field commander, a defense of Fitz John Porter, and much of interest relating to Massachusetts troops. The military analysis is enhanced by anecdotal material. Appendices cover strengths of the forces engaged, casualties, a report on Second Bull Run from Robert E. Lee, and the Fitz John Porter case. There are elaborate foldout maps but only a brief, barely adequate index.

485

Gordon, George H. **A War Diary of Events in the War of the Great Rebellion, 1863–1865** (437 pp., James R. Osgood and Co., Boston, 1882)

The story focuses on the final two years of war and is based on the author's diary, which provides a description of many anecdotes of soldier life in the Virginia peninsula, during the siege of Charleston, in the isolated theater of war in Florida, and on the lower Mississippi River. Much of the work's value arises from the unusual geography it covers. Gordon comments on his command of a division at the siege of Suffolk and the operations about Charleston, in the West, and around the Department of Virginia. His account is absorbing and hotly critical of many army officers, usually his superiors.

The writing is enthusiastic, opinionated, occasionally callous, and sometimes too partisan. The author reports some conversations with exact quotes, which stretches credibility, but for the most part the chapters in this work remain insightful. The index is adequate; six maps and illustrations highlight notable actions and places.

Ulysses Simpson Grant (1822–1885)

486

Badeau, Adam. **Military History of Ulysses S. Grant, from April 1861 to April 1865** (3 vols., 2087 pp., D. Appleton and Co., New York, 1868–1881)

These volumes are not so much a military biography of Grant as a detailed military tribute. That Badeau served on Grant's staff and deeply admired the commanding general

reduces the degree of objectivity, but it does not prevent the work from being useful. The first volume contains a brief biographical sketch on Grant's heritage and begins in earnest with his early exploits in the war. The coverage carries through early 1864. The second and third volumes cover the period of the Wilderness campaign through the end of the war and do so in elegant detail, owing to Badeau's role as aide-de-camp during the last year of the war.

Badeau's style is matter of fact without the embellishment or glorification typical of some early works. The accuracy is impressive, particularly when one considers that the work predates the *O.R.* (*q.v.*). The author does not digress or reflect on matters, so the volumes have a technical precision that is both valuable for its truthfulness and rigid because it lacks reflections on the small, interesting moments of the war. Although this account is somewhat wooden, then, it retains value for delivering an eyewitness estimation of Grant's performance during the war. It is particularly useful for the material on the 1864 campaigns and the Appomattox surrender. A later book by the same author, *Grant in Peace, from Appomattox to Mount McGregor: A Personal Memoir* (591 pp., S. S. Scranton and Co., Hartford, 1887) lacks the stature of the author's trio of volumes on Grant's Civil War career.

487

Cadwallader, Sylvanus. **Three Years with Grant** (ed. Benjamin P. Thomas, 351 pp., Alfred A. Knopf, New York, 1956)

Although almost universally regarded as a landmark narrative relating to Grant, this work is notorious for the inaccuracies that limit its usefulness. The former city editor of the Milwaukee *Daily News* and correspondent for the Chicago *Times* penned these recollections in 1896. Cadwallader spent about two and a half years in the company of Grant and his staff, beginning in August 1862. Strangely, the manuscript was originally titled *Four Years with Grant*, and this type of exaggeration sets a troublesome tone for the manuscript that follows.

Inconsistences plague parts of the text and raise suspicions about Cadwallader's credibility. He recounts the stern tale of the punishment of a fellow war correspondent, Edward Crapsey, by George Meade yet later states he never witnessed even the "slightest exhibition" of Meade's famous temper. He slips occasionally with dates, as exemplified by references to the Appomattox surrender in "May 1865." Various supposedly eyewitness accounts such as Lee meeting Grant on the porch of the McLean House, where the two "exchanged salutations," do not agree with the eyewitness testimony of many others.

Cadwallader's recollection of the date of the Chicago fire, in which he allegedly lost belongings including many of his papers, is two years off. Numerous other errors are highlighted by the editor and carry explanatory footnotes. Such problems call into question other places in the text where Cadwallader appears to be the sole witness, or thought he might have been. Such is the case with tales of Grant's drinking, particularly one escapade on 6 June 1863, where Cadwallader describes Grant as insensible from drunkenness during an active campaign. This directly conflicts with a far more reliable source, Charles A. Dana, who had no great love for Grant. Yet Dana's account squares with reality and makes no mention of the presence of Cadwallader. Suffice it to say that in many cases the newsman's penchant for a good story got the better of him. Unfortunately, Cadwallader's stories provide a partial foundation on which fables of Grant's alleged drunkenness have been built. For further review of this much-consulted but embellished book, see Ulysses S. Grant III, "Civil War: Fact and Fiction," *Civil War History* 2 (1956): 29–40.

488

Catton, Bruce. **Grant Moves South** (564 pp., Little, Brown and Co., Boston, 1960)

After Lloyd Lewis's death, the articulate and expressive writer Bruce Catton finished Lewis's biography of Grant (*q.v.*). This work shows a marked contrast to Lewis's book in that it spends much time analyzing military events and describing Grant's involvement in them as well as assessing his character. This is proper since beginning in 1861 Grant the person becomes impossible to separate meaningfully from Grant the general.

Grant Moves South opens with Grant's entrance into the war as colonel of the 21st Illinois Infantry and speedily moves on to Cairo and Belmont and Forts Henry and Donelson. The book ends with Vicksburg, after superb tellings of the trauma at Shiloh and the Vicksburg siege. This is a great amount of ground to cover, but Catton succeeds admirably in describing the Grant story. At intervals he inserts ample scene setting, reflection, and humanistic stories, preventing the big picture from clouding an understanding of what happened on a small scale. The author is able to accentuate the main presentation without reducing the reader's intellectual gain. Catton introduces an array of characters and integrates their participation well. To his credit, he uses a wide array of primary and secondary sources with care, providing a work that is balanced and varied.

489

Catton, Bruce. **Grant Takes Command** (556 pp., Little, Brown and Co., Boston, 1968)

The final act in the Lewis-Catton trilogy unfolds here. Following the title's lead, the work examines Grant's career beginning as he came east to oversee the crisis at Chattanooga, explores the politics and skirmishes of the winter of 1863 and 1864, and witnesses Grant's rise to the ultimate command position and his execution of the May campaign of 1864 in command of the Union armies. The story naturally concludes with the end of the war and the Grand Reviews and closes its curtain by delving into Grant's postwar involvement with the army and politics. The text follows the same style and quality of Catton's previous work (*q.v.*) and may be considered an impressive summary based on a wide variety of primary and secondary sources. It is reasonably documented in critical and controversial areas. The maps are adequate, providing enough detail for the general reader to follow major movements.

The chief strength, as with all of Catton's books, lies in his skillful adaption of scenes and incidents that add color to the story and deepen the meaning of significant times during the campaigns. To his credit, the author also understands Grant and the way he thought. These facts allow the book to deliver a believable and generally accurate portrait of Grant beyond the numbing capitulations of clashes with the Confederate Army. The work does not shy from analysis and shows adeptly how Grant evolved the strategy and the army that would be necessary to bring the war to a close. There is an occasional incorrect spelling, as with the names of Kennesaw Mountain, Georgia, and Polly Hundley's Corner, Virginia.

490

Catton, Bruce. **U. S. Grant and the American Military Tradition** (201 pp., Little, Brown and Co., Boston, 1954)

In this work the author helps to rescue Grant from the biographical misconceptions of the past, providing analysis and a tightly drawn portrait of Grant the man. We do not see the oversimplified and overstated hard-drinking, little-thinking soldier whose victories result from circumstance, luck, and overwhelming size of commands. This anti-intellectual characterization of Grant, though still dominant in some people's thinking, bears little resemblance to reality.

Instead, Catton paints an image of Grant in which his pure, simple logic forced actions that succeeded where far more complex plans and strategies of the day failed. The author traces Grant's determination as a commander to a childhood trait: "When the boy made a trip and accidentally drove past his destination," he writes, "he would make any kind of roundabout circuit to get back to it, even at the cost of considerable trouble. He had some deep-seated reluctance to retrace his steps." Catton suggests this as a foreshadowing of the commander whose logic dictated repeatedly turning Lee's flank during the May campaign but never retreating to old ground.

Catton argues that Grant's victory at Vicksburg and resulting rise to commander of all U.S. armies coincided perfectly with the opportunity to give the war in the East a new purpose. During the final year of war, Grant followed Sherman's advice and stayed away from Washington, commanding his armies in the field and brilliantly balancing his own nearly supreme power with a subservient role under the president and Congress. This subservience to Congress, Catton argues, helped ruin Grant's presidency.

491

Grant, Ulysses S. **The Papers of Ulysses S. Grant** (ed. John Y. Simon, David L. Wilson, J. Thomas Murphy, William M. Ferraro, Brian J. Kenny, and Sue E. Dotson, 20 vols. to date, 11,232 pp., Southern Illinois University Press, Carbondale, 1967–   )

Not only is this massive work one of the primary sets of Civil War literature, but its masterful style and scholarly, exhaustive annotation, the hallmarks of chief editor Simon, set a high standard for collected works projects throughout the field of American history.

The coverage thus far consists of the following: volume 1 (1837–1861), volume 2 (April–September 1861), volume 3 (1 October 1861–7 January 1862), volume 4 (8 January–31 March 1862), volume 5 (1 April–31 August 1862), volume 6 (1 September–8 December 1862), volume 7 (9 December 1862–31 March 1863), volume 8 (1 April–6 July 1863), volume 9 (7 July–31 December 1863), volume 10 (1 January–31 May 1864), volume 11 (1 June–15 August 1864), volume 12 (16 August–15 November 1864), volume 13 (16 November 1864–20 February 1865), volume 14 (21 February–30 April 1865), volume 15 (1 May–31 December 1865), volume 16 (1866), volume 17 (1 January–30 September 1867), volume 18 (1 October 1867–30 June 1868), volume 19 (1 July 1868–31 October 1869), and volume 20 (1 November 1869–31 October 1870). Each volume contains numerous letters and documents written by Grant, a Grant chronology covering the period, astonishingly detailed notes explaining the context of the papers and often including related correspondence, and a calendar of less important papers for each period in question.

Simon and his colleagues have remained meticulously faithful to the original documents, providing readers with an intimate and deep understanding of Grant's actions and an unparalleled view into the commander's mind. The pure and simple logic and determination that molded Grant into the supreme victor of the war appears as an always-present and slowly evolving force. Hundreds of communications sent to military superiors and subordinates depict Grant's superb understanding of the strategy and tactics of the war and help to demonstrate the reasoning behind his rapid rise to the command of all U.S. armies in the field. Many early correspondences with friends and relatives—particularly those with Julia Grant—supply a more intimate picture of Grant the man. He comes through as cautious, quiet, and analytical, yet fragile and sensitive to the feelings of others. Not only did he understand strategy—he was essentially the only one who responded to Lincoln's General Order No. 1— but this clerk also knew how to write, officiate, and organize so his troops would follow orders precisely. His men were genuinely endeared to Grant's curious persona.

The Civil War era letters and documents bring into sharp focus the many crucial campaigns and battles that marked Grant's career, such as Belmont, Fort Donelson, Shiloh, Vicksburg, the Chattanooga campaign, and the May campaign, whose trail led to Appomattox. We see the real, unembellished Grant—complete with creative spelling and other curiosities—and travel on the daring campaign for Vicksburg, witness the complex and warm relationship with Sherman as it develops, and see Grant's handling of crisis, as with Rosecrans at Chattanooga and Thomas at Nashville.

The old myths of habitual drunkenness and heartless butchery are also laid to rest in these pages. Clearly Grant imbibed rarely and almost never in excess, and certainly not during military operations. The "heartless butcher" understood the strategy needed to win the war better than any other general on either side, and he knew that the war must be won quickly to minimize the loss of life. Certainly he made mistakes, as at Cold Harbor (which he admitted dogged his conscience for years). But which other commanders so masterfully engineered winning campaigns, particularly when one had to attack and overtake enemy territory? Certainly the Confederacy's best commanders did far worse on the offensive, as at Malvern Hill, Gettysburg, and Franklin, with the exception of Longstreet's impressive frontal assault at Chickamauga. Grant understood and deplored the cost of war and wished to kill as few as possible. Could the same be said of Lee, who essentially knew the war was a lost cause but kept on fighting and sacrificing for a calendar year until surrendering?

Volumes 19 and 20, which carry the work nearly to the time of Grant's election as president, continue a valuable level of meticulous research. For more information on the Grant Papers, see William L. Richter, "The Papers of U. S. Grant: A Review Essay," *Civil War History* 36 (1990): 149. A related volume titled *Ulysses S. Grant: Essays and Documents* (ed. David L. Wilson and John Y. Simon, 145 pp., Southern Illinois University Press, Carbondale, 1981) contains some interesting primary material including the best account of Montgomery Meigs's impression of fighting around Chattanooga.

492

Grant, Ulysses S. **Personal Memoirs of U. S. Grant** (2 vols., 1231 pp., Charles L. Webster and Co., New York, 1885–1886)

Grant's memoirs comprise one of the most valuable writings by a military commander in history. The story of his driving force on writing the book against his struggle with cancer is well known, and it is fortunate indeed that he was able to finish. Although pushed into the project and supported in part by Samuel L. Clemens and others, Grant composed the work on his own, and it seems clear from the famously curious spelling that was retained that the work was only lightly copyedited. The work is genuinely that of the commander. As such, it is valuable in its scope, its plain and clear analysis and language, and its broad conclusions about the conduct of the war. Grant the person may have been terribly quiet, but he was not so on paper.

The memoirs cover Grant's life through war's end, with material in volume 1 on the commander's ancestry, birth, boyhood, West Point days, early days in the army, Mexican War career, and days on the Pacific Coast. The prewar section on private life and the peaceful days in Galena is brief. The bulk of the work carries Grant's Civil War experience up through the surrender of Vicksburg. The second volume concentrates wholly on the second half of the war up to Johnston's surrender. Maps and facsimiles of important documents illustrate the narrative.

Grant's communications are characterized by a quiet moderation, and events of great magnitude are described with a simple, calm tone. The work sets forth and analyzes the details of many campaigns and battles and the thought behind the Federal high command in the war's final year. Grant often praises the actions of commanders on both sides but rarely criticizes, and then only with softspokenness. Gentle admonishment lands on such characters as Don Carlos Buell, John M. Palmer, and Gouverneur K. Warren. Harsh rebukes are almost nonexistent, perhaps with the exception of describing Forrest's actions at Fort Pillow. Indeed, as was also the case with Robert E. Lee, Grant mostly tends to accept the blame for various failures of his campaigns, even those difficulties caused by subordinates. His description of the beginnings at Shiloh may be strained, where in reality he was caught surprised, but the details of nearly every other engagement are clear, concise, and demonstrative of the simple logic that allowed Grant such success in fighting the war to a close. A criticism of the *Memoirs* titled *The Personal Memoirs and Military History of U. S. Grant, versus the Record of the Army of the Potomac*, by Carswell McClellan (278 pp., Houghton Mifflin Co., Boston, 1887), raises some interesting points but fails with many others.

(Reprinted 1952, with an introduction by E. B. Long, 608 pp., World Publishing Co., Cleveland; 1952 edition reprinted 1982, with an introduction by William S. McFeely, 608 pp., Da Capo Press, New York)

493

Lewis, Lloyd. **Captain Sam Grant** (512 pp., Little, Brown and Co., Boston, 1950)

This story provides material on Grant's early life, covering the period from his birth to the eve of Civil War. The work is composed in the prosaic style of the newspaper journalist who penned it. Lewis's relatively thinly documented study nevertheless accomplishes a more than adequate job of separating fact from fiction and makes the most of the scanty sources covering Grant's early years. The author was the first to use a number of Grant family materials describing the family heritage and Grant's early days and presents material on the backgrounds of Grant's immediate ancestors. He treats his subject somewhat sympathetically but retains a balanced story. The straightforward treatment of Grant's childhood in Georgetown receives a storylike delivery, and the book grows in complexity and sophistication in discussing West Point and Grant's Mexican War service.

The coverage of Grant's frontier duty, his days in Oregon and California, and his resignation from the army is admirable when judged against the paucity of information the author had to work with. Lewis realistically depicts Grant's contradiction in his reasonable ambition, high character, and almost no commercial success. Without exaggerating in hindsight, the author treats the move to Galena as a significant step in which Grant seemed to be emerging from the shadows well before the crisis of war arrived. One spelling error was found, that of Barnard E. Bee's name.

(Reprinted 1991, 512 pp., Little, Brown and Co., Boston)

494

[Pulitzer Prize, 1982]

McFeely, William S. **Grant: A Biography** (592 pp., W. W. Norton and Co., New York, 1981)

McFeely offers a frustrating mixture of splendidly accomplished insight and poor characterization that somehow mirrors the uneven career of Grant. In fact this work is the philosophical inverse of Grant the man: it does quite well in assessing Grant's antebellum life, presidency, and later years but provides a significantly flawed picture of the general's Civil War years, the most important period of his life.

In this full biography the author develops strong themes of success and failure in Grant's life—mostly failure. About one-third deals with the Civil War years, a relatively small portion treats his antebellum life (including Mexican War service), and a significant amount treats Grant's presidency and last years. The brief Mexican War text does not scrutinize the apparent contradiction in Grant's disapproval of the war's basis and his enthusiastic service in it. McFeely demonstrates that after repeated failure in civilian life "some essential part of [Grant's] being was brought into play only in war," but he does not adequately suggest what that part was or why it came into being during war. The author's reproach of Grant for the concept of total war reveals an ignorance of the strategic means necessary to win the war as so eloquently outlined in *How the North Won,* by Hattaway and Jones (*q.v.*).

Many errors appear within the chapters on the Civil War that undermine the author's credibility and therefore do not help his thesis, even when it appears to be adequately supported. Such fundamentally basic errors as elevating Sherman to the immediate subordinate of Grant at Shiloh would seem to be avoidable by simple familiarity with the greatest early campaign of the western theater, or even by glancing at an order of battle. After issuing this erroneous assignment, McFeely demotes Sherman to the level of a brigade commander at Chickasaw Bluffs and cites the wrong day for the battle. He contends that Burnside replaced Buell as commander of the Army of the Ohio. He believes that Joe Johnston was in command of Confederate forces in Georgia during Sherman's march. He calls Nashville the "last great battle of the war." A check of Heitman (*q.v.*) shows that Oliver O. Howard was a brigadier general U.S.A. in 1870 but hardly the ranking officer in the army. The list of errors with regard to military history goes on and on and on.

The work more successfully treats Grant's home life and his relationship with Julia Grant and his children. The brief story of Grant's prewar life and the extensive treatment of his presidency merit reading. But the core of this work, and

indeed the core of Grant himself, require a much better and more sophisticated telling to be considered a success. For a fuller evaluation of the book, see Brooks D. Simpson, "Butcher? Racist? An Examination of William S. McFeely's *Grant: A Biography,*" *Civil War History* 33 (1987): 63.

495

Porter, Horace. **Campaigning with Grant** (546 pp., Century Co., New York, 1897)

These recollections of Grant's youthful aide who served with the commander from Chattanooga through war's end may be thought of as a companion to those by Grant himself (*q.v.*) and by Adam Badeau (*q.v.*). Although it contains interesting anecdotes and glimpses into Grant's command decisions from the May campaign through Appomattox, the work concentrates on Porter rather than Grant and is too highly embellished. Composed long after the war and allegedly based on notes that have vanished in the past century, the work is reliable in the big picture but not always so in detail. Manufactured "conversations" frequently mar the text, quoted directly and without substantiation. Specifics are fairly thin, and generalities of many events are recorded better elsewhere.

Nonetheless, Porter's book does have value. The accounts of the emergency operations about Chattanooga, personal recollections of how Grant behaved about camp and headquarters, and lengthy narratives centered on the Richmond and Petersburg operations shine with great luster. The accounts of the final weeks of war and Lee's surrender are classic. A number of misspellings appear in the text, as with the names of James Dearing and James Longstreet. The author erroneously promotes Charles Lane Fitzhugh to the grade of major general in discussing his actions at Five Forks, wrongly has William Hays a brigadier general in discussing his activities at Petersburg, and elevates Martin T. McMahon to major general.

(Reprinted 1961, ed. Wayne C. Temple, 558 pp., Indiana University Press, Bloomington; 1897 edition reprinted 1981, 546 pp., Time-Life Books, Alexandria, Va.; 1897 edition reprinted 1986, with an introduction by William S. McFeely, 546 pp., Da Capo Press, New York)

496

Simpson, Brooks D. **Let Us Have Peace: Ulysses S. Grant and the Politics of War and Reconstruction, 1861–1868** (339 pp., University of North Carolina Press, Chapel Hill, 1991)

This superb study is a must for the Grant bookshelf. Supported by peerless logic and keen insight over old—and frequently simplistically analyzed—source materials, Simpson argues that Grant's military and political abilities were intertwined. Indeed, he suggests that Grant acted as a powerful political force for reconstructing the Union during the war years themselves. Grant's reputation as a simpleminded military man receives blunt counterpoint in this work, as the author repeatedly documents how the Union's military savior understood in complex ways the political implications of his battlefield actions. Moreover, the narrative demonstrates how these political considerations played a significant part in forging Grant's grand strategy for prosecuting the war.

The political balancing act manifests itself clearly in Grant's handling of emancipation. Not only did the armies of the United States need to look after freedmen flocking to them in ever-increasing numbers, but they had to respond to the situation without adversely affecting the psychology of white Southerners, who could resort to ever more desperate reactionary measures. The author shows how Grant's actions evolved with Lincoln's. Grant did not simply follow Lincoln's stipulated orders but concocted his own strategies based on a thorough understanding of the delicate nature of the war and the necessary goals of the United States.

The author shows that Grant for a brief time held too high an estimate of Andrew Johnson's competence. In the conflict over Johnson, however, Grant's view won out. The work ends as Grant's own presidency approaches, thus leaving unexplored the failure of his two terms in the Executive Mansion. The author shrewdly demonstrates that at least throughout the war years and the early days of Reconstruction, Ulysses Grant was a master of politics as well as battle.

John Chipman Gray (1839–1915)

497

Gray, John Chipman, and John Codman Ropes. **War Letters, 1862–1865, of John Chipman Gray and John Codman Ropes** (ed. Worthington Chauncey Ford, 532 pp., Houghton Mifflin Co., Boston, 1927)

The correspondence of two educated New Englanders is collected here. Prevented from entering the service by physical disability, Ropes (later one of the founders of the Military Historical Society of Massachusetts) sustained his great interest in the campaigns of the Union Army by writing to his friend Gray. The latter served as a second lieutenant in the 3d Massachusetts Cavalry and for the last two years of the war was on the staffs of Brig. Gen. George H. Gordon and Maj. Gens. John G. Foster and Quincy A. Gillmore.

The intellectual nature of both men, Ropes's absorbing interest, and Gray's staff service make this correspondence exceedingly interesting. Occasionally, Ropes visited the front and talked with George Meade, John Sedgwick, and other influential commanders. He severely criticized George McClellan in almost every respect; by contrast, he was not so severe in evaluating Hooker, Burnside, or Halleck. The Boston blueblood did not think highly of Lincoln. The acute observational powers of these men and their precision of language and restraint of temperament make this collection valuable.

Benjamin Henry Grierson (1826–1911)

498

Leckie, William H., and Shirley A. Leckie. **Unlikely Warriors: General Benjamin Grierson and His Family** (368 pp., University of Oklahoma Press, Norman, 1984)

The overlooked Federal officer Grierson receives his turn in the spotlight in this full biography. The work describes the life and military career of Benjamin Grierson but also includes a great deal about Alice Kirk Grierson, the general's wife and a participant in her husband's wartime and postwar army career. Lucidly written and based in large part on the Grierson family papers, this biography fills a gap in bringing readers a satisfactory picture of an important but nearly forgotten Civil War officer.

About 30 percent of the book details Grierson's Civil War service. The former Illinois music teacher entered wartime service as a volunteer aide to Brig. Gen. Benjamin M. Prentiss. As colonel of the 6th Illinois Cavalry, Grierson gained experience with skirmishes in Tennessee and Mississippi. The authors engagingly describe Grierson's 1863 raid through Mississippi, a diversion that aided Grant's Vicksburg campaign and made Grierson a brigadier general. As colonel of the 10th Cavalry of "buffalo soldiers," Grierson's postwar career stretched across the plains in a series of Indian actions.

Unfortunately, the authors' assessment of Grierson is rather uncritical and the interpretation of military events rather cursory. They misspell several names and introduce some factual errors, such as the date of Wesley Merritt's commission as brigadier general U.S.A. The narrative does not describe James H. Wilson's 1864 removal of Grierson from active command. A fuller treatment of Grierson's Civil War service awaits a future scholar.

Henry Wager Halleck (1815–1872)

499

Ambrose, Stephen E. **Halleck: Lincoln's Chief of Staff** (226 pp., Louisiana State University Press, Baton Rouge, 1962)

Ambrose provides a magnificent portrayal of one of the least popular of the war's high commanders. Shy, unsociable, and bookish, Halleck garnered few friends and was difficult for most acquaintances to deal with. That notwithstanding, his reputation as a military scholar—though it may have been derived largely from embellished translations of foreign treatises—earned Halleck a position of high esteem in the army.

The author somewhat sympathetically but quite truthfully describes Halleck's ascent to command early in the war. Succeeding Frémont after the latter's political suicide, Halleck won victories in the West that made him appear to possess a significant strategic and tactical mind—demonstrating his sobriquet Old Brains. Much of the success, however, resulted from his subordinates, including Grant. After the tension with Grant eased, Lincoln smartly removed Halleck from the scene by placing him in what would be a revolutionary post, general-in-chief. The author's assessment of Halleck rightly concentrates on the subject's performance in Washington as the man who would now be considered chief of staff of the army. Taken out of field command, Halleck admirably and ably assisted Stanton and performed valuably as a link between the officers in the field and the high command. Ironically, Halleck had to leave the field and enter the office to abandon the strategic lessons of Jomini and embrace those of Clausewitz.

Halleck's part in developing the strengths of the Union Army is chronicled in this work, as is the general's role following Grant's promotion. This scholarly and well-done book places a controversial character in his significant and deserved place in history.

Charles Graham Halpine (1829–1868)

500

Hanchett, William. **Irish: Charles G. Halpine in Civil War America** (208 pp., Syracuse University Press, Syracuse, 1970)

Hanchett outlines the career of a staff officer and journalist in the Federal Army. Born in Ireland, Halpine was commissioned a first lieutenant in the 69th New York State Militia at the outbreak of war and promptly secured a commission as a staff officer for Maj. Gen. John A. Dix and then Maj. Gen. David Hunter, serving as an assistant adjutant general. After the war he was brevetted brigadier general for meritorious service. Throughout the war Halpine continued his journalistic pursuits by writing under the pseudonym Miles O'Reilly, contributing many stories and verses from the field, including commentary on the early contraband efforts on the Sea Islands off South Carolina. His witty prose was tempered by a fondness for whiskey.

The author's summary of Halpine's life makes a valuable contribution to Civil War biography. Although Halpine's war service included an integral part in the 1864 raids by Hunter into the Shenandoah Valley and other interesting actions, his greatest contribution, as the author demonstrates, was to stir Irish soldiers and civilians. Conversely, he settled the Federal government's attitudes toward Irish immigrants and black Americans too. With his pen and the voice of Miles O'Reilly, Halpine's "Sambo's Right to Be Kilt" helped establish an acceptance of black American soldiers among racist Northern citizens—if only by appealing to their visions of black soldiers as cannon fodder. Although somewhat sparsely documented, the work sympathetically but honestly chronicles and evaulates Halpine's engrossing participation in the war.

Winfield Scott Hancock (1824–1886)

501

Hancock, Almira R. **Reminiscences of Winfield Scott Hancock, by His Wife** (340 pp., Charles L. Webster and Co., New York, 1887)

This work remains useful as a lighthearted, tender collection of anecdotes and chronology of the commander. It consists of two parts, a narrative by the author and a considerable collection of appendices by others, as described below. The author traces her marriage, Hancock's antebellum duty at Jefferson Barracks, and his love of trees; she provides reminiscences of David E. Twiggs, Nathaniel P. Banks, and others, a discussion of a cholera outbreak at the post, and a recounting of Hancock's service in the Seminole war.

Considerable material bridges this period with that of the Civil War. The couple's journey to California offers interesting frontier anecdotes and recollections of Albert Sidney Johnston, Joe Johnston, and Robert E. Lee. The book contains descriptions of Los Angeles in the days before the war. With the fall of Sumter, the Hancocks traveled to Washington, and the author composed a vivid description of social activities in the capital city. She describes Hancock's preference for infantry command, his participation in the early months of the war, and a variety of special topics such as the spy system used during the conflict.

Appendices present a narrative of the operations of the 2d Corps from June 1862 to the close of the Gettysburg campaign, Andrew Johnson's message to Congress, and a lengthy set of testimonials and tributes to Hancock's record, amounting to nearly 100 pages. The work lacks an index.

502

Jordan, David M. **Winfield Scott Hancock: A Soldier's Life** (393 pp., Indiana University Press, Bloomington, 1988)

Finely composed and carefully researched, this volume fills a gap in the literature by providing a full biography of its subject. About half of the work deals with Hancock's Civil War career, a brief section treats his prewar days, and a relatively detailed set of chapters covers Hancock's postwar military exploits and his unsuccessful foray into politics.

Hancock's amazing military career supplies a biographer with a tremendous stock of interesting material to draw from, and Jordan takes full advantage of a variety of sources. Thus, we receive excellent accounts of Hancock's role in the Peninsular campaign; at Antietam, Fredericksburg, Chancellorsville, and Gettysburg; and in the Wilderness and Petersburg campaigns. The treatment of Hancock's critical participation at Gettysburg, where he essentially forged the Union strategy of holding the high ground, is particularly well handled.

The discussion of Hancock's postwar activities is somewhat less successful, as the author shows some degree of bias toward his subject for the botched 1867 plains campaign. Moreover, in an unusual twist on revisionism, the 1870 Piegan massacre appears in the text as a battle and the author apparently accepts the U.S. Army's (and Hancock's) explanation for what occurred. The general's Reconstruction policies are also treated sympathetically, contradicting a mass of more thorough analysis on the same subject. An occasional misspelling occurs, as with Samuel P. Heintzelman's name. On the whole, this study is well done, particularly its treatment of the war years.

Benjamin Harrison (1833–1901)

503

Sievers, Harry J. **Benjamin Harrison: Hoosier Warrior** (374 pp., University Publishers, New York, 1960)

Harrison's role in the war naturally eludes scrutiny by virtue of the interest in his presidency, but this work offers a readable and well-constructed narrative of the brevet brigadier general's early years and Civil War exploits. Commissioned colonel of the 70th Indiana Infantry in mid-1862, Harrison oversaw the regiment's duties in guarding railroad lines and participating in several skirmishes in Kentucky and Tennessee. Stationed at Murfreesboro after Stones River, the regiment fully participated in the battle of Chickamauga the following September. Sievers describes Harrison's prominence in the Georgia campaign of 1864 and his rise to lead a brigade in Sherman's march through the Carolinas. Particularly interesting are excerpts from Harrison's letters written from the field, a facet of the president's life poorly documented by historians (with the exception of this biography).

Franklin Aretas Haskell (1828–1864)

504

Haskell, Frank A. **Haskell of Gettysburg: His Life and Civil War Papers** (ed. Frank L. Byrne and Andrew T. Weaver, 258 pp., State Historical Society of Wisconsin, Madison, 1970)

Although he died during the war, Haskell produced one of the great contemporary accounts of battle in his classic *The Battle of Gettysburg*. This work appears along with valuable biographical material in the present discourse, which supersedes several earlier editions of Haskell's work.

A veteran of the 6th Wisconsin and, at the time of Gettysburg, aide-de-camp to John Gibbon, Haskell had the opportunity to see the climactic events of the second and third days at Gettysburg from a valuable perspective. During the events of 3 July Haskell witnessed the artillery barrage and Pickett's Charge from the front lines of the 2d Corps, at which the charge was aimed. After the wounding of both Hancock and Gibbon, Haskell was the only mounted officer issuing orders on the front line of the corps. His narrative of the battle, a long letter to his brother written just two weeks later, is a penetrating eyewitness document. (Haskell made slight revisions to the document for several months following the original writing.) Although he muffed deductions about Meade's strategy, seems not to have realized the tenuous nature of the fight for the Round Tops, and vastly overestimated the Confederate strength, the story is nonetheless spellbinding. Among the highlights is an eyewitness description of Meade's 2 July council of war in the Leister House.

The famous letter and several others describing the Gettysburg campaign comprise just under half of Byrne and Weaver's compendium. These editors have assembled a biographical essay buttressed with excerpts of other Haskell letters, 31 altogether, covering the officer's entire Civil War experience. These range from a quiet defense of Washington following Bull Run to good accounts of South Mountain and the second battle at Fredericksburg to Haskell's mortal wounding at Cold Harbor.

(Reprinted 1989, 258 pp., Kent State University Press, Kent)

Herman Haupt (1817–1905)

505

Haupt, Herman. **Reminiscences of General Herman Haupt: Giving Hitherto Unpublished Official Orders, Personal Narratives of Important Military Operations, and Interviews with President Lincoln, Secretary Stanton, General-in-Chief Halleck, and with Generals McDowell, McClellan, Meade, Hancock, Burnside, and Others in Command of the Armies in the Field, and His Impressions of These Men** (331 pp., Wright and Joys Co., Milwaukee, 1901)

A brief sketch of the volunteer officer precedes a narrative written by Haupt describing his involvement in the engineering operations relating to Second Bull Run, Fredericksburg, work in the western theater, Gettysburg, and the termination of Haupt's duties and his relationship with John A. Andrew. Along the way the author describes numerous engineering facts relating to the building and destruction of bridges and track and offers a thorough lesson in the operations of the U.S. Military Railroad.

The work's value arises from the correspondence to and from Haupt on nearly every page. Some of this material may be found in the *O.R.* (*q.v.*), but much of it appears in this work alone. By reading the narrative and military communications, one leaves with an enlightened view of the working relationship between Haupt and the War Department and how this officer felt about a number of Federal commanders and their actions.

(Reprinted 1981, 331 pp., Ayer, Salem)

506

Ward, James A. **That Man Haupt** (278 pp., Louisiana State University Press, Baton Rouge, 1973)

A full biography, this work depicts the details of Haupt's life and shows him to be a particularly skilled engineer whose entrepreneurial dabblings touched an amazing array of areas. Ward describes Haupt's early days as a mechanical prodigy in Philadelphia, follows him to West Point, and attentively illustrates his multifaceted career in railroads in the late 1840s and 1850s. Haupt's expertise in laying out a half dozen railroads in New York, Pennsylvania, and New England qualified him as one of the great engineers during a crucial expansion phase in railroading. The author's text demonstrates that Haupt's engineering genius combined with good timing to make him a much desired individual, despite his troubles with the Hoosac affair.

The author carefully describes how, as the war entered its second year, Haupt received the assignment as chief of construction and transportation for the U.S. Military Railroads and set up shop in Washington. Ward outlines Haupt's nebulous service in which he declined his grade and pay in order to continue pursuing a Massachusetts railroad contract. The work also follows Haupt's curious postwar business ventures, providing a detailed account of one of the war's more inventive minds and least appreciated engineers.

Charles B. Haydon (1834–1864)

507

Haydon, Charles B. **For Country, Cause, and Leader: The Civil War Journal of Charles B. Haydon** (ed. Stephen W. Sears, 371 pp., Ticknor and Fields, New York, 1993)

This volume chronicles the activities of an officer of the 2d Michigan Infantry. Enlisting on 22 April 1861, Haydon first experienced war in the East—First Bull Run, the Peninsular campaign, and the chaotic circumstances of Second Bull Run and Fredericksburg. In 1863 the regiment was transferred to Kentucky and then participated in the siege of Vicksburg, where the author was wounded. After being hospitalized, Haydon infrequently continued his journal. He contracted pneumonia, was moved to a military hospital in Cincinnati, and died in March 1864.

This officer's experiences in both theaters and his rise to a significant grade, lieutenant colonel, contribute to material of interest in the 20 journals that compose this book. During much of the experience Haydon was a company officer, and he found himself attempting to control the soldiers, to drill them and impose discipline. His discussion of daily events offers a great store of minute details of minor events, but he writes about them in a revealing and interesting manner. A few misspellings occur, as with the name of William B. Franklin. The accounts of battle are thin, but the reflections on soldier life in the Union Army are often enriching.

Rutherford Birchard Hayes (1822–1893)

508

Hayes, Rutherford Birchard. **Diary and Letters of Rutherford Birchard Hayes, Nineteenth President of the United States** (ed. Charles R. Williams, 5 vols., 3003 pp., Ohio State Archaeological and Historical Society, Columbus, 1922–1926)

Hayes's diary and letters contain a significant record of the presidency and other adventures of this Union officer. The second volume contains Civil War letters written to Hayes's wife, uncle, mother, niece, children, brother-in-law, and friends, together with brief selections from his diary. The work is pedestrian during his recruiting days in Cincinnati as major of the 23d Ohio Infantry, but gains interest with the descriptions of early campaigns in western Virginia, mostly in the mountains, actions that were frequently immobilized by rains and mud. The early associations with George B. McClellan, John C. Frémont, William S. Rosecrans, Eliakim P. Scammon, Philip H. Sheridan, and George Crook during this period add value to the narrative.

Hayes supplies useful discussions of camp life with a typical regiment. After a long period of little activity, he traveled east to take part in the battle of South Mountain, where he was wounded in the left arm, thereby missing Antietam. The letters illustrate his recovery in time for Cloyd's Mountain, West Virginia, in May 1864 and his participation in the Shenandoah Valley campaign of 1864, including Winchester, Berryville, Opequon, Fishers Hill, and Cedar Creek. The material herein offers good accounts of these actions and a fine study of the future president.

The coverage is as follows: volume 1, 1822–1860, boyhood, education, and law practice; volume 2, 1861–1865, Civil War; volume 3, 1865–1881, governorship and presidency; volume 4, 1881–1893, post presidency; volume 5, 1891–1893, final years, appendices, and index.

(Reprinted 1971, 5 vols., 3003 pp., Kraus Reprint Co., Millwood, N.Y.)

509

Williams, T. Harry. **Hayes of the Twenty-third: The Civil War Volunteer Officer** (324 pp., Alfred A. Knopf, New York, 1965)

Overshadowed by later considerations of politics, Hayes's military career receives careful consideration in this work. Hayes rose slowly through the ranks, thus gaining valuable experience before his brigade and temporary division commands in Sheridan's Valley campaign of 1864. He won distinction finally at Cedar Creek, for which he was brevetted major general U.S.V. Throughout the first three years of war, Hayes served as major, lieutenant colonel, and colonel of the 23d Ohio Infantry, a unit initially commanded by William S. Rosecrans.

Experiencing the war first in West Virginia, the 23d saw little action save for occasional guerrilla operations. Williams details this part of Hayes's service and makes the story, despite the inactivity, a rich portrait of Civil War military life. The author explores the unit's participation at South Mountain, where Hayes was wounded, and details Antietam, followed by the regiment's return to West Virginia. The regiment finished the war guarding Cumberland, Maryland.

Williams's analysis interweaves allied topics into the experiences of Hayes and his regiment. He is particularly fond of discussing the methods of choosing officers in the war and vigorously supports citizen-soldiers relative to their West Point brethren. This sideshow, while entertaining, runs amok, but it does not seriously detract from an otherwise expertly crafted book.

(Reprinted 1994, 324 pp., University of Nebraska Press, Lincoln)

Alexander Hays (1819–1864)

510

Hays, Alexander. **Life and Letters of General Alexander Hays** (ed. George Thornton Fleming and Gilbert Adams Hays, 708 pp., published by the editors, Pittsburgh, 1919)

The spirited and tragic story of a brigadier general killed in the Wilderness campaign comes to life in this work. Leading the 63d Pennsylvania Infantry through the Peninsular campaign, Hays was commissioned brigadier general of volunteers following Second Bull Run, where he was badly wounded. Recovering sufficiently to return to the field for the Gettysburg campaign, the Pennsylvanian distinguished himself on that battleground. Despite being well liked, he commanded only a brigade during the first days of the Wilderness campaign because he was outranked by others. Killed instantly on 5 May 1864, the general officer left a legacy of performing well in the few major campaigns he experienced.

The present volume presents a biography sufficiently detailed to satisfy anyone with a deep interest in this officer, along with tributes to his character and performance as a soldier. The work's greatest attribute is Hays's wartime letters, mostly sent to his wife, which shed light on the eastern armies and the campaigns of the Army of the Potomac in particular. The work contains a tangle of illustrations, some of great interest, and a peculiar index.

William Babcock Hazen (1830–1887)

511

Hazen, William B. **A Narrative of Military Service** (450 pp., Ticknor and Co., Boston, 1885)

This chronicle sets forth the career of an Ohio officer who rose to major general of volunteers after serving with distinction in many western campaigns. It does not cover Hazen's entire military service; rather, it is limited to the Civil War years. The author provides a recollection of the raising of the 41st Ohio Infantry, of which he was commissioned colonel, and proceeds with lengthy remarks on his participation at Shiloh, Stones River, Chickamauga, Chattanooga, the Atlanta campaign, the March to the Sea, and the Carolinas campaign. The narrative is engaging, detailed, and punctuated by frequent quotations from military dispatches and letters. Based in part on wartime notes made by Hazen, the narrative was primarily composed 20 years later. A final section, "Lessons of the War," reviews aspects of strategy and tactics, hospitals, foraging, equipment, artillery service, and newspaper reporters. Appendices cover Hazen's postwar service.

The most interesting sections treat actions at Shiloh, Stones River, Missionary Ridge, and Atlanta. Anecdotes of Hazen's close friendship with James A. Garfield surface occasionally, as do reminiscences of William T. Sherman, Don Carlos Buell, and U. S. Grant. Controversial actions or claims involving Hazen are also recorded, as with the dispute over who reached the crest of Missionary Ridge first (a disagreement with Philip Sheridan) and the animosities of David S. Stanley, who accused Hazen of cowardice at Shiloh. The story of these and other disputes is hardly covered objectively; nonetheless, the detailed material on this officer makes the work important.

(Reprinted 1993, with an introduction by Richard A.

Baumgartner and a photographic supplement, 450 pp., Blue Acorn Press, Huntington, W.Va.)

Hans Christian Heg (1829–1863)

512

Heg, Hans C. **The Civil War Letters of Colonel Hans Christian Heg** (ed. Theodore C. Blegen, 260 pp., Norwegian-American Historical Association, Northfield, Minn., 1936)

The story of a Wisconsin officer who fell at Chickamauga is captured here. Heg was colonel of the 15th Wisconsin Infantry, a unit raised at Madison and consisting primarily of Norwegians. He led the regiment in the operations against Island No. 10; in duty through Tennessee and northern Alabama; through Perryville; to Nashville; in pursuit of John Hunt Morgan; through the action at Stones River; and finally to his death near Viniard Field. The work presents a biographical essay on Heg's brief life and about 230 letters to his wife, daughter, and a few others, some of which were published during the war in the *Milwaukee Sentinel*.

The letters span the period 16 January 1862–18 September 1863. Some 125 of them are presented only in part. The work illuminates the value of Norwegian-American soldiers in the war, delivers gripping accounts of battles and marches, and outlines the incompetence of some volunteer officers and the feelings of civilians on both sides. The editing is generally sound, resulting in a collection of lasting value.

Thomas Wentworth Higginson (1823–1911)

513

Higginson, Thomas Wentworth. **Army Life in a Black Regiment** (296 pp., Fields, Osgood and Co., Boston, 1870)

A classic in black military history, this is the story of the author's role in the war, along with reminiscences of his famous regiment. Contrary to implications in the motion picture *Glory*, Col. Higginson's 1st South Carolina Infantry was the first black unit mustered into Federal service, in November 1862. That the abolitionist minister Higginson led the regiment created a first rate dramatic situation that in itself would produce a great film.

As for the book, Higginson published his diary covering the period November 1862 to January 1863 and then, after the war, composed the remaining story of his regiment's service from recollections. The result is important not so much for its descriptions of military maneuvers, which were limited in the case of his regiment, but for astutely depicting the lives of the earliest black American soldiers—their traditions, fears, and mental states. Higginson shows that the Confederate order to execute white U.S. officers commanding black troops backfired in a big way. He records many other illuminating examples of a race in the crucial moments of emerging toward freedom, and for that alone the book is worthwhile reading.

(Reprinted 1960, with an introduction by Howard Mumford Jones, 235 pp., Michigan State University Press, East Lansing; 1870 edition reprinted 1982, 256 pp., Time-Life Books, Alexandria, Va.)

Wilbur F. Hinman (1840–1905)

514

Hinman, Wilbur F. **Corporal Si Klegg and His "Pard": How They Lived and Talked and What They Did and Suffered, While Fighting for the Flag** (706 pp., N. G. Hamilton and Co., Cleveland, 1889)

This tongue-in-cheek recollection of army life is highly fictionalized and well represents wartime humor. The author, a captain in the 65th Ohio Infantry who rose to lieutenant colonel, saw wide service in Kentucky, Tennessee, Alabama, Georgia, and North Carolina throughout the war. A serious reminiscence of the author's service may be found in *The Story of the Sherman Brigade* (*q.v.*).

The fictitious characters Si Klegg and Shorty belong to the fictional unit of Company Q of the 200th Indiana Infantry. They encounter all manner of troubles and illustrate the pitfalls, dangers, difficulties, and hardships of soldier life in the Federal Army. Although the adventures of march, drill, camp life, battle, foraging, game playing, and letter writing are all hypothetical, Hinman's experience infuses a slight autobiographical content into the narrative and provides authenticity for the experiences nearly all soldiers shared. The conversational narrative becomes tiresome after many pages, but intrepid readers who brave the work's style will acquire a better feeling for the psychology of the Civil War soldier.

(Reprinted 1993, 706 pp., York Publishing Co., Galway, N.Y.)

Ethan Allen Hitchcock (1798–1870)

515

Hitchcock, Ethan Allen. **Fifty Years in Camp and Field: Diary of Major-General Ethan Allen Hitchcock, U.S.A.** (ed. W. A. Croffut, 514 pp., G. P. Putnam's Sons, New York, 1909)

This outstanding work reflects the illustrious soldier's long career. Covering the entirety of Hitchcock's life, the diary delivers much significant material on the subject's heritage, early life in the army, service in the Seminole actions in Florida and the Mexican War, and resignation from the army in 1855. It reveals his peculiar career as an amateur scholar, when he delved into diverse historical subjects and even mysticism. The material on the Mexican War is particularly valuable. The volume is filled with letters interspersed with narrative from the diary and from the editor.

The Civil War years comprise 13 percent of the book—disappointingly brief coverage, but valuable in its reflection of Hitchcock's position of importance. As confidant to Lincoln and Stanton and ultimately commissary general of prisoners, the aged major general recorded his thoughts candidly. Amusing passages recount the several attempts of the administration to place Hitchcock in field command or as a staff general-in-chief, followed by Hitchcock's persistent refusals. Less amusing are the author's accounts of the bitter quarrels throughout the various commands during each of the wars he participated in and the caustic reactions he sometimes displayed when more careful thought was called for.

(Reprinted 1971, 514 pp., Books for Libraries, Freeport, N.Y.)

Henry Hitchcock (1829–1902)

516

Hitchcock, Henry. **Marching with Sherman: Passages from Letters and Campaign Diaries of Henry Hitchcock, Major and Assistant Adjutant General of Volunteers, November 1864–May 1865** (ed. M. A. DeWolfe Howe, 332 pp., Yale University Press, New Haven, 1927)

Hitchcock's account contains an interesting record of Sherman's march and the Carolinas campaign by an intelligent staff officer. The nephew of Maj. Gen. Ethan Allen Hitchcock, the author was a leading attorney in St. Louis until he could no longer resist the urge to join the army, which he did in 1864. Receiving a staff appointment with Sherman through his uncle's influence, he set off for war, writing his first missive on 31 October 1864 from Rome, Georgia.

The many letters to his wife that follow and the diary excerpts shed light on the experience of the March to the Sea. The final letter was written after the Grand Review on 26 May 1865. The author recorded conversations with Sherman and made frequent observations about the soldiers and the countryside. The analysis of military matters is light. Hitchcock reflects cogently on the problems of destroying the railroads, of stragglers, and of destroying property in Georgia (Jefferson Davis held responsibility for the latter, according to Sherman). Property of military importance was burned; other property generally was not. The account of the burning of Columbia squares with the best modern interpretation. This work is skillfully executed and contains absorbing reflections on such diverse leaders as Grant, Wade Hampton, and Oliver O. Howard.

(Reprinted 1995, with an introduction by Brooks D. Simpson, 368 pp., University of Nebraska Press, Lincoln)

Oliver Wendell Holmes, Jr. (1841–1935)

517

Holmes, Oliver Wendell, Jr. **Touched with Fire: Civil War Letters and Diary of Oliver Wendell Holmes, Jr., 1861–1864** (ed. Mark DeWolfe Howe, 158 pp., Harvard University Press, Cambridge, 1946)

The wartime experiences of an intelligent young soldier who would become a brilliant and famous jurist are chronicled here. On Memorial Day 1884, Holmes spoke the famous words that characterize his war years: "Through our great good fortune, in our youth our hearts were touched with fire." Writing marked by equal poetic merit is contained in the diary and letters, as well as commentary of superb military value touching on the campaigns and battles Holmes weathered as a young officer who rose to captain in the 20th Massachusetts Infantry, the "Harvard Regiment." One must only lament that no more of the letters or diary exist, that this slim volume contains all that Holmes left behind on these subjects.

Nonetheless, what is here is engrossing. After letters reflecting on duties about Washington, Holmes's diary account of Ball's Bluff appears, a splendid entry that describes his wounding. Sketches of fighting and movements during the Peninsular campaign give way to the letter written after Holmes's wounding at Antietam that prompted his father to race to the battlefield, searching for his son. Further writings address Fredericksburg, subsequent woundings, and consid-

erable material on the Wilderness campaign. His recording terminates on 8 July 1864, the day before his experience of seeing Lincoln under fire at Fort Stevens. The occasional drawings reproduced as part of this collection add greatly to its appeal. The editing occasionally lacks precision, admitting errors of spelling such as those for William Woods Averell and Ambrose E. Burnside.

(Reprinted 1969, 158 pp., Da Capo Press, New York)

Joseph Hooker (1814–1879)

518

Hebert, Walter H. **Fighting Joe Hooker** (368 pp., Bobbs-Merrill Co., Indianapolis, 1944)

This is the standard Hooker biography, devoting more than 80 percent of its space to the Civil War years. Brief sections sketch the commander's background, frontier years before the sectional conflict, and postwar activities. Hebert uses the *O.R.* (*q.v.*) and a scattering of other important printed sources as well as manuscript collections including the Hooker papers. Generally sympathetic to Hooker, the author judges him more forgivingly than most historians of the past and for the most part weakly supports that defense.

The military aspects of Hooker's career are handled well, and the work remains readable. The discussion of key moments in Hooker's career, such as those on the Peninsula and at Second Bull Run, Antietam, and Fredericksburg, show him as an able and confidant commander at the divisional level. By no means does Hebert's tender portrait of his subject completely cloud Hooker's wrongdoings, however, as the author sketches Hooker's political difficulties and occasionally shows the general as his own worst enemy. The treatment of Chancellorsville is balanced although somewhat protective of the commander. The renewal of Hooker as an important commander in the western theater during the Chattanooga and Atlanta campaigns revives the book's spirit, much as it did Hooker's own psychology. Carelessness with names results in misidentifying David McMurtrie Gregg, Winfield Scott Hancock, Herman Haupt, Thomas S. Jesup, and Hector Tyndale.

(Reprinted 1987, 368 pp., R. Van Sickle, Gaithersburg)

Oliver Otis Howard (1830–1909)

519

Carpenter, John A. **Sword and Olive Branch: Oliver Otis Howard** (379 pp., University of Pittsburgh Press, Pittsburgh, 1964)

Carpenter leaves us with an impressively documented, full biography of this major general and reformer. An important picture of Howard emerges; unfortunately, however, only 63 pages of this work treat Howard's military command in the war. In this section the author rightly places his subject as a competent but unspectacular general who made errors (as at Chancellorsville, when his 11th Corps was taken by surprise) but learned from them. He was solid yet uninspired at Gettysburg, where he argued with Winfield Scott Hancock over who held command before Meade's arrival on the field. The author's narrative of Howard's military events is compact enough to read like an abbreviated tale told hastily, but the summary reads in balanced and scholarly fashion.

Howard's involvement with the Freedmen's Bureau receives substantial, if gentle, analysis. Howard's staunch Christian faith, his loss of an arm, and the will to do right by those emancipated made him a logical choice for commissioner. The author delivers a much more balanced assessment of the bureau's activities than many accounts, reducing in stature insinuations of political corruption. Those stories that echo through Howard's golden years—of involvement with Howard University and Lincoln Memorial University—round out the picture of the old commander even as the spotlight of fame faded away.

520

Howard, Oliver Otis. **Autobiography of Oliver Otis Howard** (2 vols., 1220 pp., Baker and Taylor Co., New York, 1907)

While the author sketches his career and records his thoughts on many situations and fellow commanders faithfully, this work does not stand up as one of the great memoirs of the war. Far too wordy, it might have been condensed by half. The work is tinged with the fervor of evangelical religion, and much of the writing is slow and painful to read, lacking careful copyediting. Nonetheless, the reader with patience to investigate Howard's words will discover his recollections of many important battlefields.

The portion on Chancellorsville is particularly fine. Howard had the good sense to avoid harsh criticism of Joseph Hooker despite the many troubles the two had during the war. He also has attempted to eliminate the widespread belief that he should not carry any blame for the misinterpretation of Jackson's movement on the field, and the argument is not altogether convincing. The work does ably document Howard's genuinely valuable service at Gettysburg and lays down much of interest regarding his service under Sherman. The story of Howard's postwar work in the Freedmen's Bureau is more admirable than his war record and is described with less of a hidden agenda.

(Reprinted n.d., 2 vols., 1220 pp., Ayer, Salem)

521

McFeely, William S. **Yankee Stepfather: General O. O. Howard and the Freedmen** (351 pp., Yale University Press, New Haven, 1968)

Concentrating on the political aspects of the Freedmen's Bureau, McFeely argues that Howard was an inept administrator who failed to achieve his ideals. He demonstrates that with regard to justice, protection from whites, and exploitation by plantation masters, Howard and the bureau performed badly. Howard, the author contends, was far more concerned with remaining in office and placating Andrew Johnson than carrying out his pious mission. Howard was not squarely to blame in the author's eyes, however, as he claims much of the injustice came from assistant commissioners who had yet to adopt a liberal policy toward emancipation.

The author shies away from discussing a centrally important aspect of the bureau, namely, its work in education. By doing so he creates a too-harsh picture of the failure of Howard. The general-turned-reformer was subjected to powerful political constraints that severely restricted his effectiveness. The author describes these constraints yet appears to hold his subject to a superhuman standard by expecting him to surmount them. The two modern works that treat Howard's life thus are too gentle (Carpenter, *q.v.*) or too harsh (McFeely). The reality lies somewhere in between.

(Reprinted 1994, 351 pp., W. W. Norton, New York)

Andrew Atkinson Humphreys (1810–1883)

522

Humphreys, Henry H. **Andrew Atkinson Humphreys: A Biography** (335 pp., John C. Winston Co., Philadelphia, 1924)

A work written late in life from a battery of scattered sources by the general officer's son, exactly half covers Humphreys's Civil War years. Substantial background material details the history of the subject's family in England and in the United States, his birth and early life, and his engineering duties on the Mississippi River and elsewhere in the 1840s and 1850s. These sections will hold only slight interest for students of the Civil War, though they contain excerpts from key documents describing the activities of U.S. Army officers in managing the river and formulating other internal improvements.

The real interest begins with Humphreys's assignment as chief topographical engineer of the Army of the Potomac during the Peninsular campaign. One wishes the level of detail were greater in the early sections on the war, but the narrative of Humphreys's activities is mainly objective and absorbing. The anecdotes about Antietam, Fredericksburg, and Chancellorsville all contain material of value. The text's worth is greatly enhanced by use of portions of Humphreys's letters to bolster the specifics. Humphreys's role at Gettysburg receives fair treatment, as does his subsequent acceptance as chief of staff to George Meade. As such, and as commander of the 2d Corps, as the work fairly shows, Humphreys made a significant contribution to Federal victory during the final year of the war. The work lacks an index.

(Reprinted 1988, 335 pp., R. Van Sickle, Gaithersburg)

Henry Jackson Hunt (1819–1889)

523

Longacre, Edward G. **The Man behind the Guns: A Biography of General Henry J. Hunt, Commander of Artillery, Army of the Potomac** (294 pp., A. S. Barnes Co., South Brunswick, N.J., 1977)

This is a documented, generally balanced, but extremely laudatory biography of the Army of the Potomac's chief artillerist. The cooperation of a descendant of Hunt's allowed the inclusion of several rare photographs of the subject. The greatest hindrance to fully enjoying the book is Longacre's overt worship of Hunt: the author claims that Hunt was "never accorded the rank his work demanded" and led a "unit that required the authority of a lieutenant general." Longacre confuses military grades and assignments. The author's narrative is unexceptional and lacks smooth transitions. The biography fails to place Hunt's achievements in context or to assimilate the background material necessary to understand Hunt's career. Shortcomings aside, this is the only book-length work on this important and neglected Federal general.

Richard W. Johnson (1827–1897)

524

Johnson, Richard W. **A Soldier's Reminiscences in Peace and War** (428 pp., J. B. Lippincott and Co., Philadelphia, 1886)

This autobiography of a general officer with a varied yet mostly unspectacular career is a conversational, popular account that surveys Johnson's entire life, providing background on his ancestry, early years, days at West Point, and extensive frontier duty during the antebellum years. Composed 20 years after the war, the book is based largely on memory but manages to deliver some valuable and interesting material despite occasional rambling. Of chief interest for Civil War students are the many recollections of the prewar adventures of officers who would become important commanders during the Civil War, including Phil Sheridan, William J. Hardee, Ben McCulloch, and others. The author touches on his participation in the Mormon expedition and includes many humorous anecdotes of the Mexican War, as well as memories of duty in the South, with details of the early days of New Orleans.

Johnson found himself on frontier duty in Texas during the secession crisis. Battle reminiscences describe Falling Waters, service in Kentucky with Alexander M. McCook, Mill Springs, Nashville, Corinth, Perryville, Stones River, Chickamauga, Missionary Ridge, and the Atlanta campaign. The material on Atlanta, recollections of Sherman, and details of the Franklin and Nashville campaigns are valuable. The author includes anecdotes about George H. Thomas, Alfred H. Terry, David S. Stanley, John M. Palmer, Absalom Baird, and Oliver Otis Howard. Some sections, like that on the death of William Nelson, are out of chronological order, and the index is inadequate.

Philip Kearny (1815–1862)

525

Kearny, Thomas. **General Philip Kearny, Battle Soldier of Five Wars, Including the Conquest of the West by General Stephen Watts Kearny** (496 pp., G. P. Putnam's Sons, New York, 1937)

The author recalls with some success the career of one of the most admired casualties of the Union commanders. Based on substantial research, drawing on large numbers of letters and reports, the biography sketches Kearny's wealthy New York background, horse training with his famous uncle, his early actions in Africa, and staff positions with Alexander Macomb and Winfield Scott. Kearny's Mexican War service is also explored, as is his tragic wounding at Churubusco, which necessitated amputation of his left arm.

The author delivers material of value relating to Kearny's military campaigns and battles, despite clumsy organization and poor writing. Should readers battle through the awkward prose, they can glean much about Kearny's Italian combat, his early days in the Peninsular campaign, and subsequent service at Second Bull Run. A lengthy description treats his participation at Chantilly, where he was killed in action. Despite the inadequacies of this biography, it remains the best source on this dashing officer.

Erasmus Darwin Keyes (1810–1895)

526

Keyes, Erasmus D. **Fifty Years' Observations of Men and Events, Civil and Military** (515 pp., Charles Scribner's Sons, New York, 1884)

Keyes's memoir contains the enjoyable and sometimes revealing notes of an officer who rose and fell along with George McClellan. A prominent theme in the work, which was written nearly 20 years after the war, is the author's early association with Winfield Scott. After being graduated from West Point, Keyes became an aide of Scott's, and his work relates many stories of the admired general, including a substantial amount of information drawn from Scott's autobiography. Significant antebellum coverage traces Keyes's military career in Florida, Louisiana, South Carolina, California, and Washington Territory.

The narrative accelerates as it reaches 1860 with the rise of the secession crisis and with the author's assignment as Scott's military secretary. Keyes describes much about New York society and politics. In May 1860 Scott and staff moved to Washington and tasted still more politics. The author kept a journal of events from which he drew many of the facts and anecdotes relating to this period. Through the autumn of 1860, the author shows, Scott believed war would not come. The narrative includes many letters to illustrate the range of sentiments involved. Keyes explores his involvement with Montgomery C. Meigs in planning to reinforce Fort Pickens, over Scott's opposition. On 19 April 1861 Keyes was terminated as Scott's secretary and became colonel of the 11th U.S. Infantry. He covers his participation in the First Bull Run campaign in detail, defends McClellan's "shortage" of troops on the Peninsula, and admires McClellan greatly throughout the campaign, wherein Keyes commanded the 4th Army Corps. Keyes describes his corps' actions at Fair Oaks, argues that the Army of the Potomac should have been combined with Pope's army, and concludes with the end of the Peninsular campaign. Appendices present his report on Fair Oaks and commentary from Col. C. C. Suydam, Keyes's chief of staff.

Jonathan Letterman (1824–1872)

527

Letterman, Jonathan. **Medical Recollections of the Army of the Potomac** (194 pp., D. Appleton and Co., New York, 1866)

Letterman's book is written with the dreary style of an official report, yet it contains value for patient readers. The author's key role as medical director of the Army of the Potomac from July 1862 to January 1864 enabled him to witness and oversee tremendous carnage and the resulting store of medical wisdom that arose from the great eastern battles of the middle of the war. He was appalled by the poor communication, transportation, and housing of hospital patients at the end of the Seven Days. Soldiers suffered from exposure, wet clothes, scurvy, and malaria. He quickly sent 6000 patients north in ships and put 12,000 into makeshift hospitals. He advocated digging new wells for clean drinking water, daily baths, improved tents and ambulances, and altered diets to include fresh meat, fruits, and vegetables. In short, the report shows how Letterman improved an otherwise disastrous situation for the wounded in Federal hands.

The author also effected changes in the medical corps of the army, instituting green armbands, chevrons, and shoulder straps to identify medical personnel and forcing medical purveyors, inspectors, and quartermasters to cooperate. By the time of Antietam, the medical corps was upgraded to nearly equal importance with those of food and ammunition. Nearly every house and barn in the vicinity of Sharpsburg became an aid station. By the end of 1862 the accounting of casualties and sick had been organized down to the brigade level, and a good system of distribution of medical supplies was in place. Besides outlining this important work, the narrative also describes some unusual incidents, as with Letterman's assistance to Joseph Hooker after the latter was knocked senseless at the Chancellor Tavern during the battle of Chancellorsville.

Thomas Leonard Livermore (1844–1918)

528

Livermore, Thomas L. **Days and Events, 1860–1866** (485 pp., Houghton Mifflin Co., Boston, 1920)

This curious work recalls the headlong joy and terror of the Civil War as experienced by a successful officer who rose to command the 18th New Hampshire Infantry. Composed immediately following the war and for several years thereafter, the work reflects in poorly documented but entertaining prose the common life of soldiers in the Army of the Potomac. Livermore would later become renowned for his *Numbers and Losses in the Civil War in America, 1861–65* (*q.v.*); here, his story of the war itself comes through as a gossipy hodgepodge of reminiscences.

The most valuable aspects of the work are the vivid mental images of foraging, camp life, marches, fights, and even horseracing among Livermore's comrades and inferiors. The narrative is free and open but omits the names of many people who committed less than glorious actions. The author harshly criticizes George McClellan while highly praising U. S. Grant, George Meade, Winfield Scott Hancock, Andrew A. Humphreys, and many other commmanders he observed in the field. Despite his rise in responsibility, Livermore offers only a chatty volume, primarily commenting on activities at soldier level.

John Alexander Logan (1826–1886)

529

Logan, John A. **The Great Conspiracy: Its Origin and History** (810 pp., A. R. Hart and Co., New York, 1886)

Logan has produced a lengthy and labored treatise on the political causes of the war and a running narrative of the political significance of events during the war. The first eight chapters cover the background of the war, political tensions dating back to the early days of the Republic, the slavery question, the shifting balance of power in Washington, and the sectional differences between Northerners and Southerners. The remaining 17 chapters examine the war itself, with much narration of military events and considerable analysis of the political significance behind them.

Much of Logan's source material was taken from congressional reports and other official documents, although Logan does not always make clear where he obtained various data. The work is an interesting survey, although one wishes Logan would have highlighted his own role with much greater emphasis. In most areas the presentation is bitterly partisan, and therefore the book loses some credibility it might have otherwise retained. Lengthy appendices cover the Lincoln-Douglas debates of 1858 and reports on various conspiracies against the government during the war. The work contains a poor index with more than one entry for the same person or event, and the text offers many misspellings, including the names of Barnard E. Bee, Louis Blenker, James Chesnut, Drewry's Bluff, George Meade, and Elihu B. Washburne.

530

Logan, John A. **The Volunteer Soldier of America** (ed. C. A. Logan, 706 pp., R. S. Peale and Co., Chicago, 1887)

This is a peculiar blend of materials, mostly trivial but some highly valuable. The work contains a useful sketch of Logan comprising some 73 pages, followed by Logan's long and labored history of military education in the United States and the evolution of its military system. Logan's hypothesis suggests that volunteers make excellent soldiers and that, like him, those who are not regular army officers can make superb contributions to American military organizations. The idea requires tremendous historical reviews of all the American conflicts, a lengthy narrative on why the American military system does not employ volunteers fairly, and a proposition for correcting the flaws inherent in the system.

The most useful portion of the study is a lengthy appendix titled "Military Reminiscences of the War in the West from the Journal of John A. Logan, Late Major-General of Volunteers, U.S.A." Composed of portions of Logan's wartime notes, the appendix provides a sketchy account by the author of his Civil War service. Good, short sketches of his involvement at Belmont and Forts Henry and Donelson, the movement on Corinth, the Vicksburg campaign, and the Atlanta campaign supply much detail of interest on the disposition of troops and his relations and communications with other commanders. The index is inadequate and contains duplicate entries for some individuals.

(Reprinted 1979, 706 pp., Arno Press, New York)

531

Logan, Mary S. **Reminiscences of a Soldier's Wife: An Autobiography, by Mrs. John A. Logan** (470 pp., Charles Scribner's Sons, New York, 1913)

Mary Logan offers a soft, friendly, serious reminiscence of Logan and her life with him throughout antebellum Illinois, Kentucky, and Washington, through the war years, and in postwar politics. It is conversationally written, uncritical, and occasionally wanders, yet it presents much of interest on the personal lives of the Logans and significant, often interesting background material on the author, arguably the founder of what became Memorial Day. Anecdotes relate how at the tender age of 17 the author married Logan, aided him in the legal profession, witnessed the Lincoln-Douglas campaign, traveled with Logan to the legislature, and rejoiced at his election as a U.S. congressman. She describes the journey to Washington and much about the capital city's social life, the last days of Buchanan, Lincoln's arrival, and Logan's mental transformation into a "Republican after Sumter." The work describes Logan's enlistment and the qualities that helped make him such an outstanding volunteer soldier.

The Civil War coverage spans nearly one-quarter of the book. The author describes Belmont and provides reminiscences concerning James B. McPherson, Vicksburg, the explosion of Fort Hill, befriending contrabandists back in Illinois, the Atlanta campaign, the difficulties and reconciliation between Sherman and her husband, Logan's succession by Howard, activities with the president around City Point, and Logan's journey to Nashville, where he nearly relieved Thomas. Postwar recollections center on politics and Logan's central role in the G.A.R.

(Abridged edition 1970, titled *Reminiscences of the Civil War and Reconstruction*, ed. George Worthington Adams, 324 pp., Southern Illinois University Press, Carbondale)

Charles Russell Lowell (1835–1864)

532

Emerson, Edward W. **Life and Letters of Charles Russell Lowell—Captain, Sixth United States Cavalry; Colonel, Second Massachusetts Cavalry; Brigadier-General, United States Volunteers** (499 pp., Houghton Mifflin Co., Boston, 1907)

The author sets forth the career of an expert horse soldier who perished at Cedar Creek. The offspring of accomplished New Englanders and first in his class at Harvard, Lowell was 26 when commissioned a captain in the 3d (subsequently 6th) U.S. Cavalry. The laudatory sketch of Lowell's life and his military career that makes up much of this work is skillfully, though uncritically, accomplished. The material relating to staff service for George B. McClellan is well done, as is the discussion of Lowell's heroic activities at Antietam.

The letters appended to Emerson's narrative are even more illuminating. They reveal a thoughtful individual whose focus on the military campaigns and assessments of commanders does not detract from smaller matters. Much of value exists here regarding Lowell's months protecting Washington against the likes of Jubal Early, occasionally harassing John S. Mosby, and his service in 1864 under Philip H. Sheridan. Having missed serious wounding many times, the Bostonian was mortally wounded at Cedar Creek during the critical Union counterattack that swept the field. The tribute in this work, though dated in style, retains value.

(Reprinted 1980, 499 pp., Century Bookbindery, Philadelphia)

Theodore Lyman (1833–1897)

533

Lyman, Theodore. **Meade's Headquarters, 1863–1865: Letters of Colonel Theodore Lyman from the Wilderness to Appomattox** (ed. George R. Agassiz, 371 pp., Atlantic Monthly Press, Boston, 1922)

This outstanding collection of letters is by a Federal staff officer, a Boston Brahmin who had worked as a scientific assistant to George Meade before the war. Lyman took to the field on 2 September 1863 as a volunteer aide-de-camp for the commander of the Army of the Potomac. The unusually close relationship between Lyman and his father-figure Meade (whom he called "the Great Peppery") allowed this unpaid officer to see the army's closing campaign of 1863, the ascension of Ulysses Grant, and the entire decisive campaign beginning with the Wilderness and on through Appomattox. This opportunity would not have been so great if it were not for Lyman's literate and reflective mind; his letters sent to his wife reflect on numerous military activities, battles, and skirmishes and particularly illuminate the character of many staff officers and generals in contact with Meade.

The author sketched numerous engagements and honestly set down opinions relating to the intelligence of what had occurred. His reflections on a number of actions about Petersburg are particularly valuable, as are accounts of the attack at Cold Harbor and the closing scenes of the war. Especially good reading comes from several accounts of serving as courier in hostile territory and of many discussions in a tent with Meade and others on the commander's staff. The work contains a few misspellings, as with the names of Henry Livermore Abbott, Thomas Wilburforce Egan, Charles Shiels Wainwright, and the Landram House at Spotsylvania.

(Reprinted 1994, titled *With Grant and Meade from the Wilderness to Appomattox*, with an introduction by Brooks D. Simpson, 371 pp., University of Nebraska Press, Lincoln)

Nathaniel Lyon (1818–1861)

534

Phillips, Christopher. **Damned Yankee: The Life of General Nathaniel Lyon** (287 pp., University of Missouri Press, Columbia, 1990)

This is one of the most entertaining biographies of a Union general officer in the West. Lyon, a much overlooked commander, was immensely important prior to his death at Wilson's Creek during the first summer of the war. As Phillips clearly shows in straightforward, well-written, and well-documented style, Lyon's significance extended from the military into the political arena.

The last half of the work treats Lyon's brief Civil War service; the first half details his early army career, his Mexican War service, his frontier duty, and the growth of his strong pro-Union political views. The author thus builds a psychological portrait of Lyon as a commander who could attack a superior Confederate force at Wilson's Creek fueled by the singleminded feeling that he had been charged by God to save Missouri for the Union. The author's thesis proclaims that Lyon hardly saved Missouri for the Union, however, because Union sentiment in Missouri was so strong that it likely would have chosen that course under any circumstance.

Phillips details Lyon's capture of a portion of the Missouri State Militia, the raising of the pro-Confederate State Guard, and the ensuing campaign in which Lyon captured Jefferson City, secured the central rail lines, and launched southward toward Confederates in Arkansas. The critical battle of Wilson's Creek, in which Lyon was mortally wounded, receives relatively short treatment, and maps surely would have aided readers. Nevertheless, this is a fine contribution to understanding the Civil War in the West.

Charles Porter Mattocks (1840–1910)

535

Mattocks, Charles. **"Unspoiled Heart": The Journal of Charles Mattocks of the 17th Maine** (ed. Philip N. Racine, 446 pp., University of Tennessee Press, Knoxville, 1994)

Mattocks's diary proves equally valuable for battlefield reminiscences and for reflections on prison life. The author, who rose by war's end to command of the 17th Maine as its colonel, kept a meticulous journal covering the period 18 April 1863 through 14 June 1865. Mattocks served principally in the 17th Maine but also relates his experiences with the 1st U.S. Sharpshooters. He presents details on his participa-

tion in the battles of Chancellorsville and Gettysburg, the early days of the Wilderness campaign, and his capture in the Wilderness. The diaries contain much of military interest, reflections on officers and particulars of the unit's actions, and also fine recollections of smaller moments of the war centered on associates and life in camp and march.

At one point Mattocks was imprisoned but escaped into the mountains of North Carolina. Recaptured, he recorded a wide range of thoughts during the next nine months in Confederate hands. He was exchanged prior to the battle of Sayler's Creek, where he won the Medal of Honor. His discussion of this last significant battle of the Appomattox campaign holds much of interest for students of the final weeks of the eastern war.

The book contains a few typographical errors, as with the "Kearney badge" and the misspelling of Gouverneur K. Warren's name. Generally, however, it is accurate and winningly informative.

Robert McAllister (1813–1891)

536

McAllister, Robert. **The Civil War Letters of General Robert McAllister** (ed. James I. Robertson, Jr., 638 pp., Rutgers University Press, New Brunswick, 1965)

A farmer, railroad engineer, and sometime soldier, McAllister organized and commanded a unit of Pennsylvania militia in his home county in 1839. After moving to New Jersey, he entered the war as lieutenant colonel of the 1st New Jersey Infantry and was commissioned colonel of the 11th New Jersey at the end of June 1862. He remained with this regiment throughout the rest of the war, eventually winning two brevets as brigadier general and major general.

The editor presents 936 letters written by McAllister to his wife and daughters during the war. These are filled with the minutiae of army life, sometimes entertaining and other times monotonous. Yet a comprehensive picture of this soldier emerges, one that rewards the reader for sticking with the text. McAllister's range of battle experiences included the Peninsular campaign, Fredericksburg, Chancellorsville, Gettysburg, the Wilderness campaign, and the siege of Petersburg. For this last action McAllister received his brevet brigadier general's commission for heroism at the Boydton Plank Road.

The author's poor spelling and repetitive commentary might have been corrected by the editor. The notes contain an occasional error, as with the suggestion that McAllister's brigade led Hancock's assault on the Mule Shoe at Spotsylvania.

George Brinton McClellan (1826–1885)

537

Hassler, Warren W., Jr. **General George B. McClellan: Shield of the Union** (350 pp., Louisiana State University Press, Baton Rouge, 1957)

Hassler asserts that McClellan was extraordinarily talented as a soldier, meticulous in the details of his planning, and confident in the ability of his men, who dearly loved him. The author also believes that McClellan was not a victim of his own high-mindedness and fear but of political intrigue by radical Republicans in Washington.

The argument, worked through in a rehash of McClellan's history of field command, comes close to succeeding. Hassler contends that Washington inadequately supported its commander during the Peninsular campaign. He believes that Antietam was the pinnacle of Confederate military opportunity and that McClellan's victory there thwarted the rebel war effort. McClellan transformed the Army of the Potomac into a capable and fearsome army and fought Lee when the Army of Northern Virginia was at its peak efficiency, yet his irrational actions, such as vastly overestimating his enemy's strength, prevented him from achieving more. Had he implemented the offensive tactics of a great general, he may have broken Lee's army in front of Richmond. He certainly could have achieved more success at Antietam had he used the whole army, particularly the 5th Corps. The author establishes several good points, but does not convincingly show that McClellan was as capable as he claims.

538

McClellan, George B. **The Civil War Papers of George B. McClellan: Selected Correspondence, 1860–1865** (ed. Stephen W. Sears, 651 pp., Ticknor and Fields, New York, 1989)

The editor has assembled and published an impressive selection of 813 papers, mostly letters written by McClellan, many of which were used for the successful research for his biography of McClellan (*q.v.*). The volume includes 260 McClellan papers never before printed and his 192 letters to his wife—often revealing his candid and unusual thoughts—appear uncensored.

The result is a compilation of McClellan's thoughts and ideas that transcends his own memoir (*q.v.*) because these papers were not intended for publication. If any staunch McClellan supporter is left partly intact after reading Stephen Sears's biography, then this work provides more ammunition to knock down McClellan by his own words. Perhaps the most enigmatic element of McClellan is that he

was obviously intelligent. Why should someone with so much education be terrified of unseen "evils" to a point of dysfunction? The papers herein explain why. In his complex combination of egotism, intelligence, self-righteousness, and delusion, McClellan lived in a world of his own. This work shows that although it was a strange place, it was also a fascinating one.

(Reprinted 1992, 651 pp., Da Capo Press, New York)

539

McClellan, George B. **McClellan's Own Story: The War for the Union, the Soldiers Who Fought It, the Civilians Who Directed It, and His Relations to It and to Them** (677 pp., Charles L. Webster and Co., New York, 1887)

This is in large part a reworking of McClellan's *Letter of the Secretary of War, Transmitting Report on the Organization of the Army of the Potomac, and of Its Campaigns in Virginia and Maryland, under the Command of Maj. Gen. George B. McClellan, from July 26, 1861, to November 7, 1862* (242 pp., U.S. Government Printing Office, Washington, 1864). The coverage of *McClellan's Own Story* is more extensive, however, offering a biographical sketch of McClellan, a treatise on the causes of the war, a discussion of the early months of pandemonium, a selection of letters McClellan wrote to his wife, and a narrative of McClellan's substantive part in the war from the summer of 1861 to the aftermath of his removal following Antietam.

The value of this work is reduced to a historical reflection of his psychology in the early chapters, wherein he essentially accuses Lincoln and a number of administration officials of a conspiracy to sacrifice the Army of the Potomac. As motivation for such a "treasonable conspiracy," he highlights examples of so-called evidence of a personal vendetta against him by most of those who outranked him in the army and many political advisors to Lincoln. Such an egocentric view of the army's activities and a paranoid outlook on the government are nothing more than absurdities, painfully so when the work was first published. Unfortunately, the revisionist history extends into the military narrative in this work as well, seeking to vindicate McClellan's actions, wildly overestimate the size of Confederate forces during the entire Peninsula campaign, and attack many subordinate officers as inept. Although the letters in this volume appear elsewhere in more convenient form (*q.v.*), the historical narrative retains great value for showing McClellan's amazing faults. Indeed, the book leaves him with little semblance of rationality.

The book contains a poor index with many ambiguous entries. The text includes many misspellings, as with the names of Henry Larcom Abbot, William Woods Averell, Cyrus B. Comstock, Cuvier Grover, Isaac Ferdinand Quinby, Julius Stahel, Isaac Ingalls Stevens, and Orlando B. Willcox.

540

Sears, Stephen W. **George B. McClellan: The Young Napoleon** (482 pp., Ticknor and Fields, New York, 1988)

Properly detailed, sound in its research, well documented, and analytical in its musings, Sears's biography constitutes a work of solid importance for Civil War readers. Chief in its qualities is the author's ability to avoid extremist and oversimplified interpretations. Instead, the narrative is sensible, balanced, and more realistic than most of the previous literature on this difficult personality.

A relatively brief three chapters treat McClellan's prewar life and explore the personality traits that might explain his Civil War behavior. Time and again the young soldier evaded responsibility and rationalized his problems, Sears shows, long before the war approached. After taking command of the Army of the Potomac, McClellan allowed his belief in divine selection to further his own rationalizations as well as a fatalistic view of his actions and those of others. The author rightly credits McClellan for the organizational contributions made to forging an eastern army for the Union, as well as some difficulties McClellan faced that later Federal commanders did not. He also masterfully uncovers McClellan's weird attitudes toward himself and his command, demonstrating that McClellan was wrong repeatedly as he tried to deal with his superiors, both military and civilian, and that his delusions (of Confederate military superiority, of his own grandeur, and of fearsome higher powers) clouded his judgment essentially every day. This work serves as a concise, clear, and damning indictment of the man who needed but lacked the quiet confidence of Grant.

Benjamin Franklin McIntyre (1827–?)

541

McIntyre, Benjamin F. **Federals on the Frontier: The Diary of Benjamin F. McIntyre, 1862–1864** (ed. Nannie M. Tilley, 429 pp., University of Texas Press, Austin, 1963)

This work provides a valuable account of the Civil War in the West, concentrating on Missouri, Texas, and Arkansas. The scant supply of trustworthy and well-written narratives covering this area makes this work a first-rate contribution to understanding this neglected theater of war.

The author's two-year stint covers the period September 1862–August 1864. McIntyre was commissioned a sergeant in the 19th Iowa Infantry and finished his service as a first lieutenant, experiencing along the way a blend of brief, exciting battles and a great deal of marching and camp life. After duty around Springfield, Missouri, the author and his regiment participated in James G. Blunt's campaign in Arkansas, including the battle of Prairie Grove. This marks the high point of the diary's first portion. In June 1863 the regiment moved on Vicksburg and participated in the final weeks of the siege, and the author's account of this action is superb. McIntyre then relates his experiences at Yazoo City, Port Hudson, and Carrollton before describing the regiment's advance on Brownsville and duty there. Along the way he mentions many aspects of a soldier's life among his comrades and comments on a variety of commanders, reflecting a strong dislike for John Schofield but true admiration for Ulysses S. Grant.

George Gordon Meade (1815–1872)

542

Cleaves, Freeman. **Meade of Gettysburg** (384 pp., University of Oklahoma Press, Norman, 1960)

Studious, cautious, mindful of his subordinates, and familiar with the enemy, Meade provided a real contrast to the impetuous, sometimes reckless courage displayed by other Civil War general officers. As such, he was harshly criticized during his command and has been harshly criticized since. Cleaves demonstrates that Meade's qualities were valuable to the Army of the Potomac and builds a proper case for great respect.

The author demonstrates Meade's reluctance to take command of the army by using the general's own words: how he wished to "go home and be quiet with you and the children," he wrote his wife during the war's final campaign. Part of that detachment may have stemmed from unpopularity with the troops and many junior officers. Certainly Lincoln was dismayed at Meade's lack of pursuit following Gettysburg, although clearly Meade's army was hardly fit to pursue anything at the time. Yet Cleaves documents Grant's unfailing confidence in his Potomac commander.

The author's coverage of the May campaign may be tarnished by worship of Meade, who appears to be running the show instead of Grant. Apart from this imbalance, this well-executed work accomplishes much in restoring Meade to proper historical perspective.

(Reprinted 1980, 384 pp., Morningside, Dayton)

543

Meade, George G., and George G. Meade, Jr. **The Life and Letters of George Gordon Meade, Major General United States Army** (ed. George G. Meade III, 2 vols., 821 pp., Charles Scribner's Sons, New York, 1913)

Important and underrated as a source on the operations of the Army of the Potomac, this is a key work on Northern generalship. Consisting primarily of letters from Meade to his wife and occasionally others, and supplemented by official reports and connecting narrative from Meade's son (who served on the general's staff during the war), the biography offers a great deal. The first volume examines Meade's background, delivers 178 pages of Mexican War letters, and covers the general's Civil War career up to the period immediately prior to Gettysburg. The second volume contains a wealth of material centered on Meade's assignment to command the Army of the Potomac, Gettysburg operations, the aftermath of Gettysburg, the Mine Run campaign, Meade's relationship with Grant and other commanders, and the decisive campaigns of 1864–1865.

The Civil War letters (340 pp.) sustain certain impressions of Meade as a humorless and bookish man but also clearly demonstrate his competence. Thus, that he felt "under the shadow of Grant" was an oversensitive feeling on his part, as he clearly excelled as a commander and played an important part in eventual Union military victory. A curiously omnipresent theme is Meade's worrying to his wife about the failure to destroy Lee's army following Gettysburg and the ongoing hearings of the Committee on the Conduct of the War. The series of letters shows Meade's confidence in Grant as high, waning, and then slowly recovering throughout the campaigns of 1864.

The work is not adequately documented, so that conclusions are nebulous or occasionally mysterious. The extensive appendices are sometimes useful and sometimes not. Twenty-four Gettysburg maps, poorly detailed and therefore without much value, accompany the text.

(Reprinted 1994, with an introduction by Richard A. Sauers and a photographic supplement, 2 vols., 821 pp., Butternut and Blue, Baltimore)

Montgomery Cunningham Meigs
(1816–1892)

544

Weigley, Russell F. **Quartermaster General of the Union Army: A Biography of M. C. Meigs** (396 pp., Columbia University Press, New York, 1959)

This full biography, scholarly and well-documented, spends half of its pages on the war years. Still, Weigley succeeds in using a store of Meigs family papers to establish the subject's background and early years in Philadelphia, at West Point, and on scattered engineering duty. The discussion of engineering work around antebellum Washington, including the building of the aqueduct and extension of the U.S. Capitol, is interesting and well told although not genuinely valuable to an understanding of the wartime Meigs.

Much of the documentary evidence at hand for the war years comes from the *O.R.* (*q.v.*). Occasionally the author's prose strains toward embellishment. Overall, however, Weigley convincingly and astutely casts the story of Meigs's shaping of a chaotic Quartermaster Department into one of the shining lights of efficiency of the Union war effort. Graft, theft, and shoddy manufacturing characterized the early days of supplying the Union Army. The situation under Frémont in St. Louis was perhaps the most out of hand, and Meigs found small disasters to correct everywhere. Before he could tighten the department's operation, however, Congress investigated and scandal erupted. This tale is related by Weigley in admirably detailed fashion.

Throughout the work much about the materials of war can be gleaned, and the emphasis rightly hits matters of transportation at certain key times. Meigs's involvement in the critical situation following the battle of Chickamauga is one such instance. Although at such times the author sees his subject too sympathetically, this is a credible and important biography of one of the key Union generals who is too often overlooked.

William Neal Meserve (1840–1928)

545

Meserve, William N. **Meserve Civil War Record: With the Intriguing War Story by Major William N. Meserve, the Story That Inspired His Son, the Legendary Frederick Hill Meserve, to Amass the Great "Meserve Collection" of Over 200,000 Lincoln and Civil War Era Photographs and Negatives** (ed. Richard A. Huebner, 290 pp., RAH Publications, Oak Park, Mich., 1987)

Meserve was a major in the 35th Massachusetts Infantry and 4th Massachusetts Artillery and recorded his memoirs in the 1890s. Based on a diary that was subsequently lost, this account is nevertheless believable, apparently embellished only in minor ways. It includes accounts of Antietam, Fredericksburg, the Wilderness, Cold Harbor, and engagements outside Petersburg, including the Crater and the Weldon Railroad. One reads the narrative with added interest because it inspired the author's son, Frederick Hill Meserve, to begin his great collection of Civil War photographs.

The editor is soldier Meserve's great-grandson, who thoughtfully had the first 120 pages typeset to match the original manuscript pages of the soldier's account. This is followed by a chronology of Meserve's life, a discussion of his manuscript, an outline and rosters of the two regiments, and a selection of photographs from the collection. It is a fine package that elegantly describes the service of a Massachusetts officer in the Union Army.

Nelson Appleton Miles (1839–1925)

546

Miles, Nelson A. **Personal Recollections and Observations of General Nelson A. Miles, Embracing a Brief View of the Civil War; or, From New England to the Golden Gate, and the Story of His Indian Campaigns, with Comments on the Exploration, Development, and Progress of Our Great Western Empire: Copiously Illustrated with Graphic Pictures by Frederic Remington and Other Eminent Artists** (591 pp., Werner Co., Chicago, 1896)

Miles's succinct but inspired account concentrates heavily on the Indian campaigns that followed the war. The two short Civil War chapters provide a sketch of Miles's rise from a young first lieutenant in the 22d Massachusetts Infantry to brigadier general and his final, distinguished conduct during the Appomattox campaign. A popular, patriotic, and general account, the work retains value only in that it comes across in Miles's own words. His gallantry at Fair Oaks, Antietam, Fredericksburg, and Chancellorsville receives scant treatment, as do the Wilderness campaign and Petersburg. The vast majority of this volume covers Miles's career in the 1870s and 1880s on the plains. The work lacks an index.

(Abridged edition 1911, titled *Serving the Republic: Memoirs of Civil and Military Life*, 339 pp., Harper and Bros., New York; 1896 edition reprinted 1992, with an introduction by Robert Wooster, 2 vols., 591 pp., University of Nebraska Press, Lincoln)

Edward Otho Cresap Ord (1818–1883)

547

Cresap, Bernarr. **Appomattox Commander: The Story of General E. O. C. Ord** (418 pp., A. S. Barnes and Co., San Diego, 1981)

Although it covers in degrees the subject's entire life, this work concentrates on the Civil War era, devoting about half of its narrative to those four years. Cresap suitably treats his subject's prewar years, many of which consisted of frontier duty against Indians, and describes his entrance into the active wartime Federal Army in the autumn of 1861 as a brigadier general of volunteers.

The author demonstrates that Ord's career deserves attention because he played significant roles in both theaters of the war. After jousting with Jeb Stuart at Dranesville, Ord received a commission as major general and later won a regular army brevet for Iuka, although he was not present on the battlefield. As a corps commander in the closing days of the Vicksburg campaign, Ord served Grant well. He worked his way toward Richmond and Petersburg in 1864 and was seriously wounded in September, not returning to the line until January 1865. Running the Army of the James in the wake of Ben Butler made Ord look good, as did his actions during the Appomattox campaign. While the style in this biography might have been smoother, the research is sound and presents a comprehensive picture of an important Federal major general and a capable commander.

Thomas Ward Osborn (1836–1898)

548

Osborn, Thomas W. **The Fiery Trail: A Union Officer's Account of Sherman's Last Campaigns** (ed. Richard Harwell and Philip N. Racine, 238 pp., University of Tennessee Press, Knoxville, 1986)

Chief of artillery of the Army of the Tennessee, Major Osborn kept a journal of the campaign from Atlanta to the war's end and the Grand Review in Washington. In between he managed the army's artillery throughout Sherman's activities north of Atlanta, during the battles around Atlanta, through the March to the Sea, and in the Carolinas campaign. Osborn's journal and a number of letters he penned during the period constitute this book.

The result is an excellent account of the Union penetration into Georgia in 1864. As an officer who worked for Maj. Gen. Oliver O. Howard and observed Sherman himself, Osborn adds much to an understanding of what these two important officers were doing during the campaign. Additionally, Osborn enjoyed commenting on the overall strategy of the march, including the liberal pillaging of any supplies that could be of use to Southern armies. The diary's account of the burning of Columbia squares with the most reliable information in other sources. Few excellent accounts of Sherman's march exist; this is one of them and should be considered an illuminating work on the war's western theater.

John McAuley Palmer (1817–1900)

549

Palmer, George Thomas. **A Conscientious Turncoat: The Story of John M. Palmer, 1817–1900** (255 pp., Yale University Press, New Haven, 1941)

The career of this political general is displayed from the viewpoint of his grandson. Although lightly documented and written with natural compassion for the subject, this work contributes something of value not present in the general's own recollections (*q.v.*). The passage of time allowed the grandson to place much of Palmer's apparent contradiction into perspective, sorting out the paradox of being born into slave society yet transforming into an abolitionist and sticking hard to Unionist views. This full biography provides a respectable section on the subject's antebellum life and political development before describing his role in the war. The Civil War coverage, paying close attention to both military and political aspects of Palmer's career, amounts to nearly half the book.

Quotations from many wartime letters written by Palmer add greatly to the book. The author sketches Palmer's participation at Island No. 10, in the advance on Corinth, at Stones River and Chattanooga, and in the Atlanta campaign. He sensitively treats Palmer's request for relief of command, perhaps with too much favor toward the subject, and describes faithfully his service in Kentucky. The postwar coverage transforms into a straightforward narration of Palmer's political triumphs and aspirations. The index is adequate, but a number of misspellings mar the text, as with the names of Isaac N. Arnold, John C. Breckinridge, Charlotte Cushman, and William Clarke Quantrill and the place names Kennesaw Mountain and Pittsburg Landing.

550

Palmer, John M. **Personal Recollections of John M. Palmer: The Story of an Earnest Life** (631 pp., Robert Clarke Co., Cincinnati, 1901)

This book recalls the Civil War career of an Illinois general officer and politician. A political general in the truest sense, Palmer lacked any real military experience before the war but became colonel of the 14th Illinois Infantry in large part because of his political backing of Lincoln and the Republican party in Illinois. This full account of Palmer's intersperses documents, letters, and messages throughout the narrative. The wartime period is covered well, with a discussion of the officer's initial movement with his regiment into Missouri and the subsequent discovery of how green his troops were and how inexperienced he was at command. His evolution began in earnest in December 1861 when he was commissioned a brigadier general and subsequently became a highly capable citizen-soldier.

The remarks centered on early battles along the Mississippi, the movement toward Nashville, and Stones River are particularly worthwhile, the last being the place where Palmer led a division into the thick of the battle. The author's participation in Chickamauga and the subsequent resentment toward the War Department during the Atlanta campaign form important parts of the work. Upset by Washington's removal of Thomas L. Crittenden, Palmer balked at further action but was pursuaded to remain by Lincoln. Promoted to corps command, Palmer served out the remainder of his wartime days in Kentucky, where in the war's closing days he helped to free many of the state's gathered slaves. He treats his governorship and tenure in the U.S. Senate effectively.

Ely Samuel Parker (1828–1895)

551

Armstrong, William H. **Warrior in Two Camps: Ely S. Parker, Union General and Seneca Chief** (244 pp., Syracuse University Press, Syracuse, 1978)

Armstrong recounts the life of one of the few American Indians placed in a position of influence during the war. Raised in Indian and white culture, the Grand Sachem of the Six Nations acquainted himself with Ulysses Grant in pre-war Galena, Illinois. When war erupted Parker sought Grant's help, and the Illinois general, impressed by the Indian lawyer with beautiful handwriting, eventually appointed Parker a military secretary. As such, Parker stayed by Grant's side throughout the final two years of war and wrote out the surrender terms at Appomattox. Parker was brevetted a brigadier general, to date from Lee's surrender.

The present work is a brief but full biography, with less than one-fourth of the text devoted to the wartime period. Although Armstrong provides an adequate summary of Parker's involvement as a Grant staffer, he offers little interpretation of Parker's influence or his role in the war as a whole and does little to enlighten readers about why Parker's life unfolded as it did. The work ably documents Parker's intelligence and his ability to rise above the limitations felt by most American Indians of the period, yet there is little analysis when it comes to Parker's postwar assignment as commissioner of Indian Affairs in the Grant administration.

Marsena Rudolph Patrick (1811–1888)

552

Patrick, Marsena R. **Inside Lincoln's Army: The Diary of General Marsena Rudolph Patrick, Provost Marshal General, Army of the Potomac** (ed. David S. Sparks, 536 pp., Thomas Yoseloff, New York, 1964)

This valuable memoir was composed by a high commander in the Army of the Potomac. Patrick's commission as brigadier general resulted from McClellan's request in 1862; from that point on the author participated in the entirety of the eastern campaigns. A brigade commander at Second Bull Run, South Mountain, and Antietam, Patrick was appointed provost marshal general of the Army of the Potomac shortly thereafter, serving in that capacity until promoted by Grant to the same assignment for all armies operating against Richmond.

The author's diary is exceedingly revealing and the editor has done an adequate job of annotating it. Well educated, astute in his observations, and forthright in recording details, Patrick has provided a goldmine of information not only about matters of military justice but also about the operations of the army and political matters in Washington. Sketches of military tactics and strategy abound, as do frank assessments of numerous personalities, not the least of which is Edwin M. Stanton. This work is a must on the bookshelf of any student of the Army of the Potomac.

George Whitfield Pepper (1833–1899)

553

Pepper, George W. **Personal Recollections of Sherman's Campaigns in Georgia and the Carolinas** (522 pp., Hugh Dunne, Zanesville, 1866)

An early, revealing, and occasionally unreliable account, these recollections focus on the Chattanooga campaign, actions around Atlanta, and the March to the Sea. The author served as a captain in an Ohio regiment and corresponded with several newspapers, concocting what amounts to a travel account of his adventures in the campaigns. The book is not highly informed but contains entertaining anecdotes of simple events the author experienced along the way. Pepper passed through Cincinnati in the autumn of 1863 and traveled south, reaching Chattanooga in time to participate in the subsequent actions.

Sections of the narrative straightforwardly describe military movements of the author's regiment and many others involved with assaults. Occasionally, details on important actions along the Atlanta campaign are made interesting by the author's commentary. Recollections of amusing incidents are often included, with specific conversations that the author could not possibly have recorded with such accuracy. Nonetheless, the work is enjoyable and retains the sense of urgency found in contemporary narratives, which is a refreshing quality.

William Rattle Plum (1845–1927)

554

Plum, William R. **The Military Telegraph during the Civil War in the United States, with an Exposition of Ancient and Modern Means of Communication, and of the Federal and Confederate Cipher Systems: Also a Running Account of the War between the States** (2 vols., 767 pp., Jansen, McClurg and Co., Chicago, 1882)

Plum briefly discusses the history of military communications, including those by courier, semaphore, heliostat, telegraph, flags, lanterns, and torches. He emphasizes the U.S. Military Telegraph of which he was a member during the war, ending as chief telegrapher at the Nashville office of Maj. Gen. George H. Thomas.

An important chapter describes the cipher-code systems of the Union and Confederate armies. The work explains how Confederates employed a matrix with single-letter substitutions in a series of alphabets governed by a key phrase. The principal key phrases were "Manchester Bluff," "Complete Victory," and "Come Retribution." Because word length was usually preserved and only important words in a message were ciphered, many of the Confederate cipher-code messages were read by Federal cryptanalysts.

By contrast, most of the 6.5 million Union telegraphic messages transmitted during the war were not read by Confederates, as the work describes. The U.S. Army's 12 cipher-code systems employed code words called "arbitraries" as substitutes for sensitive words or phrases. The Federal telegraphers then used a "route cipher," a word transposition matrix that utilized words in rows and columns. The ciphered message then appeared to consist of recognizable words in random order, easy to telegraph, but extremely difficult to regroup in a meaningful sequence.

The bulk of Plum's work surveys the course of the war with respect to the U.S. Military Telegraph, including the stories of many of the operators. Many proper names are misspelled, usually a result of phonetic errors, but in general the work is well done. An appendix provides a roster of 1079 operators of the U.S. Military Telegraph, the most complete list outside the records of the National Archives.

(Reprinted 1974, with an introduction by Paul J. Scheips that is part of a generalized doctoral dissertation not all of which is specifically germaine to Plum's book, reprinted from vol. 9 of *Civil War History*, 2 vols., 767 pp., Arno Press, New York)

John Pope (1822–1892)

555

Schutz, Wallace J., and Walter N. Trenerry. **Abandoned by Lincoln: A Military Biography of General John Pope** (243 pp., University of Illinois Press, Urbana, 1990)

This stands alone as a full-length biography of a controversial and unsuccessful Union commander of the Army of Virginia. The facts of Pope's career appear along with a brief section on his early life, a lengthy discussion of his Civil War exploits (particularly the period centered on Second Bull Run), a survey of his "exhile" period, and a conclusion delivering the downhill story of his later life. The prewar and postwar treatments are quite brief, but the authors are forceful when dealing with Pope's less than outstanding field performance.

While readers can discern a clear picture of the Union officer's life and his rise to the grade of major general, the biography's defensive tone steps into irrationality to revise Pope's tarnished reputation. The revisionist interpretation of Pope's victimization by numerous fellow officers and by Lincoln himself is supported rather weakly in most areas, the overwhelming bulk of the material consisting of previously published work. A few misspellings appear, as with the names of Ethan Allen Hitchcock, David Hunter, and Irvin McDowell. Those who wish to learn the details of John Pope's unhappy time in the army may read this book, awash in details of the man. But the judgments offered here are often clouded and lift their principal subject unfairly while doing injustice to others.

Fitz John Porter (1822–1901)

556

Eisenschiml, Otto. **The Celebrated Case of Fitz John Porter: An American Dreyfus Affair** (344 pp., Bobbs-Merrill Co., Indianapolis, 1950)

One of the more admirable pieces penned by this prolific author, this work has its heart in the right place. Eisenschiml tells the controversial story of Fitz John Porter's troubles with John Pope, in which Porter became the scapegoat at Second Bull Run, was cashiered, and was not cleared of wrongdoing until 16 years later. The author slyly and with great wit describes the political machinations that allowed Pope to succeed with charges of disloyalty, disobedience, and misconduct and how the board sitting for Porter's court-martial consisted of officers indebted to Edwin M. Stanton, who wished to wage political war against George McClellan, Porter's great friend.

The story amounts to high drama, including much written and courtroom testimony. An engaging narrative with light documentation that often crosses the boundary of credibility, it nonetheless shows Porter in the light he deserves, as one who acted intelligently at the embarrassing battle and who was found guilty only with the assistance of perjured or hearsay testimony. Much of the interest here lies with the story of Porter's postwar crusade to save his name for history, a battle he ultimately won with great esteem and for which Congress honored him. Porter's case is one of the more interesting postwar battles that emerged unrelated to the creation of Lost Cause folklore.

A number of areas of this work show suspicious details, where the author assumes various mental states on the part of players—something he could not possibly know. There are a few garbled errors, as with the discussion of "Adjutant General George L. Townsend," when the author meant Assistant Adjutant General Edward Davis Townsend, and an adequate index.

John Aaron Rawlins (1831–1869)

557

Wilson, James Harrison. **The Life of John A. Rawlins, Lawyer, Assistant Adjutant-General, Chief of Staff, Major General of Volunteers, and Secretary of War** (514 pp., Neale Publishing Co., New York, 1916)

Wilson provides the only competent biography of Grant's chief of staff and right-hand man on the battlefield. That the author was an important general officer who participated in many of the actions described in the work confers a sense of lasting value. Wilson does not idealize Rawlins, delivering a balanced although at times belabored assessment of Rawlins's life with suitable focus on the war years and on Rawlins's relationship with Grant.

The biography aptly demonstrates how valuable Rawlins was to Grant in the day-to-day operations of overseeing a Federal army. Closely aware of his chief's character limitations in dealing with unscrupulous people, Rawlins screened Grant's activities, helped with a mountain of details, coordinated communications, and on occasion battled with the War Department. The book examines the power balance between Grant, Halleck, and the bureau chiefs and gives us a valuable picture of how Grant's army functioned on the move. Wilson ends with a curious postwar assessment of his subject, who served briefly as secretary of war before his early death from tuberculosis.

Harvey Reid (1842–1910)

558

Reid, Harvey. **The View from Headquarters: Civil War Letters of Harvey Reid** (ed. Frank L. Byrne, 257 pp., State Historical Society of Wisconsin, Madison, 1965)

The wartime adventures of a young schoolteacher who joined the 22d Wisconsin Infantry are chronicled in these letters. This common soldier saw relatively routine service in the West and frequently wrote his parents describing his life in the regiment. Although for the most part this work lacks the drama of other collections of letters, it provides a view of the war that may have been more typical.

Reid's letters cover the period September 1862–April 1865. His 22d Wisconsin served quietly in Kentucky and Tennessee until their first action at Thompson's Station in March 1863. After surrendering to Forrest at Brentwood Station, the regiment was exchanged and henceforth served in Tennessee until participating in the Atlanta campaign, the March to the Sea, and Bentonville, ending up in Raleigh. The author's literate accounts of battle and ordinary life in the army illuminate the common soldier's experience in a western Federal army.

John Fulton Reynolds (1820–1863)

559

Nichols, Edward J. **Toward Gettysburg: A Biography of General John F. Reynolds** (276 pp., Pennsylvania State University Press, University Park, 1958)

Although this is a full biography and vividly covers Reynolds's Mexican War service, three-quarters of the work treats his Civil War career. Nichols's work is scholarly, well composed, and presents a penetrating portrait of a superb soldier who is too often overlooked because of his untimely death at Gettysburg.

The biography succeeds largely because the Reynolds family made available to Nichols a valuable store of family papers. The letters included in this collection permit a detailed understanding of Reynolds's outlook, which was not possible during his lifetime. The author describes accurately and with proper perspective Reynolds's active command during the Peninsular campaign, where Reynolds was captured on 27 June 1862. The discussion of his exchange and subsequent involvement in Second Bull Run and his disheartening command of the Pennsylvania militia during the Antietam campaign sheds new light on these clashes.

Nichols builds his story well toward Gettysburg as he describes in detail Reynolds's assignment as commander of the 1st Corps at Fredericksburg and Chancellorsville and the resulting alleged offer to Reynolds of command of the Army of the Potomac. Nichols demonstrates capably how Reynolds most likely declined this offer, recommending Meade instead. This is an important biography of a superb soldier.

(Reprinted 1988, 276 pp., Olde Soldier Books, Gaithersburg)

Elisha Hunt Rhodes (1842–1917)

560

Rhodes, Elisha Hunt. **All for the Union: A History of the 2nd Rhode Island Volunteer Infantry in the War of the Great Rebellion, as Told by the Diary and Letters of Elisha Hunt Rhodes, Who Enlisted as a Private in '61 and Rose to the Command of His Regiment** (ed. Robert Hunt Rhodes, 255 pp., Andrew Mowbray, Lincoln, R.I., 1985)

The reminiscences of an outstanding Yankee soldier are recorded, but contrary to the title, the work does not constitute a regimental history. Rather, it contains the frank recollections of a young boy who went off to war and left the service as a colonel. The author traces his journey with his regiment to Washington and participation in First Bull Run. He then focuses on the subsequent Peninsular campaign, Fredericksburg, duty in Virginia and Maryland, Gettysburg, the Wilderness campaign, the Petersburg campaign, the final weeks of war in the East, and the return to Rhode Island.

Although the diary and letters often reveal much about the temperament and psychology of the author, they are disappointingly brief in relating details of the campaigns and battles in which Rhodes participated. The entries do offer insightful and often humorous observations of a number of Federal commanders, and they succeed in providing a sketchy account of the whereabouts and experiences of this citizen-soldier. The lack of an index is a hindrance.

(Reprinted 1991, titled *All for the Union: The Civil War Diary and Letters of Elisha Hunt Rhodes*, 255 pp., Orion Books, New York)

Edward Hastings Ripley (1839–1915)

561

Ripley, Edward Hastings. **Vermont General: The Unusual War Experiences of Edward Hastings Ripley, 1862–1865** (ed. Otto Eisenschiml, 340 pp., Devin-Adair Co., New York, 1960)

The almost 500 letters between Ripley and his family constitute a complete record of this man's experience in the war from July 1862, when Ripley was commissioned a captain in the 9th Vermont Infantry, to the close of the war, when Bvt. Brig. Gen. Ripley led troops into fallen Richmond. The experiences in between are indeed unusual and very much worth reading about. Additionally, several letters from Ripley's brothers and sisters illuminate civilian life in Vermont during the war.

Ripley's writing ability permits outstanding accounts of Stonewall Jackson's capture of Harpers Ferry during the Maryland campaign and much about the action surrounding Petersburg two summers later. The editor interjects several of Ripley's postwar accounts as well. The primary value here lies in the write-ups of Harpers Ferry and Fort Harrison. A small amount of this material, titled "Final Scenes," which treat the march into Richmond, appeared in the *Papers* of the Military Order of the Loyal Legion of the United States (*q.v.*). In this paper Ripley describes warning President Lincoln about possible dangers and Lincoln's reply that he could only live "in the course marked for me."

William Starke Rosecrans (1819–1902)

562

Lamers, William M. **The Edge of Glory: A Biography of General William S. Rosecrans, U.S.A.** (499 pp., Harcourt, Brace, and World, New York, 1961)

Well documented and scholarly in its treatment, this biography provides a useful and proper account of its subject. Major General Rosecrans has always bedazzled writers: successful and influential in some ways, the commander nonetheless never quite measured up to what one imagines as his potential. He fought well early on at Rich Mountain, delivered competent performances at Iuka and Corinth, and did his best at Stones River. Of course, Rosecrans's stumbling at Chickamauga sealed his fate with the Union high command. The disaster was as much due to Longstreet's brilliance and happenstance opportunity as it was to Rosecrans's inabilities, but the tenor of the situation following the battle could not have saved Rosecrans in any event. Rosecrans's success in command, despite his valuable contributions, is a story of gradual and persistent decline.

The author treats his subject sympathetically but without blind worship. The biography focuses heavily on the Civil War years. The narrative makes excellent use of manuscript sources in addition to available printed works of value. The result is a solid and extensively researched portrait that does justice to a sometimes maligned Federal general.

John McAlister Schofield (1831–1906)

563

McDonough, James L. **Schofield, Union General in the Civil War and Reconstruction** (208 pp., Florida State University Press, Tallahassee, 1972)

Although this is not a complete biography, it does deliver a sympathetic yet analytical review of Schofield's Civil War commands and the years immediately following the close of the war. McDonough follows his subject through the early days of war in Missouri and staff service with Nathaniel Lyon before Lyon's death at Wilson's Creek. Although Schofield was stuck in a relatively unglamorous theater, the author shows that his efforts were noticed by Grant and Lincoln. Much is revealed about Schofield's western service fighting guerrillas as a brigadier general and his assignment to the Army of the Ohio in 1864. Although recognizing his subject's sometimes difficult personality, McDonough ably demonstrates his strongest qualities of administration and organization, ones that moved him into the greater spotlight of war in Georgia and Tennessee.

Throughout the discussions of Schofield's Atlanta campaign actions and his brilliant success against Hood at Franklin, the author focuses heavily on military matters. Little of Schofield the man emerges from these pages. The study analyzes the controversy between Schofield and Thomas, one that lived on long after the war, but treats Schofield's important Reconstruction activities in Virginia rather weakly. Much of interest might have been added to this work by examining Schofield's tenure as commandant of West Point, secretary of war, and general-in-chief of the army.

564

Schofield, John M. **Forty-six Years in the Army** (577 pp., Century Co., New York, 1897)

This volume recalls the long service of a man who played an increasingly important part as the Civil War dragged on and who afterward commanded the U.S. Army. But it is not so much a coherent set of recollections as a mishmash of notes and remembrances strung together chronologically in a rather disappointing fashion. The early parts of the book illuminate Schofield's youth and education at West Point. Schofield then embarks on a military narrative of service in the Civil War, outlining his participation in the western campaigns in Missouri in 1861, with particular emphasis on Wilson's Creek.

The work continues by analyzing the Atlanta campaign, sections composed in response to the publication of Sherman's *Memoirs* (*q.v.*) in 1875. The author then treats in great detail Hood's Tennessee campaign and the actions at Spring Hill, Franklin, and Nashville. Schofield presents a summary of Sherman's march before concluding with the usual reminiscences on the end of the war, Reconstruction, and his postwar exploits in the army, supported by testimonials and a retrospective chapter called "Lessons of the War." Peppered with official documents, based largely on recollections long after the war, the book contains a few adequate maps and for the most part records suitable analysis of the military campaigns Schofield witnessed, particularly the Tennessee campaign of 1864.

Carl Schurz (1829–1906)

565

Schurz, Carl. **The Reminiscences of Carl Schurz** (3 vols., 1334 pp., McClure Co., New York, 1907–1909)

Schurz's compilation contains a voluminous and incredibly detailed recollection of this soldier-politician's life. The author's narrative covers his entire life up to early service in the U.S. Senate in 1869. After Schurz's death, Frederic Bancroft and William A. Dunning completed the work by assembling letters, documents, and speeches and adding a running narrative to close out Schurz's political career. The first thick volume covers Schurz's early life, education, involvement in the revolutions of 1848, and subsequent arrival in the United States in 1852. The second volume treats the author's transformation into an antislavery politician in America, his support for John Charles Frémont and Abraham Lincoln, his post as minister to Spain, and his return to the war in 1862. The final volume contains significant material relating to Schurz's Civil War military career before centering on his remarkable postwar adventures in politics.

The military coverage is extensive. Written with great spirit and occasional unreliability, the work serves as a splendid account of Schurz's passionate defense of ideals and his ups and downs on the battlefield. The narrative glows with specifics, often based on careful notes but sometimes including concocted conversations or recollections that approach the limits of credibility. Nonetheless, the details of Schurz's activities with Lincoln and his participation at Second Bull Run, Chancellorsville, and Gettysburg are fascinating. Caught up in the debate over the poor performance by the 11th Corps at Gettysburg, the author narrates his transfer to the West and actions at Chattanooga, the conflict with Joe Hooker, and his anticlimactic service with Henry Warner Slocum as chief of staff.

This enormous work contains only a few simple mistakes, as with the names of Richard Stoddert Ewell, David Glasgow Farragut, Philip Kearny, Irvin McDowell, Alexander Schimmelfennig, and William H. Seward. A much inferior work, *The Autobiography of Carl Schurz* (ed. Wayne Andrews, 331 pp., Charles Scribner's Sons, New York, 1961) is an abridgement.

566

Trefousse, Hans L. **Carl Schurz: A Biography** (386 pp., University of Tennessee Press, Knoxville, 1983)

This full and scholarly biography presents a comprehensive picture of Schurz's life, allocating less than 25 percent of the narrative to its subject's Civil War years. Yet the survey is so well done that it sheds considerable light on Schurz's performance as a general officer and, of course, explores his evolving role as a politician after war's end.

Trefousse's analysis is on the mark as it places Schurz in the position of emergent politician and spokesman for Germans in the earliest days of the secession crisis. In exploring Schurz's military competence, the author finds him able and not worthy of blame for the confused performance of the 11th Corps at Chancellorsville and Gettysburg. He suggests that while Schurz was not responsible for disasters, he was nonetheless not a very great soldier.

Fuller analysis comes with the postwar years as Schurz's foray into politics blossoms. Although Trefousse portrays Schurz as an idealist on the surface, he shows that Schurz could abandon ideals quickly if the opportunity arose to embarrass President Grant.

Winfield Scott (1786–1866)

567

Elliott, Charles Winslow. **Winfield Scott: The Soldier and the Man** (817 pp., Macmillan Co., New York, 1937)

Elliott provides the best and most scholarly treatment of Scott's life. A full biography, the work is soundly researched, written somewhat formally, meticulous in its details, and cautious in its conclusions. The narrative briefly covers Scott's Virginia birth and early years and his days as a lawyer in Petersburg. A significant thrust of the narrative, buttressed with extensive documentation, examines Scott's illustrious participation in the War of 1812. Extensive analysis addresses Scott's role as commander-in-chief of the army beginning in 1841 and his victorious strategy employed during the Mexican War. The Civil War of course marked the twilight of Scott's career, and it receives brief but analytical and careful coverage.

The Civil War years comprise 9 percent of the work, which describes in commendable detail Scott's loyalty to the Union as contrasted with the stance taken by many Virginians. The author sensitively and expertly relates the political relations Scott maintained with Lincoln and members of the cabinet, the bureau chiefs, and general officers in the field. The relationship with George McClellan receives considerable attention and fairly shows Scott as controlled and wise and McClellan as impudent. A reading of the well-documented analysis of Scott's Anaconda Plan should settle the nonsensical claims about others' originating it.

In sum, this work is readable and with immense scholarly value, and it should stand as a cornerstone study on Scott. An occasional misspelling may be found, as with the names of William Worth Belknap, Philip Kearny, Alfred Pleasonton, and William Tecumseh Sherman.

(Reprinted 1979, 817 pp., Arno Press, New York)

John Sedgwick (1813–1864)

568

Sedgwick, John. **Correspondence of John Sedgwick, Major-General** (ed. Henry D. Sedgwick, 2 vols., 432 pp., De Vinne Press, New York, 1902–1903)

The standard source on this beloved major general who was killed at Spotsylvania, this work focuses on two primary periods of Sedgwick's career—the Mexican War and the interval 1855–1864. Each volume contains many dozens of letters relating to military affairs and personal matters. The letters were mostly written by Sedgwick to his father, mother, sister, and occasionally to officials, and family letters add greatly to the understanding of Sedgwick's personality. The letters provide commentary on a wide variety of officers and politicians, the activities of the army as a whole, and official business.

The second volume contains Sedgwick's Civil War letters, plus the oration of George William Curtis dedicating the Sedgwick statue at West Point in 1868. The work illuminates Sedgwick's activities at Fredericksburg, Second Bull Run, Chancellorsville, Gettysburg, and the Wilderness. Particular highlights of the correspondence relate to the author's severe wounding at Antietam, the brisk fight he directed at Salem Church during the Chancellorsville campaign, and his skillful victory at Rappahannock Bridge during the Mine Run campaign.

569

Winslow, Richard Elliott III. **General John Sedgwick: The Story of a Union Corps Commander** (204 pp., Presidio Press, Novato, Calif., 1982)

This study focuses on Sedgwick's Civil War career only, so it does not offer as full an analysis of its subject as many other biographies do, but it provides more complete details on the military actions of the war years than most studies. Sedgwick's career receives scrutiny from his first summer of the war to his death at Spotsylvania. Winslow carefully describes Sedgwick's involvement as a division commander during the Peninsular campaign, his glorious involvement (and multiple woundings) at Antietam, and his famous command of the 6th Corps, during which he captured Fredericksburg in the midst of the Chancellorsville campaign, provided reserve troops at Gettysburg, and skillfully executed tactical maneuvers at the Wilderness.

The author draws on the *O.R.*, newspaper accounts, and, most important, private correspondence from Sedgwick himself. Although Winslow seems occasionally oversympathetic toward his subject, the result is a satisfactory exploration of Sedgwick's significance and a capable telling of the many battles in which he bore an important part.

Robert Gould Shaw (1837–1863)

570

Shaw, Robert Gould. **Blue-Eyed Child of Fortune: The Civil War Letters of Colonel Robert Gould Shaw** (ed. Russell Duncan, 421 pp., University of Georgia Press, Athens, 1992)

These letters form a superbly produced record of the celebrated commander of the 54th Massachussetts Infantry up to the time of his death at Fort Wagner. Together with Luis F. Emilio's unit history of the 54th (*q.v.*), the work provides the real story behind the motion picture *Glory*, responsible for a great deal of popular interest in the war in recent years.

The Shaw letters cover the period of his brief experience in the 7th New York Militia through his first tastes of battle with the 2d Massachussets Infantry at Cedar Mountain and Antietam. The story intensifies with the raising of the 54th, Shaw's experiences in dealing with black soldiers (he was less of an abolitionist, initially, than the movie implies), and the regiment's journey south and the battles of James Island and Fort Wagner. Most of the letters are written to Shaw's mother and other relatives; they reveal an anti-Irish bias as well as a good deal of upper-class snobbishness. They also reveal a very young man undertaking great responsibilities and dealing effectively with the horror of combat. The letters center on Shaw's experiences, the fates of friends and acquaintances, and family matters. While there is much here of military interest, there is little about the soldiers who fought under Shaw's command.

The exceptional introduction and the wonderful job of annotating the letters substantially heightens the value of this collection. Containing the words of one of the most exhalted young officers in the Union Army, this work will stand as an important Civil War biography for ages to come.

Philip Henry Sheridan (1831–1888)

571

Morris, Roy, Jr. **Sheridan: The Life and Wars of General Phil Sheridan** (464 pp., Crown Publishers, New York, 1992)

Not a full biography, this study devotes its energy to an analysis of Sheridan's activities in the Civil War and the Indian wars. Thus, a brief introductory chapter transforms into a chronology that begins with Sheridan's unspectacular entrance into the war in the Army of Southwest Missouri. Impressively based on a clear survey of sources and well documented, the narrative spans the rapid ascension of "Little Phil" following his staff duty for Halleck and then entrance into real command as colonel of the 2d Michigan Cavalry.

Morris's descriptions of cavalry and infantry commands at Perryville, Stones River, and Chickamauga demonstrate at least partly why the young brigadier general was so highly thought of by his superior officers and in the War Department. Sheridan was abrupt, cocky, and arrogant, which only served to enlarge his image as a winning general officer. Indeed, Morris shows that this behavior, directed even at Ulysses S. Grant, did not affect Sheridan negatively. Whatever doubts politicos in Washington had were erased during the Shenandoah Valley campaign of 1864, the simultaneous maneuver that with Grant's Petersburg siege and Sherman's march ruined the Confederate will to wage war.

Lively, well written, and enjoyable, this book is a suitable companion to Sheridan's own memoir (*q.v.*). The sections on Sheridan's postwar battles in Texas and on the plains are finely worked. Further sure-footed interpretation might have cast more light on a number of controversial issues, as with the showdown between Sheridan and Gouverneur K. Warren. Two misspellings were found, for John G. Foster and John Gibbon.

572

Sheridan, Philip H. **Personal Memoirs of P. H. Sheridan** (2 vols., 986 pp. D. Appleton and Co., New York, 1888)

Sheridan's work constitutes a military classic with occasionally surprising literary content. About 10 percent of the memoirs cover Sheridan's early years and antebellum frontier duty in the West; 60 percent covers the Civil War years; and the remainder examines Sheridan's Indian wars, adventures in Europe (where he witnessed the Franco-Prussian War), and his administrative duties in the U.S. Army. The book is essentially popular because it delivers great swaths of narrative of military maneuvers and battles without much analysis or observations of commanders or events. Although providing a solid account of Sheridan's role in various operations of the war, often supplemented with official documents, the memoirs lack the opinionated criticism one might have hoped for.

Still, the book has value in its straightforward descriptions of Sheridan's early service in Missouri and the advance on Corinth and increases in interest with the author's transformation into a cavalry commander. The discussions of western fights, such as Perryville, Stones River, and Chickamauga, are valuable. A turning point is reached at Chattanooga where Sheridan's service placed him fully in view of Grant and Sherman, and the celebrated career of the commander unfolds from there. The narration of Sheridan's

activities in the Wilderness campaign is eclipsed only by his spectacular campaign to close the Shenandoah Valley in 1864 and his significant contributions to the Appomattox campaign. There are a number of misspellings, as with the names of Pierre G. T. Beauregard, John C. Breckinridge, Caspar Crowninshield, James B. Steedman, Elihu B. Washburne, and Haw's Shop and Munfordville, Kentucky.

(Reprinted 1992, 2 vols., 986 pp., Broadfoot, Wilmington; reprinted 1992, with an introduction by Jeffry D. Wert, 535 pp., Da Capo Press, New York)

William Tecumseh Sherman (1820–1891)

573

Boynton, Henry Van Ness. **Sherman's Historical Raid: The Memoirs in Light of the Record: A Review Based upon Compilations from the Records of the War Office** (276 pp., Wilstach, Baldwin and Co., Cincinnati, 1875)

A stinging rebuke to Sherman's *Memoirs* (*q.v.*), this work is so bitter that anyone reading it could conclude that Sherman played little part in the resolution of the war and had almost no soldierly qualities whatsoever. Because of the harsh tone, much credibility is lost, yet some useful facts do emerge. Boynton contends that Sherman, in his *Memoirs*, "detracts from what rightfully belongs to Grant; misrepresents and belittles Thomas; withholds justice from Buell; repeatedly loads failures for which he was responsible, now upon Thomas, now upon Schofield, now upon McPherson, and again upon the three jointly; is unjust in the extreme to Rosecrans; sneers at Logan and Blair; insults Hooker; and slanders Stanton."

The author also explores the element of surprise involving Sherman at Shiloh, the failure at Chickasaw Bayou, the difficulty of successfully attacking the northern end of Missionary Ridge, the bloody assault at Kennesaw Mountain, the escape of the Confederates at Savannah, and the difficulty of the Johnston surrender, all of which, according to Boynton, indicate Sherman's incompetence. The work reads like a legal indictment, with papers from the War Office in the words of many participants supplying the evidence. In the end, the analysis of Sherman's "slanders" and military mistakes seems reactionary. Other sources document Sherman's high esteem for Thomas and many of the others involved. His style in the *Memoirs*, however, is short and to the point, and so the concern about Thomas's slowness to act at Nashville may seem harsher than it should. In hindsight, the so-called conflicts with others appear exaggerated by Boynton.

The criticism of Sherman's generalship rests on even

shakier ground. That he did not win a large, pitched battle under his complete command, crushing the opponent army in front of his line, may be true. But such criticism ignores the end result of the war, Sherman's important contribution to it, and the changed nature of Civil War battle during the final year of the conflict, largely due to Sherman's revolutionary strategy.

574

Lewis, Lloyd. **Sherman: Fighting Prophet** (690 pp., Harcourt, Brace and Co., New York, 1932)

Although it is a full biography covering Sherman's entire life, this study concentrates on Sherman's Civil War career, devoting 60 percent of its space to the four years of war. Not only is Lewis's work meticulously researched and characterized by a balanced, commonsense view of events, but the newspaperman's writing style is superb, making this a first-rate contribution to American biographies of the 20th century. This riveting, meaningfully interpreted story remains today a pillar among works on Sherman.

Sherman comes to life as a hard-working, conscientious soldier whose life divides into three parts: the climb, the summit, and the plateau. The author deals rationally with several aspects of Sherman that tend to be exaggerated or distorted: the stormy relationship with the press, the "insanity" (read: superior foresight) of the early months in Kentucky, and the concept of total war in Georgia and the Carolinas. Because it is not documented, the work leaves itself open to criticism on many levels. Yet checking many facts and examining interpretations shows that Lewis was a responsible writer who used a vast array of sources intelligently. The result is a story of Sherman that stands as a key contribution more than 60 years after its appearance.

(Reprinted 1993, with an introduction by Brooks D. Simpson, 744 pp., University of Nebraska Press, Lincoln)

575

Marszalek, John F. **Sherman: A Soldier's Passion for Order** (635 pp., Free Press, New York, 1993)

This is the best modern biography of the Union Army's second greatest field commander. Marszalek offers a full picture of Sherman's complex life built around the concept of his subject's strong desire for order and control. Controlling events in his life and in his army meant maintaining order, and this fashioned much of Sherman's thinking regarding his early life, his family relationships, his army career, and his battlefield tactics and strategy. Although the author may push this concept too universally at times for the

sake of theme, most of the analysis based on this idea fits well into the historical record. The ordered mentality certainly explains Sherman's attitudes toward politics and the press, two areas he loathed.

The study centers on the war years and offers a more balanced and reasonable view than previous biographers have delivered. The often exaggerated ideas of Sherman's "total war" and his periods of depressive anxiety come into clearer, if less spectacular, focus. As the general's life lost drama following the war years, so also the book wanes after 1865. The author too prominently emphasizes the postwar difficulties between Sherman and Grant and oversimplifies the causes of those difficulties—the course of Reconstruction and Julia Grant's meddling over her son Fred's staff assignment played a part in the bumps in the Sherman-Grant road. However, Sherman fully supported, defended, and valued Ulysses Grant during the last years of his life.

The author provides a clear and detailed portrait of a difficult figure, earning for his book a definitive spot on the Civil War bookshelf. A few spelling errors appear, as with Quincy A. Gillmore's name.

576

Sherman, William Tecumseh. **Memoirs of General W. T. Sherman: Written by Himself** (2 vols., 814 pp., D. Appleton and Co., New York, 1875)

Penned with intelligence and passion, the volumes cover the periods of birth to the Meridian Expedition early in 1864 (vol. 1) and the remainder of the war to the commander's first decade following the war (vol. 2). A subsequent edition (2 vols., 1059 pp., Charles L. Webster and Co., New York, 1892) contains additional material and an appendix by James G. Blaine carrying the Sherman story through the general's death and funeral. The coverage of Sherman's early life is scant, although it includes significant recollections of West Point and life in and out of the army in California, New York, Kansas, and Louisiana. A generous supply of military correspondence, several maps, and appendices add to the running narrative. Sherman's somewhat careless attention to detail results in a number of inaccuracies, particularly with dates. Also the author does not admit a number of his blunders, as with the attack at Kennesaw Mountain.

The memoirs frankly describe the rights and wrongs of the Civil War campaigns Sherman experienced, without regard to stepping on the feelings of others. The work is not unduly harsh, but it is unwaveringly honest (as the author viewed these events). For a variety of reasons, the full force of Sherman's disapproval falls on Edwin M. Stanton, mostly due to difficulties with Sherman's handling of Johnston's surrender. He also finds significant fault with Henry Halleck, particularly for his early handling of Grant and his later mistakes in aiding the destruction of Johnston's army. He freely attacks, with sound logic, the generalship of Don Carlos Buell, John C. Frémont, Benjamin F. Butler, William S. Rosecrans, John A. McClernand, Joseph Hooker, and Ambrose E. Burnside. Conversely, Sherman has nothing but high praise for Grant, his best friend, and for a succession of skilled comrades, including George H. Thomas, William B. Hazen, and John A. B. Dahlgren. "Of all the men I ever met," he writes of Lincoln, "he seemed to possess more of the elements of greatness, combined with goodness, than any other." Sherman also heaps praise on the common soldiers of his western army, calling it "the most magnificent army in existence."

The writing in this work is enjoyable, more so than the average soldier's memoirs, and the enlightened opinions of the second-ranking Federal officer on a multitude of operations make the work invaluable. Hostile reaction to these memoirs criticized Sherman's handling of Thomas, Schofield, McPherson, and others, for allegedly passing off blame to them (see Henry Van Ness Boynton's *Sherman's Historical Raid* [*q.v.*]). For further analysis of the *Memoirs*, see John F. Marszalek, "Sherman Called It the Way He Saw It," *Civil War History* 40 (1994): 72–78.

(Reprinted 1957, with an introduction by B. H. Liddell Hart, 814 pp., Indiana University Press, Bloomington)

577

Sherman, William T. **Sherman at War** (ed. Joseph H. Ewing, 194 pp., Morningside, Dayton, 1992)

This study presents an untapped supply of Sherman letters written during the war to and from a number of personalities but mostly to Sherman's stepfather, Thomas Ewing, and stepbrother, Philemon B. Ewing. The letters remained in the attic of the Ewing descendants until relatively recently, when the editor, a grandson of Philemon Ewing, assembled them into the present work. The letters add considerably to the voluminous Sherman correspondence already in print and should be considered a valuable source for the western campaigns. A great deal of minutiae relating to commanders, politicians, and campaigns surfaces throughout the work. Particularly interesting portions touch on events at Shiloh, at Memphis, in the Vicksburg campaign, in front of Atlanta, and in the Carolinas.

The great bulk of the book covers the war itself, although prefatory early material appears as well as valuable missives from the Reconstruction period. Enthralling statements on a variety of topics surface, including the commentary on

Sherman's relations with the press. Other meaningful passages highlight the exploits of John A. McClernand, U. S. Grant, Lew Wallace, and George H. Thomas. A foldout map depicts the marches of Sherman's commands during the war. A number of misspellings crop up, as for Beaufort, South Carolina, and the names of Thomas L. Crittenden, Irvin McDowell, Ormsby M. Mitchel, and John A. Rawlins.

578

Sherman, William T., and John Sherman. **The Sherman Letters: Correspondence between General and Senator Sherman from 1837 to 1891** (ed. Rachel Sherman Thorndike, 398 pp., Charles Scribner's Sons, New York, 1894)

These letters provide insight into the war's evolving military and political situations. Edited by Sherman's daughter, the collection offers a private glimpse of the relationship between the two brothers who together contributed greatly toward ultimate Union victory. About 44 percent of the book covers the Civil War years, the rest touching on Ohio politics, activities at West Point, travels and adventure in the South and West, and postwar political and military Reconstruction policies. The wartime coverage is superb, with many Sherman letters examining enlistments, meetings with Washington officials including Abraham Lincoln, speculations on the activities of Southern states, and news from Congress and from the battlefield.

The letters cast much light on significant moments in the careers of both Shermans. The general's departure from Louisiana at the outbreak of hostilities demonstrates much about his philosophical makeup, as do his troubles with the press and with discouragement branded as "insanity" in the Cincinnati papers. The calm, stern eye and high influence of Senator Sherman on military affairs shows plainly throughout much of the conflict, and the correspondence between the brothers certainly played a significant part in affecting the war. Two misspellings were found, the names of George A. Custer and Philip Kearny, and the index is only adequate.

(Reprinted 1969, 398 pp., Da Capo Press, New York; 1894 edition reprinted 1972, 414 pp., AMS Press, New York)

Daniel Edgar Sickles (1819–1914)

579

Swanberg, W. A. **Sickles the Incredible** (433 pp., Charles Scribner's Sons, New York, 1956)

Swanberg's is the only full-length biography that portrays the essence of this rascally Union general. Sickles would have been great stuff for biographers even before the war; having killed Philip Barton Key for marital infidelity with his wife, he then became the first person in American jurisprudence acquitted on a defense of temporary insanity, by a team of lawyers that included Edwin M. Stanton, no less. (For an entertaining treatment of this famous affair, see Nat Brandt's *The Congressman Who Got Away with Murder*, 261 pp., Syracuse University Press, Syracuse, 1991.)

Although it is a full biography, 40 percent of Swanberg's work deals with Sickles's Civil War career. To his credit, Swanberg handles one of the most controversial figures of the wartime era with great detached objectivity. This manifests itself most strongly in the case of Sickles's disobedient march along with his 3d Corps into the Peach Orchard at Gettysburg. Of course, the action was reckless and a classic case of poor military thinking, but the biographer does not irrationally defend his subject.

Swanberg's narrative of Sickles's postwar adventures illuminates the kernel of the man. An intellectual, well versed in society and political relations and driven by ambition and a love of the spotlight, Sickles possessed enough qualities to make a fabulous general officer. Swanberg's narrative shows Sickles as a poor commander but still one of the most fascinating men of his time.

Franz Sigel (1824–1902)

580

Engle, Stephen D. **Yankee Dutchman: The Life of Franz Sigel** (333 pp., University of Arkansas Press, Fayetteville, 1993)

Engle offers a full—and the only—biography of this German veteran of the revolution of 1848 who entered Union service and inspired many German Americans to fight against the Confederacy. Placed in Missouri during the early months of the war, Sigel participated at Wilson's Creek and Pea Ridge before being transferred. The author documents the quarrelsome nature of Sigel's command (with both superiors and inferiors) and shows how his political value resulted in an eastward transfer. Barely competent to hold his own in the Shenandoah Valley, Sigel struggled to remain a part of the war effort. After a second unsuccessful round in the Valley, in 1864 opposing Jubal Early, Sigel lost his command.

Sigel was not competent as a subordinate officer or an independent commander. A marginallly successful administrator, he was really little more than a symbol—a political tool for the Germanic volunteers—and when his incompetence on the field outweighed his political value, he was dumped. The interpretation of battles and of Sigel's relationships with other officers is relatively thin. A few mistakes crop up, including misspelling Wladimir Krzyzanowski's name.

Thomas Kilby Smith (1820–1887)

581

Smith, Thomas Kilby. **Life and Letters of Thomas Kilby Smith, Brevet Major-General, United States Volunteers, 1820–1887** (ed. Walter George Smith, 487 pp., G. P. Putnam's Sons, New York, 1898)

A summary of this Federal commander compiled by his oldest son, the work is divided into three parts, each valuable. The sections include a 165-page memoir of the commander by Walter Smith, 300 pages of the general officer's letters, and a 10-page study of Kilby Smith's character by his youngest son, Theodore Dehon Smith.

The letters, written with great clarity and detail, are addressed to Smith's wife, mother, sister, daughter, and two sons, so they contain frank and revealing discussions of the ongoing campaigns, personalities, camp life, and politics. The most enthralling sections follow Smith's career as a major and, subsequently, colonel of the 54th Ohio Infantry, a unit serving under William T. Sherman at Paducah, Kentucky. The regiment saw action at Shiloh, Corinth, Arkansas Post, and Vicksburg, and fine accounts of these battles are offered. In July 1863 the author was detached as post commander at Natchez and promoted to brigadier general of volunteers. Highly interesting sections follow on the Red River campaign, the siege of Mobile Bay, and his command of Fort Gaines, Alabama.

William Farrar Smith (1824–1903)

582

Smith, William F. **From Chattanooga to Petersburg under Generals Grant and Butler: A Contribution to the History of the War, and a Personal Vindication** (201 pp., Houghton Mifflin Co., Boston, 1893)

This book consists of nearly equal parts of self-defense and criticism. Smith concludes that in July 1864 the Army of the James, consisting of the 10th and 18th Corps, utterly failed in its campaign against Petersburg. Grant subsequently wrote to Halleck suggesting that Smith be given command of the army for another effort and that Butler be transferred to departmental command of southern Virginia and North Carolina. For still-murky political reasons, Butler retained the Army of the James until 4 January 1865, when Grant finally ousted him following the first attack on Fort Fisher.

Smith reviews his association with Grant in fine detail, emphasizing his contributions to the relief of Rosecrans's army at Chattanooga. He makes a detailed and elaborate analysis of his attack on Petersburg of 15 June 1864, an assault that failed because of poor timing and Butler's lack of reinforcements. The author purports that Butler's entire force should have attacked along the Appomattox River, thus avoiding being "bottled up." The echoes of old accusations of political intrigue may be found in this book, which exposes many falsehoods in Butler's autobiography (*q.v.*) by employing data from the *O.R.* (*q.v.*). In the end, two bickering ex-commanders aided by hindsight do not resolve much, and the work, although far more on the side of right than Butler's, adds relatively little to understanding the campaigns it discusses.

Isaac Ingalls Stevens (1818–1862)

583

Stevens, Hazard. **The Life of Isaac Ingalls Stevens** (2 vols., 1010 pp., Houghton Mifflin Co., Boston, 1900)

This story of a fallen Union brigadier general was written by his son, who also served as an officer during the war. Essentially a complete biography, it covers Stevens's ancestry, his early years, education at West Point, governorship of Washington Territory, election to Congress, and revival of his military duties with the outbreak of the war. The study draws on official documents, contains many excerpts of letters, focuses primarily on military matters, and maintains objectivity.

The Civil War years are covered fully, with descriptions of the subject's controversial chairmanship of the proslavery Breckinridge ticket in the 1860 election and its nominal effects on Stevens's standing in the army. The work traces Stevens's career as colonel of the 79th New York Infantry, his participation in the Port Royal expedition, and his command of Beaufort, South Carolina, which ironically became the first area of liberation for slaves during the war. The work describes the attack on James Island in 1862. Substantial detail relates to Stevens's command of a division at Second Bull Run following his return to the Virginia front. The account of Stevens's death at Chantilly is full, well written, and detailed. Genealogical material and a photograph of the general's tomb are included. An appendix deals with Indians in Washington Territory during the antebellum years.

Leander Stillwell (1843–1934)

584

Stillwell, Leander. **The Story of a Common Soldier of Army Life in the Civil War, 1861–1865** (278 pp., Franklin Hudson Publishing Co., Kansas City, Mo., 1920)

A minor classic by a soldier who experienced an unusual and interesting set of battles and marches in the western theater, this account was composed more than 50 years after the war. The work is basically sound and consists primarily of a chronological narrative with occasional detours. Based on an extensive set of letters sent home during the war and a slim diary kept during the war's final two years, the story sometimes loses clarity but, as the author states, attempts to follow his regiment "every mile of its way." Stillwell enlisted in the 61st Illinois Infantry at Carrollton in the spring of 1862. Although the memoir was penned by "a common soldier," he was commissioned a first lieutenant at the very end of the war.

The worthwhile narrative relates experiences of battles but also contains a large amount of the minutiae of everyday soldier life having lasting value. Shortly after the author's arrival in St. Louis, his unit marched south and took part in the conflict at Shiloh. Movements and action between Corinth, Bolivar, and Jackson consumed most of the time prior to the regiment's role in the Vicksburg campaign. The author spent some time laid up with malaria in Helena before departing south for the expeditions around Little Rock and Duvall's Bluff. The closing scenes of war for Stillwell occurred in middle Tennessee, where he experienced the carnage of the battles of Franklin and Nashville and witnessed the destruction of the Army of Tennessee.

The usual misspellings and a few mistakes were found, along with an occasionally rambling narrative. The book lacks an index. An inferior edition was published three years earlier (154 pp., Press of the Erie Record, Erie, Kans., 1917).

(1920 edition reprinted 1983, 278 pp., Time-Life Books, Alexandria, Va.)

Elisha Stockwell, Jr. (1846–1935)

585

Stockwell, Elisha, Jr. **Private Elisha Stockwell, Jr., Sees the Civil War** (ed. Byron R. Abernathy, 210 pp., University of Oklahoma Press, Norman, 1958)

This entertaining memoir was penned nearly 63 years after the war by a Wisconsin soldier. Written completely from memory, the work no doubt contains embellishment and has obvious touches of creative writing such as staged "conversations." As a reminiscence, however, it retains its charm. Major aspects of the book agree well with many other sources.

As a private soldier in the 14th Wisconsin Infantry, Stockwell traveled from Milwaukee to experience action at Shiloh, Iuka, Corinth, the Vicksburg campaign, Tupelo, the Atlanta campaign, Nashville, and Spanish Fort. The battle descriptions, while interesting, are not so engaging as Stockwell's anecdotes of minor incidents of soldier life experienced as a youth. Six wartime letters Stockwell wrote to his parents appear as an appendix. One typographical error was found, a misspelling of the name of James B. McPherson.

(Reprinted 1985, 210 pp., University of Oklahoma Press, Norman)

David Hunter Strother (1816–1888)

586

Strother, David Hunter. **A Virginia Yankee in the Civil War: The Diaries of David Hunter Strother** (ed. Cecil D. Eby, 294 pp., University of North Carolina Press, Chapel Hill, 1961)

This is a terrific book. Not only was Hunter (as "Porte Crayon") a talented writer and illustrator, but as war commenced the Virginian, who possessed an intimate knowledge of the Shenandoah Valley, found himself on the staff of Maj. Gen. Nathaniel P. Banks. The result was an accomplished outlook on the war from someone who was in a position from which to observe many of the more important events in the eastern theater. Strother joined Maj. Gen. John Pope's staff in time for Cedar Mountain, joined McClellan's staff following Second Bull Run, and thereafter returned to his old commander Banks, this time in Louisiana. In 1864 he served Brig. Gen. Benjamin F. Kelley, Maj. Gen. Franz Sigel, and then Maj. Gen. David Hunter (a distant cousin) back in the Valley, resigning when Sheridan took command. Few men served so ably on so many general staffs. For his valuable war service Strother was commissioned brevet brigadier general following the war's close.

Skillfully edited and annotated, Strother's diary offers a rare glimpse into many critical actions, epitomized by the author's classic description of watching McClellan at the Pry House as Antietam raged. McClellan's comment to Strother during the battle, "It is the most beautiful field I ever saw and the grandest battle! If we win today it will wipe out Bull Run forever," somehow perfectly characterizes McClellan's detachment. Filled with similar eyewitness stories of the great and not so great, this work is one of the best of its type.

George Henry Thomas (1816–1870)

587

McKinney, Francis F. **Education in Violence: The Life of George H. Thomas and the History of the Army of the Cumberland** (530 pp., Wayne State University Press, Detroit, 1961)

As the title correctly states, this is not merely a biography of Thomas but also a biography of the Army of the Cumberland. As such, it is a standout in the field of Civil War literature. So thorough is the interpretation and description of Thomas that one reviewer declared, "The Old Warrior is between these covers." This reviewer agrees.

Thomas has always presented problems for his many biographers. His many luminary qualities make him an obvious hero—outranked in popularity after the war only by Grant, Sherman, and Sheridan. His prevention of disaster at Chickamauga and brilliant successes at Chattanooga and Nashville elevated him in the hearts of the people. Strategically and tactically he showed masterful understanding, particularly involving matters of intelligence, communications, and logistics. Yet the well-known clashes with Grant and the War Department cloud his record.

McKinney's story of Thomas's career is beautifully executed, tightly documented, and replete with well-told asides and adventurous tales. A revisionist picture of the Thomas-Grant relationship emerges in which Thomas is careful, not slow at Nashville. The author succeeds in establishing credibility for this argument, at least in part, without bashing Grant. The material providing background on the Army of the Cumberland occasionally wanders, but it also brims with the author's interesting analyses. The resulting portrait belongs on the bookshelf of everyone interested in the Civil War.

(Reprinted 1991, with an introduction by John S. Peterson, 530 pp., Americana House, Chicago)

Alfred Thomas Archimedes Torbert (1833–1880)

588

Slade, A. D. **A. T. A. Torbert: Southern Gentleman in Union Blue** (230 pp., Morningside, Dayton, 1992)

This first lengthy summary of a flamboyant cavalry commander who served under Sheridan is lightly documented but adequately researched. The volume lacks the thoroughness of a full biography but does present a sketch of Torbert's prewar ancestry, early life, and military career. The Civil War coverage receives first priority, and about 15 percent of the work is devoted to the final 15 years of Torbert's life. The narrative thus showcases the cavalry great's rise from waffling about which army to join through his commission as colonel of the 1st New Jersey Infantry and subsequent transformation late in the war to cavalry command and the grade of brevet major general.

The writing style leaves something to be desired, but the narrative is helped along with excerpts from Torbert's letters to fellow officers and official documents culled from the *O.R.* (*q.v.*) and elsewhere. Particularly interesting portions of the book treat his participation at Second Bull Run, Antietam, Chancellorsville, Gettysburg, and, as a cavalryman, in the Shenandoah Valley campaign of 1864. Slade demonstrates how this young officer shone on many battlefields and in particular at Tom's Brook and Cedar Creek. A few sloppy uses of names include those of Oliver Edwards, John McCausland, Irvin McDowell, and William S. Rosecrans. The index is adequate.

Edward Davis Townsend (1817–1893)

589

Townsend, E. D. **Anecdotes of the Civil War in the United States** (287 pp., D. Appleton and Co., New York, 1884)

The author relates material of signal importance and brief stories of the war in this casually written volume. Townsend's position early in the war as an aide to Winfield Scott, his assignment to the adjutant general's office, and his duties of virtually running the office as assistant adjutant general make him one of the better informed characters of the war. From his enlightened viewpoint, Townsend narrates his part in the early days of the crisis: the last days of the Buchanan administration, Winfield Scott's handling of military split, plans for the defense of Washington, and letters of violence to Scott.

As the war accelerates, so does the value of the anecdotes. Much material of primary importance exists regarding operations in Scott's headquarters early in the war, his development of the Anaconda plan, and the relations with Scott, his staff, and George McClellan. Sidelights illuminate many characters, such as C. P. Stone and his conduct at Ball's Bluff, the evolution of Henry Halleck's administrative role, a remembrance of Julius P. Garesché, and amused discussions of Frank Blair, Jr. A large amount of storylike material following and interspersed with the chronology relates to Confederate flags, medals, corps badges, the records of the adjutant general's office, discussions of military commissions, and extracts from official reports. The work lacks an index.

Mason Whiting Tyler (1840–1907)

590

Tyler, Mason Whiting. **Recollections of the Civil War: With Many Original Diary Entries and Letters Written from the Seat of War, and with Annotated References** (ed. William S. Tyler, 379 pp., G. P. Putnam's Sons, New York, 1912)

This significant memoir of a New England Union regimental commander, composed more than 40 years after the war from a wartime diary and letters written home during the war, captures Tyler's service from September 1862 through the taking of Petersburg. Commissioned a second lieutenant in the 37th Massachusetts Infantry, a unit raised in Pittsfield, the author served ably in Fredericksburg and most of the following eastern battles, leading his regiment as a major in the war's final weeks. He was commissioned a brevet colonel at war's end.

The book contains entertaining reflections on soldier life in a New England regiment and offers unusually rich battle accounts, as with the discussion of the Mule Shoe salient at Spotsylvania. The vivid description of the 22-hour fight is well done. The author died before completing the work, and the final section therefore contains copious reflections on Tyler by his friend Calvin Stebbins. The work details such diverse experiences as the raiding of John Tyler's home in Virginia and overseeing hordes of Confederate deserters.

Theodore Frelinghuysen Upson (1843–1919)

591

Upson, Theodore F. **With Sherman to the Sea: The Civil War Letters, Diaries, and Reminiscences of Theodore F. Upson** (ed. Oscar Osburn Winther, 181 pp., Louisiana State University Press, Baton Rouge, 1943)

A brief but illuminating memoir from a Federal soldier of the 100th Indiana Infantry, the common soldier's perspective on the war is represented solidly here, with comments on camp life, attitudes toward slavery, reflections on human nature, and thoughts on the poor training and arms of the regiment during its early days. Upson is not critical toward the enemy and he tinges passages with humor, giving this account, insubstantially modified after the war, a rare richness.

The work covers the period November 1862–May 1865. During that time the regiment moved to Memphis and participated in the Vicksburg campaign, the battles of Chattanooga, the Atlanta campaign, and the March to the Sea. Despite the title, all facets of the two and a half years are covered without special emphasis on the Georgia campaign. Upson does not always clearly indicate which portions are wartime passages or reminiscences, but he offers a satisfying story of the war from a Hoosier farmboy's perspective.

Emory Upton (1839–1881)

592

Ambrose, Stephen E. **Upton and the Army** (190 pp., Louisiana State University Press, Baton Rouge, 1964)

The greatest problem with this book is its brevity. The author's careful research, winning style, and intriguing analysis of the character of a heroic and troubled officer make this an outstanding Union biography. A mere 36 pages cover Upton's Civil War career, when the young officer displayed brilliance at Antietam, Fredericksburg, and particularly Spotsylvania and established the basis for a significant military life. Ambrose contends that Upton's ideas were ignored and that his inwardly growing personality, combined with difficult postwar experiences and illness, led to his depression and suicide.

The author's interpretation of these key points may be overdrawn. Upton's terrible headaches (perhaps indicating a brain tumor), latent sense of failure, and perhaps paranoia might have combined to rather suddenly destroy his will to live. However, Ambrose constructs a psychological interpretation of Upton's entire life. This speculation suggests that Upton believed the army must be the reformer of the nation and that his ideas were central to the national security. Although his *Infantry Tactics* was a success, Upton perceived the manuscript of *The Military Policy of the United States* to be a failure—and so, therefore, was he. Whether or not this hypothesis threads back to Upton's early life remains open to question. The author intelligently discusses Upton's influence on military thinking and leaves readers with a cogent portrait of a sad yet glorious individual.

(Reprinted 1993, 190 pp., Louisiana State University Press, Baton Rouge)

James Samuel Wadsworth (1807–1864)

593

Pearson, Henry Greenleaf. **James S. Wadsworth of Geneseo, Brevet Major General of United States Volunteers** (321 pp., Charles Scribner's Sons, New York, 1913)

Readers will find a sympathetic and mostly well-written treatment of the general's Civil War service. The explanation of Wadsworth's part in various actions is well composed, following the subject from volunteer aide to Irvin McDowell through his command of a brigade and then to service as military governor of the District of Columbia. Without straining credibility, Pearson demonstrates that despite Wadsworth's lack of military training he was an able if not outstanding battlefield tactician. The treatment of Wadsworth's brief run at political office is enlightening, as are the accounts of divisional command following Fredericksburg.

The author ably documents Wadsworth's fighting at Gettysburg on the first morning, showing how the unit fought gallantly while most of the Union Army tramped toward the field. The discussion of Wadsworth's participation in the Wilderness is skillful if not very illuminating, as it culminates quickly with the subject's fatal bullet wound in the back of the head. The author, whose literary experience still makes the book readable today, neatly summarizes the major career highlights of a general officer whose loss was a major shock as the armies maneuvered toward Richmond.

Charles Shiels Wainwright (1826–1907)

594

Wainwright, Charles S. **A Diary of Battle: The Personal Journals of Colonel Charles S. Wainwright, 1861–1865** (ed. Allan Nevins, 549 pp., Harcourt, Brace, and World, New York, 1962)

The chief attributes of this work are the intelligence and literary ability of its author and his position in the Federal army, which ranged from major of the 1st New York Artillery to brevet brigadier general in the war's third summer, serving as chief of artillery of the 1st and 5th Corps of the Army of the Potomac along the way. Reading the voluminous battle accounts from a skilled artillerist's perspective is illuminating and offers a decidedly different focus than the usual diaries of battle.

Much of the heavy action of the eastern theater appears in these pages: the Peninsular campaign, Fredericksburg, Chancellorsville, Gettysburg, the Wilderness, Spotsylvania,

Cold Harbor, the siege of Petersburg, and the closing scenes at Appomattox. Opinionated and frank in the pages of his diaries, Wainwright contributes much of value regarding the artillery branch and its evolution, including discussions of ordnance, supplies, and tactics and strategy, providing one of the better narratives from an artillerist on either side.

(Reprinted 1993, Stan Clark Military Books, Gettysburg)

Lewis Wallace (1827–1905)

595

McKee, Irving. **"Ben-Hur" Wallace: The Life of General Lew Wallace** (301 pp., University of California Press, Berkeley, 1947)

McKee has written a full biography of the Union officer who solidly played his role but never achieved greatness on the field. Son of an Indiana governor, Lew Wallace served as a volunteer officer during the Mexican War; became a lawyer, state senator, and state adjutant general; served illustriously at times during the Civil War; and at war's end became governor of New Mexico Territory, U.S. minister to Turkey, and author of one of the classic American novels. With such a varied mass of curious and interesting life experiences to write about, the author has done a credible job of assembling a worthwhile book.

The analysis of Wallace's Civil War career is at times revealing and at times scant. The result is a story of Wallace's adventures in the army without significant interpretation, which may disappoint some readers. The proudest moment of Wallace's war came with the checking of Jubal Early at Monocacy, which receives ample evaluation. But the controversial aspects of Wallace's performance at Shiloh might have received much more insightful analysis in this work. Aside from these key events, the solid narrative yields a clear overview of the Indiana general's experience in the war, his life before it, and his later diplomatic and literary career.

596

Wallace, Lew. **Lew Wallace: An Autobiography** (ed. Susan Elston Wallace and Mary H. Krout, 2 vols., 1028 pp., Harper and Bros., New York, 1906)

Published posthumously and finished by Wallace's widow and a collaborator, this autobiography serves as a useful if lavishly overdetailed account of the famous soldier-author's life experience. The first part, prepared by Wallace before his death, brings the story of his life up to the battle of Monocacy on 9 July 1864. The second part carries on the wartime story and covers Wallace's extensive postwar activities.

More than 500 pages are devoted to the war years. They contain a mountain of detail relating to the famous battles in which Wallace took part, chiefly Fort Donelson, Shiloh, and Monocacy. Unfortunately, however, many of the recollections are offered with such apologies or controversial interpretations of strategy and tactics that it is difficult to sort them out. The extensive material on Monocacy will be most useful; the coverage of Shiloh does not fully lift the veil from Wallace's poor performance. Later materials cover Wallace's participation in trying the Lincoln conspirators and his presidency of the board assembled to try Henry Wirz.

Gouverneur Kemble Warren (1830–1882)

597

Taylor, Emerson Gifford. **Gouverneur Kemble Warren** (256 pp., Houghton Mifflin Co., Boston, 1932)

The author presents a serviceable record of one of the most important engineering officers of the war. Drawing heavily on Warren's correspondence, Taylor portrays Warren as a down-to-earth, practical man whose vision and abilities enabled him to play a significant role in the Federal prosecution of the war. The work is overly sympathetic toward its subject, painting Warren as purely heroic, and is much too simplified with respect to examining Warren's contribution to battlefield strategy and tactics.

The study reflects only superficially on the contrast between Warren's sterling performance, as at Gettysburg, and his increasing troubles with George Meade, Ulysses Grant, and Phil Sheridan. The letters reveal something of a prescience of conflict with his superiors. As a corps commander, his reputation slid. Finally, given the opportunity for action, Sheridan took over at Five Forks and knocked Warren out of his command. Unfortunately, the author offers little analysis of this fascinating series of events. Warren himself spent the remaining 20 years of his life attempting to clear his name, which he finally did. It is a disappointment that this work does not make any significant attempt to understand or analyze Warren.

(Reprinted 1988, 256 pp., R. Van Sickle, Gaithersburg)

Stephen Minot Weld, Jr. (1842–1920)

598

Weld, Stephen Minot, Jr. **War Diary and Letters of Stephen Minot Weld, 1861–1865** (428 pp., Riverside Press, Cambridge, Mass., 1912)

Weld was a gifted Massachusetts officer who rose to the grade of brevet brigadier general of volunteers. A Harvard graduate, Weld was commissioned a captain in the 18th Massachusetts Infantry and served with that unit until the end of 1863, when he became lieutenant colonel of the 56th Massachusetts Infantry. He later served as colonel of the same regiment. Weld's assignments carried him through most of the important battles of the eastern theater, always a part of the Army of the Potomac and for many months a strong supporter of George McClellan. Weld's journals and letters provide sharp and clear insights into many battles and commanders, as evidenced by the harsh criticism of John Pope at Second Bull Run, the attack on Grant's bloody engagements in the Wilderness, and a lack of confidence in Joseph Hooker.

The observations of battle give way occasionally to remarks on friends, society, and politics. Although he was a Massachusetts man, Weld was too conservative for emancipation and thought that slavery would die out if left alone. He believed the Emancipation Proclamation indeed might inflame the issue to the point of jeopardizing the war effort. Many such military strategies and tactics he often presented to McClellan, even after McClellan was removed from command. Meade's failure to pursue Lee after Gettysburg, for example, exonerated McClellan's behavior in the wake of Antietam.

Important observations and documents will be found in this extensive work, a treasure of one man's career in the principal Federal Army. An occasional spelling error crops up, as with the names of Daniel Leasure and Julius Stahel. The index is rather sketchy.

(Reprinted 1979, with a foreword by David Herbert Donald, 433 pp., Massachusetts Historical Society, Boston)

Alpheus Starkey Williams (1810–1878)

599

Williams, Alpheus S. **From the Cannon's Mouth: The Civil War Letters of General Alpheus S. Williams** (ed. Milo M. Quaife, 405 pp., Wayne State University Press and the Detroit Historical Society, Detroit, 1959)

Although his career in command was marked by great accomplishments and ultimately by disappointment, Alpheus S. Williams is a superb example of a volunteer Union general. His voluminous letters are preserved in this work. Williams's service included the Shenandoah Valley campaign of 1862, Cedar Mountain, Antietam, Chancellorsville, Gettysburg, Chattanooga, Atlanta, the March to the Sea, and the Carolinas. Although Williams performed admirably during several crucial fights, most notably at Chancellorsville and Gettysburg, his lack of a West Point background prevented him from prolonged corps command or a substantive commission as a major general. (He briefly commanded the 12th Corps.)

As busy brigadier generals go, Williams wrote an astonishing number of letters, mostly to his daughters, and composed them exceptionally well. Military matters predominate, as told with the soft affection of a father. The editor of this work has eliminated many strictly family matters, leaving the bulk of what remains as historically relevant material. In this satisfying book, the sketches of various commanders and situations at large battles in the East, during the chaotic weeks of bearing down on Atlanta, or simply reflecting on the machinations of the U.S. Army, are extremely illuminating.

(Reprinted 1995, titled *From the Cannon's Mouth: General Alpheus S. Williams*, with an introduction by Gary W. Gallagher, 405 pp., University of Nebraska Press, Lincoln)

James Harrison Wilson (1837–1925)

600

Longacre, Edward G. **From Union Stars to Top Hat: A Biography of the Extraordinary General James Harrison Wilson** (320 pp., Stackpole Books, Harrisburg, Pa., 1972)

Although weakly documented, this study provides an engagingly written narrative that succeeds admirably in featuring the high points of Wilson's celebrated life, with particular emphasis on his Civil War years. Longacre describes Wilson's outstanding achievements at West Point and his youthful entrance into the war as chief topographical engineer of the Port Royal expedition and the subsequent reduction of Fort Pulaski. The author illuminates his subject's transition to the eastern theater as aide to George McClellan and his transfer to U. S. Grant's staff at Vicksburg, a position that made possible Wilson's extraordinary rise during the final two years of war.

The narrative picks up steam as Wilson, assigned to command a division of Sheridan's cavalry, enters the May campaign of 1864. The author contends that Wilson's tactical and strategic brilliance overcame his personality flaws in the months that followed. The young brigadier general emerged as one of the great cavalrymen of the war as he followed Lee's army southward toward Petersburg and participated in the Valley campaign of 1864. Appointed chief of cavalry for the Military Division of the Mississippi, Wilson commanded a corps of 17,000 that helped destroy Hood's army at Franklin and Nashville before setting off on his legendary raid to Selma and points east, one of the heroic final maneuvers of the contest.

Although Longacre is sympathetic toward his subject, touting Wilson as "the country's most successful cavalry commander," the author generally retains an objective balance, sometimes criticizing Wilson for personality traits that hindered him. The author sides squarely with Wilson in the Grant-Wilson dispute, painting an unfair picture of Grant's relations toward his sometime protégé. The analysis is sometimes strained, but this work nonetheless provides a good picture of one of the young greats of the war.

601

Wilson, James Harrison. **Under the Old Flag: Recollections of Military Operations in the War for the Union, the Spanish War, the Boxer Rebellion, etc.** (2 vols., 1162 pp., D. Appleton and Co., New York, 1912)

These reminiscences cover Wilson's entire military career. His Civil War service, which occupies a significant portion of the work, included stints on Thomas W. Sherman's staff in the South Atlantic campaign, on McClellan's staff in the Maryland campaign, and on Grant's staff in Mississippi and through the Chattanooga campaign. His Mississippi and Alabama cavalry raid in the closing days of the war fairly leaps off the pages, as do his blunt assessments of a large number of Union and Confederate commanders.

In entertaining fashion, Wilson delivers a lengthy but hazy portrait of Grant, so we are not quite clear about what he really thinks of the Union's victorious military leader. Other portraits are more straightforward: he praises George H. Thomas highly, lifting him above the abilities of William T. Sherman and Philip H. Sheridan. He also commends

Emory Upton as the "best all-round soldier of the day." On the Confederate side, the author believes Wade Hampton and Nathan Bedford Forrest were equals in ability. He believes Robert E. Lee's competence to have been greatly exaggerated. These recollections are thus still controversial in their conclusions but certainly deliver a clear if self-conscious view of Wilson himself. The index is slim and not particularly helpful.

(Reprinted 1971, 2 vols., 1162 pp., Greenwood Press, Westport)

SAILORS

William Barker Cushing (1842–1874)

602

Roske, Ralph J., and Charles Van Doren. **Lincoln's Commando: The Biography of Commander William B. Cushing, U.S.N.** (310 pp., Harper and Bros., New York, 1957)

Young Cushing's career certainly ranks as one of the most fascinating of the lower-grade officers in the Union Navy, and this popularly written account does justice to it. By using an array of contemporary sources and Cushing's letters, the authors provide an adequate story of the young officer, despite their occasional rather loose understanding of naval warfare.

Although Cushing dropped out of the Naval Academy before the war, he received another chance after capturing a blockade-runner and was commissioned a lieutenant in July 1862. The authors describe Cushing's service in the North Atlantic Blockading Squadron and particularly the Jacksonville raid in which he was forced to destroy the *Ellet*.

The book's finest narration coincides with Cushing's best performance, the destruction of the ram *Albemarle* at Plymouth, North Carolina, in October 1864. Roske and Van Doren describe Cushing's torpedo attack and the subsequent confused retreat. The *Albemarle* was ruined, Cushing's attack having blown a hole in her "big enough to drive a wagon through," and Cushing was thereafter a hero.

John Adolphus Bernard Dahlgren (1809–1870)

603

Dahlgren, Madeleine Vinton. **Memoir of John A. Dahlgren, Rear-Admiral United States Navy** (660 pp., J. R. Osgood and Co., Boston, 1882)

This excellent picture of the great naval ordnance officer was composed by Dahlgren's wife. Drawing on portions of Dahlgren's own diary and letters, the *Memoir* fairly summarizes the whole of Dahlgren's life. It contains three broad sections, the first providing a well-composed and sympathetic sketch of Dahlgren's early life, the second providing details on Dahlgren's ordnance discoveries and improvements, and the third detailing the commander's Civil War service. The latter sections examine the subject's command of the Washington Navy Yard, his relationship with President Lincoln, his staff position as chief of the Ordnance Bureau, and his command of the South Atlantic Blockading Squadron.

Much of the most valuable material comes across in Dahlgren's own tense style. Other sections written by the commander's wife are marked by eulogistic sentences and an inelegant style that occasionally leads to difficult passages. However, there is enough of value in the account to make it a lasting reference source as well as a forgivable tribute to one of the half dozen most important naval men of the Union.

Charles Henry Davis (1807–1877)

604

Davis, Charles H. II. **Life of Charles Henry Davis, Rear Admiral, 1807–1877** (349 pp., Houghton Mifflin Co., Boston, 1899)

A tender remembrance and a thorough biography of one of the ranking Union admirals by the subject's son, this work reflects carefully on a number of incidents of great interest in which Davis played a significant role. Summoned to duty from the office of the *American Ephemeris and Nautical Almanac*, the bookish Davis took over the Bureau of Detail, serving a critically important position by consulting on assignments, the purchase and construction of ships, and the operations on the Southern coast. Before the war's first year was out, however, Davis became Samuel F. Du Pont's chief of staff in the South Atlantic Blockading Squadron. The author faithfully delivers a nicely woven story of the subject's

activities during the Port Royal expedition, his relief of the wounded Andrew Hull Foote near Fort Pillow, and the subsequent attack.

The pace accelerates as Davis assaults Memphis and plays a part in the Mississippi River campaign up to the fall of Vicksburg. The narrative follows Davis's return to Washington in the autumn of 1863 and his supervision of the Bureau of Navigation, as well as his postwar exploits as director of the U.S. Naval Observatory.

Samuel Francis Du Pont (1803–1865)

605

Du Pont, Samuel Francis. **Samuel Francis Du Pont: A Selection from His Civil War Letters** (ed. John D. Hayes, 3 vols., 1540 pp., Cornell University Press, Ithaca, 1969)

This valuable collection has much to offer students of the early naval coastal war. Greatly important early in the war, a political embarrassment by 1863, and dead by war's end, Du Pont was a uniquely frustrating Federal rear admiral. His early participation in strategic planning as chief of the Blockade Strategy Board and his command of the South Atlantic Blockading Squadron make him worthy of close study despite his later falling out with the Lincoln administration.

Capably assembled and edited by Hayes, the three volumes contain 461 letters to and from Du Pont of the nearly 7000 that remain. The editor's introduction critically assesses Du Pont's career, although with a somewhat sympathetic eye. The predominantly revealing inclusions center on the triumphant capture of Port Royal and the resulting strategy of maintaining a tight blockade on Southern ports. The letters show how Du Pont's leaning toward combined operations and Assistant Navy Secretary Gustavus Fox's opposition to the policy led to disastrous downturns in Du Pont's career. The letters also document the failure of Du Pont's forces in capturing Charleston in April 1863. In the disagreement between Du Pont and Fox over the value of ironclads, Du Pont seemingly comes out on the side of right.

Du Pont had many Southern friends and employed those who stayed loyal to the Union. His correspondence with these men and with those who took up arms against the Union, particularly in the period just prior to Sumter, reveals much about his personality. He also comments on a variety of other issues, such as David Hunter's premature emancipation efforts in South Carolina and, with much resentment, the career of John A. B. Dahlgren.

David Glasgow Farragut (1801–1870)

606

Farragut, Loyall. **The Life of David Glasgow Farragut, First Admiral of the United States Navy, Embodying His Journal and Letters** (586 pp., D. Appleton and Co., New York, 1879)

This work exceeds expectations of a memoir written by a devoted son. The study leans toward autobiography in that it draws on Farragut's journals and notes to provide much of the narrative. While the author covers the entirety of Farragut's career, he devotes 55 percent of its space to the Civil War years. There is a brief history of Farragut's ancestry and his early years, followed by discussion of the young officer's naval life in the three decades prior to the Civil War. The narrative draws on many sketches of Farragut's activities made by contemporaries and contains numerous extracts from letters and official reports. The book provides valuable glimpses into Farragut's personal life, offering letters written to his family, and pieces together a coherent picture of Farragut's character.

The Civil War chapters contain little that is unique, most of the story of Farragut's exploits having been chronicled in other sources and in the *O.R.N.* (*q.v.*). However, the subject's record comes alive in this work, often in his own words, and receives serious and helpful commentary along the way. The coverage of the New Orleans expedition, the unsuccessful movements against Vicksburg, the maneuvers about Port Hudson, and the battle of Mobile Bay is thorough and excellent. Postwar recollections are less dramatic and original and include memorials written about Farragut after his death. An appendix lists vessels and officers involved in the capture of New Orleans and in the action at Mobile Bay.

607

Lewis, Charles Lee. **David Glasgow Farragut** (2 vols., 885 pp., United States Naval Institute, Annapolis, 1941–1943)

The author provides a scholarly and relatively modern treatment of Farragut's life. The two volumes, *Admiral in the Making* and *Our First Admiral*, describe Farragut's entire life with a well-documented emphasis on the boy's adventurous early start as a sailor and the man's slow rise to the top naval command. The work was carried out with capable research based on a wide variety of sources, including many Farragut papers belonging to the family, untapped in large part in the work by Farragut's son (*q.v.*). The result is a lengthy and technically accurate portrayal of Farragut the

naval strategist and tactician and the many battles and campaigns in which he participated.

The work is notable for its clear and comprehensive treatment of Farragut's early years. The subject's pseudo-adoption by David Porter and his youthful experience in the War of 1812 establish a basis for the material to come. The lengthy service of Farragut up to the time of the Civil War is carried off with charm and precision. The description of Farragut's Civil War service is clear and detailed, and the battles of New Orleans and Mobile Bay receive extensive treatment. The first volume deals only superficially with Farragut the personality; the second volume attempts a correction of that oversight, yielding much on the war and also a fair portrait of the man. As an aside, the work investigates the credibility of the "Damn the Torpedoes!" quotation, which did not appear in print until 14 years after the battle of Mobile Bay.

(Reprinted 1980, 2 vols., 885 pp., Arno Press, New York)

Andrew Hull Foote (1806–1863)

608

Hoppin, James M. **Life of Andrew Hull Foote, Rear-Admiral United States Navy** (411 pp., Harper and Bros., New York, 1874)

This detailed and enjoyable account portrays the life and career of this distinguished officer who died of wounds nearly a year after his injury at Fort Donelson. Although it is an early, thinly documented study, it provides the best summary of Foote's life to date, as well as a great deal of information regarding the construction of ironclad gunboats on the western rivers. The energetic commander played a key role in the siege of Forts Henry and Donelson and took part in the Mississippi River campaign of 1863, contributing to Federal victory on the waters and on land by bombardment.

Many of Foote's letters, both sent and received, are included. The significant coverage of Foote's antebellum naval career deals with his assignments on such vessels as the USS *United States*, the USS *Hornet*, and the USS *John Adams*, on duty in the Pacific, Atlantic, Mediterranean, Caribbean, and Indian Ocean. Promoted to captain in 1861, Foote took command of the western flotilla of river gunboats. The account of Foote's capture of Fort Henry is superb. His wounding in the left arm and left foot at Donelson is described at length, the foot wound never fully healing. The work traces Foote's participation in the attack on Island No. 10, after which he transferred his command to Henry Walke. Weakened by Bright's disease and his wound, he died in New York City in June 1863.

Alvah Folsom Hunter (1847–1933)

609

Hunter, Alvah Folsom. **A Year on a Monitor and the Destruction of Fort Sumter** (ed. Craig L. Symonds, 184 pp., University of South Carolina Press, Columbia, 1987)

Hunter provides a brief but illuminating account of service on the USS *Nahant*. The diary kept by the very youthful sailor was transformed some 60 years later into a memoir that was ably edited and annotated. Although the author lacked substantive education, he observed and commented intelligently on a multitude of things around him, and so recorded much of interest during his days on the waters. Born in New Hampshire, Hunter traveled to Boston in 1862 and enlisted in the navy, eventually being assigned to the *Nahant*, a *Passaic*-class monitor. The ship joined the South Atlantic Blockading Squadron and experienced extensive service in 1863, the crucial year of the Charleston siege.

The diary records details of the ill-fated attack on Fort Sumter of 7 April 1863. Hunter writes a splendid account of the heavy and continuous bombardment of Fort Wagner on Morris Island during the middle of July 1863, an action the *Nahant* joined. The memoir contains much of interest relating to the daily life on the ship, technological innovations, and the cooperation between land and naval forces. A few misspellings appear, as with Quincy A. Gillmore, J. Thomas Scharf, and Thomas Holdup Stevens.

Benjamin Franklin Isherwood (1822–1915)

610

Sloan, Edward H. **Benjamin Franklin Isherwood, Naval Engineer: The Years as Engineer in Chief, 1861–1869** (299 pp., United States Naval Institute, Annapolis, 1966)

Sloan has provided a full and scholarly biography of the head of the navy's Bureau of Steam Engineering. In analyzing the career of this innovative officer, the author not only relates a useful story of the wartime navy and its operations but also chronicles the development of technological gains in naval strategy. Sloan describes how Isherwood became a notable if controversial authority prior to the war and through Gideon Welles's efforts gained his high position after the war began. The author skillfully shows how Isherwood maintained a level of influence exceeding his position in detailing his relationship with John Lenthall. He also describes accurately the tremendous official burdens taken on

by Isherwood and the construction of his *Wampanoag* class of fast warships designed for blockading.

Throughout the account of Isherwood's wartime years, the author dispassionately builds the story of his subject's increasing controversy. This came to a head after the war in the feud with David Dixon Porter and the radical Republicans. Fueled by political divisions, the disagreement led to an attack on the *Wampanoag* and its sister ships as being too inefficient because of their huge engines. Isherwood's career ended as Grant took office. This biography is filled with many absorbing details of the engineering of Civil War ships and provides enjoyment for naval history buffs.

William Frederick Keeler (1821–1886)

611

Keeler, William F. **Aboard the U.S.S. *Florida*, 1863–5: The Letters of Paymaster William Frederick Keeler, U.S. Navy, to His Wife, Anna** (ed. Robert W. Daly, 252 pp., United States Naval Institute, Annapolis, 1968)

This work continues the story of Keeler's naval career. Following the loss of the *Monitor*, as described in Keeler's other work (*q.v.*), John P. Bankhead, Samuel Dana Greene, and William F. Keeler were assigned to the *Florida*. A businessman new to naval matters on the *Monitor*, Keeler now felt at home on the *Florida*. Keeler's letters, dated 8 March 1863–31 July 1865, follow his development as a naval officer. The *Florida* offered a completely different kind of Civil War shipboard life, and the resulting letters provide a stark contrast to those written from the *Monitor*. Rather than involving high-visibility actions on the water, the new assignment brought routine duty, the capture of blockade-runners, and occasional fits of boredom.

Nevertheless, the letters in this volume contain much of interest and portray sea life during the war in a more typical fashion. Keeler often thought about the ship's crew and wrote his wife about the character of Civil War sailors, often with sharp criticism. He was twice wounded during minor actions. The various highlights describing pursuits of blockade-runners contain much of interest about the effectiveness of the blockade and show that it worked magnificently considering the obstacles it had to surmount.

(Reprinted 1980, 252 pp., Arno Press, New York)

612

Keeler, William F. **Aboard the U.S.S. *Monitor*, 1862: The Letters of Acting Paymaster William Frederick Keeler, U.S. Navy, to His Wife, Anna** (ed. Robert W. Daly, 278 pp., United States Naval Institute, Annapolis, 1964)

These letters chronicle the experiences onboard a famous ship of one of her more observant crewmen. The Illinois sailor's letters cover nearly a year, from 12 January 1862 to 6 January 1863. Keeler served on the *Monitor* during its entire career, experiencing its first unusual days in the war, the storied fight at Hampton Roads, the movement up the James, and the *Monitor*'s sinking off Cape Hatteras, where he nearly lost his life. The letters to his wife, detailed, thoughtful, and filled with naval and personal matters, represent an important resource relating to the famous ironclad and to the life of a merchant turned sailor. The height of drama for Keeler came when he acted as a communication link between Lt. John L. Worden in the pilothouse and Lt. Samuel Dana Greene in the turret during the *Monitor-Virginia* fight.

Various aspects of the ship's design are also discussed, giving naval historians a valuable resource beyond the discussion of actions on the water. The letters on the fight at Hampton Roads are thrilling, and the movement up the James in the summer of 1862 in support of the Peninsular campaign provides ample opportunities for interesting discussion. The letter of 6 January 1863 from Washington contains one of the best summaries of the loss of the *Monitor*. An occasional spelling error can be found, as with "Fortress Munroe" and "George McClelland." Generally, however, the letters are exceptionally well written and edited.

Samuel Phillips Lee (1812–1897)

613

Cornish, Dudley Taylor, and Virginia Jeans Laas. **Lincoln's Lee: The Life of Samuel Phillips Lee, 1812–1897** (245 pp., University Press of Kansas, Lawrence, 1986)

This is a well-done, penetrating biography of one of the war's curious naval figures (see also the letters penned by his wife and preserved in the equally important book *Wartime Washington* [*q.v.*]). The biography's subject began his naval career in the familiar mold of one born into a prominent family with connections. He married into a very powerful family and performed ably in his long antebellum career in the U.S. Navy. Unlike his third cousin Robert, Lincoln's Lee remained loyal to the Union and embarked on a Civil War career of great luster.

The book reflects the kind of thorough scholarship that produces a solid and praiseworthy historical tome. Much of the material used came from the Blair-Lee family papers, and the authors incorporated numerous other sources in a steady and analytical fashion. The work wonderfully chronicles Lee's rise in political clout with Gideon Welles and his command of the North Atlantic Blockading Squadron. The authors do not hesitate to clearly outline their subject's weaknesses, such as a basic conservativism that prevented success in some cases or his willingness to subvert formal channels of command when he thought it necessary. The book contains a wealth of valuable information on the blockade, nicely integrating the military details with the personal investigation of Lee's character and behavior.

David Dixon Porter (1813–1891)

614

Porter, David Dixon. **Incidents and Anecdotes of the Civil War** (357 pp., D. Appleton and Co., New York, 1885)

Porter's work is an amusing but surprisingly unreliable volume penned by the Federal rear admiral. Amateurishly written, it contains spurious conversations or exact quotations that could not possibly have been recorded and in places amounts to an excessively rambling hodgepodge of material. Nonetheless, because of the author's position and range of experience, it remains a curious source worthy of investigation. Filled with scenes of local color, anecdotes about famous naval and army officers, and accounts of Porter's participation in a variety of campaigns, the book has a certain charm and interesting material that should be read with caution.

Porter recounts his experience in the secession crisis beginning at Fort Pickens, describes the attack on Fort Morgan, and details the early assault on New Orleans, punctuating such accounts with recollections of persons, such as an interview with John Ericsson. He outlines the difficulties of Butler's administration of New Orleans and takes great care to describe the movements up the Mississippi, particularly the passing of Natchez. In Washington, he recalls meetings with Lincoln, Stanton, Seward, and McClernand. Porter describes Grant at Cairo, a first meeting with Sherman, and the all-out effort on Vicksburg. The Red River expedition receives scrutiny, as does the dilemma of the gunboat fleet and the miracle of Joseph Bailey's dam. The account winds down with discussions of Butler and the plan to blow up Fort Fisher, which ended in a comic disaster. After describing Lincoln's visit to City Point and to Richmond, he concludes by stating that Lincoln was "the best man I ever knew." The book lacks an index.

615

Soley, James Russell. **Admiral Porter** (499 pp., D. Appleton and Co., New York, 1903)

This remains the best single-volume work on Porter's career. The task of assembling a careful and accurate life of Porter and his impressive naval career during the war was daunting, in part because of Porter's own sloppiness with respect to records and recollections. This problem mars Porter's own *Naval History of the Civil War* (*q.v.*). Soley, however, was a careful researcher who poured a vigorous effort into his old acquaintance's biography. The result is limited by its antiquated language but far superior to several minor works of more recent vintage.

The biography dutifully examines Porter's career and brings readers a glimpse of the man as well. The author enjoys his subject and compliments him frequently, particularly with regard to Porter's organizational, strategic, and supervisory skills. The great stories of important actions all appear, along with occasional excerpts from documents, but Soley essentially glosses over the rough edges that made Porter enemies. In the end he is too praiseful of Porter, assigning him the highest moral stature, an exaggeration. Porter did inspire the younger men he commanded, however, and that trait along with his fighting ability made him an outstanding naval commander. The index is inadequate.

Thomas Oliver Selfridge, Jr. (1836–1924)

616

Selfridge, Thomas O., Jr. **Memoirs of Thomas O. Selfridge, Jr., Rear-Admiral, U.S.N.** (288 pp., G. P. Putnam's Sons, New York, 1924)

These memoirs chronicle the career of an officer who rose to great influence after the Civil War but whose brief assignment as lieutenant commander on the USS *Cairo* and other activities during the war keep his story vital. Son of a Civil War–era commodore, the younger Selfridge served on the USS *Cumberland* in 1862 during the duel of the ironclads at Hampton Roads, Virginia, commanded gunboats on the Mississippi and on the Red River, and participated in the assault on Fort Fisher at war's end. Selfridge's memoirs include these interesting episodes and many other smaller incidents.

The work is not limited to the Civil War, however, but reflects briefly on Selfridge's early years and provides substan-

tial material on his illustrious postbellum career, including much data on scientific surveys he accompanied. Some 41 percent of the book addresses the war years, with the most engaging accounts focusing on the Hampton Roads battle and the Vicksburg campaign. His account of the sinking of the *Cairo* is disappointingly brief. A number of maps of varying quality accompany the text. The work lacks an index.

(Reprinted 1988, titled *What Finer Tradition: The Memoirs of Thomas O. Selfridge, Jr., Rear Admiral U.S.N.*, with an introduction by William N. Still, Jr., 288 pp., University of South Carolina Press, Columbia)

John Ancrum Winslow (1811–1873)

617

Ellicott, John M. **The Life of John Ancrum Winslow, Rear Admiral United States Navy** (281 pp., G. P. Putnam's Sons, New York, 1902)

The author makes a worthwhile contribution toward understanding the relatively quiet, workmanlike career of the naval officer who defeated Raphael Semmes's CSS *Alabama*. Studious and well composed, the narrative allows Winslow to speak frequently in dispatches, letters, and extracts from reports. Ellicott focuses on Winslow's baptism of fire in the Mexican War and his subsequent heroism at Frontera and in leading the landing party at Tabasco.

The Civil War coverage outlines in satisfactory detail Winslow's command of the USS *Kearsarge* despite his not being rated very highly by his fellow officers and previously being assigned relatively trivial duties. The subject's censure by being placed on furlough receives significant coverage. Winslow found himself in a poor light shortly before the assignment that would accelerate his career toward glory. Given the *Kearsarge* and the task of finding and sinking Confederate cruisers, Winslow wound his way to the English Channel and ultimately to his battle near Cherbourg, France. The well-documented story of the famous battle is superbly told and may be considered the high point of the book, which holds up well despite poor maps and diagrams.

OTHERS

George Norman Barnard (1819–1902)

618

Davis, Keith F. **George N. Barnard: Photographer of Sherman's Campaign** (232 pp., Hallmark Cards, Kansas City, Mo., 1990)

In addition to a lengthy and magnificently detailed biographical essay on Barnard and his role in midcentury photography, the book includes the complete set of 61 plates in *Photographic Views of Sherman's Campaigns, Embracing Scenes of the Occupation of Nashville, the Great Battles around Chattanooga and Lookout Mountain, the Campaign of Atlanta, March to the Sea, and the Great Raid through the Carolinas: From Negatives Taken in the Field*, by George N. Barnard (published by the author, New York, 1866), one of the primary works of Civil War photography. The images made during Sherman's campaign are reproduced far better than in earlier editions. Most of the 215 illustrations consist of the subject's artistic and revealing photographs.

Davis's background story on Barnard incorporates valuable material on the art of nineteenth-century photography. The description of Barnard's ascension to prominence as a photographer and his accompaniment of Sherman during the Atlanta campaign and the March to the Sea provides splendid reading. Additionally, the author presents an interpretation of Barnard's work in Georgia and a discussion of his subject's postwar career with a particular focus on Charleston and Chicago scenes. Missing from the 1990 edition is the text originally accompanying these images, which was written by Theodore R. Davis and adds little to the photographs themselves. The odd and erroneous spellings stand uncorrected in Barnard's original titles but are relatively obvious as they mangle names of well-known places. The work lacks an index.

Clara Barton (1821–1912)

619

Oates, Stephen B. **A Woman of Valor: Clara Barton and the Civil War** (527 pp., Free Press, New York, 1994)

The author gives us a clear and calculated portrait of an unsung hero of the Civil War, one whose fame emerged fully only in the last decades of the century. Fully researched, precise in its details, and written with great elegance, this book belongs on the shelf of anyone interested in society's changing gender roles during the war, nursing experiences on the battlefield, or studies on strength of character. As the title suggests, the work is not a full biography but focuses entirely on the activities of Barton during the war. The author employs many manuscript sources relating to Barton not used previously, conferring a freshness as well as deep insight.

Oates separates various phases of Barton's Civil War nursing activities. A full and detailed account of the subject's alarming internal call to action pervades the first two chapters, as does a marvelous account of her activities on the battlefield of Antietam. As the descriptions of Barton's field service mount, so does the realization of her determination, at such places as Fredericksburg, Fort Wagner, the Wilderness, Spotsylvania, and Petersburg. The story of her relentless pursuit to help the cause and the boys is skillfully related, approaching a crescendo with the accounts of Barton's effort to preserve the dignity of soldiers who died at Andersonville. This is a first-rate work of Civil War history.

Mathew B. Brady (1823?–1896)

620

Horan, James D. **Mathew Brady: Historian with a Camera** (244 pp., Crown Publishers, New York, 1955)

A full, scholarly, masterful volume treating Mathew B. Brady and his wonderful photographs remains to be published, but Horan's book offers a first attempt. This photographic survey presents a selection of 453 images by Brady and his collaborators, supplemented by 90 pages of text examining Brady's life and its relationship to the growth of photography in America. Some 250 of the photos illustrate the war itself, the emphasis squarely placed on portraiture.

The majority of these images are available in Miller's *Photographic History* (q.v.), or Davis's *Image of War* (q.v.), so much of the remaining value of this work consists in the author's text. (The present-day historian must be reminded of the exhaustive effort required to assemble such a work in the early 1950s compared with the relatively easy availability of the Brady images today.) The background material on Brady and the narrative of the author's research is useful and reliable, and the volume has value as a collection of many of Brady's most celebrated images as well as for portraying his spirit.

John Brown (1800–1859)

621

Oates, Stephen B. **To Purge This Land with Blood: A Biography of John Brown** (434 pp., Harper and Row, New York, 1970)

The revisionist portrait that emerges from this biography sets a modern standard. It avoids the long record of exaggeration on either side of Brown's simple and disturbed mind. The narrative follows Brown's birth and early life in Ohio, where dominating Calvinist themes forged a militant belief in the Bible and hatred of slavery. The author details Brown's westward migration and his large family and small business ventures, creating an underlying picture of someone who should have led a relatively unnoticed life.

Throughout the second and third parts of Oates's book the groundwork for Harpers Ferry is laid. The work appraises Brown moderately as simply one of many guerrilla leaders in Kansas and outlines his evolving relationships with the Secret Six. Oates discounts the notion that Brown was insane and explores in meticulous detail the poor fit between what he describes as the New Testament style of New Englanders of the day and Brown's decidedly Old Testament style. Balancing Brown's zealous spiritual and militant abolitionist views, the author shows that his subject was also a habitual liar and one whose personality severely limited his dealings with others and his ability to understand rationally mechanisms of change.

Anna Ella Carroll (1815–1894)

622

Coryell, Janet L. **Neither Heroine nor Fool: Anna Ella Carroll of Maryland** (177 pp., Kent State University Press, Kent, 1990)

Anna Ella Carroll devised the Grand Strategy that won the Civil War for the North." Such absurdities have often cropped up in the literature of wartime folklore. Coryell attempts to explore who Carroll was without the influence of mythology. She lays down Carroll's background as the daughter of a governor of Maryland; her connections with the Federal administration (often exaggerated); her correspondence with Millard Fillmore, William Henry Seward, and Abraham Lincoln; and her career as a pamphleteer.

The author provides a description of Carroll's involvement in the nativist movement of the 1850s. Her pamphlets produced in the early weeks and months of the Lincoln administration supported the president and suggested colonization for blacks. The author documents how the Mississippi River plan was not Carroll's, as she claimed for years after the war, but had previously been concocted by Winfield Scott, U. S. Grant, and Henry W. Halleck, among others. Carroll's historical claim to fame is thus shattered, but Coryell has done a superb job of taking a simplistic contest and expanding it into a meaningful life of her subject. Even without involvement in the origin of the Anaconda Plan, Carroll's life as a woman who influenced the politics of her day is worthy of careful inspection.

Thomas Morris Chester (1834–1892)

623

Chester, Thomas Morris. **Thomas Morris Chester, Black Civil War Correspondent: His Dispatches from the Virginia Front** (ed. R. J. M. Blackett, 375 pp., Louisiana State University Press, Baton Rouge, 1989)

Chester's narrative constitutes one of the best collections of writings from a relatively scarce source during the war, a black newspaperman. Assigned to cover the war for the *Philadelphia Press* in 1864, Chester commenced his journey to the Virginia front and promptly arrived at the Petersburg lines, sending his first report back on 14 August 1864, from the headquarters of the 2d brigade, 3d division, 18th Army Corps, Army of the James. The author's dispatches covered the front lines for the *Press* through June 1865, and 88 such reports appear in this volume, along with a biographical essay by the editor.

The dispatches are peculiarly interesting, not only in that they describe momentous events along the Petersburg front and mirror the army's exhausted excitement at the fall of Richmond and triumphant return home following the surrender of Lee, but because they describe these great times from the perspective of a black American. The writer's many comments on commanders include observations relating to Benjamin F. Butler, U. S. Grant, and Godfrey Weitzel. The reporting of battle actions is generally quite good, tempered frequently by an engaging sense of humor. Several errors occur, as with the spellings of Darius Couch, Stephen A. Hurlbut, and August V. Kautz, but such minor nuisances do little to detract from this fine work.

(Reprinted 1991, 375 pp., Da Capo Press, New York)

Charles Carleton Coffin (1823–1896)

624

Coffin, Charles Carleton. **Four Years of Fighting: A Volume of Personal Observation with the Army and Navy, from the First Battle of Bull Run to the Fall of Richmond** (558 pp., Ticknor and Fields, Boston, 1866)

The product of a prolific journalist, this volume records the most worthwhile thoughts of this war correspondent for the Boston *Journal*. While stylistically dated and written with a misguided aim of popularizing the author's experience, the work does contain some valuable anecdotes and observations by Coffin, a field journalist of above average ability. The author provides the usual story of the secession crisis, the political turmoil in Washington, and a scandalous state of affairs in Baltimore. He describes a visit to Fort McHenry, the attitudes of Baltimore women toward those with Northern sentiment, and the drama of officers and troops organizing around Washington.

The remainder of the work traces the author's journeys and follows anecdotes he interjects, often with humor, to illustrate episodes of the war: First Bull Run, stories of the 2d Maine Infantry, a visit to Annapolis, the state of affairs in Missouri, Mill Spring, the rise of the slavery question as a military factor, Forts Henry and Donelson, the invasions of Maryland and Kentucky, Fredericksburg, Chancellorsville, Gettysburg, the Wilderness campaign, Sherman's movements, scenes in Savannah, the fall of Richmond, and surrender. Readers will not always find clear what Coffin experienced with his own eyes and what he is merely reporting secondhand or thirdhand. The work lacks an index.

(Reprinted 1970, titled *The Boys of '61; or, Four Years of Fighting*, 558 pp., Arno Press, New York)

Jay Cooke (1821–1905)

625

Oberholtzer, Ellis Paxson. **Jay Cooke: Financier of the Civil War** (2 vols., 1248 pp., G. W. Jacobs and Co., Philadelphia, 1907)

Oberholtzer details in scholarly fashion the career of the Ohio-born financial speculator who greatly assisted the Federal war effort. The two bulky volumes provide well-researched and documented analysis of the subject's politically influential background, his financial dealings before the war, and his close association with Salmon P. Chase. The author devotes most of the first volume to the war era, during which

Cooke proposed selling government bonds in a massive scheme that would net his firm a commission, an act that became wildly successful and contributed materially to the Federal government's ability to wage war.

The work also describes Cooke's assistance in issuing greenbacks and contains much specific information on the many loans secured by Cooke and his help in raising cash for states as well as the Washington government. The author reveals that at one point Cooke and Company was moving more than $9.5 million in war bonds per day. He also describes Cooke's policing of illegal bond schemes (although he was soundly criticized for profiteering himself) and his support of such legislation as John Sherman's important Omnibus Revenue Act. The second volume loses steam with the declining fortunes of Cooke's postwar activities.

(Reprinted 1968, 2 vols., 1248 pp., Augustus M. Kelly, New York)

Pauline Cushman (1833–1893)

626

Sarmiento, Ferdinand L. **Life of Pauline Cushman, the Celebrated Union Spy and Scout: Comprising Her Early History, Her Entry into the Secret Service of the Army of the Cumberland, and Exciting Adventures with Rebel Chieftains and Others While within the Enemy Lines, Together with Her Capture and Sentence to Death by General Bragg and Final Rescue by the Union Army under General Rosecrans: The Whole Carefully Prepared from Her Notes and Memoranda** (374 pp., John E. Potter, Philadelphia, 1865)

To be read for pure entertainment, this book consists of 48 chapters about the adventures of Cushman, who was "entitled officially to be called . . . a major" in the U.S. Army. All of the information consists of "solemn truths" and is based on Cushman's notes. Many of the stories and conversations are contrived and fanciful, bordering on pure fiction. At the outset of war the young actress was playing "South Carolina" in *Uncle Sam's Magic Lantern*, a play about the states. Colonel Moore, provost marshal of Louisville, asked her to toast the Confederacy to identify rebel sympathizers. After a phony reprimand from Jeremiah T. Boyle, she was released and made her way through the lines to Nashville as a spy.

Thereafter the work introduces readers to a long series of espionage activities in which Cushman smuggled messages through the lines in bags of flour or within the craws of chickens. She informed on the identity of smugglers and reported Confederate troop dispositions. She traveled throughout Tennessee pretending to search for a brother,

A. A. Cushman, presumed to be on the staff of Braxton Bragg. She outwitted Confederate guards and charmed Confederate officers. She was arrested several times and interrogated by many, including John Hunt Morgan, Nathan Bedford Forrest, and Bragg himself, but always managed to win freedom. At last her guards abandoned her when she was ill, and the Federals sent her to Nashville in an ambulance, where James A. Garfield and William S. Rosecrans looked after her.

Frederick Douglass (1817?–1895)

627

Blight, David W. **Frederick Douglass' Civil War: Keeping Faith in Jubilee** (270 pp., Louisiana State University Press, Baton Rouge, 1989)

In this analytical work, Douglass's life is treated as a backdrop against which to explore the causes and consequences of the war, as well as the participation of Douglass in the war itself. Blight begins by establishing the antebellum breakdown of faith in America and in its political direction that Douglass experienced. Realizing that nothing for blacks could change significantly without a full-blown crisis, Douglass hoped that just such an event as the Civil War would indeed happen. He got his wish.

The author's narrative succinctly describes how Douglass acted simultaneously as a leader of black Americans and a lobbyist of white political leaders. Despite the unfolding of emancipation during the war, Douglass seemed frustrated first by the low priority of emancipation as a war aim and then, during Reconstruction, by the policies that aimed at white reconciliation before granting rights to freedmen.

Despite the work's careful and reflective tone, readers do not really learn the answers to some of the principal questions of interest: How influential was Douglass among blacks? Among political leaders such as Abraham Lincoln? Such assessments may be too difficult to quantify, and the absence of answers does little to detract from this admirable study.

628

McFeely, William S. **Frederick Douglass** (465 pp., W. W. Norton and Co., New York, 1991)

This work systematically analyzes each phase of the life of Douglass, from his Maryland years as a slave through his transformation as a speaker on the antislavery circuit to his political career following the war. Not only does a portrait of Douglass as the careful and caring reformer emerge but also a portrait of Douglass as the vain, temperamental personality.

Only 13 percent of the biography covers the Civil War period, which is proper because of the wide range of activities that Douglass engaged in before and after the war. At all phases of his subject's life, the author rightly follows the question of how Douglass perceived himself, as a leader of blacks, and how this perception shaped his behavior and affected others. The author reveals that Douglass was dominated by a quest for recognition, driving him to the lecture circuit and to a relentless hunt for government positions, three of which he finally held: marshall and then recorder of deeds for the District of Columbia and U.S. minister to Haiti.

In assessing his subject's relations with politicians, soldiers, antislavery advocates, and women, the author enters somewhat more speculative ground. McFeely's suggestion that Douglass had at least one affair with a white woman involved in the abolition movement is not well supported, nor is the speculation that he felt he was somehow different from his siblings who had somewhat darker skin. The biography cleverly investigates the disappointment that Douglass felt over the black experience in early Reconstruction years.

Edwin Forbes (1835–1895)

629

Forbes, Edwin. **Thirty Years After: An Artist's Story of the Great War, Told, and Illustrated with Nearly 300 Relief Etchings after Sketches in the Field, and 20 Half-Tone Equestrian Portraits from Original Oil Paintings** (2 vols., 319 pp., Fords, Howard, and Hulbert, New York, 1890)

These volumes contain the core of the sketch collection of one of the most productive field "special artists" of the war era. Forbes traveled with the Northern armies of the East from First Bull Run through the siege of Petersburg and never tired of producing on-site sketches of what he saw. Having produced some hundreds of drawings, many used as the basis for engravings in the papers—particularly *Frank Leslie's Illustrated Newspaper*—and later in works such as *Battles and Leaders* (q.v.), Forbes compiled two works of his own, *Life Studies of the Great Army* (1876) and *Thirty Years After*, a memoir illustrated by 320 etchings, including those from *Life Studies*.

Forbes includes 80 short essays to accompany drawings that illustrate how the common soldiers of the Army of the

Potomac lived. The art includes a few scenes of battle but focuses on the daily events of soldier life, the camp scenes, preparation of food, picket duty, marches, laying bridges, and tending horses. Although the scenes are mundane, they clearly show the common experience of the Civil War soldier, and Forbes's narrative vignettes are interestingly written. There is no index.

(Reprinted 1993, titled *Thirty Years After: An Artist's Memoir of the Civil War*, ed. William J. Cooper, Jr., 334 pp., Louisiana State University Press, Baton Rouge)

Alexander Gardner (1821–1882)

630

Katz, D. Mark. **Witness to an Era: The Life and Photographs of Alexander Gardner: The Civil War, Lincoln, and the West** (305 pp., Viking, New York, 1991)

This beautifully produced volume constitutes one of the most luxurious picture books of Civil War history. The work presents the imagery of Alexander Gardner, extending from the early years, work with Mathew Brady, the Civil War era, photographs of Abraham Lincoln made during the war, the Lincoln assassination coverage, railroading and Indians in the west, to the declining years of Gardner's photographic art and life. All of the images plus many documents are reproduced as attractive duotones, the quality of separations is superb, and many images are published quite large on the folio pages of this work, greatly enhancing readers' enjoyment. Some 106 Civil War images and 66 images of Lincoln, alone or with others, appear in the work, forming a spectacular collection. Not all of the images were made by Gardner, however; some were taken by his associate Timothy O'Sullivan.

Katz provides an excellent sketch of the life of Alexander Gardner and a running narrative of his subject's war experiences. The sections prior to and following the war are also engaging, making this work a treasure for Civil War enthusiasts. An occasional misspelling appears, as with Mathew B. Brady.

William Lloyd Garrison (1805–1879)

631

Thomas, John L. **The Liberator: William Lloyd Garrison** (502 pp., Little, Brown and Co., Boston, 1963)

While not definitively liberating Garrison's character, this work outdoes the previous works on this influential antisla-very crusader. Thomas successfully dissects the complex character of Garrison and his closest contemporaries as anti-organization radicals, showing that their crusade was really an attempt to unravel the institutions of American life in the true spirit of anarchy. The liberator certainly believed fervently in freeing the slaves, but he also wanted to "bring America to its knees." The fiery prose published in his famous newspaper over the course of 35 years demonstrates his willingness to abandon politics as a means of change. Garrison could believe in politics no more than in the government or the church.

The present work reveals that Garrison called for Northern secession to create a pure nation without slavery. In tracing his evolution of thought from the 1850s through the Civil War itself, Thomas skillfully separates the ideals at large and the man. Thus, he argues with great clarity that once the war came, Garrison could no longer champion a moral path; as the author states, when the time came for his greatest potential influence, "he had nothing to say."

Julia Dent Grant (1826–1902)

632

Grant, Julia Dent. **The Personal Memoirs of Julia Dent Grant** (ed. John Y. Simon, 346 pp., G. P. Putnam's Sons, New York, 1975)

Seldom do the memoirs of the wife of a general contribute substantially to understanding the operations of the war. This is such a work. Composed in the late 1880s and based on her remembrances, her husband's *Memoirs* (*q.v.*), and family papers and notes, Julia Grant's tale is an informal reminiscence of life in the Grant and Dent families, woven with humor and charm but as casual as dinner conversation. The editor has written an excellent introduction and peppered the text with incisive notes, which add greatly to the manuscript's value.

Julia Grant's story begins with her early life, family, and friendships. This brief section leads to discussions of antebellum life with Ulysses Grant, a narrative that sheds substantial light on the personality and everyday existence of Grant and his wife during these years of struggle inside and outside the army. The central part of the memoirs covers the war years and offers anecdotes and remembrances of numerous military personalities, including officers on Grant's staff, many of his subordinates, and commanders in Washington and in the field. The rich recollections offer much of interest on crucial periods during the war and complement the viewpoints in Grant's *Memoirs* (*q.v.*) or the Grant *Papers* (*q.v.*). She attacks

Stanton's postwar activities, outlines Grant's reluctance to accept the nomination for president, and offers many other candid and balanced assessments. The final part of the work, of somewhat lesser interest, describes life inside the Grant White House and the famous trip around the world following the Grant presidency.

(Reprinted 1988, 346 pp., Southern Illinois University Press, Carbondale)

Horace Greeley (1811–1872)

633

Van Deusen, Glyndon G. **Horace Greeley: Nineteenth-Century Crusader** (445 pp., University of Pennsylvania Press, Philadelphia, 1953)

The author provides a full story of Greeley's life based on a suitable analysis of the available sources, chronologically rendering a portrait of the man whose conservative political visions were shared with the nation through Greeley's day job as journalist. An idealist with firm roots in the Whig-Republican tradition, Greeley espoused wonderful ideas of reformation but acted little, preferring to heap the work of reform onto others. Ultimately, Van Deusen shows, Greeley was consumed by political appetite and thus compromised his ideals, which contributed substantially to his decline.

The author makes a clear case that Greeley's clout was symbolic far more than real, as the important politicians in power in his own party accorded him attention but followed almost none of his suggestions. This was the case not only with Lincoln but also with Grant, Seward, and Thurlow Weed. In the end, the author's analysis of Greeley stops short of delivering a clear picture of what made him tick and whether his actions left any lasting effects. The biography contains a few illustrations, a scant bibliography, and a rather thin index.

Cornelia Hancock (1839–1926)

634

Hancock, Cornelia. **South after Gettysburg: Letters of Cornelia Hancock from the Army of the Potomac, 1863–1865** (ed. Henrietta Stratton Jaquette, 173 pp., University of Pennsylvania Press, Philadelphia, 1937)

A Quaker girl of 23 years in 1863, Hancock traveled to Gettysburg following the battle to help care for Union wounded. She then followed the wounded to Washington and thence to Brandy Station, along the trail of the Wilderness campaign, and to City Point. Her 102 wartime letters, written mostly to her mother and sister, appeared in the 1937 first edition. Hancock did not cease activities with the close of the war, however, and a second edition with an introduction by Bruce Catton (288 pp., Thomas Y. Crowell, New York, 1956) contains 59 letters she wrote as a schoolteacher of freedmen in South Carolina.

Hancock served as a tireless aid in the best tradition of Clara Barton and won friendships and a medal from the soldiers she treated. Her descriptions of the brutalities of Civil War wounds stand with the more enlightening narratives from a nurse. Hancock clearly preferred the working atmosphere of the field hospitals compared with those in Washington, where she found less than scrupulous people in charge. Her outlook on the war is fiercely patriotic, and her observations of its casualties are shrewd. Hancock's book makes a contribution to understanding the treatment of wounded soldiers of the Union Army.

Thomas Wallace Knox (1835–1896)

635

Knox, Thomas W. **Camp-Fire and Cotton-Field: Southern Adventure in Time of War, Life with the Union Armies, and Residence on a Louisiana Plantation** (524 pp., Blelock and Co., New York, 1865)

Knox, a correspondent for the New York *Herald*, found himself in the western plains at the onset of the crisis and traveled east, observing the situation in Missouri, Arkansas, and Tennessee during the first months of the war. Therefore, this early narrative contains much of interest on the political situation in Missouri as well as dramatic, if not always completely reliable, accounts of Wilson's Creek, Pea Ridge, and Shiloh. The newspaperman focuses mainly on military activities, although he presents significant material on local citizens, the erosion of war spirit in the South, bushwhacking, and his stay on a Louisiana plantation.

The book's most valuable aspects treat the army's movement southward to Memphis and the several attempts at capturing Vicksburg. Grant's movement through Mississippi and the fall of Vicksburg transforms into a discussion of Kansas during the war, followed by accounts of Gettysburg, the Northwest Conspiracy, and a succession of chapters examining "special subjects," such as arming ex-slaves and the war's effects on agriculture. Knox provides interesting first-hand accounts, although he covers substantial ground secondhand and does not make clear at all times where his wide travels took him. The work lacks an index.

(Reprinted 1969, 524 pp., Da Capo Press, New York)

Elizabeth Blair Lee (1818–1906)

636

Lee, Elizabeth Blair. **Wartime Washington: The Civil War Letters of Elizabeth Blair Lee** (ed. Virginia Jeans Laas, 552 pp., University of Illinois Press, Urbana, 1991)

This superb collection of 368 letters offers a social, military, and political glimpse into the Federal capital. Much of the value in this work—a collection that has been called a Northern counterpart to Mary Chesnut's famous diary (*q.v.*)—lies in the writer's background, wide knowledge, and influential friendships. The daughter of Francis Preston Blair, Sr., wife of naval flag officer Samuel Phillips Lee, and sister of Montgomery Blair and Frank Blair, Jr., Elizabeth had a keen view of the war simply from the conversation inside her own family. The many missives she wrote between December 1860 and April 1865, some 900 in all and mostly to her husband, form the collection from which the present offering was selected.

The author's upbringing produced a coterie of Southern friends, and so her reflections and communications take on a multifaceted quality and are not limited to Northerners. Rather, Lee reflects with personal knowledge about many Southerners, both military and civilian, whom she knows well. Such connections often came into play to advance the career of S. P. Lee; other times they were used to advance the Union cause. The writer strongly liked or disliked certain individuals, the latter including John Charles Frémont. Some misspelled or incorrect names appear, as with Louis Blenker, Simon Cameron, Claiborne F. Jackson, George W. Cullum, H. Judson Kilpatrick, John Pegram, Lovell H. Rousseau, William B. Shubrick, Josiah Tattnall, and Godfrey Weitzel. Beyond the insight into major wartime events, the letters add a great deal to our understanding of societal and women's history in the 1860s, including discussions of child-bearing and -raising, social customs, and volunteerism.

Mary Ashton Rice Livermore (1820–1905)

637

Livermore, Mary A. **My Story of the War: A Woman's Narrative of Four Years Personal Experience as Nurse in the Union Army, and in Relief Work at Home, in Hospitals, Camps, and at the Front, during the War of the Rebellion: With Anecdotes, Pathetic Incidents, and Thrilling Reminiscences Portraying the Lights and Shadows of Hospital Life and the Sanitary Service of the War** (700 pp., A. D. Worthington and Co., Hartford, 1888)

This narrative recalls the wartime adventures of a seemingly tireless journalist and social worker. The wife of a Chicago newsman, Mary Livermore was a skilled writer and administrator who became the head of the Northwestern Sanitary Commission in Chicago. Her book contains portraits of herself and other famous women of the war, eight steel engravings of fanciful war scenes, and eight color plates of assorted battle flags not germaine to the story. The preface, introduction, descriptions of the flags, and table of contents fill the first 83 pages.

The author possesses a fine vocabulary but writes with hyperpatriotism, religious overtones, and emotional and imaginative narrative. She describes many stories of women in the war, stressing their crucial contributions, such as how Anna Ella Carroll of Maryland allegedly planned the Mississippi campaign resulting in the capture of Forts Henry and Donelson and how Carroll allegedly convinced Lincoln and his generals to carry it out. She lauds Madame Turchin, wife of the Russian volunteer, who not only nursed her husband in 1862 but allegedly took command of the 19th Illinois Infantry and led it to victory in battle. Such sections strain the credibility of even casual readers. She provides other questionable examples of women as soldiers, combat leaders, drummers, flag bearers, and nurses.

Livermore was active herself in matters relating to the Sanitary Commission, visiting hospitals in St. Louis and Memphis, aid stations at the front, and the November 1862 meeting of the commission in Washington. She comforted wounded Union soldiers, traded insults with rebel women in Memphis, and told religious stories and sang songs for the troops. In 1863 Livermore traveled down the Mississippi aboard the *Tigress* and met Ulysses Grant aboard the *Magnolia*, as he was planning the Vicksburg campaign. The more valuable parts of the work describe the author's activities with the sanitary fairs, particularly the northwestern fair in Chicago in October 1863.

(Reprinted 1972, 704 pp., Arno Press, New York; reprinted 1978, 700 pp., Corner House, Williamstown, Mass.; reprinted 1995, titled *My Story of the War: The Civil War Memoirs of the Famous Nurse, Relief Organizer, and Suffragette*, with an introduction by Nina Silber, 704 pp., Da Capo Press, New York)

Herman Melville (1819–1891)

638

Garner, Stanton. **The Civil War World of Herman Melville** (544 pp., University Press of Kansas, Lawrence, 1993)

Garner suggests that Melville was intellectually involved with the war to a high degree. The work centers on the subject's depression over the war's terrible cost, yet, drawing on an assortment of untapped archival materials, shows the war as delivering an emotional charge for Melville's creativity. Much of the analysis focuses on Melville's epic book of poetry and prose, *Battle-Pieces and Aspects of the War (q.v.)*; indeed the book contains portions of that work in its analysis of Melville's psychology, creative energy, and social and family relationships.

The scholarly inspection of Melville's contradictions is superb. The author chronicles Melville's antislavery spirit yet shows how he failed to align himself with the abolitionist movement. Although he was a staunch Democrat and sided against much of the Lincoln administration's policies, Melville vigorously supported the war effort and recorded many of its greatest moments in *Battle-Pieces*. Garner describes in vivid detail the schism between America's great writers, pitting Ralph Waldo Emerson, Henry Wadsworth Longfellow, James R. Lowell, and John G. Whittier against Melville, Nathaniel Hawthorne, and Walt Whitman. As the author shows in this engaging book, Melville believed his war writings would allow him to emerge as the great poet of the age, a hope that ultimately failed. The scholarship in this fine book is generally sound, although occasional mistakes surface, as with the names of Edward Dickinson Baker, Mathew Brady, David Ramsay Clendenin, and Henry Wager Halleck.

Timothy O'Sullivan (1840–1882)

639

Horan, James D. **Timothy O'Sullivan, America's Forgotten Photographer: The Life and Work of the Brilliant Photographer Whose Camera Recorded the American Scene from the Battlefields of the Civil War to the Frontiers of the West** (334 pp., Doubleday and Co., Garden City, N.Y., 1966)

A valuable pictorial record of the war, this work first presents substantial background material on O'Sullivan, who, as one of the employees of Mathew Brady and then a solo photographer, captured many a battlefield image. A discussion of O'Sullivan's early years contains background material on the primitive art of photography in the 1850s. Sections following the Civil War coverage document O'Sullivan's work in the King Expedition, the Darien Survey, and the Wheeler Expedition. An appendix lists O'Sullivan's images, and there is a poor index.

The central focus consists of the 203 Civil War images, which make up nearly 40 percent of the book's space. Many have appeared elsewhere, but together the collection allows one to appreciate the scope of O'Sullivan's work. The highlights include coverage of Gettysburg in the wake of the battle, many scenes of army life in Virginia, images in and around the forts at Petersburg, Fort Pulaski after the breach, Grant's council of war at Massaponax Church, railroad scenes, and the rustic church and camp of the 50th New York Engineers on the site of what is now Poplar Grove National Cemetery. Such a mass collection of important images provides hours of enjoyment.

Charles Anderson Page (1838–1873)

640

Page, Charles A. **Letters of a War Correspondent** (ed. James R. Gilmore, 397 pp., L. C. Page and Co., Boston, 1899)

The war experiences in the field of a special correspondent for the New York *Tribune* are presented here. Page traveled to Virginia in 1862 to record his impressions of the fighting on the Peninsula and sent home impressions of Gaines's Mill and White Oak Swamp. He covered the battle of Second Bull Run, the escape of Lee's army from the Gettysburg campaign, the Wilderness, Spotsylvania, Cold Harbor, Grant's move south of the James, and the operations about Petersburg. Page composed a voluminous narrative based on army life around Petersburg, including discussions of the mine explosion, reflections on the war experiences of common soldiers, the use of black troops, operations north of the James, the Weldon Railroad, a summary of the Army of the James, Five Forks, the breaking of the lines, the death of Lincoln, and the Grand Review.

The author used his wartime notes and articles to patch together much material of interest along with his extensive letters from the front lines. They offer a great deal of insight into what Page saw, deliver the gist of some notable conversations, and provide many comments on Southern civilians as well as army officers. The work lacks an index.

Allan Pinkerton (1819–1884)

641

Pinkerton, Allan. **The Spy of the Rebellion: Being a True History of the United States Army during the Late Rebellion: Revealing Many Secrets of the War Hitherto Not Made Public: Compiled from Official Reports Prepared for President Lincoln, General McClellan, and the Provost-Marshal-General** (688 pp., A. G. Nettleton and Co., Chicago, 1883)

Despite the subtitle, this is a curious work of historical fiction. Pinkerton's espionage activities, begun in 1862 when he was the chief intelligence man for George McClellan, offer the type of absorbing Civil War stories that legends are made of. Unfortunately, much of this book consists of legend rather than fact. Some of Pinkerton's official reports, as deluded as they sometimes were about Confederate troop strength and other matters, appear in the *O.R.* (*q.v.*).

The present work, presumably that of a ghostwriter, is useful merely as an oddity. Pinkerton claimed that most of his Civil War papers were destroyed in the Great Chicago Fire and thus wrote this memoir from memory. By checking Pinkerton's verifiable stories with other sources, it seems clear that many episodes are highly embellished and others are invented outright. Clearly, some of the actors in Pinkerton's story appear to be phonies, including some of his agents. Many other stories that cannot be checked in detail simply do not possess authentic characteristics.

(Reprinted 1989, titled *The Spy of the Rebellion*, with an introduction by Patrick Bass, 666 pp., University of Nebraska Press, Lincoln)

Whitelaw Reid (1837–1912)

642

Reid, Whitelaw. **A Radical View: The "Agate" Dispatches of Whitelaw Reid, 1861–1865** (ed. James G. Smart, 2 vols., 502 pp., Memphis State University Press, Memphis, 1976)

This valuable collection of material is from the pen of one of the North's greatest war reporters. Reid set out at age 24 to report for the Cincinnati *Gazette* on the war in western Virginia, using the pen name Agate. In an age characterized by haphazard, sloppy, and outright false journalism, Reid was quickly recognized for his intelligence, wit, articulate style, and candor. He rose to become Washington correspondent for the *Gazette* during the second year of the war. Despite his position he frequently traveled hard to be on the scene of action, turning in classic accounts of Shiloh and Gettysburg, as well as reporting on lesser-known actions such as Carrick's Ford, Carnifex Ferry, and the Kentucky invasion of 1862.

Reid did not limit himself to military matters. He wrote columns on a wide variety of political personalities from Lincoln and Stanton to Adam Gurowski and Clement L. Vallandigham. His discourses illuminated early Reconstruction policies, emancipation and its effects on black soldiers, censorship of the press, the wartime election, and Richmond at the close of war. The editor made good use of the Reid Papers in the Library of Congress, although his economical introduction and notes add relatively little to the radical views of the author, whose dispatches constitute one of the great published collections of wartime journalism.

Albert Deane Richardson (1833–1869)

643

Richardson, Albert D. **The Secret Service, the Field, the Dungeon, and the Escape** (512 pp., American Printing Co., Hartford, 1865)

This thrilling narrative written by a journalist at war's end is marked by the typical patriotic fervor and probable embellishment that characterized works rushed into print at the close of the war. A correspondent for the New York *Tribune*, Richardson left Cincinnati in February 1861 to write about the conflict in the South. He traveled through Kentucky, Tennessee, Alabama, Mississippi, Louisiana, Georgia, South Carolina, North Carolina, and Virginia, arriving in Washington, where he met President Lincoln. His narrative is knowledgeable but prone to the overdramatic and often reaches fanciful heights. Much of the dialogue is manufactured, with "exact quotations" provided even for private conversations where no witnesses were present.

Richardson claims to have been in New Orleans when Braxton Bragg welcomed David E. Twiggs, in Montgomery when the capture of Fort Sumter was announced, and in Richmond when the excitement of war reached its peak. The narrative covers his visits in New York, Detroit, Chicago, St. Louis, Cincinnati, and Louisville, describing the local patriotism for the Northern war effort. A particularly interesting account recorded the attack on Fort Donelson presumably aboard the USS *Benton*. He visited Shiloh, Corinth, and Memphis and describes the exaggerated reports of other journalists, citing two who reported on the battle of Pea Ridge without having been present. Richardson often uses the editorial "we," referring to journalists in general.

Ordered back to Washington, Richardson joined the Army of the Potomac about the time of Antietam. Traveling down the Mississippi past Vicksburg, he was captured in May 1863. Once paroled, he returned to Vicksburg and subsequently went to Jackson, Montgomery, Atlanta, and Richmond, where he was imprisoned in Libby Prison and Castle Thunder. In February 1864 he was transferred to Salisbury, from which he escaped on 17 December 1864, reaching the Federal lines at Knoxville on 14 January 1865.

(Reprinted 1977, 512 pp., Arno Press, New York)

William Howard Russell (1820–1907)

644

Russell, William Howard. **William Howard Russell's Civil War: Private Diary and Letters, 1861–1862** (ed. Martin Crawford, 252 pp., University of Georgia Press, Athens, 1992)

A journalistic veteran of the Crimean War, the Englishman William Howard Russell knew how to cover a war. This superior edition of his Civil War memoirs is a cornerstone narrative by a foreigner on the war and supersedes *My Diary North and South*, the 1863 first edition (2 vols., 866 pp., Bradbury and Evans, London). As correspondent for the London *Times*, Russell reported on the American war from March 1861 to April 1862. Based in Washington, he offered articulate and occasionally erroneous evaluations of soldiers and politicians. He made several trips outside Washington, the most famous of which was his journey to see First Bull Run. The present edition includes all of the original material plus correspondence that comprises one-fourth of the book.

Russell's observations show that despite a reputation to the contrary he supported the Union cause. (The criticism of Russell by Yankees evolved mainly from his Bull Run report describing the panicked Federal Army.) The author's assessments of personalities were softened for the original edition of his work. He felt that Mary Lincoln was "preposterous" and "had the devils [*sic*] temper." He describes meetings with Abraham Lincoln and other figures, including Seward, McClellan, and Jefferson Davis. Other entries show the personal side of Russell, who apparently enjoyed mingling with Americans. The editorial work for this edition is generally sound, although occasional errors occur, as with the erroneous statement that the original Willard's Hotel has been restored.

Kate Chase Sprague (1840–1899)

645

Phelps, Mary Merwin. **Kate Chase, Dominant Daughter: The Life Story of a Brilliant Woman and Her Famous Father** (316 pp., Thomas Y. Crowell Co., New York, 1935)

Phelps presents the story of the substitute hostess of wartime Washington. Supported by her husband's fortune, her father's governmental position, and her own charm and beauty, young Kate Chase enjoyed the symbolism of sitting atop the Washington social scene. Conniving and strategizing well beyond her years, Kate wished her father would become president and her husband would climb the ladder of success while still young. Mary Lincoln and many others held Chase in disdain for her youth and apparent social invincibility.

In the end, this enjoyably written story demonstrates how all unraveled for Kate Chase. Her marriage ended. Chase was shuffled out of the cabinet and into the chief justiceship, and Kate was cast out of the inner circle of Washington society. With sufficient documentation and an affection for its subjects, this work describes much about Kate and her father, although the admirable qualities of Salmon Chase are sometimes lost to the reader. The end of Kate's life, in abject poverty, stands in stark contrast to her vibrant wartime days.

George Templeton Strong (1820–1875)

646

Strong, George Templeton. **The Diary of George Templeton Strong** (ed. Allan Nevins and Milton Halsey Thomas, 4 vols., 2153 pp., Macmillan Co., New York, 1952)

Volume 3 in this set covers the period 1860–1865, during which Strong, a prominent New York lawyer and socialite, recorded his forceful and sometimes harshly critical opinions on the conduct of the war. In the summer of 1861 the author became one of the founders of the U.S. Sanitary Commission, a position that enabled him to secure a significant viewpoint on the war and on the Lincoln administration.

Strong's occasional visits to battlefield areas and with prominent governmental and military officials, including Lincoln, Grant, and Stanton, as well as his fundraising and supply activities make fascinating reading. Of equal value are his descriptions of events such as the New York draft riots and his commentaries following many major battles.

(Vol. 3 reprinted 1962, titled *Diary of the Civil War, 1860–1865*, ed. Allan Nevins, 664 pp., Macmillan, New York)

George Alfred Townsend (1841–1914)

647

Townsend, George Alfred. **Campaigns of a Non-Combatant, and His Romaunt Abroad during the War** (368 pp., Blelock and Co., New York, 1866)

This outstanding diary was written by one of the North's most celebrated wartime journalists. Although the work is a hasty compilation of a store of material published in New York papers during the war and contains a fair amount of little value, the core five chapters that focus on military matters form an outstanding contribution on the war in Virginia as seen by a young, bright reporter. (These chapters are the ones reprinted in the abridgement cited below.)

The author's narrative focuses on the spring campaign of 1862, with emphasis on movements along the Peninsula, the Seven Days battles, and the subsequent action farther north following McClellan's retreat to Harrison's Landing. Townsend's eyewitness descriptions are often powerful, such as that of Fitz John Porter's balloon ascension. A trip abroad interrupts the military narrative, which begins again near the end of the war, at Five Forks, and concludes with a penetrating description of a substantially ruined Richmond. Along the way readers receive a significant volume on material relating to common soldiers and their experiences.

(Abridged edition 1950, titled *Rustics in Rebellion: A Yankee Reporter on the Road to Richmond, 1861–1865*, with an introduction by Lida Mayo, 292 pp., University of North Carolina Press, Chapel Hill; 1866 edition reprinted 1983, 368 pp., Time-Life Books, Alexandria, Va.)

Walt Whitman (1819–1892)

648

Whitman, Walt. **Walt Whitman's Civil War: Compiled and Edited from Published and Unpublished Sources** (ed. Walter Lowenfels and Nan Braymer, 333 pp., Alfred A. Knopf, New York, 1960)

This work offers something for nearly every reader of Civil War history. The famed army nurse, poet, and journalist planned but never executed a volume of reminiscences of his Civil War activities. The editors of this work stitched together a handsome compilation of poetry (47 Civil War poems), essays, and letters by Whitman treating his experiences during the war and reflections after it. They have enhanced the flavor of this collection with 16 sketches by Winslow Homer.

Whitman's Civil War adventures began when his brother George was wounded at Fredericksburg. Not only did Whitman travel to Falmouth to locate his brother and to assist his recovery at Chatham Mansion, but shortly thereafter he began his volunteer nursing duties in Washington. The author's experiences with wounded soldiers and his observations of the president and wartime Washington resulted in his book of poems *Drum Taps* and the salute to Lincoln, "O Captain! My Captain!" Of more interest is Whitman's monograph on hospital visits, published separately as *Memoranda during the War* (68 pp., published by the author, Camden, N.J., 1875; reprinted 1993, 68 pp., Applewood Books, Old Saybrook, Conn.)

(Reprinted 1989, 333 pp., Da Capo Press, New York)

GENERAL WORKS

BLACK AMERICANS AND
THE CIVIL WAR

649

Berlin, Ira, Barbara J. Fields, Thavolia Glymph, Steven F. Miller, Joseph P. Reidy, Leslie S. Rowland, and Julie Saville, eds. **Freedom: A Documentary History of Emancipation, 1861–1867** (4 vols., 3416 pp. to date, Cambridge University Press, New York, 1982–   )

This important work offers the best collection of primary documents relating to black Americans during the wartime era. The earliest of five planned series by the Freedmen and Southern Society Project, *The Black Military Experience* (ser. 2, 852 pp., 1982) contains 267 documents, consisting of letters, reports, and testimony relating to blacks in the earliest stages of transforming from slave to free American. Chronologically arranged in five parts from 1862 through 1867, the work surveys in a fresh, firsthand way the experience of blacks who took up arms against the Confederacy. This is accomplished through their own records rather than those of the military or political entities that enabled their participation. As such, this volume is a cornerstone in the field of Civil War studies.

The second work of this set is the exceptional *The Destruction of Slavery* (ser. 1, vol. 1, 852 pp., 1985), which contains 331 documents or groups of documents tracing the collapse of slavery by two avenues, the Federal Army's military campaigns and the slaves' own attempts at breaking free. The bulk of the documents are military reports, letters, affidavits, and petitions that outline the demise of the peculiar institution in the words of the slaves themselves. As with the previous volume, this one is spectacular in its coverage and clear and successful in its aim. The other two volumes, *The Wartime Genesis of Free Labor: The Lower South* (ser. 1, vol. 3, 937 pp., 1990) and *The Wartime Genesis of Free Labor: The Upper South* (ser. 1, vol. 2, 775 pp., 1993), add further insight into the black wartime experience. The volume on the Lower South adds with great clarity documents relating to the low country in South Carolina, Georgia, and Florida, southern Louisiana, and the Mississippi Valley. The volume on the Upper South covers tidewater Virginia and North Carolina, the District of Columbia, middle and east Tennessee and northern Alabama, Maryland, Missouri, and Kentucky.

(Abridged edition 1992, titled *Free at Last: A Documentary History of Slavery, Freedom, and the Civil War*, ed. Ira Berlin, Barbara J. Fields, Steven F. Miller, Joseph P. Reidy, and Leslie S. Rowland, 571 pp., New Press, New York; supplementary volume for background reading, 1992, titled *Slaves No More: Three Essays on Emancipation and the Civil War,* by Ira Berlin, Barbara J. Fields, Steven F. Miller, Joseph P. Reidy, and Leslie S. Rowland, 243 pp., Cambridge University Press, New York)

650

Brewer, James H. **The Confederate Negro: Virginia's Craftsmen and Military Laborers, 1861–1865** (212 pp., Duke University Press, Durham, 1969)

Brewer examines the impressive and wide range of duties performed by enslaved and free blacks in wartime Virginia who aided the Confederacy as ambulance drivers, boatmen, cooks, field laborers, iron workers, miners, railroad hands, servants, and tanners. This work provides a penetrating analysis of these contributions in Virginia and helps to establish an overall view of the black contribution to the Confederate war effort.

The author describes the rules of Confederate employment of blacks in an introductory chapter and then follows the evolution of their involvement in various aspects of the war. He systematically explores their roles in quartermaster and commissary duties, naval and ordnance work, transportation, medical services, and the business of constructing fortifications. The last category, the author shows, may have employed as many as 35,000 of Virginia's blacks, many throughout the final months of war surrounding Petersburg, though few of them were involved in other types of work such as naval operations.

Despite Brewer's capable outlining of the parts played by black Virginians, he stops short of interpreting their meaning. This is a survey that does not confront the larger questions at hand, such as the attitudes of the laborers or of the Confederate government or military toward these people. Occasional errors appear, such as naming John Letcher as Virginia's governor in 1864. The greatest disappointment is the lack of context: the narrative is sterile, devoid of the desperate tenor of the times. Certainly the subjects cooperated in their work only because the alternatives might be severe punishment or death. Still, this study has much to offer those who wish to explore the role of black men and women in wartime Virginia.

651

Cornish, Dudley Taylor. **The Sable Arm: Negro Troops in the Union Army, 1861–1865** (337 pp., Longmans, Green and Co., New York, 1956)

This well-researched and impressively documented survey treats the developing role of the Union Army's use of blacks throughout the latter months of the war. As Cornish states, "it is hard to realize how revolutionary the experiment of permitting Negroes to bear arms was considered, how fraught with imagined dangers to the Union Army, how galling to white pride."

The author reflects on that difficulty and places it masterfully in the context of the times. The great success of black troops in the war is still astonishing when one considers the appalling campaign of intimidation brought on by Confederate officials to reenslave or execute black soldiers captured in the course of the war. (This, of course, is the often neglected seed of the unraveling of prisoner exchanges during the final half of the war—contrary to a mountain of simplistic rationalizations.)

Cornish judiciously assesses the barriers to arming black troops, both from a legal sense and because of the political touchiness of the possible reactions of the border states. Once initiated, the program swiftly moved forward, and Cornish deals sensitively with various military operations without derailing the book's direction. He competently focuses on the western and eastern theaters, but essentially neglects sailors and laborers, whose service was as important as that of soldiers. With the extensive analysis, little is said of how black soldiers themselves felt about all of this.

(Reprinted 1987, with a foreword by Herman Hattaway, 342 pp., University Press of Kansas, Lawrence)

652

Cox, LaWanda. **Lincoln and Black Freedom: A Study in Presidential Leadership** (254 pp., University of South Carolina Press, Columbia, 1981)

In this superbly executed and important work, Cox analyzes Lincoln's presidential policies and political wrangling and finds that he was committed both to advancing emancipation as soon as it was feasible and, through the Louisiana experiment, to extending the citizenship rights of freedmen as far as they could be made to go.

After an introductory essay, Cox examines the Louisiana policies in three broad sections. She wisely points out that emancipation was the first step toward citizenship, and until late in the war—after the results of the autumn elections of 1864, to be precise—it was not entirely clear to anyone that slavery would be completely abolished. The many historians who have criticized Lincoln and the radicals for not acting more forcefully more quickly, the author correctly contends, do not place the historical record in proper context. Clearly Lincoln compromised or avoided stands at critical times—a necessity to keep the eventuality possible. Indeed, Cox shows that Lincoln used con-

servative rhetoric only when political expediency made it unavoidable.

653

Durden, Robert F. **The Gray and the Black: The Confederate Debate on Emancipation** (305 pp., Louisiana State University Press, Baton Rouge, 1972)

Durden explores the contradiction of Confederates arming black troops in the war. This large documentary collection of newspaper accounts, official documents, correspondence between Confederate political and military leaders, and selections from the *O.R.* (*q.v.*) allows the participants in the controversy to speak for themselves. By doing so it brings to light a significant and underanalyzed storehouse of material on a sensitive issue, but it undertakes little analysis itself.

Surely the Confederate discussion of emancipating—at least temporarily—and arming slaves speaks of the desperate and depleted condition of the Southern armies toward war's end. It hardly signals a significant moral change in the philosophy of the Confederate government or any of its most important leaders. This is evidenced by Howell Cobb's significant demonstration to Jefferson Davis that if the program Davis was pushing was implemented, it would mean that the foundation of the Confederacy was flawed—words echoed by Alexander Stephens, Robert M. T. Hunter, and a battery of others. Still, the times were terribly desperate and Davis needed fighting men.

By its nature, this work provides a window into the problem. Unfortunately, the author fails to assert that the Confederacy compromised the cornerstone of its identity to achieve military success. A far more severe error is the author's suggestion that the arming of slaves would necessarily lead to emancipation—no evidence supports this. It was strictly a temporary and brutal use of available humans and promised nothing in terms of long-range policy change.

654

Glatthaar, Joseph T. **Forged in Battle: The Civil War Alliance of Black Soldiers and White Officers** (370 pp., Free Press, New York, 1990)

Examining the relationships between black troops and their white commanders can tell us not only a great deal about the regiments and how they fought but also about the emergent emancipation controversies in both the South and the North. Readers of this tightly researched book will come away with significant new insights on both soldiers and officers.

Glatthaar sketches the rise of recruiting and training black troops, the problems with discipline and racism in the North, the methods of choosing officers, and how the two groups functioned in what was at best an uneasy partnership. He sheds light on the battlefield performance of black units and finishes with an essay on "life after the U.S.C.T.," which looks ahead to the postwar era and appraises the value of service for the private soldiers. The author shows that at certain key places, Fort Wagner, Port Hudson, and Petersburg among them, the relationship worked magnificently and produced strong support for the eventual acceptance of emancipation. He also demonstrates that this bond between black and white unraveled once the war was over.

655

Jordan, Ervin L., Jr. **Black Confederates and Afro-Yankees in Civil War Virginia** (447 pp., University Press of Virginia, Charlottesville, 1995)

Focusing on the more than half a million blacks living in Virginia during the war years, Jordan reveals the wide spectrum of their roles, as slaves but also working in factories, assisting on the battlefield, as would-be soldiers in the Confederate Army, and in the field as spies or simply as workers in towns, cities, and the countryside. The result is a more complex and realistic view than historians had previously assembled, and this book should be read by anyone who desires to understand the role of blacks in Confederate Virginia.

Supported by statistical analysis and by smoothly written prose, the narrative surveys many facets of slave life and labor on the plantation, fugitive slaves, contrabands, health, education, religion, marriage, sex, race relations, and justice. The second half examines the role of blacks on the battlefield, describing body servants at war, Afro-Confederate loyalism, black troops in the Confederate Army, the effects of the Emancipation Proclamation, black Union soldiers and spies, and the collapse of Confederate society into freedom.

656

[Pulitzer Prize, 1980]

Litwack, Leon F. **Been in the Storm So Long: The Aftermath of Slavery** (651 pp., Alfred A. Knopf, New York, 1979)

This is a sterling summation of the history of blacks during the Reconstruction period. In fact, largely because of Litwack's heroic job of research into numerous sources of great importance, this is the preeminent work on the transformation of blacks from slaves to free men and women. The author describes this "epic chapter in the history of the American people" by drawing on scattered collections of manuscripts, the papers of the Federal Writers' Project, which are employed with great care, and many governmental repositories and newspaper collections. The result is a sweeping history, with its weighty and impressive conclusions, that stands as a great achievement in the documentation of 19th-century America.

Litwack clearly views freed blacks sympathetically but does not allow this to mar his judgment regarding their assimilation into new roles. The vast complexity of situations existing during the war and particularly in the years of change does not allow generalizations. "Every plantation, every farm, every town no doubt had its own version of how the slaves behaved," Litwack writes. He goes on to examine the great transformation of those who moved and took on radically different lives, but he also examines those slaves who stayed at their wartime locations. In some of the book's best prose, Litwack uncovers the self-deception that many slaveowners shared about their property and how they discovered it only after the war when everything began to change.

657

McPherson, James M., ed. **The Negro's Civil War: How American Negroes Felt and Acted during the War for the Union** (358 pp., Pantheon Books, New York, 1965)

This collection of documents—gathered during research on the editor's previous work, *The Struggle for Equality* (*q.v.*)—adds significantly to the picture of black men and women and their wartime experiences. Particularly striking accounts include a contraband witnessing the horror of Missionary Ridge and Sojourner Truth's experiences in wartime Washington. The editor has constructed a skillfully woven narrative that blends many of the materials while it carefully interprets them.

McPherson's choice of documents and analysis concentrates on how blacks felt about the war and on their eventual fate, including their attitudes toward emancipation, colonization, and fighting for their freedom. Perhaps simply because of their availability, the accounts focus mainly on the upper class of blacks during the war period. The editor's superb biographical essays provide a context so that readers can glean a lasting picture from this work, one that admirably supplements the previous book.

658

McPherson, James M. **The Struggle for Equality: Abolitionists and the Negro in the Civil War and Reconstruction** (474 pp., Princeton University Press, Princeton, 1964)

Meticulously researched and characterized by sound judgments and many insights, this work is a standard in its class. McPherson documents the evolution and success of abolitionists during the 1860s by showing their struggle for equality rather than just emancipation. The thesis builds a concrete respectability throughout the discussion of military involvement for blacks, benefits such as education and land for freedmen, and political rights for the newly liberated. The author analyzes skillfully the various problems faced by abolitionists and the delicate political balance they had to maintain.

McPherson slightly downplays the psychology of the era by claiming that abolitionists quickly earned respect and admiration across the North. Despite this contention, the work is a pillar in understanding the social and political revolution that resulted from the war.

(Reprinted 1995, with a new preface by the author, 474 pp., Princeton University Press, Princeton)

659

Mohr, Clarence L. **On the Threshold of Freedom: Masters and Slaves in Civil War Georgia** (397 pp., University of Georgia Press, Athens, 1986)

The author examines the complex and changing relationships between Georgia slaves and slaveholders during the war. Cautiously written and carefully researched, this is an outstanding study of slavery in a single state during the war. Mohr segregates his narrative into three broad areas, that of rebellion by both slaves and their masters, slaves and the changing conditions of wartime Georgia, and the final, desperate measures considered by Georgia Confederates regarding slavery to preserve antebellum Southern society. The narrative creatively explores each of these areas, weaving an interesting and highly illuminating tale of slavery's demise as it journeys through four years of war.

Slavery was transformed during the war in the urban areas of Georgia, on plantations, and in other work locales. The picture of black relations with the "invading" Union Army comes into clear view, as do refugee adventures of slaveholders and the collapse of bondage in Georgia's rural communities. The author's research shows clearly how the war ruined the slave system, rapidly destroyed it as the Union armies entered Georgia. Mohr demonstrates that freedom was indeed the preeminent concern for Georgia's

slaves and that had an offer of Confederate military service come earlier, it may have attracted a large number of slaves.

660

Ripley, C. Peter. **Slaves and Freedmen in Civil War Louisiana** (237 pp., Louisiana State University Press, Baton Rouge, 1976)

Ripley argues that the seeds of Reconstruction as it occurred were planted during the war itself. Moreover, he believes that Reconstruction policies specifically involving freedmen were initiated as much in wartime Louisiana (following the capture of New Orleans) as in the Sea Islands of South Carolina. The author further suggests that Lincoln's conservative program of Reconstruction first took hold in Louisiana as slaves remained on plantations, under control, largely to pacify landowners. That stated, Ripley compares the wartime Louisiana policies with those of postwar Reconstruction and finds great similarities.

In an effort to stay on track, the author ignores some significant changes. Postwar Reconstruction may not have brought immediate freedom to slaves, but it did lay the groundwork for the true freedom that finally arrived. Moreover, his comparisons imply that Reconstruction under the radicals was a fair test—but that requires the assumption that had Lincoln lived, he would have done exactly the same thing. Such reasoning strains the credibility of the argument in places. Still, the author's assessments of soldiers and education are particularly good, and he has supported much of his discussion with tabular material.

661

Rose, Willie Lee. **Rehearsal for Reconstruction: The Port Royal Experiment** (442 pp., Bobbs-Merrill Co., Indianapolis, 1964)

No more immediate marriage of military and societal matters arose from the war than that which transpired on 7 November 1861 in the Sea Islands of South Carolina. Attacked by Samuel F. Du Pont's fleet, the residents of the area fled and left behind 10,000 slaves. As soon as Federal soldiers landed and occupied the region, the question became what to do with the liberated slaves. The trial run for emancipation began, in its sloppy and disorganized way, before the first year of war had ended, freeing slaves, educating them, providing land for some, and ultimately allowing others to fight for universal freedom.

Rose's description of the Port Royal Experiment reads brilliantly and is meticulously researched and documented. The narrative of the collapse of plantation society in the region and the arrival of "Gideon's Band" of 50 New England abolitionists in March 1862 absorbs the intellect and paints a vivid picture of how quickly the war changed America. Although it is mired in messy and often conflicting details of what transpired, this work communicates the urgency of the freedom question and foreshadows the even more chaotic era of Reconstruction that would follow.

(Reprinted 1976, 442 pp., Oxford University Press, New York)

662

Voegeli, V. Jacque. **Free but Not Equal: The Midwest and the Negro during the Civil War** (215 pp., University of Chicago Press, Chicago, 1967)

The author explores the exodus of blacks to the Midwest before and during the war and the Republican search for policy relating to this movement. Before the war many ex-slaves migrated north to the cities and the farm fields of the fertile (and less hostile) midwest. The chaos of war in the South, accelerated by emancipation, caused this northward flow to increase dramatically. Midwestern Yankees were in large part uncomfortable with this increasing phenomenon, fueled substantially by the fear-mongering of Democratic propaganda. Voegeli's thesis examines the reactions of Northern whites and the experiences of freedmen in this slow changing of the cultural makeup of the North.

Republicans denied they wanted to make equals out of blacks, contending that ex-slaves would not stay in the Midwest because of the climate and their inability to compete for industrial jobs. As emancipation solidified into reality, Republicans mocked the Democrats' insincere concerns over freedmen and linked a lack of support for emancipation with treason. Still, as the author demonstrates, Republicans insisted that emancipation was a military necessity rather than a humanitarian social revolution.

This study succeeds in showing the effects of much of the early history of emancipation. It belongs in all collections of black history and should be read by anyone with a genuine interest in the societal fallout of the war.

663

Wood, Forrest G. **The Black Scare: The Racist Response to Emancipation and Reconstruction** (219 pp., University of California Press, Berkeley, 1968)

This author explores the white backlash against the earliest days of black freedom, drawing on a reasonable survey of Democratic newspapers and racist literature of the war and immediate postwar years to construct a delicate argu-

ment. Even though Wood asserts that Southerners and even many Northerners held white supremacy as a lofty truth, his analysis concentrates on a small, very vocal minority of Southern and Democratic racists. He surveys the reaction of this group to emancipation, the enlistment of black troops, and the resistance of many to Reconstruction policies relating to blacks. In doing so, he demolishes the statements and viewpoints he reviews—often in emotionally charged language—as irrational.

Wood erroneously states that Lincoln did not attempt to carry on with plans for black colonization. He believes the 1864 elections buried racist reaction until the postwar years, and he oversimplifies the discussion of the controversies over black suffrage, the creation of the Freedmen's Bureau, and the passage of the Thirteenth Amendment. Still, he treads ground that has been weakly investigated by others and offers a mostly useful picture of an ugly subject.

CIVIL WAR BATTLEFIELDS

664

Eicher, David J. **Civil War Battlefields: A Touring Guide** (228 pp., Taylor Publishing Co., Dallas, 1995)

This guide contains the most modern and complete set of battlefield tours, providing coverage down to individual monuments and correcting some errors extending back to the beginning of the 20th century. Based on an on-site study of the battlefields, the guide presents 41 area and detail maps covering some 22 campaigns and approximately 40 separate battles. There are 12 sections: Antietam, South Mountain, and Harpers Ferry; Bull Run; Chattanooga; Chickamauga; Fredericksburg, Chancellorsville, the Wilderness, and Spotsylvania; Gettysburg; Petersburg, Five Forks, and Appomattox Court House; Richmond and City Point; the Shenandoah Valley; Shiloh; Stones River, Franklin, and Spring Hill; and Vicksburg.

The text provides a brief summary of the strategy and tactics of each battle followed by a lengthy tour of specific sites of relevance to see on each battlefield area. The coverage includes lands owned by the Federal government, state governments, and private owners. Altogether, 1353 specific features are described, including houses, farms, bridges, fields, monuments, cemeteries, and museums. Sidebars list statistical data about the parks and cemeteries and 129 photographs illustrate key sights. The work includes maps by John H. Eicher and a foreword by James M. McPherson.

665

Kennedy, Frances H., ed. **The Civil War Battlefield Guide** (317 pp., Houghton Mifflin Co., Boston, 1990)

This work is inaccurately named, as it does not offer a guide to the battlefields. Instead, Kennedy's book consists of many short sections on battles, the text describing the action of the battle itself, accompanied by color photos of areas of some battlefields. The maps included do not show battlefields as they are today but are "blitzkrieg" maps purporting to show troop movements. They are of the most general character and lack detail, with large, sweeping arrows representing attacks and withdrawals.

Still, this book is made worthwhile by the superb text written by a large number of contributors. These include Edwin C. Bearss, Gary W. Gallagher, Herman Hattaway, Robert K. Krick, Jay Luvaas, James M. McPherson, James I. Robertson, Jr., John Y. Simon, and Richard J. Sommers.

666

Thomas, Emory M. **Travels to Hallowed Ground: A Historian's Journey to the American Civil War** (155 pp., University of South Carolina Press, Columbia, 1987)

A reflective diary of a Southern historian's battlefield journeys, this work delivers a bit of history, some personal anecdotes, and reflections on what the battlefields mean to Americans today. The result is an enjoyable and very different view of Civil War battlefields that echoes thoughts many enthusiasts experience but rarely see in print. The fields and sites covered are Harpers Ferry, Bull Run, Roanoke Island, Shiloh, Fort Pulaski, the route of Stuart's ride around McClellan, Richmond and the Kilpatrick-Dahlgren raid, Kennesaw Mountain, Mobile Bay, Petersburg, and Bennett Place. The battle areas covered are clearly not all the biggest or most commonly discussed, and this, along with the author's charming style, makes for splendid readability. Sixteen photographs—a few historical and a few modern—and seven maps accompany the text.

The author explores interesting themes such as Thomas's ancestral home outside Richmond and its wartime experiences, the odd contrast between modern America and the solemn dignity of the battlefields, and the horror of the war at Petersburg, wherein photographers purposely focused on the corpses in the hope that their images would prevent war from touching American soil again. The chapter on Stuart's ride is reworked material from the author's full biography of Stuart (*q.v.*). A number of misspellings appear throughout the book, as with Barnard E. Bee, John C. Breckinridge, Quincy Gillmore, and Irvin McDowell.

THE COMING OF THE WAR

667

Craven, Avery. **The Coming of the Civil War** (491 pp., Charles Scribner's Sons, New York, 1942)

The central revisionist statement of the causation of the war, Craven's thesis states that war could have been avoided and was essentially permitted by the neglect of Northerners and Southerners who allowed a small group of politicians to overemotionalize and distort the picture of what was happening to a level of exaggerated alarm. Moreover, Craven asserts that slavery was not the dominating cause of the war and that it "played a rather minor part in the life of the South and of the Negro."

These thought-provoking statements and many others in this work provide a basis for reinterpreting many elements of the coming of the war. Yet they dismiss much contemporary evidence to the contrary and deliver an oversimplified and distressing portrait of blacks during the Civil War era, downplaying slavery as more of a symbolic problem than a real one.

A new edition with minor changes was published in 1957 (491 pp., University of Chicago Press, Chicago). Among the changes was a toning down of the revisionist aspects of Craven's arguments. The body of evidence toward exaggeration by politicians is solid, yet the claims of exaggeration are far more easily established in the backward vision of the 20th-century historian than from the perspective of a citizen of 1861. Rational Northerners might have believed that a slavocracy would envelop the United States; and Southerners' fears of "Black Republicanism" precipitating a race war may have been rational.

668

Stampp, Kenneth M. **And the War Came: The North and the Secession Crisis, 1860–1861** (331 pp., Louisiana State University Press, Baton Rouge, 1950)

In the best summary of the sectional conflict and the North's reaction to it, Stampp skillfully documents the central cause of the war, that the South wanted slavery to expand and the North resisted it at all costs. The detail and powerful logic of this work are evident on every page. Stampp concentrates on the period of political crisis from the last weeks of 1860 to the firing on Fort Sumter. He argues that the Southern cause was tenuous because it lacked a strong central identity: "Except for the institution of slavery, the South had little to give it a clear national identity." The notion of a distinct Southern culture was, the author claims, largely a figment of the imagination. According to Stampp, religion, background, politics, and other characteristics were close to those of the North, and the romantic ideas about Southern individuality were largely the products of propaganda.

Stampp provides a first-class description of the roots of the crisis, defines the characters involved, and moves through a chronology of the major events in the weeks of paramount crisis. He keenly portrays Buchanan's ineffectiveness, credits Lincoln with a realistic, careful handling of a very difficult situation, and examines the actions of the politicians and militarists in the Southern states.

(Reprinted 1970, 331 pp., Louisiana State University Press, Baton Rouge)

669

Stampp, Kenneth M. **The Imperiled Union: Essays on the Background of the Civil War** (320 pp., Oxford University Press, New York, 1980)

Eight keenly perceptive essays provide a masterful commentary (two are new; the others appeared in journals before inclusion in this book). Stampp explores the concept of a perpetual Union, the slaves' search for identity, an analysis of Robert Fogel and Stanley Engerman's *Time on the Cross*, slavery and the Republican party of the 1850s, the Republican National Convention of 1860, Lincoln's behavior and motives during the secession crisis, the "irrepressible conflict," and the Southerners' road to Appomattox.

This volume is a summation and extension of themes raised by the author over his long career. He unravels many related issues in each of these essays to view the core problem and finds slavery the central issue that brought on the war. Indeed, in his concluding chapter Stampp suggests that Southerners, because they adhered to an archaic aristocracy that had been virtually abandoned by the rest of the world, created abolitionists. The work's final sentence reads: "The fatal weakness of the Confederacy was that not enough of its people really thought that defeat would be a catastrophe; and, moreover, I believe that many of them unconsciously felt that the fruits of defeat would be less bitter than those of success." Many historians might argue with that interpretation, but the conclusions found in the other essays, particularly those on the Republicans and slaves, are less arguable.

THE COMMON SOLDIERS

670

Barton, Michael. **Goodmen: The Character of Civil War Soldiers** (135 pp., Pennsylvania State University Press, University Park, 1981)

This is a thin and highly speculative evaluation of the character of Southern and Northern soldiers who fought in the war. Using sociological methodology, the author examines the diaries and letters of more than 400 soldiers, placing them into the following categories: Confederate officers, Confederate enlisted men, Federal officers, and Federal enlisted men. The author then interprets what he found using 82 tracers of a wide variety of information.

The work's thesis suggests that Civil War soldiers North and South were good men who shared the same values. Significant differences were found between Confederate officers and Union enlisted men, with the remaining two groups somewhere in between. While curious, the work suffers from two major problems: deriving meaning from such a small sample stretches one's credibility in an analytical sense; and interpreting complex meanings and issues from the papers of persons long dead is risky at best. While the author's conclusions merit evaluation, the work is "soft" science.

671

Burton, William L. **Melting Pot Soldiers: The Union's Ethnic Regiments** (282 pp., Iowa State University Press, Ames, 1988)

Burton examines the significant role of immigrant and foreign soldiers on the Federal side of the war. He sets the stage with an introductory chapter on ethnic politics of the prewar period so that readers may understand the significance of ethnicity for individual units. The stories of many important ethnic regiments are examined in roughly chronological fashion. Chapters deal with the performance and makeup of German regiments, Irish regiments, and others, including Scottish, Norwegian, Spanish, French, Italian, and Hungarian soldiers. In particular, regiments from New York, Cincinnati, Milwaukee, Chicago, and Philadelphia contributed much of the ethnic flavor of the Union Army. Throughout the telling of how these regiments performed, the author introduces and examines many important officers, including Louis Blenker, Franz Sigel, William H. Lytle, August Willich, Augustus Moor, Hans C. Heg, Geza Mihalotzy, and Daniel Cameron.

The work includes an overview, state by state, that introduces readers to many of the important units and their commanders, sketching their successes and failures on the canvas of Civil War history. Interpretation or analysis, however, is light. The author presents much of his information without conveying a cohesive direction or statement, so the reader is left having enjoyed the work but wondering slightly what came of it.

672

Linderman, Gerald F. **Embattled Courage: The Experience of Combat in the American Civil War** (357 pp., Free Press, New York, 1987)

Linderman provides intelligent and worthwhile observations on what motivated Union and Confederate soldiers in their four-year fight. He has carefully chosen a multitude of primary sources from common soldiers and a number of officers who rose to high grades to reflect on the meaning of the Civil War combat experience. Familiar and significant accounts are here, including those of Confederates William W. Blackford, John O. Casler, John Esten Cooke, James C. Nisbet, Elisha F. Paxton, and Robert Stiles. Union contributors include Henry Livermore Abbott, Robert Goldthwaite Carter, Joshua L. Chamberlain, Rufus R. Dawes, Theodore Lyman, Robert Gould Shaw, and Stephen Minot Weld, Jr. Most of the source writings from which the author synthesized his account appear in the original form in this work. He has chosen wisely and uses the material in clever and admirable fashion to show us something important about the soldiers who fought the war.

The author describes the various origins of courage in soldiers on both sides and demonstrates how this important commodity contributed to victories before the grueling horror of war shredded the soldiers' illusions by the perilous summer of 1864. Through the viewpoints of these significant soldiers who left worthwhile accounts, Linderman tells how, by the last year of the war, battle-hardened veterans simply wanted it to be over.

673

McPherson, James M. **What They Fought For, 1861–1865** (88 pp., Louisiana State University Press, Baton Rouge, 1994)

Why did common soldiers fight? The author has drawn on more than 1000 letters and diaries from Union and Confederate soldiers to divine an answer to this question. In the published text of a series of Walter Lynwood Fleming lectures, McPherson strikes at the generally accepted notion that Civil War soldiers had no idea what they were fighting for. ("And they fought anyway," a Civil War buff wrote recently. "That's what made them heroes.")

McPherson offers evidence that many Civil War soldiers on both sides knew exactly what they were fighting for, while others at least had a vague knowledge of the philosophical issues. Liberty and republicanism dominated the stage. According to McPherson, Confederate and Union soldiers interpreted the same documents of freedom in opposite ways: Confederates fought for liberty against a tyrannical government, while Federals fought to prevent the destruction of American liberty. This slim book's three chapters examine Confederate themes, Union themes, and the issue of slavery as viewed by both sides.

674

Mitchell, Reid. **Civil War Soldiers: Their Expectations and Their Experiences** (274 pp., Viking, New York, 1988)

The author explores the psychology of Civil War soldiers on both sides, what motivated them, and how they perceived the war effort. In an introductory section, Mitchell skillfully lays down the similarities between the Union and Confederate motivations to fight: that despite how different the causes might be in actuality, the principles at stake engendered the same emotions on both sides. Subsequent chapters investigate the psychology of Civil War service, the Union soldier and his attitudes toward the South, and the experience of combat as a Confederate soldier.

Mitchell describes each side's depiction of the other as savages, the standard rationalization of war as a mechanism of combating guilt. In contrast to other authors, including Gerald Linderman (*q.v.*), Mitchell contends that the years of war that followed Sumter hardened the men into determination. He suggests that the military conquering of the South was intended to rewrite the Southern identity into that of the North.

This book contains much of interest, some of it in conflict with similar works, and so provides a piece of the puzzle that defines the psychology of the common soldier. An occasional error occurs, as with misspellings of Kinston, North Carolina, and Thaddeus Stevens.

675

Robertson, James I., Jr. **Soldiers Blue and Gray** (340 pp., University of South Carolina Press, Columbia, 1988)

Working primarily with material that has come to light or simply been used for the first time in several decades, Robertson extends Wiley's (*q.v.*) examination of the basic social experience of being a Civil War soldier. The chapters treat such subjects as the psychology of common soldiers going off to war, the organization of units, the experience of camp life, the hardships of soldier life, discipline, medical aspects, religion, and incarceration as prisoners. The book excels because of its logical, tight organization and the extensive use of quotations from the soldiers themselves; it is on somewhat weaker ground in drawing certain conclusions, due to the scant supporting evidence presented.

Nevertheless, this is a thoroughly enjoyable work, written with zest. The goal of delivering for general readers a taste of what life was like as a Civil War soldier is achieved magnificently. Numerous enthralling anecdotes lie scattered throughout, keeping the narrative moving swiftly and delivering a clear overview. The author shows signs of Southern partisanship, as with the forgiving and rationalized description of Andersonville Prison. Several references to sources appear garbled, such as the apparent reference to Sam Clemens's *Private History of a Campaign That Failed* as if it were a factual account. The author speaks of George Gibb's tale of life as a Mississippi private as if it were composed many years after the war, but later he refers to it as if it were written during the war. He incorrectly states that Thomas Wentworth Higginson led the attack of the 54th Massachusetts at Fort Wagner, South Carolina, when the regiment's colonel was the celebrated Robert Gould Shaw. Despite these and other errors, a great deal of insight on the war's common soldiers is conveyed.

676

Wiley, Bell Irvin. **The Life of Billy Yank: The Common Soldier of the Union** (453 pp., Bobbs-Merrill Co., Indianapolis, 1952)

Like the author's earlier work on the Confederate soldier (*q.v.*), this book stands as a massive survey of the letters, diaries, and anecdotes of common soldiers and how the war experience affected them, this time from the perspective of the Yankee soldiers. After painting a portrait of the makeup of the Union soldiers and their motivation to fight the war, Wiley describes the various aspects of life in camp, on march, and in battle as the Northern soldier lived it. No important aspect of soldier life lies untouched, from food and equipment to entertainment, communication, and religion. The result is a significant synthesis that, despite more recent works on common soldiers, still stands as a monumental work.

Told in large part in the words of the soldiers themselves, the descriptions of life in the army are vivid and forceful. Readers travel to the army along with the young boys expecting a quick war; they experience harsh winter camp life, brutal imprisonment, and the joy of playing cards and writing letters around the campfire. Foraging and cooking are amply discussed, as is drilling and the relentlessness of the march. The author suggests that the Northern and Southern boys who made up most of the war's fighting forces were pretty much the same, divided only by the cultural and political issues that surfaced so violently and so unavoidably in the 1860s.

(Reprinted 1993, 453 pp., Louisiana State University Press, Baton Rouge)

677

Wiley, Bell Irvin. **The Life of Johnny Reb: The Common Soldier of the Confederacy** (444 pp., Bobbs-Merrill Co., Indianapolis, 1943)

This classic stands as the first great exploration of the common soldier in the war. Wiley surveys the variety of camp, battle, and march experiences of Rebel soldiers to provide a pure portrait of what life must have been like in the eastern and western theaters. Drawing on a great variety of sources including large numbers of soldier letters, diaries, and reminiscences, he reconstructs a glimpse not only of battle but principally of the human aspects of soldiering in the war. Readers experience the weapons, food, entertainment, communication, psychology, and personalities of Confederate soldiers. The result is a valuable addition to the usual dry accounts of marches and battles that are viewed from a commanding general's quarters.

The skillful organization and infrequent editorial intrusion of the author allows the story of the Confederate soldiers to come principally from the soldiers themselves. Clearly the majority of Southern fighters were poorly educated and labored under delusions of grandeur when it came to sizing up their Yankee opponents. The portrait of the Confederate soldier herein is not always complimentary, but it is accurate. The evolution of the spirit of the Confederate soldier is arresting, from boastful innocence to battle-hardened experience to loss of any deep care for The Cause. The treatment is realistic, to be sure, but also highly respectful toward one of the great classes of soldiers in the history of warfare.

(Reprinted 1993, 444 pp., Louisiana State University Press, Baton Rouge)

CONFEDERATE STUDIES

678

Abel, Annie Heloise. **The American Indian in the Civil War** (3 vols., 1216 pp., titled *The American Indian as Slaveholder and Secessionist: An Omitted Chapter in the Diplomatic History of the Southern Confederacy, The American Indian as Participant in the Civil War*, and *The American Indian under Reconstruction*, Arthur H. Clark Co., Cleveland, 1915–1925)

Although dated, this remains a useful work. The set is based on extensive and careful research in a variety of manuscript collections as well as the standard sources. In the first volume, Abel surveys the diplomatic alliances created between various tribes and the young Confederacy. She suggests that Indians departed from cooperation with the United States because the government neglected them.

The study contains little analysis of the internal policies of Indian nations and employs language that conjures racist, antiquated notions of minority behavior. The narrative is based on erroneous ideas about the value of slavery in the Southern states, yet it neatly summarizes the relationship between Indian tribes and the institution. The style is tedious. A number of military matters, the most important being the battle of Pea Ridge, figure prominently. Abel's discussion of the Indian participation at this western battle is well done. The work concludes by examining the abandonment of Indian policy during the war and the Reconstruction treaties of 1866.

(Reprinted 1992–1993, titled *The American Indian as Slaveholder and Secessionist* [394 pp., 1992], *The American Indian in the Civil War, 1862–1865* [403 pp., 1992], and *The American Indian and the End of the Confederacy, 1863–1866* [419 pp., 1993], with introductions by Theda Perdue and Michael D. Green, University of Nebraska Press, Lincoln)

679

Ball, Douglas B. **Financial Failure and Confederate Defeat** (329 pp., University of Illinois Press, Urbana, 1991)

This study seeks a revised answer for the military loss of the Confederacy. Dismissing the superior resources theory and others including a failure of Confederate will, poor battlefield performance, or state rights preventing cooperation with Richmond, Ball suggests that poor money management contributed significantly to Confederate defeat.

The author presents a compilation of historical economic theory and examines the personalities involved with Confederate finances. He finds Christopher G. Memminger a disastrous choice for treasury secretary and variously blames

Jefferson Davis, yet he sides with Davis against alternative might-have-been choices for a Confederate president. The powers in Richmond isolated themselves from Europe by employing a cotton embargo, neglected management of blockade-runners, wasted money by not establishing a central purchasing system, did not buy European bonds, and repeatedly bungled currency management. The failure to pay soldiers adequately or on time contributed in some cases to material disasters for the Confederate armies. Other financial oversights ruined the possibility of building ironclads in New Orleans early on, which, if they had been available, might have prevented the city's fall.

Many more such examples characterize this well-written book, which sheds a bright light on a heretofore neglected aspect of the Confederate failure but does not convincingly present this area as *the* most important factor for defeat. The most important factor, of course, was the defeat of the Confederate armies on the battlefield.

680

Brownlee, Richard S. **Gray Ghosts of the Confederacy: Guerrilla Warfare in the West, 1861–1865** (274 pp., Louisiana State University Press, Baton Rouge, 1958)

A neglected aspect of the western war comes to life in Brownlee's story of infamous rogues of the day: William Quantrill, "Bloody Bill" Anderson, Jesse and Frank James, and the Youngers. The author has adroitly woven a large amount of background material into a competent, chronological story that begins after the battle of Wilson's Creek on 10 August 1861 and ends with the violent and unglamorous deaths of Quantrill and the others.

A new, desperate, and vicious set of warriors emerges in Brownlee's portrait, combing the border war from Missouri to Texas in pursuit of glory and the Confederate cause. Although the author supports his claim that the guerrillas ably served the Confederacy, the overwhelming force of their actions informs the reader of the frequently senseless murder they introduced into warfare. The point comes home most strongly in the author's account of the Lawrence Massacre. Quantrill instructed his mob to kill every man "big enough to carry a gun," which resulted in the deaths of 150 civilians and the destruction of nearly the entire town in the two hours that followed. The retaliation from Union Brig. Gen. Thomas Ewing, Jr., included expulsion of the inhabitants of four Missouri counties. The Burnt District of western Missouri stood in silent testimony to the new, savage face of war.

(Reprinted 1984, 274 pp., Louisiana State University Press, Baton Rouge)

681

Coulter, E. Merton. **The Confederate States of America, 1861–1865** (644 pp., Louisiana State University Press, Baton Rouge, 1950)

Published as volume 7 of the series A History of the South, this is an impressively detailed, sweeping survey of the Confederate experience. Not only are summaries of the military progression of the Confederacy presented but also insightful and important summations of the secession crisis, the genesis and evolution of the Confederate government, the actions of the Confederate Congress, logistics and supply, manufacturing, patriotism, agriculture, labor, transportation and communication, trade and the blockade-runners, disloyalty, women's activities, the home front, literary activities, the press, and Southern morale and the will to fight. Such a mammoth survey might suggest poorly detailed analyses. However, this work is thorough and intelligently selective in what it chooses to highlight. The overall effect, therefore, is about as comprehensive and valuable an overview of the Confederacy as one could expect to find within a single volume.

Coulter infuses striking observations into many parts of the text. The irony of a powerful patriotic surge for the infant Confederacy at war's outset contrasts with the work's assertion that "the Confederacy never became an emotional reality to the people until Reconstruction made it so after the war had been lost." The author shows that the principle of state rights, the very heart of the Confederate cause, laid to rest hopes for success because the individual states distrusted the Richmond government. Nearly half a century after its publication, this work stands up handsomely.

682

Crofts, Daniel W. **Reluctant Confederates: Upper South Unionists in the Secession Crisis** (502 pp., University of North Carolina Press, Chapel Hill, 1989)

The author provides an exhaustive view into an important but overlooked aspect of a few months in late 1860 and early 1861. Crofts examines in detail the activities of pro-Unionists in Virginia, North Carolina, and Tennessee during the period between South Carolina's secession and Lincoln's first call for volunteers. The author contends that in these three states the party system survived the initial crisis and the states did not immediately secede. The Upper South of his study contained strong pro-Unionist sentiments in various regions because of a low number of slaveholders.

Crofts uses voting records to show that the elections of 1860 effectively separated those who did not own slaves from the mainline southern Democratic party. Thus he explores the political middle ground: a Unionist group in the Upper South that could not fully agree with the Northern Republicans yet also felt the Southern Democrats were deranged by supporting slavery staunchly enough to divide the nation. Lincoln's call effectively ended the Unionist movement in the South, but the echoes of this brief period, the author shows, continued on and helped to divide the Confederacy even as it began a long war.

683

Cunningham, Sumner Archibald, and Edith D. Pope, eds. **Confederate Veteran** (40 vols., 21,886 pp., S. A. Cunningham, Nashville, 1893–1932)

Published monthly in the interest of Confederate veterans and kindred topics," this voluminous collection spans the years during which memorializing the Confederacy transformed into celebrating the Confederacy. The *Confederate Veteran* is a potpourri of biographical reminiscences, anecdotes, poetry, random thoughts, classic advertisements, and tall stories of the war from the unreconstructed Southern point of view. A huge quantity of war reminiscences and expositions exists here, much of it valuable and much of it worthless, but taken together it conveys the spirit of the Confederate soldier in a powerful way.

The *Veteran* transformed into an official organ of the United Confederate Veterans (U.C.V.), the United Daughters of the Confederacy, the Confederate Southern Memorial Association, and the Sons of Confederate Veterans. Cunningham ably edited the project from its inception until his death in 1913, when his secretary, Edith D. Pope, assumed the editorship for the life of the publication. The content leans toward extreme editorial diversity. Reader contributions soothed the Southern mind in the years prior to the turn of the century. Each issue contains a blend of feature articles, notes, letters, editorials, poems, biographies, and advertisements, as well as departments such as book reviews and "The Last Roll," paying homage to the recently departed. The publication ceased in 1932 due to a combination of declining numbers of veterans and the onset of the Depression.

In 1986 Broadfoot Publishing Company of Wilmington, North Carolina, published a three-volume, 2387-page cumulative index to the *Veteran*. (Broadfoot also reprinted the entire *Veteran* itself, bound in cloth.) Edited by Louis Manarin, the index makes using the publication for research purposes a joy rather than a frustration. Included in the index are suggestions on how to identify Confederate soldiers, a list of battle synonyms, a roster of Confederate military organizations by local designations and by military units, and a list of U.C.V. camps and posts.

684

Current, Richard Nelson, Paul D. Escott, Lawrence N. Powell, James I. Robertson, Jr., and Emory M. Thomas, eds. **Encyclopedia of the Confederacy** (4 vols., 1916 pp., Simon and Schuster, New York, 1993)

This is a landmark work of Confederate history. The quality, depth of coverage, and wide array of topics covered in the entries are magnificent. The many contributors are experts in the fields they write about, giving the sections not only an authoritative quality but also making them a source for the latest knowledge about each of the myriad topics. There are short articles about all phases of the Confederacy, including military, political, social, and economic aspects, biographies, bibliographical references, and special subjects. The coverage is much more extensive than that of many earlier works, such as Ezra J. Warner's *Generals in Gray* (*q.v.*), so readers glean valuable details. The accounts of Jefferson Davis, Robert E. Lee, Stonewall Jackson, and Jeb Stuart set a high standard of academic excellence.

Such an encyclopedia permits exploring at length many fascinating and key aspects of the Confederacy, such as state rights, slavery, the South's preparation for war, supplies, logistics, railroads, flags, nationalism, foreign intervention, women in the Confederacy, prisons, Indians, and the reasons for Confederate defeat. All are handled beautifully, but none better than James M. McPherson's concluding essay on the explanations for Confederate failure.

In terms of high commanders of the Confederacy, the editors included 7 generals, 17 lieutenant generals, 69 major generals, 306 brigadier generals, 1 militia major general, 3 militia brigadier generals, 1 admiral, 1 rear admiral, 17 executives, 30 governors, 1 might-have-been major generals, and 35 might-have-been brigadier generals. Not included are the officials George Deas and Robert Ould and governors Rufus B. Bullock, John L. Helm, Benjamin F. Perry, Fletcher S. Stockdale, James W. Throckmorton, and James Whitfield. The work treats only 4 militia generals "nationalized" into Confederate service and erroneously includes as general officers the unconfirmed Maj. Gen. Jeremy F. Gilmer and Brig. Gens. Turner Ashby, Arthur P. Bagby, John D. Barry, Samuel Benton, Theodore W. Brevard, Thomas R. R. Cobb, James Dearing, Xavier B. DeBray, James Deshler, John Dunovant, John W. Frazer, Isham W. Garrott, Victor J. B. Girardey, Archibald C. Godwin, James M. Goggin, Benjamin F. Gordon, Robert H. Hatton, George B. Hodge, Sidney Jackman, Adam R. Johnson, John R. Jones, Wilburn H. King, Robert P. Maclay, Lucius B. Northrop, Edward A. O'Neal, James E. Rains, Horace Randal, Felix H. Robertson, Pierre Soulé, Thomas H. Taylor, Alexander W. Terrell, and Bryan M. Thomas. There are also entries for "acting" Brig. Gen. Francis S. Bartow and the unconfirmed might-have-been Brig. Gen. Basil C. Duke. The work contains a few misspellings, and D. H. Hill is erroneously listed as a lieutenant general. Four brigadier generals are listed as major generals. The editors represent 17 of the above might-have-been general officers as true generals.

As a general compendium on many widely scattered topics relating to the Confederacy, this work is invaluable. For more on it, see Joseph G. Dawson III, "The Confederacy Revisited: *Encyclopedia of the Confederacy*," *Civil War History* 40 (1994): 308.

Also of great potential interest for students of the Confederacy is *The Roster of Confederate Soldiers, 1861–1865* (ed. Janet B. Hewett, 510 pp., Broadfoot, Wilmington, 1995–   ). Only 1 of 14 proposed volumes has thus far been issued, but the set will ultimately provide names and units for all Confederate soldiers. Volume 1 contains an alphabetical listing through G. W. R. Bell.

685

Davis, William C. **"A Government of Our Own": The Making of the Confederacy** (550 pp., Free Press, New York, 1994)

This extraordinary work adds greatly to the story of the genesis of the Confederate nation. Written with skill and cheerfulness and soundly researched in primary and limited secondary sources, the book brings to life the unlikely story of the founding of Confederate politics. The author, a biographer of Jefferson Davis, naturally places the Confederate president front and center in many of the passages. But he also reflects on the secondary characters of the political experiment, including Alexander Stephens, Robert A. Toombs, and the wheeling-and-dealing Cobb brothers of Georgia.

Davis begins his narrative with the first echoes of war in May 1861 and backtracks to examine the seeds of secession fever, likening the Confederate politicians gathering in the Deep South to the original Founding Fathers. He describes beautifully the condition of Montgomery in 1861, presents his cast of characters, and allows the record to speak for itself, interspersing his reactions to the noble and not so noble as the story progresses. The writing is vivid, the facts secure. The result is an impressive story of the Montgomery Convention and the coming together of a Southern alliance. The book ends abruptly as the war itself swings into high gear. An epilogue casts a backward glance on the whole affair from the detached passion of 25 years hence.

686

Davis William C., ed. **The Confederate General** (6 vols., 1279 pp., National Historical Society, Harrisburg, Pa., 1991)

The principal photographic study of Confederate generals, this book offers a brief biography of each one and attempts to deliver a reproduction of every known wartime uniformed image of each. Several of these, however, show the commanders in civilian dress, occasionally before or after the war, or are simply engravings where no photo has come to light—one of the attributes of Ezra Warner's *Generals in Gray* (*q.v.*) criticized by Davis in his introduction. Indeed, one wonders why the stated requisite of a uniformed portrait is the goal and not portraits made during the war years, whatever the attire. Moreover, dozens of the photographs in this and earlier works feature uniforms painted on photographs, figments of an artist's imagination. The effort to assemble this work is nevertheless admirable, its exhaustive research in many repositories uncovering many little known or previously unpublished wartime images. The texts were written by a distinguished group of contributors.

Apart from the superb collection of 808 photographs, the accompanying narratives offer longer and more varied appraisals than those of Warner. Editor Davis includes 7 generals, 17 lieutenant generals, 69 major generals, 306 brigadier generals, 1 militia major general, 2 militia brigadier generals, 1 rear admiral, 1 executive, 1 might-have-been major general, and 34 might-have-been brigadier generals. A number of errors appear, as in volume 1 with the misspellings of Stephen D. Lee and Jefferson Davis and incorrect information on Rufus Barringer's place of birth, William Nelson Rector Beall's birthdate and standing in his West Point class, the battle of Kinston, North Carolina, Abraham Buford's date of birth, and the dates of the battle of Stones River.

Davis includes a section of photographs of "the generals who weren't," illustrating some of the numerous persons who claimed to be general officers although they did not go through the straightforward process that produced a general officer's commission—being appointed by President Davis and confirmed by the Confederate Senate. Any claim of a general officer's grade without that process is wrong, and the basis of the claim is simply illogical. Davis should have included many of the "legitimate" generals in his book in that class of might-have-beens. These include Turner Ashby, Arthur P. Bagby, John D. Barry, Samuel Benton, Theodore W. Brevard, William M. Browne, Thomas R. R. Cobb, James Dearing, Xavier B. DeBray, James Deshler, John Dunovant, John W. Frazer, Isham W. Garrott, Jeremy F. Gilmer, Victor J. B. Girardey, Archibald C. Godwin, Benjamin F. Gordon, Robert H. Hatton, Sidney Jackman, Adam R. Johnson, Wil-

burn H. King, Levin M. Lewis, Robert P. Maclay, Thomas T. Munford, Lucius B. Northrop, Edward A. O'Neal, James E. Rains, Horace Randal, Thomas H. Taylor, Alexander W. Terrell, and Bryan M. Thomas, none of whom were confirmed by the Senate; James M. Goggin, whose appointment was cancelled; George B. Hodge and Felix H. Robertson, whose commissions were rejected; and John R. Jones, whose confirmation was ordered postponed and never acted on. The work includes Militia Maj. Gen. Francis H. Smith and Militia Brig. Gens. Archibald S. Dobbin and Meriwether J. Thompson but omits all other militia generals "nationalized" into Confederate service.

687

DeCredico, Mary A. **Patriotism for Profit: Georgia's Urban Entrepreneurs and the Confederate War Effort** (211 pp., University of North Carolina Press, Chapel Hill, 1990)

This work sheds significant light on a minor but intriguing aspect of the Southern war experience. Given opportunities for financial gain, urban entrepreneurs flocked to the war effort in a number of Georgia cities. The author's enjoyable text outlines the antebellum foundation for enterprise in a number of Georgia cities, including Augusta's textile works, similar enterprises in Columbus, Atlanta's ventures in metals fabrication, and Savannah's shipping-related businesses.

When the war came, the author shows, the capabilities of Georgia's urban areas changed. Arsenals and quartermaster's depots sprang up in Atlanta, Augusta, and Columbus. The narrative demonstrates with precision how many private companies or citizens got into the act to produce war-related goods and how most were as motivated by money as they were by patriotism, if not significantly more so. Indeed, the entrepreneurs resisted the Confederate authorities' attempts at establishing a centralized system of control, and they got away with it largely because of the exigencies of war. As the war ended, many of the capabilities of Georgia's manufacturing were destroyed, particularly in Atlanta and Columbus. In sharp contrast to the plantation life, these wartime manufacturers, at least for a brief time, resembled their Northern counterparts.

688

DeRosa, Marshall L. **The Confederate Constitution of 1861: An Inquiry into American Constitutionalism** (182 pp., University of Missouri Press, Columbia, 1991)

This study attempts a revisionist interpretation of the chief legal document of the Confederate States. DeRosa finds that state rights and limited national government were the watchwords of the Confederate document. Thus political excesses could be constrained, the state governments could be closely watched by the populace, and the powers of the national Congress and judiciary were limited. Beyond this, save for some altered language, the Confederate Constitution strongly resembled the United States Constitution. The differences, however, represented those reasons why the South fought the war, according to the author.

While it contains some interesting perceptions, this work does not uniformly hold water. The author contends that slavery played only a minor role in bringing on the war and that the Constitution did not promote a "slavocracy." The document did indeed protect the transfer of slave property from state to state, guaranteed the existence of slavery in the territories, and prohibited antislavery laws. Although the author suggests that the states were free to autonomously decide the issues, the Richmond government clearly supported slavery in a multitude of ways.

The basis of Southern fear of a centralized government looms large in this work, but earlier studies have demonstrated how the fear of factionalism played the significant role in forging a Confederate Constitution. The author also exaggerates and oversimplifies a number of characterizations to support his view, most notably the discussions of William Henry Seward and John C. Calhoun.

689

Durrill, Wayne K. **War of Another Kind: A Southern Community in the Great Rebellion** (288 pp., Oxford University Press, New York, 1990)

This superbly well written and solidly researched examination of Washington County, North Carolina, a typical small North Carolina county, provides insight into the effects of the war on the Southern people at large. It transports the reader to Washington County and allows the chronology of the Civil War to move forward. Thus the text explores secession, the effects of the Emancipation Proclamation, Southern citizens as refugees, guerrilla warfare in the region, the battle of Plymouth, and the destruction of the local plantation lifestyle. Durrill emphasizes the war over property, between planter and working classes, and shows how plantation property could be protected only by Confederate resistance following the issuance of the Emancipation Proclamation. While he provides a superb view of the lives of those in Washington County, his efforts at extrapolating those meanings into a generalized view of others in other areas are not always successful. He takes much at face value, which leads to occasional contradictions, as with Governor Zeb Vance's apparent plotting of an assassination and

the statement, later in the work, that he "refused to sanction the use of force against opponents of the war."

690

Evans, Clement A., ed. **Confederate Military History: A Library of Confederate States History Written by Distinguished Men of the South, and Edited by Gen. Clement A. Evans** (extended ed., 19 vols., 12,585 pp., Broadfoot, Wilmington, 1987–1989)

This recently published edition, containing an introduction by Lee A. Wallace, Jr., supersedes the original (12 vol., 6600 pp., Confederate Publishing Co., Atlanta, 1899). Supplemental volumes or variants of the original published sometime later contained biographical material missing from the originals. The Broadfoot reprinting contains all of this material.

The work consists of a volume on the Confederacy, a volume on each state, a naval volume, and two index volumes. The extended edition contains significantly more material than the original, totaling 6000 biographical sketches, 500 illustrations, and 156 maps. The bulk of each volume consists of a history of the state's involvement in the Confederate war effort followed by a biographical register of important officers attached to each state. The individual volumes, written under Evans's supervision, are by Ellison Capers (South Carolina); J. L. M. Curry, William R. Garrett, and Clement A. Evans (Confederate history); Joseph T. Derry (Georgia); J. J. Dickison (Florida); John Dimitry (Louisiana); John M. Harrell (Arkansas); D. H. Hill, Jr. (North Carolina); Charles E. Hooker (Mississippi); Jedediah Hotchkiss (Virginia); Bradley T. Johnson (Maryland); J. Stoddard Johnston (Kentucky); John C. Moore (Missouri); William Harwar Parker (the Confederate Navy); James D. Porter (Tennessee); O. M. Roberts (Texas); Joseph Wheeler (Alabama); and Robert White (West Virginia).

The description of organizations, battles, movements, campaigns, and strategy throughout the narrative is generally good though frequently clouded by a strong bias. Many of the maps are completely unreliable as demonstrated by a comparison with those in the *O.R.* atlas volume (*q.v.*). Researchers should be wary of the text's many errors. For example, an analysis of the accuracy of *Confederate Military History* can be made by examining the biographical information on general officers. The level of specificity is highly variable: in the volume on Florida, for example, James Patton Anderson's birthday is given as "about 1820" rather than 16 February 1822. Outright errors are common, as the same volume demonstrates: Anderson's date of death is incorrect; Theodore W. Brevard is erroneously included as a brigadier general although his commission was never confirmed by the Confederate Senate; W. G. M. Davis's date of resignation is incorrect; the place of death for Joseph Finegan is wrong; Edward A. Perry's birthdate is incorrect; Martin L. Smith's birthplace is wrong; and William S. Walker is mysteriously and incorrectly described as having been a midshipman in the U.S. Navy.

The volume on Georgia provides another view of the careless research for this work: Howell Cobb's commission date as brigadier general is wrong, as is his brother Thomas's inclusion as a brigadier general (the younger Cobb was not confirmed as a brigadier either before or after his death); the wrong birthplace is given for Henry Rootes Jackson; incorrect birthdates are given for Philip Cook, Dudley M. DuBose, William Duncan Smith, and Pierce M. B. Young; incorrect death dates are given for Alfred H. Colquitt, Philip Cook, Dudley M. DuBose, Lafayette McLaws, Paul J. Semmes, James P. Simms, Edward Lloyd Thomas, David E. Twiggs, Claudius C. Wilson, and Pierce M. B. Young. In the fashionable practice of considering officers generals without checking the legality of their commissions, the authors include Charles C. Crews as a brigadier general, a grade he never achieved. The same holds for Victor J. B. Girardey, George P. Harrison, Jr., Bryan M. Thomas, Edward Willis, and Peter McGlashan.

Erroneous dates of legitimate commissions also appear, as with Henry Rootes Jackson, Lafayette McLaws, Gilbert Moxley Sorrel, Robert Toombs, and Ambrose R. Wright. Ironically, even chief editor Clement A. Evans's own commission as brigadier general contains an error: the book dates his commission from 19 May 1863, one year before he actually achieved the grade. Other errors of fact occur, such as the statement that Robert Toombs served as secretary of state under President Lincoln.

The same types and frequency of errors appear throughout the other volumes, so the work must be approached with caution. Nonetheless, this set continues to offer a large amount of useful information for researchers investigating the military history of the Confederacy.

691

Faust, Drew Gilpin. **The Creation of Confederate Nationalism: Ideology and Identity in the Civil War South** (110 pp., Louisiana State University Press, Baton Rouge, 1988)

In this slim book Faust outlines the problems of creating Confederate nationalism, the effects of religion on Confederate nationalistic attitudes, Confederate "sins" and their effects on nationalism, and the reform of slavery and its relationship to the Lost Cause. Her examination of social approaches to a national sense of Confederate unity is majestic, if brief. She shows clearly how Confederate leaders promoted symbols in church, in song, and in propaganda that would serve to transform the Confederacy into a redeemer nation, one that would look after the slaves and carry them up through the long journey to self-respect and intelligence. No good Confederate could disagree with such forceful ideology supported by evangelical religion.

Faust adroitly demonstrates how Confederate nationalism disintegrated practically before it got started because of numerous internal contradictions. Built on a platform that stressed class distinction, Confederate nationalism asked a great deal of the lower classes and not much of the upper classes. Risky from the start, this fragile attempt was shattered by the economic chaos that ensued shortly after the blockades and other effects of war strengthened. As the author shows, the growth of a strong Confederate national identity hardly had a prayer from the earliest days of the war.

692

Goff, Richard D. **Confederate Supply** (275 pp., Duke University Press, Durham, 1969)

In this work the author demonstrates one important way in which the Confederacy helped to defeat itself. Surveying the vast collections of the Confederate supply departments, Goff examines the methods, successes, and problems of supplying the Rebel armies, with a special eye on the various bureau chiefs whose influence helped or hindered supply operations. He also follows the politics of supply and draws some penetrating conclusions about the handicaps under which much of the Confederate system labored.

Goff finds Jefferson Davis at fault for a multitude of problems and believes he was the South's greatest encumbrance. He argues that Davis and other leaders did not evolve rationally to the changing military situation and failed to help supply the armies in the field. With the loss of Missouri, Kentucky, and Maryland, the author contends, the best possible sources for food and other supplies were gone, and the Federal armies secured invasion routes deeper into the South. According to Goff, "The greatest single supply disaster of the war" for the Confederates was Grant's capture of Forts Henry and Donelson. The various bureau chiefs entrusted with supplying the Southern armies believed they could win the war until the final days of the conflict, showing an amazing range of self-delusion.

693

Harwell, Richard B. **Confederate Music** (184 pp., University of North Carolina Press, Chapel Hill, 1950)

This unusual book covers a unique piece of ground in Civil War literature. Music played a significant part in the daily lives of soldiers in camp and on the march, and in this volume the author examines the evolution of music produced within the Confederate States during the war years. The opportunity for Southern music publishing came with the war, the author explains, because competition from Northern publishing houses kept the industry subdued in antebellum days. Not so with the explosive wave of patriotism launched during the war's early days and, needless to say, the nonexistence of Southern music published in the North.

Harwell examines the exploits of Southern publishers of sheet music and follows the effects of the creation of songs with war themes. Individuals and companies are highlighted. Many had to stay relatively mobile in the event that Federal troops might approach or capture the towns in which they conducted business. The narrative includes summaries of the activities of such publishers as A. Blackmar, the George Dunn Company, J. C. Schreiner, John H. Hewitt, and the Werleins. The analysis that follows focuses on "Dixie" and other important songs of Confederate nationalism. The work includes excerpts of lyrics from many songs but does not reproduce the sheet music.

694

Harwell, Richard B., ed. **The Confederate Reader** (389 pp., Longmans, Green and Co., New York, 1957)

An anthology of writings on a variety of Confederate subjects, this work assembles much of interest into one package. Harwell chronologically arranges 54 topics that present a short course on a wide variety of important Confederate writings. Many documents of interest are included, from the Charleston *Mercury*'s famous "Union is dissolved" broadside to Edmund Kirby Smith's farewell address to his soldiers.

Extracts from newspapers and wartime books and pamphlets treat of battles and campaigns such as Sumter, Fredericksburg, Gettysburg, Vicksburg, and the fall of Atlanta. Worshipful appraisals of commanders appear, such as those of Joseph E. Johnston, Robert E. Lee, and Leonidas Polk. Naval actions receive treatment by way of the *Alabama* and the battle of the ironclads at Hampton Roads. An excerpt from William Howard Russell's diary (*q.v.*) describes the early capital at Montgomery. Another from FitzGerald Ross's *Cities and Camps of the Confederate States* (*q.v.*) illuminates

wartime life in Mobile. Stories of soldier life are illustrated in several accounts, such as "Mule Meat at the Hotel de Vicksburg" and "Theatricals in the Army."

This is a pleasing volume. Although not all of its material is vitally important to the Confederate story, it constitutes an admirable introduction for the beginning reader. In 1958 Harwell compiled a similar volume treating Union topics (*q.v.*).

695

Hoole, W. Stanley, ed. **Confederate Centennial Studies** (27 vols., 3656 pp., Confederate Publishing Co., Tuscaloosa, 1956–1965)

This series of slim volumes published before and during the Civil War centennial offers quiet and important reflections on a number of small but illuminating topics. The quality ranges from fair to superb, and many treat subjects not adequately covered in other areas. Published in small quantity, the studies are much prized today.

The set consists of the following volumes: *Lost Generation: The Life and Death of James Barrow, C.S.A.*, by E. Merton Coulter (118 pp., 1956); *Swamp Fox of the Confederacy: The Life and Military Services of M. Jeff Thompson*, by Jay Monaghan (123 pp., 1956); *Confederate Morale and Church Propaganda*, by James W. Silver (120 pp., 1957); *Vizetelly Covers the Confederacy*, by W. Stanley Hoole (173 pp., 1957); *Confederate Engineers*, by James L. Nichols (122 pp., 1957); *A Texas Surgeon in the C.S.A.*, by John Q. Anderson (123 pp., 1957); *Rebels in the Making: Planters' Conventions and Southern Propaganda*, by Weymouth T. Jordan (135 pp., 1958); *The Confederacy and Zeb Vance*, by Richard E. Yates (129 pp., 1958); *Seven Months in the North American War, 1863*, by Justis Scheibert (166 pp., 1958); *Reconstruction in West Alabama: The Memoirs of John L. Hunnicutt*, edited by W. Stanley Hoole (145 pp., 1959); *Howell Cobb's Confederate Career*, by Horace Montgomery (144 pp., 1959); *Yankees A'Coming: One Month's Experience during the Invasion of Liberty County, Georgia, 1864–1865*, by Mary Sharpe Jones and Mary Jones Mallard (102 pp., 1959); *Lincoln's Plan of Reconstruction*, by William B. Hesseltine (154 pp., 1960); *My Ever Dearest Friend: Letters of A. Dudley Mann to J. Davis*, edited by John Preston Moore (114 pp., 1960); *Confederate Exiles in Venezuela*, by A. J. Hanna and Kathryn Hanna (149 pp., 1960); *Alabama Tories: The First Alabama Cavalry, U.S.A., 1862–1865*, by W. Stanley Hoole (141 pp., 1960); *Financial Agent for the Confederacy*, by Charles S. Davis and Colin J. McRae (101 pp., 1961); *The Peace Convention of 1861*, by Jesse L. Keene (141 pp., 1961); *The Confederate Rams at Birkenhead*, by Wilbur Devereaux Jones (124 pp., 1961); *Leroy Pope Walker, Confederate*

Secretary of War, by William C. Harris (141 pp., 1961); *A Visit to the Confederate States of America in 1863: Memoir Addressed to His Majesty Napoleon III*, by Charles Girard (126 pp., 1962); *The Confederate Veteran*, by William W. White (128 pp., 1962); *The Diplomacy of the Confederate Cabinet at Richmond and Its Agents Abroad*, by Paul Pecquet du Bellet (130 pp., 1963); *A Confederate Marine: A Sketch of Henry Lea Graves with Excerpts from the Graves Family Correspondence, 1861–1865*, edited by Richard Harwell (140 pp., 1963); *The Private Journal of Georgiana Gholson Walker, 1862–1865*, edited by Dwight Franklin Henderson (148 pp., 1963); *Lawley Covers the Confederacy*, by W. Stanley Hoole (132 pp., 1964); and *The Cruise of the CSS* Sumter, by Charles Grayson Summersell (187 pp., 1965).

696

Kerby, Robert L. **Kirby Smith's Confederacy: The Trans-Mississippi South, 1863–1865** (529 pp., Columbia University Press, New York, 1972)

This is a detailed examination of the often neglected theater of the Trans-Mississippi and its isolated existence following the Federal capture of Vicksburg. Kerby correctly demonstrates how the Trans-Mississippi became an isolated community once the Union Navy controlled the great river and how in both military and societal terms the territory degraded into also-ran status until war's end.

The author makes five assertions about the nature of the Trans-Mississippi: Confederate war planners bungled by separating military departments with the Mississippi; the Trans-Mississippi's economy endured despite its isolation; deterioration of morale rendered Kirby Smith's Confederacy impotent; Confederate authorities west of the river played a thoroughly subservient role to the Confederate government in Richmond; and concrete hopes for Confederate military victory and independence, at least in the Trans-Mississippi, evaporated early in the war.

The study admirably supports these contentions, delivering a careful narrative of the many events—military and otherwise—that transpired during the final two years of war in the Far West.

(Reprinted 1991, 529 pp., University of Alabama Press, Tuscaloosa)

697

Lester, Richard I. **Confederate Finance and Purchasing in Great Britain** (267 pp., University Press of Virginia, Charlottesville, 1975)

In this reasonably well done study of relatively over-looked Southern activities abroad, Lester looks at the band of men who worked on behalf of the Confederate government in the British Isles, showing that their influence was greater than conventionally believed. He employs a large group of primary materials, many of them from British collections, and follows the tales of constructing and purchasing ironclads, cruisers, and ordnance. He investigates how Confederate agents like James D. Bulloch financed such purchases and in close detail examines cotton as a commodity and the Erlanger loan.

The narrative contains some weak spots because of the author's reliance on outdated secondary sources, and broad conclusions are often drawn where none are warranted. Appendices cover the details of Confederate warships such as the *Alabama*, the *Florida*, the *Rappahannock*, and the *Shenandoah* and the British companies that struck deals with the Confederate government. The biographical sketches are rather pedestrian, and the index is adequate.

698

Lonn, Ella. **Foreigners in the Confederacy** (566 pp., University of North Carolina Press, Chapel Hill, 1940)

In this readable work Lonn synthesizes valuable material on a relatively untouched subject. Disputing contemporary notions, she demonstrates that, like the armies of the North, the Confederate armies contained significant numbers of soldiers born in foreign countries. She shows that at the outbreak of war about 250,000 such persons resided in the secession states—mostly English, Irish, and German—and that many of these individuals contributed materially to the Confederate war effort.

Although some of the foreign-born men in the Confederate States claimed exemption from service or fled at the outbreak of hostilities, the majority took up arms in the name of their adopted states, even as plans for coercion of aliens into service surfaced in the Richmond government and at state and local levels. The author reveals that many foreigners in the army and the small Confederate Navy were accepted with some degree of suspicion, and relatively few of them rose to army grades higher than that of captain. The text occasionally draws on anecdotal material of suspect authenticity, but overall this study contributes significantly toward a clear understanding of this area.

(Reprinted n.d., 566 pp., Peter Smith, New York)

699

Lonn, Ella. **Salt as a Factor in the Confederacy** (324 pp., Neale Publishing Co., New York, 1933)

Salt was a necessity during the war for the general health of people and animals and particularly for curing and preserving meat. A shortage of salt would be disastrous for either side. Lonn discusses the salt shortage that plagued the Confederate armies and the Southern home front and the attempts to rectify it. She describes how imported salt was plentiful before the war, but the blockade changed that and pushed Southerners into extracting salt from local deposits in Saltville, Virginia, southwestern Alabama, southeastern Kentucky, northeastern Texas, and northwestern Louisiana. Evaporating the brine over furnaces produced salt crystals, but the supplies were scant beginning in the autumn of 1861.

Lonn describes in detail the difficulty of the salt extraction procedures and the increasing harassment of those working on the problem by the encroachment of Federal troops. Many of the most valuable sites were captured during the first year or two of the war, and places such as Saltville were beleaguered by internal arguments over the railroad line. A poorly detailed map and inadequate index do little to damage the fine job of research that supports this volume.

(Reprinted 1965, 324 pp., University of Alabama Press, Tuscaloosa)

700

Massey, Mary Elizabeth. **Ersatz in the Confederacy: Shortages and Substitutions on the Southern Home Front** (233 pp., University of South Carolina Press, Columbia, 1952)

The only study of its kind, this genuinely intriguing book examines the causes of shortages and governmental reactions to them and provides a sweeping narrative investigation of the creative responses Southerners employed to continue life as more or less normal. The chapters cover food and drink, clothing, household goods, drugs and medicine, transportation, industry, agriculture, and "the little things in life." Eight photographs illustrate some of the homespun goods concocted during the war.

The author examines with tenderness and journalistic ardor the evolution of Southern inventiveness, from stretching old materials and methods to inventing entirely new ones. Scraps and oddball natural substitutes played an increasingly important role as the blockade tightened and the armies demanded more goods. Massey's brief overview does not probe deeply but surveys quantitatively. Thus, short summations of some of the substitute clothes, shoes, coffees,

alcoholic drinks, and household devices are utterly amazing but present a catalog more than an investigation.

(Reprinted 1993, with an introduction by Barbara L. Bellows, 288 pp., University of South Carolina Press, Columbia)

701

Massey, Mary Elizabeth. **Refugee Life in the Confederacy** (327 pp., Louisiana State University Press, Baton Rouge, 1964)

Massey explores a fascinating and underdeveloped aspect of the Southern wartime experience. The prongs of Union military invasion unsettled whole regions of Southern civilians and slaves, driving them to peculiar and faraway places to avoid the dangers or the oppression of war. A scholarly study interpreting the effects of transforming Southern people into Confederate refugees strikes the imagination as a wonderful thing, and indeed much of this work fills a wide gap in the literature. The author describes the qualities and circumstances that made some refugees fly past the war and others sink into it.

Unfortunately, the work lacks sufficient detail in its studies of individual cases to attach a human face to all of the suffering and despair. Although the author consulted a wide range of materials, the resulting book lacks the kind of meaningful analysis that would make it a cornerstone in Confederate studies. As such, it is a curiously intriguing work, but it stops short of being definitive.

702

Moore, Albert Burton. **Conscription and Conflict in the Confederacy** (367 pp., Macmillan, New York, 1924)

This aged work stands as a relevant and useful contribution to an infrequently examined aspect of the Confederate war effort. The bulk of the narrative represents Moore's doctoral dissertation from the University of Chicago. The author surveys the Confederate military system to April 1862, the First Conscription Act, substitution, statutory exemptions, courts and conscription, Confederate versus state authority in various regions of the South, and the concluding year of conflict. He provides an essay evaluating the success of conscription as a procedure.

Moore outlines the immediate conflict between Confederate and state authority that hampered success with conscription efforts. The First Act of 16 April 1862 called for conscription of men 18 to 35 years of age for service of 3 years. The act was instituted to establish uniformity and lengthen the duration of service, the author shows. The Second Act of 17 September 1862 increased the age range to 18 to 45 years, attempted to limit substitution, and sparked argument over the exemption of principals who furnished substitutes under the First Act. Legal opinions over the constitutionality of the acts were divided. Fraud, bribery, desertions, and other difficulties magnified the problems. Congress attempted to abolish substitutions, which amounted to 50,000 to 150,000 men lost by their furnishing others to take their place. The first list of exemptions was long: professionals and industrialists, ministers, teachers, pharmacists, miners, mailmen, transportation workers, telegraphers, hospital employees, government employees, militiamen, the handicapped, overseers of 20 or more slaves, and others. This amounted to about 29 percent of the total pool of conscripts.

As the war effort became more desperate, the rules changed: the Conscription Act of 17 February 1864 retained draft ages of 18 to 45 but added Junior Reserves (ages 17 to 18) and Senior Reserves (45 to 50) while abolishing many classes of exemptions. In the spring of 1865, Congress dissolved the Bureau of Conscription. As the number of available men waned, Congress considered arming the slaves. After much debate the measure was voted for, but it was never implemented. The author ably handles conflicts between Confederate authorities and state governors, most notably those of Joseph Brown of Georgia and Zeb Vance of North Carolina. Further exploration of related topics can be found in *Disloyalty in the Confederacy,* by Georgia Lee Tatum (176 pp., University of North Carolina Press, Chapel Hill, 1934).

(Reprinted 1963, 367 pp., Hillary House, New York)

703

Neely, Mark E., Jr., Harold Holzer, and Gabor S. Boritt. **The Confederate Image: Prints of the Lost Cause** (257 pp., University of North Carolina Press, Chapel Hill, 1987)

The authors offer 140 Confederate engravings and a skillful and balanced interpretation of their significance as propaganda during the war and afterward. Two large sections contain 14 chapters that touch on a variety of topics related to the engravings and the engravers. The first section presents material relevant to the war period itself; the second explores the postwar significance of Confederate images up to the year 1907.

The famous and predictable images are all here, from portraits of Davis, Jackson, and Lee to the "Burial of Latane" to battle scenes and an amazing array of nationalistic Confederate icons. The backgrounds of a large number of artists, engravers, and lithographers come to light, including the well-known individuals Adalbert J. Volck, Allen C. Redwood, and William Sartain and the productive firms of Hoyer and

Ludwig, Blelock and Company, and Currier and Ives. Meaningful text and a fine selection of images produced primarily but not exclusively in the South make this work a valuable survey of how the Confederacy saw itself.

704

Owsley, Frank Lawrence. **State Rights in the Confederacy** (289 pp., University of Chicago Press, Chicago, 1925)

Long considered a classic of Confederate literature, this book has some inherent defects that have been frequently attacked by later scholarship. The work purports that state rights attitudes in the Southern state governments weakened the central government of Jefferson Davis so that it materially caused the collapse of the Confederacy. The thesis echoes that put forth by Jefferson Davis himself, that the Confederate government "died of state rights."

Owsley examines the records of governors, state legislatures, and the courts, showing that many withheld arms, men, and supplies necessary for the Confederate armies. Moreover, they interfered with Confederate troops on their soil. They fought against impressment measures and suspension of the writ of habeas corpus. That this occurred is plain, and an exhaustive search of source materials such as Owsley's makes the point well. The difficulty comes in the overly aggressive interpretation of the consequences of the states' actions.

The author presents isolated examples of such troubles and extrapolates them into sweeping generalizations of doom. He reads much into the statements of various sources that does not seem, on closer inspection, to be there. He has also selectively ignored evidence that contradicts his argument. Much of the narrative naturally focuses on Joe Brown and Zeb Vance. Both offer examples of mishandling. He misquotes Vance in letters to Jefferson Davis and suggests that Vance "swung the state into a position of violent opposition to the suspension of the writ of habeas corpus," an extreme exaggeration. The author's contempt for other governors is more damning to this work than the record of the state politicians. The index is inadequate, and a few typographical errors, such as "Lucius Northup" appear.

(Reprinted 1961, 289 pp., Peter Smith, New York)

705

Pollard, Edward A. **Southern History of the War** (4 vols., 1486 pp., West and Johnson, Richmond, and C. B. Richardson, New York, 1862–1866; consisting of: *The First Year of the War* [Richmond, 1862], *The Second Year of the War* [Richmond, 1863], *The Third Year of the War* [New York, 1865], and *The Last Year of the War* [New York, 1866])

This famous work is a wonderful historical curiosity. The narrative strongly reflects Pollard's background, position of employment, relationship with the Richmond government, and the time of composition. Written immediately after the war in the heat of passion, the book is a revisionist Southern attempt to attack the Northern credibility and to blame a long list of Southerners who failed in defeat, chiefly Jefferson Davis himself.

The author edited the Richmond *Examiner* during the war but was no friend of the administration. Some interesting observations relate to the Southern side of the slavery issue as it developed during the war, but the work is marked by incomplete information, poor judgment, and a bloated oratorical style. The narrative is too centered on Virginia and Virginians, and the author's journalistic background proves detrimental to his writing intelligently about campaigns and battles. The narrative retains some value as representing the views of many Southerners in the immediate aftermath of the conflict, though the most lasting accomplishment of the work may have been popularizing the phrase "the Lost Cause."

The first volume contains a vitriolic attack on the political history of the United States and a justification for secession. Pollard covers the election of 1860, the Lincoln administration, and the "strength of the revolution." Then he turns to a military narrative of the war's events. The first volume carries the story through to Second Bull Run. It is a straight narrative, undocumented, with battle summaries that roll on for many pages. Pollard is highly critical of many commanders on both sides yet could praise even Federal generals on occasion. The second volume covers activities from the fall of New Orleans through Vicksburg and Gettysburg. The third volume extensively discusses the great Confederate failures of 1863 with a scathing review of Northern political ideals. The author also covers Chattanooga, Chickamauga, the Wilderness campaign, and Atlanta. An appendix describes his imprisonment in Fort Warren in Boston Harbor. The final volume wraps up the coverage with the conclusion of the war and continues attacking various parties on both sides of the conflict. In the end, the author declares: "Any contact, friendly or indifferent, with the Yankee, since the display of his vices, would be painful to a free and enlightened people. It would

be vile and unnatural to the people of the South if extended across the bloody gulf of a cruel war, and unspeakably infamous if made in the attitude of submission."

(Abridged edition 1866, titled *The Lost Cause: A New Southern History of the War of the Confederates, Comprising a Full and Authentic Account of the Rise and Progress of the Late Southern Confederacy: The Campaigns, Battles, Incidents, and Adventures of the Most Gigantic Struggle of the World's History: Drawn from Official Sources, and Approved by the Most Distinguished Confederate Leaders*, 752 pp., E. B. Treat and Co., New York, 1866; abridged edition reprinted n.d., titled *The Lost Cause*, 752 pp., Bonanza Books, New York)

706

Potter, David M. **The South and the Sectional Conflict** (321 pp., Louisiana State University Press, Baton Rouge, 1968)

This collection of 11 stimulating essays on Southern identity and a large array of related questions probes issues central to Civil War history. The result is a precisely and eloquently written volume that raises many questions, solves others, and offers tantalizing reading.

The essays touch a range of subjects including understanding the South, the literature of the war, the Lincoln theme in historiography, John Brown, Horace Greeley, Republican behavior, Jefferson Davis, and assessing the war in the modern world. Potter argues that despite the many characteristics that made the South different it never forged a distinctive culture of its own. He compares the adherence to Old South views by modern Southerners with their adoption of modern urban living. He suggests that John Brown's lack of black friends and consultants demonstrates his irrationality more than any other single factor. According to the author, Greeley probably did not intend to let the "erring sisters go" into their own confederation despite his famous editorial.

Potter meaningfully surveys the political disasters that beset the Confederacy's success and suggests that the war "fused the cause of nationalism with the cause of liberalism." This work, though dated in some small respects, still offers readers significant insights.

707

Rable, George C. **The Confederate Republic: A Revolution against Politics** (416 pp., University of North Carolina Press, Chapel Hill, 1994)

This wonderfully original study is grounded in impressive research and a splendid knowledge of the background characters and events. Moreover, it is written with great enthusiasm. The result is a first-class work that adds much new and enlightening material on the Confederacy as an independent unit.

Rable's cornerstone argument claims that the Confederacy represented a revolution against politics that would purify the sectional partisanship and evils of party politics and return the citizens to a nation like that immediately following the American Revolution. Drawing on a succession of documentary evidence, the author's story mounts as the idea spun out of control. Indeed, Confederate nationalists backing Jefferson Davis and his administration's war policies found themselves fighting dissension that worked against a unified government, some of the dissenters in very high places, like Davis's own cabinet. The irresolvable conflict resulted from the claim that each side was representing the true interests of the new nation. The conflict spilled outside of politics and into the Confederate Army and Navy, education, societal functions, and religion.

This work neatly reconstructs the details of Confederate political culture. The author argues that despite the disagreements, the culture helped the Confederacy's chances of survival. Moreover, it shaped Southern politics for many years following the defeat of Confederate armies in the field.

708

Radley, Kenneth. **Rebel Watchdog: The Confederate States Army Provost Guard** (340 pp., Louisiana State University Press, Baton Rouge, 1989)

Radley furnishes a unique assessment of one element of the Confederate military organization, the Provost Guard, which performed many difficult and thankless tasks in the Confederate Army, from rounding up stragglers to overseeing prisoners to enforcing martial law to hunting down spies and dissenters. The framework of the book comprises investigations into these areas as well as biographical glimpses into the lives of some of the men attached to the provost service, including John H. Winder, Benjamin J. Hill, and Charles Livenskiold.

The author's research is admirable and includes a large number of primary and secondary sources organized into a generally cohesive narrative. The organization of the book—examining aspects in "watertight containers"—presents some problems with repetition, as with the discussion of Charles A. Davidson on pages 44 and 241. Moreover, the author has drawn on a variety of highly embellished and problematic sources for some of his assertions, including such unreliable records as the *Confederate Veteran* and the *Southern Historical Society Papers*, and many questionable memoirs—all apparently taken at face value. Additionally, spelling errors oc-

casionally mar the text, as for Castle Pinckney and Centreville. The index also gives some incorrect page numbers and such inclusions as "Pierre G. T. de Beauregard," "Moxley G. Sorrel," and "John B. Breckinridge." Although this work contains much of value, its content must be sorted out and the unreliable material ignored.

709

Ramsdell, Charles W. **Behind the Lines in the Southern Confederacy** (ed. Wendell H. Stephenson, 136 pp., Louisiana State University Press, Baton Rouge, 1944)

An intriguing set of three lectures addressing the reasons for Confederate defeat, this work was published posthumously and therefore without the author's intended revision. Ramsdell argues that Confederate failure was due in significant part to the collapse of morale behind the Confederate lines. Without proposing a single cause of the disintegration of Confederate nationalism, the author suggests hoarding, inflation, profiteering, and extortion as contributing factors. After careful analysis of the economic system in place at the time, Ramsdell declares that the financial problems of the Confederacy were all but insoluble. In attempting to work through the debt problem as well as others, the actions of the Confederacy usually compounded, rather than eased, the initial difficulties.

710

Randall, James G. **Lincoln and the South** (161 pp., Louisiana State University Press, Baton Rouge, 1946)

In this brief but meaningful analysis of the relationship between the Union war leader and the people of the states in rebellion, Randall clearly shows how Lincoln, a Southerner by birth, avoided treating the rebellious states as the enemy wherever possible. Because of his sentimental attachment to the South and its people, Lincoln did not include destruction of Southern institutions or culture in his military portfolio. Instead, he pushed to welcome the Southern states back into the Union—he maintained on legal grounds they had never really left—as evidenced by his plans for reuniting the nation as the war drew to a close.

The author devotes a significant amount of attention to the Emancipation Proclamation. He details the political necessity of astutely handling the situation by issuing a proclamation affecting only the states in rebellion, and affecting those only on paper. The four lectures presented survey these themes and other lesser ones, and with sharp scholarship the author reveals much about Lincoln's aims and his handling of the war.

711

Robinson, William M., Jr. **Justice in Grey: A History of the Judicial System of the Confederate States of America** (713 pp., Harvard University Press, Cambridge, 1941)

This scholarly study examines a wide landscape of justice throughout all aspects of the Confederate States. Robinson describes the Southern courts and the way they operated, the efforts toward establishing a Confederate Supreme Court and Court of Claims, outlines the relationships between the Confederate Justice Department and its subagencies, the Patent Office and Bureau of Printing, and defines the South's commissions and quasi-judicial agencies. The work is entirely successful, providing a large collection of well-documented source material assembled into a rather dry narrative. The author lays down a background history of the function of the courts and the system and illustrates his conclusions by citing sections of cases. By doing so, he clarifies the operations of the legal system in the ordinary course of law, in settling legal situations arising from the war, in punishing crimes, in enforcement of conscription, and in settling civil disputes.

The work broadly divides into seven parts. The first surveys the collapse of Federal judgeships in South Carolina and in other Southern states and examines the judicial powers of the Confederate States, the classification of courts, powers and jurisdiction of district courts, and the "superiority" of Confederate courts to the older Federal system. Part 2 examines the structure and business of state courts, with special emphasis on Virginia, Kentucky, Missouri, Texas, Arkansas, and Louisiana. The author also surveys hostile competition among state courts. The third part deals with the organization and operation of district courts, citing many examples of cases and devoting a section to Georgia decisions. The fourth treats special subjects such as the rebellion and invasion in eastern Tennessee, maritime jurisdiction at Key West, legal wranglings in Indian territories, martial law and the suspension of the writ of habeus corpus, and courts-martial. Part 5 explores the proposed Supreme Court of the Confederate States. Part 6 covers bureaus, departments, and the office of attorney general. The final section examines the relationship of the courts to the collapse of the Confederacy and Reconstruction.

712

Roland, Charles P. **The Confederacy** (218 pp., University of Chicago Press, Chicago, 1960)

An excellent brief history of the South during the Civil War era, well written and ably documented, this study offers an integrated presentation of the military aspects of the war along with the most important portions of political, economic, and social activities in the Confederacy. The military history does not dominate, but the author does interpret the impact of the battles on the other issues that represent the Confederacy as a whole. Thus a portrait of Southerners during the war years, their changing lives, and how they withstood the experience of patriotic fervor and, ultimately, defeat lies within easy grasp of the reader.

The author does not judge harshly but tends to present both sides of controversies, allowing readers to consider the outcome for themselves. Roland believes Jefferson Davis was not able to play his part effectively in the situation as it unfolded, yet he delivers in the end a rather sympathetic treatment of Davis's personality and his attempts at solving difficult and impossible problems. Although Roland believes the Confederacy lacked sufficient resources to win the war, he also concludes that disloyalty contributed significantly to a catalog of unsolvable problems that beset the would-be nation.

713

Thomas, Emory M. **The Confederacy as a Revolutionary Experience** (150 pp., Prentice-Hall, Englewood Cliffs, N.J., 1971)

Thomas offers an intriguing thesis to explain the Southern meaning of the war. He asserts that Southerners employed radical means to preserve their conservative lifestyle. Rural agrarian ways, state rights, slavery, and Southern individualism, the author suggests, had come under attack during the period before the war. To preserve these valued attributes of the Southern existence, Confederates launched a revolution.

The book's seven chapters define the revolutionary nature of the Confederate movement. Thomas explores secessionists, the unusual strategy of the Confederate military, the abrupt shift from state rights to a centralized government, the economic growth of Southern industry, and the social revolution in the South caused by the war. He claims that these factors portend great change in the Southerners' way of life, but he only partially admits that this change was a temporary aspect brought on by the exigencies of war. Some of the characterizations are too forgiving, as with Jefferson Davis, and some odd misspellings appear, as for Albert Sidney Johnston. For the most part, though, the thesis holds together well, and this work deserves wide acclaim for its originality of thought.

(Reprinted 1987, 150 pp., University of South Carolina Press, Columbia)

714

Thomas, Emory M. **The Confederate Nation, 1861–1865** (384 pp., Harper and Row, New York, 1979)

Thomas contends that the Confederacy developed from the seeds of a political movement empowered by the plantation identity of the Old South. The idea supposes that Southerners valued most highly a sense of place—of belonging—and maintained personal friendships as a high ideal. The Confederacy went to war to preserve these ideals, the author finds, so that by definition the Confederacy was a conservative movement in the face of an awesome, inevitable revolution occurring around it.

With this in mind, the author explores the birth and evolution of the Confederate States in political and military terms, secondarily providing summaries of social and economic aspects. The author finds that by 1862 the Old South mentality was transforming into a Confederate South as the central government in Richmond increased its control. Not only did the war pull the Confederacy into a revolution of its own, but Southerners on all fronts including at home felt the change. Women and slaves found their roles radically altered. The author shows that if the Confederacy had lived, it would have been a fundamentally different entity than the one its early leaders set out to create.

Thomas's skill at discussing military campaigns and political personalities is first rate, and his writing style makes for absorbing reading. Nevertheless, careless errors often crop up in the text, as with the misspellings of Barnard E. Bee, Beriah Magoffin, Irvin McDowell, Wilmer McLean, Colin J. McRae, Thomas T. Munford, Lucius B. Northrop, Robert Patterson, Roswell S. Ripley, and Louis T. Wigfall.

715

Tidwell, William A. **April '65: Confederate Covert Action in the American Civil War** (264 pp., Kent State University Press, Kent, 1995)

The author continues his investigations into the subject initiated in *Come Retribution* (*q.v.*) with an in-depth description of the Confederate States Secret Service and its activities throughout the war, uncovered by meticulous research in the National Archives and many other institutions. Tidwell delivers cogent portraits of the many personalities involved. He describes the establishment of Confederate irregular operations and traces the plans and plots to disrupt the Northern war effort and promote a Northern peace movement.

The author suggests that the Confederate government planned to strike a blow at the Federal military high command in Washington. The attack that never occurred transformed slowly into the Lincoln assassination, accomplished by Booth, a relative lackey in the system of volunteer assailants cooperative with various Confederate agents. The work sketches the level of detail of Confederate governmental involvement in the plots that eventually resulted in the assassination. Along the way it delivers a mountain of minutiae, some of it striking and some merely speculative, that casts new and significant light on all aspects of the Confederate secret war. A few minor errors of spelling appear, as with John C. Breckinridge, Edwin Gray Lee, and Raphael Semmes. The photographs of documents on pages 128 and 163 were switched.

716

Vandiver, Frank E. **Their Tattered Flags: The Epic of the Confederacy** (362 pp., Harper's Magazine Press, New York, 1970)

A concise, well-written, carefully assembled introductory history characterized by an economy of language and brief summaries of many aspects, the work manages to include a full survey of the birth, life, and death of the Confederacy. Not limited to military aspects, it examines political, social, and economic issues while inquiring into the meaning of the secession movement.

Vandiver begins with the story of the secession winter and quickly explodes into the first months of war. He carries the reader through a visitation of the embattled South. Military aspects are handled best, although some questionable assertions appear, such as the portrayal of Earl Van Dorn as competent, the generous evaluations of Jefferson Davis and commanders such as John Hunt Morgan, and the supposed Northern allegiance of Beriah Magoffin.

As the war continues and begins to destroy the South, the author's narrative delivers a useful and penetrating, although brief, description of the deterioration of Southern life and Southern armies. The Confederate political system grinds into shambles, and diplomatic maneuvers go wildly astray. Blockades create shortages that demolish the civilian will to support the war. The armies gradually lose men they cannot replace. The author delivers a winning introductory survey, cleverly relating the important details in a brief text that does not fail its audience.

717

Wiley, Bell Irvin. **The Plain People of the Confederacy** (104 pp., Louisiana State University Press, Baton Rouge, 1943)

This brief, penetrating essay examines the wartime experience and perseverance of the hard-working commoners of the Confederacy. Given his broad range of expertise and impressive research, Wiley's sweeping summations of the difficulty of life in the Confederacy are indeed valuable. Important themes rise out of the narrative of hard work and strife, particularly with regard to the material treating Southern blacks and the Southern soldier.

The author cleverly introduces humor to lighten the story of despair. In the discussion of how painful shortages developed, he analyzes inflation and speculation, describing the Confederate government's ill-fated attempts at remedying these already out of control processes. He shows how the cure was often disastrously worse than the problem and how life on the Southern home front turned from inconvenient to dangerously ill-supplied rather quickly.

718

Wiley, Bell Irvin. **The Road to Appomattox** (121 pp., Memphis State University Press, Memphis, 1956)

This splendid essay should be read by all students of the Confederacy. The author establishes a modern platform for viewing the probabilities of Confederate success by conceding that the North indeed had superior resources but rejecting the old notion that Southern defeat was an essential outcome of the war. He discusses intelligently how the Northern armies faced a far larger task in militarily conquering the South, one that would require many more men and resources than fighting a defensive war on familiar ground. Because of the South's defensive position, it could simply outlast the North.

Wiley explains that Southern defeat was more an outcome of errors and shortcomings in the Confederacy. He examines the errors of Jefferson Davis, the "reluctant helmsman," the influential political and military figures who opposed Davis, critical failures that hurt the Confederate war effort, and the eroding of the Southern will to fight. The classic Wiley graph of Confederate morale as a function of time appears in this volume. Most important, the work shows how Southerners underestimated the Northern will to fight as well as the abhorrence of slavery by foreigners.

(Reprinted 1994, 121 pp., Louisiana State University Press, Baton Rouge)

719

Yearns, Wilfred Buck. **The Confederate Congress** (293 pp., University of Georgia Press, Athens, 1960)

This study provides a tale of function and dysfunction in Richmond. The story begins filled with the hope and esprit de corps of the early congressional sessions and degrades into the political infighting and hopelessness of the later sessions, a progression one can follow in detail by reading the *Journal of the Congress of the Confederate States of America (q.v.)*. Yearns describes the challenges and limitations placed on the Confederacy's great governing body and describes in detail—and with amusement—some of the most famous incidents and personalities in it. In collaboration with Ezra J. Warner, Yearns produced an excellent companion volume, *Biographical Register of the Confederate Congress (q.v.)*.

720

Yearns, W. Buck, ed. **The Confederate Governors** (295 pp., University of Georgia Press, Athens, 1985)

This compilation contains essays by 13 specialists on the wartime governors of Alabama, Arkansas, Florida, Georgia, Kentucky, Louisiana, Mississippi, Missouri, North Carolina, South Carolina, Tennessee, Texas, and Virginia. The authors capably summarize their subjects and the events that surrounded them, although the brevity of the compilation minimizes detail. Occasionally authors do not provide specific dates for the incumbencies of their subjects, and they do not mention or explain the status of various "acting" or interim governors, an analysis of which would be useful.

Yearns concludes that as a group the Confederate governors acted well under trying conditions that arose from poor planning and a lack of resources. As the war progressed they were usually successful in supporting the military requirements of the Confederacy, which explains why the Confederate States lasted as long as it did.

EQUIPMENT

721

Hazlett, James C., Edwin Olmstead, and M. Hume Parks. **Field Artillery Weapons of the Civil War** (322 pp., University of Delaware Press, Newark, 1983)

As the principal study of Civil War field pieces, this work systematically reviews the many types of field artillery used in the war. The volume includes numerous statistical tables, drawings, photographs of many cannon in parks, detailed descriptions covering the makers and qualities of the guns, and appendices covering ordnance officers, gun makers, and a catalog of the locations of surviving Civil War tubes. The text is expertly written and the production value high, making this work an absolute necessity for the bookshelves of those who study Civil War equipment or venture to the battlefields.

The types of light artillery pieces covered are Federal 6-pounder guns and 3.67-inch rifles, Confederate 6-pounder guns and 3-inch rifles, Federal 12-pounder field howitzers, Confederate 12-pounder field howitzers, Federal Napoleon guns, Confederate Napoleon guns, Parrott rifles, 3-inch ordnance rifles, false Napoleons and Gettysburg replicas (this book is the best source for detecting fake cannon on battlefields), small guns, boat howitzers, James smoothbore guns and rifles, rare guns, large guns, and British rifled cannon. Throughout the chapters the authors rightly suggest that guns should be referred to by their bore diameters rather than the confused system of shot and shell weight.

722

Ripley, Warren. **Artillery and Ammunition of the Civil War** (384 pp., D. Van Nostrand Reinhold Co., New York, 1970)

Ripley's book makes a satisfying companion volume to the work of Hazlett, Olmstead, and Parks (*q.v.*) and should be considered a mainstay on the reference shelf of Civil War buffs. Compiled by an ordnance enthusiast and editor of Edward Manigault's diary (*q.v.*), this prodigious picture book—660 images in all—showcases artillery and ammunition. Aimed at buffs and collectors, it will delight anyone with an interest in Civil War cannon. Organized by type of gun, the work provides a historical introduction to howitzers, mortars, Columbiads, Dahlgrens, Parrotts, Brookes, and British rifles. Subsequent chapters investigate gun carriages and the artilleryman's art, and detail the many types of smoothbore and rifled balls, shells, and other ammunition. Tabular statistics follow.

(Reprinted 1981, 384 pp., Battery Press, Charleston)

723

Sylvia, Stephen W., and Michael J. O'Donnell. **The Illustrated History of American Civil War Relics** (Rev. ed., 319 pp., Moss Publications, Orange, Va., 1986)

Of the many books showcasing relics for buffs, this is by far the best and should be the centerpiece of any collection of books on relics. This luxuriously produced book (a first edition appeared in 1978) documents the history of Civil War relic collecting from the firing on Fort Sumter to the mid-1980s. Hundreds of illustrations and a well-written text describe numerous collections. Early chapters describe and depict pieces of the Fort Sumter flagstaff, a piece from E. Elmer Ellsworth's bloodstained shirt, swords, guns, knives, canteens, plates, bullets, uniforms, hats, and numerous other personal items from Chancellorsville, Gettysburg, the Wilderness, Vicksburg, Bull Run, and many other sites. The bulk of the work showcases postwar collections such as those of J. Howard Wert, John Rosensteel, A. E. Brooks, and Charles F. Gunther.

724

Woodhead, Henry, ed. **Echoes of Glory: Arms and Equipment of the Civil War** (3 vols., 951 pp., Time-Life Books, Alexandria, Va., 1991)

Although it contains much material of little value, this book does present a powerful set of images. Many of the photographs of Civil War relics collected for the Time-Life work *The Civil War* (*q.v.*) are used here, including some that do not appear in that multivolume set. The photography is superb, the captions are often informative, and the value of such a collection in handy books easily pulled off the shelf is evident.

The work's first two volumes present images of arms and equipment of the Confederacy and of the Union, categorizing the material by small arms, uniforms, equipment (miscellaneous), music, flags, and artillery. The third volume presents a rehash of the maps used in the Time-Life series (*q.v.*). They were not especially helpful in that work, and do nothing here to increase the value of the photographs of relics.

FICTION

725

[Pulitzer Prize, 1929]

Benét, Stephen Vincent. **John Brown's Body** (377 pp., Doubleday, Doran and Co., New York, 1928)

This is the epic elegy of the Civil War. Recognized as a classic almost immediately after publication, the work consists of a history of the war from Brown's blundered attack on Harpers Ferry to the surrender of Joe Johnston delivered in more than 15,000 lines of poetry. Although decidedly different from standard works of history, it can nevertheless be classified as a historic work as well as a poetic one. Most of the major events of the war appear in one of the eight books comprising the work, and fictional characters mingle with real ones to touch on the experience of war in America.

Composed by the son of a West Pointer who served with distinction during the war, the book may be the strongest identifier of the conflict as an intimate experience of American history. Both North and South and those along the spectrum of beliefs can identify with the rhythm and the delicate introspection of the sadness and the glory all felt in the war. Taken as a literary contribution to the war's memory, Benét's work is a masterpiece and will stand as a cornerstone in capturing the emotional spell of the war. It has been reissued many times.

726

Bierce, Ambrose. **Tales of Soldiers and Civilians** (300 pp., United States Book Co., New York, 1891)

This outstanding work of fiction was composed by a first lieutenant in the 9th Indiana Infantry. As authentically as any writer before or since, Bierce knew Civil War battle, the psychology of its effects on soldiers, and how war touched civilians. His classic volume on the war contains 26 stories as stunning today as they were a century ago for deploring war's carnage and for their surprise, shock endings. Nowhere is this better illustrated than in "An Occurrence at Owl Creek Bridge," Bierce's most famous Civil War short story. Of those focusing on soldiers, "Chickamauga," "One of the Missing," "The Coup de Grâce," and "Killed at Resaca" are all superb tales with carefully woven themes and subthemes. Fifteen of the stories focus on the war's themes and will be of the most interest to Civil War students. The tales of civilians are no less absorbing, though they lack the Civil War themes of the first group.

The complete text may also be found in *The Collected Writings of Ambrose Bierce* (810 pp., Citadel Press, New York, 1994). Variants include *Ambrose Bierce's Civil War* (ed. William McCann, 257 pp., Henry Regnery Co., Chicago, 1956), and *The Civil War Short Stories of Ambrose Bierce* (ed. Ernest J. Hopkins, 139 pp., University of Nebraska Press, Lincoln, 1988).

(Reprinted 1943, 222 pp., Limited Editions Club, New York; reprinted 1970, 300 pp., Books for Libraries, Freeport, N.Y.)

727

Crane, Stephen. **The Red Badge of Courage** (233 pp., D. Appleton and Co., New York, 1895)

The greatest of the early post–Civil War novels, though written by a young man who was born after the war, this relatively short work magically solidifies the experience of terror felt by a young soldier prior to and during a battle. Created not from the battlefield but from reading *Battles and Leaders* (*q.v.*), Crane's characters and descriptions have a realistic feel. Serialized in the Philadelphia *Press* and published in book form shortly thereafter, the story bears a strong antiwar stance. The main character is a boy soldier, Henry Fleming, who experiences an unnamed action that bears a resemblance to Chancellorsville.

The novel's revolutionary quality lies in the unromanticized viewpoint of the story and the primary character. The work's orchestrated understatement accentuates the death, destruction, grime, and futility of battle, seen as a whirlwind of chaos surrounding the untested soldier. The heroism of the war comes through in a more mature way than earlier works by others, showing that determination and long, difficult, dangerous fighting turned the tide of battle rather than simple boldness of the moment. In the end, after the battle, Fleming's understanding of war and of humanity expands as he realizes the inglorious nature of the fight. This novel delivers the message as powerfully today as it did a century ago. It has been reprinted many times.

728

Keneally, Thomas. **Confederates** (427 pp., Harper and Row, New York, 1979)

In convincing Southern prose, the author reflects on the Confederacy's struggle during the long, hot summer of 1862. Four primary characters dominate the novel, presenting readers with a wide range of personalities. Usaph Bumpass of the Shenandoah Volunteers is a combat soldier whose exploits allow readers to see the horror and struggle of the war on the front lines. Hardships of all kinds pepper the experiences of this soldier and his mates, ranging from dysentery to sheer exhaustion and galling boredom. The soldier's relationship with Decatur Cate, a fellow Confederate who also knew his wife, provides some of the story's tension. A succession of others contribute in small part to the military affairs but none as centrally as Stonewall Jackson, whom Keneally uses to symbolize the Confederacy itself.

The novel is grounded in large part in history but of course takes off with literary adventures unrestrained by truth. Other major characters, Horace Searcy and Dora Whipple, provide the contrasting roles of a British newsman and a nurse and spy who cares for Southern boys while providing intelligence for the Union. The work is wholly enjoyable, written with flair, and one of the finest on the period.

(Reprinted 1994, 427 pp., HarperCollins, New York)

729

Melville, Herman. **Battle-Pieces and Aspects of the War** (272 pp., Harper and Bros., New York, 1866)

Although it was essentially overlooked on publication, this is one of the war's literary treasures. The work presents 52 poems forming a chronological story of the war and 21 inscriptive and memorial verses. "Misgivings" foretells war, and many outstanding and stirring poems follow. Among the choicest are "A Utilitarian View of the *Monitor*'s Fight," "Shiloh," "Battle of Stone River," "The March to the Sea," "The Surrender at Appomattox," and "Aurora Borealis." Other pieces relate to individuals. "Stonewall Jackson" and "Stonewall Jackson (ascribed to a Virginian)" contrast Northern and Southern views of the great commander and of the war. Other poems record special topics such as "The Swamp Angel," "In the Prison Pen," "On the Photograph of a Corps Commander," and "America." The verses include such outstanding pieces as "Inscription for Graves at Pea Ridge, Arkansas," "An Epitaph," "Lee in the Capitol," and "On a Naval Monument in a Field of Georgia."

Melville provides an enlightening and at the time novel approach to summarizing the myriad feelings and attitudes produced by the war. It failed to respark his career, as he had hoped, but now can be recognized as a monumental work.

(Reprinted 1960, with an introduction by Sidney Kaplan, 272 pp., Scholar's Facsimiles and Reprints, Gainesville, Fla.; 1866 edition reprinted 1963, titled *The Battle-Pieces of Herman Melville*, ed. Hennig Cohen, 302 pp., Thomas Yoseloff, New York; 1866 edition reprinted 1995, titled *Battle-Pieces and Aspects of the War: Civil War Poems*, with an introduction by Lee Rust Brown, 272 pp., Da Capo Press, New York)

730

[Pulitzer Prize, 1937]

Mitchell, Margaret. **Gone with the Wind** (733 pp., Macmillan Co., New York, 1936)

Thoroughly researched by Mitchell, who grew up hearing stories from elderly veterans, in many ways the story fairly rings with realism as its heroine, Scarlett O'Hara, sees the Old South fall to pieces in the wake of Sherman's army and sees a New South emerge. Despite universal adoration of the work, it is not particularly good history. The treatment of slavery is far from accurate. Mitchell's blockade of the South takes effect long before the Union Navy's actually did. She omits Antietam completely and makes small mention of Grant's victory at Vicksburg while emphasizing Lee's victories at Fredericksburg and Chancellorsville. She highlights Chickamauga as a great Confederate victory, which is fair enough, but she ignores the Union capture of Missionary Ridge two months later.

Nonetheless, the book is influential fiction. By 1983 some 25 million copies had been sold in 27 languages. The story does give readers and cinema buffs—the motion picture *Gone with the Wind* stands as the most successful film in history—a pseudo-authentic taste of what life must have been like for a certain class of Southerners during the war. The story is cloaked heavily in emotional ties and rifts between Scarlett, the men in her life, and especially Rhett Butler. The battlefield realities of the war are for the most part far away from the daily action. But the fictional format allows the author to communicate to a wide range of readers much about the hardships of life in the South, the enormous suffering of the Confederacy, and the downward spiral of its hopes and dreams into the New South. Ignore the historical flaws in this work: read it as a great immersion into the feeling of the war era. The novel has been reprinted many times.

731

[Pulitzer Prize, 1975]

Shaara, Michael. **The Killer Angels: A Novel** (374 pp., David McKay Co., New York, 1974)

This work focuses on several "killer angels" on both sides of the tumultuous battle but particularly on Col. Joshua Lawrence Chamberlain of the 20th Maine and Lt. Gen. James Longstreet, 1st Corps commander of the Army of Northern Virginia. Inspiration of the motion picture *Gettysburg*, the book invariably must be compared with the actual history of the battle because it stays so close to reality in many respects.

The author focuses on four days, 29 June, 1 July, 2 July, and 3 July 1863, and moves back and forth between the Union and Confederate heroes, who are searching for greater relevance in the face of a terrible battle and the cost of many human lives. The portrayal of Chamberlain and Longstreet reveals a clear understanding of the two men, although Shaara's Longstreet may be too revisionistic, going too far to eliminate the unfair stereotyping of Lee's disagreeable commander. Many other characters make appearances and discuss the war, tactics, and the meaning of civilization; they include Lee, George Meade, Winfield Scott Hancock, Dick Ewell, John Buford, Tom Chamberlain, Moxley Sorrel, A. P. Hill, John Reynolds, Isaac Trimble, Richard Garnett, and J. Johnston Pettigrew. Although closer participation occurs with the Confederate characters, the author's conclusions side strongly with Chamberlain and his Union compatriots, and the interpretation of Lee is rather harsh.

What this work lacks in understanding and believability, it makes up for in entertainment. While not all of its conversation and interpretation is faithful to history, it succeeds in allowing an understanding of the times that one cannot feel as strongly from the officers' reports.

(Reprinted 1993, 374 pp., Random House, New York)

732

Slotkin, Richard. **The Crater** (558 pp., Atheneum, New York, 1980)

This well-executed and sensitive portrayal of characters involved with the Petersburg siege, and particularly the mining operations, lends a human element to an infamous and dramatic wartime event. The work begins with a very brief synopsis of the armies' settlement into siege lines at Petersburg, and the story proceeds with Lincoln's conference with Grant and his generals on 21 June 1864. The work receives a frequent infusion of credibility from the author's use of many dispatches, most of them real and taken from the *O.R.* (*q.v.*), which provide a basis of understanding and a supporting superstructure for the smaller-scale story.

The three parts center on the creation of the Federal mine, the battle of the Crater, and the aftermath and consequences up to the burial of the dead from the tragic explosion. Slotkin spends much time on members of the 48th Pennsylvania and spins a believable narration relating to their work, while paying attention to the Confederate countermine and the mounting drama toward the attack. As the author readily admits, he takes a few liberties for the sake of the story, such as substituting an imaginary 22d North Carolina Infantry for the 18th South Carolina. Some of the dispatches were edited to conform to the narrative, but the overall effect is satisfying, creating a deeply understandable story centered on this fascinating incident in the war's final months on the eastern front.

733

Stowe, Harriet Beecher. **Uncle Tom's Cabin; or, Life among the Lowly** (2 vols., 634 pp., J. P. Jewett and Co., Boston, 1852)

The original Civil War novel, this is a work that predates the firing on Sumter by nearly a decade. First serialized in the *National Era*, the novel sold 300,000 copies in its first year of publication in book form—an unprecedented success in its day. Indeed, Lincoln allegedly told Mrs. Stowe on her visit to the White House that she had caused the war. William Henry Seward claimed the book triggered Lincoln's emergence into national politics. While these were good-natured exaggerations, the novel did powerfully affect the national (and international) thinking about slavery in the United States far more than any other literary work, despite the fact that nearly 30 novels dealing with slavery were published in the 1850s.

Although stylistically difficult for today's readers, *Uncle Tom's Cabin* must be recognized as the powerful force that it is. Stowe skillfully manipulates characters Tom and Eliza to engender a spiritual kinship within the reader. The simplicity of the story line does not prevent the reader from feeling the horror of the slave system and its evil embodiment in Simon Legree. Fittingly, the novel presents the whole story of slavery, including the classic defenses of slaves being better off chained than free, slavery as the ideal management system for a backward race, and slavery as a biblical fact of creation. The pathos of slavery shines through precisely because of this whole-picture scenario—were it one-sided propaganda, the effect would have been immeasurably lessened. The work has been reprinted many times. Readers who wish to investigate Stowe's life may consult Harriet Beecher Stowe's own *Life of Harriet Beecher Stowe: Compiled from Her Letters and Journals, by Her Son Charles Edward Stowe* (530 pp., Houghton Mifflin Co., New York, 1889).

734

Thomason, John W., Jr. **Lone Star Preacher: Being a Chronicle of the Acts of Praxiteles Swan, M.E. Church South, Sometime Captain, 5th Texas Regiment Confederate States Provisional Army** (296 pp., Charles Scribner's Sons, New York, 1941)

The author presents a fictional tale of life in Hood's Texas brigade. This strange yet well-composed novel consists of eight vignettes centered on Praxiteles Swan, a Methodist preacher and chaplain in the Texas brigade. The subject finds his mission as a warrior during the Seven Days on the Peninsula when he picks up a musket and goes to battle, relinquishing the Lord's work because of the hot fight surrounding him. Swan continues his soldierly activities at Second Bull Run, where he enjoys whipping John Pope's army, and at Antietam, Gettysburg, Chickamauga, the Wilderness, Spotsylvania, and Cold Harbor. The wonderful vignettes give us a skillfully re-created dialogue as authentic as could be expected and cast a glowing light over the special nature of the Texans, blends of an old Andy Jackson type of rough, western, primordial cowboy.

Thomason delivers memorable scenes of Swan's antebellum life in addition to the lengthy treatment of his wartime transformation. The Louisiana Tigers play chess on a dead Yankee's chest. Swan skampers up Little Round Top facing a hail of lead. He preaches. He beats a Northern soldier to death. He helps a young boy at the battle of Antietam. Such contradictory signals provide readers with much insight into war and about the rough-hewn nature of the Texans who fought in it.

735

Wicker, Tom. **Unto This Hour** (642 pp., Viking Press, New York, 1984)

Wicker offers a well-composed and massively detailed story of Second Bull Run. The author sets out to use a multitude of characters, mostly fictional or fictionalized, to explore the effects of a major battle whose traditional interpretation relegates it to a meaningless slugfest. The work's complex and shifting viewpoints of commanders, common soldiers, and civilians provide a good approximation of the battle. Wicker suggests how Second Bull Run touched the lives of many individuals, influenced the course of the war, and helped to direct politics and society.

The characters in this novel range from the familiar—John Pope, Robert E. Lee, and Stonewall Jackson—to fantasy characters such as Yank and Reb privates who view the battle and the war from radically different perspectives. One of the book's more valuable qualities is the depiction, for the most part convincing, of farmers and slaves caught in the grip of two armies.

Wicker certainly succeeds in forcing a contemplation of the battle and of the aims of the war from both sides. His writing is sometimes jarring, as with the overdone use of stereotypical dialect and the improbable—in some cases impossible—employment of modern attitudes and behavior by a wide variety of characters. However, he does not attempt to recreate Second Bull Run but asks readers to reflect on the carnage of war and its meaning for the survivors. In that he succeeds.

GENERAL HISTORIES

736

Catton, Bruce. **The Centennial History of the Civil War** (3 vols., 1683 pp., titled *The Coming Fury* [1961], *Terrible Swift Sword* [1963], and *Never Call Retreat* [1965], Doubleday and Co., Garden City, N.Y., 1961–1965)

This work is masterfully written simple history, lightly documented and sweeping in its overview of a multitude of complex events. Catton walks a dangerous line that sinks most authors of such populist method, but he succeeds with a tremendous background knowledge of the facts, a sharp intuitional sense of when to pull the story into focus and when to push it back, and the valuable research assistance of E. B. Long.

The story opens in Charleston in the spring of 1860 and closes with the capture of Jefferson Davis in May 1865. *The*

Coming Fury sees the war through First Bull Run; *Terrible Swift Sword* follows it until the aftermath of Antietam; *Never Call Retreat* covers a too-vast amount of ground, the war's final two and a half years.

In his race to include the whole story with scant interpretation or context, Catton sends some troubled messages. In *The Coming Fury* he suggests that slavery was doomed before the war began, and he misinterprets and elevates Stephen A. Douglas's role in prewar politics. In the predictable and sensible portraits of other major figures, Catton adds nothing new to older visions. The words in the works are deftly manipulated, but the message is often predictable.

Terrible Swift Sword forges the theme weakly foreshadowed in the first volume. The author portrays the war as a struggle on both sides to preserve the past. The emergence of emancipation signals a revolution to free all Americans—black and white—from the imperfections of the past. The framework of battle narrative serves well to carry out this story, and although the spotlight speedily scans from event to event, the author successfully recounts the major events of the war's middle years.

Never Call Retreat races through a lengthy and critical period of the war. The resulting compression of details significantly damages the work's usefulness. Taken together, though, Catton's trilogy succeeds in delivering a concise, balanced narrative.

737

Commager, Henry Steele, ed. **The Blue and the Gray: The Story of the Civil War as Told by Participants** (2 vols., 1201 pp., Bobbs-Merrill Co., Indianapolis, 1950)

The coverage in this wonderful collection of memorable documents relating to the great events of the war emphasizes military events but is not limited to them. Thus, significant material bearing on political, social, economic, religious, and other issues appears. Some of the finest excerpts treat the experiences of common soldiers in the field and the home-front conditions on both sides.

Material from many well-known sources may be found here, including passages from Northerners John D. Billings, Wilder Dwight, Theodore Gerrish, U. S. Grant, John Chipman Gray, Oliver Wendell Holmes, Abraham Lincoln, Thomas L. Livermore, George B. McClellan, William Pittenger, Alfred Pleasonton, William T. Sherman, and Gates P. Thruston. Outstanding Confederate accounts originate from Pierre G. T. Beauregard, Heros von Borcke, John O. Casler, Jefferson Davis, John B. Gordon, D. H. Hill, Joseph E. Johnston, Robert E. Lee, Carlton McCarthy, William C. Oates, Stephen Dodson Ramseur, and Richard Taylor.

Superb accounts relate to prisons and hospitals, and naval actions are covered with great sensitivity. The work contains a wonderful section treating the popular songs of the Civil War era. Illustrations and maps round out this useful volume. Some of the material is unreliable, such as Augustus Buell's writing from *The Cannoneer*. A misspellings appear, as for David Hunter Strother. Generally, however, the editing is exceptionally good.

(Reprinted 1982, 1 vol., 1201 pp., Fairfax Press, New York)

738

Early, Jubal A., J. William Jones, Robert A. Brock, James P. Smith, Hamilton J. Eckenrode, Douglas Southall Freeman, and Frank E. Vandiver, eds. **Southern Historical Society Papers** (52 vols., 20,382 pp., 1876–1959: Southern Historical Society, Richmond, vols. 1–38, 1876–1910; "New Series," Southern Historical Society, Richmond, vols. 39–49, 1914–1943; Virginia Historical Society, Richmond, vols. 50–52, 1953–1959)

This is a landmark set on Confederate history, containing a huge number of valuable resources and papers of special interest. Among the standard fare are many official reports, wartime newspaper accounts, comments on controversies, and a virtual who's who of authors and topics covering the entirety of the Confederate experience, with special emphasis on the eastern theater and the Army of Northern Virginia in particular. The pages of many early volumes are the primary source in creating the heroic postwar stature of Robert E. Lee.

Several volumes contain works of special interest. For example, volume 2 (1876) contains a significant Confederate roster of general officers by Charles Colcock Jones, Jr. (pp. 321–455), predating Marcus Wright's valuable efforts. In this list, some confusion in names and 22 spelling errors appear. Some mistaken grades are provided: John B. Hood is listed as a general; D. H. Hill, Joseph Wheeler, and John B. Gordon appear as lieutenant generals; Jeremy F. Gilmer is listed as a major general; 11 brigadier generals are listed as major generals; inexplicably, Raphael Semmes appears as captain C.S.N. rather than rear admiral C.S.N; 66 militia generals and might-have-beens are listed as brigadier generals; Robert Bullock, Henry Gray, and William R. Peck are wrongly omitted as brigadier generals.

Volume 15 (1887) contains a complete list of Appomattox paroles of the Army of Northern Virginia, with an explanatory introduction by R. A. Brock. Volume 43 (1920) contains complete reprintings of James Power Smith's *With Stonewall Jackson in the Army of Northern Virginia* and William Allan's *History of the Campaign of Gen. T. J. (Stonewall) Jackson in*

the Shenandoah Valley of Virginia from November 4, 1861, to June 17, 1862 (q.v.). James I. Robertson, Jr., edited an index (2 vols., 1612 pp., Kraus International Publications, Millwood, N.Y., 1980).

(Reprinted 1990–1992, with a 3-vol. index [1460 pp.], 55 vols., 21,842 pp., Broadfoot, Wilmington, and Morningside, Dayton)

739

Flaherty, Thomas H., ed. **The Civil War** (28 vols., 4926 pp., Time-Life Books, Alexandria, Va., 1983–1987)

This set is in some ways successful. Richly illustrated, usually competently written, and summarizing a vast store of material without oversimplification, the collection serves as an ordinary reference for casual browsing. The maps are not particularly valuable, most consisting of the usual "blitzkrieg" style with low accuracy. But as a collection of historic photographs and images of Civil War relics, peppered throughout a generally successful introductory history, the book succeeds.

The coverage is as follows: *Brother against Brother: The War Begins,* by William C. Davis (176 pp., 1983); *First Blood: Fort Sumter to Bull Run,* by William C. Davis (176 pp., 1983); *The Road to Shiloh: Early Battles in the West,* by David Nevin (175 pp., 1983); *Decoying the Yanks: Jackson's Valley Campaign,* by Champ Clark (176 pp., 1984); *Forward to Richmond: McClellan's Peninsular Campaign,* by Ronald H. Bailey (176 pp., 1983); *Lee Takes Command: From Seven Days to Second Bull Run,* by the editors of Time-Life Books (176 pp., 1984); *The Bloodiest Day: The Battle of Antietam,* by Ronald H. Bailey (176 pp., 1984); *The Struggle for Tennessee: Tupelo to Stones River,* by James Street, Jr. (176 pp., 1985); *Rebels Resurgent: Fredericksburg to Chancellorsville,* by William K. Goolrick (176 pp., 1985); *Gettysburg: The Confederate High Tide,* by Champ Clark (176 pp., 1985); *War on the Mississippi: Grant's Vicksburg Campaign,* by Jerry Korn (176 pp., 1985); *The Fight for Chattanooga: Chickamauga to Missionary Ridge,* by Jerry Korn (176 pp., 1985); *The Killing Ground: Wilderness to Cold Harbor,* by Gregory Jaynes (176 pp., 1986); *Battles for Atlanta: Sherman Moves East,* by Ronald H. Bailey (176 pp., 1985); *Death in the Trenches: Grant at Petersburg,* by William C. Davis (176 pp., 1986); *The Shenandoah in Flames: The Valley Campaign of 1864,* by Thomas A. Lewis (176 pp., 1987); *Sherman's March: Atlanta to the Sea,* by David Nevin (175 pp., 1986); *Pursuit to Appomattox: The Last Battles,* by Jerry Korn (176 pp., 1987); *The Assassination: Death of the President,* by Champ Clark (176 pp., 1987); *The Nation Reunited: War's Aftermath,* by Richard W. Murphy (176 pp., 1987); *The Blockade: Runners and Raiders,* by the editors of Time-Life Books

(176 pp., 1983); *The Coastal War: Chesapeake Bay to Rio Grande,* by Peter M. Chaitin (176 pp., 1984); *Confederate Ordeal: The Southern Home Front,* by Steven A. Channing (176 pp., 1984); *Tenting Tonight: The Soldier's Life,* by James I. Robertson, Jr. (176 pp., 1984); *Spies, Scouts, and Raiders: Irregular Operations,* by the editors of Time-Life Books (176 pp., 1985); *Twenty Million Yankees: The Northern Home Front,* by Donald Dale Jackson (176 pp., 1985); *War on the Frontier: The Trans-Mississippi West,* by Alvin M. Josephy, Jr. (176 pp., 1986); and *Master Index: An Illustrated Guide* (176 pp., 1987).

740

Foote, Shelby. **The Civil War: A Narrative** (3 vols., 2934 pp., consisting of *Fort Sumter to Perryville* [1958], *Fredericksburg to Meridian* [1963], and *Red River to Appomattox* [1974], Random House, New York, 1958–1974)

A stylistic masterpiece, this is one of the best popular histories of the war. The study is a useful counterpart to Catton's trilogy (*q.v.*) because it offers a sweeping overview of the war from a decidedly different perspective. Foote views the war predominantly from the Confederate side and emphasizes the western campaigns, whereas Catton is primarily concerned with the Northern side and the eastern campaigns. Both writers employ a winning style and weave many human interest stories throughout the long pages of battle lore. From an academic (and factual) standpoint, Catton clearly wins out: Foote's work is undocumented, and although the author claims to resist interpretation, he frequently interprets and judges a multitude of situations and personalities, many times with dubious results, nearly all of these glorifying or embellishing Southern Civil War mythologies.

Foote is nonetheless a master storyteller of the war, and his accounts are riveting. The first volume presents the story of secession, the firing on Sumter, and the organization of war, and ends with an examination of Antietam and Perryville. The second volume surveys the war's middle period, with emphasis on Fredericksburg, Prairie Grove, Stones River, and the great contests of 1863, Chancellorsville, Gettysburg, Vicksburg, Chickamauga, and Chattanooga. The final volume draws the war to a close, examining the various western campaigns in the last year, the Grant-Lee campaign from the Wilderness to Appomattox, Sheridan's Valley campaign, and the thrust into the Deep South by Sherman.

Spectacular as story and generally sound in fact, Foote's *Narrative* nonetheless suffers from some problems. Apart from a lack of documentation, which the author generally surmounts due to his great knowledge of the war, the sources relied on are often pedestrian and offer little beyond those of much earlier basic accounts. His characterizations are often unfair, if not outright silly: he attacks the savagery of Sherman's march to the point where one wonders how any antebellum structures happen to remain in Georgia to this day. He mercilessly portrays Joe Johnston and Braxton Bragg as complete incompetents, exaggerating realities into oversimplified stereotypes. By contrast, he shows his bias toward a local hero by exaggerating the significance of many of Nathan Bedford Forrest's activities.

(Reprinted 1986, 3 vols., 2934 pp., Vintage, New York)

741

Greeley, Horace. **The American Conflict: A History of the Great Rebellion in the United States of America, 1860–65: Its Causes, Incidents, and Results: Intended to Exhibit Especially Its Moral and Political Phases, with the Draft and Progress of American Opinion Respecting Human Slavery, from 1776 to the Close of the War for the Union** (2 vols., 1430 pp., O. D. Case and Co., Hartford, 1864–1866)

A contemporary history of the war steeped in the emphatic ideals of slavery and freedom exists in this rancorous newspaper editor's volumes. The first enables Greeley to record his version of the entire history of the nation from 1776 to the second year of the Civil War. The second analyzes the final three years of the war and includes substantial material on emancipation and the crushing of the rebellion. The prose is sticky and turgid and the passions of the time race through on every page, yet the work is entertaining if for no other reason than to allow the reader to analyze Greeley's influential psychology.

The author traces the seeds of the war and includes a large cache of public documents and speeches to make his case. Failed compromise is the predominating theme. The treatment of wartime personalities is generally balanced, yet there is no pretense in attacking or praising those who in the writer's opinion deserve special judgment. Composed during the war, the work is particularly notable for the presentation of predictions about the years to come, particularly regarding the slavery question.

(Reprinted 1969, 2 vols., 1430 pp., Greenwood Press, Westport)

742

Henderson, G. F. R. **The Civil War, a Soldier's View: A Collection of Civil War Writings** (ed. Jay Luvaas, 322 pp., University of Chicago Press, Chicago, 1958)

The English soldier Henderson is best known for his biography of Stonewall Jackson (*q.v.*), but in this volume editor Luvaas has selected a miscellany of Henderson's other material that offers insights not only into the subjects at hand but also the British interpretation of the Civil War and the Confederacy. The principal essay, "The Campaign of Fredericksburg, Nov.–Dec., 1862," was published in book form (145 pp., K. Paul Trench Co., London, 1886). Also appearing is a lengthy review of *Battles and Leaders of the Civil War* (*q.v.*) and several chapters from Henderson's book *The Science of War* (1905), providing an overview of the war, an analysis of Gettysburg, a review of the Wilderness campaign, and an evaluation of Stonewall Jackson written for the second edition of Mary Anna Jackson's *Memoirs of Stonewall Jackson* (*q.v.*).

This is an odd assemblage of material, but many items of interest can be found scattered throughout. The description of Fredericksburg is useful because of the sparse amount of writing on that battle. Designed as a tactical text for British officers, the work serves as testimony to the value of the Civil War as seen by foreign officers. Indeed, so much about the two sides is perfectly balanced that the study of the tactics and strategy of what occurred was judged highly important by overseas analysts. From the lessons of Fredericksburg Henderson argues that modern warfare required greater roles for junior officers. He underestimates the importance of rifled and breechloading weapons, however, and his historical analysis of the battle shows inflated casualty figures, errors of fact one would expect from a writer not equipped with the *O.R.*

The chapters on Gettysburg and the Wilderness exhibit the same characteristics, and throughout the work Henderson displays a peculiar bias toward the Confederacy. This is at its strongest, of course, in the material relating to Jackson. An able, closing chapter by editor Luvaas assesses Henderson's legacy, developing the themes of volunteer and professional soldiers and evaluating Henderson's influence on later military thinking.

743

Johnson, Robert Underwood, and Clarence Clough Buel, eds. **Battles and Leaders of the Civil War, Being for the Most Part Contributions by Union and Confederate Officers: Based upon "The Century" War Series** (4 vols., 3091 pp., Century Co., New York, 1887–1888)

Collected and published in the *Century* magazine between November 1884 and November 1887, *Battles and Leaders* appeared in book form, with some changes from the serial edition, to the delight of the American reading public. Chronologically covering the war's military events and written by dozens of its leading participants (including many general

officers), this work sheds light on many major battles and minor skirmishes, as well as revealing much about the strategy and tactics of numerous campaigns. Both naval events and land operations receive lengthy and skillful treatment.

The 388 articles by 226 authors are accompanied by 197 well-drawn maps, nearly 1500 engraved illustrations, statistical summaries, orders of battle, and editorial notes inserted by Johnson and Buel. The engravings are among the best relating to Civil War history and were done by a team of artists and illustrators that includes Edwin Forbes, Winslow Homer, Allen C. Redwood, William L. Sheppard, James E. Taylor, and Alfred R. Waud.

Major players who were alive in the 1880s contributed significant articles, and coverage includes articles on the same battle or campaign from both viewpoints. So we have Pierre G. T. Beauregard describing First Bull Run as well as James B. Fry's description of the Federal advance. Beauregard, Grant, Buell, and Albert Sidney Johnston's son William Preston Johnston all describe Shiloh. Johnston's article is a piece of his biography of his father (*q.v.*). Many participants cover Gettysburg, including E. Porter Alexander, John Gibbon, Henry J. Hunt, John D. Imboden, Joseph B. Kershaw, James Longstreet, George G. Meade, Daniel E. Sickles, and Francis A. Walker. This multiplicity of views is especially helpful because, as is sometimes the case with battlefield reports and postwar recollections, conflicting stories reflect rationalizations or outright distortions made to cover an individual's actions. Heated exchanges sometimes ensue, as with the Meade-Sickles controversy at Gettysburg, Longstreet and his detractors over Gettysburg, the Pope–Rufus King and Pope–Fitz John Porter arguments over Second Bull Run, the Jefferson Davis–Joe Johnston debate over the Mississippi campaign of 1862–1863, the Sheridan-Warren dispute at Five Forks, the Beauregard–William Preston Johnston debate over Shiloh, the Beauregard–Joe Johnston differences over First Bull Run, and various fiery disagreements over Jeb Stuart's role at Gettysburg.

Numerous accounts by general officers make this work a necessary, primary source for all Civil War libraries. They also make the work somewhat dry and lifeless, however, a problem the editors lessened a century ago by balancing the military narratives, most in the style of official reports, with a number of lighter articles written by common soldiers and civilians. These constitute a less historically important contribution but make the volumes more readable and enjoyable. They include William Lee Goss's stories of common soldier life constituting part of his book, George W. Cable's description of New Orleans, Constance Cary Harrison's descriptions of wartime Richmond, and Charles C. Coffin's "Antietam Scenes."

The success of the *Battles and Leaders* articles increased the *Century*'s circulation to 225,000 and helped to heal many of the lingering sectional wounds in the minds of participants. The book version makes permanent this collection, with minor changes. It should be read carefully and often. For more on *Battles and Leaders*, see Stephen Davis, "'A Matter of Sensational Interest': The *Century* Battles and Leaders Series," *Civil War History* 27 (1981): 338.

(Reprinted 1991, 8 vols., 3091 pp., Archive Society, Harrisburg, Pa.)

744

McClure, Alexander K., ed. **The Annals of the War Written by Leading Participants North and South: Originally Published in the Philadelphia *Weekly Times*** (800 pp., Times Publishing Co., Philadelphia, 1879)

Beginning in 1877 the Philadelphia *Weekly Times* published an extensive series of articles on the Civil War written by key military figures on both sides. In 1879, under the direction of McClure, the paper published a compilation of 55 of the best articles from the series. Many important subjects are covered in this work, and it is similar in style and an excellent companion to the *Century* magazine's *Battles and Leaders* set (*q.v.*).

Although many of the annals overlap in coverage, this allows intriguing comparisons. For example, one can read about the flight and capture of Jefferson Davis from the viewpoints of both Confederate Postmaster General John H. Reagan and Union Maj. Gen. James H. Wilson. Eyewitness accounts of John Morgan's Indiana and Ohio raids appear by both Brig. Gen. Basil W. Duke, who was Morgan's brother-in-law, and Union Bvt. Brig. Gen. John E. McGowan. Excellent papers on Lee and his army appear by Lt. Gen. James Longstreet, Maj. Gen. Cadmus M. Wilcox, Brig. Gen. Armistead L. Long, and the Reverend J. William Jones. Jackson and his Valley campaign are the focus of articles by Col. William Allan and Maj. Henry Kyd Douglas.

Several more articles show exceptional merit. Union Navy Secretary Gideon Welles describes the genesis of the USS *Monitor*. Gettysburg papers cover both viewpoints especially well, particularly those by Confederates James Longstreet, Brig. Gen. John McCausland, and Col. Walter H. Taylor, and by Union participants Bvt. Maj. Gen. David M. Gregg, Bvt. Col. James C. Biddle, and Maj. J. E. Carpenter.

(Reprinted 1988, with an index added, 839 pp., Morningside, Dayton; 1879 edition reprinted 1994, with an introduction by Gary W. Gallagher, 800 pp., Da Capo Press, New York)

745

[Pulitzer Prize, 1989]
McPherson, James M. **Battle Cry of Freedom: The Civil War Era** (904 pp., Oxford University Press, New York, 1988)

The preeminent single-volume history of the war, this exhaustively researched and meticulously documented tome explores the many facets of the war era. The work covers not simply the story of the military or political activities but also the approach of sectional crisis, the psychology of Northerners and Southerners before the war, the societal experience of the Civil War, the emancipation of slaves, and a number of other areas such as industry, education, agriculture, transportation, supply, and logistics. But the emphasis is squarely on the military activities that touched 10,000 places over the four-year struggle.

McPherson emphasizes the four crucial periods of the war in which events might have produced results of a very different nature—the bloody summer of 1862, the North's hopeful growth toward military competence after Antietam, the horrors and strategic importance of the great battles of 1863, and the long, hot summer of 1864 in which the noose tightened around the eastern Confederate Army while Sherman's great raid struck at the Southern will to resist defeat.

In providing a dramatically composed narrative of the war's great battles and what they meant, McPherson eliminates a great deal of nonsense contributed by earlier Civil War literature. He maintains and clearly demonstrates that the Confederate Army lost the war on the battlefield and offers brief but convincing analysis damning other rationalizations. He convincingly portrays Lee the man rather than Lee the legend and capably shows how various Southern general officers foolishly wasted opportunities for success—most notably John Bell Hood. He straightforwardly describes Lincoln's slow discovery of the proper commanders and makes clear the difference between the North's need to militarily conquer and hold territory and the South's less-formidable task of defending its own lands.

The author contends that the South struck a "pre-emptive counterrevolution" to stop the changing winds of Washington from altering its way of life. The basis for this begins in the Mexican War era and evolves toward the 1860 election. In delivering this creative approach to the secession crisis, the author describes in abundant detail the sudden rise of the ongoing political adventures of Lincoln and Davis. The politics of the war itself receives substantial and meaningful treatment, although readers spend most of the time understanding the war's military events, as they should. Covering all of this material in fewer than 1000 pages was a tremendous undertaking, and McPherson has accomplished this brilliantly. This work will endure as an important contribution to Civil War studies.

746

McPherson, James M. **Ordeal by Fire: The Civil War and Reconstruction** (694 pp., Alfred A. Knopf, New York, 1982)

The author emphasizes the evolution of Northern thought, business, and industry beginning in the 1840s and how the lack of a similar process in the South produced a regional schism. The work details the Southern response to increasing Northern political power as a counterrevolution and suggests that not only did it fail but it virtually ensured the success of the Northern revolution. McPherson closely follows the fortunes of blacks and other minorities along the pathway to conflict, producing a clear and comprehensive understanding of how slavery served as a catalyst for war.

The author covers a vast amount of ground and therefore compresses much but loses little as a result. McPherson presents Abraham Lincoln as a revolutionary leader who worked within the means at hand, often frustrated by poor generalship. The work is too harsh in some cases, however, as with Meade's understandably drowsy pursuit of Lee after Gettysburg. It shines particularly brightly in dealing with Reconstruction and offers a balanced and weightily supported view of the treatment of ex-slaves. This work stands as a significant, progressive companion to the older and still useful study by James G. Randall and David Donald (*q.v.*).

747

[Military Order of the Loyal Legion of the United States.] **Papers of the Military Order of the Loyal Legion of the United States, 1887–1915** (66 vols., 29,215 pp., Broadfoot, Wilmington, 1991–1996)

The Broadfoot republication supersedes the original set, produced by many publishers between 1887 and 1923 and subdivided as follows: *Biographical Sketches of Contributors* (ed. William Marvel, 325 pp., Broadfoot, Wilmington, 1995); *Sketches of War History, 1861–1865: Papers Read before the Ohio Commandery of the Military Order of the Loyal Legion of the United States* (ed. Theodore F. Allen, Robert Hunter, W. H. Chamberlin, Edward S. McKee, J. Gordon Taylor, George A. Thayer, and A. M. Van Dyke, 9 vols., 3235 pp., Robert Clarke and Co., Cincinnati, 1888–1903, and Monfort and Co., Cincinnati, 1908); *Military Essays and Recollections: Papers Read before the Commandery of the State of Illinois, Military Order of the Loyal Legion of the United States* and *Memorials of Deceased Companions of the Commandery of the State of Illinois, Military Order of the Loyal Legion of the*

United States (8 vols., 4493 pp., A. C. McClurg and Co., Chicago, 1891–1894, Dial Press, Chicago, 1899, and Cozzens and Beaton Co., Chicago, 1907–1923); *War Papers and Personal Reminiscences, 1861–1865: Read before the Commandery of the State of Missouri, Military Order of the Loyal Legion of the United States* (451 pp., Becktold and Co., St. Louis, 1892); *War Talks in Kansas: A Series of Papers Read before the Kansas Commandery of the Military Order of the Loyal Legion of the United States* (391 pp., Franklin Hudson Printing Co., Kansas City, Mo., 1906); *War Papers Read before the Commandery of the State of Maine, Military Order of the Loyal Legion of the United States* (4 vols., 1373 pp., Thurston Print, Portland, 1898, and Lefavor-Tower Co., Portland, 1902–1915); *Personal Recollections of the War of the Rebellion: Addresses Delivered before the New York Commandery of the Military Order of the Loyal Legion of the United States* (ed. A. Noel Blakeman, Titus Munson Coan, and James Grant Wilson, 4 vols., 1626 pp., published by the commandery, New York, 1891, and G. P. Putnam's Sons, New York, 1897–1912); *War Papers Read before the Indiana Commandery, Military Order of the Loyal Legion of the United States* (521 pp., published by the commandery, Indianapolis, 1898); *Civil War Sketches and Incidents: Papers Read by Companions of the Commandery of the State of Nebraska, Military Order of the Loyal Legion of the United States* (277 pp., published by the commandery, Omaha, 1902); *Glimpses of the Nation's Struggle: A Series of Papers Read before the Minnesota Commandery of the Military Order of the Loyal Legion of the United States* (ed. Edward D. Neill, 6 vols., 3153 pp., St. Paul Book and Stationery Co., St. Paul, 1887–1890, D. D. Merrill Co., New York, 1893, H. L. Collins Co., St. Paul, 1898, Review Publishing Co., St. Paul, 1903, and August Davis, Publisher, Minneapolis, 1909); *Personal Narratives of the Rebellion, Being Papers Read before the Rhode Island Soldiers and Sailors Historical Society* (10 vols., 4567 pp., Sidney S. Rider, Providence, 1878–1879, N. Bangs Williams and Co., Providence, 1880–1883, published by the society, Providence, 1883–1915); *War Papers, Being Papers Read before the Commandery of the District of Columbia, Military Order of the Loyal Legion of the United States* (4 vols., 1960 pp., published by the commandery, Washington, 1887–1918); *War Papers, Being Papers Read before the Commandery of the State of Wisconsin, Military Order of the Loyal Legion of the United States* (4 vols., 1920 pp., published by the commandery, Milwaukee, 1891–1914); *War Papers, Being Papers Read before the Commandery of the State of Michigan, Military Order of the Loyal Legion of the United States* (2 vols., 880 pp., published by the commandery, Detroit, 1886–1898); *Civil War Papers Read before the Commandery of the State of Massachusetts, Military Order of the Loyal Legion of the United States* and *The Other Side of the War: Letters from the*

Headquarters of the United States Sanitary Commission during the Peninsular Campaign in Virginia in 1862, by Katherine Prescott Wormeley (3 vols., 838 pp., published by the commandery, Boston, 1888–1900); *War Sketches and Incidents as Related by the Companions of the Iowa Commandery, Military Order of the Loyal Legion of the United States* (2 vols., 907 pp., P. C. Kenyon, Des Moines, 1893, and published by the commandery, Des Moines, 1898); *War Papers of Vermont and Miscellaneous States Papers and Addresses* (421 pp., Broadfoot, Wilmington, 1994); *Companions of the Military Order of the Loyal Legion of the United States: An Album Containing Portraits of Members of the Military Order of the Loyal Legion of the United States* (337 pp., L. Hammersly Co., New York, 1901); *Military Essays and Recollections of the Pennsylvania Commandery of the Military Order of the Loyal Legion of the United States* (2 vols., 1074 pp., Broadfoot, Wilmington, 1995); and *Civil War Papers of the California Commandery and the Oregon Commandery of the Military Order of the Loyal Legion of the United States* (466 pp., published by the commanderies, San Francisco and Portland, 1888–1910).

The massive Broadfoot reprinting brings everything together, provides some material not originally published in book form, and will include a 3-volume index. The material ranges greatly in quality and includes papers contributed by both common soldiers and high officers. The coverage touches all aspects, all theaters, all phases of the war. Much of inestimable value lies within the set, and its literary quality is far greater overall than other, similar reminiscences. Valuable papers by important authors are interspersed throughout the set, including those by Daniel Ammen, Ezra Carman, Joshua Lawrence Chamberlain, Augustus L. Chetlain, Jacob D. Cox, Rufus R. Dawes, Manning F. Force, Rutherford B. Hayes, William B. Hazen, Oliver O. Howard, John Page Nicholson, Philip H. Sheridan, William T. Sherman, William F. Smith, David S. Stanley, Benjamin F. Stevenson, and James Grant Wilson.

The reprint coverage includes an introduction (1 vol.); photographs (1 vol.); California and Oregon (1 vol.); District of Columbia (4 vols.); Illinois (8 vols.); Indiana (1 vol.); Iowa (2 vols.); Kansas (1 vol.); Maine (4 vols.); Massachusetts (3 vols.); Michigan (2 vols.); Minnesota (6 vols.); Missouri (1 vol.); Nebraska (1 vol.); New York (4 vols.); Ohio (9 vols.); Pennsylvania (2 vols.); Rhode Island (10 vols.); Vermont (1 vol.); and Wisconsin (4 vols.). The introduction contains material by William Marvel. The 10 Rhode Island volumes are a republication of the *Personal Narratives of Events in the War of the Rebellion, Being Papers Read before the Rhode Island Soldiers and Sailors Historical Society* (originally published in 100 vols., 4567 pp., Rhode Island Soldiers and Sailors Historical Society, Providence, 1878–1915).

748

Moore, Frank, ed. **The Rebellion Record: A Diary of American Events, with Documents, Narratives, Illustrative Incidents, Poetry, etc.** (11 vols., 6769 pp., G. P. Putnam's Sons, New York, 1861–1863, and D. Van Nostrand Co., New York, 1864–1868; supplemental volume, 759 pp., published by G. P. Putnam's Sons and Henry Holt, New York, 1864)

This is an entertaining hodgepodge of valuable documents and worthless material. While it provides authentic flavor of the reporting of the war, the work contains little worth reading that does not appear elsewhere in more accessible form. Still, it is an interesting period piece loaded with browsing material, including newspaper reports from North and South, addresses, poetry, documents, engravings, maps, sketches, and facsimile autographs.

The coverage is as follows: volume 1: Edward Everett address, diary and correspondence to 20 June 1861, poetry, and documents; volume 2: diary to 22 August 1861, poetry, and documents; volume 3: diary to 4 January 1862, poetry, and documents; volume 4: diary to 30 April 1862, poetry, and documents; volume 5: diary to 9 October 1862, poetry, and documents; volume 6: diary to 31 May 1863, poetry, and documents; volume 7: diary to 31 October 1863, poetry, and documents; volume 8: diary to 30 April 1864, poetry, and documents; volume 9: documents and poetry; volume 10: documents (military measures of Congress); volume 11: documents; volume 12 (supplemental): documents omitted from previous volumes.

749

Nevins, Allan. **Ordeal of the Union** (8 vols., 4152 pp.; consisting of: *Ordeal of the Union* [2 vols., 1183 pp., 1947], *The Emergence of Lincoln* [2 vols., 996 pp., 1950], and *The War for the Union* [4 vols., 1973 pp., 1959–1971], Charles Scribner's Sons, New York, 1947–1971)

This incomparable work delivers a massive, heavily documented, and detailed story of the secession crisis and the Civil War written by one of the master historians of the modern era. Nevins begins by exploring the "fruits of Manifest Destiny" that followed the Mexican War period and thus sets a credible and detailed stage for the many actors and actions to follow. Expertly and with wry analysis, he details the nation's growth and the inevitable movement toward war with itself, detailing primarily not military events but the entire scope of American life at mid-19th century—political, economic, social, and industrial. The two sections emerge with stark clarity in the reader's mind, and the narrative follows the many crucial events that successfully form a basis for understanding the path to war.

The final four volumes demonstrate the author's thesis that the war provided a catalyst for forging modern America. The details of military events are skillfully recounted, and the careful reader may glean a valuable strategic and tactical understanding of why many events unfolded as they did. The transformation of modern American society leaps off the pages as the author examines such diverse topics as agriculture, education, literature, music, railroads, finance, industry, immigration, and technology. The result is a stunning walk through the Civil War era that teaches an immense amount, all carefully documented.

Errors occasionally appear, as with Nevins's assertion that James A. Seddon served the Confederacy to the bitter end as war secretary. The author harshly attacks radical Republicans such as Charles Sumner and makes the glaring misstatement that after the war Southerners adopted a "change in racial attitudes." The errors are few and far between, however, and the great accomplishment of this narrative will remain valuable for decades to come.

750

Paris, Louis Phillipe Albert d'Orléans, comte de. **History of the Civil War in America** (ed. Henry Coppée and John Page Nicholson, 4 vols., 3003 pp., Porter and Coates, Philadelphia, 1876–1888)

One of the valuable early histories of the war, this study is still admirable for its great insight. Published originally as *Historie de la guerre civile en Amérique* (7 vols., Michel Lévy Frères and Calmann Lévy Frères, Paris, 1874–1890), the work's first English edition supplied the version widely circulated in the United States. The four bulky volumes were supplemented with a useful set of maps. Paris's nationality gave him something of an impartial viewpoint for the massive undertaking, despite his service on George McClellan's staff as a volunteer aide-de-camp.

The level of detail in this study is highly impressive. With the insight of European culture and military tradition, the author sketches the military history of the war beginning with a synopsis of the Mexican War, the organization of the regular army, the rise of volunteer officers, and the organizational differences between the Union and Confederate armies. His sympathies are of course with the Union, but he does not allow this to obscure the judgment of the narrative of military operations that follows. The coverage, roughly chronological, bounces back and forth between the eastern and western theaters.

Paris believes Irvin McDowell was too harshly criticized,

blames McClellan for squandering opportunities in October 1861 by inactivity, praises Lincoln's military judgment despite some disastrous political-general commissions, and lays blame on Grant and Sherman for their surprise at Shiloh. The treatment of Fredericksburg and of Burnside's ineptitude is extensive. The estimation of a multitude of events and commanders at Chancellorsville and Gettysburg is outstanding. Characterizations sometimes contradict earlier statements, however, providing conflicting images of high and low esteem, as with George Stoneman and Joseph Hooker. The work is somewhat too harshly unappreciative of George Meade. A subsequent work by the same author, *The Battle of Gettysburg, from the History of the Civil War in America* (315 pp., Porter and Coates, Philadelphia, 1886) consists only of the Gettysburg material.

751

Randall, James G., and David H. Donald. **The Civil War and Reconstruction** (2d ed., 820 pp., D. C. Heath and Co., Boston, 1961)

Long hailed as the classic Civil War textbook, this compilation still deserves a place on the shelf. The first edition, published in 1937 and written by Randall alone, has been supplanted by the second edition, which substantially improves and updates the work. The book provides a sober and factual chronology of the causes of the war, political considerations, the war itself (with fair and balanced assessments of military, political, social, and economic considerations), and Reconstruction through the Grant era. The treatise is still useful as a reference because Donald scoured through it to update various portions bringing it in line with centennial-era scholarship.

Donald's changes reveal much about the evolution of thinking on the war. The second edition tones down the extremist picture of the abolitionists, analyzes more fully the issues tied to slavery, diminishes the stature of Jefferson Davis and George McClellan, dims critical views on the Port Royal Experiment, and includes a substantially altered version of Reconstruction, in large part lessening the evil influences of the radical Republicans. A variant titled *The Divided Union* (572 pp., Little, Brown and Co., Boston, 1961) omits the material on Reconstruction.

(Reprinted 1969, with an expanded bibliography, 866 pp., D. C. Heath and Co., Boston)

752

Rhodes, James Ford. **History of the United States from the Compromise of 1850 to the Final Restoration of Home Rule in the South in 1877** (7 vols., 3793 pp., Macmillan Co., New York, 1892–1906)

For years a classic reference work, this study retains value as the preeminent turn-of-the-century summary of the secession crisis, the war, and Reconstruction. It is solidly grounded on numerous primary and secondary sources and capably sorted and interpreted by Rhodes, who writes chiefly from his vantage point as a Northerner. The fair and objective coverage of many events is infused by the moral hatred of slavery. The treatment of the antebellum topics is weaker than that of the war and Reconstruction. The significance of westward expansion in the United States before the war is lightly covered. The admission of western states in the antebellum period warrants only brief mention, while subjects like John Brown's raid and captures of fugitive slaves are detailed at length.

Volumes 3, 4, and 5, covering the military aspects of the war itself, although at times drawing heavily on the *O.R.* (*q.v.*), come across as having greater value than coverage of other aspects of the war such as diplomacy, economics, and social conditions. The numerous characterizations of significant figures are generally well done, although Andrew Johnson receives a blunt and unsympathetic treatment. The work is fascinating in its stupendous scope and for recalling how, for many years, students of the Civil War perceived the conflict and its influence. Volume 8, covering the period 1877–1896, was published in 1919. In 1920 the set was republished with a general index in volume 8.

(Abridged edition 1966, ed. Allan Nevins, 576 pp., University of Chicago Press, Chicago)

753

Roland, Charles P. **An American Iliad: The Story of the Civil War** (289 pp., University Press of Kentucky, Lexington, 1991)

Although scholars may disapprove of the absence of documentation in this work, Roland's deep understanding of the subject allows for a sterling product. Not only does he explain the coming of the war, the military history of the two sides, the political situations in the two capitals, and the significant players in the drama, but he does this with a wonderful sense of balance and confidence.

The author plays no favorites in the bulk of his work, which addresses the military history of the war's campaigns and battles. The eastern, western, and Trans-Mississippi theaters all receive clear and penetrating coverage, as do the field commanders in most of the warring major armies. Statistics and analysis provide backing for the author's conclusions, and his experienced style dictates just when and how much to include. The slim number of pages typical of a sweeping general history do not disable this author. Rather, he makes expedient use of them and in the process produces an outstanding introduction to a very complicated subject, tightly presented and admirable in its enriching style.

754

Ropes, John Codman, and Theodore F. Dwight, eds. **Papers of the Military Historical Society of Massachusetts** (15 vols., 6638 pp., Broadfoot , Wilmington, 1990)

New material in the Broadfoot reprinting supersedes that in the original volumes of this work, published by the Military Historical Society of Massachusetts, Boston, 1895–1918. Among the new material is an index and a group of brief biographies of the contributing authors by William Marvel.

The Bostonian group of war survivors included some of the finest minds of the Union Army, permitting their reminiscences to be accurate, balanced, and generally valuable resources for a variety of campaigns and related subjects. Several of the final volumes contain some material unrelated to the Civil War. Included are 186 papers and 66 maps. The books cover campaigns in Virginia in 1861–1862; Pope's Virginia campaign; campaigns in Virginia, Maryland, and Pennsylvania in 1862–1863; the Wilderness campaign; Petersburg, Chancellorsville, and Gettysburg; the Shenandoah and Appomattox campaigns; campaigns in Kentucky and Tennessee, 1862–1864; campaigns in the Mississippi Valley, Tennessee, Georgia, and Alabama, 1861–1864; operations on the Atlantic coast, 1861–1865, Virginia in 1862 and 1864, and Vicksburg; some Federal and Confederate commanders; naval actions and operations against Cuba and Puerto Rico, 1593–1815; naval actions and history, 1799–1898; Civil and Mexican wars, 1861, 1846; and Civil War and miscellaneous papers.

The contributors were soldiers or prominent historians and include editors Ropes and Dwight, Adelbert Ames, George L. Andrews, Francis Channing Barlow, Henry Van Ness Boynton, Henry S. Burrage, William B. Franklin, George H. Gordon, Lewis A. Grant, John C. Gray, Jr., Norwood P. Hallowell, Thomas L. Livermore, John C. Palfrey, Francis W. Palfrey, William F. Smith, Hazard Stevens, Francis A. Walker, Alexander S. Webb, Stephen Minot Weld, Jr., and James H. Wilson. Coverage is not limited to the Union perspective, as superb papers by William Allan, McHenry Howard, William Lamb, and James Power Smith also appear.

Many papers contain outstanding analyses of various actions. Among these are Livermore's assessment of the Appomattox campaign (vol. 6), Smith's paper on Jackson at Chancellorsville (vol. 8), Francis Palfrey's recollections of Antietam (vol. 3), Boynton's explanation of the Chickamauga campaign (vol. 7), and Ames's account of the capture of Fort Fisher (vol. 9). Groups of related papers allow readers to draw their own conclusions about disagreements, as with Barlow's and Baldy Smith's versions of the capture of the Mule Shoe at Spotsylvania (vol. 4).

The works are generally well edited and the Broadfoot edition contains a page of errata for each volume. These amount to typographical errors, a few transcription errors, and several more severe problems, such as sections of misplaced text. A number of errors exist in Marvel's short biographies, such as misspelling William Allan's name (B-5), providing erroneous birthdates for George H. Gordon and Lewis A. Grant (B-24 and B-25), and miscalculating Henry J. Hunt's age (B-33).

755

Ropes, John Codman, and William Roscoe Livermore. **The Story of the Civil War: A Concise Account of the War in the United States of America between 1861 and 1865** (4 vols., 1270 pp., G. P. Putnam's Sons, New York, 1895–1913)

This work remains valuable as a well-done early summary of a portion of the war's military operations. It consists of three parts in four volumes, as follows: part 1 (by Ropes), *To the Opening of the Campaigns of 1862* (274 pp., 1895); part 2 (by Ropes), *The Campaigns of 1862* (475 pp., 1895); part 3, book 1 (by Livermore), *Chancellorsville, Vicksburg, and So Forth* (270 pp., 1913); part 3, book 2 (by Livermore), *Vicksburg, Port Hudson, Tullahoma, Gettysburg, and So Forth* (251 pp., 1913).

This is the most balanced and authoritative turn-of-the-century account of the strategic and tactical operations of the war, with the authors taking great pains to remain impartial. The narrative consists of an analytical military story with extensive discussions of troop movements, strategy, tactics, numbers engaged and as casualties, results of the battles, and interpretations of the events in Washington and Richmond. The first volume is essentially an introduction, describing the armies, characters, and the early campaigns, with emphasis on First Bull Run. The second volume covers Forts Henry and Donelson, Shiloh, the Peninsular campaign, the offensives of Lee and Bragg, Stones River, and Fredericksburg. The third volume tackles Fort Pillow, the third advance on Vicksburg, Baton Rouge, Iuka, Corinth, the fall of Vicksburg, the armies along the Rappahannock, and

Chancellorsville. The final volume assesses the fall of Vicksburg, operations in Pennsylvania and Tennessee, and contains extensive coverage of Gettysburg.

The authors are too severe in criticizing the military capabilities of Lincoln and Stanton. They bitterly, and usually correctly, attack Halleck's treatment of the early western campaigns. They admonish Bragg and Kirby Smith for essentially incompetent behavior in Kentucky in 1862 wherein Buell was allowed to establish a base and resume the offensive. The authors severely chastise McClellan for his performance on the Peninsula. They attack Pope without mercy but point out several handicaps he labored under, such as the composition of his reconstituted army. The authors caustically attack Burnside for his failures at Antietam and during his command of the army, when he committed an "unbroken chain of errors." They deplore the high-grade appointments of Butler, Banks, and Frémont. The maps are too primitive to be of much use. An early, one-volume edition of the same work, later expanded, was titled *The Story of the Civil War: A Short History, Mainly Military, of the War in the United States of America, Between 1861 and 1865* (182 pp., published by the author, 1893).

756

Smith, Edwin Conrad. **The Borderland in the Civil War** (412 pp., Macmillan Co., New York, 1927)

Smith offers a compilation of moderately detailed information on a theme either lost in general works or scattered in specialized works. He surveys the effects of the war on the southern parts of Ohio, Indiana, and Illinois, the Trans-Allegheny portion of Virginia, and most of Kentucky and Missouri. The population of white males in this delicate region, according to the author, nearly equaled that of the seceding states. Because of the unified nature of the economies, politics, and societies in this area, the author contends, whatever route the region took, the membership would stay together.

Therefore, as Smith somewhat overzealously states, "the attitude of this section afforded easily the most important problem of the war." The narrative begins with a discussion of the 1860 election and a proposition that the borderland acted as a mediator during the possible compromises that followed. Although many of the borderland's inhabitants were Southern in origin, the region generally held fast to strong Union sentiment. The borderland residents blamed abolitionists for provoking the South and felt unwilling to wage war for the defeat of slavery. Yet, when pushed, the region supported the North, largely through Lincoln's diplomacy. The author overstates the case by claiming that if this region had remained neutral "the division of the United States into two Republics was certain." Despite such occasionally overblown rhetoric, the work is worth reading.

(Reprinted 1969, 412 pp., Books for Libraries Press, Freeport, N.Y.)

757

Swinton, William. **Twelve Decisive Battles of the War: A History of the Eastern and Western Campaigns, in Relation to the Actions That Decided Their Issue** (520 pp., Dick and Fitzgerald, New York, 1867)

This is one of the earliest works for popular consumption that summarizes the major battles. A journalist who traveled on occasion with the Federal Army, Swinton composed a popular "analysis" of the following engagements: First Bull Run, Fort Donelson, Shiloh, Antietam, Stones River, the naval fight between the USS *Monitor* and the CSS *Virginia*, Vicksburg, Gettysburg, the Wilderness, Atlanta, Nashville, and Five Forks. What he means by "decisive" is not entirely clear, but for the battles he has chosen he offers a prefatory statement, a discussion of the action itself, and a look at the aftermath.

The author leans heavily toward the Union side on matters of strategy and tactics but for the most part offers fair assessments of individual commanders and a reasonable discussion of the battles. The writing is clear, often dramatic, and sometimes exaggerated. The early date of composition means that a number of small errors appear that, if consulted, the *O.R.* (*q.v.*) would have corrected. The work retains the flavor of an early journalistic report on each of these important actions. Seven portraits of Federal commanders and seven maps are included.

(Reprinted 1986, 520 pp., Promontory Press, New York)

MEDICAL ASPECTS

758

Adams, George Worthington. **Doctors in Blue: The Medical History of the Union Army in the Civil War** (253 pp., Henry Schuman, New York, 1952)

Compact and only occasionally analytical, Adams's work draws on a wide range of sources from army records, the publications of the U.S. Sanitary Commission, and writings by a relatively large number of doctors and nurses. The author describes the initial confusion and incompetence in assembling a Medical Bureau and carrying out the gruesome work necessary on the battlefield. The bureau's leaders re-

ceive fair analysis, as with the ineffective reign of Clement A. Finley and the far more valuable service of William A. Hammond, whose successor, Joseph K. Barnes, brought the bureau to a level of professional competence by carrying out the plans laid down by Hammond.

In addition to succinct descriptions of the logistics and organization of the Medical Bureau, readers will also find a more human story of medicine in the Union Army. The rise of talented women nurses, assembly of battlefield hospitals, and care for the wounded and ailing are treated admirably. The author adequately demonstrates how many surgeons gained professionalism only as their experience mounted and war's end approached. A few omissions, such as discussion of the Western Sanitary Commission and the Christian Commission, are forgivable, as are occasional misspellings.

(Reprinted 1985, 253 pp., Morningside, Dayton)

759

Cunningham, H. H. **Doctors in Gray: The Confederate Medical Service** (339 pp., Louisiana State University Press, Baton Rouge, 1958)

In this general survey, Cunningham describes the way the Confederate Army and Navy created and administered medical services. The Confederacy had a large and, for its day, competent pool of doctors to draw on, and despite inadequacies of supply, its medical services provided a reasonably adequate level of care. The roles of prison hospitals, medical officers in the field, medical supplies, causes of disease, treatments for disease, and surgical operations are examined, and a final chapter provides an appraisal of Confederate doctors and surgeons.

The often overlooked surgeon general of the Confederacy, S. P. Moore, receives fine treatment here, the author crediting Moore with introducing the pavilion type of hospital that because of its healthy environment became the standard structure well into the next century. Cunningham's arguments are balanced, and he uses many anecdotal examples to illustrate his points and add interest to the work.

(Reprinted 1993, 339 pp., Louisiana State University Press, Baton Rouge)

760

Schroeder-Lein, Glenna R. **Confederate Hospitals on the Move: Samuel H. Stout and the Army of Tennessee** (226 pp., University of South Carolina Press, Columbia, 1994)

Stout, who began as a country physician and ended his Civil War career as medical director of hospitals of the Army of Tennessee, provides a fascinating subject for this well-executed book. After a thorough education, Stout became a farmer, schoolteacher, and doctor who quietly practiced in rural Tennessee. At the outbreak of war, however, he joined the army and by the autumn of 1861 was in charge of a hospital in Nashville. When Federal forces pressed into the city, he removed to Chattanooga. A brilliant administrator, he caught the attention of Gen. Braxton Bragg, who assigned Stout administrative charge of the hospitals of the Army of Tennessee surrounding Chattanooga.

Schroeder-Lein takes full advantage of Stout's voluminous writings—which he published in the *Medical Practitioner* and elsewhere—to assemble an interesting narrative. The topics covered invite an insider's view of the workings of Confederate hospitals and the need to keep hospitals relatively mobile as Federal armies drew closer. The author presents such topics as the assignment of surgeons, doctors, matrons, and so forth; the treatment of patients; supplying the hospitals; and selecting and building hospital sites. This is a highly unusual and valuable book of Confederate medical history.

761

Steiner, Paul E. **Medical-Military Portraits of Union and Confederate Generals** (342 pp., Whitmore Publishing Co., Philadelphia, 1968)

This work offers a fascinating glimpse into the case histories of 10 general officers who suffered from various maladies during the war and hints at the effects that their illnesses had on battlefield performance. Among the diseases in question are bilious fever, cholera, acute enteritis, typhoid fever, and yellow fever. The study focuses on commanders Dick Ewell, Nathan Bedford Forrest, John Bell Hood, Joseph Hooker, Stonewall Jackson, Joe Johnston, George B. McClellan, James B. McPherson, and John F. Reynolds.

Steiner does not limit himself to physical ailments, ascribing McClellan's poor performance to a "neuropsychiatric disorder" that he believes was exacerbated by a series of previous medical problems. While he stops short of specific claims relating to physical diseases and their effects on individual commanders at particular times, his work raises questions about the behavior of a sick individual and how it can affect the lives of many in an extraordinary circumstance such as war.

762

Steiner, Paul E. **Physician-Generals of the Civil War: A Study in Nineteenth Mid-Century American Medicine** (194 pp., Charles C. Thomas, Springfield, Ill., 1966)

In this statistical study, which provides brief biographical sketches of each of the officers and a synopsis of various characteristics before, during, and after the war, Steiner examines 33 general officers who were physicians and served outside the medical corps. He employs control groups and attempts to find characteristics that might explain why these physicians sought to fight rather than heal. The author presents some rather unsurprising conclusions, such as that many of these physicians had abandoned medicine before the war.

The author provides an interesting survey of an unusual group of combat officers, and the material on James Patton Anderson, Samuel Wylie Crawford, Nathan Kimball, Albert J. Myer, Lucius B. Northrop, and Edward A. Wild is especially enjoyable. But as an attempt to find deep meanings within a scattered group of individuals linked by one trait, the work does not fare particularly well. The author also confuses categories of company, field, and general officer grades with types of "corps," line and staff.

763

[U.S. Surgeon General's Office.] **The Medical and Surgical History of the War of the Rebellion (1861–65), Prepared, in Accordance with the Acts of Congress, under the Direction of Surgeon General Joseph K. Barnes, United States Army** (2 vols. in 6 serials, 5579 pp., U.S. Government Printing Office, Washington, 1870–1888)

This work consists of numerous statistical summaries relating to diseases, wounds, and deaths in both the Union and Confederate armies, with the overwhelming bulk of material formed from the reports of U.S. medical directors, surgeons, doctors, and hospital staff. In addition to the statistical summaries, excerpts are presented from case studies of tens of thousands of victims of disease and injury during the war. Not only is this account the basic source for medical data, but it comprises one of the finest collections of material relating to individual soldiers. Hundreds of engravings, charts, and tables, as well as many color plates accompany the text.

The coverage is as follows: part 1, volume 1, medical history: an introduction, a statistical summary of illnesses for each year of the war, and an appendix of medical reports; parts 2 and 3, volume 1, medical history: diarrhea and dysentery, medical statistics for prisoners, malaria, and typhoid fever, smallpox, scarlet fever, measles, mumps, yellow fever, scurvy, pneumonia, bronchitis, consumption, poisoning, alcoholism, and a summary of the general hospitals; part 1, volume 2, surgical history: incised and puncture wounds, head injuries, and gunshot wounds of the skull, wounds and injuries of the face, plastic surgery following gunshot face wounds, spinal injuries, and chest wounds; part 2, volume 2, surgical history: injuries of the abdomen, pelvis, back, and upper extremities, including techniques of arm and hand amputations; part 3, volume 2, surgical history: wounds and injuries of the lower extremities, including techniques for amputating legs and feet, miscellaneous injuries, wounds and complications, anaesthetics, and transportation of the wounded.

(Reprinted 1990–1992, titled *The Medical and Surgical History of the Civil War*, with a valuable 3-vol. index that lists names alphabetically and also by state and by unit, 15 vols., 7505 pp., Broadfoot, Wilmington)

764

Welsh, Jack D. **Medical Histories of Confederate Generals** (297 pp., Kent State University Press, Kent, 1995)

Following Ezra Warner's lead in *Generals in Gray* (*q.v.*), Welsh has included 425 general officers in this superbly interesting account of a poorly documented area. Although the author creates a number of fake general officers and excludes some authentic ones, the coverage is generally good and the care with facts is excellent. Welsh's background in medicine allows him to formulate a clear understanding of the various conditions and traumas Confederate general officers experienced and to communicate their complexities to readers in a lucid, direct way.

We learn in a paragraph or two about the antebellum, postbellum, but primarily wartime medical histories of each man. More extensive write-ups appear for renowned officers or those with complex medical problems. The author analyzes with great care the famous incidents of woundings and deaths on the battlefield, as with Albert Sidney Johnston at Shiloh, Stonewall Jackson at Chancellorsville, James Longstreet in the Wilderness, Earl Van Dorn at Spring Hill, and Patrick Ronayne Cleburne at Franklin. The result is a unique reference volume that should be kept handy for browsing.

PICTORIAL WORKS

765

Davis, William C., ed. **The Image of War, 1861–1865** (6 vols., 2809 pp., Doubleday and Co., New York, 1981–1984)

A necessary companion to Miller (*q.v.*), this work sets a modern standard for accuracy and provides a lively group of well-conceived texts and impressive photographic reproduction. Moreover, a survey prior to beginning work on this set uncovered a huge number of previously unpublished or little-known images, which alone make these volumes a necessity for seeing the war as it was.

The 4017 photographs are assembled in thematic chapters important and varied enough to catalog. Volume 1, *Shadows of the Storm*, contains "The Coming of the War" (T. Harry Williams), "The Guns at Fort Sumter" (W. A. Swanberg), "The Boys of '61" (Bell I. Wiley), "The First Bull Run" (Joseph P. Cullen), "The Navies Begin" (Virgil Carrington Jones), "The War Moves West" (Albert Castel), "Photographer of the Confederacy: J. D. Edwards" (Leslie D. Jensen), "The North at War" (Maury Klein), and "The Photographers of the War" (Frederic E. Ray).

Volume 2, *The Guns of '62*, presents "Yorktown: The First Siege" (Warren W. Hassler, Jr.), "The New Ironclads" (William N. Still, Jr.), "Mr. Cooley of Beaufort and Mr. Moore of Concord: A Portfolio," "The Peninsular Campaign" (Emory M. Thomas), "In Camp with the Common Soldiers" (Bell I. Wiley), "The Conquest of the Mississippi" (Charles L. Dufour), "Jackson in the Shenandoah" (Robert G. Tanner), "The Second Bull Run" (David Lindsey), and "The War on Rails" (Robert C. Black III).

Volume 3, *The Embattled Confederacy*, holds "The Bloodiest Day: Antietam" (James I. Robertson, Jr.), "The Fury of Fredericksburg" (Peter J. Parrish), "Strangling the South" (James M. Merrill), "New Bern in North Carolina, Slaves No More" (Dudley T. Cornish), "Washington at War," "Chancellorsville, Lee's Greatest Triumph" (Frank E. Vandiver), "The South at War" (Charles P. Roland), and "The Guns at Gettysburg" (William A. Frassanito).

Volume 4, *Fighting for Time*, contains "Jewels of the Mississippi" (Herman Hattaway), "Following the Armies: A Portfolio," "Raiders of the Seas" (Norman C. Delaney), "The Siege of Charleston" (Rowena Reed), "Caring for the Men" (George W. Adams), "The Camera Craft: A Portfolio," "War on Horseback" (Dee Brown), "The Sailor's Life" (Harold D. Langley), and "Prison Pens and Suffering" (Frank L. Bryne).

Volume 5, *The South Besieged*, features "The War for Tennessee" (Edwin C. Bearss), "Squadron of the South" (Frank J. Merli), "Partners in Posterity: A Portfolio," "Into the Wilderness" (Robert K. Krick), "The Atlanta Campaign" (Richard M. McMurry), "Back into the Valley" (Everard H. Smith), "A Campaign That Failed" (Ludwell H. Johnson III), and "The Forgotten War: The West" (Maurice Melton).

Volume 6, *The End of an Era*, contains "The Modern Army" (Russell F. Weigley), "'Damn the Torpedoes!'" (Charles R. Haberlein, Jr.), "Houghton at the Front: A Portfolio," "The Great March" (John G. Barrett), "Petersburg Besieged" (Richard J. Sommers), "Richmond, City and Capital at War" (Emory M. Thomas), "An End at Last" (Louis Manarin), and "The 'Late Unpleasantness'" (William C. Davis).

A reading of the titles suggests that the organization and coverage of this set does not present a comprehensive picture of the war, a fact discussed by the editor in his introduction. However, a systematic reading of the work bends this warning because, taken together, the sections very nicely present an overall look at the war, from start to finish. In his introduction Davis suggests that the work is simply an extension of the important, though flawed, Miller set. Despite occasional minor errors and frequently underpowered captions that link pictures only loosely, Davis's book is an outstanding model for Civil War photographic history.

766

Davis, William C., ed. **Touched by Fire: A Photographic Portrait of the Civil War** (2 vols., 644 pp., Little, Brown, Boston, 1985–1986)

This continuation of Davis's *Image of War* set (*q.v.*) is a skillfully assembled book that reproduces many rarely seen Civil War images. Davis enlisted historians to contribute essays on subjects that establish the basis for the 1040 photos chosen from a variety of collections (499 in vol. 1 and 541 in vol. 2). The photographic reproduction is excellent, with all images appearing as light-brown duotones.

Although some familiar photos appear, many are previously unpublished. The photos are arranged in unusual and captivating categories, including a portfolio of the Louisiana photographer A. D. Lytle's work, uncommon views of Union and Confederate commanders, photography of Camp Nelson, Kentucky, and sections on the ravages of war and the final years of the participants. Contributors include Herman Hattaway, Harold M. Hyman, Robert K. Krick, Richard J. Sommers, and Emory M. Thomas. Despite occasional errors in captions and the structural dilemma of a sequence of images often loosely tied together, this is a valuable contribution to Civil War photographic history.

767

Gardner, Alexander. **Gardner's Photographic Sketch Book of the War** (2 vols., 100 plates, each with a letterpress description, Philip and Solomons, Washington, 1865)

As the earliest important photographic collection on the war widely distributed to the public, this work is not only important as a historical force and curiosity but also delivers some of the most powerfully evocative images of the war. In it we find scenes of the war in the East, including activities around Washington, battlefield dead from Antietam and Gettysburg, many famous houses and river crossings, portraits of soldiers ranging from those on picket duty to Confederate prisoners, and photographs of the countryside at war. Coverage extends down the decisive campaigns in Virginia, presenting material on Richmond, Petersburg, and Appomattox.

Among these 100 well-reproduced photos are some famous images, as with the dead Confederate sharpshooter at Gettysburg (a contrived photo), views of the Lacy Estate near Fredericksburg, and the huge wagon park at Brandy Station in May 1863. Although the captions often contain errors—for example, the Trostle House at Gettysburg appears as Trossel's House—this work is a monument to the immediacy of news photography in some of its earliest days.

(Reprinted 1959, 1 vol., 100 plates, Dover, New York)

768

Guernsey, Alfred H., and Henry M. Alden. **Harper's Pictorial History of the Great Rebellion in the United States** (2 vols., 836 pp., Harper and Bros., New York, 1866–1868)

This is the classic early pictorial history of the war. Drawn from the pages of *Harper's Weekly*, the most popular journal of its day, the work offers not only a chronology of the war but a briefer treatment of the history of the United States with emphasis on the causes of the war. Nearly 125 pages bring readers up to Sumter; thereafter the story comes alive in copy taken from the periodical with minimal re-editing and written shortly after the war. Thus, the work seems fresh and exciting to read. It is also wildly inaccurate in many cases.

As with Frank Leslie's illustrated history (*q.v.*), much of the pleasure here comes from the engravings. There are 998 engravings, mostly scenes of battles, camps, marches, soldier life, and portraits of officers, with a few maps and plans included. The compilation strives for authenticity but clearly a good many of the scenes are embellished. Nonetheless, this work delivers the news of the war much as the civilians during the conflict experienced it, and it is therefore both touching and memorable.

(Reprinted n.d., 2 vols., 836 pp., Arno Press, New York; reprinted 1985, 1 vol., Fairfax Press, New York)

769

Holzer, Harold, and Mark E. Neely, Jr. **Mine Eyes Have Seen the Glory: The Civil War in Art** (336 pp., Orion Books, New York, 1993)

The more than 250 works of art included herein range from miniatures to giant cycloramas, from brushy primitives to meticulously crafted oil portraits in the best European tradition. The subjects include the whole interpretive canvas of Civil War art in the last decades of the 19th century: battle pieces, studies of camp scenes and picket duty, portraits of officers and private soldiers, naval scenes and actions, and reflective art centered on the home front and civilian experience. All show us how artists attempted to synthesize the Civil War experience for posterity.

The accompanying text provides a reasonably detailed analysis of the military history behind the paintings as well as a lighter discussion of the art history at play. The production value of this book, so critical in a work of this nature, is splendid: the photographs are sharp, the color separations well done, the printing and the paper first rate. All the great pieces are here, including the Gettysburg cyclorama by Paul Phillippoteaux and many works by Albert Bierstadt, Winslow Homer, and Eastman Johnson. This is a necessary volume for anyone interested in the history of Civil War art.

770

Lossing, Benson J. **A History of the Civil War, 1861–1865, and the Causes That Led Up to the Great Conflict, by Benson J. Lossing, LL.D., and a Chronological Summary and Record of Every Engagement: Showing the Total Losses and Casualties Together with War Maps of Localities, Compiled from the Official Records of the War Department: Illustrated with Facsimile Photographic Reproductions of the Official War Photographs, Taken at the Time by Mathew B. Brady, under the Authority of President Lincoln and Now in the Possession of the War Department, Washington, D.C.** (512 pp., War Memorial Association, Washington, 1912)

This sweeping general history of the entire war serves as an important memento of the earliest days of photographic Civil War histories. The text is ultrapatriotic and both celebrates Union victory and welcomes the two sections together (as was fashionable at the time).

The work was originally issued in 16 sections, each with a color plate made from an oil painting, mostly by Henry A.

Ogden. The real value lies in the photographs, some 744 in all (many plates are montages, however, so more than 744 individual images appear). The text is interesting primarily because it reflects the pre–World War I perception of the Civil War. Several maps, diagrams, and other illustrations appear. Occasional errors surface, as with the switched captions on page 264, and the work lacks an index.

(Reprinted n.d., 512 pp., Fairfax Press, New York)

771

Miller, Francis Trevelyan, ed. **The Photographic History of the Civil War** (10 vols., 3497 pp., Review of Reviews Co., New York, 1911)

The grandfather of pictorial histories, this mammoth work is a necessary part of any Civil War library. The photographs are thematically arranged in sections of text as follows: *The Opening Battles* (vol. 1); *Two Years of Grim War* (vol. 2); *The Decisive Battles* (vol. 3); *The Cavalry* (vol. 4); *Forts and Artillery* (vol. 5); *The Navies* (vol. 6); *Soldier Life and Secret Service* (vol. 7); *Prisons and Hospitals* (vol. 8); *The Armies and Leaders* (vol. 9); and *Poetry and Eloquence* (vol. 10).

Published on the 50th anniversary of the war's start, Miller's work brings together written contributions from soldiers and historians on both sides. Among the authors are William C. Church, S. A. Cunningham, Frederick Dent Grant, Charles King, Thaddeus S. C. Lowe, Randolph H. McKim, George H. Putnam, Allen C. Redwood, Theodore F. Rodenbaugh, T. M. R. Talcott, Marcus J. Wright, and John A. Wyeth. The texts are generally well done and unusually spirited, in some cases allowing biases to shine through. Overall, however, the authors are successful in their attempts to describe aspects of the war as detached, objective history.

The work contains 3389 images that constitute an important source work on the war's appearance—its battlefields, common soldiers, officers, forts, diseases, camp scenes, army movements, and materiel. Virtually all the classic icons of the Civil War are contained in this work, along with hundreds of lesser-known images. The reproduction quality is good in terms of 1911 printing technology, although recent reprintings contain images degraded substantially by making plates from the printed pages of an original copy.

The captions must be used judiciously, as many speculate poetically on the accompanying scenes or contain outright errors, some of which originated with the photographers themselves. An examination of the volume on armies and leaders shows it to be factually untrustworthy. Strong Vincent is identified as Vincent Strong (p. 137). Fitz Henry Warren is misidentified as colonel of the 1st Iowa Infantry

(p. 205). John B. Gordon is erroneously identified as a lieutenant general (p. 247), as is Joseph Wheeler (p. 249). A photograph purporting to show Confederate Brig. Gen. Laurence S. Baker depicts Union Brig. Gen. Lafayette C. Baker (p. 281). Many names are misspelled, as with Barnard E. Bee (p. 147), Lawrence O'Bryan Branch (p. 149), John C. C. Sanders (p. 155), Otho F. Strahl (p. 157), George W. Deitzler (p. 207), Catharinus P. Buckingham (p. 235), John Cabell Breckinridge (p. 251), Jones M. Withers (p. 253), Francis A. Shoup (p. 261), Gilbert Moxley Sorrel (p. 265), Dudley M. DuBose (p. 265), Hylan B. Lyon (p. 269), Allen Thomas (p. 271), Collett Leventhorpe (p. 281), Laurence S. Baker (p. 281), James Chesnut, Jr. (p. 283), James Conner (p. 285), Alexander Schimmelfennig (p. 293), John C. Vaughan (p. 299), Frank Wheaton (p. 305), Armistead L. Long (p. 317), and David A. Weisiger (p. 319).

The practice of misidentifying officers as generals who never legally achieved the grade is rampant, as with Francis S. Bartow (p. 147), Turner Ashby (p. 149), Thomas R. R. Cobb (p. 151), James E. Rains (p. 151), James Deshler (p. 153), Samuel Benton (p. 155), James Dearing (p. 157), John Dunovant (p. 157), Victor J. B. Girardey (p. 157), Archibald C. Godwin (p. 157), Isham W. Garrott (p. 255), Theodore W. Brevard (p. 261), Bryan M. Thomas (p. 265), George B. Hodge (p. 269), Adam R. Johnson (p. 269), Edwin H. Stoughton (p. 307), and Felix H. Robertson (p. 315).

Other errors occur, such as incorrect dates of commissions, as with George B. McClellan (p. 164), and dates of death, as with Ambrose E. Burnside (p. 168). The tables of officers who attained various grades are flawed. The Union data include 84 misspellings, 18 inadvertent duplications, and the reversal "Bvt. BGen. Frank Paul"; the Confederate data include 17 spelling errors and the phantom name A. M. W. Sterling in addition to Sterling A. M. Wood. John Bell Hood is listed as a general; and William Wirt Allen, John S. Bowen, William Dorsey Pender, and Jeremy F. Gilmer are listed as major generals. Altogether, 24 might-have-beens are listed as brigadier generals.

(Reprinted 1987, 5 vols., 3497 pp., Blue and Grey Press, Secaucus)

772

Moat, Louis Shepheard, ed. **Frank Leslie's Illustrated Famous Leaders and Battle Scenes of the Civil War: The Most Important Events of the Conflict between the States Graphically Pictured, Stirring Battle Scenes and Grand Naval Engagements, Drawn by Special Artists on the Spot, Portraits of Principal Participants, Military and Civil, Famous Forts, Pathetic Episodes, etc., etc.** (544 pp., published by Mrs. Frank Leslie, New York, 1896)

This collection of material published during the war in *Frank Leslie's Illustrated Newspaper* was reworked and repackaged in book form. Some 869 engravings with extensive accompanying captions present a running narrative of the war, its events, and the military and political leaders of both sides.

The approach is of course highly partisan and patriotic, reflecting the Northern outlook. Evaluations of battles and their numerical analysis are often distorted. The illustrations are sometimes enchanting but more often highly exaggerated and unreal. Still, the work is entertaining for its delivery of a near-contemporary narrative of operations, something that delights despite its deficiencies. Subsequent printings contain an appendix on the Spanish-American War.

(Abridged edition 1992, titled *Leslie's Illustrated Civil War*, with an introduction by John E. Stanchak, 256 pp., University Press of Mississippi, Jackson)

773

Muench, David, and Michael B. Ballard. **Landscapes of Battle: The Civil War** (141 pp., University Press of Mississippi, Jackson, 1988)

Although the text serves primarily as filler to separate the photographs, this work presents a gorgeous collection of colorful images of fields, markers, and monuments. Superior in color, composition, and contrast, these images will be admired by both casual buffs and scholars. There are 99 scenic color shots, as well as a sprinkling of historic images and some poorly done "blitzkrieg" maps. The chronological coverage includes Fort Sumter, Bull Run, Wilson's Creek, Fort Donelson, Pea Ridge, Shiloh, Fort Pulaski, the Seven Days, Antietam, Fredericksburg, Stones River, Chancellorsville, Vicksburg, Gettysburg, Chickamauga, Chattanooga, the Wilderness, Spotsylvania, Cold Harbor, Kennesaw Mountain, Petersburg, and Appomattox.

By necessity, just a few images appear for each site. Some are magnificent scenes, as with the overview of Moccasin Bend, the sweeping panorama of Little Round Top, the crisp portrait of the Sunken Road at Antietam. Still others are striking because of prominent foregrounds, as with the series of monument studies at Vicksburg. Others are generic views of water, fields, and flowers and might as well have been taken anywhere. However, the majority of these beautiful photographs form a remembrance of the major battlefields of the war as they appear today.

774

Roberts, Bobby, Carl Moneyhon, and Richard McCaslin. **Portraits of Conflict** (4 vols., 1339 pp., consisting of *A Photographic History of Arkansas in the Civil War* [242 pp., 1987], *A Photographic History of Louisiana in the Civil War* [356 pp., 1990], *A Photographic History of Mississippi in the Civil War* [396 pp., 1993], and *A Photographic History of South Carolina in the Civil War* [345 pp., 1994], University of Arkansas Press, Fayetteville, 1987–1994)

These volumes, the first three written by Roberts and Moneyhon and the fourth by McCaslin, assess the Civil War as it happened in each of the states and those states' participation and contribution to the war. Topics covered in the first volume include Arkansas's preparation for war, the Civil War in northwest Arkansas, Helena, Little Rock, medicine in Civil War Arkansas, and Camden and the legacy of guerrilla warfare. The work on Louisiana emphasizes the fall of New Orleans, Baton Rouge, the Port Hudson campaign, and the Red River campaign. The Mississippi volume covers the struggle for northeastern Mississippi, the Vicksburg campaign, and the Meridian Expedition. The volume on South Carolina covers the secession crisis and Fort Sumter, South Carolinians in the Army of Northern Virginia, the naval and land assaults on Port Royal and Charleston, the siege of Charleston, South Carolinians in the West, Sherman's march, and Reconstruction. The Arkansas volume contains 212 images; those on Louisiana and Mississippi present 293 and 296, respectively, and the South Carolina volume has 251.

The photographic reproduction in these works is superb. The images are varied enough to provide a balanced view of the war as it relates to each state, with many wartime scenes of places, commanders, and common soldiers on both sides. An appendix briefly describes the fate of many of the primary characters discussed in the volumes. Errors occur in the captions, and some captions are so vague as to be only obliquely related to the photos they describe. But overall these volumes are valuable by virtue of making such a large collection of enjoyable images—many of them quite rare—widely available.

775

Sears, Stephen W., ed. **The American Heritage Century Collection of Civil War Art** (400 pp., American Heritage Publishing Co., New York, 1974)

This fine collection of Civil War art presents a broad sampling of the work created in the 1880s for *Century* magazine's Battles and Leaders series, an extremely influential and popular collection of articles that became *Battles and Leaders of the Civil War* (*q.v.*). The editors collected more than 1000 engravings to be considered for the series, in addition to their previous holdings, and this work offers superb reproductions of 378 of them, as well as an appendix of the entire American Heritage collection, which numbers 679. Many additional examples are shown as small black-and-white photos in the appendix. Prominent artists are represented, including Edwin Forbes, Allen C. Redwood, Charles W. Reed, William L. Sheppard, Walton Taber, and James E. Taylor.

776

Taylor, James E. **With Sheridan Up the Shenandoah Valley in 1864: Leaves from a Special Artist's Sketchbook and Diary** (ed. George F. Skoch, Martin F. Graham, and Dennis E. Frye, 637 pp., Morningside Dayton, 1989)

This soldier-artist's more than 600 drawings, along with notes from his wartime diary, furnish an intriguing collection. Taylor served with the 10th New York Infantry for two years before joining *Frank Leslie's Illustrated Newspaper* as a special correspondent. The finely crafted realistic style of this artist and his battle-hardened eye for the soldier's life make for an enriching combination.

The work traces Sheridan's Valley campaign of 1864 and includes observations on the great and the trivial. The accuracy of the material ranges from concrete to speculative, so certain scenes must be viewed through the filter of embellishment. But overall this massive archive of art captures one of the critical final campaigns of the war in a unique way and deserves wide circulation.

POLITICS AND SOCIETY

777

Ash, Stephen V. **Middle Tennessee Society Transformed, 1860–1870** (299 pp., Louisiana State University Press, Baton Rouge, 1988)

Ash argues that a special region of central Tennessee, a tobacco-growing region surrounding Nashville and extending south to the edge of the state, constituted a "Third South." Set apart significantly from other Tennessee regions, the 13 Tennessee counties represented here were characterized by wealth, significant slave ownership, and advanced society. The author analyzes this society and its changes from the secession crisis through the war years, three-fourths of which were characterized by Federal occupation, to the early years of postwar Reconstruction.

Census data and a mountain of sources relating to local history are used to portray a united white Southern front that vigorously supported the Confederacy but cracked somewhat after the fall of Forts Henry and Donelson and after the earliest visions of emancipation touched the area's slave population. The author skillfully describes how Federal occupation held the territory and prevented Confederate resistance while it ruined the region's economy and estranged the local whites. He also contends that most of the former slaves simply left without significant assistance from the Union Army. This work adds substantially to the literature on wartime society by clearly showing the evolution of one important section of a very influential state.

778

Baker, Jean H. **The Politics of Continuity: Maryland Political Parties from 1858 to 1870** (239 pp., Johns Hopkins University Press, Baltimore, 1973)

The author provides a rigorous analysis of the political system in the complex and splintered state of Maryland during the war years and early Reconstruction—no easy task, given that the state's western region remained loyal to the North, whereas the eastern counties possessing strong economic and social ties to the South split in their voting patterns and support of candidates in Democratic, Republican, and Know-Nothing parties. Governor Thomas Holliday Hicks, a Know-Nothing, teetered on the fence as the secession crisis mounted but ultimately prevented secession from spreading in Maryland.

Baker shows through county voting patterns that the Democratic party survived and reemerged after the war as the power base of the "Union as it was." But political patterns that formed in the antebellum years continued to dominate the state's politics, and loyalties, distrust, and hatreds endured. Although she documents the state's electoral divisions, Baker does not fully interpret them. Still, she sheds light on the confused and often confusing competition behind Maryland politics and shows how the state held an essentially neutral position during the war.

779

Bernstein, Iver. **The New York City Draft Riots: Their Significance for American Society and Politics in the Age of the Civil War** (363 pp., Oxford University Press, New York, 1990)

This work places into context the greatest single episode of unrest in the wartime North. Thoroughly and creatively researched, it stands as a significant contribution to the social history of the war. Bernstein follows the political and economic history of New York from midcentury through the early Reconstruction years, analyzing events through the perspective of the July 1863 riots. He begins with a detailed and well-written summary of the riots and their relationship to the war as it stood in the summer of 1863; subsequent chapters investigate the roles played by various groups in the riots and their significance measured against a backdrop of the city's antebellum social history.

The author's probe into the parts played by different groups is scholarly and well supported. He shows that Irish Catholics, seemingly the most threatened by blacks, were the most violent participants in the riots. Other ethnic groups joined in to varying degrees, and before the riots were over German workers entered the fray as self-appointed police, settling the crowds before the arrival of exhausted troops from Gettysburg. The narrative also explores the reaction of New York's elite social classes, painting a sharp contrast in a city that at wartime was already a huge blend of many different classes from many different places. If the author sometimes exaggerates the influence of the riots, particularly after the war, it is a small defect in an otherwise superb book.

780

Bogue, Allen G. **The Congressman's Civil War** (189 pp., Cambridge University Press, New York, 1989)

This brief, illuminating view of the Federal Congress during the war years is an offshoot of Bogue's earlier work on Republican senators of the war period (*q.v.*). The work divides into five sections: the career paths of congressmen and the coming of the war, the relationship between Lincoln and the Congress, the investigative process in the U.S. House, the institution's authority structures, and a conclusion. An appendix lists representatives and senators who died in office during the period 1844–1865.

Bogue succeeds admirably in throwing new light on the meaning of the role of Congress during the Civil War. Because those senators and representatives who died between 1844 and 1865 were eulogized in Congress, Bogue presents evaluations of them as prepared by their colleagues; then he provides his own analysis of what seemed to make successful congressional careers, contrasting the effects of Southerners and Northerners as the secession crisis erupted. He successfully explores what congressmen hoped to gain from President Lincoln and how Lincoln dealt with the situation. Investigations and authority structures in Congress reveal much about the way the body worked during those turbulent times. In the end, the author argues that no individual or group was able to establish control of the legislation that passed through the Civil War Congress.

781

Bogue, Allen G. **The Earnest Men: Republicans of the Civil War Senate** (369 pp., Cornell University Press, Ithaca, 1981)

This study explores the record of radicals in the wartime Senate, with appendices that document roll-call voting patterns. Bogue examines the committees and leaders of the Senate, radicals and moderates, the issues of slavery, emancipation, punishment, the judiciary, border states, and human rights to provide an assessment of Senate radicals and how they performed during the war. Much of the interpretation rests on an analysis of the voting record, and the author surveys issues pertinent to Southern politics to place senators on a scale judging their degree of radicalness.

Fifty-two roll-call votes provide the basis for the author's ranking of senators as radicals or moderates. The narrative further investigates this ranking throughout four additional sessions of the Senate. The author then explores other issues that may be tested in the same manner. The result agrees with the longstanding contention that radicals sought revenge as well as victory. Also not surprisingly, Bogue finds that Federal authority and abolitionist tendencies are characteristics of radicalism. The radicals found fewer constitutional limits than did their moderate counterparts. The result is a scholarly study that will remain useful for many years.

782

Carroll, Daniel B. **Henri Mercier and the American Civil War** (396 pp., Princeton University Press, Princeton, 1971)

Carroll shows that although the French minister to the United States was primarily aligned with Southerners, his actions during the wartime years centered on avoiding war with the United States. He focused on this goal while holding French interests above all else, maintaining ties to the South, and believing that the disunion between the two American factions was irreversible. Indeed, although Mercier wanted to avoid sliding his own country into the war,

he did propose a common market system between Europe and both warring parties in which the Confederacy would be able to sell cotton and other exports and the North would gain strong economic advantages. Washington would not listen.

The author's probing research in this narrow but important area illuminates much about Franco-American relations during the war years. We read excellent accounts of the blockade, the French recognition of the Confederacy's hostile status, the famous interview of June 1861, the *Trent* affair, and the peace offerings of 1862 and 1863. The author exposes Mercier's rather self-centered attitudes toward the economic value of America and the Emancipation Proclamation. Carroll agrees with the view put forth by Case and Spencer (*q.v.*) that the influence of France during the Civil War years was rather limited. Further narrative describes the intervention in Mexico and the American reaction to it.

783

Case, Lynn M., and Warren F. Spencer. **The United States and France: Civil War Diplomacy** (747 pp., University of Pennsylvania Press, Philadelphia, 1970)

Exhaustively researched and marked by systematic objectivity, this work examines Franco-American relations from both sides of the Atlantic. The early chapters treat the developing relationship between the three players—France, the United States, and the Confederate States—during the war's first several months. Case and Spencer's portrayal of William Henry Seward is heavy handed, to say the least. They exaggerate Seward's actions as bullying maneuvers and reduce the intelligence and stamina of Henri Mercier and British Minister Lord Lyons in their relationship with Seward. To heighten the drama, the authors have Seward shouting, and they even invent a quotation to buttress their lurid depiction of the American secretary of state.

The chapters that follow are more balanced and accurately recount the French role in mediating the *Trent* affair and the ever-fluctuating possibility of France's intervention in the war. (In a peculiar hypothesis, however, the authors suggest the Confederacy may have staged the *Trent* crisis to draw European powers into the war.) The remaining analysis of France's diminishing influence in the American war is admirably executed, and many nuggets of information, like those treating the activities of Confederates in Europe, are skillfully brought to light.

784

Cimprich, John. **Slavery's End in Tennessee, 1861–1865** (191 pp., University of Alabama Press, Tuscaloosa, 1985)

The author straightforwardly examines slavery in Tennessee during the war with an analysis of the changing lives of slaves under the Confederacy and subsequent Federal occupation. Cimprich draws on a large base of documents, including records of the Union Army, the Freedmen's Bureau, and newspaper accounts. In evaluating the termination of slavery in Tennessee, he examines the seeds of Reconstruction, the role of contraband camps and ghettos, and the participation of blacks in state and local politics of the chaotic wartime period. Additionally, he surveys military service experienced by Tennessee slaves in both the Federal and Confederate armies.

The work deftly shows that blacks exhibited a surprising degree of control over their destiny as the war unfolded. Cimprich describes the efforts of both paternalists and laissez-faire adherents to provide a transition period in which blacks could find their new lives. He usefully shows that Andrew Johnson could be both relatively racist and a proponent of emancipation. Careful in its conclusions, this work provides a balanced and objective look at the end of one of Tennessee's oldest institutions.

785

Cook, Adrian. **The Armies in the Streets: The New York City Draft Riots of 1863** (323 pp., University Press of Kentucky, Lexington, 1974)

In contrast to Bernstein's work on the subject (*q.v.*), Cook's study focuses not on the political and social aspects of antebellum and postbellum New York City but squarely on the story of the riots themselves. The work therefore provides an excellent account of the problem that began when a volunteer fire department, incensed by the draft law and the existence of an exemption, forced the shutting down of a local draft office. The resulting spiral of street violence receives careful documentation in this work, which artfully describes the lack of law enforcement and the military's more pressing engagement at Gettysburg. The horror and destruction that resulted from the riots, with mobs looting and burning at will, marked the most extreme such activities in American history until nearly another century had passed.

Cook's description of the quelling of mob rule by exhausted veterans of Gettysburg days after the battle and the lasting significance of the riots is splendid. He demonstrates that the goal of ethnic peace rose in significance in the minds

of Tammany politicians and that the riots may even have prolonged the war because of lingering European beliefs that such riots might respark an antigovernment revolution.

786

Curry, Leonard P. **Blueprint for Modern America: Nonmilitary Legislation of the First Civil War Congress** (302 pp., Vanderbilt University Press, Nashville, 1968)

This work contributes a significant analysis of an overlooked aspect of wartime politics. As Curry correctly contends, pure politics of the war era molded much of the structure of America today, although he confusingly refers to modern America as both the present and the end of the last century. By undertaking a systematic survey of a dizzying array of sources, the author has produced a work that competently outlines a variety of subjects, examines them, and formulates concrete conclusions about the way the war's first Congress changed the politics of the nation.

Curry's sources range from the *Congressional Globe* to newspapers, books, periodicals, and important government documents. Other works relied on—perhaps in unwarranted fashion—include the old edition of Gideon Welles's diary (*q.v.*) and Nicolay and Hay's obsolete edition of Lincoln's works. The author examines slavery, confiscation, taxation, currency, public improvements, and the increased dominance of Congress over the executive branch. This last discussion is clouded by a thin examination of Lincoln's relations with Congress during its first term. Curry's thesis also concentrates heavily on Republicans; he examines voting records in a somewhat perplexing way and suggests that the Committee on the Conduct of the War overstretched its authority. Still, the work has solid merit that makes it valuable for any consideration of wartime politics.

787

Ferris, Norman B. **Desperate Diplomacy: William H. Seward's Foreign Policy, 1861** (265 pp., University of Tennessee Press, Knoxville, 1976)

Through a systematic, logical, and admirable analysis, Ferris reconstructs the wartime actions of the enigmatic Seward and establishes a clear picture of his actions relating to foreign powers. In the process, he unravels a number of earlier, more cynical views of Seward's behavior. Ferris leans toward sympathy for his subject but in no way misrepresents the facts as he shows many earlier works have. His interpretations are solid, precise, and well supported.

Ferris describes how Seward cleverly dealt with the early months of war in a statesmanlike fashion, using Britain's preoccupation with European matters to full advantage. He restores great credit to Seward's role in averting crises with Britain and France without diminishing the parts played by Minister Adams and others. He also shows how Seward made the case that exigencies of the war were solely an American matter. Ferris documents the secretary's actions fully while demonstrating that Seward was not, as has often been charged, driven by expansionism. The machinations that allowed Seward to convince foreign ministers that the American war was purely an internal affair were often complex and, in many cases, succeeded by a slim margin. The author paints a superbly detailed, valuable portrait of Seward's balancing act during the first months of war.

788

Ferris, Norman B. **The *Trent* Affair: A Diplomatic Crisis** (280 pp., University of Tennessee Press, Knoxville, 1977)

The author's re-creation of the period in which the *Trent* crisis occurred is key to understanding its significance. According to Ferris, the Lincoln administration had settled for a long war and was exasperated and preoccupied with its army generals. In a classic case of poor thinking and bad timing, Charles Wilkes seized the *Trent* and Commissioners Mason and Slidell and infuriated the British government. The author demonstrates that the British were angry enough to consider violent actions against the United States, which had little to gain, if not everything to lose, from another war involving Britain. Moreover, British recognition of the Confederacy would certainly markedly increase the latter's chances for survival. Realizing this, Lincoln and Seward blinked.

This clear, factual account sets down the story of the *Trent* crisis and examines the roles of Lincoln and Seward, the Confederate commissioners and government, and a battery of British officials. Drawing on an impressive number of archival sources, the author's narrative is complete and well documented. Ferris may give slightly too much credit to Seward and not quite enough to Lincoln, but this is understandable considering his previous work, *Desperate Diplomacy* (*q.v.*). By analyzing the British reactions, the author shows that indeed the *Trent* affair was a diplomatic crisis that, even if it had been handled less skillfully by the Americans, probably would not have escalated into another war.

789

Gates, Paul W. **Agriculture and the Civil War** (383 pp., Alfred A. Knopf, New York, 1965)

Gates takes a penetrating look at a neglected aspect of the war. Impressively researched and soundly executed, this work sets the standard for analyzing the impact of the war on agriculture and of agriculture on the war.

The author follows agriculture in both the South and the North and examines the influence and activities of the U.S. government on agriculture during the war years. Gates successfully portrays the problems with shifting Southern farmers away from cotton production and the limited success of growing crops to supply the Confederate Army. The plantation structure had partly changed by the middle of the war but not sufficiently, largely due to the blockade. Not only were soldiers suffering from want of food but also civilians, and this substantially impacted the Southern will to fight.

The author demonstrates how Northern farmers far more successfully answered the necessities of the war, in part because numerous small farms growing a wide variety of foodstuffs already existed. Moreover, he shows that they employed one-quarter as many workers to achieve the same result, in part because of a greater use of technology on the farm. The diversity of agriculture in the North, with widespread dairy and livestock enterprises, led during the war to the rise of commercial farming.

790

Hammond, Bray. **Sovereignty and an Empty Purse: Banks and Politics in the Civil War** (400 pp., Princeton University Press, Princeton, 1970)

This work describes the financial crisis interposed on the American economy by the Civil War. Hammond carefully surveys the crisis of the Union in terms of dollars and the response and creative solutions investigated by Secretary of the Treasury Chase, members of Congress, the wealthy, fundraisers, and the public at large. The core of the work focuses on legislation relating to finances, encompassing the Independent Treasury Act, the Legal Tender Act, and the National Bank Act, all of which the 37th Congress enacted.

The picture that emerges is the clearest and most sensible account of Civil War finances on the Union side. The author treats Chase harshly, documenting the secretary's draining of the government's gold reserves rather than more intelligently converting to a check and deposit system. In demolishing Chase's competence, he suggests alternative actions that the secretary might have pursued more wisely. Yet the author has the advantage of historical hindsight and therefore may be judging Chase too severely in various places. This work does refine the picture of Chase, much to his discredit, and documents the sloppy story of the government's financing of the war—something that deeply affects the nation today.

791

Hesseltine, William B. **Lincoln and the War Governors** (405 pp., Alfred A. Knopf, New York, 1948)

This detailed evaluation of the various tensions and conflicts between the executives of the Union states and the Federal government is impressively researched and thoroughly documented. Hesseltine spends considerable effort outlining the stories behind the relationship between Lincoln and the war governors, with special emphasis on problematic situations. He pays special attention to John A. Andrew, Austin Blair, William A. Buckingham, Andrew G. Curtin, William Dennison, Samuel J. Kirkwood, Edwin D. Morgan, Oliver H. P. T. Morton, Edward Salomon, William Sprague, David Tod, Israel Washburn, and Richard Yates. Nor does he neglect the various cabinet officials in Lincoln's administration, delivering cogent analysis of the activities of Simon Cameron, Edwin M. Stanton, and Salmon P. Chase.

Hesseltine argues persuasively that Lincoln's political mastery of his governors played a significant role in the Federal victory and that the balance of power shifted immensely from the start to the end of the war. At first, he shows, the power of raising troops and commanding them lay almost completely with the state executives. But Lincoln's mastery of people and of politics eroded this control and transferred it to his own door, allowing the Federal armies to become efficient fighting machines.

(Reprinted 1972, 405 pp., Peter Smith, Gloucester, Mass.)

792

Hyman, Harold M. **A More Perfect Union: The Impact of the Civil War and Reconstruction on the Constitution** (562 pp., Alfred A. Knopf, New York, 1973)

Outstanding as a probe of the legal aspects of the war, the book is unique in its approach of surveying the effects of the Constitution as a document on the thought processes of the war's participants. Arguing that the war and its outcome indeed helped to shape the meaning of the Constitution for Americans, Hyman maintains that perhaps more important, and certainly of more interest to Civil War scholars, the Constitution helped to shape the meaning of the war for those living it.

The author analyzes and compares the stationary view of the Constitution held by most Democrats with the evolving view held by most Republicans. He contends that despite playing the role of revolutionaries, the Republicans held fast to the legal limitations provided by the Constitution. Indeed, the leading Republican, Abraham Lincoln, believed the Constitution was sacred, knew it better than perhaps any president before or since, and used its legalities to the upper limit in his prosecution of the war. He was both a "nationalist and a constitutionalist," the author shows, and demonstrated that a constitutional democracy could cope with a national crisis of unparalleled severity.

Agreeing with the bulk of recent historiography, the author believes that Reconstruction began immediately following the attack on Sumter. Military governorships, conquered territories, liberated slaves, and regions surrounding armies in "enemy territory" became, in the words of the author, "laboratories" for experimenting with Reconstruction methods. Hyman shows, in this masterful and classic work, that Congress aimed to restore governments to as near a state of prewar existence as it could, even as the war raged on in the Southern states.

793

Jenkins, Brian. **Britain and the War for the Union** (2 vols., 785 pp., McGill-Queens University Press, Montreal, 1974–1980)

The author persuasively suggests that rather than a long list of other factors, the "turmoil in Europe" during the Civil War era prevented British intervention in the American war. During the war's early days, as Jenkins carefully demonstrates, British authorities believed the war would end relatively quickly. The documentation of Franco-British relations and Jenkins's discussion of the clever diplomacy of William Seward reveal that Britain came to worry over possible French gains in Europe and even a possible American-Russian partnership that could influence the European balance of power. In the end, the British ministry sought to protect Canada and simply deal with the Northern and Southern factions in America without any extensive involvement.

Jenkins documents the complex British attitudes toward American slavery's role in the war. The majority of British people apparently assumed the American war was about slavery from the outset and displayed surprise at Lincoln's emphasis on the preservation of the Union. However, Jenkins shows that after the issuance of the Emancipation Proclamation, British reaction was mixed, and often hostile in the British press. This section belies or at least reduces much of the stature of previous claims about the significance of Britain's abolitionist tendencies. For the most part, however, this soundly researched and well-written study confirms the longstanding notions about Britain's reaction to the war.

794

Jimerson, Randall C. **The Private Civil War: Popular Thought during the Sectional Conflict** (270 pp., Louisiana State University Press, Baton Rouge, 1988)

The many ways in which participants in the war viewed its effects on their lives are skillfully and engagingly discussed in this study. Jimerson focuses on why Northerners and Southerners endorsed the war, how each viewed the other side, the changing attitudes toward slavery and race, and dissent on each side. Because he carefully analyzes a large number of well-known and little-known accounts, he provides an important glimpse into the minds of Americans during the war period.

The narrative succinctly explains how two very different outlooks produced a very similar type of patriotic support for warfare. To investigate the perceptions of the enemy, the author presents selections from the writings of particular subjects in the Confederacy (Alexander Cheves Haskell, William King, and Sarah Morgan) and the Union (Robert McAllister, Nathan B. Webb, and Charles Wills) that include both soldiers and civilians. The sections dealing with the rising alarm among Confederates regarding emancipation are particularly striking, and the handling of the internal divisions within each section forms a nice introduction to that specialized area.

795

Jones, Howard. **Union in Peril: The Crisis over British Intervention in the Civil War** (300 pp., University of North Carolina Press, Chapel Hill, 1992)

Jones views the American Civil War through British eyes and examines the British response to what appeared to them to be destruction on a scale disproportionate to the issues at hand. He places into proper interpretive context the mass of details of political wrangling back and forth across the Atlantic. The characters are clearly portrayed: Lincoln, Seward, and Charles Francis Adams make their case to the British government that the problem is an internal insurrection. Yet Palmerston and Russell wait and watch while they extend some hope of diplomatic recognition and perhaps support for the Confederacy.

The author shows that the Emancipation Proclamation may have actually increased the chances for British intervention because foreigners feared a resulting race war on a mass scale. So why did the British government fail to intervene? The doubly crushing blows at Gettysburg and Vicksburg during the first days of July 1863 convinced Palmerston and his government that the South could not win the war. More-

over, the author suggests, any outside settlement would have been unrealistic. How could it be enforced? The story of the British involvement in the war comes to light in this well-told and detailed narrative.

796

Jordan, Winthrop D. **Tumult and Silence at Second Creek: An Inquiry into a Slave Conspiracy** (391 pp., Louisiana State University Press, Baton Rouge, 1993)

The author documents in impressive detail the planning and execution of a slave conspiracy near Natchez, Mississippi, in May 1861. The paranoia that swept the land in the wake of the John Brown raid at Harpers Ferry lingered and even worsened by the outbreak of war. Seldom did slave rebellions occur. The Second Creek insurrection was foiled, as were most. Discovered by plantation owners from an overseer's son who overhead the slaves plotting, the conspiracy fell apart. The revolt did produce a violent (and illegal) backlash by the white owners, however, and marks a low point in Natchez-area history. Within four months, 27 slaves had been hanged without trial.

The incident receives very fine examination in this work, which reproduces in full the key document recording the details of the event, an account of slave testimony. This appears along with extracts of letters and other testimony relating to the Second Creek conspiracy. The editing on these source documents, along with Jordan's own well-crafted story, provides a beautifully reconstructed look at a shameful event.

797

Kirkland, Edward Chase. **The Peacemakers of 1864** (279 pp., Macmillan and Co., New York, 1927)

After an analysis of the various factions involved, Kirkland describes a number of specific peace missions, including that of Horace Greeley, the efforts of Jeremiah S. Black to negotiate via his old Buchanan cabinet mates, the mission of Frank Blair, Sr., to Richmond, the Hampton Roads Conference, Clement Vallandigham's efforts to discredit the Lincoln administration and bring about peace, and the ridiculous Gilmore-Jaquess mission to Richmond. While the descriptions of these well-intentioned but occasionally near-comical efforts are adequate, the author's focus is the people involved in them.

The narrative is well woven, and the author has a rich mine of peculiar personalities to describe at length. Certainly those in the North, such as Clement Vallandigham and Horace Greeley, were evangelistic in their fervor. Discussions of Fernando Wood, James R. Gilmore, William C. Jewett, and the Blair clan add to the flavor of the Yankee side. Southerners like Jacob Thompson, Clement Clay, John A. Campbell, and Robert M. T. Hunter attempted confused and feeble progress toward peace but seemingly all had ulterior motives. Of course, Jefferson Davis and Abraham Lincoln would have nothing to do with peace on anything but their own terms, and so the whole attempt reads like a perverse, but very interesting, waste of time.

(Reprinted n.d., 279 pp., AMS Press, New York)

798

Klement, Frank L. **The Copperheads of the Middle West** (341 pp., University of Chicago Press, Chicago, 1960)

Klement provides a solid overview of the Copperhead movement. Drawn together by common hatred, the opponents of the war in the Midwest comprised a handful of worrisome, desperate men who nearly gained power in the 1864 elections.

The author aptly demonstrates that organizations such as the Knights of the Golden Circle and the Sons of Liberty were driven by fanatics without a competent basis for existence. Hatred and fear of blacks, railroad power, big business, and northeastern industrialism formulated and thrust forward their ideals. Not all met the fate of Vallandigham—some, such as George Pendleton and S. S. Cox, empowered themselves in postwar political careers. But for the most part the Copperheads were a small and pathetic movement, and the author occasionally overestimates their strength and influence on contemporary events. Indeed, a careful analysis of their claims of the Lincoln "despotism" and their vision of an emerging racial war might make an astute observer write them off as crazies. Instead, the author elevates them to counterpart status with the radical Republicans.

Although their importance during the war and after has been exaggerated, the Copperheads are worthy of calm study. This work provides an excellent summary of the movement even if it takes the people behind it somewhat too seriously.

799

Klement, Frank L. **Dark Lanterns: Secret Political Societies, Conspiracies, and Treason Trials in the Civil War** (263 pp., Louisiana State University Press, Baton Rouge, 1984)

Eight sections offer analyses of major and minor organizations and incidents involving antiwar sentiment in the North, with a particular interest in the Knights of the Golden Circle, the Order of American Knights, the Sons of Liberty, and the pro-Lincoln Union Leagues. Unlike Klement's treatment of the

Copperheads as serious threats to the Lincoln administration (q.v.), he shows here that the secret antiwar societies were primarily weak and almost laughable organizations.

The author demonstrates that antiwar societies amounted to little throughout the entire course of the war, although their influence was exaggerated for political purposes by both Republicans and Democrats. The work discredits the much-publicized Indianapolis conspiracy and the plot to free Confederate prisoners from Camp Douglas. Its accounts of the Indianapolis and Cincinnati treason trials are filled with minute details that substantiate a massive job of researching little-known figures. In assembling this work, the author has left us a concrete and systematic examination of civil liberties in the North during the war as well as a fascinating book full of intriguing stories.

800

McWhiney, Grady. **Southerners and Other Americans** (206 pp., Basic Books, New York, 1973)

These 12 essays aim to analyze and dispel myths that maintain a lingering hold on Southern culture. The topics in this collection, held together by the theme of antebellum to Reconstruction Southern mythology, span a fairly wide range. They include an attack on the notion of an irrepressible conflict, an exposé of the sex lives of Old Army officers, two reports on Jefferson Davis, three essays on the Reconstruction period, and a petition for writers to stop propagandizing while delivering revisionist history.

Some of the essays are more successful than others; these include the papers on Davis, which convincingly depict the Confederate president's role in bringing on the war and botching much of the Confederate war effort once it began. The Reconstruction essay dealing with the Ku Klux Klan suggests that the effectiveness of its use of the symbolism of dead Confederate soldiers is overdrawn. Other essays do not work so well, and the thread that binds them together is often weak. Nevertheless, they contribute some valuable ideas to old themes and thus illuminate, in places, many topics of considerable interest to Civil War readers.

801

Monaghan, Jay. **Diplomat in Carpet Slippers: Abraham Lincoln Deals with Foreign Affairs** (505 pp., Bobbs-Merrill Co., Indianapolis, 1945)

This work remains valuable for assessing Lincoln's role in several international incidents during the war years. Written in a popular and eventful style, the narrative is nonetheless scholarly and sound in its conclusions. A range of subjects including the *Trent* affair, Confederate plans to emancipate slaves in exchange for foreign recognition, the British involvement in creating a Confederate Navy, Napoleon III's interference in Mexico, and many incidents of lesser importance receive superb and meaningful treatment.

The development of characters is central to the author's success. A balanced portrayal of Lincoln's attitudes and actions predominates, although occasionally Monaghan, without documentation, suggests that Lincoln overstepped his authority. He is too harsh on Seward, perhaps for the result of a good story. Others, including Cassius M. Clay, Charles Sumner, Palmerston, Russell, and Bright, receive competent and admirable portrayals.

802

Montgomery, David. **Beyond Equality: Labor and the Radical Republicans, 1862–1872** (508 pp., Alfred A. Knopf, New York, 1967)

The laborer's view of the transformation of American society is a significant and virtually neglected aspect of the war's wide-ranging effect. In this unique study Montgomery examines the influence of the changing character of the labor movement on the Republicans of the Civil War and Reconstruction era.

With diligent research and a sweeping narrative, the author outlines the nature of wage earners and their various struggles during the wartime years. Vivid portraits of many labor leaders and industrialists emerge, as do accounts of the significant conflict between laborers and their employers, the many organizations formed, the stories of strikes, and other problems. Continuing the survey beyond the war years, the author shows how the labor movement helped to thwart radical Republicanism. The connection between the radicals' views on slavery and those on monetary issues like greenbacks is hard to establish, however, and the interpretation of radicals such as Sumner and Chandler as different from their ultraradical counterparts is questionable. Filled out by much statistical data on laborers and their unions, this work offers a refreshing and important glance into a specialized aspect of society's changing nature during and after the war.

(Reprinted 1981, with a bibliographical afterword, 535 pp., University of Illinois Press, Urbana)

803

Murdock, Eugene Converse. **Patriotism Limited, 1862–1865: The Civil War Draft and the Bounty System** (270 pp., Kent State University Press, Kent, 1967)

This study, confined to New York State, documents the failure of many New Yorkers to respond to the call for military service. Murdock examines the conscription law of 1863 and the bounty act and offers a clear portrait of the many abuses inherent in the systems at work. He employs a variety of sources, primarily New York newspapers, to explore the history of draftees paying their way out of service and also bounty jumpers illegally collecting multiple financial rewards. The system was much abused, and the author contends—but does not fully support—that the history of the draft in New York may be generalized to apply to the other Northern states. Additionally, he suggests that draftees in poor districts paid commutation fees as frequently as those in wealthy districts and concludes, therefore, that the war was not "a rich man's war, but a poor man's fight."

The author offers a great service in his portrayal of Horatio Seymour's incompetence during New York's draft riots and his meddling and uncooperative attitudes toward the Lincoln administration's enforcement of the laws. He also ably depicts the important role played by Brig. Gen. James B. Fry as provost marshal general. Fry made outstanding contributions in directing the Bureau of the Provost Marshal General in enforcing the conscription acts, suppressing desertions, and prosecuting bounty jumpers. Murdock tells this last story well.

804

[Pulitzer Prize, 1992]

Neely, Mark E., Jr. **The Fate of Liberty: Abraham Lincoln and Civil Liberties** (278 pp., Oxford University Press, New York, 1991)

Neely argues that poor historiography has characterized the debate over Lincoln's use of constitutional power during the war. Did the chief executive go too far in suspending habeas corpus and trying civilians by military commission? This and other issues of civil liberty are explored as they played out during the Lincoln administration. Neely uses an extensive collection of previously unanalyzed records to sort through the myriad questions that have lingered since the war.

The author found that Lincoln's administration arrested a large number of civilians indeed, and that the policy for detaining them was often incoherent and motivated solely by political or military goals. However, the suspension of habeas corpus, he documents, did not lead to arbitrary arrests. Moreover, the trials by military commission came off with generally competent results and with respect for due process and organized methodology. Neely shows that some famous cases such as 1863's *Ex parte Vallandigham* and 1866's *Ex parte Milligan* were important symbolically but unrepresentative.

This thorough and well-researched book therefore shows that Lincoln's use of constitutional power was not an abuse, however confused and irregular it might have been. After all, there were no precedents, and the cases had to go on during the exigencies of civil war.

805

Owsley, Frank Lawrence. **King Cotton Diplomacy: Foreign Relations and the Confederate States of America** (617 pp., University of Chicago Press, Chicago, 1931)

The author's thesis establishes the primary explanation for a lack of British and French intervention during the war. The fledgling Confederacy's diplomats believed that a free supply of Southern cotton would no doubt bring about such intervention. Owsley maintains that the Confederate government should have carefully controlled the sale of cotton from the war's outset, thereby increasing its bargaining power, whether real or perceived. On the other side of the Atlantic, British interpreters feared war with the United States, Owsley contends, and believed for a time that the South would gain independence of its own accord.

Other themes permeate the work. Perhaps most important, the author argues that Confederate policy should have incorporated plans for emancipation early on, something the historical record shows could not possibly have occurred given the composition of the government. Owsley asserts that the British interference in Confederate shipbuilding in England was "unnecessary." He also downplays the real significance of the Federal blockade.

(New edition 1959, ed. Harriet Chappell Owsley, 614 pp., University of Chicago Press, Chicago)

806

Palladino, Grace. **Another Civil War: Labor, Capital, and the State in the Anthracite Regions of Pennsylvania, 1840–1868** (221 pp., University of Illinois Press, Urbana, 1990)

A revisionistic exploration of an underinterpreted Civil War event emerges in this work. Traditional views hold that the Lincoln administration dispatched Federal troops to the coal-mining regions of Pennsylvania to put down activities by Copperheads interfering with conscription and supplies of anthracite. Palladino, who declares herself pro-labor, takes issue with this idea. She places the incidents within the context of a longtime "war" between labor and capital that gives the wartime events new meaning.

The author provides a disappointingly thin amount of information about soldiers from these areas of Pennsylvania or about other wartime activities connected to the region. What she does offer is an analysis of the growth of coal mining in the area and an outline of the factions involved in it. She draws heavily on a variety of sources, including newspaper editorials and the records of a number of mining companies. The uneasy partnership between workers and managers becomes clear in this study. However, one wishes that the author offered more analysis of the meaning of wartime incidents as well.

807

Paludan, Philip S. **A Covenant with Death: The Constitution, Law, and Equality in the Civil War Era** (309 pp., University of Illinois Press, Urbana, 1975)

This study offers a fresh approach to wartime psychology. Believing that the Civil War did not represent a second American Revolution and that most Northerners in power viewed the war conservatively, Paludan analyzes the writings of Thomas M. Cooley, Sidney George Fisher, Francis Lieber, and John Norton Pomeroy. The author shows that these mid-19th-century intellectuals stuck to conservative themes. Such traditional Jacksonian perceptions checked the radical stimulus for revolutionary change and controlled the chaotic situation that was unfolding.

Moreover, the author contends, such thinkers viewed the war as predominantly a crusade for preserving the Union rather than for furthering social change. Those under analysis believed in a decentralized government after the war as they had before it, and Paludan argues that the views of these intellectuals represent those guiding the nation as a whole. Such a jump in logic is dangerous at best, as examining such subjects is not equivalent to analyzing the views of important governmental officials, military commanders, or the public at large. Thus, this study offers a valuable legal analysis of the views of some influential men, but it cannot pretend to override other viewpoints in different and even more significant places.

808

Paludan, Philip Shaw. **Victims: A True Story of the Civil War** (144 pp., University of Tennessee Press, Knoxville, 1981)

This work has a split personality. First, it is a straightforward account of the Shelton Laurel Massacre, wherein 13 Unionist mountaineers were killed in North Carolina. This odd tale has an appeal of its own, being a little-known aspect of the war. Fortunately, Paludan finds enough detail and substantiation to discuss the event clearly and offer some speculative interpretation to go along with the story. Second, he places the massacre into the context of the war's effect on small towns.

In his wide-reaching analysis of the event, Paludan enters the arena of Appalachian society and delivers an intriguing exposé of Civil War guerrilla activities. He explores the minds of the victims and the killers, suggesting what may have driven the perpetrators to commit the crime and what it means in today's America. In presenting this thought-provoking tale, however, he offers conversations as if they had been recorded on the spot, occasionally cites highly unreliable sources (such as Daniel Ellis's embellished book *Thrilling Adventures of Daniel Ellis*), and advances strange comparisons that bridge the gulf of 130 years from past to present.

809

Potter, David M. **Lincoln and His Party in the Secession Crisis** (408 pp., Yale University Press, New Haven, 1942)

Concentrating on the Lincoln-Seward relationship, Potter contends that on Lincoln's inauguration the president believed the Union could be saved without war. The rapidly changing roles of Lincoln and his cabinet form a backdrop for analyzing the events that followed. Although Lincoln did not initially assert his prerogatives—allowing Seward and other Republican leaders to momentarily overshadow him—the crisis at Sumter forced Lincoln's hand.

In stark contrast to other works on the same subject, Potter asserts that Lincoln would have given up Sumter if Fort Pickens were made the leading symbol of national authority. That failing to happen, Lincoln had no choice but to attempt a resupply mission to Anderson at Sumter, and then the war came. Potter's argument is difficult to counter and remains authoritative on the first days of Lincoln's administration and its initiatives to preserve the Union.

(Reprinted 1996, with an introduction by Daniel W. Crofts, 408 pp., Louisiana State University Press, Baton Rouge)

810

Pressly, Thomas J. **Americans Interpret Their Civil War** (347 pp., Princeton University Press, Princeton, 1954)

Pressly attacks the many and changing views of the war from the earliest days following Sumter to the revisionist era following World War II and concentrates primarily on analyzing the causes of the war and a multitude of political aspects. His thesis is that by 1870 all possible interpretations of the war had been made. He outlines the evolution of the major areas of these interpretations, starting with the pro-Northern and pro-Southern governmental views and the third major group consisting of citizens on both sides who believed the war was forced upon them needlessly.

The chapters on postwar developmental themes nicely outline the many views as they evolved, but the author does not critically analyze. Although he considers himself a "new nationalist" in philosophical agreement with Allan Nevins, he does not fully explain or summarily evaluate the competing ideas. He does, however, occasionally jab at prominent Southern historians in an effort to illuminate their biases, sometimes correctly and sometimes not. The midcentury revisionists followed by James G. Randall are dismissed completely. This book, while valuable as a guide to the growth of Civil War historiography, is not the objective study it might have been.

(Reprinted 1962, 384 pp., Collier Books, New York)

811

Randall, James G. **Constitutional Problems under Lincoln** (580 pp., Appleton and Co., New York, 1926)

Written by the ambitious revisionist historian Randall several years after the close of World War I, this work delivers coded commentary on the course of that war while directly confronting the legal issues of Lincoln's administration. Civil war raised the most complex tests of U.S. constitutional law we have seen. Certainly Lincoln did not hesitate to use his power to the fullest in the areas of suspending the writ of habeas corpus, branding Confederate officials traitors, instituting martial law, ignoring Roger Taney's Supreme Court, conscripting soldiers, emancipating slaves, and creating the state of West Virginia.

Randall shows that because of the exigencies of war Lincoln did not violate or exceed his presidential powers. In contradiction to critics who have not fully researched their position, Randall demonstrates that Lincoln strictly followed the limits of the Constitution, in fact delaying measures until they could be implemented legally, and spent great energy explaining and justifying his actions under the law. A revised edition of this work was published in 1951 by the University of Illinois Press.

(1951 revised edition reissued 1996, 596 pp., University of Illinois Press, Urbana)

812

Rose, Ann C. **Victorian America and the Civil War** (304 pp., Cambridge University Press, New York, 1992)

This study provides an intriguing synthesis based on the experiences of 75 men and women who lived through the war. Rose attempts to portray the effects of the war on the lives of these individuals, many of whom were well known and others less prominent, and to glean something about the character of Victorian society in the United States through this project. One criterion for the "participants" is that they were born between 1815 and 1837 and had experiences into the last years of the century. The samples thus includes some familiar names: those of important military service, such as Ulysses S. Grant, Pierre G. T. Beauregard, Wade Hampton, William Tecumseh Sherman, George E. Pickett, Thomas Wentworth Higginson, John Bell Hood, Oliver O. Howard, James A. Garfield, and Lew Wallace; politicians and intellectuals, such as Richard Henry Dana, "Long John" Wentworth, Henry David Thoreau, and George Templeton Strong; and accomplished women, such as Mary Boykin Chesnut, Charlotte Cushman, Virginia Clay-Clopton, Elizabeth Cady Stanton, Louisa May Alcott, Julia Grant, and Mary Todd Lincoln.

The resulting narrative focuses on the people, as in collective biography, rather than on the nation. The real analysis here hits religion, politics, family, work, and leisure. The author demonstrates that many Victorians found it increasingly hard to maintain their religious views in light of what was happening in their world. Politics, then, served as a kind of religion for many individuals, and the author shows that the war brought a belief that a higher meaning might be restored to their lives.

813

Shattuck, Gardiner H., Jr. **A Shield and a Hiding Place: The Religious Life of the Civil War Armies** (161 pp., Mercer University Press, Macon, 1987)

This too-brief but excellent work on the role of religion in the armies contains valuable glimpses of the religious revival that swept the camps in 1863 and 1864. The author clearly divides aspects of Northern and Southern society by his documentation of the significance of religion in the two armies. Moreover, he casts light on the value of religion for the fighting troops, particularly those in the Confederacy and toward the end of the war, and shows in amazing detail how the defeat of the Confederacy sparked a rejuvenation of religious participation in the postwar South.

The study does not downplay the significance of religion in the Federal armies, however. Shattuck expends careful research on demonstrating the involvement of Northern religious leaders in the war effort. The wave of revival spread over the Union Army as victory became more certain, empowering the Federal soldiers with the moral belief that God was on their side. The author paints a very different portrait of Southern evangelicalism, however, showing it to be nearly a self-fulfilling prophecy of defeat. Once suspicions of defeat arose among the religious, the moral dilemmas were overpowering.

814

Silbey, Joel H. **A Respectable Minority: The Democratic Party in the Civil War Era, 1860–1868** (267 pp., W. W. Norton and Co., New York, 1977)

The author examines in admirable detail the "other" party of the wartime North. Neglected primarily because of the minimal influence it held during the war and the first years of Reconstruction, the Democratic party nonetheless warrants close inspection on several grounds. In this book, Silbey goes a long way toward providing a complete picture of a party that was shattered before the 1860 election, often stood for racist views, and leaned peacefully toward the wartime enemy bent on separating the United States. Such an analysis does not come easily but only by carefully weighing the actions of the important participants in the Democratic party during the period in question. Such unlikely personalities as George B. McClellan, Horatio Seymour, and Clement L. Vallandigham contribute much toward defining the wobbly activities of the party in this study.

Silbey separates his party members into Legitimists and Purists, defined, respectively, as those who developed legitimate opposition to the Lincoln administration but essentially backed the war and those who held old-party ideas and sanctioned peace as an attainable goal. The author believes that the Democrats were not as fragmented as history has contended and that they maintained some degree of strength because of partisan activities and the historical voting records of certain areas. He does not refrain from criticizing the Northern Democrats, who may have been "wrong-headed," and on a number of levels he demonstrates the value in preserving the two-party system through the greatest crisis in American history.

815

Wayne, Michael. **The Reshaping of Plantation Society: The Natchez District, 1860–1880** (226 pp., Louisiana State University Press, Baton Rouge, 1983)

Wayne provides a significant case study of the evolution of plantation society—one surrounding Natchez, a region that epitomizes Southern plantation life—from the war itself through Reconstruction. He considers the region of Mississippi and Louisiana from Vicksburg and Richmond in the north to Fort Adams in the south, placing Natchez and Vidalia centrally within the area studied. An introductory chapter examines plantation life in the area before the war; subsequent sections deal with the transition to wartime life and the emergence of a postwar planter's lifestyle.

The author uses a wellspring of data to show that although considerably reduced in wealth by the war, the region's planters retained the social upper hand in the New South. They often kept land via tax evasion or simply because there was little demand for their devalued property. The author also shows that after the war the welfare of blacks dissolved as an issue in the minds of Natchez area planters. Despite this, he suggests, plantation workers gained influence in the postwar district because they could shift to a new employer if dissatisfied during a given season. The conclusions drawn in this impressive study can, with some caution, be applied to other parts of the South as well.

(Reprinted 1990, 226 pp., University of Illinois Press, Urbana)

816

Williams, T. Harry. **Lincoln and the Radicals** (413 pp., University of Wisconsin Press, Madison, 1941)

Although solidly researched, this work has undergone recent attacks as numerous as those fired by the radicals at Lincoln himself. Nonetheless, this traditional view of the relationship between Lincoln and prominent radical Republicans in the legislative branch of government and within Lincoln's cabinet remains an important work.

Williams closely examines the relationships of Lincoln and radicals including Edwin M. Stanton, Salmon P. Chase, Zachariah Chandler, Thaddeus Stevens, Benjamin Wade, and even the army officers Ambrose E. Burnside, Benjamin F. Butler, John Charles Frémont, and Joseph Hooker. Clearly, the actions of these and many other radicals worked politically against Lincoln, and Williams concludes that in essence most of the radicals came out victorious. Yet drawing such a conclusion is analogous to stating that small victories are greater than large ones. After all, in the end, Lincoln's war aims and grand strategy convincingly dominated the war effort and led to victory.

Despite the harsh conclusion on Lincoln's ability, the work contains insightful analysis and much useful material. It stands as a valuable study on Washington politics, a well-documented view of a dirty part of the war.

(Reprinted 1972, 413 pp., University of Wisconsin Press, Madison)

817

Wolseley, Garnet Joseph, Viscount. **The American Civil War: An English View** (ed. James A. Rawley, 230 pp., University Press of Virginia, Charlottesville, 1964)

This trio of peculiar essays—the second and third being the most intriguing—is largely useful as a historic relic.

The work incorporates a narrative of Wolseley's 1862 visit to Richmond; an 1887 eulogistic appraisal of Robert E. Lee; and a lengthy and curious commentary, written in 1889, on *Battles and Leaders of the Civil War* (*q.v.*).

The essay written after Wolseley's return to England and published in *Blackwood's* magazine stings with the most simplistic pro-Confederate rhetoric of the times. It savagely attacks the Lincoln administration and provides a misinterpretation of American constitutional law while it reports cockeyed analysis of the military campaigns of the ongoing struggle. It is a propaganda piece written with the usual overtones that appear silly viewed from modern times. Similarly, the appraisal of Lee is so slanted as to be useless except as a curiosity. In his characterizations, the author clearly subscribes to the Lee mythology in all its glory and sees brushstrokes of black and white rather than shades of gray.

The seven commentaries that scrutinize *Battles and Leaders* are worthy of attention, even if they contain marked biases and lack the necessary knowledge of the *O.R.* (*q.v.*). Wolseley contends the Confederacy lost its chances for success by not promoting Lee sooner (in fact, Lee was *assigned*). As good Lee supporters do, he savagely attacks Longstreet. Although he points out shortcomings in McClellan, he lays the blame for McClellan's failure on Stanton's doorstep. Despite his attacks on Washington, he ends by weakly praising Lincoln. Many errors lie scattered throughout the book.

THE PRESS

818

Aaron, Daniel. **The Unwritten War: American Writers and the Civil War** (402 pp., Alfred A. Knopf, New York, 1973)

Aaron surveys the literary effects of the war on writers in the last decades of the 19th century. He shows how the war infiltrated the literature of the Gilded Age in a variety of ways and the responses to it, ranging from reflections on the war's horror to celebrating a patriotic rebirth of the nation to recognizing and recording the pathos and irony that saw so much good wrapped in so much bad. The authors covered include most of the very famous, such as James Russell Lowell, Ralph Waldo Emerson, Nathaniel Hawthorne, Walt Whitman, Herman Melville, Henry Adams, Mark Twain, Henry James, Ambrose Bierce, Stephen Crane, Sidney Lanier, George Washington Cable, and William Faulkner.

Suitable emphasis appears on Northern (particularly New England) authors and those of the South, and coverage includes postwar writers who did not experience the war firsthand. The chapter on antebellum writers accomplishes a clean setup for the change to follow. The work thus adds greatly to the interpretation of the effect of the war on literature and the effect of this literature on the understanding of the war by later generations. A final chapter views the influence of Southern writers on Confederate mythology and historiography. The author laments the general lack of literary epics produced by the war, a notion presented in his title.

(Reprinted 1987, 402 pp., University of Wisconsin Press, Madison)

819

Andrews, J. Cutler. **The North Reports the Civil War** (813 pp., University of Pittsburgh Press, Pittsburgh, 1955)

In an engaging story, Andrews builds a credible case for the competence and energy necessary to attempt to report on the war and provides an analysis of the correspondents who covered it. Danger certainly lurked in the shadows for reporters, occasionally as much as for soldiers. For example, the reporters Albert Deane Richardson and Junius Henri Browne were captured and spent time in Confederate prisons. Andrews also reports that a New York *Herald* correspondent, crossing a battlefield, came upon a Confederate officer on the ground. The Rebel raised his rifle at the reporter only to be shot dead by the quick draw of the reporter's sidearm. If Confederates did not give them trouble, Union officers might. Aside from the legendary anger of Sherman, other Union generals punished reporters who revealed too much and sometimes banished them from camp.

The author maintains that the underlying character of Civil War reporting, its wild inaccuracy, arose from the intense competition to file stories. No doubt the chaos and confusion of battle contributed to poor-quality information. By contrast, the story Andrews tells us is well done.

(Reprinted 1985, 813 pp., University of Pittsburgh Press, Pittsburgh)

820

Andrews, J. Cutler. **The South Reports the Civil War** (611 pp., Princeton University Press, Princeton, 1970)

This work furnishes a look into the experiences of Southern wartime journalists. As with Andrews's Northern press study (*q.v.*), the author follows events chronologically and introduces readers to a varied cast of characters that made up the working press in question. These include George William Bagby, John Esten Cooke, Felix Gregory de Fontaine, John Forsyth, Henry Hotze, Gustave Meyer, Sam-

uel Chester Reid, Jr., William G. Shepardson, Henry Timrod, and Henry Watterson.

Andrews surveys the whole of Southern reporting, highlighting several key periods of the war. These include First Bull Run, Peter W. Alexander's coverage of Shiloh, John Forsyth's reporting of the 1862 Kentucky campaign, the Gettysburg campaign, quiet desperation after the fall of Atlanta, and the war's end in Virginia. The viewpoint is predominantly that of the newsmen, making heros of many and pseudo-villians of some army officers including Joe Johnston and the caustic Braxton Bragg.

Appendices include a discussion of the identity of "Shadow," an anonymous correspondent who may have been Henry Watterson. The scholarly tone of the volume does not preclude exciting narrative, and the story draws in a large cast of characters aside from the protagonists, those reporters who brought color, if not always accuracy, to the hometown version of the war's progress.

(Reprinted 1985, 611 pp., University of Pittsburgh Press, Pittsburgh)

821

Freidel, Frank, ed. **Union Pamphlets of the Civil War** (2 vols., 1233 pp., Harvard University Press, Cambridge, 1967)

This collection of documents reveals much about certain influential politicians of the war period. Complete texts of 52 pamphlets follow an introduction by the editor. Eight facsimile title pages are included. Among the notable works are: *The Causes of the American Civil War,* by John Lothrop Motley; *Captain Maury's Letter on American Affairs. Also the Address of Hon. John C. Breckinridge to the People of Kentucky,* by Matthew Fontaine Maury and John C. Breckinridge; *The Contest in America,* by John Stuart Mill; *Our Domestic Relations: or, How to Treat the Rebel States,* by Charles Sumner; *The President's Policy,* by James Russell Lowell; and *Lincoln or McClellan. Appeal to the Germans in America,* by Francis Lieber.

822

Lively, Robert A. **Fiction Fights the Civil War: An Unfinished Chapter in the Literary History of the American People** (230 pp., University of North Carolina Press, Chapel Hill, 1957)

This study succeeds admirably in assessing fictional works on the war up to the time of its publication. In an area historians have traditionally avoided like a minefield, Lively ventures forth to assess many of the major literary works treating the war, and this alone makes the book worth reading. The author is overly apologetic in his introduction for taking on such a study, a reaction that occasionally colors the text. "Historians, my customary associates, have been suspicious of the work's legitimacy," claims the author.

The chief dilemma inherent in such a work is the meager amount of fiction relating to the Civil War that is of value to readers. Moreover, by current standards, nearly half of the existing fictional works of interest have been published since Lively's study. Despite this, his book is well done and merits consultation by anyone who seeks the story of fictionalized accounts of the war. Lively's examining of more than 500 novels allows him to compile a list of 15 "best" works and 30 "well-done" efforts.

823

Masur, Louis P., ed. **The Real War Will Never Get in the Books: Selections from Writers during the Civil War** (301 pp., Oxford University Press, New York, 1993)

A superb companion volume to Daniel Aaron's survey of Civil War fiction (*q.v.*), this work reprints and analyzes the works of 14 writers who produced material of significance during the war years. The selections and accompanying analyses are presented in greater depth than those in Aaron's work but are far more limited in scope. The authors are weighted toward New Englanders although a number of distinguished Southern writers appear as well: Henry Brooks Adams, Louisa May Alcott, Lydia Maria Child, John Esten Cooke, John William De Forest, Frederick Douglass, Ralph Waldo Emerson, Charlotte Forten, Nathaniel Hawthorne, Thomas Wentworth Higginson, Herman Melville, William Gilmore Simms, Harriet Beecher Stowe, and Walt Whitman.

The most significant portions consist of letters from Adams, passages from Alcott's wartime journal, the thoughts of Frederick Douglass on the unfolding emancipation, portions from Melville's *Battle-Pieces*, and several of Whitman's historic writings and poems, particularly those from the close of the war. This valuable volume allows easy access to fascinating and contemplative reflections on the war by some of the era's greatest literary figures.

824

Starr, Louis M. **Bohemian Brigade: Civil War Newsmen in Action** (367 pp., Alfred A. Knopf, New York, 1954)

A competent general survey of Northern war reporting, though sketchy on background information necessary for interpreting the actions of the press, this work provides a useful glimpse at some of the war's most influential reporters. These include Sylvanus Cadwalader, Charles C. Coffin, Charles A.

Dana, Charles A. Page, Whitelaw Reid, Albert D. Richardson, William Swinton, George Alfred Townsend, and Henry Villard.

Drawing on the previously untapped papers of Sydney Howard Gay, Dana's successor as managing editor of the New York *Tribune*, Starr describes the relationships and incidents of these newsmen in chronological fashion. Illuminations of several well-known stories are made: the Cincinnati papers and Sherman's "insanity," Samuel Wilkeson's manipulation of Simon Cameron to gain an inside look at administration politics, and the forged "correspondence" between Lincoln and Stanton that appeared in two New York papers.

(Reprinted 1987, with an introduction by James Boylan, 387 pp., University of Wisconsin Press, Madison)

825

Wilson, Edmund. **Patriotic Gore: Studies in the Literature of the American Civil War** (816 pp., Oxford University Press, New York, 1962)

Both stimulating and uninformed, this study may be read by those looking for a different interpretation of military and political events. The undocumented exposé attempts to construct a truthful portrait of important persons of the war by surveying the literature covering Civil War history in the first century following the conflict. Some of those thrust into the spotlight were vitally important to the war effort, others not: Harriet Beecher Stowe, Abraham Lincoln, Ulysses S. Grant, William T. Sherman, Frederick Law Olmsted, Charlotte Forten, Thomas Wentworth Higginson, Sarah Morgan Dawson, Mary Chesnut, Robert E. Lee, John S. Mosby, Richard Taylor, Hinton R. Helper, Alexander H. Stephens, and Oliver Wendell Holmes, Jr.

The introduction is so vitriolic as to verge on the comic for anyone with a thorough reading knowledge of the war. So formulaic is the approach in the chapters that follow that one feels the sometimes damning conclusions of the author were preconceived and the material was simply chosen to support his thesis. Balance is definitely missing from many of the essays, and Wilson shows a lack of judgment in choosing evidence. Moreover, much of the interpretation is overdrawn and viewed outside the context of the times. In an exaggerated and misunderstood telling of Sherman's approach on Atlanta, the author contends that Sherman "was anticipating the *Schrecklichkeit* exploited by the Germans in the first World War as well as the *Blitzkrieg* of the second." Sherman was doing no such thing.

(Reprinted 1994, 816 pp., W. W. Norton and Co., New York)

PRISONS

826

Futch, Ovid L. **History of Andersonville Prison** (146 pp., University of Florida Press, Jacksonville, 1968)

This slim book presents a concise, meaningful, and skillfully executed tale of the war's most notorious lockup. Futch surveys the origin of Camp Sumter, the management of its early days, life within the stockade, the camp's horrible disease and death rates, stories of the Andersonville raiders, medical care for the prisoners, and the prison's dissolution. He closes with a summary of the trial and execution of Capt. Henry Wirz.

The author combed a sizable group of reminiscences, letters, diaries, and official records to prepare this impartial and balanced evaluation. He lays blame for the deteriorated conditions at Andersonville on Brig. Gen. John H. Winder, who died before Federal authorities caught up with him. He also faults Wirz and Maj. Gen. Howell Cobb. Yet he documents that much of the suffering was out of control of the Confederate authorities because of the poor resources available and the ailing nature of the Confederate nation as a whole. Overcrowded and isolated, Andersonville was doomed to disaster from the beginning. Yet Futch refuses to make unrealistic apologies for the South and maintains that the lack of prisoner exchange could not rationalize the treatment of Yankee soldiers in Southern prisons.

(Reprinted 1992, 146 pp., University of Florida Press, Jacksonville)

827

Hesseltine, William Best. **Civil War Prisons: A Study in War Psychology** (290 pp., Ohio State University Press, Columbus, 1930)

This impartial and objectively assembled study examines the inadequate capacities for handling prisoners both North and South in the early months of the war and how both sides reacted to the problem. During the war Federal armies captured more than 215,000 Confederate prisoners and the Rebel armies detained a slightly smaller number of Northerners. The need for prisons was overwhelming from a logistical point of view and worsened, particularly in the South, as resources shrank. Hesseltine describes the acquisition and handling of prisoners during the first year before an exchange system was established. He surveys the construction of prisons and takes a detailed look at a number of important and notorious prisons.

Heavily dependent on the *O.R.* (*q.v.*), the study highlights the inept handling of prisoners at Confederate institutions such as Andersonville, Libby Prison, and other places, yet it does not hesitate to cite the difficult conditions at Northern prisons as well. The author draws on reminiscences with care, as many are highly embellished or fictionalized, but does not employ a number of important sources such as the *Journal of the Confederate Congress* (*q.v.*). Despite its age, the work stands up well as an introduction to the difficult dilemma of handling captured troops. It should not be confused with *Civil War Prisons*, edited by William B. Hesseltine (123 pp., Kent State University Press, Kent, 1972; reprinted 1993), which is a collection of essays reprinted from *Civil War History*.

828

Marvel, William. **Andersonville: The Last Depot** (337 pp., University of North Carolina Press, Chapel Hill, 1994)

Sifting through a considerable store of documents, letters, and diaries, Marvel offers a more apologetic assessment of Henry Wirz than the traditional portrait. He nicely describes the background of prisoner of war exchanges and the military situation facing the Confederacy in the months preceding the establishment of Camp Sumter. In sketching the development of the camp as a prison, the author allows the story to gain momentum as the prisoners arrive and the chaos of the camp spirals.

The argument is made that Wirz and most other Confederates associated with Andersonville were not responsible for the suffering of Federal prisoners. Disease and shortages of proper food and medical supplies afflicted many of the thousands who died there, and Wirz could hardly have improved the situation. Moreover, Marvel argues, the Federal refusal to exchange prisoners was the real cause of the trouble. But this line of reasoning falls short because it downplays the Confederacy's role in the failed exchange. The Confederacy's refusal to exchange black soldiers, indeed its legislation to return them to slavery or execute them, fueled much of the exchange problem. Moreover, that the South could not adequately handle the Union prisoners because the Confederates "could not even supply their own army" does not rationalize the mistreatment, lack of medical attention, or poor food administered at Andersonville or other prisons. Marvel concludes with the Wirz trial, an account that is highly colored in its viewpoint that the government severely mistreated the accused. Such a revisionist essay provides food for thought and a compelling story of the prison itself, but it does not succeed in delivering a balanced account of the facts.

RAILROADS AND THE WAR

829

Black, Robert C. III. **The Railroads of the Confederacy** (360 pp., University of North Carolina Press, Chapel Hill, 1952)

The author argues persuasively that Confederate military authorities failed to use effectively the valuable interior railroad lines scattered throughout the South that were available to support numerous campaigns. Not only did ineffectual military planning cause this problem, but it was exacerbated by profiteering by railroad owners and workers with Union sympathies. Moreover, state rights worked against the Confederate war effort in this area. Further problems were inherent in the system: for example, many of the lines in the South were built so cheaply that they could not be adequately maintained during the exigencies of war and so diminished opportunities for maximizing Confederate rail transport.

A mountain of material from the National Archives, including military documents, rail company reports, state archives, newspapers, and periodicals, appears in this soundly documented study, and the maps effectively add to the narrative of this confused story. Black shows how ingenuity had to be brought into play simply to maintain the most vital lines in the South and that "expansion" was essentially limited to building four short lines and linking routes coming into important cities. The work coexists nicely with Thomas Weber's study of the Northern railroads in the war (*q.v.*).

(Reprinted 1987, 360 pp., Broadfoot, Wilmington)

830

Johnston, James Angus II. **Virginia Railroads in the Civil War** (336 pp., University of North Carolina Press, Chapel Hill, and the Virginia Historical Society, 1961)

This volume has much to offer those even casually interested in the eastern theater of war. Johnston's thesis promotes the clearly correct view that rail transport played a vital role in the various military operations in Virginia from the first large battle onward and even in the skirmish at Vienna that preceded it. The Confederate commanders' reliance on rail transport, the author shows, limited their options and even constrained their successes throughout the war. By contrast, Union armies resupplied and transported via water, and this transformed ultimately into a significant tactical flexibility. The author's documentation is inspiring and the strong background research supports his contention that, although it required months to evolve, the Federal system of waging war ultimately strengthened its military might.

831

Lash, Jeffrey N. **Destroyer of the Iron Horse: General Joseph E. Johnston and Confederate Rail Transport** (228 pp., Kent State University Press, Kent, 1991)

This study illuminates Confederate Gen. Johnston's use and misuse of railroads. Lash explores how Johnston's neglect of protecting and repairing the railroads around Jackson and Grenada, Mississippi, resulted in the loss of most of the rail equipment to Sherman and Grant after the fall of Vicksburg. Johnston wanted the railroad companies rather than his own corps of engineers to take responsibility for railroad maintenance, and the author suggests this was a fatal policy flaw.

Although it contains some intriguing analysis, in the end the argument that a major failing of Johnston's generalship was his inability to make good use of the Confederate railroad system is not very convincing. The author magnifies the unconcern of Johnston for railroad operations and protection and gives too much credit to others such as Polk and Bragg. At one point, Lash makes the startling statement that Leonidas Polk was "easily the Confederacy's ablest railroad general." Some errors occur, such as misspelling the names of Laurence S. Baker, Benjamin F. Cheatham, and Arthur J. L. Fremantle, and an index entry for Josiah "Borgas" (instead of Gorgas).

832

Turner, George Edgar. **Victory Rode the Rails: The Strategic Place of the Railroads in the Civil War** (419 pp., Bobbs-Merrill Co., Indianapolis, 1953)

This thorough, scholarly treatment of the value of rail lines to the Northern and Southern armies does not break new ground. Turner relies primarily on previously published works and ties them together in a sweeping overview of the significance of railroads in the strategy and tactics of Civil War battle. The volume thus has few remarkable insights, but it does provide a competently executed, reasonably detailed summation of its subject.

Particular emphasis relates to the organization of Confederate and Union high commands and how they viewed the importance of railroads. The author covers a string of campaigns and battles, including First Bull Run, Bragg's Kentucky invasion, the "Great Locomotive Chase," the Maryland campaign of 1862, raiding and the railroads, Gettysburg, Vicksburg, the Atlanta campaign, the role of the various rail lines in and near Petersburg, and the final significance of how each side used the rails. Many stories deal with engineers and their activities, as with Herman Haupt.

(Reprinted 1992, with an introduction by Gary W. Gallagher, 419 pp., University of Nebraska Press, Lincoln)

833

Weber, Thomas. **The Northern Railroads in the Civil War, 1861–1865** (318 pp., King's Crown Press, New York, 1952)

A significant companion to Robert Black's study (*q.v.*), this work analyzes the effects of railway transportation on the Union war effort and examines the war's effect on the railroad industry. In stark contrast to the Southern lines, the Northern railways were well constructed and in the midst of a great conversion from iron to steel during the war. Moreover, railway companies in the North turned a profit, and suitable supplies for repair and expansion were readily available. This careful study sets forth and summarizes the record of Northern rails during the war, drawing on a large cache of archival material from government repositories that includes military papers and those of private companies.

The nature of the Union's railroads in the war was of course radically different from that of the lines in the Confederacy. An increased usage was the most significant effect the war brought to most Northern lines. Urgent supply routes were identified and maintained. Occasionally emergency situations arose, as with the transportation of significant reinforcements southward following the battle of Chickamauga, but mostly these lines existed in comparative peace.

REFERENCE WORKS

834

Allardice, Bruce S. **More Generals in Gray** (301 pp., Louisiana State University Press, Baton Rouge, 1995)

This ambitious work gathers data on 137 officers considered "other Confederate generals" who have been overlooked by previous historians. The format follows that of Ezra J. Warner's classic *Generals in Gray* (*q.v.*), the author providing biographical sketches (several paragraphs each) and photographs for 111 of the officers. Additionally, Allardice offers an appendix of 134 additional, "less credible" officers who are often referred to as generals. Thus, the work provides valuable biographical data on a large number of interesting and relatively obscure figures who nonetheless played important roles in the Confederate war effort.

The effort might have been more clearly defined, and errors abound. The author confuses the meanings of the terms *appointment* and *nomination* as well as *rank* and *grade*, which leads to problems and inaccuracies throughout. On page 1 the author refers to "officers who became generals through the regular procedure—*appointment* to that *rank* by Confederate President Jefferson Davis." On page 2 he states, "The laws . . . required *appointment* by the president, and . . . subsequent *nomination* by the president of the Senate." On page 3 he states, "All presidential appointments to general, by law, were supposed to go through the *nomination* and *confirmation* process," and he refers to "President Davis' *nominees.*" On page 5 he states, "By strict definition, only those officers *nominated* by the president . . . should be considered a Confederate general." On the same page, he claims, "[Daniel H.] Hill's July 11, 1863 *appointment* to Lieutenant General had lapsed because of the subsequent failure of President Davis to *nominate* him to that *grade.*" On the following page, the author asserts, "Kirby Smith would *assign* an officer to duty pending approval of that *appointment* by President Davis . . . and President Davis would independently *nominate* that officer." Allardice defends Kirby Smith's actions because of his relative isolation in the Trans-Mississippi Department, but further states, "President Davis did not delegate to Smith the presidential authority to appoint and nominate general officers." (That denial of delegation was so stated in a letter of 19 July 1880 from Jefferson Davis to Marcus J. Wright.) See the entry for Warner's *Generals in Gray* (*q.v.*) for a discussion of the procedure that created bona fide general officers.

Some other areas of confusion also appear throughout the work. In a footnote on page 2, the author states, "The Union army . . . had only two grades of general officers—brigadier general and major general." The author overlooked Lt. Gen. U. S. Grant. In another footnote on page 2, the author confuses the meaning of brevet commissions. "Although Confederate army regulations (following the regulations of the United States Army) allowed the award of 'brevet' (honorary) rank, it appears that no award of brevet was ever made," he asserts. However, a brevet is not an award—nor is it a synonym for honorary—but rather a commission. A brevet is not a rank, but a grade. Brevet Brigadier General Charles Dimmock, commissioned by Governor Letcher, was apparently accepted in that grade by the Confederate States Army when the Virginia Provisional Army was absorbed by the PACS. All parties continued to address Dimmock as "general."

Allardice's argument that there were "six main categories of (more or less legitimate) claimants to the title 'Confederate general'" is ludicrous, as five of the six categories given are by definition illegitimate and unlawful. Discussions on pages 3 and 5 mention the "one exception" of appointments without nomination or confirmation, the author's category 3. The lack of mention of the usual "advise and consent" phrase in the Confederate law of 21 May 1861, the so-called Volunteer Troops Act, was an oversight. However one considers the category 3 group, this act applied to only one major general and four brigadier general appointments. The major general, Joseph Wheeler, was appointed and confirmed in the regular manner only three days later. One of the brigadier generals, George W. C. Lee, had his appointment dropped and was soon promoted to major general in the conventional manner. The other three brigadier general appointments, George B. Cosby, William Dorsey Pender, and Henry H. Walker, were all reappointed, nominated, and confirmed as brigadier generals in the conventional manner, thus correcting the category 3 problem.

In a footnote on page 5, the author states, "(though of course, a militia general would not be held in as high a regard as a military man as would a regularly appointed general)." General officers were not held in high or low regard, but rather were ranked according to their grades and within their grades according to their dates of commission. The ACSA grade of general and later the PACS grades of general, lieutenant general, and major general were all legislated so that Confederate officers would outrank state militia officers, as well as to allow a system of promotions for more competent officers ahead of less qualified senior officers.

His claim that "by early 1862 these state armies (and/or militia) had either disbanded or had been absorbed into the PACS" is easily dismissed, as the militia, provisional state armies, state guard, and local guard units, while diminished in size as the war progressed, were not necessarily disbanded or absorbed—for example, the state units of M. Jeff Thompson in Missouri were among the last Confederate troops to surrender in 1865. A few dates are in error, such as that for the battle of Atlanta, mentioned as 22 June 1864 rather than 22 July 1864. Two especially dubious inclusions are those of Samuel Preston Moore as a "general" because he was surgeon-general C.S.A. and was mentioned as a general in the *Confederate Veteran*, and Thomas Grimké Rhett, who is included as a militia general from South Carolina even though the author states that he "never served as a general."

835

Amann, William F., ed. **Personnel of the Civil War** (2 vols., 749 pp., Thomas Yoseloff, New York, 1961)

Users of this often-cited reference for data on armies and general officers should know that this work is a virtual copy of earlier works, chiefly those by former Confederate Brig. Gen. Marcus J. Wright. Astonishingly, Amann does not attribute material from these earlier sources, although parts of his book do not simply draw from earlier works but are exact copies made from plates from the earlier works.

The publication consists of two volumes, one on the Confederacy and one on the Union. Volume 1 (parts 1, 2, and 3) contains local designations of Confederate units, a memorandum of armies, corps, and geographical commands in the Confederate States, and a memorandum of Confederate general officers. Volume 2 (parts 4 and 5) consists of a record of Union general officers and a list of synonyms of volunteer organizations in the service of the Union Army.

Parts 1 and 2 were compiled in 1876 by Brig. Gen. Wright. These were "discovered" in a secondhand bookstore by Amann, but nowhere does he inform the reader that they were originally published in 1890 and 1881, respectively. Part 3 was also compiled by Wright and published in 1881, and has been augmented several times since. Unfortunately, Amann fails to use the later works but provides the "valuable and rare" early edition, laden with errors. The list of errors is long: Samuel Cooper, M. C. Butler, and 78 brigadier generals are missing; John B. Hood is listed as a brigadier general; Edmund Kirby Smith, D. H. Hill, and J. E. B. Stuart are listed as lieutenant generals; Henry W. Allen, John S. Bowen, Jeremy F. Gilmer, William D. Pender, and William B. Taliaferro are listed as major generals; Thomas J. Churchill, Edward C. Walthall, and Pierce M. B. Young are listed as brigadier generals; 39 might-have-beens or "acting" brigadier generals are listed as brigadier generals.

Part 4 is a hopelessly inaccurate list of Federal generals taken from Frederick Phisterer's volume in the Scribner's *Campaigns* series (*q.v.*). Although the plates from the Phisterer work were copied for this section, the final four pages were dropped. Part 5 was written in 1885 by John T. Fallon. Neither part 1 nor part 5 has anything to do with personnel, although they are convenient for checking unit designations.

In his introduction, which reviews the literature of the Civil War, Amann failed to distinguish between the *Official Records of the Union and Confederate Armies* (*q.v.*) and the *Official Records of the Union and Confederate Navies* (*q.v.*). He makes the astounding statement that these records, along with the Fallon list (part 5) and a report by the quartermaster general in 1887 entitled *Tabular Statements Showing the Names of Commanders of Army Corps, Divisions, and Brigades, United States Army, 1861–1865*, "have to this day constituted the sole official source of information dealing with the War of the Rebellion." Strangely, the book contains no Union equivalent to part 2, although the quartermaster report mentioned constitutes just such a section.

836

Boatner, Mark M. III. **The Civil War Dictionary** (974 pp., David McKay Co., New York, 1959)

One of the most used references by historians and armchair buffs alike, a revised edition of this work was published in 1988 (974 pp., David McKay Co., New York). Much of the data in this volume is useful and appears in a form convenient for checking facts. The work consists of 4186 entries including terms, summaries of battles and campaigns, and brief biographies of general officers, naval flag officers, politicians, and other important individuals. However, users should be aware that Boatner's work contains a large number of errors and omissions. A few of these errors were caught and corrected for the second edition; most were not.

In his introduction Boatner states that "all of the generals on both sides are covered." Yet there are many omissions, especially brevet commissions. He states, "I identify men as 'Union (or C.S.A.) Gen.' only if they were bona fide generals." Yet 25 of Boatner's Union generals and 52 of his Confederate generals were not general officers. He claims to provide birth and death dates for persons given biographical entries but supplies only the years of birth and death. Often he does not include even that, although in many cases the years were well known from other sources decades before Boatner's first edition appeared. Examples include the death dates of William Birney (p. 65), Luther P. Bradley (p. 77), and Edward S. Bragg (p. 79)—hardly obscure data. Boatner's coverage of individuals is unsystematic. He provides complete names for some, partial names for others. He also misspells the names of prominent general officers in some cases, as with William F. Brantley (p. 82). More disturbing, his data on important figures are sometimes dead wrong: for example, he writes that Daniel E. Sickles was commissioned Colonel of the 20th New York to rank from 20 June 1861. Sickles was in fact commissioned Colonel of the 70th New York to rank from 29 June 1861. Had I not owned Sickles's commission, I might not have suspected.

Boatner is one of the worst offenders of misinterpreting the grades of officers. Although he calls numerous Union brevet brigadier generals "Union officers," he includes as legitimate generals many officers who were in fact not generals because their appointments were never confirmed. This is the case with Turner Ashby (p. 28), John D. Barry (p. 47), Samuel Benton (p. 60), Joseph L. Brent (p. 83), Theodore W. Brevard (p. 83), Thomas R. R. Cobb (p. 161), James Dearing (p. 228), James Deshler (p. 237), John Dunovant (p. 252), John W. Frazer (p. 310), Henry S. Gansevoort (p. 323), Isham W. Garrott (p. 326), Jeremy F. Gilmer (p. 343), Victor J. B. Girardey (p. 344), Archibald C. Godwin (p. 346), Benjamin

F. Gordon (p. 347), George P. Harrison, Jr. (p. 378), Robert H. Hatton (p. 385), George B. Hodge (p. 403), Adam R. Johnson (p. 436), John R. Jones (p. 442), Thomas M. Jones (p. 444), Levin M. Lewis (p. 481), Robert P. Maclay (p. 500), Peter A. S. McGlashan (p. 532), Thomas T. Munford (p. 574), Edward A. O'Neal (p. 608), Nicholas B. Pearce (p. 627), James E. Rains (p. 677), Horace Randal (p. 678), Felix H. Robertson (p. 702), Pierre Soulé (p. 778), Edwin H. Stoughton (p. 810), David Stuart (p. 812), Frederick S. Stumbaugh (p. 816), Alexander W. Terrell (p. 830), Bryan M. Thomas (p. 835), John B. S. Todd (p. 840), Edward W. West (p. 902), and David H. Williams (p. 927).

Other errors are more serious. Consider the case of William Montrose Graham, Sr. (c. 1798–1847), a veteran of the Florida and Mexican wars who was killed at Molino del Rey, and his son, William Montrose Graham, Jr. (1834–1916), a nephew of Franklin Pierce and of George G. Meade and an officer commissioned brevet brigadier general for his Civil War service, particularly as a captain of the 1st U.S. Artillery at Gettysburg. One can almost feel the wonder as Boatner, writing of the elder Graham, claims, "although he was killed in 1847 in the battle of Molino del Rey in the Mexican War as Lt. Col. 11th U.S. Inf., he was breveted B.G. USA 13 Mar. '65." Any militarist would judge this story highly unlikely. Indeed, Boatner confused father and son.

In his discussion of Charles D. Anderson (p. 13), Boatner says, "Heitman lists him as Col. 21st Ala., then B.G. Wood says he was appointed B.G. in May '64. C.M.H., Warner, and Wright find he never was a general. In the Atlanta campaign, however, he moved up from command of his 21st Ala. to lead the 3d Brigade of Polk's Corps (B&L). This position made him an acting B.G. addressed as 'general.'" Boatner, himself a U.S. Army colonel, should have known that an assignment does not create a commission. Shying away from analysis, however, Boatner usually hedges in the face of conflicting data. He shows no evidence of understanding the criteria for determining military grades. This shows again, for example, in the discussion of C. C. Gilbert (p. 342), where Boatner confuses Gilbert's commission and appointment.

On page 350, in discussing the terms *grade* and *rank*, Boatner writes that "these words along with *office* and *title*, differ in ways important primarily to law courts and military scholars." Boatner, as a potential military scholar, should explain the difference between *grade* and *rank*, and should not confuse the terms *appointment, nomination, commission, confirmation,* and *assignment.*

The use of the term *ponton* (p. 658) is incorrect. Says Boatner: "Scott's *Military Dictionary* (1862) uses the form 'pontoon' as does most Civil War literature; Wilhelm's *Military Dictionary* (1881) uses the form 'ponton' which is the correct modern military usage." This is wrong. Boatner should consult *Webster's* to see *pontoon*, a modern military agreement with the Civil War era spelling.

Boatner lists Union Brevet Brig. Gen. Willoughby Babcock as "Babcock Willoughby" (p. 930) following the entry for August Willich. Benjamin F. Partridge is listed out of place (p. 623). He wonders in type why Rollin V. Aukeny is "not listed by Heitman" (p. 35). Yet Boatner simply misspelled Ankeny, who *is* listed by Heitman. He repeats Phisterer's error of misspelling William C. Talley as Tulley (p. 851). Similarly, he repeats the error of the phantom "Nicholas J. Vail" (p. 864). He mistakes the name of George Paul Harrison, Jr., as "George P. J. Harrison" (p. 378). In the discussion of Cheat Mountain (p. 148), he refers to Colonel Rush, meaning Albert Rust. He describes George B. Crittenden as serving "without rank" on J. S. Williams's staff (p. 208), whereas Crittenden was a colonel in the Department of S.W. Virginia and E. Tennessee at the time; he mentions the wounding of Gen. G. H. Stuart (p. 211) meaning G. H. Steuart; he misdates Albert Sidney Johnston's commission as colonel 2d U.S. Cavalry in 1849 (p. 440) rather than 1855; he misspells Wladimir Krzyzanowski's name (p. 469); and lists Gilman Marston as colonel of the 10th New Hampshire rather than the 2d New Hampshire (p. 514).

On page 837 Boatner states: "Thompson, James M. Although listed by Phisterer as Lt. Col. 107 Pa. and Bvt. B.G. USV 13 Mar '65, he does not appear in Heitman or Dyer." However, Heitman lists the officer as James MacThompson. Neither is correct—they refer to James McLean Thomson. Various sources misspell the surname five different ways.

Boatner describes John C. Moore's participation in the Atlanta campaign and activities in Selma in 1864 (p. 564) although in reality Moore had resigned his commission and returned to Texas on 3 February 1864; he reports Richard L. Page was a nephew of Robert E. Lee (p. 615) rather than a cousin; he mistakes Stephen D. Ramseur's unit as the 29th North Carolina (p. 677) rather than the 49th North Carolina; and describes the capture of "Gen. Anderson" at Spotsylvania (p. 788), although neither Confederate generals George T. Anderson or Richard H. Anderson, present at Spotsylvania, was so captured. Boatner errs by stating that Earl Van Dorn was killed on 8 May 1863 (p. 867); pronounces Israel Vogdes dead in 1873, although the Union brigadier general lived until 1889; erroneously lists William S. Walker as a midshipman in the Mexican War (p. 886); and mistakenly provides John E. Wool's year of birth as 1789 (p. 948) rather than 1784. At least 35 spelling errors of the names of general officers appear. Apparently he did not consult four primary sources for information on generals: *Journal of the Executive Proceedings of the Senate of the United States of America* (q.v.), *Journal of the Congress of the Confederate States of America, 1861–1865* (q.v.), *Memorandum Relative to the General Officers Appointed by the President in the Armies of the C.S.A.* (1908), and *Memorandum Relative to the General Officers in the Armies of the United States during the Civil War* (1906).

837

Callahan, Edward W. **List of Officers of the Navy of the U.S. and of the Marine Corps from 1775–1900** (750 pp., L. R. Hamersly and Co., Philadelphia, 1901)

Callahan attempts to duplicate for the U.S. Navy what Heitman's *Historical Register* (q.v.) accomplished for the U.S. Army. The work begins with lists of secretaries of the navy, bureau chiefs, and a brief discussion of the organization from 1775 to 1798. The great register then commences, containing names of officers and dates of commission. Unfortunately the meticulous and detailed information contained in Heitman's work is not repeated here. The book contains a liberal sprinkling of typographical errors as well, limiting its usefulness. Appendices contain summaries of Thanks of Congress, errata, and a list of U.S. warships of the period 1797–1900.

Disappointingly brief, the biographical entries contain a surname and initials (sometimes the full name) and some of the appointments, grades, and terminations. Very little additional information appears.

(Reprinted 1989, 750 pp., Olde Soldier Books, Gaithersburg)

838

Cogar, William B. **Dictionary of Admirals of the U.S. Navy, Vol. 1: 1862–1900** (217 pp., Naval Institute Press, Annapolis, 1989)

Although many reference works are assembled without a thorough background knowledge of the subjects they discuss or a respect for precision, such is fortunately not the case with Cogar's splendid work. In terms of completeness of coverage, the book surveys 211 men who were commissioned admiral, from David Glasgow Farragut (the first, in 1862) to the year 1900. The author assembles the primary data (birth, death, education, and career summary) for each of them and also includes a photograph of each.

One of the few faults of this work is omitting two rear admirals placed on the retired list during the Civil War, Henry Eagle and William Smith. A few other errors appear, as with the misspelling of James Grant Wilson in the bibliographical essay. But such minor problems pale in comparison to this work's valuable qualities. That the author thoroughly understands the complexities of naval grades, assignments, and various actions is immediately apparent: the data are systematically thorough, precise, and correct. This is a reference book one can have solid faith in using.

839

Crute, Joseph H., Jr. **Confederate Staff Officers, 1861–1865** (267 pp., Derwent Books, Powhatan, Va., 1982)

This is a reworked expansion of the rare *List of Staff Officers of the Confederate States Army, 1861–1865,* by Marcus Wright (186 pp., U.S. Government Printing Office, Washington, 1891). Crute provides an alphabetical list of general officers with years of birth and death, grade, assignment, the origin of appointment, and date of rank. The staff officers are listed along with each general, although the information provided for them is variable and often missing. Coverage is far from complete. The work provides appointment dates and length of service "if available." Thus, one learns about tenure on a particular staff only in rather hazy terms. Still, until significant research furnishes a more definitive replacement, the book offers something of value.

840

Crute, Joseph H., Jr. **Units of the Confederate States Army** (423 pp., Derwent Books, Midlothian, Va., 1987)

The rare work *List of Field Officers, Regiments, and Battalions in the Confederate States Army, 1861–1865,* by Marcus J. Wright (131 pp., U.S. Government Printing Office, Washington, 1891), is revised and expanded here. State by state, Crute provides very short summaries of the origin and activities of each Confederate regiment and battalion he could uncover and adds this material to Wright's volume. The coverage is too brief to constitute short regimental histories like those for Union units in Dyer's *Compendium* (*q.v.*). Instead, the work acts as a bare-bones reference for identifying the simplest of data about a particular Confederate unit. A fuller treatment of the same ground is much needed.

841

[C.S. Senate.] **Journal of the Congress of the Confederate States of America** (7 vols., 5695 pp., U.S. Government Printing Office, Washington, 1904–1905 [58th Cong., 2d sess., S.Doc. 234, 1 February 1904])

The set consists of volume 1, *Provisional Congress* (982 pp.); volume 2, *Senate of the First Congress* (541 pp.); volume 3, *Senate of the First Congress* (886 pp.); volume 4, *Senate of the Second Congress* (797 pp.); volume 5, *House of Representatives of the First Congress* (606 pp.); volume 6, *House of Representatives of the First Congress* (917 pp.); and volume 7, *House of Representatives of the Second Congress* (966 pp.). The work also appears in the U.S. Government Serial Set as #s4610–4616.

One of the premier early reference works on Civil War history, now virtually ignored, this set offers a view of Confederate legislation of inestimable value. Its content defines numerous military and social laws and events of the Confederacy. The two necessary steps for commissioning officers were nomination by the president and confirmation by the Senate, and so here historians may find the full record of who was or was not a general officer. Additionally, many confirmations of officers were made and not specified, particularly in the 5th Session of the Provisional Congress. Examples of this occurred on 13 December 1861, 24 December 1861, 31 December 1861, 2 January 1862, and 17 February 1862.

The Senate occasionally confused records, as with Joseph Finegan. On 19 September 1862, Finegan was nominated as brigadier general, and the nomination was debated several times until withdrawn on 3 October 1862, when someone pointed out that Finegan had already been nominated and confirmed on 5 April 1862. The Congress sometimes confused names. On 3 October 1862, a nomination for M. S. Perry was withdrawn when the body found the nomination was confused with that of E. A. Perry, whose nomination had been made on 19 September 1862 and who was confirmed on 30 September 1862.

Occasional misspellings reduce the clarity of the proceedings. For example, the Senate misspelled the name of Bryan Grimes as "B. Grymes" and that of C. M. Shelley as "C. M. Shelby." Complications of rank also cloud Senate issues. On 1 June 1864, the Senate debated the rank of Stephen Dodson Ramseur relative to William Mahone. A War Department list stated that Ramseur ranked Mahone, but the Senate list had Mahone ranking Ramseur. Presumably the War Department list was correct.

One should not confuse other sources of coverage of the Confederate Senate with these official documents. The coverage in the *Southern Historical Society Papers* (*q.v.*), for example, consists of often poorly executed newspaper reports on Congressional actions. The *Journal* offers a wealth of significant data and should be reprinted and made more widely available.

842

[C.S. War Department.] **Regulations for the Army of the Confederate States, 1864** (423 pp., J. W. Randolph, Richmond, 1864)

Of fundamental value for studies of the Confederate Army, this work is closely similar to the *Regulations* of the U.S. Army (*q.v.*). The regulations consist of 47 articles comprising 1536 numbered paragraphs, followed by the Confederate States Articles of War, consisting of 101 articles. All aspects of army life are necessarily covered, and the work thus provides a view of common soldier life in the Confederate Army. Important topics covered include organization, grades, ranks, discipline, drills, camp layouts, a soldier's daily routine, patrols, work of the staff departments, army pay, procurement, contracts and supply, recruiting and training, and uniform regulations. Examples of forms for records, returns, and reports are included. The 1864 edition advises that "over 3,000 errors from earlier editions of West & Johnson have been corrected."

843

Dyer, Frederick H. **A Compendium of the War of the Rebellion: From Official Records of the Union and Confederate Armies, Reports of the Adjutant Generals of the Several States, the Army Registers, and Other Reliable Documents and Sources** (1796 pp., Dyer Publishing Co., Des Moines, 1908)

This book belongs in every Civil War library. It is the result of a massive private study conducted by a veteran who ran away from home to join the war as a drummer boy in the 7th Connecticut Infantry (under the false name Frederick H. Metzger) and later served as a private in the same regiment.

The work consists of three parts. Part 1 provides statistics of Union Army organizations, including troops furnished, losses, deaths, national cemeteries, unit organizations listed alphabetically and by states of origin, commanders of units, geographical divisions and departments, and tabular lists of the departments, armies, corps, divisions, brigades, and regiments. These lists are invaluable for tracing movements of component units, which are difficult to find in any other comprehensive source.

Part 2 contains lists of 10,455 actions, affairs, assaults, battles, campaigns, captures, combats, contacts, events, expeditions, occupations, raids, reconnaissances, scouts, sieges, and skirmishes during the war, arranged alphabetically and also chronologically by state—including mentions of the Union forces engaged and a pictorial section of maps.

In 1959 Bell I. Wiley categorized the duplication of some actions and suggested 8700 as a more accurate number of separate events.

Part 3 offers the most important single volume collection of capsule histories for 2494 Union regiments. It focuses on their itineraries, together with those of over 1000 associated units arranged by state organization, with the addition of regular army and general service units.

Despite the subtitle, virtually all the information relates to Union units and commanders. Statistics generally lack the completeness of those in the *O.R.* (*q.v.*). For example, Dyer lists the total number of Union deaths as 359,258 rather than the later figure of 360,022. Despite the fact that Dyer worked with materials from the Adjutant General's Office, the work contains misspellings of 181 names of general officers. Dyer listed a few incorrect dates, a number of incorrect assignments, and omitted some commanders. If the book is used with proper caution, however, these defects are more than offset by the convenience of having the data compiled in a single place. Because of the generally high quality of Dyer's research, this work is among the most comprehensive, important, and useful of its type.

(Reprinted 1978, with an extensive introduction that provides a capsule history of Dyer and his project, 1 vol., 1796 pp., Morningside, Dayton)

844

Esposito, Vincent J., ed. **The West Point Atlas of the Civil War** (308 pp., Frederick A. Praeger, New York, 1962)

This atlas was adapted from *The West Point Atlas of American Wars* (vol. 1, 1959). Few works on the Civil War offer maps with precise locations and accurate numbers of troops assigned to armies, corps, divisions, and brigades. Fewer still discuss tactics and strategy coherently, fairly, and meaningfully. All this is offered here as well as maps and interpretation that are presented more conveniently (and with more modern and intelligent analysis) than those in the atlas volume of the *O.R.* (*q.v.*) and other, older sources. Because of this, Esposito's *West Point Atlas* is a book that should be in every Civil War library no matter what its size. Moreover, it is a book that students of the Civil War should read and understand thoroughly before they plunge into the sea of specialized studies on battles and campaigns.

The book contains 154 pages of detailed topographical maps with overprinted blue (Union) and red (Confederate) indicators showing troop positions. (The work contains 242 separate maps.) The first 16 map pages treat Colonial wars, the Revolution, the War of 1812, and the Mexican War. The final 138 map pages depict the major campaigns of the Civil

War, including First Bull Run, Forts Henry and Donelson, Shiloh, the Peninsular campaign, Jackson's Valley campaign, Second Bull Run, Antietam, Fredericksburg, Stones River, Chancellorsville, Gettysburg, Vicksburg, Chickamauga, Chattanooga, the Wilderness, Spotsylvania, Petersburg, Atlanta, and Franklin and Nashville.

Although the maps showing action are done in "blitzkrieg" style with sweeping arrows, they are more accurately and tastefully executed than most. With the exception of a few errors (Hood's army termed "The Army of the Tennessee" on the page facing map 154, for example), the precise text permits a clear understanding of how and why elements of the campaigns unfolded.

(Reprinted 1995, with revisions and a foreword by John R. Galvin, 308 pp., Henry Holt and Co., New York)

845

Faust, Patricia L., ed. **The Historical Times Illustrated Encyclopedia of the Civil War** (850 pp., Harper and Row, New York, 1986)

Although this important reference work contains only 57 percent as many entries as Boatner's (q.v.; 2380 vs. 4186), Faust's dictionary is far superior in accuracy and includes balanced coverage of the most significant terms, battles and campaigns, and individuals. The entries are generally longer and more analytical than Boatner's, although Faust covers vastly fewer junior grade officers.

The relatively limited number of general officers, flag officers, and junior officers listed prevents this work from standing alone as a primary dictionary of the war. Common errors relating to general officers appear, such as claiming grades of brigadier general for Turner Ashby (p. 26), Samuel Benton (p. 55), Theodore W. Brevard (p. 79), James Deshler (p. 217), John Dunovant (p. 230), Isham W. Garrott (p. 300), Jeremy F. Gilmer (p. 311), Victor J. B. Girardey (p. 312), Archibald C. Godwin (p. 313), James M. Goggin (p. 313), Robert H. Hatton (p. 351), James E. Rains (p. 611), Felix H. Robertson (p. 637), Edwin H. Stoughton (p. 724), Thomas H. Taylor (p. 744), and Bryan M. Thomas (p. 753). The number of these might-have-beens is smaller than in other references. Altogether, about 30 errors of grade appear for various general officers.

Although the biographer correctly states that George B. Hodge's commission as brigadier general was not confirmed by the C.S. Senate, he amazingly contradicts the earlier statement by claiming that Hodge was "paroled as a Brigadier General" (p. 364). The discussion of Alexander Watkins Terrell's appointment as brigadier general not being "ratified" (p. 748) suggests again a poor understanding of the commis-

sioning process. Astonishingly, a biographer claims that James S. Wadsworth served at Spotsylvania (p. 795), although he had been killed at the Wilderness earlier in the same month. A contributor demotes Abner Doubleday to brigadier general during the Gettysburg campaign (p. 224).

A survey of the naval personnel shows a similar percentage of minor errors, such as date of birth for Daniel Ammen (p. 11), death dates for Theodorus Bailey (p. 33) and Louis M. Goldsborough (p. 314), and problems with correct names, as with James Dunwoody Bulloch (p. 89), Thomas Tingey Craven (p. 191), John Adolphus Bernard Dahlgren (p. 202), Edward Saloman (p. 654), and Meriwether Jeff Thompson (p. 755). Thomas O. Selfridge, Jr. (p. 665), is not identified with his famous father, which could lead to confusion. Errors of naval grade appear as well. A discussion of George H. Preble's wartime troubles and subsequent promotions is garbled (p. 600). Most dates involving Silas H. Stringham's career are wrong (p. 727). The entry for Daniel Ammen states that "by 1861 he had risen to the rank [sic] of commander" (p. 11). In fact he was commissioned commander U.S.N. to rank from 26 July 1862. Similar errors appear with Samuel P. Carter (Lt. Comdr., p. 117), Thomas Tingey Craven (Commodore, p. 191), John Adolphus Bernard Dahlgren (Acting Midshipman, p. 202) Samuel Francis Du Pont (Comdr., p. 230), and David Glasgow Farragut (Lt. and Comdr., p. 254). The erroneous statement that Theodorus Bailey was commissioned "admiral" 25 July 1866 (p. 33), suggests carelessness with terms. A similarly misleading statement appears regarding Andrew Hull Foote (p. 266).

Curiously, a contributor makes the bizarre statement that "on their shoulder boards major generals commanding armies wore three stars, the center star being larger than the others" (p. 771). This arose from a misunderstanding from a uniform maker for Bvt. Lt. Gen. Winfield Scott's uniform. On the whole, the overwhelming bulk of material this encyclopedia contains is reliable and constitutes the best one-volume multifaceted reference dictionary to date.

846

Fox, William F. **Regimental Losses in the American Civil War, 1861–1865: A Treatise on the Extent and Nature of the Mortuary Losses in the Union Regiments, with Full and Exhaustive Statistics Compiled from the Official Records on File in the State Military Bureaus and at Washington** (595 pp., Albany Publishing Co., Albany, N.Y., 1889)

Although the most reliable of the early numerical studies, Fox's important statistical work is by definition rather limited in scope. Using muster rolls and morning reports from the offices of adjutant generals from the various states,

Fox assembled tables of mortality rates and numerical strengths of various regiments. He then statistically compared them, drawing conclusions on a variety of matters including losses in battle and deaths from disease and during imprisonment. Although relatively trustworthy and entertaining to scan, the analysis is limited by the very nature of the records it draws on, as they are far from perfect.

(Reprinted 1985, 595 pp., Morningside, Dayton)

847

Heitman, Francis B. **Historical Register and Dictionary of the United States Army, from Its Organization, September 29, 1789, to March 2, 1903** (2 vols., 1695 pp., U.S. Government Printing Office, Washington, 1903)

This work is unparalleled for checking data on Federal regular army officers and volunteer generals. Heitman's coverage is vast, and the execution, with data carefully copied from records in the Adjutant General's Office, is as accurate as it can be, given the source. The work fully supersedes earlier compilations such as Thomas Holdup Stevens Hamersly's *Complete Army Register of the United States* (1880) and William Henry Powell's *Officers of the Army and Navy (Regular) Who Served in the Civil War* (1892) and *Officers of the Army and Navy (Volunteer) Who Served in the Civil War* (1893).

Volume 1 (1069 pp.) consists primarily of a biographical register of regular army officers and volunteer general officers. Full names and dates of substantive and brevet commissions are provided, along with special data such as award citations, information on woundings, and sometimes dates of death. The detail varies but generally is quite complete, reflecting the War Department's records at the turn of the century. The volume also contains a list of U.S. presidents and vice presidents, secretaries of war, and commanding generals of the army, plus a list of general officers by rank, a chronology of bureau chiefs, a list of the recipients of awards, and an analysis of West Point classes.

Although Heitman's research was meticulous, a few errors do occur. There are 10 spelling errors among the generals, and he includes 270 names of Confederate officers from a list that is not incorporated into his biographical sketches. He erroneously lists John Bell Hood as a general, D. H. Hill, Joseph Wheeler, and John B. Gordon as lieutenant generals, and Jeremy F. Gilmer as a major general. He lists 12 Confederate brigadiers as major generals and 61 officials, militia generals, and might-have-beens as brigadier generals. In addition to listing Martin W. Gary, he includes "M. W. Gray" as a separate entry. Heitman also erroneously demotes four Confederate major generals, listing Robert E.

Rodes, John A. Wharton, Jones M. Withers, and Pierce M. B. Young as brigadier generals. He incorrectly lists 45 Union volunteer brigadier generals who were never confirmed as such, and he includes 23 volunteer brevet brigadier generals who were not confirmed in that grade.

Heitman's second volume contains a wealth of data. Included is a list of officers killed, wounded, or captured, Mexican War volunteer regiments, Civil War volunteer and militia field officers, Civil War captains of light batteries, U.S. and C.S. general officers who were killed or died of wounds during the war, Confederate generals, U.S. officers who joined the Confederate Army, and volunteer officers and units in the Spanish-American War. Particularly valuable sections are those on the strength of the army with battle losses from the Revolution to 1901, a chronological list of battles for that period, a list of U.S. military establishments, and a register of organizational tables. This work also appears in the U.S. Government Serial Set as #s4535 and 4536.

(Biographical register reprinted 1965, 2 vols., 1069 pp., University of Illinois Press, Urbana; 1903 edition reprinted 1988, 2 vols., 1695 pp., Olde Soldier Books, Gaithersburg)

848

Hunt, Roger D., and Jack R. Brown. **Brevet Brigadier Generals in Blue** (700 pp., Olde Soldier Books, Gaithersburg, 1990)

This reference work fills a major gap in the literature and does so with an admirable depth of research. One of its strongest qualities is the collection of photographs of the brevet generals, although the image of Daniel White (p. 666) is really George W. Randall, and the authors could not locate a photograph of Henry L. Scott, who should not have been included anyway (see below), or Edward W. West.

The book provides basic career data (places and dates of birth and death, commissions received, and notes on occupations, education, civil offices held, and interments) for 1400 officers. Of these, 22 are brevet major generals U.S.A., 78 are brevet major generals U.S.V., 142 are brevet brigadier generals U.S.A., and 1148 are brevet brigadier generals U.S.V. The coverage is skewed somewhat because the authors erroneously include 1 substantive brigadier general of volunteers and 9 might-have-been brevet brigadier generals, the latter officers never having been confirmed as general officers. Moreover, brevet general officers whose commissions were issued prior to the war but were still in force when the war began are not included; nor are those officers whose brevet commissions were issued after the war for wartime service, some of which came as late as 1869 for active officers and as late as 1904 for retired officers. The work omits regular army brevet brigadier generals Joseph B. Brown, Sylvester Churchill, John Garland, Thomas Lawson, Thomas A. McParlin, John J. Milhau, Orlando M. Poe, William J. Sloan, and Ebenezer Swift, and volunteer brevet brigadier generals Alexander Chambers, George M. Geigler, Wladimir Krzyzanowski, James McClurg, Benjamin Parker, and Gustavus A. Smith.

Those listed who should not be considered general officers are Henry B. Van Rensselaer, who was appointed brigadier general U.S.A. but never confirmed yet is listed by Hunt and Brown as a volunteer brevet brigadier general; Eli S. Bowyer, James C. Briscoe, Albert Erskine, Rufus E. Fleming, Henry S. Gansevoort, Henry L. Scott, Isaac C. B. Suman, and Daniel White, who were appointed brevet brigadier general U.S.V. but were never confirmed. The authors include James Oakes as a brevet brigadier general, although he was commissioned a brigadier general of volunteers (and declined it). Despite these errors, this is a valuable collection of data and images that should be part of all major Civil War collections.

849

Krick, Robert K. **Lee's Colonels: A Biographical Register of the Field Officers of the Army of Northern Virginia** (3d ed., 520 pp., Morningside, Dayton, 1991)

This work, previous editions of which contain less material, provides a much-needed roster of the subordinate officers in the great Confederate Army of Northern Virginia. The author supplies brief statistical information followed by a lengthy alphabetical register filled with short biographies of some 1976 of the army's field grade officers. An appendix lists some 3524 Confederate field grade officers who did not serve in the Army of Northern Virginia. A geographical index allows one to look up an individual based on the unit in which he served. The author notes that 482 of these officers of the Army of Northern Virginia died while in the service of the army.

Krick does not include those officers who rose to the grade of general officer, citing an ample body of literature already covering them. He also omits staff officers because of their large numbers. However, these exclusions are not strictly followed at least with respect to the appendix, which contains numerous officers who became generals, particularly outside the Army of Northern Virginia. The list also omits some field grade line officers within that army. Despite this, the work is immensely valuable as a specialized reference aid.

850

Livermore, Thomas L. **Numbers and Losses in the Civil War in America, 1861–65** (150 pp., Houghton Mifflin Co., Boston, 1900)

The most-cited statistical analysis on the war, this work is the outgrowth of a paper read to the Military Historical Society of Massachusetts on 23 February 1897. Livermore's work is based on data published in the *O.R.* (*q.v.*), Kennedy's *Population of the United States in 1860* (*q.v.*), Fox's *Regimental Losses* (*q.v.*), and muster rolls and pension records. A subsequent, related paper by Livermore, "The Numbers in the Confederate Army," appears in volume 13 of the *Papers* of the Military Historical Society of Massachusetts (*q.v.*) and was read at a meeting on 7 March 1905.

Limited by the means at hand, Livermore's numbers reflect the best estimates as of the turn of the century of troops serving in various campaigns, as well as those killed, wounded, or captured. Of course, the primitive and often wholly lacking nature of Confederate records precludes specific knowledge in many cases. But Livermore accurately estimates that 2.9 million enlistments occurred in the Federal service and approximately 1.5 million in the Confederate Army. The latter is a number more than 100 percent greater than that claimed by Jubal Early, Alexander H. Stephens, Marcus Wright, and others writing principally in the *Southern Historical Society Papers* (*q.v.*).

How do the numbers stack up for a large battle? Livermore's analysis, which uses the best available materials at the time and fudge factors to reduce effective strengths or estimate casualties, certainly produces occasionally questionable results, but the numbers work essentially as well as they could now, given the increase in our knowledge over the past century. The book is still useful as a source for estimating the strengths of both armies.

(Reprinted 1957, 150 pp., Indiana University Press, Bloomington; rev. ed. 1986, ed. Ken Bandy and Steve Ward, 150 pp., Morningside, Dayton)

851

Long, E. B., and Barbara Long. **The Civil War Day by Day: An Almanac, 1861–1865** (1135 pp., Doubleday and Co., Garden City, N.Y., 1971)

This valuable work belongs in every Civil War collection. The daily entries vary considerably in size and scope, covering most major actions exceedingly well and documenting in brief numerous minor events useful for Civil War students. The coverage begins in November 1860; lengthy chapters treat 1861, 1862, 1863, 1864, 1865, and two events in

1866, the final one being President Johnson's proclamation declaring the insurrection in Texas at an end. Useful appendices cover supplementary topics such as statistical capitulations of the population in North and South, slavery, immigration, city populations, sizes of the armies, casualties, desertion, prisoners, the blockade, and the economics of war. An exhaustive bibliography remains one of the better simple compilations of many useful works for scholars and readers.

The focus is squarely on military campaigns, which leaves out much of related importance that restricts the reader's understanding of the chronology of the war. Occasionally the entries are so condensed that they provide little information on a given event, but they nonetheless serve as signposts for checking fuller information from a wide variety of other sources. One wishes there had been a more exhaustive effort—a multivolume set—to summarize in greater detail the daily activities at the various headquarters and political nerve centers involved. But the purpose of this work is not to offer a narrative for reading but a fact-checking tome for quick reference. In this capacity the Longs' massive effort makes a tremendous and important contribution to the literature of the war.

(Reprinted 1985, 1135 pp., Da Capo Press, New York)

852

McPherson, James M., ed. **The Atlas of the Civil War** (223 pp., Macmillan Co., New York, 1994)

This may at first glance appear to be a knockoff work but its value lies in maps that stand above the typical "blitzkrieg" efforts. Carefully redrawn from the *Atlas to Accompany the Official Records* (q.v.) and other contemporary sources, the maps display army corps, divisions, brigades, and sometimes regiments in an effort to show clearly the disposition of units at crucial times during each of 98 battles or campaigns. The detail often matches that of the *O.R.* maps, providing precise coverage of large areas with geographical features and timed movements or very detailed depictions of smaller areas such as battlefields, often showing individual houses and farms. The color coding of the maps is natural, and the "motion" of individual units is shown by ghosting rectangles and coupling them with arrows.

The narrative is nicely composed and written with enthusiasm, and general readers will come away with a fine summary of the tactical and strategic importance of the various actions. Photographs and illustrations add to the maps. Unfortunately, the work is marred by a number of errors in the text, captions, and map labels. For example, misspelled names include those of Lawrence O'Bryan Branch, Simon

B. Buckner, Don Carlos Buell, John C. Caldwell, Samuel F. Du Pont, Winfield Scott Hancock, William B. Hazen, Stephen A. Hurlbut, Wladimir Krzyzanowski, Gideon J. Pillow, Alexander Schimmelfennig, Albin F. Schoepf, William Sooy Smith, Alexander H. Stephens, Emory Upton, Horatio P. Van Cleve, Godfrey Weitzel, and Gideon Welles. Still, this work will be consulted even by old hands alongside Esposito's *West Point Atlas* (q.v.).

853

Phisterer, Frederick. **Statistical Record of the Armies of the United States** (vol. 13, "supplementary volume," in Scribner's series Campaigns of the Civil War, 343 pp., Charles Scribner's Sons, New York, 1883)

Although frequently cited as an important reference work, this book is dangerously unreliable and should not be used for modern studies. The first part provides numbers and organization of the U.S. armies, including organizations mustered into Federal service, military divisions, departments, and districts, principal armies, army corps, strengths of the armies, honors awarded by Congress, losses, and a list of national cemeteries. The second section offers a chronological list of battles. The third section lists general officers of the U.S. regulars and volunteers, arranging them by rank in each grade, and general officers who died during war service.

Phisterer's book suffers from two fatal problems: the data used are in many cases inaccurate or incomplete, and typographical and factual errors abound. The work includes rank tables for 2549 names, which reduces to 1968 individuals after removing duplicate entries. Phisterer misspells the names of 116 general officers and also lists some generals in the wrong grades (6 brigadier generals are listed as major generals and 42 major generals, militia generals, and might-have-beens are listed as brigadier generals. He includes the phantom "Bvt. Brig. Gen. Nicholas J. Vail." The volume's inclusion in the Scribner's set warrants its review here, but principally as a warning to avoid its unreliable information and to read it only for historical curiosity.

(Reprinted 1989, with an introduction by Peter S. Carmichael, 343 pp., Broadfoot, Wilmington)

854

Richardson, James D., ed. **A Compilation of the Messages and Papers of the Confederacy** (2 vols., 1403 pp., U.S. Publishing Co., Nashville, 1904)

A cornerstone work of Confederate military and diplomatic history, this volume contains many papers of fundamental importance that are difficult to locate elsewhere, ranging from messages and papers of Jefferson Davis to congressional actions, diplomatic correspondence, biographical material relating to a spectrum of Southern leaders, and official acts of the Confederate government. The work's great value as an historical source is nearly equaled by its chronological view of the Confederacy as a nation. The preparations for combat appear in official sources, as do the crises on the Southern home front, the glorious victories on the battlefield, and the slow ebb of Confederate morale. Many tales of personality conflict may be found here and add much to the understanding of difficulties within the Southern government itself.

(Reprinted 1966, titled *The Messages and Papers of Jefferson Davis and the Confederacy, Including Diplomatic Correspondence, 1861–1865*, with an introduction by Allan Nevins, 2 vols., 1403 pp., Chelsea House, New York)

855

[Pulitzer Prize, 1929]
Shannon, Fred Albert. **The Organization and Administration of the Union Army, 1861–1865** (2 vols., 671 pp., Arthur H. Clark Co., Cleveland, 1928)

Uninspired and based in some cases on thin source material, this work retains some usefulness as a reference on the logistics of the Federal war effort. Surveying the methodology of raising and equipping the Federal armies in 1861, Shannon covers organizing and supplying the Northern troops and ventures into a discussion of the daily life and discipline of the Federal soldiers. Much of the information supplied here is correct, but the author often makes judgmental assertions about the poor record of organizing and supplying men, one built on the early days of the war, and he does not adequately explain that conditions improved markedly over the months that followed.

The discussion of regular army and volunteer officers is based largely on a paper written by Federal Col. Thomas Wentworth Higginson. The author vigorously argues that no general or staff officers should have been appointed who were not West Point graduates. While the majority of talented commanders were regular army material, this rule is negated by the superior records of many volunteer officers who rose to high levels of command, John A. Logan being just one example.

(Reprinted 1965, 2 vols., 671 pp., Peter Smith, Gloucester, Mass.)

856

Sifakis, Stewart. **Compendium of the Confederate Armies** (10 vols., 1943 pp., Facts on File, New York, 1992–1995)

This compilation aims to be a Confederate equivalent to the coverage of Union regiments in Dyer's *Compendium* (*q.v.*). The volumes cover Alabama; Florida and Arkansas; Kentucky, Maryland, Missouri, Confederate units, and Indian units; Louisiana; Mississippi; North Carolina; South Carolina and Georgia; Tennessee; Texas; and Virginia. The list for each unit typically provides alternative names, a statement of organization, the first commander, a list of field officers, a list of assignments, and a list of battles in which the unit participated. The coverage is disappointingly brief compared with that in Dyer, the list of officers does not even cover the entire period of the war, and many spelling errors occur. The incomplete nature of this work prevents it from being significant, although it is somewhat helpful until more precise research produces a true companion to Dyer.

857

Thian, Raphael P. **Notes Illustrating the Military Geography of the United States, 1813–1880** (203 pp., U.S. Government Printing Office, Washington, 1881)

This specialized and important reference work for tracing information on the Federal armies was composed by a lifelong staff officer in the Adjutant General's Office. Thian compiled lists fundamental to military command and geography that include presidents, vice presidents, secretaries of war, generals-in-chief, and adjutants general for the period 1789–1880; a chronology of military commands in the U.S. Army from 1813 to 1880; a history of military commands; states and territories of the United States, including the military departments and districts they contained at various times; a list of maps in the military atlas of the United States, 1813–1818; and a complete index of commands. Four foldout charts provide a chronological summary of military divisions, districts, and departments from 1813 to 1880 and data for U.S. states and territories.

Although its scope is limited, this is the primary source for the material it does cover. The most valuable portion is the largest: the chronological summary of commands that presents a capsule history of each along with a listing of commanders and their dates of tenure. For those researching the technical aspects of the prewar and wartime U.S. Army, this is a necessary source.

(New edition 1979, with notes by Francis B. Heitman, ed. John M. Carroll, 203 pp., University of Texas Press, Austin)

858

[U.S. House of Representatives.] **Population of the United States in 1860** (ed. Joseph C. G. Kennedy, 694 pp., U.S. Government Printing Office, Washington, 1864)

Valuable background statistics on the population and regional resources of the United States on the eve of war are contained in this encyclopedic reference, the product of the eighth census (1860) and additional data gathering. The work documents the 31,148,047 people in the United States and its territories in 1860, 3,950,531 of whom were slaves and 476,536 of whom were free blacks. The geographical distribution of persons is given, as are the previous census figures. The population figures are also given for each state by county.

A mountain of other data also appears. Tables cover mortality in the United States, information on banks, agriculture, the manufacture of beer, canals and river improvements, clothing, coal, petroleum oil, the printing industry, musical instruments, mining, schools, railroading, slavery, real estate, tonnage, wheat, wool, firearms, flax, fisheries, the deaf and mute, diseases, immigration, fruits and vegetables, furniture, and lumber production. The list goes on and on.

859

[U.S. Senate.] **Journal of the Executive Proceedings of the Senate of the United States of America** (5 vols., 5815 pp., consisting of vol. 11 [6 December 1858–6 August 1861, 961 pp.], vol. 12 [2 December 1861–17 July 1862, 684 pp.], vol. 13 [1 December 1862–4 July 1864, 1290 pp.], vol. 14, pt. 1 [5 December 1864–6 February 1866, 542 pp., plus 533 pp. index], and vol. 14, pt. 2 [13 February 1866–28 July 1866, 1805 pp.], U.S. Government Printing Office, Washington, 1858–1866)

These volumes of the continuing U.S. Government *Journal* are crucially valuable as a source of Civil War military as well as political history. They contain a daily record of appointments, confirmations, treaties, resolutions, and committee reports while in executive session. Thus they must be consulted as a principal primary source for a multitude of research tasks. Caution must sometimes be used, however, as they do contain errors, especially in their indices. For example, the set contains the phantom "Bvt. Brig. Gen. G. E. Tourtelloute" and omits several confirmations, such as James H. Wilson's confirmation as major general of volunteers. The set was "declassified" by Anson G. McCook on 28 June 1886 and reprinted by the Johnson Reprint Co., New York, in 1969. The five volumes discussed here form part of a set published consistently from close to the founding of the nation and continuing today.

860

[U.S. War Department.] **Official Army Register, 1861–1866** (9 vols., 1150 pp., U.S. Government Printing Office, Washington, 1861–1866)

Valuable for checking grades and ranks for regular U.S. Army officers, the register lists general officers of the regular army, officers of the adjutant general's department, the judge advocate general's department, the inspectors general, the quartermaster's department, the subsistence department, the medical department, the paymaster general's department, the corps of engineers, the topographical engineers, the ordnance department, and the regular army units of the cavalry, artillery, and infantry. The state of birth, state of appointment, previous commissions, and date of original entry into service appears for each officer.

The back of each volume contains a list of retirees, additional aides-de-camp, signal corps officers, hospital chaplains, general and staff officers, assistant adjutants general of volunteers, assistant quartermasters of volunteers, commissaries of subsistence of volunteers, surgeons of volunteers, additional paymasters, the lineal rank of field officers and captains of cavalry, artillery, and infantry, a list of casualties, a pay table, data on West Point, an index, and an errata page. Despite the issuance of these documents from the Adjutant General's Office, one must be wary of occasional errors. The registers most relevant to Civil War officers were issued on 1 January 1861, 1 September 1861, 1 January 1862, August 1862, 1 January 1863, 1 April 1863, 1 January 1864, 1 January 1865, and 1 January 1866.

861

[U.S. War Department.] **Official Army Register of the Volunteer Force of the United States Army: For the Years 1861, '62, '63, '64, '65** (8 vols., 3822 pp., U.S. Government Printing Office, Washington, 1865)

This valuable work, which belongs in every Civil War collection, lists all officers who served in volunteer regiments and battalions of the U.S. Army. The compilation is organized by state, and the coverage is as follows: volume 1, Maine, New Hampshire, Vermont, Massachusetts, Rhode Island, and Connecticut; volume 2, New York and New Jersey; volume 3, Pennsylvania, Delaware, Maryland, and the District of Columbia; volume 4, West Virginia, Virginia, North Carolina, South Carolina, Georgia, Florida, Alabama, Mississippi, Louisiana, Texas, Arkansas, Tennessee, and Kentucky; volume 5, Ohio and Michigan; volume 6, Indiana and Illinois; volume 7, Missouri, Wisconsin, Iowa, Minnesota, California, Kansas, Oregon, and Nevada; volume 8, Washington, Utah, New Mexico, Nebraska, Colorado, Indian, Dakota, Arizona, Idaho, and Montana territories, plus the following U.S. troops: Veteran Reserve Corps, 1st Army Corps (veterans), miscellaneous units, and black troops.

The list of officers includes the date of muster out, with notes on officers who resigned, were discharged, mustered out on expiration of term of service, were promoted, or died. Grades and appropriate dates are given for each officer. Summary lists of each unit's prominent battles are provided with many of the histories. A list of errata is appended in each volume, but users must be wary of other misspellings, omissions, and similar errors. The early date of compilation, use of phonetic spellings of many names, and other problems sometimes detract from the work's credibility.

(Reprinted 1987, 8 vols., 3822 pp., Olde Soldier Books, Gaithersburg)

862

[U.S. War Department.] **Revised Regulations for the Army of the United States, 1861** (559 pp., J. B. Lippincott and Co., Philadelphia, 1861)

This work contains the rules of the U.S. Army at the outbreak of the war. The many topics covered provide an accurate picture of textbook military life in the army and so furnish a valuable background for students of the armies (the Confederate regulations [*q.v.*] did not differ substantially). Military laws cover grade, rank, discipline, succession in command, appointment and promotion of commissioned officers (a section more Civil War authors should read), resignations, exchanges and transfers, staff appointments, and other personnel matters.

The survey includes policy regarding forts, camps, training, discharges, leaves of absence, furloughs, chaplains, sutlers, arrests, publications, inspections, musters, parades, guards, courts-martial, recruiting, and regulations of the ordnance, pay, medical, quartermaster, subsistence, and engineer departments. Sections on flags, uniforms, and volunteer and militia service precede the articles of war, pertinent acts of Congress, and an army pay table. Other editions with changes, additions, and appendices were issued by a variety of publishers during the war.

863

[U.S. War Department.] **The War of the Rebellion: A Compilation of the Official Records of the Union and Confederate Armies** (70 vols. in 128 serials, 138,579 pp., U.S. Government Printing Office, Washington, 1880–1901)

The most important work in the literature of the Civil War, the *O.R.* is the official government compilation of Civil War records, orders, dispatches, messages, and correspondence relating to the military operations of the war. It is not perfect, however: the reports reflect the fallibility of the officers who wrote them, some conflicting and many attempting to justify actions after the fact. To be meaningfully analyzed, records in the *O.R.* must be compared with each other and with other sources to gain a clear picture of events as they actually happened.

The publication's nomenclature is somewhat confusing: it consists of 70 so-called volumes in 128 individual books (separate bindings or serials), containing 4 series, an index, and an atlas. The individual books are numbered through 130 because volumes 54 and 55 (serials 112 and 113) were never compiled or printed. As with most important government documents, the complete *O.R.* was also published as part of the U.S. Government Serial Set of official papers.

Series 1 consists of Union and Confederate reports, returns, orders, and correspondence relating to military operations; it appears in 53 volumes, arranged in chapters by campaigns and by chronology. Tables of contents and a chronology of events precede the text in each volume. Tables of alternate unit designations are appended. Series 2 consists of 8 volumes of Union and Confederate reports, returns, orders, and correspondence relating to prisoners of war. Series 3 consists of 5 volumes of Union records not included in series 1 or 2. Series 4 consists of 3 volumes of Confederate records not included in series 1 or 2.

The index volume contains the principal preface; a synopsis of the contents of each volume; an index of the principal armies, army corps, military divisions, and departments; tables of chronological concordance of the volumes; tables of additions and corrections for each volume; and the general index, which refers readers to the detailed indices in individual books. The atlas consists of 821 maps and charts, 106 engravings, and 209 drawings of equipment, uniforms, insignia, and flags. This volume also contains tables of contents, authorities, references to maps and sketches in the other volumes, and an index.

The monumental task of compiling records of the Civil War began with a joint resolution of Congress on 19 May 1864 and was continued by many individuals under the supervision of 16 successive secretaries of war. Congress funded the project beginning with an act of 23 June 1874. An astonishing staff attached to the U.S. War Department undertook the compilation of the *O.R.*, supervised by three successive editors: Lt. Col. Robert N. Scott, Lt. Col. Henry M. Lazelle, and Brig. Gen. Fred C. Ainsworth. Supporting personnel who played key roles in working on the project included such luminaries as Bvt. Maj. Gen. and Adj. Gen. Edward Davis

Townsend; the military jurist Dr. Francis Lieber; W. T. Barnard, secretary to the secretary of war; Joseph W. Kirkley, clerk to the adjutant general; H. T. Crosby, chief clerk of the War Department; Thomas J. Saunders, clerk in the office of the secretary of war; Brig. Gen. and Judge Advocate Gen. George B. Davis; Leslie J. Perry, member of the publication board; Brig. Gen. George W. Davis; Capt. Calvin D. Cowles, who compiled the atlas; and principal indexer John S. Moodey. Former Confederate Maj. Gen. Marcus J. Wright helped with locating Confederate records and was assisted by such notables as ex-Confederate Maj. Gens. Cadmus M. Wilcox, Charles W. Field, Lunsford L. Lomax, and Henry Heth, and by ex-Confederate Col. Edwin J. Harvie and ex-Confederate Maj. Jedediah Hotchkiss.

The *O.R.*'s contents represent only a small fraction of the contemporary Civil War literature. Many records were misplaced, deliberately destroyed, discarded as worthless, or withheld. The existence of the *O.R.* is even more astonishing considering that many documents were issued in multiple copies as sent, received, and distributed to various individuals. All documents located for the series had to be examined to avoid omissions and duplications and to verify authenticity. Records available for the project buried the War Department in paper. Union records of discontinued volunteer commands filled a large four-story warehouse. The "Rebel Archives," papers not destroyed but captured in Richmond at the end of the war, crowded a three-story building. Records of the Adjutant General's Office occupied one-third of the floor space of the War Department building. A single collection of U.S. military telegrams numbered over two million items. Several thousand private collections were donated or loaned to the War Department for inclusion in the *O.R.*

To make the *O.R.* a feasible project, the compilers selected only what they considered to be the best of the most important material and refrained from making editorial corrections because most of the information, later in dispute, could be found to exist in the original documents. The compilers did make corrections in spelling, grammar, and dates when the corrections could be verified. For homogeneity, the compilers made the style of orders and reports uniform and omitted irrelevant material. To avoid a never-ending cycle of writing and rewriting, revisions of reports, orders, and correspondence were not permitted.

The *O.R.* has been republished several times (National Historical Society, Broadfoot, and Morningside). The *O.R.* is available on CD-ROM from Broadfoot, Guild Press of Indiana, and H-Bar Enterprises in Oakman, Alabama. The atlas volume has been republished separately several times and is usually scaled at approximately 90 percent of the original. The most easily available edition is titled *The Official Military Atlas of the Civil War* (Fairfax Press, New York, 1983).

A useful companion to the *O.R.* is *A User's Guide to the Official Records of the American Civil War*, by Alan C. Aimone and Barbara A. Aimone (139 pp., White Mane Publishing Co., Shippensburg, Pa., 1993), which contains information about how to use the *O.R.* properly. A shorter version of this work appeared in 1977 as *The Official Records of the American Civil War: A Researcher's Guide* (U.S. Military Academy Library Bulletin No. 11A). For further criticism of the *O.R.*, see Joseph L. Eisendrath, Jr., "The *Official Records*—Sixty-three Years in the Making," *Civil War History* 1 (1955): 89, and Neil E. Salisbury, "The Official Atlas of the Civil War," *Civil War History* 5 (1959): 325. Between 1894 and 1927 the U.S. Government Printing Office issued an analogous set of official records of the Union and Confederate navies (*q.v.*).

In 1994 Broadfoot Publishing Company of Wilmington, North Carolina, initiated an ambitious project to extend the coverage and availability of official reports. The *Supplement to the Official Records of the Union and Confederate Armies* (ed. Janet B. Hewett, Noah Andre Trudeau, and Bryce A. Suderow, 20 vols., 15,963 pp., and continuing, Broadfoot, Wilmington, 1994–   ) contains a wealth of data that missed inclusion in the *O.R.* itself. The material varies somewhat in quality and differs significantly from the *O.R.* in that it includes postwar materials. The publisher suggests the *O.R. Supplement* may comprise as many as 100 volumes. Coverage thus far in this valuable set includes a multitude of reports not included in the *O.R.*, reports and records of events for Alabama, Arizona Territory, Arkansas, California, Colorado Territory, Connecticut, Dakota Territory, Delaware, District of Columbia, Florida, Georgia, and Illinois units, and a reprint of *Proceedings, Findings, and Opinions of the Court of Inquiry Convened by Order of the President of the United States in Special Orders No. 277, Headquarters of the Army, Adjutant General's Office, Washington, D.C., Dec. 9, 1879, in the Case of Gouverneur K. Warren, Late Major-General U.S. Volunteers.*

864

Wakelyn, Jon L. **Biographical Dictionary of the Confederacy** (603 pp., Greenwood Press, Westport, 1977)

This work attempts to provide a single-volume reference on important aspects of the Confederate state and its military commanders. Four early chapters offer a collective overview and shallow analysis of personalities in the Confederacy. The biographical sketches that follow summarize 651 politicians, military commanders, and notable personalities of the Confederacy. They include 7 generals, 17 lieutenant generals, 68 major generals, 158 brigadier generals, 1 militia major general, 2 militia brigadier generals, 1 admiral, 1 rear admiral, 17 executives, 24 governors, one might-have-been major general, 6 might-have-been brigadier generals, and 1 "acting" brigadier general.

One gets a sense of the peculiar criteria for inclusion in this work. The author omits Maj. Gen. David E. Twiggs, along with no less than 148 brigadier generals, officials George Deas and Henry T. Ellett, and 12 Confederate governors. He includes might-have-been Maj. Gen. Jeremy F. Gilmer, who was never confirmed, and the false brigadier generals Turner Ashby, Thomas R. R. Cobb, George B. Hodge, Lucius B. Northrop, Edward A. O'Neal, and Pierre Soulé, as well as "acting" Brig. Gen. Francis S. Bartow, who was never confirmed.

Errors abound: Wakelyn states that Thomas J. Jackson died at Chancellorsville, that William H. Jackson was wounded at Belmont, that William Mahone was promoted "for the battle of the crater where he captured Warren's Corps," that Edmund Kirby Smith was "never confirmed as a General," and that Jeb Stuart was "mortally wounded at the Yellow Tavern during the battle of Cold Harbor during the Wilderness campaign." He claims that Jones M. Withers "in 1855 was elected to the U.S. House," that James Patton Anderson "never sought a parole" (he was paroled on 1 May 1865), and similarly that William R. Boggs "never surrendered" (he was paroled on 9 June 1865). He erroneously states that Braxton Bragg "in January of 1862 was promoted to Lt. Gen" and that Isham G. Harris was a U.S. representative from Tennessee. In perhaps the most bizarre of his many errors, Wakelyn says that Harry T. Hays, "in May of 1865, after the war had ended, was promoted to Maj. Gen."

This work may be useful for checking facts for some Confederates. However, it lacks the detailed and confident precision that would have made it truly dependable and useful for a broad range of reference tasks.

865

Warner, Ezra J., and W. Buck Yearns. **Biographical Register of the Confederate Congress** (352 pp., Louisiana State University Press, Baton Rouge, 1975)

This study documents the ability of a wide range of Southerners from diverse backgrounds to achieve political success in the most chaotic time in the nation's history. Capsule biographies are provided for the 267 men who served in the Confederate congresses throughout the conflict, many of whom are now little-known figures. In a wonderful essay, Warner and Yearns analyze the makeup of the Confederate Congress, survey its accomplishments, and set the stage for the biographies that follow. Readers of Warner's two volumes on general officers (*q.v.*) will understand and appreciate the depth and intellectual rigor contained within these sketches. The authors have carefully selected meaningful facts for each person, giving the biographies lasting value for researchers. They provide significant summaries of the congressmen's voting records, as well as basic data such as birth and death dates and places, marriages, families, occupations, wealth, and education.

The work does have limitations, however. Many dates are nonspecific or are at variance with other references without apparent explanation. Errors also occur, as with the statement that Francis S. Bartow is buried in Savannah's Bonaventure Cemetery (he rests across town in Laurel Grove Cemetery).

866

Warner, Ezra J. **Generals in Blue: Lives of the Union Commanders** (680 pp., Louisiana State University Press, Baton Rouge, 1964)

A companion to Warner's earlier work on Confederate generals (*q.v.*), this volume presents basic data for the Federal commanders. In an attempt to cover all Union general officers, the author provides 583 capsule biographies and photographs for those generals who received substantive commissions and an appendix consisting of the names of 1367 general officers by brevet. One officer, Joseph Hayes, appears twice; his substantive commission as brigadier general U.S.V. warrants inclusion in the main work, but he also appears in the brevet list.

Warner has compiled an impressive list, missing only a small number of general officers. There are few errors compared with other such lists, but those who use the work for reference should be aware of such slips. Warner omits regular Bvt. Maj. Gens. George Gibson and William A. Nichols and volunteer Bvt. Maj. Gens. Milton Cogswell and Thomas Wilhelm. He leaves out the following brigadier generals of volunteers: James H. Lane, Thomas L. Price, William A. Richardson, Friend S. Rutherford, and J. Napoleon Zerman. The following regular army brevet brigadier generals are missing: Timothy P. Andrews, Levi C. Bootes, Joseph B. Brown, Sylvester Churchill, Beekman DuBarry, Franklin F. Flint, Delancey Floyd-Jones, John Garland, Thomas Lawson, Robert Macfeely, Daniel McClure, Thomas A. McParlin, John J. Milhau, Allan Rutherford, William J. Sloan, Ebenezer Swift, Augustus C. Tassin, John M. Taylor, and Henry C. Wood. Warner omits the following volunteer brevet brigadier generals: Henry L. Abbott, James L. Bates, John W. Beazell, James W. Britt, John T. DeWeese, Richard Dillon, George

M. Geigler, Isaac R. Hawkins, Lewis C. Hunt (of Ohio), James McClurg, Benjamin Parker, Daniel C. Rodman, John Scott, Henry A. Smalley, Alfred B. Smith, John T. Sprague, Edwin V. Sumner, Jr., Eugene L. Townsend, William P. Wainwright, and Edward W. West.

The author also chooses a number of officers who do not warrant designation as confirmed general officers. These include Ohio militia Brig. Gen. Melancthon S. Wade, whose substantive commission as brigadier general was never confirmed. Also erroneously included are the following brigadier generals of volunteers, who were appointed but not confirmed: Richard Busteed, Gustave P. Cluseret, Robert Cowden, Charles C. Gilbert, Isham N. Haynie, James L. Kiernan, Justis McKinstry, William P. Sanders, Isaac F. Shepard, Edwin H. Stoughton, David Stuart, Frederick S. Stumbaugh, Charles M. Thruston, John B. S. Todd, Strong Vincent, Stephen H. Weed, David H. Williams, and Nelson G. Williams. Additionally, the author should not have included the following unconfirmed brevet brigadier generals of volunteers: Eli Bowyer, James C. Briscoe, Albert Erskine, Rufus E. Fleming, Henry S. Gansevoort, and Daniel White. A number of officers are listed as substantive generals who were in fact brevet brigadier generals: Alexander Chambers (U.S.V.), Wladimir Krzyzanowski (U.S.V.), Orlando M. Poe (U.S.A.), and Gustavus A. Smith (U.S.V.).

More trivial errors also occur, such as the misspelling of the name of John McAuley Palmer. Warner occasionally embellishes his usually excellent texts, such as the exaggerated story of Alexander Schimmelfennig hiding in a "pigsty" rather than a woodshed at Gettysburg. Nonetheless, this is a fine standard for checking information on Union generals, even if is not the precisely correct set.

867

Warner, Ezra J. **Generals in Gray: Lives of the Confederate Commanders** (420 pp., Louisiana State University Press, Baton Rouge, 1959)

The information in this gem of Civil War history is usually highly reliable and the research solid. A paramount, widely used reference for Confederate general officers, this book matches the format of *Generals in Blue* (*q.v.*) in that each officer receives a biographical sketch as well as a photograph. Most photographs are wartime views; others are postwar or prewar poses. (Three officers, Robert Houstoun Anderson, William Henry Carroll, and Henry Gray, are depicted with a sketch, and only one photo is omitted, that of John B. Grayson, whose photo appears in Faust's *Historical Times Illustrated Encyclopedia of the Civil War* [*q.v.*] and in later printings of Warner's book.) Warner includes 425 gen-

erals plus 9 "Trans-Mississippi" generals. He apparently took his total from Marcus Wright's *Memorandum Relative to the General Officers Appointed by the President in the Armies of the C.S.A.* (1905).

In his introduction, Warner correctly warns readers about the vagaries of general officers. "Almost from the closing days of the war," he says, "controversies have raged about who was and who was not a 'general' in the armies of the Confederate States. Through ignorance, prejudice, or sentiment, many officers have been promoted to grades which they themselves would not have laid claim. It is also true that some officers, as old men, in the shimmering haze of retrospect, have indulged in self-promotions. Southern writers, and especially southern newspapers, have been loath to dispute such claims, however tenuous their basis. The result has been the attribution in otherwise excellent biographies of totally unverifiable rank." But in discussing some of his 434 generals, Warner commits the same infraction. He reports that all laws regarding the creation of general officers required confirmation by the Senate except for the act of 21 May 1861, the Volunteer Forces Act. However, this act does not set aside Senate confirmation; in fact, it does not mention it. Of the nine generals appointed under this act, six were soon reappointed under other acts and only three—Jeremy F. Gilmer, James Dearing, and Bryan M. Thomas—were not reappointed. The act of 28 February 1861 states "the President shall appoint by and with the advice and consent of the Congress [Senate], such general officer or officers for said forces as may be necessary for the service." A Judiciary Committee report of 22 September 1862 offered the opinion that only the president has the right to nominate general officers and the Senate may only confirm or not confirm the commission. After discussion, the Senate sustained this opinion. Furthermore, a resolution of 25 May 1864 made clear that all unconfirmed nominations not acted on by a session of the Senate must be resubmitted during a subsequent session. The Confederate Senate adopted this resolution five days later.

Without complete acknowledgment of these laws, Warner includes four "groups" of generals: (1) those appointed, nominated, and confirmed; (2) those appointed and nominated but not confirmed; (3) those assigned by Edmund Kirby Smith or others; and (4) those referred to as "general" because of assignment to important commands. Warner correctly accepts the validity of group 1 and rejects the validity of group 4. He hedges on groups 2 and 3, stating that those in group 2 "have a very positive claim to their respective ranks" and that the promotions for group 3 were aided by poor communications with Richmond after July 1863. This is the kernel of Warner's mistake. On the legal authority of Jefferson Davis and the Confederate Senate, no such commissions were valid unless both nominated by the president and confirmed by the Senate.

Warner often ignores the differences among appointments, nominations, promotions, and commissioning of various general officers, which leads to incorrect listings of grades for 27 generals. Moreover, he lists the following might-have-beens whose commissions were never confirmed and who therefore do not count as general officers: as major general, Jeremy F. Gilmer; and as brigadier generals, Turner Ashby, Arthur P. Bagby, John D. Barry, Samuel Benton, Theodore W. Brevard, William M. Browne, Thomas R. R. Cobb, James Dearing, Xavier B. DeBray, James Deshler, John Dunovant, John W. Frazer, Isham W. Garrott, Victor J. B. Girardey, Archibald C. Godwin, James M. Goggin, Benjamin F. Gordon, Robert H. Hatton, George B. Hodge, Sidney Jackman, Adam R. Johnson, John R. Jones, Wilburn H. King, Levin M. Lewis, Robert P. Maclay, Lucius B. Northrop, Edward A. O'Neal, James E. Rains, Horace Randal, Felix H. Robertson, Thomas H. Taylor, Alexander M. Terrell, and Bryan M. Thomas. A corrected record of general officers for both the Confederate and Union armies is much needed.

868

Welcher, Frank J. **The Union Army, 1861–1865: Organization and Operations** (2 vols., 2073 pp., consisting of vol. 1, *The Eastern Theater* [1065 pp., 1989], and vol. 2, *The Western Theater* [1008 pp., 1992], Indiana University Press, Bloomington, 1989–1992)

Based largely on the *O.R.* (*q.v.*), this work brings together much information that would require tedious searching with regard to the structure, command, and activities of many Federal units, including armies, corps, divisions, and brigades. Although beset by some organizational difficulties of its own and judged harshly by critics after its publication, the work offers considerable quantities of useful material. Unfortunately, the volumes are difficult to use and marred by some inconsistencies, omissions, and a great deal of repetition. The reader will find that many references suggest checking other areas but do not provide page numbers, making finding specific information elsewhere in the work difficult. The work is undocumented, which prevents this massive reference book from being definitive and completely trustworthy.

Volume 1, which lacks an index (readers must refer to the index in volume 2 to use either volume), focuses on the eastern theater. Welcher lays down the organization and command of the armies of the United States, the military divisions, military departments, field armies, army corps, miscellaneous organizations, and a summary of battles and campaigns. The

sketches of battles are thin but provide a tracking of various units through eastern engagements. Indeed, none of the material is highly original, but it is handy to have it gathered in one place. The coverage is somewhat peculiar, as the author includes the Savannah and Carolina campaigns in the eastern volume. There are some outright omissions, such as the artillery reserve units of the Army of the Potomac.

Volume 2 covers the western theater. As with the first volume, it provides for the major units dates of organization, commanders, the hierarchy of command, and an itinerary of engagements and assignments for each of the units. Welcher includes some regiments in the section on miscellaneous organizations—and ones that served in the eastern armies, at that.

869

Wright, Marcus J. **General Officers of the Confederate Army, Officers of the Executive Departments of the Confederate States, Members of the Confederate Congress by States, Compiled and Prepared by General Marcus J. Wright** (188 pp., Neale Publishing Co., New York, 1911)

Long a standard source on Confederate generals, this remains an interesting historical curiosity. Effectively superseded by Warner's *Generals in Gray* (*q.v.*), this work by the Confederate brigadier general was the first systematic and competently executed attempt at cataloging the Confederate general officers—an area littered with fakes.

The author created 16 categories for his officers, thus establishing a somewhat confusing system, and some of the data on birth and death dates and places, dates of appointment, confirmation, and other basic factual information are in error. The officers are listed in order of appointment so that one can glean ranks within each grade. An index certainly would have helped the user. The compilation is an extension of two primary, early works by Wright: *Memorandum Relative to the General Officers Appointed by the President in the Armies of the C.S.A.* (1908), and *Memorandum Relative to the General Officers in the Armies of the United States during the Civil War* (1906).

(Reprinted 1983, with an introduction by John M. Carroll, 188 pp., J. M. Carroll and Co., Mattituck, N.Y.)

STATE AND TERRITORY PARTICIPATION

Alabama

870

Brewer, Willis. **Alabama: Her History, Resources, War Record, and Public Men, from 1540 to 1872** (712 pp., Barret and Brown, Printers, Montgomery, 1872)

This remains somewhat useful for its regimental histories. Despite its marginal quality, the work has no modern descendant, so the 116 pages of wartime coverage retain some reference value. The war record, regimental histories, and lists of field and staff officers constitute a history of Alabama during the war as well as an illumination of the exploits of its soldiers. Records for the Alabama infantry, cavalry, and artillery units (mostly regiments, battalions, and batteries) list field officers and captains. Biographies of many state and county officers appear, but the records of most are incomplete because the subjects were still living.

(Reprinted 1975, 712 pp., Reprint Co., Spartanburg, S.C.)

871

Fleming, Walter L. **Civil War and Reconstruction in Alabama** (815 pp., Columbia University Press, New York, 1905)

Long the standard source, Fleming's study retains its value as a reference and sound overview of the state's wartime and immediate postwar experience. The fourth state to secede, Alabama at first hosted the Confederate capital and then lost prominence when the center of Southern politics moved to Richmond. Nonetheless, the state made significant financial contributions to the Confederate war effort, with its 16 ironworks and large numbers of fighting men. Thwarting the state's activities was the area of northern Alabama demonstrating pro-Union sentiment and, by the second year of the war, the growing areas under Federal occupation.

Written with a decidedly pro-Southern tone, the book effectively sets the stage for Alabama's wartime role. The author describes in detail the antebellum conditions in Alabama, the economic, political, and social issues that existed, and the state's reaction to the growing secession crisis. The differences between plantation owners and non-slaveholders are made clear, as are the necessities of homebuilt industrial businesses and manufacturing companies during the war—an effect of being isolated in large part from the rest of the world. The maps aid significantly in understanding the evolution of Alabama during the war, and the author describes at length the various aspects, many exceedingly

unpleasant, of Alabama's experiences under Reconstruction government.

(Reprinted 1949, 815 pp., Peter Smith, New York)

872

McMillan, Malcolm Cook, ed. **The Alabama Confederate Reader** (468 pp., University of Alabama Press, University, 1963)

The editor presents a compilation of diaries, newspaper accounts, military reports, and correspondence relating to Alabama's wartime experience. Not only does this detailed work provide a story of the war inside Alabama, but it also supplies readers with a capsule history of the Confederacy as seen through the microcosm of wartime life in Alabama. For example, the study shows the difficulties that developed between the governments in Richmond and Montgomery and documents how areas fell under Federal occupation and, in some cases, how local civilians welcomed the Union Army as a liberator.

The documents in this sourcebook reveal much about the dynamics of wartime Alabama, such as the political and social tensions between the northern and southern sections of the state. In the process, a number of minor stories unfold: the terror inflicted by Federal Brig. Gen. Ormsby M. Mitchel, the heroic efforts of ordnance works run by Brig. Gen. Josiah Gorgas, and the irony of state rights as a sacred principle and one that interfered with the Confederate war aims. Slavery receives a fair amount of space, but the issue is delivered secondhand, through the words of white Southerners.

(Reprinted 1992, with an introduction by C. Peter Ripley, 468 pp., University of Alabama Press, Tuscaloosa)

873

McMillan, Malcolm C. **The Disintegration of a Confederate State: Three Governors and Alabama's Wartime Home Front, 1861–1865** (152 pp., Mercer University Press, Macon, 1986)

An impressive scope of research supports this brief, valuable look at the wartime helm of this Confederate state and its influence on Alabama's people. McMillan consulted more than 1000 letters and documents of wartime Governors Andrew Barry Moore, John Gill Shorter, and Thomas Hill Watts. He demonstrates that each of the three was handicapped by unpopular policies that fueled class strife and sectional division within the state. Moore comes across as unable to handle almost all the crises through the period of secession. Shorter cooperated fully with Richmond but lost to the state rights advocate Watts, who oversaw the final disintegration of the state. As the author convincingly shows, by 1863 the people of Alabama had lost the will to wage war, many longing for the old Union.

Arkansas

874

Bishop, Albert W. **Report of the Adjutant General of Arkansas, for the Period of the Late Rebellion, and to November 1, 1866** (278 pp., U.S. Government Printing Office, Washington, 1867)

As an early summary of the role of Arkansas in the war and data on Union troops raised from its boundaries, this brief report of the state's condition during the war in political and military terms is very general but does contains some useful facts. The bulk of the volume consists of a lengthy appendix, which offers a roster of Arkansas volunteers that includes name, grade, date of enlistment, date of rank, and remarks. Bishop provides data on field and staff officers, noncommissioned officers, and enlisted men. The Federal units covered are the 1st–4th Cavalry, 1st Infantry, 2d Infantry, 4th Infantry, and artillery units. The regimental sketches are brief, most of the coverage having gone into the rosters. Other appendices cover the evacuation of Fort Smith, disbursements by the Adjutant General's Office, and the Arkansas Militia organized by J. J. Reynolds.

875

Christ, Mark K., ed. **Rugged and Sublime: The Civil War in Arkansas** (207 pp., University of Arkansas Press, Fayetteville, 1994)

This volume offers five penetrating essays written by four contributors who outline the major events in the state during the war. Carl Moneyhon's evaluation of 1861 shows a unified state at war's outset but unveils a developing condition of unrest on the home front at the conclusion of the first year of war. William L. Shea's fine treatment of 1862 contains a superb summary of the battle of Prairie Grove and illustrates the failure of Thomas C. Hindman's strategic objectives. He also describes in concise narrative the social, economic, and political chaos unleashed in the state as the war crept onto Arkansas soil. Thomas A. DeBlack attacks the middle year of the war and finds that in Arkansas, as for the Confederacy at large, it was a disaster. The Union control of parts of the state was beginning to choke the morale from the populace, and the author conveys the events at

Arkansas Post, Fort Smith, and Little Rock with admirable excitement.

The final two chapters nicely summarize the collapse of the war movement in Arkansas. Daniel E. Sutherland's discussion of events in 1864 highlights Steele's campaigns and the many small resultant battles and shows the Confederate Army to have been virtually run out of the state. Chaos resulted and the refugee problem grew. Moneyhon's work on 1865 describes a state in anarchy that would require months to dissipate. An appendix lists Civil War sites of interest in Arkansas.

876

Moneyhon, Carl H. **The Impact of the Civil War and Reconstruction on Arkansas: Persistence in the Midst of Ruin** (288 pp., Louisiana State University Press, Baton Rouge, 1994)

This work constitutes the most intellectually valid and modern synthesis of the role of Arkansas in the Civil War. The author broadly divides the work into three parts, exploring the state's antebellum, wartime, and postwar situation. Moneyhon explores issues of the economy, society, slavery, and politics. The most significant analysis treats the war years, surveying both areas that remained under Confederate authority and those under Federal occupation. Other sections treat emancipation and the efforts toward reestablishing a pro-Union government within the state. The coverage of Reconstruction includes essays on the political machinations of the period, the postwar economy, and the lives of the freed slaves.

Moneyhon finds that by 1874 the powers that controlled Arkansas before the war—cotton, Democrats, and landlords—regained authority within the state, and that an elite aristocracy regained control of many of the state's societal systems. He has based his research on considerable reading and statistics. The maps are fair but include some errors.

877

Woods, James M. **Rebellion and Realignment: Arkansas' Road to Secession** (277 pp., University of Arkansas Press, Fayetteville, 1987)

Woods demonstrates that Arkansas backed away from internal secession impulses during the crises of the early 1850s but that as the inauguration of Lincoln approached, the political ties between state Democrats and ex-Whigs splintered. He takes careful aim at analyzing the two classes of Arkansas population: uplanders, who tended toward pro-Union sentiment; and lowlanders, who leaned toward the

Confederacy. He also shows that the southern regions of Arkansas most strongly bonded with the other Southern states and adhered to slavery as an economic force.

The author not only carefully documents the economic rifts among the common people of Arkansas but also spends considerable time focusing on the political factions within the state and among state and national figures. The role of the leading newspapers in polarizing sentiment receives careful analysis. This work adds a great deal to the understanding of how a prominent Southern state worked its way toward a place in the Confederacy.

878

Wright, Marcus J. **Arkansas in the War, 1861–1865** (ed. A. C. McGinnis, 104 pp., Independence County Historical Society, Batesville, Ark., 1963)

A useful hodgepodge of data relating to the contributions of Arkansas to the Confederacy, this work was prepared in 1909 by the former Confederate general officer but waited 54 years for publication. Wright follows the format used in his studies on Tennessee and Texas (*q.v.*). For Arkansas, he offers a list of battles, campaigns, and skirmishes fought within the state during the war, a list of its Confederate units, local designations of of state's units, Confederate general officers and naval officers appointed, a partial list of Confederate quartermasters, and a summary of U.S. troops from the state.

California

879

Orton, Richard H. **Records of California Men in the War of the Rebellion, 1861 to 1867** (887 pp., J. D. Young, State Printer, Sacramento, 1890)

A valuable source of data on a relatively thinly covered geographical area, this volume presents a historical summary of the proposed invasion of California and Texas by Confederate forces and the reactions of California troops. It also offers a history of the California column and regimental histories and rosters of all California units—these include field and staff officers and enlisted men by companies, providing names, ranks, dates of enrollment, enlistment, muster, and remarks. A regimental history preceeds each roster. The coverage includes the 1st Cavalry, 2d Cavalry, Native Cavalry, 1st–8th Infantry, special infantry organizations, mountaineers, the California Hundred, and a list of war dead from the state. J. Carlyle Parker edited *A Personal Name*

Index to Orton's "Records of California Men in the War of the Rebellion, 1861 to 1867" (153 pp., Gale Research Co., Detroit, 1978).

Connecticut

880

[Connecticut Adjutant General's Office.] **Record of Service of Connecticut Men in the Army and Navy of the United States, during the War of the Rebellion** (1071 pp., Press of the Case, Lockwood and Brainard Co., Hartford, 1889)

This compilation, which provides significant data on units from this state, contains well-written regimental histories, lists of engagements, and rosters of members, including both officers and men. Names, residences, dates of enlistment, dates of muster, and remarks about services, promotions, and terminations of service are included for all Connecticut infantry, artillery, and cavalry units. Supplementary tables list Connecticut men in the regular army, Connecticut men in the U.S. Navy, records of wounded men, Connecticut men in regiments from other states, and a revised table of casualties. A complete name index is included.

881

Croffut, William A., and John M. Morris. **The Military and Civil History of Connecticut during the War of 1861–1865: Comprising a Detailed Account of the Various Regiments and Batteries through March, Encampment, Bivouac, and Battle: Also Instances of Distinguished Personal Gallantry and Biographical Sketches of Many Heroic Soldiers: Together with a Record of the Patriotic Action of Citizens at Home, and of the Liberal Support Furnished by the State in Its Executive and Legislative Departments** (891 pp., Ledyard Bill, New York, 1868)

Although saturated with the fire of postwar passions, the book retains some value as a statistical source on this important Northern state. The authors present an early history of Connecticut with a running, approximately chronological narrative on a variety of subjects composed with patriotic fervor. They discuss the exploits of the state's regiments, with much attention focused on important commanders. The survey contains some engravings and a name index.

882

Niven, John. **Connecticut for the Union: The Role of the State in the Civil War** (493 pp., Yale University Press, New Haven, 1965)

Niven contends that Connecticut boys were so bored by their home life that they flocked to the call when war came more to escape their state than to save the Union. Might that not have been largely the case in any state at the outbreak of war? In any event, the author goes on to explore the activities of Connecticut's regiments and believes they fought well despite poor officership at the brigade and division levels. He portrays the many battle experiences of Connecticut soldiers, their camp and drill life (at least as boring as life back at home), and shows that they did particularly well in coastal operations because of their nautical skills.

The author displays prowess in his outlining of the Republican-dominated state politics and the activities of Governor William A. Buckingham and the political echoes left by Gideon Welles and Joseph R. Hawley. He traces the interactions of moderate Republicans, War Democrats, and Peace Democrats and suggests that the last group bordered on criminal disloyalty to the Lincoln administration. He concludes by citing compelling evidence that the war significantly delayed rather than accelerated the developing industrial role of the state. He shows that certain industries like munitions grew rapidly, while others, like railroads, dried up until Reconstruction.

District of Columbia

883

Brooks, Noah. **Washington in Lincoln's Time** (328 pp., Century Co., New York, 1895)

Although it is a hodgepodge of sketches on Lincoln's actions, military affairs, political gossip, and Washingtonian social life, Brooks's narrative is readable and credible. Readers gain not only an insight into Lincoln but also can gauge the wartime mood of the capital city. Fearsome panic swept Washington's streets following First Bull Run, Fredericksburg, Chancellorsville, and Early's 1864 raid. Jubilation permeated the city following Vicksburg and Gettysburg and of course at war's end, until it was shattered by the assassination. Lincoln's close association with the newsman for the *Sacramento Union* might have resulted in an appointment for Brooks as presidential secretary had Lincoln lived. Their friendship allowed Brooks to witness numerous important

wartime events, particularly during the final two years of the war. Excerpts from the 258 dispatches sent to his California paper form the core of this work.

(Reprinted 1958, with an introduction by Herbert Mitgang, 309 pp., Rinehart and Co., New York; abridged edition 1967, titled *Mr. Lincoln's Washington*, ed. P. J. Staudenraus, 481 pp., Thomas Yoseloff, New York)

884

[Pulitzer Prize, 1942]

Leech, Margaret. **Reveille in Washington, 1860–1865** (483 pp., Harper and Bros., New York, 1941)

Long recognized as a classic for its smooth writing and dramatic storytelling, this wonderful book suggests better than any other the state of societal and political affairs in Washington City. Composed like a novel, it offers a you-are-there vision of the many personalities dominating the capital during the secession crisis and the war years, not the least of whom are the Lincolns, but also many members of Congress, army officers, common citizens, spies, and riffraff. The aura of rumors, deals, and suspicions hangs thick in the air. Leech skillfully reconstructs the many human details of her characters, from the stiff demeanor of Seward to the homely realism of Lincoln to the military spit-and-polish of McClellan. The portraits that emerge, buttressed by an appendix of capsule biographies, support the wonderful story they help create.

Given the author's literary objective, she sets forth the military story of the war superbly well. But she treads on weak ground factually and employs some embellished sources, so the book should be read with a discriminating eye. Various incidents cited are undocumented and may be of dubious or secondary origin, but this rarely affects the larger purpose of the book.

Florida

885

Johns, John E. **Florida during the Civil War** (265 pp., University of Florida Press, Gainesville, 1963)

Limited only by the relative inactivity characterizing Florida's wartime role, this is a first-rate, scholarly appraisal on many levels. Johns discusses the state's secession movement and Confederate efforts to take Federal forts in Florida, outlining the successful operations at St. Augustine and Chattahoochee and the continuous Union occupation of Fort Pickens and Fort Zachary Taylor at Key West. He describes accurately the battle of Olustee, Florida's only engagement of any importance (and relatively minor at that).

According to Johns, apart from these actions and several Union raids in 1862, Florida was a state that contributed substantially to the Confederate cause but changed little during the war years. He contends that the raids battered Floridians' morale considerably and shows that the state's contributions waivered as the war dragged on. Subjects of logistics and supply were of little importance for geographical and psychological reasons.

886

Nulty, William H. **Confederate Florida: The Road to Olustee** (273 pp., University of Alabama Press, Tuscaloosa, 1990)

This work centers on the battle of Olustee even as it provides an excellent summary of the early war years in Florida and a discussion of Florida's role in the declining Confederacy during the war's final year. Nulty capably sketches the reasons for the Federal invasion that resulted in the clash at Olustee, the significance of the battle, and the Confederate reaction to the movements in Florida. He correctly describes how the Union's interest in Florida, after securing Fort Pickens, Key West, and St. Augustine, was to tighten the blockade. The state's importance to the Confederate war machine grew as the war dragged on and more and more supplies made their way north from Florida. The burgeoning rail line constructed by Confederate forces threatened to increase the efficiency of Florida's main supply route, necessitating a Yankee response to shut down the flow of supplies.

The discussion of the battle itself is superb. Brig. Gen. Truman Seymour's activities are well described, as is the tactical response of the Confederates. A few misspellings appear, as for the name of Gustavus V. Fox, and the index includes duplicate entries for General Seymour, but these are minor problems.

887

Robertson, Frederick L. **Soldiers of Florida in the Seminole Indian, Civil, and Spanish-American Wars: Prepared and Published under the Supervision of the Board of State Institutions** (368 pp., Democrat Book and Job Printer, Live Oak, Fla., 1909)

Useful for its contribution to a thinly documented area, this work consists primarily of rosters of organizations raised in Florida, about 83 percent of which cover the Civil War, 8 percent the Seminole War, and 8 percent the Spanish-American War. Robertson also offers a brief overview of the state's role in the war as well as a discussion of miscella-

neous organizations. The focus falls on the rosters of the 1st–11th Florida Infantry, the 1st–5th Florida Cavalry, artillery units, and naval actions in Florida. The rosters typically present names, dates of muster in and out, and remarks and describe officers and enlisted men. Robertson also provides short biographies of commanders associated with the state, including Edmund Kirby Smith, William W. Loring, James Patton Anderson, and Martin Luther Smith. The work has no index.

Also of great value is *Biographical Rosters of Florida's Confederate and Union Soldiers, 1861–1865,* by David W. Hartman and David Coles (6 vols., 2543 pp., Broadfoot, Wilmington, 1995). The work contains a mountain of data, organized by unit, including a summary of each soldier's service.

(Reprinted n.d., 368 pp., Richard J. Ferry, Macclenny, Fla.)

Georgia

888

Bryan, T. Conn. **Confederate Georgia** (299 pp., University of Georgia Press, Athens, 1953)

This is a competent review that draws on a multitudinous array of facts. The author burdens readers with a thick narrative that is difficult to plod through, but the many facets of Georgia's role in the war not thoroughly explored elsewhere make this reference a worthwhile contribution to Confederate history.

889

Henderson, Lillian. **Roster of the Confederate Soldiers of Georgia, 1861–1865** (6 vols., 6030 pp., Longino and Porter, Hapeville, Ga., 1959–1964)

This useful source for raw data on Georgia troops covers infantry only, providing a roster of regiments giving field and staff, band, and line companies, typically including officers listed by grade, noncommissioned officers, and private soldiers. The data include name, grade, date of enlistment, and miscellaneous information for some entries. The information appears in paragraph form rather than as a statistical table, preventing easy use, and the original volumes lack an index. Little information appears relating to the regiment's histories, something that would have added great value. The coverage is as follows: volume 1, 1st–9th Infantry; volume 2, 10th–23d Infantry; volume 3, 24th–36th Infantry; volume 4, 37th–46th Infantry; volume 5, 47th–57th Infantry; and volume 6, 59th–66th Infantry. A later index volume titled *Roster of the Confederate Soldiers of Georgia, 1861–1865,*

Index (ed. Juanita S. Brightwell, Eunice S. Lee, and Elsie C. Fulghum, 513 pp., Reprint Co., Spartanburg, S.C., 1982) is a typescript addition to the set that enhances its value.

890

Jones, Charles Edgeworth. **Georgia in the War, 1861–1865** (167 pp., Foote and Davies, Atlanta, 1909)

This handbook of lists relating to Georgia in the war, culled from the author's library, contains sufficient data to make it worthwhile for those deeply interested in Georgia's Confederate participation. (For more on the author's historian-father, see *The Children of Pride* [*q.v.*].) Sifting through the *O.R.* (*q.v.*), the war records of Marcus J. Wright, and the archives of veterans' organizations, Jones offers lists of general officers from Georgia (including militia generals), an abstract of Georgia units in the war, the "high commanders of the state of Georgia, and the campaigns and battles fought on Georgia soil." The book is partisan and eulogistic but does offer a superb summary of material that is not easily available elsewhere.

(Reprinted 1988, 167 pp., Freedom Hill Press, Jonesboro, Ga.)

Illinois

891

Hicken, Victor. **Illinois in the Civil War** (391 pp., University of Illinois Press, Urbana, 1966)

Primarily a military study, this book is the result of sound research, thorough documentation, and a careful reading of many sources including a substantial number of soldiers' letters. The author examines the character and performance of the large number of soldiers and influential officers from Illinois who fought during the conflict, fairly assessing the capabilities of such general officers as U. S. Grant, Benjamin H. Grierson, John A. Logan, and John A. Rawlins.

Strangely, Hicken supports the contention that McClernand was a capable officer who was underrated. In discussing the latter's capture of Arkansas Post, for example, he suggests that McClernand showed his true abilities. Yet the relatively simple mission at that battle pales in comparison with the tasks of other Illinois generals, particularly Grant. Moreover, Hicken does not fully appreciate the political damage inflicted by McClernand that extended his poor career as a military commander as far as it went. He fares better with the accounts of common soldiers, whom he describes as fighting for the preservation of the Union with little interest in abolition or other considerations. Illinois troops fought aggressively and well, the author shows, and provided a backbone throughout many of the conflicts of the western theater.

(Reprinted 1991, 391 pp., University of Illinois Press, Urbana)

892

[Illinois Adjutant General's Office.] **Report of the Adjutant General of Illinois Containing Reports for the Years 1861–66** (8 vols., 5674 pp., H. W. Rokker, State Printer, Springfield, 1886)

The first volume (705 pp.) contains the adjutant general's reports for the years 1863, 1864, and 1865. All manner of valuable and trivial information is included, from the records of state officials and officers to lengthy official reports to a general history of the state's participation in the war to a list of flags captured by Illinois regiments, as well as data for the 1st–15th Illinois Infantry. The other volumes contain a capsule history of each Illinois unit and a roster of members by company. The information is sketchy and consists primarily of name, grade, date of enlistment, date of muster, and occasional brief remarks. The coverage is as follows: volume 2 (715 pp.), 16th–35th Infantry; volume 3 (720 pp.), 36th–55th Infantry; volume 4 (680 pp.), 56th–77th Infantry; volume 5 (694 pp.), 78th–105th Infantry; volume 6 (616 pp.), 106th–131st Consolidated Infantry; volume 7 (692 pp.), 132d–156th Infantry, 1st–5th Cavalry; and volume 8 (852 pp.), 6th–17th Cavalry, artillery, special units, and Illinois recruits for the regular army.

Indiana

893

[Indiana Adjutant General's Office.] **Report of the Adjutant General of the State of Indiana** (8 vols., 5904 pp., Alexander H. Conner, State Printer, Indianapolis, 1865–1869)

This report comprises a lengthy and detailed record of Indiana's participation in the war effort and a roster of its troops. Volume 1 (838 pp.) contains a general summary of the condition of the state at the outbreak of hostilities, the organization of volunteer units, the draft, appointments, internal troubles, military departments, a war history, and appendices and documents. Volume 2 (690 pp.) contains a roster and regimental history of the 6th–74th Infantry, including field and staff officers, and presents names, ranks, residences, dates of commission, dates of muster, and comments. Volume 3 (687 pp.) contains a roster for the 75th–156th Infantry, miscellaneous infantry units, 1st–26th Artillery, naval officers, and Indiana Legion officers. Volume 4 (680 pp.) gives enlisted men in each unit. The volume covers the 6th–29th Infantry. Volume 5 (698 pp.) covers the 30th–59th Infantry. Volume 6 (699 pp.) presents a roster of enlisted men for the 60th–110th Infantry. Volume 7 (781 pp.) continues the roster with the 111th–156th Infantry, U.S.C.T. units, and the 1st–26th Artillery. Volume 8 (831 pp.) contains a supplemental report on officers, an addendum, and Indiana's roll of honor.

894

McCormick, David I. **Indiana Battle Flags and Record of Indiana Organizations in the Mexican, Civil, and Spanish-American Wars, Including the Movements of Troops in the Civil War, as Follows: Actions, Affairs, Attacks, Battles, Campaigns, Defenses, Expeditions, Marches, Movements, Raids, and Reconnaissances, by the Indiana Battle Flag Commission** (ed. Mindwell Crampton Wilson, 682 pp., Indiana Battle Flag Commission, Indianapolis, 1929)

A record of the Hoosier regiments, this volume contains a significant number of speeches made by various dignitaries at the presentation of Indiana battle flags to the state. It also contains capsule regimental histories of Indiana units, partly composed of accounts from the *Indianapolis Journal*, along with a roster of battles and duties of the regiments. The bulk of the work treats the Civil War, although as the title states the Mexican and Spanish-American wars receive coverage. The volume is not documented and the index is rather brief. The quality of the summaries is variable, but the book does provide some interesting accounts, not easily found in other sources, of the activities of Indiana troops.

895

Thornbrough, Emma Lou. **Indiana in the Civil War Era, 1850–1880** (758 pp., Indiana Historical Bureau, Indianapolis, 1965)

A thorough survey of wartime aspects of Hoosier life, this work systematically contends with prewar conditions, shifting political attitudes, the war itself, the state's military contribution, disloyalty during the war, Reconstruction, and a myriad of affected areas such as transportation, agriculture, industrialization, education, demographic changes, religion, and the societal fallout from the war. This is a huge amount of a ground for one volume to cover, with only about 30 percent of the work devoted to the war itself.

Thornbrough has created a sourcebook that, while it may not be entertaining reading, serves as an adequate reference to the changing face of Indiana during the mid-19th century. Indiana stands as the most Southern of the Yankee states, and the author shows why this was the case and how it slowly changed following the war. After 1870, railroad development and an emerging population pushed Indiana into a more modern configuration, but it still lagged behind most of the North in terms of industrial and social liberalism. Although few surprises lurk within these pages, the author offers a clear, concise view of numerous aspects of Indiana's journey through the wartime experience.

(Reprinted 1989, 758 pp., Indiana Historical Society, Indianapolis)

Iowa

896

Ingersoll, Lurton Dunham. **Iowa and the Rebellion: A History of the Troops Furnished by the State of Iowa to the Volunteer Armies of the Union, Which Conquered the Great Southern Rebellion of 1861–5** (743 pp., J. B. Lippincott and Co., Philadelphia, 1866)

This extensive, turgid narrative offers a history of the state's role in supporting and prosecuting the war and a history of Iowa's military organizations, comprising data on the 1st–40th Infantry and the 1st–9th Cavalry. Ingersoll presents some correspondence, lists of important officers from Iowa, a register of casualties at various engagements, crude maps, a narrative describing the sufferings of those incarcerated in Southern prisons, and a list of black troops from the state. The tone is highly partisan, often bitter, and retains the fervor of wartime patriotism. The volume lacks an index.

897

[Iowa Adjutant General's Office.] **Roster and Record of Iowa Soldiers in the War of the Rebellion, Together with Historical Sketches of Volunteer Organizations, 1861–1866** (6 vols., 8977 pp., Emory H. English, State Printer, Des Moines, 1908–1911)

A brief historical sketch of the state's regiments is followed by a lengthy roster of each regiment grouped by company and with soldiers in a given company randomly listed within each letter starting a family name. Thus, the organization makes looking up a particular soldier relatively inconvenient, but this is the only compilation of its kind. Field officers are listed with each regiment, along with records of outstanding officers tucked in throughout the listings of data. The typically minimal information for each soldier includes name, grade, date of enlistment, date of muster, and occasional notes. Coverage is as follows: volume 1 (1222 pp., 1908), 1st–8th Infantry; volume 2 (1199 pp., 1908), 9th–16th Infantry; volume 3 (1795 pp., 1910), 17th–31st Infantry; volume 4 (1794 pp., 1911), 1st–9th Cavalry and two independent companies of cavalry; volume 5 (1799 pp., 1911), 32d–48th Infantry, 1st African Infantry, and 1st–4th Battalion Artillery; and volume 6 (1168 pp., 1911), miscellaneous troops and those serving in the Mexican, Indian, and Spanish-American wars.

Kansas

898

[Kansas Adjutant General's Office.] **Report of the Adjutant General of the State of Kansas, 1861–'65** (2 vols., 948 pp., Kansas State Printing Co., Topeka, 1896)

Material is presented relevant to checking on units and individuals from this western frontier state. The work contains a summary of the state's military history, a discussion of the Executive Department, officers from Kansas, and a roster of officers and enlisted men in the Federal armies from Kansas that include field and staff officers, noncommissioned officers, bands, and enlisted men by companies. The data typically provided includes name, rank, residence, date of enlistment, date of muster, and remarks. The coverage includes the 1st–17th Infantry, 1st and 2d Kansas Colored Volunteers, 1st–3d Kansas Battery, men from Kansas in the 18th U.S.C.T., and cavalry battalions. The military history of Kansas regiments is useful, as are portions of the appended official reports.

Kentucky

899

Harrison, Lowell H. **The Civil War in Kentucky** (115 pp., University Press of Kentucky, Lexington, 1975)

Harrison provides a fair and lightly documented overview of the several campaigns and battles that touched the bluegrass state. Although only a brief, cursory treatment, this work is admirably executed. A short introductory chapter outlines the peculiar split existing within Kentucky as the war approached and defines the political realities at play. The author shows that the prevailing sentiment in Kentucky was toward the Union, save for the southern fifth of the state. Subsequent chapters detail early actions in Kentucky, including the Union recruiting and drilling at Camp Dick Robinson and Albert Sidney Johnston's occupation of Bowling Green. The author surveys the Kentucky campaign of 1862 and provides a dispassionate assessment of Braxton Bragg's role in it, as well as a brief summary of the battles at Mill Spring and Perryville. He then focuses on John Morgan's activities and delivers an excellent summary of the war's impact on this key border state. The work lacks an index.

900

[Kentucky Adjutant General's Office.] **Annual Report of the Adjutant General of Kentucky, 1861–1866** (2 vols., 2144 pp., John H. Harney, Public Printer, Frankfort, 1866–1867)

Typical of postwar state summaries, this work offers a lengthy roster of Kentucky organizations serving in the Union Army, consisting primarily of a brief summary for each man: name, grade, where and when enlisted, date of muster out, and occasional notes that range from a word or two to lengthy passages. A substantial appendix in volume 2 contains a list of black troops raised in Kentucky. The work also includes an alphabetical list of officers.

(Reprinted 1984, with an index, 2 vols., 2201 pp., McDowell Publications, Utica, Ky.)

901

[Kentucky Adjutant General's Office.] **Report of the Adjutant General of the State of Kentucky: Confederate Kentucky Volunteers, War, 1861–1865** (2 vols., 1182 pp., State Journal Co., Printers, Frankfort, 1915–1918)

This is a simple and straightforward roster of Kentucky troops by unit with the following annotation: grade, where and when the soldier enlisted, data on mustering out of service, and occasional remarks, which range from a word or two to some extensive passages. The work lacks an index.

(Reprinted 1979, with an index, 2 vols., 1352 pp., Cook and McDowell Publications, Hartford, Ky.)

902

Speed, Thomas, R. M. Kelly, and Alfred Pirtle. **The Union Regiments of Kentucky: Published under the Auspices of the Union Soldiers and Sailors Monument Association** (741 pp., Courier-Journal Job Printing Co., Louisville, 1897)

This work, which retains value a century after its appearance, contains a general history of Kentucky's role in the war. The authors focus on the political background in Kentucky prior to and during the first months of war, the military campaigns within the state, and biographical sketches of important Union commanders from Kentucky. The volume also contains capsule histories of Kentucky's Union cavalry, artillery, and infantry regiments, descriptions of the state militia, maps of important battlefields, rosters, and a useful name index. Speed contributed the regimental histories, Kelly the political material, and Pirtle the biographical sketches.

903

Townsend, William H. **Lincoln and the Bluegrass: Slavery and Civil War in Kentucky** (392 pp., University Press of Kentucky, Lexington, 1955)

Far more than an analysis of Lincoln, this book takes readers through the changing attitudes toward slavery and Union in Lexington as well as the experiences of the Kentuckian Todds and Lincolns. Only the final third of the work deals with the war years themselves, for to understand the complex nature of such a border state's position, one must be thoroughly immersed in the antebellum ways of the region.

Readers are offered much information about Lexington and the Todds, the Breckinridges, and the Clays. Sifting through the innumerable small details of the personages from Lexington allowed Townsend to construct a narrative that skillfully conveys both a better sense of what gave the Lincolns their peculiar flair and what provided Kentucky with an ultimately ironic and conflicting sense of identity. Lincoln's own correspondence and mannerisms that infuriated certain members of his cabinet illustrate the former. Events such as the purchase of a slave who happened to be the Pleasant Green Baptist Church's pastor by the congregation of Lexington's First Baptist Church illustrate the latter. By virtue of the extensive ground covered in a work of this nature, one comes away with a strong flavor of the times, no small feat for a book of fewer than 400 pages.

(Reprinted 1989, 392 pp., University Press of Kentucky, Lexington)

Louisiana

904

Bartlett, Napier. **Military Record of Louisiana, Including Biographical and Historical Papers Relating to the Military Organizations of the State: A Soldier's Story of the Late War, Muster Rolls, Lists of Casualties in the Various Regiments (So Far as Now Known), Cemeteries Where Buried, Company Journals, Personal Narratives of Prominent Actors, etc.** (252 pp., L. Graham and Co. Printers, New Orleans, 1875)

This record contains background on the formation of the Louisiana Confederate brigades, capsule histories of many regiments, discussion of Louisiana troops in the western theater, journals from a number of officers, a story of the Trans-Mississippi theater, discussions of the Army of the West, and a section on the Washington Artillery. The text is accompanied by interesting statistical summaries and narrative anecdotes, as well as portraits and muster rolls.

(Reprinted 1964, 259 pp., Louisiana State University Press, Baton Rouge)

905

Bergeron, Arthur W., Jr. **Guide to Louisiana Confederate Military Units, 1861–1865** (256 pp., Louisiana State University Press, Baton Rouge, 1989)

This well-researched volume lists basic data for each of Louisiana's 111 artillery, cavalry, and infantry units that participated in the war. Following the format of successful works pertaining to other states, Bergeron provides a list of officers for each unit and a brief history of the activities of each unit throughout the war.

906

Booth, Andrew B. **Records of Louisiana Confederate Soldiers and Louisiana Confederate Commands** (3 vols. in 4 serials, 3507 pp., published by the State, New Orleans, 1920)

Indispensable for research on the Confederacy in Louisiana, this alphabetical register of over 900 Confederate Louisiana organizations provides basic data for more than 50,000 Confederate soldiers who fought in Louisiana units. The entries are brief, typically providing name, grade, unit, a sketchy service record, parole data, and information on those who died or were captured.

(Reprinted 1984, 3 vols., 3507 pp., Reprint Co., Spartanburg, S.C.)

907

Winters, John D. **The Civil War in Louisiana** (534 pp., Louisiana State University Press, Baton Rouge, 1963)

Winters's studious, documented narrative focuses on the rich variety of military actions that occurred in Louisiana. After systematic and well-explained sections on the Louisiana secession movement and the blockade, the author follows battles and campaigns throughout the state while not losing touch with political measures. The coverage of the fall of New Orleans, Baton Rouge, operations associated with the Vicksburg campaign, actions around Port Hudson, and the Red River campaign is well executed. Major figures of interest come alive throughout the text, including Mansfield Lovell, Nathaniel Banks, Edmund Kirby Smith, and Benjamin F. Butler. The author steadily reinforces his theme that crucial cities and river strongholds regularly falling into Union hands—including the South's largest city—inflicted immeasurable real and psychological damage on the Confederate war effort.

(Reprinted 1991, 534 pp., Louisiana State University Press, Baton Rouge)

Maine

908

Whitman, William E. S., and Charles H. True. **Maine in the War for the Union: A History of the Part Borne by Maine Troops in the Suppression of the American Rebellion** (637 pp., Nelson Dingley Jr. and Co., Lewiston, 1865)

This early compilation retains value for its storehouse of data. Extraordinarily patriotic, as most publications of the 1860s were, it offers a generalized narrative of the war and the involvement of Maine organizations in various battles. The authors provide details on the whereabouts and engagements of various regiments, battalions, and batteries and give lists of field and staff officers as well as company officers. The coverage includes 1st–15th Infantry, sharpshooters, 1st Cavalry, light artillery units, artillery batteries, 16th–30th Infantry, 2d Cavalry, 31st and 32d Cavalry, 1st D.C. Cavalry, and 1st Veteran Infantry. Misspellings are spread liberally throughout the work, which lacks an index.

Maryland

909

Cottom, Robert I., Jr., and Mary Ellen Hayward. **Maryland in the Civil War: A House Divided** (126 pp., Maryland Historical Society, Baltimore, 1994)

Although brief, thinly documented, and unsystematic, this overview offers a suitable introductory summary of Maryland's role in the war. The authors present a medley of facts and stories associated with the state that includes the (nearby) raid on Harpers Ferry in 1861, a good summary of the Baltimore Riots, and a description of battles, skirmishes, and movements within Maryland, with an emphasis on Antietam. The work includes many important photographs and reproductions of pieces of art, as well as short summaries of a variety of subjects. A few misspellings occur, as for Mathew Brady, John C. Breckinridge, and Wade Hampton. The volume will be especially useful to those Civil War students with a particular interest in Maryland.

910

Goldsborough, William W. **The Maryland Line in the Confederate States Army** (357 pp., Kelly, Piet and Co., Baltimore, 1869)

This war record of four Maryland Confederate units was composed from a variety of sources by a major in the 2d Maryland Infantry, C.S.A. It consists of early sketches of the 1st Maryland Infantry (100 pp.), the 2d Maryland Infantry (95 pp.), the 1st Maryland Cavalry Battalion (97 pp.), and the Baltimore Light Artillery (65 pp.). The work is exclusively a military history of the campaigns of these units and provides a spirited description of many adventures during the war. "Conversations" are reported throughout the text, along with portraits of some of the most prominent officers described, including Goldsborough, Arnold Elzey, George H. Steuart, and Bradley T. Johnson. There are interesting descriptions of fighting in the Shenandoah Valley campaign, Gettysburg, Mine Run, and operations about Petersburg, but no index.

(New edition 1900, with additional material on the 2d Maryland Cavalry by Bradley T. Johnson and on the 3d Maryland Artillery by W. L. Ritter, 397 pp., Guggenheimer, Weil and Co., Baltimore; reprinted 1972, with an introduction by Jean Baker and a 74-page index published in Annapolis in 1944, 371 pp., Kennikat Press, Port Washington, N.Y.; reprinted 1983, 371 pp., Butternut Press, Gaithersburg)

911

Wilmer, L. Allison, J. H. Jarrett, and George W. F. Vernon. **History and Roster of Maryland Volunteers, War of 1861–5, Prepared under Authority of the General Assembly of Maryland** (2 vols., 1119 pp., Press of Guggenheimer, Weil and Co., Baltimore, 1898–1899)

This important work on Maryland Civil War history covers all Maryland units of the Union Army and Navy. It provides a brief narrative history of the raising of each regiment, its composition, a general history of its marches and battles, anecdotes, and a full roster of field and staff officers and enlisted men arranged alphabetically in companies, generally giving name, grade, date of enlistment, date of muster out, and remarks. The authors cover naval forces in admirable detail and offer a complete unit history of Maryland U.S.C.T. regiments.

(Reprinted 1990, with an index volume compiled by Martha and Bill Reamy, 3 vols., 1272 pp., Family Line, Westminster, Md.)

Massachusetts

912

Bowen, James L. **Massachusetts in the War, 1861–1865** (1029 pp., Clark W. Bryan and Co., Springfield, Mass., 1889)

In this extensive history of the state's organizations, the tone is generally controlled, avoiding both overly sensationalizing events or reporting them with partisan bitterness. Thus, the study remains useful as a collection despite the author's inability to draw on most of the material that went into the *O.R.* (*q.v.*). Bowen provides a lengthy general summary of the role of Massachusetts during the war, followed by generalized regimental histories and a list of officers. The narrative is matter-of-fact in style and reports a great deal of military minutiae relating to each of the state's organizations, making it a necessary resource for checking into individual actions of Massachusetts regiments. The work covers the 1st–62d Infantry, heavy artillery units, the 1st–5th Cavalry, artillery batteries, and sharpshooters and provides sketches of general officers from Massachusetts. Engraved portraits accompany the text.

913

Higginson, Thomas Wentworth. **Massachusetts in the Army and Navy during the War of 1861–1865** (2 vols., 1452 pp., Wright and Potter Printing Co., Boston, 1895–1896)

This volume contains a valuable record of the state's war effort. Higginson, the Massachusetts state military and naval historian, is a fine writer with an excellent style who used good sources to compile the information. The first volume includes a survey of Massachusetts during the war, the organization of its state militia and volunteer forces, data on companies and regiments, and a narrative of their participation in the major battles. The author discusses the difficulties created by the government's action in commissioning politicians to high grades at the war's outset. He points out the serious consequences of employing raw troops at Big Bethel, Bull Run, and Ball's Bluff early in the war, as well as the folly of placing recruits into newly created regiments rather than as replacements in established units.

Higginson provides a condensed history of each Massachusetts regiment, cavalry unit, and battery, with lists of their commanding officers and the numbers of men in each grade. Casualties are listed by battles. There follow lists of officers who were killed in action, died of wounds, or died as prisoners. A list of regimental flags preserved in the State House accompanies this data. The second volume contains lists of Massachusetts naval officers, general officers of the state, field officers, company officers, officers from the state in the regular army, and brevet grades given to Massachusetts officers. A chapter is devoted to Massachusetts women in the war, and there is a state bibliography.

914

[Massachusetts Adjutant General's Office.] **Massachusetts Soldiers, Sailors, and Marines in the Civil War** (9 vols., 7459 pp., Riverdale Press, Brookline, 1931–1935)

An indispensable guide to the state's wartime organizations, this set constitutes a massive roster of field and staff officers, noncommissioned officers, bands, and enlisted men by companies. Each entry provides names, residences, dates of commission and muster, and notes. The coverage is as follows: volume 1 (816 pp.), 1st–11th Infantry; volume 2 (833 pp.), 12th–24th Infantry; volume 3 (824 pp.), 25th–37th Infantry; volume 4 (874 pp.), 38th–57th Infantry; volume 5 (847 pp.), 58th–62d Infantry, unattached militia, 1st–16th Artillery, and 1st–3d Heavy Artillery; volume 6 (838 pp.), 4th Heavy Artillery, unattached heavy artillery, 1st–5th Cavalry, and miscellaneous officers and soldiers, U.S.A. and U.S.V., with surnames from A to L; volume 7 (875 pp.), officers and soldiers, U.S.A. and U.S.V., with surnames from M to Z, Veteran Reserve Corps, U.S.C.T., officers of the navy, and naval enlisted men with surnames from A to E; volume 8 (918 pp.), naval enlisted men with surnames from F to Z and U.S. Marine Corps; volume 9 (634 pp.), general index.

Michigan

915

[Michigan Adjutant General's Office.] **Record of Service of Michigan Volunteers in the Civil War, 1861–1865** (45 vols., 6783 pp., Ihling Bros. and Everard, Printers, Kalamazoo, 1905)

A massive collection of regimental histories is provided for virtually all Michigan units serving in the war. Each volume contains a history of the unit discussed, a list of officers, and an alphabetical roster of enlisted men with a short sketch, dates of enlistment, muster, grades achieved, brevets, deaths, wounds, and remarks.

The coverage is as follows: volume 1 (151 pp.), 1st Infantry; volume 2 (189 pp.), 2d Infantry; volume 3 (211 pp.), 3d Infantry; volume 4 (197 pp.), 4th Infantry; volume 5 (136 pp.), 5th Infantry; volume 6 (158 pp.), 6th Infantry; volume 7 (117 pp.), 7th Infantry; volume 8 (148 pp.), 8th Infantry; volume 9 (164 pp.), 9th Infantry; volume 10 (126 pp.), 10th Infantry; volume 11 (177 pp.), 11th Infantry; volume 12 (178 pp.), 12th Infantry; volume 13 (163 pp.), 13th Infantry; volume 14 (130 pp.), 14th Infantry; volume 15 (181 pp.), 15th Infantry; volume 16 (180 pp.), 16th Infantry; volume 17 (116 pp.), 17th Infantry; volume 18 (109 pp.), 18th Infantry; volume 19 (102 pp.), 19th Infantry; volume 20 (104 pp.), 20th Infantry; volume 21 (127 pp.), 21st Infantry; volume 22 (160 pp.), 22d Infantry; volume 23 (118 pp.), 23d Infantry; volume 24 (164 pp.), 24th Infantry, volume 25 (82 pp.), 25th Infantry; volume 26 (83 pp.), 26th Infantry; volume 27 (148 pp.), 27th Infantry; volume 28 (70 pp.), 28th Infantry; volume 29 (71 pp.), 29th Infantry; volume 30 (64 pp.), 30th Infantry; volume 31 (109 pp.), 1st Cavalry; volume 32 (178 pp.), 2d Cavalry; volume 33 (188 pp.), 3d Cavalry; volume 34 (165 pp.), 4th Cavalry; volume 35 (157 pp.), 5th Cavalry; volume 36 (155 pp.), 6th Cavalry; volume 37 (146 pp.), 7th Cavalry; volume 38 (173 pp.), 8th Cavalry; volume 39 (112 pp.), 9th Cavalry; volume 40 (155 pp.), 10th Cavalry; volume 41 (109 pp.), 11th Cavalry; volume 42 (274 pp.), 1st Artillery; volume 43 (232 pp.), 1st Engineers; volume 44 (182 pp.), 1st Sharpshooters; and volume 45 (324 pp.), miscellaneous units, including Merrill's Horse, 1st Michigan Lancers, Chandler Horse Guards, and Provost Guard.

An index volume, *Alphabetical General Index to Public Library Sets of 85,271 Names of Michigan Soldiers and Sailors Individual Records* (1097 pp., Wynkoop, Hallenbeck, Crawford and Co., State Printers, Lansing, 1915), adds greatly to the work's usefulness (reprinted 1984, 1097 pp., Michael Hogle and Ray Walsh, East Lansing).

916

Robertson, John. **Michigan in the War** (Rev. ed., 1039 pp., W. S. George and Co., State Printer, Lansing, 1882)

This work supersedes an inferior edition of 859 pages published in 1880. It is a lengthy general history written in the light of sectional animosity and therefore infused with glorifying stories and patriotic fervor. Much of value lies within the book, however, as the general history contains important and enlightening facts in addition to less-useful rambling reflections. The bulk of the volume consists of a massive collection of capsule histories of all the Michigan units. The chapters generally contain a field and staff roster of officers, documents relating to the units' origins, and a narrative regimental history highlighting important accomplishments, battles experienced, and so on. A lengthy roster of commissioned army and navy officers follows, along with an appendix covering the War of 1812 and early Indian skirmishes.

Minnesota

917

Carley, Kenneth. **Minnesota in the Civil War** (168 pp., Ross and Haines Co., Minneapolis, 1961)

This brief, popular introduction to the state's participation in the war has virtually nothing to say about Minnesota itself but is limited to brief sketches of the actions of Minnesota troops in major battles, mostly in the western theater. The narrative centers on Gettysburg, the battles around Chattanooga, the capture of Little Rock, the Vicksburg campaign, the battle of Nashville, and the battle of Corinth. Appended is a chronology of important wartime events and a partial roster of Minnesota regiments mentioned in the work, listing the top field officers of the regiments.

The book is written in a fairly simple style and illustrated with a few photographs and crude maps. It is not documented but does offer a short bibliography. The battle accounts, while not particularly inventive, summarize the Minnesotans' experiences. As a starting point for those interested in prominent Minnesota units, this work may suffice.

918

[Minnesota Indian and Civil Wars Commission.] **Minnesota in the Civil and Indian Wars, 1861–1865: Prepared and Published under the Supervision of the Board of Commissioners, Appointed by the Act of the Legislature of Minnesota of April 6, 1889** (2 vols., 1496 pp., Pioneer Press Co., St. Paul, 1890–1893)

A fine summary is provided of Minnesota's troops in the field and the state's role in the war. Volume 1 (844 pp.) contains a history and roster of Minnesota troops. The regimental histories provide a summary of battles, field and staff officers, and enlisted men by companies, giving the following information for each: name, age, dates of muster, and remarks. The coverage includes the 1st–11th Infantry, 1st and 2d sharpshooters, mounted rangers, various cavalry units, heavy and light artillery units, general officers from Minnesota, staff corps, regular army appointments, U.S.C.T. troops, and the Indian Wars. Volume 2 (652 pp.) presents a chronological history of Civil War battles and the participation of Minnesota troops. A later index volume was prepared by Irene B. Warming (488 pp., Minnesota Historical Society, St. Paul, 1936).

Mississippi

919

Bearss, Edwin C. **Decision in Mississippi: Mississippi's Important Role in the War between the States** (636 pp., Mississippi Commission on the War between the States, Jackson, 1962)

Drawing heavily on the *O.R.* (*q.v.*), Bearss focuses his battle narrative on the various actions that occurred in Mississippi during the conflict, with emphasis placed squarely on Vicksburg. Readers receive not only a great summary of that vital siege but careful and systematic treatment of the clashes at Champion's Hill (the author prefers Champion Hill), Iuka, and Van Dorn's Holly Springs raid. The author expends great energy telling the story of Van Dorn's raid but features next to nothing about a far more important action, the battle of Corinth.

Many of the battle accounts are replete with a dazzling array of detail in which novice readers may get lost. In telling the story of Grant's campaign for Vicksburg, Bearss exaggerates the importance of Champion's Hill, raising it to the level of a decisive battle of the war. He contends that Grant's army was supplied by trains during the campaign, contradicting Grant's memoirs and many other sources. He

delivers a favorable assessment of Grant and judges Pemberton, Johnston, and McClernand less positively. At times the writing slips, but the work nonetheless stands as a fine achievement in state histories of the war.

920

Bettersworth, John K. **Confederate Mississippi: The People and Policies of a Cotton State in Wartime** (386 pp., Louisiana State University Press, Baton Rouge, 1943)

This standard narrative history draws on a wide variety of sources, both primary and secondary, to construct a sweeping overview of Mississippi's politics, economy, social aspects, religious nature, and military effort during the war years. Among the sources used are letters, diaries, journals, newspaper accounts, and governmental documents. Bettersworth's treatment of this mass of material is splendidly organized; his selections are intelligent, and the linking narrative is well-composed.

The author aptly demonstrates how war touched Mississippi once it spilled onto the state's soil. All semblance of a normal home front shattered; refugees filled the woods and swamps, schools closed, most newspapers shut down, the state government faltered, and the economy unraveled. The fall of Vicksburg crushed the state's will to prosecute the war. The work deals insufficiently with blacks in Mississippi but does an admirable job discussing disloyalty in the state.

(Reprinted 1979, 386 pp., Porcupine Press, Philadelphia)

921

Bettersworth, John K., and James W. Silver, eds. **Mississippi in the Confederacy** (2 vols., 681 pp., Louisiana State University Press, Baton Rouge, 1961)

A rich store of contemporary writings relating to Mississippi and her role in the Confederate war effort is found in the first volume, *As They Saw It* (362 pp.), and the second, *As Seen in Retrospect* (319 pp.). Containing excerpts from diaries, reminiscences, letters, and military documents, the volumes allow a glimpse of how Mississippians felt about the war as they lived through it and in its immediate wake. The effect is powerful and touches on nearly all aspects of the Confederate experience in the Deep South. Although the materials are local in a strict sense, they allow readers to extrapolate a picture of Confederate nationalism. Such volumes are valuable in understanding the state's influence on the war as a whole.

The editors purport that Mississippians were drawn to secession because the Yankees failed to follow the order of the U.S. Constitution, regarding slavery in particular. Although he was a local, Jefferson Davis did not universal praise from Mississippians on his acceptance of the provisional presidency. When war touched Mississippi, the populace lost control. Refugee life, the loss of the river, everyday hardships, and frequent deaths of kin and friends became too much to bear. Repairing the bitter anguish of defeat came slowly. These volumes document the whole experience and stand as a worthwhile contribution.

(Reprinted 1970, 2 vols., 681 pp., Kraus Reprints, Millwood, N.Y.)

922

Rietti, John C. **Military Annals of Mississippi: Military Organizations Which Entered the Service of the Confederate States of America, from the State of Mississippi** (196 pp., published by the author, Jackson, 1895)

This product of a grand plan that produced only one volume remains an interesting curiosity. Rietti planned a set of works describing all of the state's Confederate units, but this volume contains only a few introductory documents pertaining to Mississippi's secession and raising of militia troops, followed by a numerical discussion of regiments, from the 1st Infantry to the 15th Infantry. Included are a roster of officers, a list of companies, a short summary of the regiment's experience, and various tributes and anecdotes of variable quality. The book is amateurishly written, and the material is not altogether reliable.

(Reprinted 1976, with an index, 245 pp., Reprint Co., Spartanburg, S.C.)

Missouri

923

Parrish, William E. **Turbulent Partnership: Missouri and the Union, 1861–1865** (242 pp., University of Missouri Press, Columbia, 1963)

A peculiar blend of noninvolvement and terrifying, murderous raids characterized this distant state's role in the war. This odd sense of belonging to the conflict, in addition to a long list of peculiar characters active in the state's wartime years, provides an unusual challenge to anyone wishing to chronicle Missouri's Civil War history. Parrish has succeeded in relating the story.

This author does not focus squarely on military aspects but primarily on the political history of Missouri's wartime experience. He examines Provisional Governor Hamilton R. Gamble's support of the Lincoln administration, his crucial

interplay in keeping Missouri within the Union, and his frustrating occasional lack of cooperation with Federal authorities over the Missouri State Militia. He also looks at the early careers of officers in Missouri who would later rise to prominence, including Henry Halleck, John M. Schofield, and Samuel R. Curtis. The author's treatment of Nathaniel Lyon, whose career was cut short at Wilson's Creek, and John Charles Frémont, who terminated his own career, is balanced and noteworthy.

Nebraska Territory

924

[Nebraska Adjutant General's Office.] **Roster of Nebraska Volunteers, from 1861 to 1869, Compiled from Books, Records and Documents on File in the Office of the Adjutant General of State** (236 pp., Wigton and Evans, State Printers, Hastings, 1888)

This work covers the contributions of men raised from Nebraska Territory during the war years. The roster includes field and staff officers and enlisted men, grouped by companies, and delivers names, ages, residences, dates of enlistment, dates of muster, and remarks. The coverage includes the 1st Infantry, 1st Battalion of Infantry, 2d Regiment (Cavalry), miscellaneous cavalry units, and other miscellaneous units.

New Hampshire

925

Ayling, Augustus C., ed. **Revised Register of the Soldiers and Sailors of New Hampshire in the War of the Rebellion, 1861–1866** (1347 pp., Ira C. Evans, Public Printer, Concord, 1895)

This basic roster for New Hampshire troops includes regimental histories and enlisted men and officers listed alphabetically rather than by companies, plus an index. The data provided are names, ages, residences, dates of enlistment, dates of rank, and remarks. The summary of each regiment sketches its activities, deaths, woundings of officers and men, and captures. The coverage includes 1st–18th Infantry, 1st Cavalry, 1st Light Artillery, miscellaneous artillery units, heavy artillery, sharpshooters, miscellaneous units, Veteran Reserve Corps, U.S.C.T., members of naval and marine corps units, state units, and Medals of Honor awarded.

926

Waite, Otis F. R. **New Hampshire in the Great Rebellion, Containing Histories of the Several New Hampshire Regiments, and Biographical Notices of Many of the Prominent Actors in the Civil War of 1861–65** (608 pp., Tracy, Chase and Co., Claremont, 1870)

This early, highly partisan, but nonetheless useful compilation on units from this New England state incorporates summaries of units raised in the state along with a lengthy discussion of New Hampshire's role in the various events of the war. The summaries are reasonably well done, covering the 1st–18th Infantry, 1st Cavalry, light and heavy artillery batteries, and sharpshooters. The discussion of battles and campaigns emphasizes the parts New Hampshire units and commanders played in them. The biographical sketches of officers include sections on Gilman Marston, Joseph H. Porter, Haldimand S. Putnam, and John G. Foster. Illustrations of some officials and officers appear, including Ichabod Goodwin, Simon G. Griffin, and Edward E. Cross. The work lacks an index.

New Jersey

927

Foster, John Y. **New Jersey and the Rebellion: A History of the Services of the Troops and People of New Jersey in Aid of the Union Cause** (872 pp., Martin R. Dennis and Co., Newark, 1868)

An early, enthusiastic report on this state's wartime activity, the book remains useful despite its tone of extraordinary patriotism. After surveying the causes of the war, the uprising in New Jersey, and troops sent forward, Foster delivers a history of the war as it relates to New Jersey. He surveys New Jersey troops at Bull Run, describes the activities of the 1st New Jersey Brigade, and details much about Philip Kearny. The author highlights the Peninsular campaign, Antietam, Fredericksburg, Chancellorsville, Gettysburg, the Wilderness, Cold Harbor, and Petersburg.

Material on the 2d New Jersey Brigade is followed by a section that delivers sketches of regiments, including the 9th–40th Infantry, the 1st–5th Artillery, cavalry units, and miscellaneous organizations. The work details the invasion of Pennsylvania, the support of New Jersey citizens for the war, the role of the church, general officers of the state, chaplains and surgeons, and other military matters.

928

Gillette, William. **Jersey Blue: Civil War Politics in New Jersey, 1854–1865** (389 pp., Rutgers University Press, New Brunswick, 1995)

The author attacks the popular notion that New Jersey's citizens had strong pro-Southern feeling before the war or were relatively unsupportive of the war when it came. Backed by a substantial research effort and precise documentation, Gillette surveys the state politics of New Jersey during the middle 1850s and finds that as the war approached, many New Jersey residents considered themselves part of a "border" state only in the sense that they stood on middle ground on the issues. The author concedes that New Jersey's trade with the South played a role in shaping the state's attitudes but finds that the state's economy, politics, and society reveal a region solidly behind the war effort.

Gillette examines many small facets of New Jersey's role in the approaching secession crisis and in the war itself. He explores the nomination and election processes of the 1860 contest, the reaction of many New Jerseyans to the outbreak of war, the politics of patriotism at the beginning of war, and Democratic factionalism as the war continued. The pace quickens with an adept handling of the various crises of the middle part of the war and the coming of the 1864 election. The author places war's end into a thoughtful context as he recalls the meaning of New Jersey's contributions to the Union Army. Finding the state "not ambivalent" and its war record "admirable," Gillette shows that New Jersey in no way resembled border slave states. An appendix provides political statistics.

929

Miers, Earl Schenck. **New Jersey and the Civil War** (135 pp., D. Van Nostrand Co., Princeton, 1964)

Although slim and far from comprehensive, this book serves as an adequate introduction to the state's participation in the war. The curiously different stand taken by state politicians toward slavery and peace movements made it a standout among Northern states early in the war. New Jersey's voting population twice defeated Abraham Lincoln, and the politically charged newspapers throughout the state routinely criticized the administration. As the war developed, however, New Jersey supplied more than 80,000 troops and stood for the Union. Governors Charles S. Olden and Joel Parker supported the war more vigorously than they opposed Lincoln.

Miers's volume illustrates New Jersey's role by presenting 31 accounts touching on a great many aspects of the war as experienced by participants, mostly from New Jersey. A wide spectrum of battles and campaigns, politics, societal matters, and personality profiles receives attention. The work lacks an index.

930

Stryker, William S., ed. **Record of Officers and Men of New Jersey in the Civil War, 1861–1865** (2 vols., 1934 pp., John L. Murphy, Printer, Trenton, 1876)

This volume, which may still be consulted for information on the activities of many New Jersey units, is primarily a roster that includes data on field and staff officers, noncommissioned officers, bands, and enlisted men by companies. Names, ranks, dates of commission, dates of enlistment, dates of muster, and comments are provided. Volume 1 covers general and staff officers and the 1st–32d Infantry; volume 2 covers the 33d–40th Infantry, 1st–3d Cavalry, artillery units, miscellaneous organizations, the Veteran Reserve Corps, the 1st Army Corps, U.S.C.T., U.S. Regulars, naval officers and men, New Jersey troops interred in U.S. national cemeteries, and an index.

New York

931

McKay, Ernest A. **The Civil War and New York City** (336 pp., Syracuse University Press, Syracuse, 1990)

This well-written and exhaustively documented account of the Civil War's effect on New York includes many reflections on prominent New Yorkers, both civilians and military officers and soldiers, and much about Northern urban existence during the war years. The author provides a detailed slice of urban culture in a unique period, treating New York's recruiting activities, financing of war materiel, the city's mayoral election, the effect of emancipation on New York, loyalty and dissent among the populace, the draft riots of July 1863, political wranglings, Lincoln's 1864 election, and the victorious celebrations of the war's end.

One of the work's strengths is its analysis of the nonobvious. McKay outlines Horace Greeley's attempts to mediate a peace and James Gordon Bennett's work on annexing Canada, Mexico, and Cuba. We also discover an undercurrent of New York society and merchants who ultimately supported the Union despite their amazing diversity. Throughout the war years, New Yorkers seemingly embraced emancipation as an obvious outcome of the war; this is the case even for those who stood firmly against it in 1861 or

1862. A few misspellings appear, as with the names of Mathew Brady and Wladimir Krzyzanowski. But generally the text is free of errors and enlightens readers by showing how the citizens of the North's largest city transformed themselves into relatively more modern thinkers by the glorious and painful year of 1865.

932

Phisterer, Frederick. **New York in the War of the Rebellion** (3d ed., 6 vols., 4871 pp., J. B. Lyon and Co., State Printers, Albany, 1912)

This work retains great value for its storehouse of data. The present set supersedes a crude first edition—a single volume of 532 pages published in 1890—and the second edition that appeared in 1891. Phisterer, who died in 1909, had served as acting adjutant general of New York and was brevetted brigadier general of volunteers at the close of the war. Although some errors (mostly typographical) appear scattered throughout, the volumes form a useful reference tool for New York units and commanders.

Volume 1 (896 pp.) consists of four large parts. Part 1 surveys events in the state during the war and covers calls for men, credits due the state, drafts, ages of the volunteers, periods of service, organizations raised, cost of the war, and military relics (flags). Part 2 covers events in the field and includes maps, a chronology of battles and campaigns, and a summary of casualties. Part 3 supplies the roll of honor, a list of brevets, Medals of Honor, and deaths in the service. Part 4 contains a register of officers and sketches of New York units. The registers are usually presented by company, battalion, regiment, or other unit and provide short biographies, including ages, service records, and awards for each officer. The coverage includes New York Militia and National Guard units and 1st–9th New York Cavalry.

Volume 2 (911 pp.) continues the unit histories from the last portions of the 9th New York Cavalry through the 26th Cavalry, 1st and 2d Mounted Rifles, 1st Dragoons, 1st and 2d Veteran Cavalry, independent cavalry units, artillery units, engineer units, sharpshooters, and 1st through part of the 7th Infantry. Volume 3 (895 pp.) continues with the 7th Infantry and proceeds through part of the 69th Infantry. Volume 4 (911 pp.) covers the final part of the 69th Infantry through part of the 140th Infantry. Volume 5 (882 pp.) covers the remainder of the 140th Infantry through the 194th Infantry, independent infantry units, U.S. Colored Troops from the state, Veteran Reserve Corps units, general and staff officers from New York, officers of volunteer units, volunteer naval officers, New York officers in the regular army, and New York officers in the Marine Corps. Appendices cover statistics of death in the army and numbers of men furnished the army. Volume 6 (376 pp.) is an index.

North Carolina

933

Barrett, John G. **The Civil War in North Carolina** (484 pp., University of North Carolina Press, Chapel Hill, 1963)

The Tarheel State played a tremendously important role in the Confederacy, and this work does not back away from the significant challenge of conveying a survey of the state's military operations, its troops, and its government's relations with the Confederacy. Barrett documents the minor role that North Carolina played in the secession crisis before plunging into an examination of the state's participation throughout the war years.

The author contends that despite early Union attempts to blockade the Atlantic Coast, blockade-runners operating in and out of North Carolina's ports contributed immensely to the Confederate war effort. The state provided significant manpower, the author argues, to the point where one-sixth or so of the Confederate Army hailed from North Carolina and one-fourth of those lost in battle were North Carolinians. The author further suggests that the open nature of Wilmington throughout the war enabled the Army of Northern Virginia to carry on as far as it did and that the fall of Fort Fisher sealed its doom.

(Reprinted 1990, 484 pp., University of North Carolina Press, Chapel Hill)

934

Clark, Walter, ed. **Histories of the Several Regiments and Battalions from North Carolina, in the Great War, 1861–'65** (5 vols., 3982 pp., State of North Carolina, Raleigh, 1901)

These capsule histories of North Carolina units were written by regimental members long after the war. Although parts of the work are superficial and others certainly embellished, this mass of assembled recollections retains value. The coverage is as follows: volume 1, organization of the state troops, 1st–16th Infantry; volume 2, 17th–42d Infantry; volume 3, 43d–69th Infantry; volume 4, reserves, 70th–83d Infantry, 16th and 10th Infantry, 1st–25th Battalions, special units, brigades, and military prisons; volume 5, concluding material and summaries of battles, the state's role in naval warfare, and addenda. Artillery and cavalry data are scattered throughout.

A number of units have more than one contribution, and each is accompanied by a photograph of regimental officers. The text is florid and at times awkwardly written, but it contains a mountain of information not easily available in compact form elsewhere. The appendices in the final volume hold considerable value, particularly with regard to matters such as the Appomattox paroles, the activities of various educational institutions in the war, and the indices.

(Reprinted 1991, 5 vols., 3982 pp., Broadfoot, Wilmington)

935

Hill, D. H., Jr. **Bethel to Sharpsburg: A History of North Carolina in the War between the States** (2 vols., 893 pp., Edwards and Broughton, Raleigh, 1926)

This chronological narrative of North Carolina's war experience was penned by the son of an argumentative Rebel major general. The first volume focuses on the secession movement in North Carolina and the battles of Big Bethel, First Bull Run, operations on the Virginia coast, the North Atlantic Blockading Squadron's attack on the Carolina coast, the progress of Federal troops moving into the state, and the efforts of blockade-runners. The second volume carries the story through the Peninsular campaign, Cedar Mountain, Second Bull Run, and the early days of the Antietam campaign. Hill's death stopped the work before he completed a full discussion of Antietam.

Although the range of discussion extends into many eastern battles (and even beyond that theater), the work concentrates on the activities of North Carolinians, or at least periodically revisits them. The account is largely grounded in the *O.R.* (*q.v.*) but also draws on a number of other valuable sources. It is on the whole objective, though glimmers of partisanship frequently shine through. The overall result is a useful work when coordinated with other efforts relating to this well-covered state.

(Reprinted 1992, 2 vols., 893 pp., Broadfoot, Wilmington)

936

Manarin, Louis H., and Weymouth T. Jordan, eds. **North Carolina Troops, 1861–1865: A Roster** (13 vols., 9049 pp., and continuing, North Carolina Archives and History Division, Raleigh, 1966–   )

Perhaps the finest state roster of Civil War troops, this thoroughly researched and carefully edited assemblage resulted from countless hours spent in the National Archives sorting through and compiling muster rolls and soldiers' records. Included with organizational tables are comprehensive rosters of each unit and a capsule unit history. Long introductions and useful indices round out these works, which are necessary for checking data on individuals who fought for North Carolina.

The organization of volumes follows: volume 1 (738 pp.), artillery units; volume 2 (847 pp.), cavalry units; volume 3 (739 pp.), 1st–3d Infantry, miscellaneous units; volume 4 (763 pp.), 4th–8th Infantry; volume 5 (752 pp.), 11th–15th Infantry, 13th Battalion; volume 6 (786 pp.), 16th–18th and 20th–21st Infantry; volume 7 (730 pp.), 22d–26th Infantry; volume 8 (580 pp.), 27th–31st Infantry; volume 9 (662 pp.), 32d–35th and 37th Infantry; volume 10 (563 pp.), 38th–39th and 42d–44th Infantry; volume 11 (557 pp.), 45th–48th Infantry; volume 12 (580 pp.), 49th–52d Infantry; and volume 13 (752 pp.), 53d–56th Infantry.

937

Yearns, W. Buck, and John G. Barrett, eds. **North Carolina Civil War Documentary** (365 pp., University of North Carolina Press, Chapel Hill, 1980)

This is a superb compilation of contemporary documents relating to the state's war effort and the effect of the war on North Carolina. Twenty sections cast light on principal areas of interest, as follows: the secession crisis, North Carolina's secession, the early invasion of the state, war in eastern North Carolina, blockade-running, Fort Fisher, war in the central and western counties, the call to arms, problems of procurement, state socialism, the costs of the war, the war and North Carolina's railroads, the economy, churches and schools, the victims of attrition, life on the home front, state rights, the peace movement, wartime politics, and Sherman's campaign in the Carolinas. The sources range from the predictable to the unlikely and uncover a great range of meaning relating to the Confederate state.

Among the more striking passages are a description of the powder boat explosion at Fort Fisher in December 1864, difficulties of the conscription and exemption systems, details of state taxation, the sacrifice of minor railroads, the fear of local despotism, and the chaotic flight from Sherman's onslaught. Good summaries of battles fought in the state appear, particularly with regard to the spring of 1865, such as Bentonville. One wishes such a valuable reference work, which reads so entertainingly, were available for more states of the Confederacy.

Ohio

938

Brandt, Nat. **The Town That Started the Civil War** (336 pp., Syracuse University Press, Syracuse, 1990)

Although its title exaggerates significantly, this work presents an enthralling story of the abolition center of Oberlin, Ohio. The progressive attitudes fostered early on in this home of Oberlin College allowed the town to act as a microcosm of abolition sentiment. Brandt describes the town's background and some influential characters associated with it in a superbly written and very well researched narrative. The work reflects on the town's importance as an underground railroad stop and the spark of passion unleashed by the 1858 kidnapping of the Kentucky fugitive slave John Price.

The Price case became an intense focus of polarization, the author shows, in a way smaller but similar to that generated by the John Brown raid a year later. Many citizens of the town, including professors and students from the college, assisted in freeing the slave, and this story symbolizes much of the sectional tension that followed. The author's sparkling narrative and liberal use of quotations not only enliven an antebellum picture of abolition sentiment but bring readers back to the moment to understand it concretely.

939

[Ohio Adjutant General's Office.] **Official Roster of the Soldiers of the State of Ohio in the War of the Rebellion, 1861–1866** (12 vols., 9369 pp., Werner Printing and Lithography Co., Akron, vols. 1, 4–6, and 11; Wilstach, Baldwin and Co., Cincinnati, vol. 2; Ohio Valley Co., Cincinnati, vols. 3 and 7–10; and Laning Co., Norwalk, vol. 12; 1886–1895)

Although it is marred by typographical errors and data of variable quality, this is a valuable research tool for Buckeye troops. The two primary aspects of reports by state adjutant generals are here: a full roster of Ohioans who fought in the war and a summary capsule history of Ohio's units. The set contains a record of each unit's service, including regiments, independent companies, artillery units, cavalry units, United States Colored Troops, and navy units. The summaries incorporate discussions of participation in important battles. The set also includes a roster of officers and enlisted men and an honor roll of Ohioan deaths during the war. The final volume provides data on Ohio's participation in the Mexican War and errata and additions.

940

Reid, Whitelaw. **Ohio in the War: Her Statesmen, Her Generals, and Soldiers** (2 vols., 1999 pp., Moore, Wilstach, and Baldwin, Cincinnati, 1868)

This work records the history of the state during the war, offers short biographies of general officers from Ohio, and provides a history of the regiments from Ohio that participated in the war. Reid's experience as a wartime journalist adds greatly to the value of this work and places it among the better state histories. It is marked by the typical qualities, focusing on state officials and the experience of Ohio's population during the war, but is notable for its careful and extended treatment of Chase and Stanton as well. The episodes detailing Morgan's raids through the state offer absorbing reading.

The final two parts are the most valuable. The biographies of generals are engaging and balanced, save for Reid's special feelings toward some commanders. Of the three greatest Ohioans in the war, Sheridan fares especially well; the treatment of Grant is somewhat lackluster, and the author criticizes some of Sherman's actions although he praises his overall conduct. McClellan fares especially poorly, while the author bolsters the evaluations of Rosecrans, Gillmore, McPherson, Garfield, and Mitchel. The material on Ohio regiments is well done, with a roster of officers and their dates of appointment, subsequent commissions, discharges, and deaths. The work also provides a neatly succinct regimental history for Ohio units.

Pennsylvania

941

Bates, Samuel P. **History of Pennsylvania Volunteers, 1861–5, Prepared in Compliance with Acts of the Legislature** (5 vols., 6722 pp., B. Singerly, State Printer, Harrisburg, 1869–1871)

As the most complete and valuable reference on troops from the Keystone State, this work provides a brief sketch of the units from Pennsylvania followed by a roster covering field and staff officers, band, and enlisted men by companies. The data supplied include name, rank, date of muster, term of service, and remarks.

The coverage is as follows: volume 1 (1321 pp.), three-month infantry regiments, 1st–50th regiments, reserve corps units, and miscellaneous infantry; volume 2 (1356 pp.), 51st–84th regiments; volume 3 (1376 pp.), 85th–118th regiments; volume 4 (1305 pp.), 119th–179th regiments; volume 5 (1364

pp.), 180th–215th regiments, miscellaneous cavalry and artillery units, U.S.C.T., officers appointed from Pennsylvania, and independent militia companies.

(Reprinted 1993–1994, with a highly useful index, ed. Janet Hewett, 4 vols., 4279 pp., containing more than 380,000 entries, 14 vols., 11,001 pp., Broadfoot, Wilmington)

942

Gallman, J. Matthew. **Mastering Wartime: A Social History of Philadelphia during the Civil War** (354 pp., Cambridge University Press, New York, 1990)

Gallman offers a detailed view of an important Northern city and its relationship with the war. His study is particularly valuable for two reasons: he has chosen a city of paramount importance for its long-standing character, wealth, and social traditions; and he has analytically approached a wide variety of subjects relating to the city. The result is a systematic attempt at showing how the war changed Philadelphia and its citizens, and the author succeeds admirably. In doing so he discusses Philadelphia's preparation for war, civic celebrations of the war, responses of the citizenry to death of loved ones, order and disorder in the wartime city, the Sanitary Fair of 1864, workers in wartime Philadelphia, the direction of Philadelphia's economy and manufacturing during the war, and the resulting city that emerged and evolved toward the Centennial years.

Although Gallman outlines the tremendous changes thrust on people during the war, he believes that Philadelphia itself was changed little by the experience of war. The change mainly came about in the lives of individual people, not in the life of a great Northern city. He explores recruiting and the draft at length and finds that the war was not a "poor man's fight." Indeed, many lower-class whites purchased substitutes or commutation, as he shows. Gallman accomplishes some of his best writing in detailing how Philadelphians dealt with the deaths of relatives and friends.

943

Sauers, Richard A. **Advance the Colors: Pennsylvania Civil War Battleflags** (2 vols., 608 pp., Capitol Restoration Committee, Harrisburg, 1987–1991)

These volumes are unique among modern works dealing with state participation and will be greatly appreciated by students who know how important Civil War flags were to men facing the enemy. Sauers presents in exhaustive detail the histories of Pennsylvania's Civil War battle flags, those of all 215 regiments. The work is lavishly produced, with color throughout and printed on heavy, glossy paper.

Color photographs present the flags as they appeared at the time of publication, more than a century after being carried home from battle.

The first volume contains a chapter on prewar Pennsylvania battle flags, an introductory discussion of the wartime flags, and a postwar history of the flags and how they were preserved. The final section is composed of a regiment-by-regiment description of the flags and their histories within the war. Appendices include attractive campaign maps and an authoritative analysis of the composition of Pennsylvania regiments. Volume 2 includes a page of corrections to the first volume.

944

Taylor, Frank H. **Philadelphia in the Civil War, 1861–1865** (360 pp., City of Philadelphia, 1913)

As a summary of the city's responses to the war, this narrative provides a useful story of the patriotic fervor that struck Northern urban areas at the outset of the war and the challenge to organize troops and supply the war effort with money and materiel. The book is well endowed with a variety of illustrations, including scenes of camps, arsenals, barracks, hospitals, forts, and veterans organizations. The most valuable aspect of Taylor's study resides in the descriptions of units organized in Philadelphia, with rosters of their officers in many cases. He provides summary regimental histories, location of Philadelphia-related regimental monuments on battlefields, an army necrology of Philadelphians, a discussion of general officers from Philadelphia who fought for the Union, both substantive and brevet, and officers from Philadelphia who earned brevets.

Rhode Island

945

Dyer, Elisha, ed. **Annual Report of the Adjutant General of the State of Rhode Island and Providence Plantations for the Year 1865** (2 vols., 2301 pp., E. L. Freeman and Sons, Printers to the State, Providence, 1893–1895)

Providing a valuable record of the state's units and soldiers who served in them, these volumes contain a regimental history for each unit as well as a roster presenting data on field and staff officers, noncommissioned officers, and a name roster of enlisted men arranged alphabetically. Data include names, companies, residences, dates of enrollment, dates of muster, and remarks. Volume 1 (867 pp.) contains a regimental history and roster of the infantry units, includ-

ing the 1st detached militia, the 2d–4th Infantry, 7th Infantry, 9th–12th Infantry, U.S.V. officers from Rhode Island, naval officers from the state, U.S.C.T., and an appendix presenting extracts from the reports of the state adjutant general. Volume 2 (1434 pp.) contains a similar treatment for cavalry and artillery units and material on officers who received promotions, Medals of Honor, lists of killed and wounded, regular army officers from the state, Rhode Island volunteer officers, U.S.C.T., deaths and burials, and corrections and additions to the first volume.

Tennessee

946

Durham, Walter T. **Reluctant Partners: Nashville and the Union, July 1, 1863 to June 30, 1865** (327 pp., Tennessee Historical Society, Nashville, 1987)

Durham surveys the experience of occupation in wartime Nashville. He makes clear the extraordinary importance of the city as a Federal supply depot during the final two years of war, delivers a crisp summary of events during that period, and examines the personalities involved with the occupation and the campaign that led to it.

The author delivers a sound narration of the transformation of Nashville as a community. The discussions of supply, logistics, hospitals, and dissent are keenly composed. The treatment of Hood's campaign and the battle of Nashville is of course not as detailed as some other accounts, but the context gives it added meaning. Durham uses military grades loosely, calling any general officer "general." The text is well documented, the maps are nicely executed, and the many stories of Nashvillians and local landmarks such as Traveller's Rest add a great deal of enjoyment to the work. Durham's related title, *Nashville the Occupied City: The First Seventeen Months, February 16, 1861 to June 30, 1863* (324 pp., Tennessee Historical Society, Nashville, 1985), is a companion volume focusing on the months preceding the period covered in *Reluctant Partners*.

947

Maslowski, Peter. **Treason Must Be Made Odious: Military Occupation and Wartime Reconstruction in Nashville, Tennessee, 1862–65** (164 pp., KTO Press, Millwood, N.Y., 1978)

The author offers a succinct analysis of the wartime Reconstruction policies that molded Nashville during the final three years of war. Not only does Maslowski propose, as have many others, that Reconstruction began shortly after the firing on Sumter, but he also provides a documented study of the effects of wartime Reconstruction in and around Nashville. He contends that the army accomplished far more than simply fighting battles; it also assumed a role in politics and society that provided protection and even health care for citizens. He compares Andrew Johnson's wartime Reconstruction government with that of the president's postwar policies and notes that Lincoln allowed Johnson to carry out his own agenda that was more in line with the Wade-Davis Bill than Lincoln's Reconstruction agenda as experimentally tested in Louisiana. This work sheds much light on local activities in wartime Tennessee, the wartime policies of Andrew Johnson, and of course the model of Reconstruction as it was carried out in Nashville.

948

[Tennessee Civil War Commission.] **Tennesseans in the Civil War: A Military History of Confederate and Union Units with Available Rosters of Personnel** (2 vols., 1079 pp., Tennessee Civil War Centennial Commission, Nashville, 1964–1965)

This superb work is necessary for any library dealing with Tennessee's Civil War participation. One of the more accurate and accomplished state works, the set provides splendid military histories and rosters for all Tennesseeans in the war in both armies. Volume 1 includes histories for all Tennessee units, Union and Confederate. Each generally consists of a short summary of how and when the unit was raised, the companies, company officers, and a brief survey of service. The accuracy is very high. Volume 2 is an alphabetical roster of all Tennessee soldiers in the war, with highest grade achieved and unit of service, often down to company level. The roster is segregated into Confederate and Union lists.

(Reprinted 1989, 2 vols., 1079 pp., University of Tennessee Press, Knoxville)

Texas

949

Gallaway, B. P., ed. **Texas, the Dark Corner of the Confederacy: Contemporary Accounts of the Lone Star State in the Civil War** (3d ed., 286 pp., University of Nebraska Press, Lincoln, 1994)

From a trove of interesting material, and by piecing together 42 vignettes written by soldiers and civilians between the 1850s and the end of the war, editor Gallaway delivers a cohesive picture of wartime Texas. The work is carefully conceived, tightly edited, and functions beautifully as a sourcebook of Texas Civil War tales. David Carey Nance's boyhood recollections open the volume and recall farm life southwest of Dallas in the early 1850s. Antebellum descriptions of El Paso and San Antonio, coupled with travel narratives of the Texas frontier, demonstrate the hard life in the wilderness that Texans knew before the war. Sections describe the secession of Texas, Twiggs's surrender of San Antonio, and army adventures in a great variety of situations. Among the most pleasing accounts are those that describe riding with Lane's rangers, the battle of Sabine Pass, Texas, railroads during the war, and Northerners' assessments of Texas during the conflict. Useful appendices include a bibliographical essay and a chronology of events.

950

Marten, James. **Texas Divided: Loyalty and Dissent in the Lone Star State, 1865–1874** (246 pp., University Press of Kentucky, Lexington, 1990)

This study seeks to explore the rugged individualism that separated Texas from the other Confederate states. The Lone Star State faced a different set of worries in that it contended with Indian problems, large groups of Mexican Americans, a sprawling western frontier, and isolation from its eastern brethren. Indeed, Richmond seemed incredibly distant to Texans in 1861. According to Marten, these factors plus the usual difficulties contributed to a special brand of dissent in wartime Texas.

The author examines various factions that existed in Texas and their relationships, including Germans (a group divided on the issue of secession), Anglo-Texans (most of whom sided with the Confederacy), and Mexican Americans (many of whom did not care one way or the other). Marten forges a cohesive look at antebellum dissent in Texas, "Confederate Unionists," speculators, bandits, deserters, ethnic Texans, black Texans, and the dissenters during Reconstruction. He covers an immense amount of ground in relatively few pages, and thus sweeping generalizations sometimes color the conclusions he presents. For the most part, however, this insightful study probes an area little discussed before and makes a worthwhile contribution in doing so.

951

Smith, David Paul. **Frontier Defense in the Civil War: Texas' Rangers and Rebels** (237 pp., Texas A&M University Press, College Station, 1992)

This work explores the changing relationships between Indians, the Union, and the Confederacy in the Texas frontier during the war years. After the evacuation of Texas by Federal soldiers, the area fell to the Confederate forces. The threat to civilians by Indians intensified in some areas, particularly by the Kiowas and Comanches. The present work focuses on the Indian frontier, a line stretching from west of San Antonio to Wichita Falls, and the soldiers who defended it. He describes the rangers who kept the order in a rough area: members of local militia, state militia, or Confederate organizations. They patrolled the changing settlements and guarded against the marauding bands of Indians always posing a threat to frontier defense. Smith's analysis does not stretch far enough to tie the significance of these relatively obscure frontier duties to the rest of the Confederacy, but he does supply a detailed look at a small number of men who provided a needed service in a distant part of the Confederacy.

952

Wright, Marcus J. **Texas in the War, 1861–1865** (ed. Harold B. Simpson, 246 pp., Hill Junior College Press, Hillsboro, 1965)

This valuable set of data is taken from Wright's research on the *O.R. (q.v.)*. Most of the work consists of statistical compilations on Texas units and commanders obtained from the War Records Office in the 1880s and 1890s and follows the formulation used for Wright's similar works on Arkansas (*q.v.*) and Tennessee. A biographical mine of Texans appears, as does a compilation of Texas battles and skirmishes and the basic data on Texas forts. Sketchy data for Federal officers in Texas is included. Wright's original information is enhanced by helpful biographical notation, appendices, and a photographic supplement added by the editor.

Utah Territory

953

Long, E. B. **The Saints and the Union: Utah Territory during the Civil War** (310 pp., University of Illinois Press, Urbana, 1981)

This is the first work to analyze the anomalous and peculiarly influential situation in Utah Territory during the war

years. Two central characters rise out of the haze in this story—the Mormon leader Brigham Young and Union Bvt. Maj. Gen. Patrick E. Connor. The focus of the story is really the relationship between the persecuted church that leaned toward supporting the Confederacy and the tenuous Union military rule in this island territory of the West. The author inserts long and sometimes labored quotations throughout much of the text, which detracts from the book's appeal. However, his research is well documented and the story well told. He shows how Connor acted to bring Utah Territory closer to the normal Union sentiment. In the end, one could say that a victory was achieved for both the Saints and the Union.

Vermont

954

Benedict, G. G. **Vermont in the Civil War: A History of the Part Taken by the Vermont Soldiers and Sailors in the War for the Union, 1861–5** (2 vols., 1428 pp., Free Press Association, Burlington, 1886–1888)

Three brief chapters treat Vermont's response to the secession crisis and the organization of state troops. The overwhelming bulk of the work consists of unit histories that provide discussions of raising the regiments, batteries, and battalions and of the officers serving with each unit, as well as a reasonably detailed chronological narrative of the unit's service in the field. The tone is matter-of-fact, strictly military, and fairly well composed in that it sticks to a serious monologue free from embellished side trips. A few poorly done maps accompany each volume, as do engravings of important officers associated with the Vermont regiments, including William F. Smith, William H. T. Brooks, Lewis Addison Grant, George J. Stannard, and William Wells. The coverage is as follows: volume 1 (620 pp., 1886), 1st–6th Infantry and the 1st Vermont Brigade; volume 2 (808 pp., 1888), 7th–17th Infantry, 1st Cavalry, 1st Artillery, 1st and 2d U.S. Sharpshooters, Vermonters in other organizations, and naval officers from Vermont.

955

Coffin, Howard. **Full Duty: Vermonters in the Civil War** (376 pp., Countryman Press, Woodstock, 1993)

Coffin delivers a long chronological essay on Vermont during the Civil War and the participation of its men in major battles. Undocumented and written in workmanlike fashion, this book will not suffice for serious researchers, but it does offer an agreeable glimpse into Vermont's Civil War for casual readers. The early chapters explore the state's reaction to Lincoln's election and call for volunteers, Vermont's history of abolition sentiment, Stephen A. Douglas, and John Brown. The chapters treating the period following the commencement of the war fall into a formula of describing the major battles and using excerpts from prominent Vermont soldiers' diaries, letters, or reminiscences. This approach succeeds in creating an overview of some of the characters involved, a few of the regiments, and some of their deeds. The focus is on major actions, although a number of lesser battles and skirmishes surface on occasion.

956

Peck, Theodore S., ed. **Revised Roster of Vermont Volunteers and Lists of Vermonters Who Served in the Army and Navy of the United States during the War of the Rebellion, 1861–66** (863 pp., Press of the Watchman Publishing Co., Montpelier, 1892)

A good basic list of the state's participants in the war, this roster includes field and staff officers, noncommissioned officers, and enlisted men, and it provides name, residence, date of enlistment, date of muster, and remarks for each man. The coverage spans the 1st–17th Infantry, sharpshooters, light artillery units, heavy artillery, recruits for the 54th Massachusetts Infantry, miscellaneous organizations, naval officers from the state, sailors and marines, Vermonters in other state organizations, and Vermont soldiers' graves in national cemeteries. There is an errata page and an index.

Virginia

957

Thomas, Emory M. **The Confederate State of Richmond: A Biography of the Capital** (227 pp., University of Texas Press, Austin, 1971)

This study outlines Richmond's triple importance to the Confederate cause as political center of the government, a major manufacturing facility crucial to the Confederate war effort, and the psychological focus of hopes for a Confederate life beyond war. The population of Richmond swelled even as military raids and campaigns threatened its safety. Thomas's chronological organization allows readers to see how Richmond grew enormously during the war. He expertly discusses the people and events of wartime Richmond and blends political, military, economic, and social issues with great ease. The work's brevity precludes treating many top-

ics relating to Richmond and the war effort in great depth, but the author has nevertheless skillfully laid down the story of the young Confederacy's capital and its influence on and involvement in military affairs—something that should be done for other cities in both South and North. The author's map of Richmond's wartime features is one of the best created for any such study.

958

[Virginia Regimental Series and Virginia Battles and Leaders Series.] **Virginia Regimental Series** and **Virginia Battles and Leaders Series** (H. E. Howard Inc., Lynchburg, 1982–   )

Students of the war in Virginia must investigate the Virginia Regimental Series, an ambitious, ongoing set of nearly 100 volumes that will include regimental histories of all Virginia units in the war, including artillery, cavalry, and infantry units, each with a roster. The Virginia Battles and Leaders Series is made up of volumes on cities, battles, and personalities. There are several dozen titles in this growing set. The works are generally short and without great detail—many constitute mere sketches of their subjects—and the quality of the material varies considerably, but most of these works offer information not easily found elsewhere. Some of the regimentals have been reprinted and slightly revised. The primary volume of importance from this publisher is Lee A. Wallace Jr.'s *A Guide to Virginia Military Organizations, 1861–1865* (2d ed., 372 pp., 1986), which lists capsule tables of organization for each of Virginia's Confederate units. The first edition (348 pp.) was published by the Virginia Civil War Commission, Richmond, in 1964.

West Virginia

959

Lang, Theodore F. **Loyal West Virginia from 1861 to 1865, with an Introductory Chapter on the Status of Virginia for Thirty Years prior to the War** (382 pp., Deutsch Publishing Co., Baltimore, 1895)

The author, a major in the 6th West Virginia Cavalry, examines all the campaigns in western Virginia as well as major engagements in the Shenandoah Valley, Second Bull Run, and actions associated with the defenses of Washington. He also describes in detail the various political meetings that led to the creation of West Virginia. The text provides lists of company and field officers from West Virginia, with their dates of service.

A brief introduction sets the stage for the differences in

political culture in antebellum Virginia. Lang examines George McClellan's early operations in western Virginia before launching into a lengthy section of personal reminiscence that contains much of value. He surveys the Pierpoint administration and the importance of the Baltimore and Ohio Railroad to the state. The author then shifts focus to offer perhaps his most valuable contribution, a running account of the cavalry, infantry, and artillery units from West Virginia during the war. A lengthy summary presents famous commanders associated with the state, including Benjamin F. Kelley, Robert H. Milroy, William W. Averell, and George Crook. Thirty-two portraits and three maps accompany the text, which lacks an index.

960

Stutler, Boyd B. **West Virginia in the Civil War** (304 pp., Educational Foundation, Charleston, 1963)

This competent study offers 58 stories that chronicle the birth of West Virginia during the first three years of war and its inhabitants' participation within and far away from the new state. Stutler's narrative describes the mountaineers' opposition to secession and their cultural and economic ties to the North, or at least to Pennsylvania and Ohio. Vignettes of the early battles in West Virginia, the emerging roles of Lee and McClellan, and Francis Pierpoint's election as "governor of Virginia" highlight portions of the text. Despite border warfare and divided loyalties in the region, West Virginia supplied 32,000 troops to the war effort, and the author carefully shows how these men fought in a wide range of battles in the eastern and western theaters of war and nobly earned statehood for their home region. See also *A House Divided: A Study of Statehood Politics and the Copperhead Movement in West Virginia,* by Richard O. Curry (203 pp., University of Pittsburgh Press, Pittsburgh, 1964).

Wisconsin

961

Love, William DeLoss. **Wisconsin in the War of the Rebellion: A History of All Regiments and Batteries the State Has Sent to the Field, and Deeds of Her Citizens, Governors and Other Military Officers, and State and National Legislators to Suppress the Rebellion** (1140 pp., Church and Goodman, Chicago, 1866)

This early recounting of the state's participation in the war is marked by strong partisan feeling, but it is valuable as a historical sampling of the times. Love offers material

on the early history of Wisconsin, the rise of antislavery sentiment in the state and the growing significance of clashes over slavery, religion in the state and how it affected the coming war, and a history of the politics of the state before the war and at the time of the secession crisis. More useful are the chapters on the press in Wisconsin and its handling of the emergency and the swell of patriotism in the heat of crisis.

The most valuable parts of this work reside in the capsule regimental histories of Wisconsin units, divided by service in the eastern and western theaters, a narrative of battles and field officers, an honor roll of wounded and dead, descriptions of prisons and hospitals, and a regimental index. Illustrations include crude battlefield maps and engravings of politicians and commanding officers.

962

Quiner, Edwin B. **The Military History of Wisconsin: A Record of the Civil and Military Patriotism of the State in the War for the Union, with a History of the Campaigns in Which Wisconsin Soldiers Have Been Conspicuous, Regimental Histories, Sketches of Distinguished Officers, the Roll of the Illustrious Dead, Movements of the Legislature and State Officers, etc.** (1022 pp., Clarke and Co., Chicago, 1866)

This is a reasonably well done study considering its early date of publication. A state history in the truest sense, it focuses on Wisconsin's activities during the war, examining the records of state officials and what occurred within its borders during the war years. Much attention falls on the governors, the state's adjutant and surgeon generals, and important officers such as Rufus King and Carl Schurz. Writing with patriotic zeal, the author further presents sections on general military operations in the eastern, central, and western divisions and extensive regimental histories with rosters, sketches of service, and discussions of officers. Biographical sketches follow, including material on Charles S. Hamilton, Cadwallader C. Washburn, Lysander Cutler, Frederick Salomon, Halbert E. Paine, Lucius Fairchild, Edward S. Bragg, and John C. Starkweather.

963

[Wisconsin Adjutant General's Office.] **Roster of Wisconsin Volunteers, War of the Rebellion, 1861–1865** (2 vols., 1808 pp., Democrat Printing Co., Madison, 1886)

This list of the Badger State's Civil War soldiers consists of a roster by company of each man, identifying field and staff officers, followed by a record of companies by letter designation for each unit. The data typically include name, residence, date of enlistment, and remarks. Volume 1 covers the 1st–4th Cavalry, 1st–13th Artillery, 1st Heavy Artillery, and 1st–15th Infantry; volume 2 includes the 16th–53d Infantry, Wisconsin citizens commissioned by the president, the Milwaukee Cavalry, sharpshooters, brigade bands, permanent guard, 1st U.S.V.V. engineers, commissioned officers of the U.S.C.T., members of Company F, 29th U.S.C.T., unassigned black troops, members of Hancock's corps, enlistees in the Veteran Reserve Corps, and recruits for the regular army. Another edition may assist research: *Wisconsin Volunteers, War of the Rebellion, 1861–1865, Arranged Alphabetically* (1137 pp., Democrat Printing Co., Madison, 1914).

STRATEGY AND TACTICS

964

Adams, Michael C. C. **Our Masters the Rebels** (256 pp., Harvard University Press, Cambridge, 1978)

Highly original and engagingly written, this work attempts to alter the standard reasoning for early Union military failures—but in the end provides only selective information and a partial explanation. Adams contends that a psychological elevation of the Southern warlike culture existed in the minds of Northerners, that most Yankees believed their Southern brethren—farmer-planter-hunters who were deeply rooted in military and aristocratic tradition—would make natural and fearsome soldiers. Coupled with the Federal rout at First Bull Run, the author believes, this fear developed into an inferiority complex as personified by George McClellan, who was loathe to commit his army into battle against the Virginians he faced.

While elements of this thesis are admittedly true, generalizing an attitude felt by some to a dominating national psychology is ridiculous. The notion that First Bull Run was a "stunning loss" is mostly due to the Federal government's high expectations for easy victory. The slow achievements of Union armies resulted more from the necessary goal of attacking, conquering, and holding vast areas rather than simply defending them. The behavioral patterns of Northern commanders, in and out of the Army of the Potomac, were hardly significantly influenced by McClellan's poor tactics. If anything, McClellan helped future generalship by demonstrating how *not* to manage a campaign. The author's portrait of poor morale and disputes of rank and grade in the Army of the Potomac could certainly be equaled, if not exceeded, by an investigation of the Army of Northern Virginia. Similar infighting existed with its prominent command-

ers, as with Stonewall Jackson versus A. P. Hill and D. H. Hill versus nearly everyone.

(Reprinted 1992, titled *Fighting for Defeat: Union Military Failure in the East, 1861–1865*, 256 pp., University of Nebraska Press, Lincoln)

965

Ballard, Colin R. **The Military Genius of Abraham Lincoln** (246 pp., Oxford University Press, London, 1926)

Before 1926, Abraham Lincoln was generally accorded a poor assessment as a military mind. This changed with the publication of Ballard's work. Appearing the same year as Maurice's *Statesmen and Soldiers of the Civil War* (*q.v.*), the British general's book set the stage for a new evaluation of Lincoln as self-taught military strategist.

A key example of Lincoln's alleged misunderstanding of military capabilities was his outrage and disappointment at Meade's failure to attack Lee following the Gettysburg retreat, when the Army of Northern Virginia faced a Potomac River hindering its escape. Ballard argues that despite the weary and depleted condition of the Army of the Potomac, Lincoln correctly "interfered" with his generals on that and on other occasions. (The term "interfere" is hard to justify, as Lincoln was in fact commander-in-chief of the armies.)

Ballard documents the growth of Lincoln as one who increasingly understood military strategy better than most of his commanders in the field. In fact, Ballard offers a convincing argument that Lincoln himself, unintentionally at first, pioneered what would become the military system of high command. In a simplistic sense, Lincoln's problem was twofold. First, he had to convince most of the commanders that their objective was to destroy the opposing army, not capture "enemy territory." Second, once that appeared to be understood by officers in the field, Lincoln had to prod most of them to implement a coordinated strategy to achieve that goal. In the end, the commanders who instinctively and independently did just those things, principally Grant and Sherman, won the war. Ballard's thesis remains valid and important today.

(Reprinted 1952, with a foreword by Fletcher Pratt, 246 pp., World Publishing Co., Cleveland)

966

Beringer, Richard E., Herman Hattaway, Archer Jones, and William N. Still, Jr. **Why the South Lost the Civil War** (582 pp., University of Georgia Press, Athens, 1986)

In this wonderful companion work to Hattaway and Jones's *How the North Won* (*q.v.*), the authors employ a vast array of references, manuscripts, previous analyses, statistics, and psychology to put forth their long and critical evaluation of the Confederate war effort. The result is a penetrating and insightful work that towers over previous attempts and delivers a clear view of the disaster of the Confederacy.

Beringer and his coauthors offer a multiplicity of reasons for Confederate defeat. The tried and true causes are all here, such as inadequate resources and manpower, poor manufacturing capability, shortages of funds, the loss of the Mississippi River, the blockade, and so on. But they rightfully place other causes front and center such as a destruction of Southern civilian support for the war. The South may have continued on with the struggle past the spring of 1865, the authors suggest, but realized that doing so was hopeless. Slavery could not be continued in any case, and the similarities of the two sections were so strong that maintaining separate nations would be illogical. As Howell Cobb and others alarmingly stated in the war's final weeks, without slavery the Confederacy's central supporters would no longer retain an interest in prosecuting the war.

The authors skillfully describe the Confederate military situation throughout the war and offer fair and sometimes revisionist—but highly substantiated—analyses of general officers such as Pierre G. T. Beauregard, Braxton Bragg, John Bell Hood, Joe Johnston, and Robert E. Lee. Additionally, they examine in critical and marvelous detail the role of psychology and religion in Southerners' minds throughout the changing war. Once it became apparent that God did not ordain a Southern victory, a psychological paralysis took hold and Confederate aims shifted from slavery and victory to state rights and white supremacy. Masterful in its contentions, this work belongs in every collection.

967

Boritt, Gabor S., ed. **Lincoln's Generals** (245 pp., Oxford University Press, New York, 1994)

Five excellent essays explore the relationships between Lincoln and U. S. Grant, William T. Sherman, George B. McClellan, Joseph Hooker, and George Meade, contributed by John Y. Simon, Michael Fellman, Stephen W. Sears, Mark E. Neely, Jr., and Boritt, respectively. The essays offer penetrating insights into the relationships between Lincoln and these commanders and shed new light on some of the key actions involved, even if the insights are sometimes aided significantly by historical hindsight.

Boritt outlines Lincoln's careful relationship with Meade, who was difficult to oversee and remarkably sensitive about a variety of issues. The work on Grant is first-rate, with an examination of the anxieties at work between the two men,

adding a layer beyond the classic well-oiled team one thinks of. Neely's revisionistic look at Chancellorsville faults Lincoln for ordering Hooker to the offensive. Fellman's piece nicely contrasts Lincoln and Sherman, whose conservative traits prevented him from being a full partner in the revolutionary overtones of the war. The McClellan-Lincoln difficulties are well known, but Sears offers a fine, compact summary.

968

Boritt, Gabor S., ed. **Why the Confederacy Lost** (209 pp., Oxford University Press, New York, 1992)

The result of a 1991 symposium of the Gettysburg Civil War Institute, this work offers insightful analysis on Confederate failure and adds much of real value to subjects that have been visited many times before but without such clarity. James M. McPherson outlines the military leadership of Lincoln, Grant, Sherman, Stanton, and Meigs, citing examples of its superiority to that of Davis, Lee, and Johnston. Following a similar theme, Gary W. Gallagher describes the relative accomplishments of Grant, Sherman, and Lee. Archer Jones attacks the complex issues of military versus political strategy, combat versus logistical strategy, and persisting versus raiding offenses. He further describes the concentration of forces in terms of space and time, turning versus frontal attacks, and comparisons of casualties as percentages of effective forces available.

Two specialized essays shed further light on the successful battlefield formulas of the Union military-political machine. Reid Mitchell elegantly describes the perseverance of the Northern soldiers, especially during the second half of the war, compared with the decline in morale of Confederate troops. Such a wide gulf in spirit was a huge factor in the war's ultimate outcome. Joseph T. Glatthaar describes faithfully the contributions and influence of black soldiers in the conflict.

969

Connelly, Thomas Lawrence, and Archer Jones. **The Politics of Command: Factions and Ideas in Confederate Strategy** (235 pp., Louisiana State University Press, Baton Rouge, 1973)

In an important work, Connelly and Jones reflect in a scholarly, thoughtful way on the successes and failures of Confederate strategy. The authors deliver a thorough discourse on the European origins of 19th-century strategic thought, examining the importance of Baron Jomini's influence on West Pointers who ascended to Civil War command, especially Pierre G. T. Beauregard and Henry W.

Halleck. The authors critically expose the differences between Jomini's work, his interpretation of Napoleonic ideas, and the American views of these intertwined branches of thought. They rightly contend that the Jominian influence was not terribly important, as evidenced by the American preoccupation with forts.

Connelly and Jones paint a picture of Confederate grand strategy as localized, evolving toward grand concentration and cooperation (with Chickamauga as a high point), and moving back to local dominance toward the end. They examine the departmental command system emphasized by Jefferson Davis and find it full of defects. Unlike the harshly critical picture of Lee, Davis is portrayed as one who came to see the importance of cooperation and concentration even if he did not always implement it successfully. As with the authors' other works (*q.v.*), the emphasis is squarely on the western campaigns. Their important analysis is not limited to that theater, however, and the book deserves wide reading by all students of Confederate military strategy.

970

Donald, David H., ed. **Why the North Won the Civil War** (128 pp., Louisiana State University Press, Baton Rouge, 1960)

This brief, stimulating work gathers essays by five distinguished Civil War historians who probe the reasons that support the book's title. The editor suggests that the contributions may complement more than contradict each other, but they do no such thing—and it is the conflict between the essays that makes the book a success.

Donald details the North's objectives of preserving the Union and abolishing slavery. He suggests that the Union paid only token support to democracy in time of war and that the South stressed democratic principles and adhered to Constitutional law in preserving state rights, damaging itself in the process. Richard N. Current believes that the old stereotype of greater Northern resources won the war for the Union. Norman Graebner suggests a large component of Northern success was diplomacy, which kept European powers neutral. He contends that the South might have succeeded had it attracted the support of a foreign power. David M. Potter points out that the North had two political parties engaged in compromises while the monolithic system in the South, complicated by the problematic personality and character of Jefferson Davis, led to infighting and dissension that helped to seal the Confederacy's fate. T. Harry Williams may strike closest to the truth with his thesis of an evolving, masterful redefinition of the war by the Federal high command.

971

Freeman, Douglas Southall. **Lee's Lieutenants: A Study in Command** (3 vols., 2395 pp., Charles Scribner's Sons, New York, 1942–1944)

One of the epic works on the Confederate armies, these exhaustively researched and brilliantly written volumes deserve to be read by all Civil War students. Freeman employs an amazing quantity of information, much of it gleaned from Confederate sources in Richmond, and he is an interesting and intelligent writer, offering insights into a multiplicity of actions and personalities. The three hefty volumes cover the period following Sumter to the end of the Peninsular campaign (vol. 1), Second Bull Run to Chancellorsville (vol. 2), and the Gettysburg campaign to war's end (vol. 3). Each contains a section introducing the major characters, including a few photographs, nicely executed maps, and useful appendices covering many subjects.

Freeman acts as an apologist for the Southern defeat, blaming mainly a lack of human and material resources for the collapse of the Confederacy. The exposition is written from the viewpoint of the Virginians, with little reference to the Union, to the western theater, or to the Deep South. As Freeman outlines the major campaigns involving the Army of Northern Virginia, he ascribes a number of secondary causes for Confederate defeat. These include attrition of trained and experienced officers and the inferior nature of political appointees compared with professional militarists. Moreover, the quality of military leadership could not be tested but had to be discovered under battle conditions. Confederates did not stress the importance of instruction in strategy and tactics from the top downward. Junior officers were often left to make their own decisions. Further, training and proper logistics counted for more than patriotism, élan, and individual bravery, and the Confederacy typically lacked the former. Finally, the Confederate tendency to initiate offensive operations such as at Malvern Hill and the final day at Gettysburg cost them a very high number of casualties compared with defensive operations such as at Fredericksburg and Chancellorsville. Freeman also stresses that Lincoln was a far better politician than Davis.

The author's arguments successfully explain many troubles plaguing Lee's army, yet the same problems often marred the Union operations. As explanations, they do not always succeed in excusing the Confederate Army from better performance. At a detail level, the work contains several disturbing errors, as with the botched explanation of the organization of Pickett's Charge wherein the author attributes Scales's position to that of Lane (vol. 3, p. 183). These shortcomings notwithstanding, this is a masterpiece of Confederate history that offers one of the finest insights into Lee's army and its many campaigns.

972

Fuller, John F. C. **Grant and Lee: A Study in Personality and Generalship** (323 pp., Eyre and Spottiswoode, London, 1933)

One of the ablest Civil War monographs by a British officer, this work contains a clear presentation of the primary military campaigns of the war and sketches examining the personalities of Grant and Lee. The author accomplishes much in leveling mythologies that touch both commanders. When Fuller first read the standard biographies of Grant and Lee, he concluded that Lee was one of the world's great generals and that Grant was an inexperienced "butcher." After 50 years of study and reading an additional 250 works on his subjects, says Fuller, his original ideas were completely shattered. In revising his outlook on Grant and Lee, he argues that courage, tenacity, audacity, and leadership are the major elements of great generalship. He thus concludes that Grant was a brilliant general officer and that Lee was "one of the most incapable generals in history."

(Reprinted 1982, 323 pp., Indiana University Press, Bloomington)

973

Glatthaar, Joseph T. **Partners in Command: The Relationships between Leaders in the Civil War** (286 pp., Free Press, New York, 1994)

This is a wonderfully insightful study in contrasts. Glatthaar compares the themes of success and failure in command relationships, analyzing the successful teams of Lee and Jackson, Grant and Sherman, Lincoln and Grant, and Grant, Sherman, and Porter. He also probes the unsuccessful partnerships of Lincoln and McClellan as well as Davis and Joe Johnston. Glatthaar explores the various military campaigns that utilized these teams, what happened, and why they worked or failed. The thinking behind his conclusions is sound, carefully supported by a variety of evidence, and nicely documented.

The author finds the successful teams composed of complementary partnerships. Lee was inspiring, patriarchal, audacious, and intelligent; Jackson was demanding, unpredictable, eccentric, and a superb tactician. Grant and Lincoln complemented each other as the skilled soldier and the savvy politician. The psychology of command worked to thwart goals, too. Davis was opinionated, experienced, and argumentative; Johnston was temperamental, defensive, accomplished in tactics and logistics, and a poor administrator.

Glatthaar shows how through experience gained on the battlefield, Grant and Sherman evolved a strategy to win the war, prepared penetrations to Richmond and Atlanta, and hatched raids through the Shenandoah Valley and Georgia as well as closing Wilmington and Mobile. A few spelling errors were found, as for the names of Simon Cameron, Catharinus P. Buckingham, and David Hunter.

974

Griffith, Paddy. **Battle Tactics of the Civil War** (237 pp., Yale University Press, New Haven, 1989)

Although it proposes an interesting thesis and contains some ideas of real value, this study also exhibits some major flaws. Disputing many other historians, Griffith contends that rifled muskets and artillery provided only a marginal advantage over smoothbore weapons and that armies on both sides performed poorly in a tactical sense because of the defensive-minded education received by most Civil War commanders at West Point. The author further states that battles were typically chaotic struggles in which tactics were generally lost and results were rarely decisive. Had Civil War leaders stuck to the offensive doctrines of Napoleon, such as concentrated artillery barrages, blitz infantry attacks, and large forces of saber-armed cavalry, the war would have ended sooner and more decisively.

The problem with this approach is that it is poorly supported in the present work and vigorously and convincingly shown to be wrong elsewhere. True, at short range smoothbore guns could be effective; but rifled muskets were far more effective, and at longer ranges they were the only effective weapons. To support the idea of frontal attacks seems more than odd, as only rarely and under special circumstances (as with Longstreet at Chickamauga and Thomas at Missionary Ridge) did they work. Normally they failed disastrously, as Lee learned at Gettysburg and Hood learned at Franklin.

Many smaller aspects of the argument also do not pass muster. The characterizations of scores of personalities do not ring true, particularly those of Joe Johnston, Ambrose Burnside, John Bell Hood, and Braxton Bragg. Occasionally, the author draws on unreliable material as casually as that which is certain to be reliable, further weakening his argument. This work contains some interesting passages, but its major theme is just not credible.

975

Hagerman, Edward. **The American Civil War and the Origins of Modern Warfare: Ideas, Organization, and Field Command** (366 pp., Indiana University Press, Bloomington, 1988)

Hagerman explores the complex questions of why the Civil War was fought the way it was and the structural and organizational lessons it left for later military commanders. He finds the contradictory military theory of the war based on both quick offensive Napoleonic tactics and the tactics of careful defense taught at West Point by Dennis Hart Mahan. Further, he finds this contradiction befuddled by a detachment of thought about tactics and careful planning of strategy. The bulk of the work then examines how the armies met three great challenges: supply, communication, and dealing with the rapid and shocking transformation of war caused by the rifled musket.

The origins of modern warfare were present in these three areas during the Civil War. Mule-drawn wagons used in unprecedented numbers supplied the troops well, particularly on the Union side, and Federal quartermasters had soldiers carry a larger amount of supply personally as the war dragged on, to unencumber the supply train problems. The communication problems were dealt with by the invention of signal systems and busy telegraphs, although scouts, couriers, and aides still performed much of the message delivering. Hagerman devotes a great amount of analysis to the effect of rifled muskets, the most significant new weapon used en masse, particularly during the middle and last years of the war. He demonstrates how the armies shifted from the offensive to the defensive to deal with the tremendous casualties inflicted by the rifled weapons.

The author's thesis is not always well supported, and many factual mistakes and spelling errors (with important figures such as William F. Barry, John C. Breckinridge, Albert Sidney Johnston, Albert J. Myer, and Sylvanus Thayer) detract from the text. The author contends that Grant defeated Earl Van Dorn at the battle of Corinth in 1862 and errs when providing a description of the geography of the West, as with the distances between Murfreesboro and Nashville as well as Chattanooga and Atlanta. He refers to the great Confederate Army of the West as the Army of the Tennessee and bungles basic facts relating to the strategic and tactical outcome of Missionary Ridge, Sherman's Meridian Expedition, and Stones River. Such errors—and there are many—mar a work that nonetheless contains a great deal of valuable information on the logistics, supply, communication, and strategy and tactics of the war.

976

Hattaway, Herman, and Archer Jones. **How the North Won: A Military History of the Civil War** (762 pp., University of Illinois Press, Urbana, 1983)

One of the finest works on strategy and tactics of the Civil War literature, superbly written and illustrated by useful, if simple, maps showing important movements, this volume offers a comprehensive survey of Union and Confederate strategy and tactics during the war. Hattaway and Jones explore chronologically the many campaigns and battles throughout the four-year struggle and in doing so demonstrate how the Union had a better political administration and a much better organization within the War Department than did the South.

Aside from providing a wonderful narrative of the war's major events and an examination of their significance, the authors bring to light many topics touched on weakly by others. They outline the contributions of the War Board as a forerunner of modern special staff organization and liaison functions. They show in detail how Grant became an unparalleled tactician, solving many of his own supply problems. They depict Grant's and Sherman's attempts to damage the logistics of the South. The authors skillfully describe the military policy that ultimately brought Union success. To counter the Confederate raids into the North (such as those by Lee, Forrest, Wheeler, and Early), Grant and Sherman devised massive raids of their own and those carried out by A. J. Smith, James H. Wilson, and Philip H. Sheridan. Sherman's raid, the authors argue, transformed into a penetration when it reached Savannah, as did his raid into the Carolinas after meeting Schofield moving inland from Wilmington. Both Grant and Sherman repeated the strategy of exhaustion, the authors show, rather than that of annihilation or stalemate, as had previous Union commanders.

The work contains relatively few errors: some misspelled names, as with Zealous B. Tower; repetition of the fallacy that Lee was offered command of "the Union Army"; and reference to the "Confederate Army of the Mississippi." The authors confuse S. H. M. Byers's "Sherman's March to the Sea" with Henry Clay Work's "Marching through Georgia." They claim that Jefferson Davis was graduated from Transylvania University and that Mobile and Wilmington were the "Confederacy's two final ports." The maps contain some errors, such as the misspelling of Ft. DeRussy. These are generally minor inconveniences, however. *How the North Won* is a winning analysis of the war and particularly of its strategic victors, Grant and Sherman.

977

Jones, Archer. **Civil War Command and Strategy: The Process of Victory and Defeat** (338 pp., Free Press, New York, 1992)

This well-executed, fluently written elementary treatise on organization, command, strategy, and tactics is accomplished without documentation, leaving the author to deal with a complex set of information and conclusions "without a net." Such a task would overawe some historians, but Jones's superb qualifications enable him to complete this popular treatment in very fine style.

Beginning Civil War readers will surely appreciate this volume. The author surveys preparations for war, the balance of power in the war's early days, strategic considerations, the evolution of command structures in both armies, strategic and tactical thought on the battlefield, logistics and supply, and various important campaigns. He uses First Bull Run, Chickamauga, and Chattanooga to supply case studies of the points he makes, and these military summations work effectively. The work can thus be recommended highly as an overview of the complexities of the Union and Confederate operations in the field.

978

Jones, Archer. **Confederate Strategy from Shiloh to Vicksburg** (259 pp., Louisiana State University Press, Baton Rouge, 1961)

In his thought-provoking and admirably executed specialized study, Jones begins by recounting the Confederate high command's chief strategic principle, that of defending its territory. He shows that Confederates believed secession was a Constitutional right, and given that it was already accomplished, they considered the Union forces aggressors. Confederate commanders rarely strayed from this simple rule; not only did they believe it reflected Southern honor, but they were mostly incapable of doing anything else. Jones believes that George Wythe Randolph far exceeded the importance of the other war secretaries in formulating strategy and argues that it was a terrible moment when Randolph resigned in protest against Davis's refusal to consolidate the western departments to oppose Grant and Buell.

Jones presents elaborate and forceful evidence to proclaim, as many other historians have, that the western theater was the decisive area of battle. He vigorously attacks the Confederate high command and its armies in Virginia for inadequately participating in the western battles while increasing their eastern armies and supplies as much as possible. He also rightly contends that Jefferson Davis and his generals should have given far more support to the operations in Tennessee and Mississippi, "where the war was being lost."

The analysis of the shortcomings of organization and unbalanced emphasis in Richmond is fair and defensible. After establishing these facts, however, Jones contends that Davis and other members of the high command "bear scrutiny well." He further suggests that the Confederate system of decentralized authority worked effectively. These last conclusions seem to be at least partly contradicted by the evidence appearing earlier in the book and certainly in numerous places elsewhere. The war in the western theater, particularly the Vicksburg campaign, documents the *ineffective* use of Confederate strategy and should fairly condemn Davis and his advisors for mishandling the situation.

(Reprinted 1991, 259 pp., Louisiana State University Press, Baton Rouge)

979

Luvaas, Jay. **The Military Legacy of the Civil War: The European Inheritance** (253 pp., University of Chicago Press, Chicago, 1959)

This work explores the significance of the Civil War in America from the viewpoint of foreign military observers. Of great interest to Europeans during that time and since, the Civil War saw large armies composed of men from the same nation who spoke the same language, worshiped the same God, and indeed often trained in the same institutions. Thus, the war offers a splendid study ground for tactics and strategy, and Luvaas demonstrates the importance of this and the recognition of it even during the war's first months. Leadership was scarce during the war and reliance on volunteers and amateur-level militia was great, with ineffective staff work at practically every level of command.

Prussian, British, and French observers—some of whom became participants—made the most of analyzing the American war. The views of Charles C. Chesney, Francois DeChenal, Henry C. Fletcher, FitzGerald Ross, and Justis Scheibert are included, and Luvaas also describes the later writings of John F. C. Fuller, George F. R. Henderson, and Frederick Maurice. Although the Europeans studied the war in meticulous detail, he argues that few learned its tactical and strategic lessons until a revival of interest following World War I.

As the first large-scale war following the industrial revolution, the Civil War brought many innovations. The author shows that rifled muskets, railroads, armored steamships, and the telegraph, among other developments, laid the groundwork for the European wars to come. Massed infantry assaults and shock cavalry charges gave way to entrenched infantry and artillery barrages. Cavalry degraded into mounted, mobile infantry, and heavily wooded areas limited rifled artillery and maneuvers.

(Reprinted 1988, University Press of Kansas, Lawrence)

980

Maurice, Frederick. **Statesmen and Soldiers of the Civil War: A Study of the Conduct of the War** (173 pp., Little, Brown and Co., Boston, 1926)

This study, which originated as a lecture series at Trinity College and first appeared in print in the *Atlantic Monthly* and the *Forum*, retains its value. An eminent British military authority, Maurice undertook an examination of how Jefferson Davis and Abraham Lincoln evolved a policy of marshaling their armies during the war and how these policies translated into successful and unsuccessful strategies and tactics on the battlefield. He explores the different approaches the two leaders took, probing into the conditions they had to live with, at least during the earliest months of the conflict.

The author finds that at the outbreak of hostilities Lincoln "had little administrative and less military experience [and] was far from being master in his own house." But Lincoln devised his own system of analysis so that he could accomplish "that which might have baffled the skill of a very practiced statesman." His policy of exerting the maximum military pressure on the South never wavered, but he lacked the field commanders who could coordinate such a large group of armies into a unified, coordinated movement. Over time Lincoln developed a system to find his men and translate his strategy onto the battlefield, an achievement that President Davis never clearly matched.

981

McWhiney, Grady, and Perry D. Jamieson. **Attack and Die: Civil War Military Tactics and the Southern Heritage** (209 pp., University of Alabama Press, University, 1982)

In this novel interpretation of Confederate defeat, McWhiney and Jamieson suggest that Confederate losses were unusually high because of the Confederates' predilection to attack. The authors ascribe this to the Southerners' Celtic heritage. They also suggest that the Confederacy undid itself because of the appallingly high casualties it sustained by sheer force of attack—only at Fredericksburg did the Confederacy lose a lower percentage of men than the Union. The authors contend that Confederate generals relied too heavily on Mexican War tactics and underestimated the improvements in rifled muskets and artillery weap-

ons, only slowly realizing that cavalry charges were outmoded, as were sword and bayonet actions.

Despite the labored thesis that Confederates predominantly attacked, which downplays or even ignores numerous examples of Union offensive operations, McWhiney and Jamieson show that by 1864 the Confederacy was less likely to take the offensive due to an increasing shortage of manpower. Support for their arguments comes in the form of statistical tables, which are necessarily sketchy and perhaps open to overinterpretation. Placing the South's military performance into the ancient Celtic tradition is certainly peculiar if not illogical. They also err by suggesting that Winfield Scott may have functioned as a spiritual source of attack mongering. These shortcomings aside, the book does successfully shed light on the casualty rates and strategies of several Confederate campaigns.

982

Reed, Rowena. **Combined Operations in the Civil War** (468 pp., Naval Institute Press, Annapolis, 1978)

This work examines the cooperative role of army-navy ventures during the war. Reed demonstrates how Scott's Anaconda Plan recognized the importance of combined operations in blockading the East Coast, launching amphibious assaults on selected coastal areas, and surging ahead with a Mississippi River campaign against Columbus, New Madrid, Island No. 10, Memphis, Vicksburg, Port Hudson, Baton Rouge, and New Orleans. She examines how combined operations unfolded throughout the war and contends that such strategy, particularly offensive operations employing both the army and navy, were not understood or appreciated at the time. One could cite examples beyond the second assault on Fort Fisher that might argue against such a conclusion, however.

The author displays a remarkable inclination toward George McClellan and defensively asserts that his problems in cooperating with the Lincoln administration pale in comparison to Washington's (and the navy's) lack of support for him. She contends that the failure of the Peninsular campaign rests more with Wool, McDowell, and Franklin than McClellan, a difficult argument to support in detail. She further states that McClellan's ideas on combined operations greatly influenced the navy and the administration, although she does not support this claim. Her portrayal of Grant as one who came to the same conclusions regarding strategy and tactics as McClellan had two years earlier is ridiculous.

Errors of fact occasionally mar the text. Reed erroneously believes that David Hunter ranked Henry W. Halleck and confusingly asserts that McClellan continued to "wear the three stars of his command." Still, she contributes much of value on a neglected aspect of the war despite the fact that her thesis is weakly supported and she shows peculiar biases toward or against some of her subjects.

(Reprinted 1993, with an introduction by John D. Milligan, 504 pp., University of Nebraska Press, Lincoln)

983

Royster, Charles. **The Destructive War: William Tecumseh Sherman, Stonewall Jackson, and the Americans** (523 pp., Alfred A. Knopf, New York, 1991)

This revisionist work offers intriguing reading even if one fails to agree with its conclusions or detects an occasional exaggeration for the sake of the story. Promotional copy for the book suggests an astonishing treatment: "zealots in both camps, patriots all, driven by their need for a national identity, set out to validate their own regional definition of America by destroying those who had a differing vision." Well, in most wars the opposing forces set out to destroy each other, and in that respect the Civil War was hardly unique.

Royster does explore some penetrating themes by analyzing Jackson and Sherman's use of aggression in a modern-war sort of way. He offers generally balanced analysis of specific actions in battles, though a general Southern bias runs through the text, perhaps because most battles were fought on Southern soil, with the considerable destruction brought on by any warfare. The author's treatment of the Grand Review in Washington is particularly thorough, and his chapter on the war as viewed by nonparticipants and postwar authors is refreshing. However, the strain of molding a thesis compelling enough for hot press releases stretches the interpretation of some material in this work. The treatment of the burning of Columbia fails to point out that most of the destruction was accidental, courtesy of stores of liquor and cotton left behind by Confederate quartermasters.

Dispassionate balance is required in such cases to appreciate the historical truth. In Sherman's own words, the destruction accomplished by his army and by other Federal armies had one purpose: to deprive the Confederates of useful supplies. (Witness the famous photograph of a burned-out Atlanta bank next door to an intact billiard hall.) Terrorism had a beneficial side effect in that it worsened an already crippled Southern home-front morale. But the extent of the premeditation of wholesale destruction offered by this book belies a thorough understanding of the Civil War in its own time—a critical error in a book containing many enlightening passages.

984

Tilley, John Shipley. **Lincoln Takes Command** (334 pp., University of North Carolina Press, Chapel Hill, 1941)

This influential but flawed work on the war's genesis, composed by a lawyer who carefully reviewed the evidence of the war of words before Sumter, attempts to show that Lincoln and other Northern politicians deceived their Southern brethren and maneuvered them into firing the first shot in Charleston Harbor. Tilley claims that "these many years the South has stood before the bar under indictment for recklessly firing on the flag" but that "a mass of evidence seems to point in a different direction." He then proceeds to construct an argument to justify trickery on the part of Lincoln and friends in the communications relating to Forts Pickens, Moultrie, and Sumter. In the final third of the work he examines closely Lincoln's role in assessing the slowly changing focus of a "hot spot" where a war might begin.

Writing in the fashion of a legal brief, Tilley emphasizes the promises made by Buchanan's administration not to resupply Pickens and Sumter if the South would not attack them. Statements and actions by Ward Lamon and William Henry Seward suggest that some Southerners believed the Lincoln administration would carry out the same "policy," perhaps evacuating Sumter altogether. The betrayal then came, according to Tilley, when Lincoln ordered the Sumter resupply mission—that act pushed the would-be Confederates into the single option of firing on the fort.

Unfortunately, Tilley's thesis is selectively illogical. Suppositions made by citizens about what a leader may or may not do based on anecdotal evidence of an administration's subordinates are hardly legally binding. Lincoln could scarcely be expected to honor a pledge of Buchanan's or to carry on an unofficial "policy" toward a touchy area, particularly when that area is an armed rebellion against the government. Should the commander-in-chief of the U.S. Army give away Federal installations based on the unhappiness of local constituents? Such a response as pulling Anderson's men out of the fort would surely concede the issue at hand.

Moreover, the author is guilty of an error common with amateur historians: viewing events in an oversimplified manner that does not take into account the nature of the times in which those events occurred. This volume has influenced the thinking of many since its publication, chiefly those who wanted to have their thinking influenced in just such a way. But the distinguished historian James G. Randall's wisdom most succinctly answers Tilley: "To say that Lincoln meant that the first shot would be fired by the other side *if a first shot was fired* is by no means the equivalent of saying that he deliberately maneuvered to have the shot fired."

985

Vandiver, Frank E. **Rebel Brass: The Confederate Command System** (143 pp., Louisiana State University Press, Baton Rouge, 1956)

In outlining the many problems that constrained the South's system of high command, the author does not provide a thorough analysis of the Confederacy's high command. He does, however, sketch the modern aspect of the war and the outmoded ways of thinking that the South's politicians and generals often applied to it. Vandiver briefly investigates the relationship between civilian and military leaders and the logistical problems that plagued the Confederacy throughout the war. He shows how the principle of state rights dictated against a centralized and efficient Confederate command system, which covered a large area, employed large armies, and required a comprehensive and co-operative logistics program.

In exploring political considerations, Vandiver finds that Jefferson Davis relied heavily on his friendships for advice and service, a propensity that often led to trouble. He also analyzes the various war secretaries and shows that Randolph and Seddon contributed significantly. The author argues that the crucial system of logistics for production, distribution, and vitalization broke down early on because of a lack of overall planning and management. He touches on some Confederate successes, as with Josiah Gorgas's direction of ordnance activities and the blockade-running effort of the early and middle years. However, the successes were few and far between and could not have materially resulted in overall success.

(Reprinted 1993, 143 pp., Louisiana State University Press, Baton Rouge)

986

Williams, Kenneth P. **Lincoln Finds a General: A Military Study of the Civil War** (5 vols., 2498 pp., Macmillan Co., New York, 1949–1959)

This is a masterful review of the Union search for a successful grand strategy and the commander who could implement it. Intended to be a 6- or 7-volume set running the course of the entire war, Williams's lengthy work describes the painful, early days of the war through to the discovery of Ulysses Grant as the general who would prosecute the war successfully. Because of the author's untimely death, the final volume ends before the battles of Chattanooga and Grant's promotion to lieutenant general. Despite this, the massive narrative functions well as a treatise that demonstrates the many difficulties besetting the Union armies up to nearly the end of 1863.

Based largely on the *O.R.* (*q.v.*) but also on an array of other contemporary sources, the work far more cleverly assesses the hows and whys of much of the Union trouble than most works treating strategy and tactics. Much of the early narrative centers on attacking George McClellan, frequently with a solid base of logic but occasionally too harshly criticizing the great organizer of the Army of the Potomac. Such is also the case with the negative evaluation of Antietam, which in terms of grand strategy did wonders for the Union cause. Strikingly, while Williams spares no ammunition on McClellan, he gingerly appraises other poor commanders, including John Pope.

The middle volumes of the set lose some credibility owing to a pronounced bias toward Grant. This is somewhat understandable in such a work and certainly mirrors the complementary bias of Douglas Southall Freeman in his monumental biography of R. E. Lee (*q.v.*). Still, it is disturbing to see an author shielding Grant in places from the historical record in order to see him come out heroically in the end. The handling of Belmont, for example, suggests such insight into Grant's decision making that it must have been clear he was the Union's greatest general officer before the first year of the war expired.

Errors occur in the text, as when the author incorrectly uses the famous letter of Abraham Lincoln to Joseph Hooker, placing the latter in command of the Army of the Potomac. The discussion of Ethan Allen Hitchcock's role in Stanton's War Department is clouded and leads to ambiguous inferences. The narrative states that James Shields "almost" challenged Lincoln to a duel. Occasional sloppiness surfaces, as with Adjutant General "Alonzo Thomas," the "Confederate ship *Merrimac*," the assertion that George Cadwalader commanded "Pennsylvania volunteers," and the statement that the "Confederacy had a number of four-star generals." In speaking of Joe Johnston at First Bull Run, the author bungles his understanding of Confederate grades by claiming that Johnston's "four stars exceeded Beauregard's one." He mistakenly claims that McClellan entered service as a major general of volunteers and that Joe Johnston outranked Robert E. Lee.

The final two volumes show far more care with scholarship and with the interpretation of facts and actions. The handling of Iuka, Corinth, and Perryville, Stones River, Vicksburg, various minor actions in Louisiana and Mississippi, and Chickamauga, is top-notch and a welcome piece of analysis on the western campaigns. Lengthy appendices throughout the volumes analyze various special areas of study. Not only does the handling of Grant crystallize into a more mature portrait in these volumes, but the author's discussion of Henry Halleck is also among the best (and most forgiving!) treatments in print. In the end, despite some early carping and unevenness in his portrayals, Williams succeeds nicely in showing how and why Lincoln found his general.

987

Williams, T. Harry. **Lincoln and His Generals** (370 pp., Alfred A. Knopf, New York, 1952)

Williams clearly and coherently examines the complex relationships between the Federal leader and his many field commanders. He begins with an introductory chapter exploring the "pattern" of command and proceeds to examine the record of Federal generalship in chronological fashion, all the while exploring Lincoln's own evolving role. The work solidifies as Lincoln builds a command team led by Grant, who was a superb strategist in agreement with Lincoln's ideals. Both Lincoln and Grant learned by experience how to select increasingly competent subordinates and staffs.

The author demonstrates that, although Lincoln had no military education and little military and administrative experience prior to the war, he showed an astonishing grasp of strategy and tactics. Lincoln's early ideas of directly invading the seceded states and directly attacking the Southern armies as the military objectives were ultimately borne out. The author documents Lincoln's early mistakes and his reliance on political expediency in early appointments but shows that this record improved with time. The Confederate command system worked quite differently, Williams contends. Although Jefferson Davis had considerable experience in the military and with governmental administration, he ultimately was a mediocre strategist and tactician. Often hesitant in delegating authority, Davis was prone to micromanage military problems, often leading to poor results.

988

Woodworth, Steven E. **Jefferson Davis and His Generals: The Failure of Confederate Command in the West** (380 pp., University Press of Kansas, Lawrence, 1990)

The author convincingly argues that the relationship between the Confederate president and his western commanders contributed significantly to the South's downfall. He chronologically traces the western war with a keen eye on Davis and the various commanders who fell in and out of favor, ranging from the early battles in Kentucky, the loss of Albert Sidney Johnston, Bragg's Kentucky campaign, the difficult winter of 1862–1863, the bungled Vicksburg campaign, the devastating losses of Tennessee and northern Georgia, and the final destruction of the Army of Tennes-

see. Marked by thoughtful research and careful writing, this volume makes important and clear pronouncements about the strengths and shortcomings of the president and his field commanders while maintaining an enviable balance in tone. Although it may occasionally lean too heavily on secondary sources, it is necessary reading for those interested in the western theater.

Woodworth's conclusion places Davis well above average when one considers the mighty task at hand and the strategic significance of the western theater. The author prefers to blame a series of commanders for the various setbacks, from the obvious slings at John Hood, Leonidas Polk, Gideon Pillow, and John B. Floyd to more carefully evaluated flaws that surface in the performances of Braxton Bragg and Joe Johnston. The latter comes under considerable attack for his lack of offensive plans and for difficulty in sharing the plans he did formulate with superiors, including Davis. Woodworth assigns much of the blame to Polk for losing Perryville, by virtue of that general's failure to carry out his orders. Harsh judgment also arrives at the doorstep of Edmund Kirby Smith.

UNION STUDIES

989

Belz, Herman. **Reconstructing the Union: Theory and Policy during the Civil War** (336 pp., Cornell University Press, Ithaca, 1969)

The early seeds of Reconstruction that began during the war years themselves, in addition to the well-accepted notion that Reconstruction began the day after Sumter and evolved throughout the war, receive a thorough survey in this highly original work. Even as Belz analyzes with a sharp eye the political fallout of various acts during the war, he shows that the army was the only body capable of enforcing the reconstruction of the nation. After the military victory of the North, the author shows, Reconstruction developed with the goal of equality in all aspects and for all peoples, not just freedmen.

The bulk of the work consists of a penetrating discussion of wartime policies and the evolution of constitutional and moral opportunities for normalizing the chaos of war. Belz shows how attempts at policy change developed from the Crittenden Resolution to emancipation. He compares Lincoln's 1863 proclamation on pardons and restoration to Congress's 1864 Wade-Davis bill, finding the documents remarkably similar. He also skillfully demonstrates how the Union philosophy and its attendant rights for the emancipated became the dominating and necessary theme for those who wished to end the war. After Appomattox, the end was a forgone conclusion, and only Lincoln's assassination helped to unravel its lofty execution.

990

Catton, Bruce. **This Hallowed Ground: The Story of the Union Side of the Civil War** (437 pp., Doubleday and Co., Garden City, N.Y., 1956)

This is perhaps the best known attempt at an accessible military history of the Union. Certainly many students of the Civil War first experienced the story of the Northern war effort in these pages.

Catton begins in 1856 by listening in on Charles Sumner and his colleagues on the floor of the U.S. Senate. This approach—introducing beginning readers to the coming struggle and the kaleidoscope of events before Sumter—is both helpful and dizzying in its rapid and superficial nature, yet by the time the war erupts the reader basically comprehends the issues at hand. In Catton's story the Northern impetus for waging war is based on the idealistic destruction of slavery; other significant issues, such as economics and politics, receive short shrift.

Once up to speed, Catton's narrative focuses primarily on military matters and generally delivers a balanced and perceptive view. Covering so much ground, however, severely limits the author's ability to describe the complexities of various characters and situations that would make them truly meaningful. For all the brilliance of Catton's literary style, readers may often find themselves feeling empty in pursuit of substantial meaning behind the story. The maps are wholly inadequate, consisting of ultrasimplified topography annotated by "blitzkrieg" arrows that can only hint at a meaning in the broadest sense.

991

Current, Richard Nelson. **Lincoln's Loyalists: Union Soldiers from the Confederacy** (253 pp., Northeastern University Press, Boston, 1992)

In an expert examination of a hitherto sketchily documented area, Current discusses those persons living in the Confederacy who did not support The Cause, had little stake in slavery, and even fought for the Union. They were concentrated in western Virginia, eastern Tennessee, and in the mountains of North Carolina, Alabama, and Georgia. He shows that Southerners disloyal to the Confederacy played a more significant role than they have previously been credited for. Rather than passively sitting out the war, isolated by geography, these pro-Union Southerners actively supported the Union war effort.

The work documents how every Southern state but South Carolina provided white soldiers for the Union Army before the signing at Appomattox. Thousands of Southern men went North and enlisted in Federal regiments, providing more than 100,000 Union soldiers from the Southern states. Current clearly details the story of these soldiers and describes the terrible price they paid if caught by Confederate authorities. Tragedies such as the Fort Pillow massacre and the execution of members of the 2d North Carolina (U.S.A.) on charges of desertion bring to light the brutality of the Confederate response to disloyal persons from the Confederate States.

992

Fite, Emerson David. **Social and Industrial Conditions in the North during the Civil War** (318 pp., Macmillan and Co., New York, 1910)

This standard background volume on the Northern war effort remains a useful summary of an important area neglected by modern works. It surveys the classic areas defining the growth of the Northern industrial revolution expanded by the war effort, including agriculture, mining, lumbering, transportation, manufacturing, labor, public improvements, education, luxuries, and charity—in short, nearly all commercial aspects of life in the North during the war. The study is grounded in scholarly research in the early sources it employs, and the author's conclusions are sound and well supported.

Fite shows that large Northern grain crops contributed to stemming Britain's potential support of the Confederacy, how various arms contracts altered the course of the war, how vigorous work on the home front contributed substantially to Northern victory, and who made fortunes from the war. Although stylistically dated, the book deserves careful reading.

(Reprinted 1968, 318 pp., Frederick Ungar, New York; reprinted 1983, 318 pp., AMS Press, New York)

993

Frederickson, George M. **The Inner Civil War: Northern Intellectuals and the Crisis of the Union** (277 pp., University of Illinois Press, Urbana, 1965)

Frederickson explores the emotions of war as experienced by two distinct groups of Yankees, conservatives and reformers. The unusual aspects of this study make it appealing and revealing in certain ways. The author analyzes the thought processes of two groups that still exist, those who believed the nation is controlled by a dominant, tightly knit group of authoritarians and those who felt the war offered the opportunity to transform the nation into a utopian future society. Examples of the former class include Henry Bellows, Horace Bushnell, and Francis Parkman; examples of the latter include Ralph Waldo Emerson, William Lloyd Garrison, and Walt Whitman.

The author neatly shows how the war disappointed at least the extremists of both groups—it changed too much for the conservatives and too little for the reformers. The abolitionists were disheartened because slavery was eradicated, not by the spirit of the masses, but by the iron hand of the government. Frederickson oversteps his bounds by asserting that the war "turned the genuine radicalism of the prewar period into an obvious anachronism." He unfairly assesses the changing role of James Russell Lowell's views on the war and misspeaks of many abolitionists by claiming they "abandoned" their roles as reformers once the Emancipation Proclamation was issued. The author also errs when he says the war thwarted "the drive for 'humanitarian democracy.'" Much useful analysis does appear in this volume, however, and the misestimation of the reformers' wartime and postwar roles should not mar this otherwise excellent work.

(Reprinted 1993, with a new preface, 277 pp., University of Illinois Press, Urbana)

994

Geary, James W. **We Need Men: The Union Draft in the Civil War** (264 pp., Northern Illinois University Press, DeKalb, 1991)

Geary offers the best comprehensive treatment of the Federal draft and its significance to the war effort. The text is well written and delivers a large amount of material in a relatively brief synthesis, in addition to making a relatively unengaging subject quite interesting.

An introductory chapter describes the volunteer system. Sections that follow investigate the bounty system, the Militia Act, the 1862 draft, the Enrollment Act of the 37th Congress, the Federal Conscription Act, the mid-war experience of conscripts, quotas, and credits, and commutation and class discrimination. The author also provides a summary on alienation and the draft. Volunteerism continued unabated throughout the war, and the draft itself raised relatively few troops (about 1 percent of the total), so a question arises over its significance. The author contends that it held great symbolic significance in shifting power to the Federal government. Moreover, he argues convincingly that the mech-

anisms in place were fairer than those used in the 20th century and created an army more representative of the U.S. population than more recent conflicts have seen.

995

Harwell, Richard B., ed. **The Union Reader** (362 pp., Longmans, Green and Co., New York, 1958)

A companion to Harwell's earlier book on the Confederacy (*q.v.*), this volume presents a miscellany of material that introduces the general reader to the Union side of the war. Chronologically arranged, the excerpts cover a wide range of aspects relating to the Union war effort, from the firing on Sumter to raising the flag over Sumter at war's end. Altogether, 40 documents illustrate battles and campaigns, the lives of common soldiers, the medical service, and naval actions.

Among the work's highlights are battle accounts and orders relating to Port Royal, New Orleans, Fredericksburg, Chancellorsville, Gettysburg, Vicksburg, Chattanooga, and Winchester. The author has included much of interest relating to the western as well as the eastern theater, as evidenced by the 2d Colorado Infantry's story of bushwhackers in Kansas. We also see glimpses of scarce works, such as Louisa May Alcott's *Hospital Sketches*, and well-known ones, such as Lincoln's Gettysburg Address and Second Inaugural Address. In addition, the author has included song lyrics, where appropriate, for such tunes as George F. Root's "Grafted into the Army" and George Henry Boker's "Tardy George." A highlight of the book is Q.M. Gen. Montgomery C. Meig's report to Stanton on the battle of Chattanooga. Meigs witnessed the climactic and unexpected assault on Missionary Ridge from Grant's command post on Orchard Knob, and the account is one of the finest from a Union high commander.

996

Hess, Earl J. **Liberty, Virtue, and Progress: Northerners and Their War for the Union** (154 pp., New York University Press, New York, 1988)

Hess attempts a synthesis of how a broad cross section of Union citizens and soldiers felt about the war. His thesis, which emerges from an extensive sampling of the writings of his many subjects, proclaims that these works were not simply rhetorical disguises. Instead, they show a common ideology of self-government, democracy, and individualism, and those qualities represented the core issues over which Yankees were fighting the war.

The sampling of writings extends from common soldiers to general officers to civilians on the home front to progressive thinkers. Some of the more powerful passages come from such writers as George Templeton Strong and Ralph Waldo Emerson. These two intellectuals certainly pondered the mighty philosophical issues at stake as the battles raged. Whether or not the majority of common soldiers did is somewhat open to question. Still, this work gathers a large amount of interesting and useful material and presents it in a coherent and suggestive way.

997

Lonn, Ella. **Foreigners in the Union Army and Navy** (725 pp., Louisiana State University Press, Baton Rouge, 1951)

Following the formula in her earlier study *Foreigners in the Confederacy* (q.v.), Lonn analyzes the composition and contributions of foreign-born soldiers and officers in the Union cause. Unlike its Confederate counterpart, this study limits itself to the military without examining the effects of foreign-born civilians. The focus here is squarely on the army; a brief chapter treats the naval forces and does not go into nearly as much interpretive detail as does the analysis of foreigners in the Union Army.

The narrative describes the many Union units composed largely or wholly of foreigners and also follows the careers of many important commanders born outside the United States. The author suggests that slightly more than 500,000 foreigners served for the Union and that the most significant groups were Germans and Irishmen. Many of the important officers who acted as topographers, engineers, surgeons, and field commanders underwent a process of Americanization during the conflict, building a strong bond with their adopted country. The survey is engagingly written, well supported, and makes a fine contribution to the literature.

(Reprinted 1979, 725 pp., Greenwood Press, New York)

998

Mitchell, Reid. **The Vacant Chair: The Northern Soldier Leaves Home** (201 pp., Oxford University Press, New York, 1993)

This study attempts an analysis of why and how Northern soldiers fought, based on the psychology and social backgrounds they knew at home. The author liberally draws on memoirs, letters, and diaries, allowing the participants to speak for themselves with clarity and force. Mitchell has woven these pieces into a readable narrative that offers intelligent reflections on the motives of Yankee soldiers and how they differed materially from their brethren in the Southern armies.

Women exerted a great influence on the attitudes of Union soldiers, the author shows. He writes that Union soldiers despised Confederate ladies and that in a peculiar sense Federal soldiers saw their wartime activities as family extensions in a way that Southerners did not. The argument may seem tenuous in places, but it is certainly thought provoking. The supporting material in this work fills out a very enjoyable volume.

999

Murdock, Eugene C. **One Million Men: The Civil War Draft in the North** (366 pp., State Historical Society of Wisconsin, Madison, 1971)

Murdock examines the political and military logistics of the Conscription Act, describing the reasons for the act, the military situation in 1863 that created it, and the many administrative duties and personnel involved in implementing the draft. Employing a careful writing style and a thorough understanding of the unpopularity of conscription, the author surveys the many related aspects of substitution, bounty jumpers, resistance to the draft, bounty brokers, and commutation. In doing so, he creates a vivid picture of the nonuniform way in which conscription touched people's lives, including the meeting of local quotas, get-rich-quick schemes initiated by brokers, the various checkered (and sometimes successful) careers of jumpers, and the significance of purchasing a substitute. He shows that, despite these quirks and the riots of July 1863, the draft succeeded overwhelmingly in furnishing a vastly enlarged army for the Union.

The book's occasional repetition and somewhat shallow investigation of the Lincoln administration, Congress, and the Provost Marshal General's Bureau and their roles in conscription are relatively minor criticisms. Overall this work is successful and important.

1000

Paludan, Philip Shaw. **"A People's Contest": The Union and Civil War, 1861–1865** (486 pp., Harper and Row, New York, 1988)

Paludan describes the war as Northerners lived it. With a high degree of professionalism and a beguiling style of writing, he masterfully chronicles the various ways in which the war transformed the Northern people. The book is divided into three large sections—"Learning War," "Making War," and "Finding War's Meanings"—in which the author investigates a long list of social and political subjects while providing a chronological history of the war, principally from the Northern point of view. The impressive array of subjects covered in some detail includes making and distributing weapons, the early political aspects of the Union, congressional actions, agriculture, industry, emancipation, religion, and the development of modern war by Grant and Sherman.

The author contends that the Northern war effort resulted from a large and powerful society built of communities whose watchwords included "law" and "order." Thus they prosecuted the war to keep America morally in the right and to continue the growth of the republic on the road to its destiny. The North's politics of war enforce this thesis, as Paludan describes how the South's "breaking of the law" could not be allowed to stand without a struggle. The military aspects are treated lightly; logistics and the psychology of war, by contrast, receive a fairly detailed analysis, as do the North's two principal officers, Grant and Sherman. The author's great skill in providing a sweeping and correct overview of the North's reaction to the sectional crisis is evidenced in the many tales of individuals that illustrate points in the text. Nowhere does the human element of the war, its glory and terrible suffering, get lost in these pages.

1001

Smith, George Winston, and Charles Judah, eds. **Life in the North during the Civil War: A Source History** (397 pp., University of New Mexico Press, Albuquerque, 1966)

This illustrated collection of contemporary source materials provides a useful compilation of materials relating to the Union war effort. The work consists of speeches, letters, essays, sermons, newspaper accounts, and diary entries arranged by topics into a survey of Northern attitudes toward various facets of the war. The editors have added linking paragraphs that set these documents into a meaningful order and provide sufficient background information for most users. But the bulk of the material consists of the original documents themselves, illuminating many areas of the war.

The parts played by a number of politicians, soldiers, slaves, businessmen, clergy, farmers, and economists are explored. The authors survey the Northern response to secession, political wrangling in Washington, the volunteer army and its citizen-soldiers, slavery and blacks during the war, the social experience of the wartime North, agriculture during the war, religion, and the arts. They successfully treat a wide array of topics and include intelligent choices to initiate careful reflection by readers.

1002

Starr, Stephen Z. **The Union Cavalry in the Civil War** (3 vols., 1649 pp., Louisiana State University Press, Baton Rouge, 1979–1985)

Starr creates a masterful and exhaustive summary of the emergence of the Federal cavalry during the wartime period. The three thick volumes chronicle the cavalry's involvement in major actions in the eastern theater from Fort Sumter to Gettysburg (vol. 1), eastern battles from Gettysburg to Appomattox (vol. 2), and the western cavalry operations (vol. 3). Establishing a clear and correct basis for slow progress (faulty equipment, shoddy training, and amateurish organization), the author describes in the first volume the gradual experience gained by cavalry in the war's early eastern actions. The clashes at Kelly's Ford, Brandy Station, and the trio of Aldie, Middleburg, and Upperville receive particularly thorough treatment. Starr also provides succinct and meaningful portraits of many of the Federal cavalry commanders, including John Buford, Judson Kilpatrick, Alfred Pleasonton, George Stoneman, and James H. Wilson.

The second volume continues this successful treatment, examining the Wilderness campaign, raids by Sheridan and Averell, operations in the Shenandoah Valley, Cedar Creek, Five Forks, and the closing scenes at Appomattox. The final volume details Grierson's Raid, operations in Tennessee, Chickamauga, the Meridian Expedition, Brice's Cross Roads, Atlanta, Nashville, and Wilson's Raid. Throughout the well-documented narrative, the author evaluates the performance of Union cavalry, suggesting that it performed poorly until the summer of 1863, when at Brandy Station it began to contribute substantially to the success of Federal strategy.

1003

[The Union Army.] **The Union Army—A History of Military Affairs in the Loyal States, 1861–65: Records of the Regiments in the Union Army, Cyclopedia of Battles, Memoirs of Commanders and Soldiers** (8 vols., 3707 pp., Federal Publishing Co., Madison, 1908)

This scarce set offers a peculiar blend of statistical information woven with ultrapatriotic Northern prose and substantially useful data difficult to find in other sources. Half of this work offers a group of brief regimental histories comparable to those in the third volume of Dyer's *Compendium* (*q.v.*). Volume 1 (526 pp.) contains regimentals for Maine, New Hampshire, Vermont, Massachusetts, Rhode Island, Connecticut, Pennsylvania, and Delaware troops. Volume 2 (483 pp.) contains regimentals for New York, Maryland, West Virginia, and Ohio. Volume 3 (433 pp.) provides regimentals for New Jersey, Indiana, Illinois, and Michigan. Volume 4 (463 pp.) supplies regimentals for Wisconsin, Minnesota, Iowa, Kansas, Missouri, Kentucky, Tennessee, California, Oregon Territory, and the District of Columbia.

Volumes 5 (496 pp.) and 6 (467 pp.) comprise an encyclopedia of battles, 7 (330 pp.) deals with the U.S. Navy, and 8 (509 pp.) contains biographical sketches of Union generals and, curiously, biographies of notable officers of lower grade from Ohio only. The publishers of *The Union Army* compiled the work using contributions from numerous soldiers and employed section editors, including Union generals Joshua L. Chamberlain, Joab N. Patterson, David M. Gregg, Daniel E. Sickles, Joseph W. Keifer, Benjamin H. Grierson, and Byron R. Pierce.

WAR'S AFTERMATH

1004

Connelly, Thomas L., and Barbara L. Bellows. **God and General Longstreet: The Lost Cause and the Southern Mind** (158 pp., Louisiana State University Press, Baton Rouge, 1982)

In this perceptive and often amusing work, Connelly and Bellows argue that the Lost Cause is the spiritual essence of the Southern identity. The work begins with an introductory exploration of the Lost Cause mentality in which Longstreet emerges as the chief villian of Confederate defeat. Subsequent chapters detail "How Virginia Won the Civil War" and Robert E. Lee's evolving image. A concluding chapter ties up much of the Lost Cause mindset and speculates on its effects on modern Southern culture.

The authors capably outline the construction of the Lee mythology by members of the Southern Historical Society and the simultaneous attacks on Longstreet as the villain of Gettysburg. They trace the treatment of Lee by the generation of Southern writers who created the endearing portraits of Lost Cause mythology, crumpling the historical record in the process. Their documentation and analysis is thorough and difficult to counter. However, the final chapter rests on shaky ground, with its assertions that country music, the rise of Jimmy Carter, the enduring popularity of Elvis Presley, and "good ol' boy" movies all hark back to an internalized attachment to the Lost Cause. The authors misspell Albert T. Bledsoe's name.

1005

Foster, Gaines M. **Ghosts of the Confederacy: Defeat, the Lost Cause, and the Emergence of the New South, 1865 to 1913** (306 pp., Oxford University Press, New York, 1987)

This excellent work examines Lost Cause mythology and its effects on Southern culture. Based on creative and thorough research, the book surveys the three primary periods of Confederate identity following the war: the defeat and aftermath (to 1885), the celebration and memorialization of the Confederacy (to 1907), and the decline of Confederate tradition prior to World War I.

Foster convincingly emphasizes the sense of tradition that permitted white Southerners to forge a repaired identity in the wake of the loss of the Confederacy even as he deemphasizes the more traditional themes of Confederate mythology and religious fervor. The author traces the efforts of Confederates to sanctify Confederate heroes—particularly R. E. Lee—by the Virginians in the Southern Historical Society as early as the 1870s, reflecting an analysis similar to that offered by Thomas Connelly and Barbara Bellows (*q.v.*) and Alan T. Nolan (*q.v.*). Foster skillfully documents the rise of Confederate celebration a decade later by veterans groups such as the United Confederate Veterans, led by John B. Gordon and others. The waning importance of the Confederate tradition after the first decade of the new century provides a sad ending for this scholarly work, even as it demonstrates the springboard from which later Confederate remembrances were launched.

1006

McConnell, Stuart. **Glorious Contentment: The Grand Army of the Republic, 1865–1900** (312 pp., University of North Carolina Press, Chapel Hill, 1992)

In the late 1860s the G.A.R. arose as a political extension of the Republican party and was composed largely of political supporters of U. S. Grant. It evolved rapidly into a less-political fraternal organization promoting veterans' affairs. This work traces the evolution of the G.A.R. and explores several characterizations of the group as it changed during the 1870s, 1880s, and 1890s. Membership peaked shortly after 1890; as the new century turned, the declining memberships in G.A.R. camps whittled away the influence and activities of the organization.

McConnell presents a clear story of the G.A.R.'s role in memorializing the war, influencing postwar politics, and bringing deserved benefits to the surviving Union soldiers. He splendidly sets these themes against the societal background of late 19th-century America, arguing that the

G.A.R.'s goal is that of trying to preserve an older America in the face of astonishing change. The organization was antiprogressive to the point of excluding immigrants, minorities, blacks, and women—it was a giant and, for a time, powerful machine benefiting white men of middle- and lower-class backgrounds. An occasional error occurs, as with the misspelling of William S. McFeely's name.

1007

Rosenburg, R. B. **Living Monuments: Confederate Soldiers' Homes in the New South** (240 pp., University of North Carolina Press, Chapel Hill, 1993)

This study documents one of the more fascinating outcomes of the Lost Cause: the celebration of the surviving Confederate veterans in postwar Southern society. In this illuminating glance at a topic covered poorly in earlier literature, the author establishes the unusual nature of deep love for the survivors in a society that had been conquered. He explores the character of the men who fought for the Confederacy and hence the character of the men who aged in Confederate soldiers' homes. Significant detail accompanies the discussion, provided by several key archive collections in repositories and from the remnants of the various homes themselves. Additional material from a large number of veterans rounds out a fine, skillfully crafted, and well-documented picture of life inside these homes which stood in the former Confederate states plus California, Kentucky, Maryland, Missouri, and Oklahoma. The work focuses on the period between 1880 and 1920, although, as the work shows, a few veterans remained in the homes until the early 1950s.

Rosenburg further explores the relationship between the welfare system providing for these old soldiers and the state governments involved with administering their care. He shows that organizations promoted the Lost Cause in Southern postwar society in large part to foster their own goals, and, as a by-product, the care of the aging soldiers had peculiar side effects. Decrepit and far from their youth, the Johnnies were often escorted outdoors to "entertain" visitors or to sit in trucks and cars to withstand parades.

1008

Silber, Nina. **The Romance of Reunion: Northerners and the South, 1865–1900** (257 pp., University of North Carolina Press, Chapel Hill, 1993)

The author of this study of sectional reconciliation argues that gender played a significant role in transforming the American psyche in the years following the assassination of Lincoln. For the remainder of the century, according to the author, Northerners sought reconciliation by imagining a Northern "husband" and a Southern "wife" in a "remarriage." This feminine image of the South persisted until the 1890s, when the Spanish-American War created a more mature reconciliation on the new battlefields where Yankees and Rebels and their sons fought together.

Such a metaphorical view of the sections and Northerners' attitudes toward them is highly peculiar. Nonetheless, the framework, whether literally true to history or not, contains a mine of useful information on the attitudes prevailing during the three decades following the war. Everywhere in this analysis gender issues dominate. Still, the author describes adequately the Northern racism that marked the century's last decades and shows clearly the reunion that occurred in the 1890s, as Northerners embraced a new image of Dixie. Silber does not always clearly describe how the South itself changed.

1009

Wilson, Charles Reagan. **Baptized in Blood: The Religion of the Lost Cause, 1865–1920** (256 pp., University of Georgia Press, Athens, 1983)

The evolution of Lost Cause mythology is examined as it relates to Southern evangelical religion. The author surveys the attempts to rationalize the South's war aims, preserve its memories, and construct mythologies based on a uniquely Confederate religious doctrine. To accomplish this task, Wilson examines rituals and ceremonies of the Lost Cause and documents the behavior of so-called Crusading Christian Confederates; he also touches on the theology of the Lost Cause, analyzing the relationship of race and the emerging philosophy of the former Confederates, provides a detailed look at the well-known propagandist J. William Jones, and probes the methods of educating Southern children in Lost Cause mythology.

Wilson illustrates how ministers came to be the conservators of Lost Cause mythology and how the ideas and ideals involved were perpetuated through organizations, ceremonies, and schools. The revisionist history of the Confederacy was bolstered, the author shows, by the powerful influence of Southern evangelical Protestantism to produce a unique doctrine for the decades that followed the war. The study is limited to examining the mainstream churches and so leaves out many related analyses that could shed further light on this topic. But it provides a solid grounding by examining the primary Christian churches of the South and how they reacted to Confederate defeat.

WOMEN AND THE WAR

1010

Clinton, Catherine, and Nina Silber, eds. **Divided Houses: Gender and the Civil War** (418 pp., Oxford University Press, New York, 1992)

This study examines the relationships between women and men during the Civil War era. Essays contributed by 18 historians make up this thought-provoking work, each seeking to examine how gender affected a multitude of actions and outcomes of the Civil War era. Some are more successful than others; all, however, have important things to say about a specialized branch of Civil War history that has only recently developed into a serious area of analysis. In some areas gender as operant is crucial; in others it is only peripheral. Unfortunately, the work lacks an index.

Kristie Ross contributes a fine essay on nurses on hospital ships operated by the U.S. Sanitary Commission, showing how the perceptions of women were greatly affected by the wartime years. In a paper originally published in the *Journal of American History*, Drew Gilpin Faust suggests that the attitudes of Southern women contributed to the failure of the Confederate war effort. Stephanie McCurry argues that small farmers of the South needed to employ their wives and children to pull themselves into economic stability and therefore felt a bond with plantation owners who held slaves. Jeanie Attie compares the grueling work done by women to support the Union Army and the Sanitary Commission. Others, including LeeAnn Whites, Reid Mitchell, David W. Blight, George Rable, and Michael Fellman, touch on similarly interesting themes, all of which should inspire scholars to further explore these issues.

1011

Culpepper, Marilyn Mayer. **Trials and Triumphs: The Women of the American Civil War** (427 pp., Michigan State University Press, East Lansing, 1992)

This readable and useful work examines women in the Union and Confederacy, on the home front and assisting in the war effort. Culpepper's narrative draws on a wide range of sources, from the obvious (the Mary Chesnut diary) to the obscure, giving readers a broad overview of her subject. Unfortunately, readers must draw their own conclusions about what the wartime experience of various women means. Interpretation is shallow when present, and so we are left to wonder about the significance of the fundraising woman in Columbia, South Carolina, and others. Indeed, such diverse topics as the female black experience, the plight of poor women, and those women who worked for the governments receive almost no coverage. The documentation is often tenuous, and the author is apparently unsure of when to take the source seriously and when not to. Further, the book lacks an index. Despite these problems, this summary of women's experiences as refugees, nurses, and simply survivors deserves attention.

1012

Massey, Mary Elizabeth. **Bonnet Brigades** (371 pp., Alfred A. Knopf, New York, 1966)

The author surveys the impact of the war on women's roles in American society and finds that the momentous event propelled women some 50 years ahead. Massey's book is a collection of vignettes tied together rather loosely save for the introductory and closing chapters, which affirm the new responsibilities women found as the war commenced and especially as Reconstruction emerged. Between these periods, the author takes a sweeping look at the various aspects of involvement by women. Her solid and enviable research brings these portraits of different domains together to form a worthwhile overview.

The Civil War allowed women to emerge in many areas, including nursing, teaching, fundraising, writing, working in industry, spying, and even fighting. The author illustrates with occasional vivid examples the areas where women contributed, such as Clara Barton's adventures on the battlefield. The summary chapter evaluates the new woman in America following the war and her evolution through the remainder of the century. This last chapter lacks the spark of earlier accounts, yet it answers many questions and supports, in the main, the author's contention that the war was a significantly progressive event for American women.

(Reprinted 1994, titled *Women in the Civil War*, with an introduction by Jean V. Berlin, 371 pp., University of Nebraska Press, Lincoln)

1013

Rable, George C. **Civil Wars: Women and the Crisis of Southern Nationalism** (391 pp., University of Illinois Press, Urbana, 1989)

Rable's summary of the changed roles of Southern white women during the wartime period is tightly envisioned, written in a precise style, and carefully researched. This volume has much to say about an area lightly skimmed by earlier, shorter works. The author explores the upsetting predicaments of rapid change presented to Southern women at the outset of war, the responsibilities thrust upon them with the absence of many men, their relationship to Confederate authorities, the dilemmas of Confederate women's patriotism, the horrors of refugee life, and the transformation of Southern women's psychology with the realization of Confederate defeat. Such a large number of complex themes may overwhelm many an author, but this work stands up beautifully, with specific examples to support the author's contentions.

Drawing on a large number of contemporary diaries and letters, Rable shows how Confederate women's lives were transformed by the war. Education and the opportunities for expansion outside the home came through necessity and produced a rising level of experience in the lives of many. The author treats the experience of life under Union occupation especially well and, ironically, concludes that although the experiences of Confederate women blossomed during the war, their roles sank to a level substantially in line with antebellum tradition following the emotional shock of defeat.

UNIT HISTORIES

ARMIES

Army of Northern Virginia

1014

Allan, William. **The Army of Northern Virginia in 1861–1862** (537 pp., Houghton Mifflin Co., Boston, 1892)

This book expands on Allan's earlier work on the Valley campaign (*q.v.*), setting down in eyewitness detail a superb description of the movements and activities of the much-feared Southern army in bloody 1862. The early date of the study precluded the use of much valuable material that could have forged a great work, yet this volume remains important as a source of contemporary material from inside the Confederate Army. Allan's description of the battles of the Army of Northern Virginia are must reading for any student of the Confederacy. The year 1861–1862 saw the Peninsular campaign, Second Bull Run, Antietam, and Fredericksburg, and Allan's narrative casts a steady, focused light on the activities of Johnston's and Lee's army throughout that period.

(Reprinted 1984, 548 pp., Morningside, Dayton; reprinted 1995, with Allan's *History of the Campaign of Gen. T. J. [Stonewall] Jackson [q.v.]*, with an introduction by Robert K. Krick, 537 pp., Da Capo Press, New York)

1015

Jones, J. William. **Army of Northern Virginia Memorial Volume** (347 pp., J. W. Randolph and English, Richmond, 1880)

This assortment of papers originating at the memorial meeting in Richmond following General Lee's death also presents six years' worth of papers from the meetings of the Virginia division of the Army of Northern Virginia Association, provides brief organizational tables of the army for the period of the Peninsular campaign and the month preceding Gettysburg, and supplies an unreliable discussion of the relative strengths of the Army of Northern Virginia and the Army of the Potomac at various engagements.

The work consists almost entirely of addresses delivered by former officers of the army at the various reunions. The bulk of the book, then, is replete with the early revisionist history of the Lost Cause, with many tales of superhuman Southern bravery and overwhelming Northern numerical strength. The many tributes to Robert E. Lee helped to form the basis of some of the later works on Lee by Jones and others (*q.v.*). Among the more enjoyable addresses are those by Charles Venable (the Virginia campaigns of 1864), William Allan (Jackson's Valley campaign), and Fitzhugh Lee

(Fredericksburg and Chancellorsville). The tone is typically defensive of Lee, placing blame on others and belittling the Federal military efforts that opposed the great Southern army. The statistical discussion of strengths is highly distorted, magnifying the size of the Union forces employed while reducing those of the Confederate Army.

(Reprinted 1976, with an introduction by James I. Robertson, Jr., 347 pp., Morningside, Dayton)

1016

Jones, J. William. **Christ in the Camp; or, Religion in Lee's Army** (528 pp., B. F. Johnson and Co., Richmond, 1887)

Jones describes the role of religion in the Army of Northern Virginia and the great revival of 1863 that swept through it. He makes no attempt at balance, as this well-known secretary of the Southern Historical Society considered himself an unreconstructed Rebel who continued to fight for the Confederate cause on paper. This aside, the work has much to offer and is a remarkable narrative of the effects of religion on the soldiers and the religious rituals practiced in camp and prior to battle. The author examines the religious spirit of the Confederate armies at the outset of war, the influence of good Christian officers (focusing on Jefferson Davis, Robert E. Lee, and Stonewall Jackson), the work to secure and distribute Bibles among the soldiers, hospital work, the roles of chaplains and missionaries, and the "eagerness of the soldiers to hear the gospel."

The most enthralling portions of the book recall the great religious revivals of the Lower Shenandoah Valley, around Fredericksburg, and along the Rapidan River among many brigades and provide many fascinating reports and letters. The remaining sections trace the evolution of the religious spirit of what would become the Lost Cause in 1864 and 1865 and a discourse on the "proof of its genuineness." This is a significantly fascinating work on the Army of Northern Virginia. A valuable and extraordinarily long appendix contains letters of reminiscence from many field chaplains written just after the war. Unfortunately, the work lacks an index.

(Reprinted 1904, 624 pp., Martin and Hoyt Co., Atlanta; 1904 edition reprinted 1986, 624 pp., Sprinkle Publications, Harrisonburg, Va.)

1017

Jones, Terry L. **Lee's Tigers: The Louisiana Infantry in the Army of Northern Virginia** (274 pp., Louisiana State University Press, Baton Rouge, 1987)

The author describes the contributions made by Louisiana soldiers in the Confederacy's principal eastern army.

Jones begins with a brief description of the onset of war and the organization of Louisiana units before launching into a chronology of the various battles experienced by the soldiers. The approximately 13,000 Louisiana infantrymen in the Army of Northern Virginia became known as the Tigers and gained a reputation for fierce fighting as well as for unruly behavior. This work portrays the battles in a winning, overview fashion as well as interposes stories of many exploits by officers and enlisted men. The author shows how many immigrants and rough countrymen from Louisiana learned to fight as well as loot, riot, and generally raise hell.

The narrative describes the Tigers' important contribution of stopping the initial Federal attack at Bull Run, its intense participation in Jackson's Valley campaign, and the drudgery of fighting it experienced in the Wilderness campaign, outside Petersburg, and at Appomattox as the Confederacy dissolved around it. The battle reporting is well documented and written in an engaging style that will delight readers. The author traces the war experiences of many small units as well, including Maj. Roberdeau Wheat's 1st Special Battalion and the notorious 14th Louisiana Infantry, famous for its depredations.

1018

McMurry, Richard M. **Two Great Rebel Armies: An Essay in Confederate Military History** (204 pp., University of North Carolina Press, Chapel Hill, 1989)

This study contrasts the Army of Northern Virginia with the Army of Tennessee. Artfully written and filled with insightful assertions, it is one of the best recent works on Confederate military history. McMurry set out to examine why the Army of Tennessee could not successfully defend Atlanta; indeed, why it had so many difficult times relative to Lee's army before John Bell Hood finally shattered it at Franklin and Nashville. His points are many but include judgments that Lee used his army more intelligently, until the last year of the war faced less fearsome Federal commanders, and, perhaps most important, that the Army of Northern Virginia's subordinate officers were far superior to those of the western army. One might add another related point: Jefferson Davis and the Confederate high command supported Lee's army far better than they did the Army of Tennessee, particularly when Joe Johnston commanded the latter.

McMurry asserts a great Confederate military irony: the weakly supported Army of Tennessee with its many defects fought the battles that ultimately supported Confederate war strategy. The eastern battles were less conclusive, perhaps strategically less important, yet the Army of Northern Virginia received the cream of the personnel and logistical support.

The author's contention that Federal armies in the East felt inferior to the enemy is erroneous (see Michael C. C. Adams's *Our Masters the Rebels*, [*q.v.*]), as is the generous assessment of Henry W. Halleck's competence. The author also wrongly describes Turner Ashby, Thomas R. R. Cobb, James Dearing, Isham W. Garrott, Jeremy F. Gilmer, and John C. C. Sanders as general officers, none of whom were confirmed by the Confederate Senate. Despite these and other minor flaws, this work is significant, particularly for students of the West.

1019

Wise, Jennings Cropper. **The Long Arm of Lee; or, the History of the Field Artillery, Army of Northern Virginia, Its Organization, Personnel, Material, and Tactics, with a Sketch of the Operations of the Confederate Bureau of Ordnance** (2 vols., 995 pp., J. P. Bell Co., Lynchburg, 1915)

This basic source book was compiled and written by an astute lawyer and professor at the Virginia Military Institute who was also a grandson of a governor of Virginia, Henry A. Wise. Although several important narratives written by officers of artillery in Lee's army exist, Wise's book offers an enlightened survey of the organization, logistics, tactics, and equipment of this important branch of service. A skilled artillerist himself, Wise supplemented his research by interviewing many old soldiers from Lee's army. The result is a book that after 80 years still dominates others on this topic.

Wise uses as mainstay characters two of the most important officers among Lee's artillerists, William N. Pendleton and Edward Porter Alexander. As Lee's chief of artillery, Pendleton figures most prominently, and Wise's treatment of him is generally well done. The author's discussions, however, show a marked subscription to the Lee mythology created by members of the Southern Historical Society in the 1870s. This diminishes the effect of some of his conclusions but does not prevent an effective description of the campaigns. Porter Alexander, though not directly tied to the Lee myths, perplexes the author. He admires the young officer's artillery skills but also downplays Alexander's importance owing to his role on Longstreet's staff.

A great amount of analysis occurs in the Gettysburg chapters, wherein Wise essentially brushes the blame for failure onto Stuart. Similar defenses of Lee and his closest associates mar other judgments, but these are forgivable considering the writer's background. In all, the work is a grand review of Lee's artillery branch that rightly shows its value and effectiveness in many a battle. The text is buttressed by many useful statistical tables.

(Reprinted 1991, with an introduction by Gary W. Gallagher, 995 pp., University of Nebraska Press, Lincoln)

Army of Tennessee

1020

Connelly, Thomas Lawrence. **Army of the Heartland: The Army of Tennessee, 1861–1862** (305 pp., Louisiana State University Press, Baton Rouge, 1967) and **Autumn of Glory: The Army of Tennessee, 1862–1865** (558 pp., Louisiana State University Press, Baton Rouge, 1971)

Together, these volumes form a magnificently successful history of the Confederacy's greatest western army and belong in every Civil War collection. In a wonderful style and with much scholarly documentation in support, Connelly shows that this fighting unit was as strategically important as the Army of Northern Virginia. He demonstrates that the army, even with its smaller numbers, was charged with defending a much larger area and often with poor supplies and infrastructure such as rail systems. Despite the enormity of its task, the Army of Tennessee under its various commanders succeeded admirably in most of its assignments and held together until Hood's disastrous campaign in late 1864.

The first volume traces the formation of the Army of Tennessee and sheds light on the role of Isham Harris in its origin. The author shows how concentrating forces along the Mississippi made possible Grant's success at Forts Henry and Donelson. He cleverly and rightly assesses a multitude of personalities, including several of the army's commanders, and rejects the mythology about Albert Sidney Johnston, exposing him as weak and indecisive. Connelly demonstrates in detail how Bragg has been too harshly treated by historians and that much of the blame for the Perryville campaign must be placed elsewhere. The author perhaps extends his thesis too far in attacking Edmund Kirby Smith. He also errs by stating that Sterling Price refused to support Earl Van Dorn by launching a march through western Tennessee.

By the time Connelly picks up the narrative in the second volume, the fortunes of war are falling squarely against the Army of Tennessee. More detailed than its predecessor, this second volume chronicles the army's experiences through Stones River, Chickamauga, Chattanooga, the Atlanta campaign, Hood's Tennessee campaign, and the final days in North Carolina. The author depicts Bragg as lacking the moral courage to confront tough decisions and Johnston as pessimistic to a fault. He shows that Johnston's replacement with Hood, though it may not have improved the command, did little to harm it during the Atlanta campaign, as Johnston had no coherent plan of action ready.

1021

Daniel, Larry J. **Cannoneers in Gray: The Field Artillery of the Army of Tennessee, 1861–1865** (234 pp., University of Alabama Press, University, 1984)

Daniel's book provides a chronology of the activities of the western artillerists and includes a substantial amount of material on the artillery branch and notable personalities. The result is a work that documents the difficulties experienced by artillerists, the Army of Tennessee, and the Confederate military as a whole. Daniel lays as groundwork a well-documented assertion that Confederate artillery in the Army of Tennessee was poorly supplied, utilized slipshod equipment, and was often short of horses and mules. Shot, shell, and cannon were often poorly made, leading to uncertain or even dangerous results.

The work is based primarily on the *O.R.* (*q.v.*) and many sources such as diaries and letters. Written with an inventive approach and adequately documented, this work has something to offer students of the Army of Tennessee and of artillery operations in the West. The characterizations are fair, particularly those of Braxton Bragg, Joe Johnston, Felix Robertson, and Francis A. Shoup, and the battle narratives are well done. The author shows that the western Confederate army ineffectively used its artillery for the most part, even poorly organizing it into chains of command whereby infantry line officers commanded batteries in action. The work is a fine contribution to western theater Civil War history.

1022

Daniel, Larry J. **Soldiering in the Army of Tennessee: A Portrait of Life in a Confederate Army** (231 pp., University of North Carolina Press, Chapel Hill, 1991)

This well-executed study of the common soldiers in the Confederacy's great western army supports the earlier contention of Thomas L. Connelly that the western soldiers maintained unit identities at brigade and regimental levels. Daniel finds that the common soldiery of the Army of Tennessee consisted of a ragged bunch lacking in discipline and rather low in morale.

The author summarizes a handful of areas relating to the common soldier's experience in the Army of Tennessee, including marches, camp life, morale, desertions, medical aspects, discipline, religion, and communication. The western soldiers lacked the army spirit of the Army of Northern Virginia, the author shows, but they equaled the easterners in fighting spirit. The battles of Shiloh, Stones River, and Chickamauga slowly gave these men their confidence throughout the first three years of war, and the army fought desperately at Franklin and Nashville before being effectively eliminated. The author's commentary on the observations made by these soldiers is well worth remembering.

Army of the Cumberland

1023

Cist, Henry M. **The Army of the Cumberland** (vol. 7 in Scribner's series Campaigns of the Civil War, 289 pp., Charles Scribner's Sons, New York, 1882)

This book falls short of its potential as one of the better volumes of the Scribner's set. As a well-liked and capable staff officer under Rosecrans and Thomas, Cist had the opportunity to deliver a lively narrative full of anecdotes, interpretations, and inside information about the army's campaigns. Unfortunately, the narrative bogs down in minutiae and drags the reader through an uninventive description of the army's activities through the battles of Mill Springs, Perryville, Stones River, Chickamauga, and Chattanooga. Cist's reading of events is skewed by his admiration of Rosecrans and contempt for McCook's action at Stones River. Seven maps, reprinted and reduced in size from Thomas Van Horne's study of the same subject (*q.v.*), accompany the text.

(Reprinted 1989, with an introduction by Peter Cozzens, 289 pp., Broadfoot, Wilmington)

1024

Van Horne, Thomas B. **History of the Army of the Cumberland: Its Organization, Campaigns, and Battles, Written at the Request of Major-General George H. Thomas Chiefly from His Private Military Journal and Official and Other Documents Furnished by Him** (2 vols., 932 pp., plus atlas volume of 22 maps, Robert Clarke and Co., Cincinnati, 1875)

Despite its faults, this is the best summary of the operations of a celebrated Federal Army of the West. The work consists chiefly of a chronology of the operations of the Army of the Cumberland, provided in minute detail, and contains a succession of carefully collected reports, orders, dispatches, and letters woven into a functional narrative. The narrative is highly sympathetic toward George Thomas—indeed, was essentially worked on by Thomas himself—but as a whole accomplishes little criticism or independent judgment of the various campaigns and battles engaged by the Army of the Cumberland.

Van Horne brings forth an exhaustive and generally objective record of battle employing the journal kept by Thomas during his command of the army, which gives the book great life and high value. The accounts of Van Horne and other officers are in part aimed at vindicating Thomas's record and staving off criticism of the general by such senior commanders as Grant and Sherman, but the work fails to accomplish that. It does provide a great record of a great army, even if it does not fully restore one's confidence in Thomas's slowness at Nashville.

(Reprinted 1992, without the atlas volume but with an introduction by Peter Cozzens, 2 vols., 932 pp., Broadfoot, Wilmington)

Army of the Potomac

1025

[Pulitzer Prize, 1954]

Catton, Bruce. **The Army of the Potomac** (3 vols., 1190 pp., consisting of *Mr. Lincoln's Army* [1951], *Glory Road* [1952], and *A Stillness at Appomattox* [1953], Doubleday and Co., Garden City, N.Y., 1951–1953)

In slightly less than one page per day of the war, Catton re-creates the story of the preeminent Union armed force of the East, its battles, commanders, soldiers, and spirit. Naturally, the discussion centers on the battles and, in the first volume, on the building of Mr. Lincoln's army, which for a time could have been called Maj. Gen. McClellan's army. The author describes the detailed and exhaustive work of raising the force, equipping it, and drilling it until McClellan found it partially satisfactory. The story of the early battles is well told, with sufficient detail to understand the strategy and tactics of what was unfolding as the commanding general lost his credibility with the president.

The second and third volumes present a readable and absorbing version of the battles conducted by Burnside, Hooker, and Meade. The difficulties of undertaking an offensive war while occupying vast swaths of territory come alive in this work, as do the reckless decisions that sometimes issued from less than qualified commanders. The third volume witnesses the army under the personal direction of Grant, though the narrative turns more to the story of the common soldier as the vision of victory solidifies. Many human interest stories and brilliant writing add to the drama of what actually happened. Mistakes do show up, as with the misspellings of John A. B. Dahlgren, Solomon Meredith, Joseph A. Mower, Marsena R. Patrick, and the misspelled place names for Fort De Russy and Haws's Shop.

1026

Hassler, Warren W., Jr. **Commanders of the Army of the Potomac** (281 pp., Louisiana State University Press, Baton Rouge, 1962)

The author provides an overview and evaluation of the seven men Hassler contends "commanded the North's Army of the Potomac." Much insightful analysis of the roles of McDowell, McClellan, Pope, Burnside, Hooker, Meade, and Grant appears on these pages. Yet the author's credibility is in question because of his choice of characters: Irvin McDowell never commanded the Army of the Potomac, nor did John Pope, nor did Ulysses S. Grant. A major general who did temporarily command the army in the winter of 1864–1865, John G. Parke, does not appear in the book. One must wonder about the precision of the discussion.

Hassler also compiled a study of George B. McClellan (*q.v.*), and his bias of leniency toward the man shows clearly. The narrative focuses heavily on battle tactics and strategy and in the main is successful. Few surprises lie in the typical assessments of failure on the parts of McDowell, Burnside, Pope, and Hooker. In drawing conclusions, however, the author limits himself to the microverse of the battlefields without properly informing readers of the larger questions of politics and society at hand. Eight photographs and 12 crude maps supplement the text.

(Reprinted 1980, 281 pp., Greenwood Press, Westport)

1027

Joinville, François Ferdinand Philippe Louis Marie d'Orléans, prince de. **The Army of the Potomac: Its Organization, Its Commander, and Its Campaign** (118 pp., Anson D. F. Randolph, New York, 1862)

These impressions of McClellan's army and the Peninsular campaign are by an aristocratic volunteer aide on McClellan's staff. The work was originally published as "Campagne de l'Armée du Potomac" in the *Revue des Deux Mondes* for 15 October 1862, under the pseudonym A. Trognon, and is here translated and annotated by William Henry Hurlbert. The author presents four salient points: that McClellan lacked boldness, Washington constantly interfered with his plans, Southern field commanders were more able than those in McClellan's army, and McClellan's plan was a good one that was not carried off well.

The author is high-handed and judgmental, and overall he leans far too compassionately toward McClellan. Joinville overestimates McClellan's achievements, underestimates those of the Southern army, and is far too harsh with the Lincoln administration in supporting his defense of the

commanding general. The work contains a handsome early map of the Peninsula but lacks an index. It is useful as a wartime piece of propaganda and may afford entertaining diversions by comparing its conclusions with the record in the *O.R.* (*q.v.*).

1028

Naiswald, L. Van Loan. **Grape and Canister: The Story of the Field Artillery of the Army of the Potomac, 1861–1865** (593 pp., Oxford University Press, New York, 1960)

Singular as a study of the Army of the Potomac's artillery, this scholarly work offers much of value and can be considered a Union counterpart to Wise's *The Long Arm of Lee* (*q.v.*), treating the Army of Northern Virginia's artillery. Two superb elements impress the reader: the history of the artillery operations of the Army of the Potomac and the many characters who made it happen. Naiswald succinctly describes McClellan's early frustrations with long-range guns and the resulting strategy of arming units in the field with 12-pounder Napoleons, 3-inch ordnance guns, and 10-pounder Parrotts. Readers also receive a brief but meaningful lesson in the techniques of using field pieces and the types of balls and shells they most frequently fired. Indeed, spherical shot, shells, and canister were used almost exclusively, and the title reference to grapeshot is nearly a misnomer.

The evolution of artillery use peaked at Gettysburg. Before that date the artillery service lacked superior officers or simply operated under often careless infantry commanders. After that date the era of open-field fighting had waned. The war's final months in Virginia and much of the western theater did not always lend itself to the advantage of using artillery. Shining stars do emerge from this story, however, particularly in Henry Jackson Hunt and William F. Barry.

(Reprinted 1992, 593 pp., Olde Soldier Books, Gaithersburg)

1029

Stine, James H. **History of the Army of the Potomac** (752 pp., J. B. Rodgers Printing Co., Philadelphia, 1892)

This is a collection of battle histories and anecdotal material relating to the Army of the Potomac compiled by the historian of the 1st Army Corps. It is a relatively dry description of the eastern battles, with analysis of movements, and documents utilized to support assertions on the significance of the action. The viewpoint is of course Northern, and much information of variable quality appears. Perhaps the most valuable aspects of the work are eulogies of enlisted men and officers who performed bravely, observations on many campaigns and battles given by officers of varying grade, and opinions of Confederate officers.

The author covers in some detail First Bull Run, Dranesville, the Peninsular campaign, the interval between First and Second Bull Run, Second Bull Run, South Mountain, Antietam, Antietam to Rectortown, Fredericksburg, Chancellorsville, Fredericksburg to Frederick, Gettysburg, Gettysburg to the Rappahannock, Mine Run, the Wilderness, Spotsylvania, Sheridan's raid in the Valley, Richmond, Cold Harbor, various cavalry battles, the siege of Petersburg, Wilson's raid, Deep Bottom, Five Forks, the Appomattox campaign, and the organization of the Society of the 1st Corps, Army of the Potomac. Many illustrations of officers highlight the work, which lacks an index.

1030

Swinton, William. **Campaigns of the Army of the Potomac: A Critical History of Operations into Virginia, Maryland, and Pennsylvania, from the Commencement to the Close of the War, 1861–1865** (640 pp., Charles B. Richardson, New York, 1866)

This is an important early work that, among other things, contains the first discussion in print of the dissension between Lee and Longstreet at Gettysburg. The author talked at length with Longstreet, who cataloged the errors that Lee made during the campaign. The publication of this material helped to spark the long controversy that followed. Composed by a journalist who accompanied the Army of the Potomac during part of its history, the impartiality of the narrative and balanced objectivity marking most of the text give this book a lasting value.

Swinton chronicles the evolution of the army from the early days in West Virginia to the organization of the Army of the Potomac at Washington, through First Bull Run, the Peninsular campaign, Pope's campaign in Virginia, Antietam, Fredericksburg, Chancellorsville, Gettysburg, Mine Run, the May campaign, Petersburg, and Appomattox. The criticism is relatively balanced, with analysis and details of the army's movements and the tactical and strategic significance of the battles given at every step. That the study was so well done gives it the status of an important historical work even now, despite the fact that its early composition necessitates errors one would expect before the publication of the *O.R.* (*q.v.*). The index is poor, and the work contains a number of misspellings, as with the names of Arthur J. L. Fremantle, Henry Wager Halleck, Philip Kearny, and Fort Stedman, Virginia.

(Reprinted 1988, 640 pp., Blue and Grey Press, Secaucus)

ARMY CORPS

1031

Hyde, Thomas Worcester. **Following the Greek Cross; or, Memoirs of the Sixth Army Corps** (269 pp., Houghton Mifflin Co., Boston, 1894)

This is essentially a unit history of the 6th Corps. Hyde entered service as major of the 7th Maine Infantry and served continuously throughout the eastern battles in the 6th Corps of the Army of the Potomac, rising to command of the 1st Maine Infantry by war's end. Commissioned brevet major general of volunteers for war service, the author not only fought bravely at many of the actions but served on the staffs of William F. Smith, John Sedgwick, and Horatio G. Wright. This experience and a competent and entertaining literary style gave him the ability to pen a work that is not only a memoir of his own service but an overview of the corps. The result is an excellent work that retains its value today.

The narrative incorporates extensive discussions of both battles and commanders. Some re-created "conversations" stretch the authenticity of certain sections, but on the whole the work is highly reliable. The narrative utilizes official documents and anecdotes of common soldier life to recall First Bull Run, recruiting the 7th Maine, war fever in Boston, life at Camp Griffin in Virginia, Williamsburg, Custer's first skirmish, Gaines's Mill, Savage's Station, Malvern Hill, Second Bull Run, Chantilly, sharpshooting at Antietam, and the author's arrest and subsequent return to the army after Fredericksburg.

Worthwhile recollections give the book character, especially the discussion of Gettysburg, descriptions of civilians in Warrenton, the "cold and disgusting" Mine Run campaign, the Wilderness, Sedgwick's death, the Mule Shoe attack, life in the Shenandoah campaign of 1864, Sayler's Creek, and the Grand Review. The author incorporates much material on Sedgwick, Baldy Smith, William B. Franklin, George Meade, Martin T. McMahon, and Phil Sheridan. The work lacks an index.

(Reprinted 1988, 269 pp., Olde Soldier Books, Gaithersburg)

1032

Powell, William H. **The Fifth Army Corps (Army of the Potomac): A Record of Operations during the Civil War in the United States of America, 1861–1865** (900 pp., G. P. Putnam's Sons, New York, 1896)

This hefty tome records much of the military campaigns of the 5th Corps from First Bull Run to Appomattox. Powell was lieutenant colonel of the 11th U.S. Infantry during the war, assigned to the 5th Corps, so he writes with the first-hand knowledge of one who lived through the majority of the campaigns and with the insider's knowledge of how the corps organization worked. The volume consists of a running narrative of the organization and operations of the 5th Corps and is buttressed with statistical tables of organization, casualties, and so forth. Many excerpts from official reports appear throughout. As the elite army corps of the Army of the Potomac, the 5th Corps contained the regular army units as well as a large number of highly professional, choice field officers.

One would expect that this narrative would be among the finest unit histories on either side of the war. While the work contains a fair summary of most of the activities of the 5th Corps, it does not live up to its potential. The author is highly and unrealistically favorable to George McClellan in his evaluations of that general's performance, and he focuses almost exclusively on the major eastern campaigns, concentrating on a small part of the army without providing much context. His statements regarding the political relationship between the army's commanders and the Lincoln administration are often confounding. Thirty-eight maps, including large, folding diagrams, depict the strategically most pertinent actions, and there is an adequate index.

(Reprinted 1993, 902 pp., Morningside, Dayton)

1033

Stevens, George T. **Three Years in the Sixth Corps: A Concise Narrative of Events in the Army of the Potomac, from 1861 to the Close of the Rebellion, April, 1865** (436 pp., S. R. Gray, Albany, N.Y., 1866)

Although broadly offering a narrative of the author's experience, this work supplies in effect a sketchy history of the activities of the 6th Army Corps. The work reflects life in the 77th New York Infantry, a regiment brigaded into the 6th Corps in 1862, after which the narrative expands its sights and includes much useful information. As regimental surgeon, Stevens wrote intelligently and in a calm, detached manner the year following the close of the war, drawing on his own experience and the diaries of regimental comrades.

The coverage includes First Bull Run, the Peninsular campaign, army life at Harrison's Landing, Second Bull Run, Antietam, Fredericksburg, Chancellorsville, Gettysburg, the Mine Run campaign, the May campaign of 1864, Cold Harbor, the earliest days at Petersburg, and the closing campaigns. This last material was included despite the author's muster out in December 1864. Antiquated or erroneous spellings betray a poor knowledge of many place names, but

this is natural in a work so closely following the war. Some of the more valuable narration covers the period in 1864 during which the 6th Corps was transferred to Sheridan's command and participated in resisting Jubal Early at Fort Stevens and in the Shenandoah Valley campaign of that summer. The account of Cedar Creek is noteworthy. The book lacks an index.

(Reprinted 1982, 436 pp., Time-Life Books, Alexandria, Va.)

1034

Walker, Francis A. **History of the Second Army Corps in the Army of the Potomac** (737 pp., Charles Scribner's Sons, New York, 1886)

This military chronicle of one of the most distinguished corps of the primary eastern Federal army is a straightforward battles-and-campaigns narrative that nevertheless carefully analyzes a variety of issues and retains a measure of balance despite its strong focus on the corps. The author outlines the corps' organization, command, and participation in a long list of battles that includes the Peninsular campaign, Antietam, Fredericksburg, Chancellorsville, Gettysburg, Mine Run, the Wilderness campaign, Petersburg, and Appomattox. Superb analysis of Hancock's activities at Gettysburg may be found, as well as impressively extensive details of the numerous operations about Petersburg.

Thirty maps, most of them poorly executed, accompany the text. Five "appendices" serve as an index and are poorly done. A number of misspellings occur, as with the names of Charles Edward Hazlett, Samuel Peter Heintzelman, Philip Kearny, Ranald Slidell Mackenzie, Irvin McDowell, Albert Sidney Johnston, and David Addison Weisiger.

(Reprinted 1988, 737 pp., Olde Soldier Books, Gaithersburg)

DIVISIONS

1035

Blessington, Joseph P. **The Campaigns of Walker's Texas Division, by a Private Soldier: Containing a Complete Record of the Campaigns in Texas, Louisiana, and Arkansas, the Skirmish at Perkins' Landing and the Battles of Milliken's Bend, Bayou Bourbeux, Mansfield, Pleasant Hill, Jenkins' Ferry, etc. etc., Including the Federals' Report of the Battles, Names of the Officers of the Division, Diary of Marches, Camp Scenery, Anecdotes, Description of the Country through Which the Division Marched, etc. etc.** (314 pp., published by the author, New York, 1875)

This early yet entertaining discourse focuses on the division commanded by Maj. Gen. John G. Walker that saw wide service in the West, including actions in Texas, Arkansas, and Louisiana. Blessington served as a private in the 16th Texas Infantry, as an aide to Brig. Gen. William R. Scurry, and fought through many small and a few significant actions in the western and Trans-Mississippi theaters. His account did not have the advantage of using the *O.R.* (*q.v.*) as a resource, so it is sketchy and embellished in areas, but it offers a sweeping campaign history of Walker's division that will delight students of the Far West.

The work is supported by a wartime diary kept by Blessington, official reports, and materials from fellow members of the division gleaned in the first decade after the war. The writing retains a striking freshness in the accounts of many battles, particularly those of the Red River campaign, in which Walker's division helped thwart the inept movements of Nathaniel P. Banks. The coverage of Mansfield, Pleasant Hill, and Jenkins' Ferry is particularly good. There are many misspellings, as with the names of Elias Smith Dennis, Francis Fessenden, J. A. Guppey, Horace Haldeman, James M. Haws, William B. Kinsey, William J. Landram, Herman Lieb, William T. Mechling, Benjamin A. Philpot, Horace Randal, David Porter Smythe, and A. Testand.

(Reprinted 1994, titled *The Campaigns of Walker's Texas Division*, with introductions by Norman D. Brown and T. Michael Parrish and an ambiguous index, 332 pp., State House, Austin)

1036

Georg, Kathleen R., and John W. Busey. **Nothing but Glory: Pickett's Division at Gettysburg** (728 pp., Longstreet House, Hightstown, N.J., 1987)

This volume focuses on Pickett's command and its disastrous charge and provides a statistical summary of the unit, including a detailed roster. Georg and Busey draw on a dizzying array of sources, and the result is a blow-by-blow account of the third day's action as recorded by many participants in the division. This lengthy and at times almost overwhelming presentation of important material and minutiae occasionally makes sorting the former from the latter something of a challenge.

The spotlight on Pickett's division produces a mountain of information for those interested in the fight from that perspective. However, the exclusion of material on the other divisions that participated in the charge, the Confederate high command and its rationale for ordering the action, and the Union defense along Cemetery Ridge withholds interpretation of the events from readers. The roster of 6288 Virginians who served in Pickett's division includes basic data (ages, occupations, etc.) for most of the soldiers and information on those who were killed, mortally wounded, or captured and died in the third day's fight.

1037

Losson, Christopher. **Tennessee's Forgotten Warriors: Frank Cheatham and His Confederate Division** (352 pp., University of Tennessee Press, Knoxville, 1989)

This study chronicles the career of Benjamin Cheatham and the service record of his famous and feared division. The author was challenged by a relatively small number of papers relating to Cheatham from which to draw. Thus, the sections discussing the prewar and postwar years are somewhat brief, but they adequately summarize Cheatham's role in the Mexican War, as a major general of the Tennessee Militia, and his latter duties as superintendent of Tennessee prisons and postmaster of Nashville. The height of Cheatham's career came during the war, of course, and Losson's text concentrates on that period.

Wartime sources relating to Cheatham are scarce, particularly those dealing with the Atlanta campaign and Hood's Tennessee campaign of 1864. To surmount this obstacle, the author has carefully drawn on a large number of reminiscences, diaries, letters, and (mostly) official reports from others involved with Cheatham's division. The result is a well-written and significant contribution to understanding the western campaigns. The author does especially well with the discussions of Stones River, Chattanooga, Kennesaw Mountain, and Spring Hill and Franklin, and he clearly demonstrates Cheatham's competence compared with some other commanders close to him.

1038

Schenck, Martin. **Up Came Hill: The Story of the Light Division and Its Leaders** (344 pp., Stackpole Co., Harrisburg, Pa., 1958)

One of the most celebrated divisions in wartime history is certainly that of A. P. Hill, and a solid, balanced history of the Light Division would be much valued. This work travels part of the way toward that goal. The study is likable in that its chief protagonist, Powell Hill, is a fascinating character, and the exploits of his division carried it through much of the eastern theater's greatest actions. Schenck's narrative reiterates much prior work and assembles it into a coherent discussion of the division's accomplishments. The study is not without problems, however. The author claims early in the book: "There is no record as to exactly why this unique name was selected." But it is well known that the division's name derived from the fact that it "traveled light," without the usual baggage and quartermaster's supplies in wagon trains. The author's naïveté infects the text to follow.

The book is weakly supported by scant documentation, and those sources consulted by the author beyond the *O.R.* (*q.v.*) often are secondary in nature. Moreover, Schenck's praise of Hill comes at the expense of those who squabbled with him, most notably Stonewall Jackson. While he renders harsh criticism of Hill's superiors and subordinates alike, he uncritically examines Hill's own lackluster performance at key times, such as at the battle of Mechanicsville.

(Reprinted 1985, 344 pp., Butternut Press, Gaithersburg)

BRIGADES

1039

Caldwell, J. F. J. **The History of a Brigade of South Carolinians, Known First as "Gregg's" and Subsequently as "McGowan's Brigade"** (247 pp., King and Baird, Printers, Philadelphia, 1866)

Caldwell, who served as an officer in the 1st South Carolina Infantry, composed this very early but still useful history that chronicles the activities of his brigade. Beginning in 1862, the brigade was comprised of the same five regiments and saw action throughout the complete record of the Army of Northern Virginia. The five regiments commanded by Maxcy Gregg and then by Samuel McGowan were the 1st, 12th, 13th, and 14th South Carolina Infantry and Orr's Rifles.

The author provides a general description of the battles the brigade experienced, its organization, officers of the reg-

iments, casualties, and excerpts of reports on various actions. He includes a substantial amount of material on the brigade's second commander, McGowan. The coverage spans most of the major eastern battles, including battles around Richmond in the Peninsular campaign, Second Bull Run, Antietam, Fredericksburg, Chancellorsville, Gettysburg, the Wilderness campaign, Petersburg, and Appomattox. The writing is clear, entertaining, and devoid of sectional animosity; the primary flaws of the narrative might be expected from a work that predates the *O.R.* (*q.v.*). Errors include the misspelling of Maxcy Gregg and such common names as Manassas and Culpeper. The work lacks an index.

(Reprinted 1987, 326 pp., Morningside, Dayton)

1040

Conyngham, D. P. **The Irish Brigade and Its Campaigns: With Some Account of the Corcoran Legion, and Sketches of the Principal Officers** (599 pp., P. Donahoe, Boston, 1867)

This is a valuable albeit early and occasionally confused treatment of a famous unit of the Army of the Potomac. The unit consisted of the 63d, 69th, and 88th New York Infantry, the 28th Massachusetts Infantry, and the 116th Pennsylvania Infantry. Heavily Irish in composition, the brigade assembled a glorious record of fighting at many of the eastern battles and was well known for some colorful characters within it, not the least of whom was Bvt. Maj. Gen. Thomas Francis Meagher, the unit's onetime commander. Brig. Gens. Michael Corcoran and Thomas A. Smyth also contributed materially to the brigade's fighting reputation, if not its unusually colorful exploits in camp and on the march. Coverage includes the brigade's record on the Peninsula, at Antietam, Fredericksburg, Chancellorsville, Gettysburg, and in the Virginia campaigns of 1864 and 1865. The discussion is generally good and written with great style, but a preponderance of re-created "conversations" weakens the book's credibility.

An appendix provides a sketch of the battles experienced by the brigade, biographies of Meagher, Corcoran, and Smyth, and summaries of the officers in each of the regiments. The work has a poor, ambiguous index. Conyngham misspells a large number of names, including those of William Woods Averell, Romeyn Beck Ayres, Philip Kearny, Alfred Pleasonton, James Brewerton Ricketts, and David Sloan Stanley. Many ambiguous references to officers pepper the text.

(Reprinted 1994, titled *The Irish Brigade and Its Campaigns*, with an introduction by Lawrence Frederick Kohl, 616 pp., Fordham University Press, New York)

1041

Davis, William C. **The Orphan Brigade: The Kentucky Confederates Who Couldn't Go Home** (318 pp., Doubleday and Co., New York, 1980)

Davis relates the story of the 1st Kentucky Brigade, formed under the watchful eye of John C. Breckinridge in the autumn of 1861 and consisting of the 2d, 4th, 5th, 6th, and 9th Kentucky Infantry C.S.A. Recruited from a broad band of counties from eastern Kentucky through Lexington and Frankfort to Louisville and scattered western areas, the brigade experienced a wide range of combat in the war's western theater. Following Kentucky's alignment with the Union, the Orphan Brigade assembled at Camp Boone, Tennessee, under Breckinridge's direction. The brigade's 4000 soldiers came to admire Breckinridge greatly, the author shows, and Breckinridge was endeared to his men who had already lost their home state.

The author's skillful narrative, written in a spritely style, is well grounded in an impressive variety of sources. The story follows the exploits of the brigade throughout the major western battles, including Shiloh, Vicksburg, Baton Rouge, Stones River, Atlanta, the March to the Sea, and the Carolinas campaign. Davis details the record of the many commanders of the brigade and its regiments and provides ample anecdotal material on many common soldiers in the unit. He documents the wild life of a western soldier and leaves readers with a taste for more.

1042

Dickert, D. Augustus. **History of Kershaw's Brigade, with a Complete Roll of Companies, Biographical Sketches, Incidents, Anecdotes, etc.** (583 pp., E. H. Aull Co., Newberry, S.C., 1899)

Dickert presents the unusually interesting record of the brigade variously consisting of the 2d, 3d, 7th, 8th, 15th, 20th, and 3d Battalion South Carolina Infantry. One of the earliest units organized, the brigade and its first commander, Col. Joseph B. Kershaw, experienced a wide range of service in the East. The battles covered in this lengthy and detailed narrative include First Bull Run, the Peninsular campaign, Second Bull Run, Antietam, Fredericksburg, Chancellorsville, Gettysburg, Chickamauga, the Wilderness campaign, Cold Harbor, Petersburg, and the Shenandoah Valley campaign of 1864.

The author's experience allowed him to pen a worthwhile volume. Serving first as a private soldier and later an officer of the 2d South Carolina (Kershaw's first regiment), Dickert was close enough both to the common soldiers and, late

in the war, to commanders to convincingly communicate both sides of the war to readers. An alphabetical roster lists 8800 names of members of the brigade. The volume contains an eight-page list of errata. A large number of misidentifications appear, as with "General Curtis" rather than Governor Curtin, and misspellings of Paul J. Semmes and Robert E. Rodes. Errors of fact occur throughout the text, and not all of them are corrected by the errata list.

(Reprinted 1990, with an introduction by Mack Wyckoff, 730 pp., Broadfoot, Wilmington)

1043

Gaff, Alan D. **Brave Men's Tears: The Iron Brigade at Brawner Farm** (209 pp., Morningside, Dayton, 1985)

The author examines the participation of a single brigade in a single battle. The Iron Brigade, consisting of the 2d, 6th, and 7th Wisconsin Infantry, the 19th Indiana Infantry, and Battery B of the 4th U.S. Artillery, centrally participated in a clash with Stonewall Jackson's corps at John C. Brawner's farm near Groveton, south of the old Bull Run battlefield, on 28 August 1862. The fight was an opening action in Second Bull Run but here receives examination on its own grounds, with a pointed emphasis on the three-hour battle on the farm. The brigade, commanded by Brig. Gen. John Gibbon, served alongside Abner Doubleday's brigade to stave off Ewell's and Taliferro's soldiers in a tactical draw.

Although the consequences of the fight may have contributed but slightly relative to the major battle that followed, Gaff skillfully and with considerable research and sound interpretation draws a portrait of this small conflict. The material is presented in an interesting fashion, from the various command decisions of Pope and Ewell to the soldiers' fight in the field. The author proficiently demonstrates that a small fight can produce superb history, and this book thus deserves wide reading. Photographs of participants, a carefully composed order of battle, and a small number of helpful maps add value to this study.

1044

Gottschalk, Phil. **In Deadly Earnest: The History of the First Missouri Brigade, C.S.A.** (562 pp., Missouri River Press, Columbia, 1991)

This volume is the outgrowth of the author's energetic research into the embattled unit whose commanders included Lewis H. Little, John S. Bowen, and Francis M. Cockrell. Grounded in approximately 150 primary sources—35 brigade members, 64 Confederates outside the brigade, and nearly 50 Union soldiers and officers—Gottschalk's history traces the unit from its raising during the war's first months to the final defensive war in the trenches at Fort Blakely. Twelve chapters focus on the major phases of the brigade's fighting career, including interesting accounts of service at Pea Ridge, Shiloh, Grand Gulf, the Vicksburg campaign, and the Atlanta campaign. Simple maps with "blitzkrieg" arrows denoting attacks supplement the major battles, and photographs illustrate the most significant commanders and a handful of common brigade members.

Gottschalk provides a mesmerizing amount of detail in small snippets from a wide variety of manuscript sources and letters. The result is a powerful and voluminous running narrative that succeeds in documenting the activities of the brigade but lacks the controlled rhythm to sort the important from the trivial and weave tangential side trips into a cohesive flow. Many errors appear, the simplest of which are misspellings, evidenced with the names of John C. Breckinridge, Abraham Buford, Benjamin F. Cheatham, Matthew D. Ector, Daniel M. Frost, Claiborne F. Jackson, John P. McCown, Randal McGavock, Joseph Mower, and Emerson Opdycke.

1045

Hinman, Wilbur F. **The Story of the Sherman Brigade: The Camp, the March, the Bivouac, the Battle: And How "the Boys" Lived and Died during Four Years of Active Field Service** (1104 pp., published by the author, Alliance, Ohio, 1897)

The "Sherman Brigade" was organized in the spring of 1861 by John Sherman as colonel and consisted of the 64th and 65th Ohio Infantry, the 6th Ohio Artillery, and McLaughlin's cavalry squadron. Abraham Lincoln talked Sherman into resigning in December 1861 to serve in the U.S. Senate. Hinman, who rose to lieutenant colonel of the 65th Ohio Infantry and composed one of the best unit histories of the war, covers the wartime exploits of the four units, which were sometimes separated during the war.

The work presents not only a detailed history of the units but also a comprehensive roster of the 3224 men who served in the brigade and 371 portraits of personnel. The roster supplies ages, promotions, dates of service, wounds, and terminations. The 79 chapters of narrative provide details on a mass of activities, including the raising of the units, early adventures in wartime Kentucky, the advance to Nashville, the campaign and battle of Shiloh, the siege of Corinth, Bragg's Kentucky campaign, Stones River, Chickamauga, Chattanooga, the Atlanta campaign, Franklin, Nashville, and the closing days of the war. This is a monumental unit history.

1046

Nolan, Alan. **The Iron Brigade: A Military History** (412 pp., Macmillan and Co., New York, 1961)

Composed of the 2d, 6th, and 7th Wisconsin Infantry, the 19th Indiana Infantry, and attached artillery, the Iron Brigade received its baptism of fire during the campaign of Second Bull Run. At John C. Brawner's farm, the brigade held off a surprise attack from soldiers of Stonewall Jackson's corps. Shortly thereafter, as it encountered D. H. Hill's troops at Turner's Gap, the unit punched through the mountain pass and earned its illustrious nickname. The brigade then saw action at Antietam, Fredericksburg, Chancellorsville, and Gettysburg, as its composition changed by the contribution of the 24th Michigan.

The author vividly and precisely describes the encounters of the brigade and the contributions of many of its famous soldiers, including commanders Rufus King and John Gibbon. Nolan's choice was a superb one, as the sterling record of this unit provides an ideal story. This work ought to be required reading for anyone interested in unit histories, and it most assuredly deserves the reputation of being one of the finest of its genre.

(Reprinted 1983, with an introduction by James I. Robertson, Jr., 412 pp., Historical Society of Michigan, Ann Arbor, and Hardscrabble Books, Berrien Springs; reprinted 1994, with an introduction by Gary W. Gallagher, 412 pp., Indiana University Press, Bloomington)

1047

Polley, Joseph B. **Hood's Texas Brigade: Its Marches, Its Battles, Its Achievements** (347 pp., Neale Publishing Co., New York, 1910)

Written by a member of the brigade, Polley's work constitutes an eyewitness account of the many battles experienced by Hood's Texans throughout their eastern and briefer western service. The author was a private soldier who became quartermaster sergeant of the brigade before war's end. As such, he was intelligent and literate enough to pen a good book, although the tales of camp and battle sometimes drone on in a folksy style, perhaps because much of the source material comes from letters and reminiscences of other members. Many dates and times, as well as the significance of some of the actions the brigade witnessed, are in error, probably because much of the work was created from memory long after the war.

The book contains valuable muster rolls for the 1st, 4th, and 5th Texas Infantry and intriguing biographical sketches of many of the members, a list of Appomattox paroles, and a smattering of photographs. Unfortunately, it lacks a much-needed index.

(Reprinted 1988, with an introduction by Richard M. McMurry, 347 pp., Morningside, Dayton)

1048

Robertson, James I., Jr. **The Stonewall Brigade** (271 pp., Louisiana State University Press, Baton Rouge, 1963)

A first-rate study of one of the legendary units of the Confederate Army, meticulously researched and skillfully crafted, this work offers the story of the brigade's personalities, effectiveness on the battlefield, and context in the war as a whole. Not only does the reader receive a substantial amount of battle narrative but also microbiographies of the brigade's leaders, a fascinating set of Virginians including Jackson himself, Brig. Gen. Richard B. Garnett, Brig. Gen. Charles S. Winder, Col. William S. H. Baylor, Brig. Gen. Elisha F. Paxton, Brig. Gen. James A. Walker, and Brig. Gen. William Terry.

Robertson follows the raising of the 2d, 4th, 5th, 27th, and 33d Virginia Infantry, the components of the brigade, and tells the story of its action on Henry House Hill and Jackson's rise to fame. The unit participated in a long list of the major eastern battles: Jackson's Valley campaign, the tail end of the Peninsular campaign, Second Bull Run, Antietam, Fredericksburg, Chancellorsville, Gettysburg, the Wilderness, and Spotsylvania, where the brigade was so battered that it was splintered and consolidated with other units. Such was the brigade's participation in these battles that all but three of its commanders were killed or mortally wounded. Robertson's work is splendid, and one only wishes the compilation were longer.

(Reprinted 1987, 271 pp., Louisiana State University Press, Baton Rouge)

1049

Simpson, Harold B. **Hood's Texas Brigade: Lee's Grenadier Guard** (512 pp., Texian Press, Waco, 1970)

Commanded for fewer than six months by the glory-seeking Hood, the brigade consisted of the 4th and 5th Texas Infantry and the 18th Georgia Infantry. Later the composition changed to include the 1st, 4th, and 5th Texas Infantry and the 3d Arkansas Infantry. The brigade served as part of the Army of Northern Virginia and experienced most major eastern battles from the Peninsular campaign onward, with the exception of service under Longstreet in the West, which included Chickamauga, Chattanooga, and Knoxville.

Simpson tells the story of this brigade in stirring fashion.

He explores the personalities of its long string of commanders, including Hood, Col. Jerome B. Robertson, Col. P. A. Work, Brig. Gen. John Gregg (killed at Petersburg), Col. C. M. Winkler, Col. F. S. Bass, and Col. R. M. Powell. Many stories of the men in the brigade appear interwoven with accounts of the numerous battles the brigade experienced. This leaves the reader with a solid sense of this unit's participation in the war and an appreciation of the terrible casualties it suffered. These qualities make this one of the better brigade histories of Civil War literature. Over a period of several years, Simpson completed an array of works that supplement this study, all relating to Hood's Texas brigade.

1050

Thompson, Edwin Porter. **History of the Orphan Brigade** (1104 pp., Lewis N. Thompson, Louisville, 1898)

A valuable firsthand view of the Kentucky Orphan Brigade comes through in this work. Thompson served as sergeant and subsequently 1st lieutenant in the 6th Kentucky Infantry, a regiment belonging to the brigade, and so experienced the wide range of actions in the western theater under John C. Breckinridge and the brigade's other commanders. Wounded twice, he was captured at Stones River and after exchange served as a commissary officer for the Orphan Brigade. Before war's end the author began collecting material for this work, both from his own notes and the contributions of many other members. Thus, the work is close to its subjects, and its narrative is authentic and straightforward.

The story is thoroughly grounded in the brigade's official papers. Better than most brigade histories, the narrative contains a mountain of extracts from official reports and rich collections of anecdotal material at the ends of individual chapters. Additionally, the book offers many valuable sketches of individual soldiers. An earlier, inferior edition titled *The History of the First Kentucky Brigade* was published in 1868.

(Reprinted 1973, with an introduction by William C. Davis, 1104 pp., Morningside, Dayton)

REGIMENTS AND BATTERIES

Alabama

1051

Oates, William C. **The War between the Union and the Confederacy, and Its Lost Opportunities: With a History of the 15th Alabama Regiment and the Forty-eight Battles in Which It Was Engaged: Being an Account of the Author's Experiences in the Greatest Conflict of Modern Times: A Justification of Secession, and Showing That the Confederacy Should Have Succeeded: A Criticism of President Davis, the Confederate Congress and Some of the General Officers of the Confederate and Union Armies: Praise of Line Officers and Soldiers in the Ranks for Their Heroism and Patriotism, and Including the Author's Observations and Experiences as Brigadier-General in the War between the United States and Spain** (808 pp., Neale Publishing Co., New York, 1905)

Oates may be best remembered as the colonel who faced Joshua Lawrence Chamberlain's regiment in the hollow between the Round Tops at Gettysburg. This story and many others of value find a worthwhile place in this work, the most valuable part of which is the author's history of his 15th Alabama Infantry, which fought in the Shenandoah Valley campaign of 1862, the Peninsular campaign, Cedar Mountain, Second Bull Run, Antietam, Gettysburg, Chickamauga, Chattanooga, and the Virginia campaigns of 1864. Such widespread experience in both theaters toughened the soldiers of the 15th into hardened veterans.

The battle accounts in this work are highly variable in quality, ranging from accurate to completely uninformed. Despite being written long after the war, the work leans on the recollections and accounts of its members, which ensures a lasting merit. The same may not be true of other parts of the work, which grind various axes and offer little of value.

(Reprinted 1985, with an introduction by Robert K. Krick, 808 pp., Morningside, Dayton)

Colorado Territory

1052

Hollister, Ovando J. **History of the First Regiment of Colorado Volunteers** (178 pp., Thomas Gibson and Co., Denver, 1863)

Hollister offers a glimpse of the New Mexico campaign of 1861–1862 as recorded in the diary and wartime notes of a private and later a noncommissioned officer of the regiment. Although crude, marked by gaps of understanding and incomplete information, and embellished for the sake of dramatic story, this work contains a fair account of Henry Hopkins Sibley's ill-fated campaign. The narrative ranges from the formation of the 1st Colorado in Denver, the pro-Union sentiment in the city, and the early exploits of a raw set of soldiers who had largely been miners before the summer of 1861. After the author recalls Sibley's advance, the work transforms into a combination unit history and narrative of the resistance to Sibley's campaign.

The primary value of this history rests in the soldier's eye view of a scantily documented set of actions. Although Sibley's campaign was the pinnacle of Confederate aspirations in the distant West, it was ultimately a disaster. The viewpoint of a well-informed Federal private soldier illuminates not only soldier life at Fort Laramie and Denver but evaluations of commanders John P. Slough and John M. Chivington and the battles of Valverde and Glorieta Pass. The book contains a roster by companies.

(New edition 1962, titled *Colorado Volunteers in New Mexico, 1862*, ed. Richard B. Harwell, 309 pp., Lakeside Press, Chicago)

Connecticut

1053

Hamblen, Charles P. **Connecticut Yankees at Gettysburg** (ed. Walter L. Powell, 152 pp., Kent State University Press, Kent, 1993)

This succinct but entertaining patchwork account records the activities of Connecticut soldiers in a variety of units during Gettysburg's three days. The various Connecticut units participating in the battle, their assignments, field commanders, and the routes they marched during the early phase of the Gettysburg campaign are outlined. Seven chapters examine critical regiments and the actions they encountered during the battle, focusing on the 17th Connecticut Infantry at Barlow's Knoll, the 27th Connecticut Infantry in the Wheatfield, the 17th Connecticut Infantry on East Cemetery Hill, the 5th and 20th Connecticut Infantry on Culp's Hill, the 14th Connecticut Infantry on Cemetery Ridge, and the aftermath of the battle.

Much of the appeal comes from the diaries, battle accounts, and letters excerpted throughout and arranged to form a coherent story. Maps sketch the positions of the units during critical phases of the battle, and photographs highlight important officers and common soldiers cited in the text. The unusual approach of focusing on a particular state's units at a single battle gives this work a peculiar appeal and could be used in volumes on other states' participation at Gettysburg and on other fields. An appendix lists Connecticut soldiers killed, mortally wounded, wounded, or captured at Gettysburg.

Georgia

1054

Andrews, William Hill. **Footprints of a Regiment: A Recollection of the 1st Georgia Regulars, 1861–1865** (ed. Richard M. McMurry, 220 pp., Longstreet Press, Atlanta, 1992)

Although McMurry shies away from presenting this standout work as a significant Civil War memoir and regimental history, the array of anecdotes it contains provides delightful commentary on the life of a common soldier. Originally written in the 1890s, the book draws on a smattering of sources, including the memories of fellow soldiers, yet it hangs together with a fair degree of credibility.

Andrews excitedly supported secession and state rights and enlisted in the Fort Gaines Guards in January 1861. Soon incorporated into the 1st Georgia Regulars, Andrews's company traveled to Fort Pulaski and served in the Savannah area until removing to the Peninsular campaign and then the battle of Antietam. Thereafter, the 1st Georgia Regulars returned to their home state and ended up by retreating to North Carolina before Sherman's march. The reminiscence of this service includes ample recollections of camp life, battles, and the monotony of drill and march. Occasional glances of commanders like Robert E. Lee and Robert Toombs add flavor to the narrative.

Indiana

1055

Brown, Edmund R. **The Twenty-seventh Indiana Volunteer Infantry in the War of the Rebellion, 1861 to 1865, First Division, 12th and 20th Corps: A History of Its Recruiting, Organization, Camp Life, Marches, and Battles, Together with a Roster of the Men Composing It, and the Names of All Those Killed in Battle or Who Died of Disease, and, as Far as Can Be Known, of Those Who Were Wounded** (640 pp., published by the author, Monticello, Ind., 1899)

The author presents a relatively complete and well-composed account of a Hoosier regiment. Organized at India-

napolis, the unit followed Col. Silas Colgrove to action throughout the Shenandoah Valley campaign of 1862, Antietam, Chancellorsville, and Gettysburg. In late 1863 the regiment transferred to the western theater and experienced action in the Tullahoma campaign, Chattanooga, and the battles for Atlanta before being mustered out.

Brown, a private in the regiment, pieced the text together from the diaries and letters of several comrades and his own recollections. The work contains a fair amount of reflection on the lives of common soldiers in addition to the normal narrative of battle and march, adding some material of value to the literature on both theaters of war. The portions describing the draft riots in New York following Gettysburg, the maneuvers around Chattanooga, and the attitudes of various soldiers in his company give the work a certain historical value. A fair number of minor errors appear, as with the misspellings of many place names and proper names, but the author has crafted this work with honest intent and for the most part delivers a memorable work. An excellent roster by companies follows the text.

(Reprinted 1985, 640 pp., Olde Soldier Books, Gaithersburg)

1056

Rowell, John W. **Yankee Artillerymen: Through the Civil War with Eli Lilly's Indiana Battery** (320 pp., University of Tennessee Press, Knoxville, 1975)

Organized at Indianapolis in August 1862, the 18th Independent Battery of Indiana Light Artillery experienced widespread service within the western theater. Capt. Eli Lilly, later the great chemist, led the battery until the spring of 1864, when Capts. Joseph A. Scott and then Moses M. Beck took command. The unit served in the Kentucky campaign of 1862, the middle Tennessee campaign, Chickamauga, Chattanooga, Knoxville, the Atlanta campaign, and Wilson's raid during the final weeks of the war.

Accomplished in the same style as the author's *Yankee Cavalrymen (q.v.)*, this work utilizes the diaries and letters of 17 of the unit's soldiers. Because of this, the work carefully and meticulously describes life within an artillery battery and details much about the war in the West. Anecdotes of commanders, the several battles the unit experienced, and minutiae relating to soldier life fill the pages. Rowell probably overestimates the battery's importance within the war, but that does not obscure the story of what was certainly a capable and confident group of artillerists in camp and in battle.

Iowa

1057

Scott, William Forse. **The Story of a Cavalry Regiment: The Career of the Fourth Iowa Veteran Volunteers from Kansas to Georgia, 1861–1865** (602 pp., G. P. Putnam's Sons, New York, 1893)

The history of a hard-fighting western unit is recorded by Scott, who served as a private soldier and subsequently sergeant-major of the regiment, ending his Civil War days as regimental adjutant, finally making 1st lieutenant in June 1865. As a youthful and energetic paper shuffler, he took up with great enthusiasm the task of recording the regiment's exploits and composed this work nearly 30 years after Appomattox by drawing on his own experience and the diaries, memoirs, and letters of fellow members of the regiment.

Unlike the majority of regimental histories, this work is carefully researched and offers a balanced narrative generally free of self-glamorization. Under the command of Cols. Asbury Porter and Edward Winslow, the unit participated in a dozen skirmishes and battles in Missouri and Arkansas early in the war and subsequently saw action during the Vicksburg campaign, harassing Forrest at Brice's Cross Roads and Tupelo, counteracting Sterling Price's Missouri raid, and sharing in Wilson's Selma raid during the final days of the war. The work draws on the *O.R.* (*q.v.*) in addition to the single collections of its members and can be recommended for achieving a superb level of history and personal narrative relative to most regimental histories. An appendix lists engagements and casualties.

(Reprinted 1992, 602 pp., Press of the Camp Pope Bookshop, Iowa City)

Kansas

1058

Starr, Stephen Z. **Jennison's Jayhawkers: A Civil War Cavalry Regiment and Its Commander** (405 pp., Louisiana State University Press, Baton Rouge, 1973)

The author explores the life and times of a Kansas unit that saw action in the western theater. Organized at Fort Leavenworth in October 1861, the 7th Kansas Cavalry was commanded by Charles R. Jennison, Albert Lindley Lee, and Thomas P. Herrick. Jennison led the regiment for a short time through some insignificant operations in western Missouri and Kansas, resigning in May 1862. Afterward the unit, commanded by Lee, saw action at Iuka and Corinth before

participating in Grant's operations about Vicksburg. Reconnaissance duty in Mississippi and Tennessee followed, as did action at several minor engagements before pursuing Sterling Price through Missouri.

Starr shows that the regiment included several companies of Ohioans who considered themselves abolitionists—including John Brown's son John Jr.—and that Jennison recruited the regiment at the encouragement of Kansas politicians, including James H. Lane. Although they may have been abolition-minded, the men of the 7th Kansas Cavalry hardly lived up to the reputation of jayhawkers during their war service. The author describes how battles and skirmishes weeded out incompetent officers in the unit, and his biographical information intertwined with the unit history provides ample background information to make the study interesting.

Kentucky

1059

Brown, Dee. **The Bold Cavaliers: Morgan's 2d Kentucky Cavalry Raiders** (353 pp., J. B. Lippincott and Co., Philadelphia, 1959)

This is a competently woven story of Morgan's exploits by the author of the Union study *Grierson's Raid* (*q.v.*). Although the work is loosely documented, Brown has used facts carefully and taken only minor liberties for literary effect. The result is a useful history of Morgan's cavalry that rings true despite its storylike trappings. Throughout the description of Morgan's unit the author skillfully dispenses general information on cavalry fighting and the challenge of the Southern horseman in the war. The story begins with Morgan's raising of the Lexington Rifles in September 1861, examines Morgan's command of the 2d Kentucky Cavalry, and takes a sweeping tour of Morgan's Civil War duty. High points of the narrative include Shiloh, the Ohio raids, and Morgan's dramatic death.

(Reprinted 1993, titled *Morgan's Raiders*, 353 pp., Konecky and Konecky, New York)

1060

Duke, Basil W. **History of Morgan's Cavalry** (578 pp., Miami Printing and Publishing Co., Cincinnati, 1867)

This is a classic work about John Hunt Morgan's legendary cavalry exploits, written by Morgan's brother-in-law and a brigadier general in his own right. The narrative is conversational in tone, praiseful of Morgan, and describes many soldiers of Morgan's command and their adventures in Kentucky, Ohio, Tennessee, and elsewhere. A focused military narrative of Morgan's operations, the work is valuable for Duke's eyewitness recollections recorded soon after the war. The author provides brief background information on Morgan, surveys the political situation in Kentucky in 1861, and proceeds with the unit's advance on Bowling Green. Throughout the military narrative, he seeks to diminish the destruction allegedly carried out by Morgan.

Various chapters describe outstanding or unusual aspects of Morgan's campaigns or major activities in the theater, as with the evacuation of Nashville, the Confederate concentration at Corinth, the battle of Shiloh, Morgan's movement into Tennessee, and episodes of night attacks, cotton burning, and other wild escapades. The author recalls the unit's reorganization at Chattanooga, the practice of cutting telegraph lines, bushwhacking in Kentucky, and the actions at Cynthiana, Gallatin, and Cairo. The dramatic element increases with the discussion of the great Ohio raid, the detour around Cincinnati, Morgan's capture and prison life, the escape, and Morgan's subsequent return to the field. The recollection of Morgan's death precedes a movement to Charlotte, duty as an escort for Jefferson Davis, and surrender at Woodstock. The book "sets the record on Morgan straight," according to the author, but is highly worshipful, overly dramatic, and contains many misspellings. It also lacks an index.

(New edition 1906, titled *Morgan's Cavalry*, 441 pp., Neale Publishing Co., New York; 1867 edition reprinted 1960, ed. Cecil Fletcher Holland, 595 pp., Indiana University Press, Bloomington)

Louisiana

1061

Owen, William M. **In Camp and Battle with the Washington Artillery of New Orleans: A Narrative of Events during the Late Civil War from Bull Run to Appomattox and Spanish Fort** (467 pp., Ticknor and Co., Boston, 1885)

Composed in large part from Owen's diary, this is a strictly military narrative of this famous artillery unit peppered with a few official documents and recollections of many commanders. The author presents a history of the formation of the Washington Artillery in New Orleans and proceeds down the path of the typical regimental history. He describes the unit's travel via Lynchburg and Richmond to McLean's Ford, Union Mills, and First Bull Run, where he presents glimpses during battle of Stonewall Jackson, Fran-

cis S. Bartow, and Barnard E. Bee. After a discussion of life in camp with the unit, Owen details Ball's Bluff, the Peninsular campaign, fighting near Richmond, and the exchange of prisoners. A great deal of value lies in the small details of soldier life that are revealed.

The artillerists experienced Rappahannock Station, Second Bull Run, Thoroughfare Gap, and the Maryland campaign, where Owen refers to James Longstreet and his staff as impromptu gunners. Descriptions of unpleasant winter quarters give way to victory at Chancellorsville, Gettysburg, and a change of venue to participate at Chickamauga. The discussions of Grant's shelling of Petersburg and the depressing, starving march to Appomattox Court House are particularly vivid. The final section outlines the activities of members of the Washington Artillery after the war. The work includes a full roster but lacks an index.

(Reprinted 1964, with an introduction by Kenneth Trist Urquhart, 467 pp., Pelican Publishing Co., New Orleans; 1885 edition reprinted 1983, 467 pp., R. Van Sickle, Gaithersburg)

1062

Tunnard, William H. **A Southern Record: The History of the Third Regiment, Louisiana Infantry** (393 pp., published by the author, Baton Rouge, 1866)

This compilation documents the war experiences of a much-traveled Confederate unit. Written shortly after the war, it relies on notes kept by soldier-author Tunnard along with reminiscences and documents provided by fellow members of the regiment. Organized in New Orleans, the 3d Louisiana Infantry participated in a wide range of actions in the western theater and in the Trans-Mississippi, including Wilson's Creek, Pea Ridge, Iuka, Corinth, and the Vicksburg campaign, after which most members were captured and paroled. The unit reorganized at Pineville in the summer of 1864 and spent most of the war's duration on guard duty.

Tunnard details with great clarity the actions he and other members of the regiment experienced. He describes such topics as camp life and observations of Indians and civilians; the unit's commanders, who included Cols. Louis Hébert and Frank C. Armstrong; and many places of unusual interest, including Baton Rouge, Little Rock, Fort Smith, Corinth, and Shreveport. This is an important and finely accomplished story of a Southern regiment in the Far West.

(Reprinted 1988, with an introduction, notes, a roster, and an index by Edwin C. Bearss, 581 pp., Morningside, Dayton)

Maine

1063

Mundy, James H. **Second to None: The Story of the 2nd Maine Volunteers, "The Bangor Regiment"** (280 pp., Harp Publications, Scarborough, 1993)

Mundy chronicles the adventures of the 2d Maine Infantry, a regiment commanded by Cols. Charles D. Jameson, Charles W. Roberts, and George Varney. The regiment, raised at Bangor, participated in many early clashes of the Army of the Potomac until being mustered out and absorbed into the well-known 20th Maine three weeks before the battle of Gettysburg. This work surveys the background of the Maine men in camp and battle, their war experiences, and the peculiar breakup of the unit. The author's slow and deliberate pace nearly avoids a clear explanation of the charges of dereliction of duty on 125 of the members of the 2d Maine, those transferred to Chamberlain's 20th Maine. Succumbing in part to avoiding any criticism of the local boys, Mundy casts an accepting light on the mutinous attitudes of these soldiers who fought at Gettysburg anyway, most of whom continued in their service as they were obligated to.

The author briefly recounts the battles fought by the 2d Maine at First Bull Run, the siege of Yorktown, the Seven Days, Second Bull Run, Antietam, Fredericksburg, and Chancellorsville. The narrative is not particularly deep in terms of military matters, and interpretation is lacking almost entirely, yet a story worth telling emerges. The text is complemented by photographs, a few "blitzkrieg" maps, and a roster. A number of misspellings occur, as with "Fortress Munroe" and "Centerville." The index is far too thin to serve researchers adequately.

1064

Pullen, John J. **The Twentieth Maine: A Volunteer Regiment in the Civil War** (338 pp., J. B. Lippincott and Co., Philadelphia, 1957)

This is a work that begins with a great advantage over most regimental histories in that the story of the 20th Maine and its heroic commanders provides Pullen with superb material. A skillful writer, he has produced a model history that is insightful and well documented, and it should be counted among the better regimental histories in Civil War literature.

Pullen describes the roles of sterling officers of the unit, including Adelbert Ames, Joshua Chamberlain, and Thomas Chamberlain. The exploits of the regiment are presented in enthralling fashion, from the muster-in at Portland to battle experiences at Fredericksburg, Chancellorsville (where it was quarantined with smallpox), Gettysburg, the Wilderness campaign, and Petersburg. Of particular interest are the regiment's activities at Fredericksburg, about which the author provides an excellent account of the frontal assault on Marye's Heights, and at Gettysburg, where they held the Union left flank on Little Round Top. He describes the regiment's activities at Appomattox and the subsequent march to Washington via Fredericksburg. At the latter place, Lt. George H. Wood was accidentally but mortally wounded on 10 May 1865, becoming one of the last officers to die in the war. Throughout the history the author nicely weaves in discussions of tactics, strategy, weaponry, and anecdotes of the lives of the common soldiers. The work is supplemented by a well-done bibliography, notes, and index.

(Reprinted 1991, 388 pp., Morningside, Dayton)

1065

Tobie, Edward P. **History of the First Maine Cavalry, 1861–1865** (735 pp., published by the author, Boston, 1887)

Organized at Augusta in the first autumn of the war, the 1st Maine Cavalry was led by a collection of well-known officers, including Cols. Charles H. Smith, Samuel H. Allen, and Calvin S. Douty, as well as Lt. Col. Jonathan P. Cilley. Tobie rose to 2d lieutenant and served as regimental historian, thus drawing the task of composing this record, which benefits from the author's own experience as well as a number of diaries, letters, and recollections of comrades. The regiment served with the Army of the Potomac through most of the pitched battles of the eastern theater.

The narrative is well composed, resists straying into glorification, and interjects many contemporary accounts as well as reliable recollections written during the two decades following the war. Highlights include coverage of Cedar Mountain, Second Bull Run, South Mountain, and Antietam and an awakening of cavalry tactics at Brandy Station. The Gettysburg campaign follows, as do the experiences of horse soldiers attempting to weather the grueling Virginia campaigns of 1864. Many interesting accounts center on minor actions about Petersburg, and the regiment reaches a zenith along the Boydton Plank Road, at Dinwiddie Court House, and at Sayler's Creek and Farmville. A detailed roster by companies follows the text. These two components make for a superb unit history.

(Reprinted 1987, 735 pp., R. Van Sickle, Gaithersburg)

Massachusetts

1066

Billings, John D. **A History of the Tenth Massachusetts Battery of Light Artillery in the War of the Rebellion: Formerly of the Third Corps, and Afterwards of Hancock's Second Corps, Army of the Potomac** (400 pp., Hall and Whiting, Boston, 1881)

One of the better New England unit histories, this work relies on a wartime diary and a collection of nearly 300 letters written by Billings during the war. Such a solid foundation provides an excellent story of service with the Army of the Potomac in Virginia and Maryland from late August 1862 through the end of the war. The author describes much about soldier life in the battery, the Southern people and the countryside in war, and the officers of the unit. He also speculates about commanders on both sides. The account is well written and a worthy companion to his classic *Hardtack and Coffee* (*q.v.*).

The best material focuses on camp life on the outskirts of Washington, the Antietam campaign, Brandy Station, and the Wilderness campaign. The unit participated in the latter actions of the war, from Cold Harbor to many engagements and movements about Petersburg to the Appomattox campaign.

(Reprinted 1987, 496 pp., Butternut and Blue, Baltimore)

1067

Bruce, George A. **The Twentieth Regiment of Massachusetts Volunteer Infantry, 1861–1865** (519 pp., Houghton Mifflin Co., Boston, 1906)

This well-written history of a superb regiment chronicles the so-called Harvard Regiment, organized at Camp Meigs in Readville in August 1861. The 20th experienced the entirety of the significant battles in the eastern theater from Ball's Bluff to the final actions around Petersburg. The regiment's senior officers included William R. Lee, Francis W. Palfrey, George N. Macy, Paul J. Revere, and Henry Livermore Abbott; its junior officers included William F. Bartlett, Caspar Crowninshield, Edward Needles Hallowell, Norwood P. Hallowell, Oliver Wendell Holmes, Jr., and William Lowell Putnam. With such a preeminent cast of volunteer soldiers, the regiment's story deserves this spectacular accounting.

Bruce "never saw the regiment" but nonetheless has assembled a summary of the men and officers of the 20th and their wartime experience. The work relies on the regimental association's great collection of papers, which allows the author

to portray the actions of the 20th in vivid detail. Among the highlights are descriptions of carrying the Mule Shoe salient at Spotsylvania, Pickett's Charge at Gettysburg, the attack on the right at Fredericksburg, and the dreary Mine Run campaign. The maps are rather poor and the book lacks an index.

(Reprinted 1988, with a photographic supplement, 519 pp., Butternut and Blue, Baltimore)

1068

Emilio, Luis F. **History of the Fifty-fourth Regiment of Massachusetts Volunteer Infantry, 1863–1865** (410 pp., Boston Book Co., Boston, 1891)

This is the principal source of information on the celebrated regiment that attacked Fort Wagner on Morris Island in July 1863. One of the first black fighting units to see action in the field, the 54th was commanded by Col. Robert Gould Shaw, who left a collection of letters that form a valuable companion to this work (*q.v.*). Emilio served throughout the war as a captain in the regiment, and his insights on the peculiar origin of the regiment, its national composition, and the youthful commander who was killed at Wagner are valuable.

The work was composed from Emilio's own notes and recollections as well as the diaries, letters, and remembrances of many other members of the regiment, mostly within the two decades following the war. The narrative is tight and factual, and the author offers resplendent detail covering drilling at Camp Meigs in Readville, the rather astonishing parade through the streets of Boston, and the unit's journey southward. Superbly detailed recollections of the fighting on James Island and Morris Island offer a highlight, although the history covers the regiment's entire service as it fought under Col. Edward Needles Hallowell in many other minor actions, including Olustee in Florida.

(Reprinted 1990, titled *A Brave Black Regiment: History of the Fifty-fourth Regiment of Massachusetts Volunteer Infantry, 1863–1865*, with introductions by James M. McPherson and Edwin Gittleman, 452 pp., Ayer, Salem; 1990 edition reprinted 1995, with an introduction by Gregory J. W. Urwin, 452 pp., Da Capo Press, New York)

1069

Waitt, Ernest Linden. **History of the Nineteenth Regiment, Massachusetts Volunteer Infantry, 1861–1865** (456 pp., Salem Press, Salem, 1906)

The campaigns of the 19th Massachusetts carried it through most of the major eastern fights (and some minor ones), including Ball's Bluff, the Peninsular campaign, Second Bull Run, Antietam, Fredericksburg, Chancellorsville, Gettysburg, the Mine Run campaign, the May campaign, and the siege of Petersburg. The regiment's commanders, Cols. Edward W. Hinks and Arthur F. Devereaux and Lt. Col. Edmund Rice, assembled a distinguished record for themselves as well as their unit. The regiment's front-and-center position on the receiving end of Pickett's Charge, where Rice won the Medal of Honor, is one of the book's highlights.

Waitt presents a chronology of the regiment's marches, battles, and encampments, punctuating it with recollections of members, official correspondence, and excerpts from letters and diaries. The portions reflecting on the failures at Fredericksburg and Chancellorsville are valuable, as are the remembrances of anguish on the slow grind around Petersburg. This generally well done work contains a number of the usual misspellings, as with the names of Philip Kearny and Alfred Pleasonton and the names of structures such as Fort Stedman and the Landram House. An appendix provides an alphabetical roster. The index is very poor and contains many ambiguous references.

(Reprinted 1988, 456 pp., Butternut and Blue, Baltimore)

1070

Wilkinson, Warren. **Mother, May You Never See the Sights I Have Seen: The 57th Massachusetts Veteran Volunteers** (665 pp., Harper and Row, New York, 1990)

This study chronicles a Yankee regiment's experiences in tremendous detail. Wilkinson's great-great grandfather served in this unit, which was raised in Worcester and Readville on 6 April 1864. Commanded by Cols. William F. Bartlett and Napoleon B. McLaughlin, both of whom would end the war as brigadier generals of volunteers, the 57th Massachusetts saw action during the Wilderness campaign, along the North Anna River, and at Cold Harbor. During the siege of Petersburg it participated in the actions at the Mine explosion, along the Weldon Railroad, at Poplar Spring Church, and along Hatcher's Run. Subsequent actions included a role in the Appomattox campaign. The narrative of major battles is rather thin, but the author presents a dazzlingly vast array of snippets from soldiers and officers, drawing on diaries, letters, journals, and official papers.

Wilkinson successfully portrays the lives and experiences of many common soldiers in camp, march, and battle and conveys the sensation of knowing a regiment's members and activities thoroughly. Along with 10 maps, 85 photographs supplement the text. This respectable modern unit history, executed in remarkable detail, provides the type of compilation that would be useful for other units of longer wartime service.

Michigan

1071

Bacon, Edward. **Among the Cotton Thieves** (299 pp., Free Press Steam Book and Job Printing House, Detroit, 1867)

This early memoir by the colonel of the 6th Michigan Infantry effectively serves as a history of the unit's most important activities. The regiment formed at Kalamazoo and, strangely, was reformed and redesignated as the 1st Michigan Heavy Artillery in July 1863. Bacon's narrative begins in July 1862 as the unit withdrew from the failed attempt at capturing Vicksburg and concludes with the Confederate surrender at Port Hudson, prior to the reformulation of the regiment. Thus, the bulk of the narrative concentrates on the 6th Michigan's role in the siege of Port Hudson, a rather overlooked affair whose recounting will delight students of the Mississippi River campaign.

The narrative, often charged with emotion, usually contains significant details regarding the unit's actions and also carries some hidden and open agendas. The author despised the West Point officers he served under and ultimately was discharged over several clashes, most notably with Brig. Gens. William Dwight and Thomas Williams. Bacon's dislike of these men results in some caustic recollections, and a bias against regular army discipline permeates the work. Still, he offers a keen and factually cohesive account of a regiment's participation in several unsuccessful campaigns and one triumphant effort resulting in the fall of Port Hudson.

(Reprinted 1989, with an introduction by Arthur W. Bergeron, Jr., 310 pp., Everett Co., Bossier City, La.)

1072

Smith, Donald L. **The Twenty-fourth Michigan of the Iron Brigade** (312 pp., Stackpole Co., Harrisburg, Pa., 1962)

In composing this very fine regimental history, Smith mined a variety of sources. Whenever possible, the participants are allowed to do the talking in superbly chosen quotations. The author traces the regiment's genesis at Detroit and its exploits around the capital and later on guard duty in the wake of Antietam. Significant action came at Fredericksburg, when four regimental color-bearers were killed during the melee. Of particular interest is the gripping description of the regiment's participation, as a part of the Iron Brigade, in the first day's action at Gettysburg. The Wilderness campaign and duty around the Petersburg lines fills out the excellent survey, which deserves a place in the regimental section of every library.

Minnesota

1073

Moe, Richard. **The Last Full Measure: The Life and Death of the First Minnesota Volunteers** (345 pp., Henry Holt and Co., New York, 1993)

Moe's fine work details the war record of the regiment that suffered one of the highest casualty rates of the war, at Gettysburg. Splendidly written, with great charm and vision, the volume covers the organization of the regiment at Fort Snelling and the long career of this fighting unit at First Bull Run, on the Peninsula, at Antietam, Fredericksburg, Chancellorsville, Gettysburg, Mine Run, Petersburg, and Appomattox. The unit's full career in the Army of the Potomac with such a distinguished group of regimental leaders—including Willis A. Gorman, Napoleon J. T. Dana, Alfred Sully, and William Colvill—provides opportunity for dramatic storytelling, and the author comes through in entertaining fashion. He draws on a variety of diaries, letters, newspaper accounts, and printed sources, the result being a suitable summary of the regiment's activities in battle and one that provides glimpses of the lives of the common soldiers in tent, camp, and on the march.

The author concludes his story of the regiment following Gettysburg, where the 1st Minnesota suffered such heavy casualties. A too-brief epilogue describes the remaining almost two years of service in Virginia—Moe missed the opportunity to discuss the recharged unit's experiences as the nature of war shifted and the fruits of fighting finally paid off for the boys from Minnesota. The work misidentifies Edward Dickinson Baker, and the index is brief but usable. A roster would have made this history more instructive.

New Hampshire

1074

Haynes, Martin A. **A History of the Second Regiment, New Hampshire Volunteer Infantry, in the War of the Rebellion** (350 pp., published by the author, Lakeport, 1896)

The author offers a relatively well-composed narrative of a unit that saw action in the eastern theater. Written shortly after the collapse of the Confederacy, the narrative reflects a sense of immediacy and does not rely on distant recollection for detail. Haynes was a private in the regiment and writes intelligently about the Peninsular campaign, Fredericksburg, Gettysburg, and the Virginia campaigns of 1864. He devotes a chapter to Gilman Marston, the regiment's

colonel who in 1862 was promoted to brigadier general. Anecdotes of camp and army life add to this work, which focuses on military aspects.

Brief biographical sketches of prominent officers associated with the regiment, including Francis Fiske, Edward Bailey, Joab N. Patterson, Simon G. Griffin, and Henry E. Parker, are included. Supplemental material covers the 2d New Hampshire Monument at Gettysburg, regimental reunions, farewell orders, and a roster of the regiment. A first, much inferior edition is titled *History of the Second Regiment New Hampshire Volunteers: Its Camps, Marches, and Battles* (223 pp., C. F. Livingston, Printer, Manchester, 1865).

New Jersey

1075

Marbaker, Thomas B. **History of the Eleventh New Jersey Volunteers, from Its Organization to Appomattox: To Which Is Added Experiences of Prison Life and Sketches of Individual Members** (364 pp., MacCrellish and Quigley, Printers, Trenton, 1898)

Marbaker chronicles the activities of a regiment raised in Trenton and commanded by Col. Robert McAllister, who penned a fine memoir (*q.v.*). Between August 1862 and the war's end, the 11th New Jersey participated in Fredericksburg, Chancellorsville, Gettysburg, the Wilderness campaign, and the battles around Petersburg. Their unit history is a comprehensive analysis of the battles and incidents of camp life and marches, drawing on the writer's recollections, the records and papers of fellow members of the regiment, and McAllister's material. The result is a relatively balanced, reasonably credible narrative that provides adequate detail relating to most of the major actions.

The accounts relating to Chancellorsville, Gettysburg, and Locust Grove are particularly appealing. An account of the imprisonment of Aaron Lines at Belle Isle and many brief sketches of officers, the best of which treat McAllister and Lt. Col. John Schoonover, are appended.

(Reprinted 1990, with an introduction by John W. Kuhl, a photographic supplement, roster, and index, 470 pp., Longstreet House, Hightstown, N.J.)

1076

Pyne, Henry R. **The History of the First New Jersey Cavalry (Sixteenth Regiment, New Jersey Volunteers)** (350 pp., J. A. Beecher, Trenton, 1871)

This unit, which participated in many important battles

of the eastern theater, counted among its field officers the curious and admirable characters Col. Percy Wyndham and Bvt. Brig. Gen. Joseph Kargé. Pyne's account comprises a complete war history of the unit from the Valley campaign of 1862 to Appomattox. The author, who was the regiment's chaplain, includes full, careful, and at times humorous accounts of Cedar Mountain, Second Bull Run, Fredericksburg, Brandy Station, Gettysburg, Mine Run, Haws's Shop, Trevillian Station, and Deep Bottom. The result is a great representative story of a Union cavalry regiment's exploits during battles and in times of lesser anxiety. The reflections on army life are enriching; so too are anecdotes such as that of the capture of some of Mosby's troopers engaged in less than saintly behavior. The work lacks an index.

(New edition 1961, titled *Ride to War: The History of the First New Jersey Cavalry*, ed. Earl Schenck Miers, 340 pp., Rutgers University Press, New Brunswick)

New York

1077

Curtis, Newton Martin. **From Bull Run to Chancellorsville: The Story of the Sixteenth New York Infantry Together with Some Personal Reminiscences** (384 pp., G. P. Putnam's Sons, New York, 1906)

This volume offers a history of a skilled fighting unit of the Army of the Potomac, along with the author's entertaining and often humorous recollections of army life. Curtis began his Civil War career as captain of Company A of the 16th and rose by war's end to brevet major general of volunteers. The author's background and raising of the regiment are described, followed by a detailed chronological journey of the 16th up through the time of Chancellorsville. Skillfully cast versions of the fights at First Bull Run, the Peninsular campaign, Antietam, Fredericksburg, and Chancellorsville take up much of the book, and they are fully described with the keen eye of a militarist. The single thematic fault of the work in this sense may be an overly generous appraisal of George McClellan's generalship, which along with the irrational support of Joe Hooker's abilities occasionally mar the judgment of the author.

The book offers more of value in the minor incidents and anecdotes related by Curtis. Much of the feeling for the lives of ordinary soldiers and of the relationship between privates and their field officers emerges in these scenes. In Virginia, Curtis befriended George Mason, a descendant of the Revolutionary War patriot. The author's clear vision of the Civil War, supported by his contemporary notes and the many recollections and letters of others—Union and Confederate—helps to give this work a richness lacking in many other unit histories. An occasional slip appears, as with the claim that George Washington attended William and Mary College.

1078

Tevis, C. V., and D. R. Marquis. **The History of the Fighting Fourteenth** (366 pp., Brooklyn Eagle Press, New York, 1911)

A hodgepodge of materials is used to describe the record of the 84th New York (14th Brooklyn Militia) Infantry, a celebrated regiment that was in the thick of the battle on the first day's field at Gettysburg, at Second Bull Run, and in many other actions. Led by Cols. Alfred M. Wood and Edward B. Fowler, the unit fought through the major eastern battles as part of the Army of the Potomac, collecting a record at First Bull Run, Cedar Mountain, Second Bull Run, South Mountain, Antietam, Fredericksburg, Chancellorsville, Gettysburg, Mine Run campaign, May campaign, and Spotsylvania.

Compiled by journalists to commemorate the 50th anniversary of the formation of the regiment, the work is based on a spectrum of sources, from the *O.R.* (*q.v.*) to a large collection of materials from the members of the unit. The quality is highly variable, but much of interest relating to certain campaigns will be found buried among the less revealing material. The section on the fighting around the railroad cut at Gettysburg is especially noteworthy. An alphabetical roster follows the text, but the work lacks an index.

(Reprinted 1994, with an introduction by James M. Madden and a photographic supplement, 366 pp., Butternut and Blue, Baltimore)

Ohio

1079

Cope, Alexis. **The Fifteenth Ohio Volunteers and Its Campaigns, War of 1861–5** (863 pp., published by the author, Columbus, 1916)

This is a massively detailed account of a unit commanded by Moses R. Dickey, William Wallace, and Frank Askew. Raised throughout the state, the regiment experienced a typical progression in the western theater, fighting at Shiloh, Corinth, Stones River, Chickamauga, Chattanooga, the Atlanta campaign, and Hood's Tennessee campaign. Cope rose to the grade of captain in the regiment and performed a capable service by compiling a mountain of material into this exhaustive narrative account.

The author combines a number of diaries kept by members of the regiment, including those of Lt. Andrew J. Gleason, Nathaniel Mumaugh, John G. Gregory, Frank L. Schreiber, William McConnell, and Randall Ross. He makes substantial use of the *O.R.* (*q.v.*) and excerpts of letters written by many members of the regiment. The result is a narrative that focuses on battles and places the 15th Ohio in the context of the larger war around it, in addition to providing entertaining anecdotes of camp life and the sore tedium of marches. Particularly good accounts describe the regiment's activities at Shiloh, Stones River, and in a host of actions in northern Georgia. Misspellings occur throughout the text, including the names of Philemon P. Baldwin, John C. Breckinridge, Gordon Granger, Joseph F. Knipe, and Benn Pitman. The work contains a thorough roster by companies.

(Reprinted 1993, 863 pp., General's Books, Columbus)

1080

Curry, William L. **Four Years in the Saddle: History of the First Regiment, Ohio Volunteer Cavalry, War of the Rebellion, 1861–1865** (401 pp., Champlin Printing Co., Columbus, 1898)

This story of a midwestern cavalry unit typifies the hard experience of riding through battle in the western theater of war. Organized at Camp Chase and commanded by Cols. Owen P. Ransom, Thomas C. H. Smith, Minor Milliken, Beroth B. Eggleston, and others, the regiment served in Kentucky, on the perimeter of Shiloh, at Corinth, Perryville, Stones River, Chickamauga, Chattanooga, the Atlanta campaign, in Wilson's raid, and in the capture of Jefferson Davis. Many minor forays in Tennessee, Georgia, and Kentucky punctuated these major activities and involved pursuits of Braxton Bragg and Joe Wheeler as well as numerous reconnaisance activities.

Curry served as 1st lieutenant in the regiment until being mustered out in December 1864. He used his own wartime diary as well as many accounts from fellow soldiers of the regiment, official reports, and letters to construct this history some 30 years after the war. In the true spirit of a regimental history, the narrative sometimes exaggerates the adventures of the unit and its significance and serves up a great deal of rather unimportant material. Balancing these shortcomings, however, are clear accounts of many of the battles Curry himself witnessed and a voluminous cache of material on the everyday life of Federal horse soldiers in the

West. The author shows that Union cavalry clearly had its competent members early in the war, despite Confederate legends to the contrary.

(Reprinted 1984, 462 pp., Freedom Hill Press, Jonesboro, Ga.)

1081

Hannaford, Ebenezer. **The Story of a Regiment: A History of the Campaigns and Associations in the Field of the Sixth Regiment, Ohio Volunteer Infantry** (639 pp., published by the author, Cincinnati, 1868)

The campaigns of one of the celebrated fighting regiments of southern Ohio are described. Hannaford served as a common soldier in the 6th from its early marches through the Atlanta campaign, when the regiment was mustered out of service. Subsequently a 1st lieutenant and regimental adjutant of the 197th Ohio Infantry, he was competent as a historian of the regiment and an author, and his work stands as one of the best Ohio regimental histories from the period immediately following the war.

As a chronology of the regiment's activities, the account is frank, modest, and sufficiently detailed to merit value. It traces the unit's participation in the Grafton campaign, camp life near Hodgenville, Buell's jaunt to Nashville, Shiloh, Perryville, Stones River, Chickamauga, Knoxville, and the early phases of the Atlanta campaign. The author clearly describes many commanders of note along the way, including Col. Nicholas Longworth Anderson and one he clearly admired, Brig. Gen. William Nelson. The work also includes a compendium of reminiscences, letters, and sketches of regimental members.

Pennsylvania

1082

Craft, David. **History of the One Hundred Forty-first Regiment, Pennsylvania Volunteers, 1862–1865** (270 pp., Reporter-Journal Printing Co., Towanda, 1885)

Craft summarizes the exploits of a regiment raised in Harrisburg in early autumn 1862. The regiment was commanded by Col. Henry J. Madill and fought at Fredericksburg, Chancellorsville, Gettysburg, the Mine Run campaign, the Wilderness campaign, and around Petersburg. Craft, the regiment's chaplain, compiled this book based on his own notes, recollections of members of the regiment, and such early reference works as Swinton's *Campaigns of the Army of the Potomac* (*q.v.*) and the Comte de Paris's *History of the*

Civil War in America (q.v.). The writing is occasionally turgid and military movements are often dryly recounted , but the author does occasionally provide interesting anecdotes of the common soldiers in the ranks.

The most enthralling sections treat Chancellorsville, Gettysburg, and the collapse of the Confederate lines at Petersburg. The work is typical of the many regimental histories published in this period in that it offers some really absorbing material surrounded by much of minor interest and numerous misspellings. There is a roster by company and a woefully inadequate index.

(Reprinted 1991, 270 pp., Butternut and Blue, Baltimore)

1083

Gavin, William Gilfillan. **Campaigning with the Roundheads: The History of the Hundredth Pennsylvania Veteran Volunteer Infantry Regiment in the American Civil War, 1861–1865** (773 pp., Morningside, Dayton, 1989)

The history of a Pittsburgh regiment that saw action in the eastern and western theaters is presented. Commanded by Cols. Daniel Leasure and Norman J. Maxwell, the unit fought on James Island, at Second Bull Run, Antietam, Fredericksburg, Vicksburg, Knoxville, the Wilderness, Spotsylvania, and Petersburg. Such an interesting mixture of activities provides much for the author to discuss, and his sound job of research allows for a fine narrative supplemented by excerpts from diaries, letters, and official reports.

The author focuses strictly on the chronology of battle, march, and camp experienced by the unit and provides nice descriptions of some of the officers and men. The sections treating the South Carolina expedition, Antietam, the Wilderness campaign, and Fort Stedman are particularly enjoyable. Appendices provide photographs of many of the regiment's officers and soldiers, a complete roster taken from Samuel P. Bates's *Pennsylvania Volunteers (q.v.)*, and a summary of the regiment's monument at Antietam. The index is fairly accomplished, the maps variable in quality. A number of spelling errors appear, as with the names of Ellison Capers, Thomas L. Crittenden, John G. Parke, Richard J. Sommers, and Fort Sedgwick, Virginia, and the McCoull House at Spotsylvania.

1084

Judson, Amos M. **History of the Eighty-third Regiment Pennsylvania Volunteers** (139 pp., B. F. H. Lynn, Erie, 1865)

Although brief, this book offers an enjoyable look inside a celebrated Pennsylvania regiment. Written shortly after the war, it recounts Judson's experiences in the 83d

from 13 September 1861 to 26 September 1864, at which time the author was mustered out. Organized at Erie and commanded by John W. McLane (killed in the Peninsular campaign), the celebrated Strong Vincent (killed at Gettysburg), Orpheus S. Woodward, and Chauncey P. Rogers, the unit saw action across the eastern front. Assigned to the Army of the Potomac, the 83d participated in the Seven Days battles, Second Bull Run, Antietam, Fredericksburg, Chancellorsville, Gettysburg, the Wilderness campaign, the Petersburg campaign, and the final approach to and surrender at Appomattox.

With such varied experience behind the author, the narrative is useful for its commentary on a Pennsylvania infantry regiment in the thick of numerous actions. The author rose to captain, which allowed him to observe the regiment's activities from a position high enough to understand the strategy and tactics at play. His candid recollections are often tragic but sometimes humorous and show a range of discussion, from common soldiers to company commanders to regimental commanders, from inside the regiment that suffered the second greatest number of casualties of any unit in the Army of the Potomac.

(Reprinted 1986, with an introduction by John J. Pullen, 333 pp., Morningside, Dayton)

1085

Mark, Penrose G. **Red, White, and Blue Badge: Pennsylvania Veteran Volunteers, a History of the 93rd Regiment, Known as the "Lebanon Infantry" and "One of the 300 Fighting Regiments" from September 12th, 1861, to June 27th, 1865** (577 pp., Aughinbaugh Press, Harrisburg, 1911)

The author recalls the story of a unit that served in the eastern theater. Mark, a captain of the 93d Pennsylvania Infantry, draws on the *O.R. (q.v.)*, correspondence from members of the regiment (some of which was published in the Lebanon *Courier*), and newspaper accounts from a variety of Pennsylvania dailies. The narrative details the interesting scandal centered on Col. James M. McCarter, who was court-martialed in late 1862 but commissioned again in 1863 and who finally left permanently several months later. During the colonel's absence, the junior officers vied for influence, and so the thread of regimental politics runs through the volume.

The quality of the material varies somewhat, and the most interesting recollections center on the Peninsular campaign, Antietam, Gettysburg, the Wilderness, and the Shenandoah Valley campaign of 1864. Other lengthy sections detail the regiment's experiences at Fredericksburg, Spotsylvania, Cold Harbor, and Petersburg. A complete roster by companies appears. A large amount of material relating to regimental reunions may be found, but the book lacks an index.

(Reprinted 1993, with an introduction by Richard A. Sauers, 577 pp., Butternut and Blue, Baltimore)

1086

Rowell, John W. **Yankee Cavalrymen: Through the Civil war with the Ninth Pennsylvania Cavalry** (280 pp., University of Tennessee Press, Knoxville, 1971)

The author provides a skillfully executed and enticing picture of a Union cavalry regiment. Based in part on the diaries of Cornelius Baker and William Thomas, members of the regiment, the story follows the 9th Pennsylvania (variously known as the 92d Volunteers and the Lochiel Cavalry) throughout its exploits in the western theater. Mustered in at Harrisburg and commanded by Cols. Edward C. Williams and Thomas J. Jordan, the unit saw a wide range of action beginning in the spring of 1862. The regiment participated in Perryville, Chickamauga, the March to the Sea, and the Carolinas campaign. As cavaliers, they harassed John Hunt Morgan, served variously throughout the Atlanta campaign, and performed duty in central Tennessee.

Rowell's narrative nicely captures the flavor of life in a cavalry regiment. The portions treating the war against Morgan in Kentucky, the battle of Thompson's Station, and Bentonville are particularly intriguing. They offer a decidedly different view of some familiar actions, and the author's careful documentation and wide range of viewpoint—from commanders to common soldiers—make the book particularly engaging.

Rhode Island

1087

Denison, Frederic. **Sabres and Spurs: The First Regiment, Rhode Island Cavalry in the Civil War, 1861–1865: Its Origin, Marches, Scouts, Skirmishes, Raids, Battles, Sufferings, Victories, and Appropriate Official Papers, with the Roll of Honor and Roll of the Regiment** (600 pp., First Rhode Island Cavalry Veteran Association, Central Falls, 1876)

Denison, the regiment's chaplain, provides an early and enjoyable history of a cavalry unit raised in Providence in late 1861 and early 1862. Led by Cols. Robert B. Lawton and Alfred N. Duffié, the regiment traveled to Washington in March 1862 and subsequently engaged in the battles at

Front Royal, Cedar Mountain, Second Bull Run, Chantilly, Fredericksburg, Kelly's Ford, Middleburg, Deep Bottom, the Shenandoah Valley campaign of 1864, and operations around Richmond.

The author utilized diaries, official reports, letters written by members of the regiment, and miscellaneous postwar recollections to assemble the book. The many fine accounts of march and battle are peppered with stories of picket duty, camps and bivouacs, recruiting duty, and numerous tidbits from the prison journals of E. E. Chase, J. R. Umfreville, W. A. Johnson, E. D. Guild, and others. A complete roster of the regiment by companies appears as an appendix, along with a list of members who were killed, mortally wounded, or died of disease. The work lacks an index.

(Reprinted 1994, with an introduction by R. D. Madison, 600 pp., Butternut and Blue, Baltimore)

Tennessee

1088

Barber, Flavel C. **Holding the Line: The Third Tennessee Infantry, 1861–1864** (ed. Robert H. Ferrell, 281 pp., Kent State University Press, Kent, 1994)

Barber narrates the war record of the Confederate regiment assembled at Lynnville in the spring of 1861. The author served as major of the regiment, fighting gallantly at Fort Donelson, where he was captured and imprisoned on Johnson's Island, Ohio. During the imprisonment, Barber began writing this memoir, which was not published until more than 130 years later. The account of prison conditions at Johnson's Island is valuable, as are a cache of observations about Barber's regiment, the men it contained, and the Federal attack on Fort Donelson viewed with careful retrospection. The author's recollections of the previous autumn include comments on Bowling Green, where the regiment saw its initial duty.

After exchange, Barber traveled south with the regiment and saw action at the battle of Chickasaw Bayou, where Sherman met stiff resistance. The subsequent activity in the siege of Vicksburg and the battles of Port Hudson, Raymond, and Jackson provide much for Barber to discuss. Thereafter the unit traveled to Georgia in time to participate at Chickamauga, although the diary for this period is missing. The story continues with the Atlanta campaign, during which Barber was mortally wounded at Resaca. The intelligently written narrative is a treasure of Confederate histories relating to the western theater. A full alphabetical roster is included.

1089

Carter, W. R. **History of the First Regiment of Tennessee Volunteer Cavalry in the Great War of the Rebellion, with the Armies of the Ohio and Cumberland, under Generals Morgan, Rosecrans, Thomas, Stanley, and Wilson, 1862–1865** (335 pp., Gaut-Ogden Co., Knoxville, 1896)

This history recalls the activities of a unit that was first known as the 4th Tennessee Infantry before its reorganization in 1862. Under Col. Robert Johnson, son of Andrew Johnson, and James P. Brownlow, son of William G. Brownlow, the unit fought through a wide area of western service in Kentucky, Ohio, Tennessee, and Georgia. Among the actions the regiment participated in were the Tullahoma campaign, Chickamauga, Wheeler's raid, Mossy Creek, the Atlanta campaign, and Franklin and Nashville. The work reflects a great deal about the eastern Tennessee Unionist spirit that prevailed and that contributed substantially to reintroduce the state into Federal occupation.

The military narrative is straightforward and factual without the significant embellishment or minutiae often found in such histories. The author, a sergeant in Company C of the regiment, waited long enough in assembling the history to make use of the *O.R.* (*q.v.*) and other official source materials. The narrative is useful particularly for illuminating a succession of minor actions rarely encountered in the literature. The work lacks an index.

(Reprinted 1992, 351 pp., Overmountain Press, Johnson City, Tenn.)

Texas

1090

Bailey, Anne J. **Between the Enemy and Texas: Parsons's Texas Cavalry in the Civil War** (355 pp., Texas Christian University Press, Fort Worth, 1989)

The author describes a neglected but interesting wartime unit of the Far West. Despite being hampered by the relative inaction in this area, Bailey has created a workable study of Col. William H. Parsons's 12th Texas Cavalry regiment and its participation in the war. The narrative centers on a number of battles fought between 1862 and 1864 in which the 12th Texas helped Confederate resistance in Arkansas, Louisiana, and Missouri, principally aiding Confederate armies in thwarting Nathaniel P. Banks's Red River campaign of 1864.

Despite the sequences of action, much of the book reflects the inactivity that pervaded life in the far western theater after Pea Ridge. Superposed on this difficulty is the author's tendency to focus narrowly on Parsons's activities without placing them in context. Readers may receive a distorted impression of the overall war and how these relatively minor incidents related to it. Nonetheless, the research is sound, the writing generally successful, and the study adds an incisive picture of one of the lesser areas of the final two years of the war.

1091

Hale, Douglas. **The Third Texas Cavalry in the Civil War** (347 pp., University of Oklahoma Press, Norman, 1993)

This is a worthwhile regimental history of a Texas unit. Written by a descendant of a member of the 3d Texas Cavalry, this account offers a chronological story of the camp life and battle experienced by the unit. Hale clearly views his subject passionately, yet this does not cloud his view of the regiment's importance. He documents the backgrounds of members of the 3d Texas Cavalry, finding that many came from upper-middle-class families in eastern Texas. Some 1097 men enlisted in what became the 3d Texas, and more than half the men's families owned slaves—a surprisingly high percentage for a Texas unit. The men staunchly supported secession, state rights, and slavery.

Organized into helter-skelter service that shifted them from east to west, the men experienced campaigning in Georgia, Mississippi, and even Indian Territory. The unit's 72 engagements included the Vicksburg and Atlanta campaigns, and the men served occasionally as infantry as well as performing the standard duties of cavalry. As a cavalry unit, the 3d Texas avoided the most intense fighting on the field and therefore had a relatively high survival rate. The experience of this Texas unit comes through vividly in this history, with its abundant use of letters, diaries, and journals. This volume effectively supersedes S. B. Barron's semiclassic *Lone Star Defenders: A Chronicle of the Third Texas Cavalry, Ross' Brigade* (276 pp., Neale Publishing Co., New York, 1908).

United States Volunteers

1092

Stevens, Charles A. **Berdan's United States Sharpshooters in the Army of the Potomac** (555 pp., Price-McGill Co., St. Paul, 1892)

This lengthy unit history is seen partly through the eyes of a regimental member and partly through the eyes of others in the unit. Stevens served as 1st lieutenant in the innovative regiment, which consisted of members from Michigan, New Hampshire, New York, Vermont, and Wisconsin, and was mustered in between the summer of 1861 and spring of 1862. Led by Col. Hiram Berdan, Lt. Col. William Ripley, and Maj. George G. Hastings, the 1st U.S. Sharpshooters served in most of the major and many minor battles fought by the Army of the Potomac from Big Bethel to Hatcher's Run, after which the unit was mustered out. The unusual nature of the sharpshooters' mission and the regiment's storied performance on several fields—notably Gettysburg, where they worked well into the Confederate lines along Seminary Ridge—makes for absorbing reading.

The story works well during the times when Stevens participated in the battles and actions described. He occasionally relies on the accounts of fellow members of the regiment and supplies linking material and further commentary by borrowing from the *O.R.* (*q.v.*). The commentary bears the marks of occasional embellishment or at least self-aggrandizement, but for the most part the narrative offers a relatively straightforward and detailed account of a most unusual fighting unit. The author's literate and thoughtful reflections on personalities and battles add greatly to this history's lasting value.

(Reprinted 1985, with a foreword by Stuart G. Vogt, 555 pp., Morningside, Dayton)

Virginia

1093

Krick, Robert K. **Parker's Virginia Battery, C.S.A.** (400 pp., Virginia Book Co., Berryville, 1975)

The author chronicles an adventuresome artillery unit. Capt. William Watts Parker was a physician who wished to raise an infantry unit but nevertheless succeeded in the artillery branch, his battery of young men from the Richmond area being mustered in on 14 March 1862. Assembled for a unit of artillery that never materialized, the battery served in 19 battles, beginning with Second Bull Run. During its illustrious service the unit's 200 young artillerists served in the battalions of S. D. Lee, E. Porter Alexander, and Benjamin Huger. The battery performed with distinction throughout the war up to the Confederate disaster at Sayler's Creek.

Krick provides a careful and interesting narrative, thoroughly backed by research into official documents, dispatches, and letters. The book is in typescript form, which may disappoint those interested in production value, but the information within is solid and reliable. A fine map and roster fill out the effort, creating a worthwhile Virginia unit history.

(Reprinted 1989, typeset, 487 pp., Broadfoot, Wilmington)

1094

Wert, Jeffry D. **Mosby's Rangers** (384 pp., Simon and Schuster, New York, 1990)

The exploits of John Singleton Mosby's battalion of rangers and their guerrilla-like tactics in Virginia are explored in an enthusiastically written narrative that makes use of a wide variety of sources. The vibrant style allows readers to appreciate the desperate nature of the guerrilla war in Virginia and the Federal response to it. The character development of Mosby and his many associates is handled adequately, bringing to light details of a little-known group of men who influenced the psychology of the war in the east.

Wert frequently overinterprets his material, and his predilection for the Mosby legend tarnishes much of his commentary. His contention that Mosby's rangers constituted the "most famous command of the Civil War" is patently ridiculous. Students who know the war well know that Mosby's importance has been embellished heavily since the war (largely in his own *Memoirs* [*q.v.*] as well as in the works of associates) and that a number of other guerrilla cavalry leaders had more strategic and tactical significance during the war, the first of whom was John Hunt Morgan. Wert thoroughly advances "combat" as Mosby's most important goal and then proceeds to describe small-scale raids as the rangers' central activities. He writes about engagements in which Mosby's rangers participated, but the descriptions are overblown, as is the exaggerated story of the Federal reaction to Mosby's activities.

1095

Wood, William N. **Reminiscences of Big I** (107 pp., Michie Co., Charlottesville, 1907)

The author enlisted in Company A of the 19th Virginia Infantry in the summer of 1861 and experienced action at Williamsburg, Seven Pines, the Seven Days, Second Bull Run, Antietam, Gettysburg, and Cold Harbor. Wood was captured along with his regiment at Sayler's Creek, and a brief description treats his short stay in the Old Capitol Prison in Washington. The author's narrative of battles and camp life is decidedly unemotional and straightforward, providing a limited but entertaining anecdotal view of life in the regiment. One wishes the text were fuller, but the book delivers some insight on common soldier life in the Army of Northern Virginia and is therefore useful.

Big I was serialized in the Charlottesville *Progress* in 1895. The book's original printing was limited to 200 copies, but this work became widely available when Bell I. Wiley edited a new edition containing an introduction (138 pp., McCowat-Mercer Press, Jackson, Tenn., 1956).

(1956 edition reprinted 1987, 138 pp., Broadfoot, Wilmington)

Wisconsin

1096

Dawes, Rufus R. **Service with the Sixth Wisconsin Volunteers** (330 pp., E. R. Alderman and Sons, Marietta, Ohio, 1890)

Not only did this unit form part of the core of the famed Iron Brigade, but its author advanced from company commander to colonel of the regiment and, following the war, to brevet brigadier general for his illustrious wartime service. Dawes's book consists mainly of his diary and various letters written from the battlefields which together eloquently depict the story of this celebrated Wisconsin regiment.

Vivid commentary on many major eastern clashes is included, as with the author's descriptions of Second Bull Run, Antietam, Fredericksburg, Chancellorsville, Gettysburg, the Wilderness campaign, Cold Harbor, and duty along the Petersburg lines. The writer's own materials are merged with other writings and material gleaned from conversations with members of the regiment. The result is a classic and wonderfully executed memoir of a western regiment that tasted battle in the east.

(Reprinted 1962, with an introduction by Alan T. Nolan, 330 pp., State Historical Society of Wisconsin, Madison; reprinted 1984, with an introduction by Gregory Coco, 367 pp., Morningside, Dayton)

1097

Herdegen, Lance J., and William J. K. Beaudot. **In the Bloody Railroad Cut at Gettysburg** (389 pp., Morningside, Dayton, 1990)

This exciting account of the early hours of the Gettysburg fight focuses on the 6th Wisconsin Infantry, which formed part of the Iron Brigade of the 1st Corps that arrived on the field early on the morning of 1 July as the first cracks of infantry fire exploded west of the town along the Chambersburg Pike. A fine general history of the regiment by Rufus R. Dawes (*q.v.*) chronicles the unit's service throughout the war; Herdegen and Beaudot examine its participation in the early action at Gettysburg in minute detail. They utilize an impressive number of primary sources, including diaries, reminiscences, letters, and newspaper accounts to reconstruct the charge of the 6th Wisconsin into the railroad cut. The authors argue persuasively that the minor action played a significant role in stemming the tide of the onrushing Confederates at that early stage of the battle and that therefore it played a significant part in the events to follow.

A fine writing style and a store of material relating to minor officers and private soldiers belonging to the unit characterize this account. The authors examine the postwar disputes that arose among members of the 6th Wisconsin, the 84th New York (14th Brooklyn) Infantry, and the 95th New York Infantry involving which units should have claimed responsibility for the success of the charge. An appendix by Howard Madaus describes the uniforms of the Iron Brigade. A number of misspellings appear throughout the work, as with Christopher Columbus Augur, and many other misspellings appear in the index. The authors erroneously assign John Blair and Judson Warner the grade of "general." Readers who wish to further explore this area may wish to consult *An Irishman in the Iron Brigade: The Civil War Memoirs of James P. Sullivan, Sergt., Company K, 6th Wisconsin Volunteers*, by James P. Sullivan (ed. William J. K. Beaudot and Lance J. Herdegen, 189 pp., Fordham University Press, New York, 1993).

1098

Otis, George H. **The Second Wisconsin Infantry** (ed. Alan D. Gaff, 372 pp., Morningside, Dayton, 1984)

This work first appeared serially in the Milwaukee *Sunday Telegraph* in 1880. Its author, a New Yorker who moved to Wisconsin to join the printing trade, rose to the grade of captain before being mustered out in June 1864. His loyalty to the regiment and intense interest in recording the unit's history produced this enjoyable and competently edited reminiscence of a Yankee regiment often in the thick of battle.

Otis's recollections of the 2d Wisconsin's commanders offer some of the best commentary in print, particularly for Col. Lucius Fairchild. Treatment of the unit's service at First Bull Run, Brawner's Farm, Antietam, and Gettysburg is significant and well composed, and several contributions from other regimental soldiers appear, particularly the letters of Charles C. Dow. Elisha R. Reed's paper on his imprisonment in Richmond is enlightening. Although it lacks a cohesive, continuous narrative and the reliability of postwar newspaper accounts remains much in question, this history contributes a fair understanding of the majority of service of the 2d Wisconsin, an enviable fighting unit.

COMPANIES

1099

Bean, William G. **The Liberty Hall Volunteers: Stonewall's College Boys** (227 pp., University Press of Virginia, Charlottesville, 1964)

This narrative follows the company formed mostly from students at Washington College who enlisted during the secession months and removed to Harpers Ferry during the war's first summer. Bean provides more than a chronological essay on the achievements of the Liberty Hall volunteers; indeed, he also successfully provides a glimpse into the experiences and attitudes of individual soldiers in the unit as the war unfolded. His characterizations of many members' experiences makes this a valuable unit history with a considerably fresh approach.

The commanders of Company I of the 4th Virginia Infantry were James J. White, Henry R. Morrison, Hugh A. White, and Givens B. Strickler. The company's soldiers served in the Army of the Shenandoah, the Army of the Potomac, the Stonewall brigade of the Army of Northern Virginia, and in Terry's Consolidated Brigade of the Army of the Northern Virginia. The unit experienced virtually the entire run of major battles in the East: First Bull Run, Jackson's Valley campaign, the Peninsular campaign, Second Bull Run, Antietam, Fredericksburg, Chancellorsville, Gettysburg, the Wilderness campaign, Sheridan's Valley campaign, and the surrender at Appomattox. With such an array of experiences, the unit suffered heavily, and the author's narration of the men's suffering strikes a heavy chord. As headquarters guard before Antietam, the men saw much of Jackson and admired him strongly. War took its toll, however, and only 3 of 73 original members were left after Gettysburg.

1100

Watkins, Sam. **"Co. Aytch," Maury Grays, First Tennessee Regiment; or, a Side Show of the Big Show** (236 pp., Presbyterian Printing House, Nashville, 1882)

One of the most charming Confederate memoirs outlines the author's experiences with Company H of the 1st Tennessee Infantry. Watkins penned the book in 1881 and 1882 and first published it serially in the *Columbia Herald* in Tennessee. In late 1882 Watkins published his stories as a paperbound book; the press run was 2000. In 1900 the *Chattanooga Times* republished the book, printing another 2000 copies.

Undoubtedly, a good many of Watkins's tales are spurious or exaggerated, yet he provides a great glimpse of the life of a common soldier in the Army of Tennessee. Watkins's experiences included arriving at Bull Run too late for the battle and "feeling like the war was over and we would have to return home without seeing a Yankee soldier." His anecdotes of Shiloh let us appreciate the terror of battle: "I remember a man by the name of Smith stepping out of the ranks and shooting his finger off to keep out of the fight." Of the battle itself, Watkins paints a picture of chaos: "The air was full of balls and deadly missiles. The litter corps was carrying off the dying and wounded. We could hear the shout of the charge and incessant roar of the guns, the rattle of musketry, and knew that the contending forces were in a breast to breast struggle."

Co. Aytch reveals the common soldier's Civil War as well as any other work available. Watkins himself stated it most powerfully in an advertising blurb: "The Generals, and President, and Vice-President, and other high officials have published their accounts of the war, but Sam Watkins is the first high private who has written up the common soldier side of the matter."

(Reprinted 1952, with an introduction by Bell I. Wiley, 231 pp., McCowat-Mercer Press, Jackson, Tenn.; 1882 edition reprinted 1982, 236 pp., Morningside, Dayton; 1952 edition reprinted 1987, 231 pp., Broadfoot, Wilmington)

APPENDIX 1

PROLIFIC PUBLISHERS OF CIVIL WAR BOOKS

Americana House
357 West Chicago Avenue
Chicago, IL 60610

Ayer Co. Publishers
Box 958
Salem, NH 03079

John F. Blair, Publisher
1406 Plaza Drive
Winston-Salem, NC 27103

Broadfoot Publishing Co.
1907 Buena Vista Circle
Wilmington, NC 28405

Butternut and Blue
3411 Northwind Road
Baltimore, MD 21234

Cambridge University Press
40 West 20th Street
New York, NY 10011

Camp Pope Bookshop
Box 2232
Iowa City, IA 52244

Stan Clark Military Books
915 Fairview Avenue
Gettysburg, PA 17325

Dover Publications
31 East 2d Street
Mineola, NY 11501

Facts on File
460 Park Avenue South
New York, NY 10016

Fordham University Press
University Box L
Bronx, NY 10458

The Free Press
866 Third Avenue
New York, NY 10022

Genealogical Publishing Co.
1001 North Calvert Street
Baltimore, MD 21202

The General's Books
522 Norton Road
Columbus, OH 43228

Greenwood Press
Box 5007, 88 Post Road West
Westport, CT 06881

HarperCollins Publishers
10 East 53d Street
New York, NY 10022

Heritage Books
1540-E Pointer Ridge Place
Bowie, MD 20716

Indiana University Press
601 North Morton Street
Bloomington, IN 47404

Kent State University Press
P.O. Box 5190
Kent, OH 44242

Kraus Reprint Co.
Route 100
Millwood, NY 10546

Little, Brown and Co.
34 Beacon Street
Boston, MA 02108

Longstreet House
Box 730
Hightstown, NJ 08520

Louisiana State University Press
P.O. Box 25053
Baton Rouge, LA 70893

McFarland and Co.
Box 611
Jefferson, NC 28640

Mercer University Press
Macon, GA 31207

Michigan State University Press
1405 South Harrison Road, Suite 25
East Lansing, MI 48823

Morningside Book Shop
258-260 Oak Street
Dayton, OH 45401

National Historical Society
6405 Flank Drive
Harrisburg, PA 17112

Naval Institute Press
118 Maryland Avenue
Annapolis, MD 21402

W. W. Norton and Co.
500 Fifth Avenue
New York, NY 10110

Olde Soldier Books
18779B North Frederick Avenue
Gaithersburg, MD 20879

Oxford University Press
200 Madison Avenue
New York, NY 10016

Pelican Publishing Co.
Box 3110
Gretna, LA 70054

Random House
201 East 50th Street
New York, NY 10022

Rutledge Hill Press
211 Seventh Avenue North
Nashville, TN 37219

Simon and Schuster
1230 Avenue of the Americas
New York, NY 10020

Southern Illinois University Press
P.O. Box 3697
Carbondale, IL 62902

Syracuse University Press
1600 Jamesville Avenue
Syracuse, NY 13244

Taylor Publishing Co.
1550 West Mockingbird Lane
Dallas, TX 75235

Texas A&M University Press
Drawer C
College Station, TX 77843

University of Alabama Press
Box 870380
Tuscaloosa, AL 35487

University of Arkansas Press
201 Ozark Avenue
Fayetteville, AR 72701

University of Georgia Press
330 Research Drive
Athens, GA 30602

University of Illinois Press
1325 South Oak Street
Champaign, IL 61820

University of Missouri Press
2910 LeMone Boulevard
Columbia, MO 65201

University of Nebraska Press
312 North 14th Street
Lincoln, NE 68588

University of North Carolina Press
P.O. Box 2288
Chapel Hill, NC 27515

University of Oklahoma Press
1005 Asp Avenue
Norman, OK 73019

University of South Carolina Press
Carolina Plaza, 8th floor
937 Assembly Street
Columbia, SC 29208

University of Tennessee Press
293 Communications Building
Knoxville, TN 37996

University of Texas Press
P.O. Box 7819
Austin, TX 78713

University of Wisconsin Press
114 North Murray Street
Madison, WI 53715

University Press of Kansas
2501 West 15th Street
Lawrence, KS 66049

University Press of Kentucky
663 South Limestone Street
Lexington, KY 40508

University Press of Mississippi
3825 Ridgewood Road
Jackson, MS 39211

University Press of Virginia
Box 3608, University Station
Charlottesville, VA 22903

White Mane Publishing Co.
Box 152
Shippensburg, PA 17257

APPENDIX 2

A SHORT LIST OF CIVIL WAR BIBLIOGRAPHIES

GENERAL BIBLIOGRAPHIES

Bartlett, John Russell. *The Literature of the Rebellion: A Catalogue of Books and Pamphlets Relating to the Civil War in the United States and on Subjects Growing Out of That Event, Together with Works on American Slavery, and Essays from Reviews and Magazines on the Same Subjects.* 447 pp. Draper and Halliday, Boston, and Sidney S. Rider and Bros., Providence, 1866.

Bridges, Hal. *Civil War and Reconstruction.* 2d ed. 25 pp. American Historical Association, Washington, 1962.

Broadfoot, Tom. *Civil War Books: A Priced Checklist with Advice.* 3d ed. 560 pp. Broadfoot Publishing Co., Wilmington, N.C., 1990.

Cole, Garold L. *Civil War Eyewitnesses: An Annotated Bibliography of Books and Articles, 1955–1986.* 400 pp. University of South Carolina Press, Columbia, 1988.

Coulter, E. Merton. *Travels in the Confederate States: A Bibliography.* 289 pp. University of Oklahoma Press, Norman, 1948.

Cox, Jacob D. "Period of the Civil War, 1860–1865," in *The Literature of American History: A Bibliographic Guide,* ed. J. N. Larned. 588 pp. Houghton Mifflin Co., Boston, 1902.

Donald, David H. *The Nation in Crisis.* 92 pp. Appleton-Century Crofts, New York, 1969.

Dornbusch, Charles E. *A Military Bibliography of the Civil War.* 4 vols., 1441 pp. Vols. 1–3: New York Public Library, New York, 1971–1982; Vol. 4: Morningside, Dayton, Ohio, 1988.

Freemon, Frank R. *Microbes and Minié Balls: An Annotated Bibliography of Civil War Medicine.* 253 pp. Fairleigh Dickinson University Press, Rutherford, N.J., 1994.

Long, E. B. *The Civil War Day by Day: An Almanac, 1861–1865.* 1135 pp. Doubleday and Co., Garden City, N.Y., 1971.

Menendez, Albert J. *Civil War Novels: An Annotated Bibliography.* 192 pp. Garland Publishing Co., New York, 1986.

Mugridge, Donald H. *The American Civil War: A Selected Reading List.* 24 pp. U.S. Government Printing Office, Washington, 1960.

Nevins, Allan, James I. Robertson, Jr., and Bell I. Wiley, eds. *Civil War Books: A Critical Bibliography.* 2 vols., 604 pp. Louisiana State University Press, Baton Rouge, 1967–1969.

Nicholson, John Page. *Catalogue of the Library of Brevet Lieutenant Colonel John Page Nicholson Relating to the War of the Rebellion, 1861–1866.* 1022 pp. John T. Palmer Co., Philadelphia, 1914. Reprint: 1022 pp., Maurizio Martino, Storrs-Mansfield, Conn., 1995.

Randall, James G., and David H. Donald. *The Civil War and Reconstruction.* 2d ed. 820 pp. D. C. Heath and Co., Boston, 1961.

Sabin, Joseph. *A Dictionary of Books Relating to America,* ed. Wilberforce Eames and R. W. G. Vail. 29 vols., 16,321 pp. Joseph Sabin, New York, 1868–1936.

Smith, Myron J., Jr. *American Civil War Navies.* Vol. 3 of *American Naval Bibliography.* 347 pp. Scarecrow Press, Metuchen, N.J., 1972.

GOVERNMENT BIBLIOGRAPHIES

Arnold, Louise, ed. *Special Bibliography #11: The Era of the Civil War, 1820–1876.* 704 pp. U.S. Army Military History Institute, Carlisle Barracks, Pa., 1982.

Beers, Henry P. *Guide to the Archives of the Government of the Confederate States of America.* 536 pp. National Archives, Washington, 1968.

Munden, Kenneth W., and Henry P. Beers. *Guide to Federal Archives Relating to the Civil War.* 721 pp. National Archives, Washington, 1962.

Sellers, John R., ed. *Civil War Manuscripts in the Library of Congress.* 391 pp. U.S. Government Printing Office, Washington, 1985.

U.S. War Department. *Bibliography of State Participation in the Civil War, 1861–1866.* 3d ed. Document #432. 1140 pp. U.S. Government Printing Office, Washington, 1913.

BATTLE BIBLIOGRAPHIES

Hartwig, D. Scott. *The Battle of Antietam and the Maryland Campaign of 1862: A Bibliography.* 117 pp. Meckler Corp., Westport, Conn., 1990.

Sauers, Richard A. *The Gettysburg Campaign, June 3–August 1, 1863: A Comprehensive, Selectively Annotated*

Bibliography. 277 pp. Greenwood Press, Westport, Conn., 1982.

CONFEDERATE BIBLIOGRAPHIES

Crandall, Marjorie Lyle. *Confederate Imprints: A Checklist Based Principally on the Collection of the Boston Athenaeum.* 2 vols., 1318 pp. Boston Athenaeum, Boston, 1955.

Freeman, Douglas Southall. *A Calendar of Confederate Papers: With a Bibliography of Some Confederate Publications: Preliminary Report of the Southern Historical Manuscripts Commission, Prepared under the Direction of the Confederate Memorial Literary Society.* 620 pp. Confederate Museum, Richmond, 1908.

————. *The South to Posterity: An Introduction to the Writing of Confederate History.* 235 pp. Charles Scribner's Sons, New York, 1939.

Harwell, Richard B. *The Confederate Hundred: A Bibliophilic Selection of Confederate Books.* 58 pp. Beta Phi Mu Fraternity, Urbana, Ill., 1964.

————. *Cornerstones of Confederate Collecting.* 35 pp. Bibliographical Society of the University of Virginia, Charlottesville, 1952.

————. *In Tall Cotton: The 200 Most Important Confederate Books for the Reader, Researcher, and Collector.* 82 pp. Jenkins Publishing Co. and Frontier America Corp., Austin, Tex., 1978.

————. *More Confederate Imprints.* 2 vols., 345 pp. Virginia State Library, Richmond, 1957.

Krick, Robert K. *Neale Books: An Annotated Bibliography.* 234 pp. Morningside, Dayton, Ohio, 1977.

Parrish, T. Michael, and Robert M. Willingham, Jr. *Confederate Imprints: A Bibliography of Southern Publications from Secession to Surrender (Expanding and Revising the Earlier Works of Marjorie Crandall and Richard Harwell).* 991 pp. Jenkins Publishing Co., Austin, Tex., and Gary A. Foster, Katonah, N.Y., 1984.

UNION BIBLIOGRAPHIES

Mullins, Michael, and Rowena Reed. *The Union Bookshelf: A Selected Civil War Bibliography.* 81 pp. Broadfoot's Bookmark, Wendell, N.C., 1982.

Murdock, Eugene C. *The Civil War in the North: A Selected, Annotated Bibliography.* 765 pp. Garland Publishing Co., New York, 1987.

STATE BIBLIOGRAPHIES

Black, Patti C. *Guide to Civil War Source Material in the Department of Archives and History, State of Mississippi.* 71 pp. State of Mississippi, Jackson, 1962.

Bradley, Isaac S. *A Bibliography of Wisconsin's Participation in the War between the States, Based upon Material Contained in the Wisconsin Historical Library.* 42 pp., Wisconsin History Commission, Madison, 1911.

Burton, William L. *Descriptive Bibliography of Civil War Manuscripts in Illinois.* 393 pp. Northwestern University Press, Chicago, 1966.

Jordan, William B. *Maine in the Civil War: A Bibliographic Guide.* 75 pp. Maine Historical Society, Portland, 1976.

May, George S., ed. *Michigan Civil War History: An Annotated Bibliography.* 128 pp. Wayne State University Press, Detroit, 1961.

Ryan, Daniel Joseph. *The Civil War Literature of Ohio.* 518 pp. Burrow Brothers Co., Cleveland, 1911.

Shetler, Charles. *West Virginia Civil War Literature: An Annotated Bibliography.* 184 pp. West Virginia University Library, Morgantown, 1963.

Sinclair, Donald A. *The Civil War and New Jersey: A Bibliography of Materials of New Jersey's Participation in the American Civil War.* 186 pp. Friends of the Rutgers University Library, New Brunswick, 1967.

LINCOLN BIBLIOGRAPHIES

Angle, Paul M. *A Shelf of Lincoln Books: A Critical, Selective Bibliography of Lincolniana.* 142 pp. Rutgers University Press, New Brunswick, in association with the Abraham Lincoln Association, Springfield, Ill., 1946.

Fish, Daniel. *Lincoln Bibliography: A List of Books and Pamphlets Relating to Abraham Lincoln.* 380 pp. Francis D. Tandy Co., New York, 1906.

Monaghan, Jay. *Lincoln Bibliography, 1839–1939.* 2 vols., 1079 pp. Illinois State Historical Library, Springfield, 1943–1945.

Oakleaf, Joseph B. *Lincoln Bibliography: A List of Books and Pamphlets Relating to Abraham Lincoln.* 424 pp. Torch Press, Cedar Rapids, Iowa, 1925.

Ritchie, George T. *A List of Lincolniana in the Library of Congress.* Rev. ed. with supplement. 86 pp. U.S. Government Printing Office, Washington, 1906.

BIBLIOGRAPHIES LISTING MAPS AND PHOTOGRAPHS

Ashby, Charlotte M., ed. *Civil War Maps in the National Archives.* 127 pp. National Archives, Washington, 1964.

Bosse, David. *Civil War Newspaper Maps: A Cartobibliography of the Northern Daily Press.* 253 pp. Greenwood Press, Westport, Conn., 1993.

Gottschall, Irwin. *A Bibliography of Maps of Civil War Battlefield Areas.* U.S.G.S. Circular #462. 33 pp. U.S. Department of the Interior, Washington, 1962.

Milhollen, Hirst D., and Donald H. Mugridge. *Civil War Photographs, 1861–1865: A Catalog of Copy Negatives Made from Originals Selected from the Mathew B.*

Brady Collection in the Prints and Photographs Division of the Library of Congress. 74 pp. Library of Congress, Washington, 1961.

National Archives and Records Administration. *A Guide to Civil War Maps in the National Archives.* 2d ed. 140 pp. U.S. Government Printing Office, Washington, 1986.

Stephenson, Richard W., ed. *Civil War Maps: An Annotated List of Maps and Atlases in Map Collections of the Library of Congress.* 2d ed. 410 pp. Library of Congress, Washington, 1989.

Italic page numbers denote an author or editor of a secondary reference work or a reprint edition rather than a primary book reviewed in detail.

INDEX OF TITLES

Italic page numbers denote a title cited as a secondary reference work (rather than a primary book reviewed in detail) or as a variant title used for a reprint edition.

DAVID J. EICHER is managing editor of *ASTRONOMY* magazine. An avid student of the Civil War since being given wartime papers and relics of his great-great grandfather, an Ohio soldier, he enjoys studying battlefields and general officers. Eicher is the author of *Civil War Battlefields: A Touring Guide.* He lives in Waukesha, Wisconsin, with his wife and son and approximately 3000 Civil War books and assorted memorabilia.

GARY W. GALLAGHER is a professor of American history at Pennsylvania State University. He has published widely on the Civil War, including *Stephen Dodson Ramseur: Lee's Gallant General, Fighting for the Confederacy: The Personal Recollections of Edward Porter Alexander,* and *Lee the Soldier.*